Communications
in Computer and Information Science

235

Min Zhu (Ed.)

Information and Management Engineering

International Conference, ICCIC 2011
Wuhan, China, September 17-18, 2011
Proceedings, Part V

 Springer

Volume Editor

Min Zhu
Nanchang University
235 Nanjing Donglu
Nanchang, 330047, China
E-mail: minzhu2012@yeah.net

ISSN 1865-0929   e-ISSN 1865-0937
ISBN 978-3-642-24021-8   e-ISBN 978-3-642-24022-5
DOI 10.1007/978-3-642-24022-5
Springer Heidelberg Dordrecht London New York

Library of Congress Control Number: Applied for

CR Subject Classification (1998): C.2, H.4, I.2, H.3, D.2, J.1, H.5

Typesetting: Camera-ready by author, data conversion by Scientific Publishing Services, Chennai, India

Printed on acid-free paper

Springer is part of Springer Science+Business Media (www.springer.com)

Preface

The present book includes extended and revised versions of a set of selected papers from the 2011 International Conference on Computing, Information and Control (ICCIC 2011) held in Wuhan, China, September 17–18, 2011.

The ICCIC is the most comprehensive conference focused on the various aspects of advances in computing, information and control providing a chance for academic and industry professionals to discuss recent progress in the area. The goal of this conference is to bring together researchers from academia and industry as well as practitioners to share ideas, problems and solutions relating to the multifaceted aspects of computing, information and control.

Being crucial for the development of this subject area, the conference encompasses a large number of related research topics and applications. In order to ensure a high-quality international conference, the reviewing course is carried out by experts from home and abroad with all low-quality papers being rejected. All accepted papers are included in the Springer LNCS CCIS proceedings.

Wuhan, the capital of the Hubei province, is a modern metropolis with unlimited possibilities, situated in the heart of China. Wuhan is an energetic city, a commercial center of finance, industry, trade and science, with many international companies located here. Having scientific, technological and educational institutions such as Laser City and the Wuhan University, the city is also an intellectual center.

Nothing would have been achieved without the help of the Program Chairs, organization staff, and the members of the Program Committees. Thank you.

We are confident that the proceedings provide detailed insight into the new trends in this area.

August 2011   Yanwen Wu

Organization

Honorary Chair

Weitao Zheng   Wuhan Institute of Physical Education,
Key Laboratory of Sports Engineering of
General Administration of Sport of China

General Chair

Yanwen Wu   Huazhong Normal Universtiy, China

Program Chair

Qihai Zhou   Southwestern University of Finance and
Economics, China

Program Committee

Sinon Pietro Romano   Azerbaijan State Oil Academy, Azerbaijan

International Program Committee

Ming-Jyi Jang	Far-East University, Taiwan
Tzuu-Hseng S. Li	National Cheng Kung University, Taiwan
Yanwen Wu	Huazhong Normal University, China
Teh-Lu Liao	National Cheng Kung University, Taiwan
Yi-Pin Kuo	Far-East University, Taiwan
Qingtang Liu	Huazhong Normal University, China
Wei-Chang Du	I-Shou University, Taiwan
Jiuming Yang	Huazhong Normal University, China
Hui Jiang	WuHan Golden Bridgee-Network Security Technology Co., Ltd., China
Zhonghua Wang	Huazhong Normal University, China
Jun-Juh Yan	Shu-Te University, Taiwan
Dong Huang	Huazhong University of Science and Technology, China
JunQi Wu	Huazhong Normal University, China

Table of Contents – Part V

Robust Exponential Stability Analysis for Uncertain Stochastic Neural
Networks 1
    Xinhuai Tang and Li Xie

Low Computational Complexity Pitch Based VAD for Dynamic
Environment in Hearing Aids 10
    Yu-Jui Chen, Cheng-Wen Wei, Yi-Le Meng, and Shyh-Jye Jou

Design of a Programmable CCI Filter with Attenuation
Compensation 18
    *YuJing Li, LinTao Liu, YouHua Wang, RuiTao Zhang, and
    RuZhang Li*

Application of Risk-Oriented Audit in the Process of Informatization in
SMEs of Anhui Province 24
    Li Xia and Liu Qingling

Design of DRM Middleware Player System in IPTV Based on JSE 30
    Xie Weihua and Huang YaChao

A New Scheme for Detecting Faulty Sensor Nodes and Excluding Them
from the Network 36
    Shahram Babaei, HamidehJafarian, and AliHosseinalipour

Integrated OLAP Architecture in Harbor Logistics 43
    Xixu Fu, Xizhang Gong, Kaijun Wu, Shu Zhang, and Dongming Pan

Innovative Education Practice of Heat Transfer Based on
Constructivism Instructional Model 50
    Li Xuemei and Ding Lixing

Research of Identity Metasystem Based Authentication Mechanism in
SOA 56
    Jun Hao Wen, Peng Li, Hai Jun Ren, and Fang Fang Tang

Practice and Exploration of College-Enterprise Cooperation on Major
Establishment 64
    Guohong and Liuxiaoning

The Exploration of the Training Mode for Undergraduate
Application-Oriented Engineering Creative Professionals 69
    Hua Meng, Ran Zhen, Xue-li Wu, and Jianhua Zhang

The Design and Implementation of Budget Management System Based
on ExtJS and ASP.NET   74
    Wu Bo and Peng Yan

Experimental Simulations of Flow Fields within Air-Conditioning
Aircraft Cabin   82
    Wang Jin, Pang Liping, Gong Mengmeng, Cui Yi, Xu Jie, and
    Wang Jun

Reformation and Study on Practical Teaching in Mechanical
Manufacturing Technology   89
    G.H. Qin and H.C. Ye

Reform and Exploration on Professional Personnel Training System of
Geotechnical Engineering   94
    Zheng Da

Discussion on Improving the Safety Training Effect of Three Categories
of Staff   100
    Zhong-qiang Sun, Wei-min Dai, Jing Wang, and Xu Han

XML Webpage Design Teaching Method Application: A Study   105
    Li Yuxiang, Bi Danxia, Shao Lijun, Wang Shi, and Geng Qingjia

Research on Applied Teaching Pattern of University Designing Lessons
in the Major of Architecture   111
    Bojia Liu and Jianqing Wang

Design and Analysis of a New Undergraduate Curriculum for
Information Technology Degree at Universities in West China   117
    Xiaoying Wang, Weitong Huang, and Xiaojing Liu

The Study on Management Design Education Concept in Engineering
Management Major   125
    Guangshe Jia and Lingling Chen

Bilingual Teaching Mode Combined Top-Down with Down-Top
Method   133
    Wang Yun, Xu Zhenying, Dai Yachun, Zhang Kai,
    Jiang Yinfang, and Ren Naifei

The Exploration of "Electro-Hydraulic Control Technology" Course
Teaching   137
    Jilin He, Shuibing Rao, and Song Jun

Reform Practice in Experimental Contents and Methods of Plant
Protection Specialty   143
    Ming-wang Shi and Ju-huai Zhai

A Probe on Teaching Model of Course-Certificate Combination for
Programmable Logic Controller Course in Institutions of Higher
Education   148
    Shi Xuhua

Discussion on Cultivating Model of Multimoda Innovation Capability
for Students of Electric Automation Major   153
    Shi Xuhua

Does the Missing of the Inflectional Morphology Imply the Impairment
of Interlanguage Grammar? – A Study Based on the Pro-drop
Parameter   158
    Tang Xuemei

Innovation on Practical Teaching of Graphics Mapping for
Comprehensive Ability Cultivation   164
    Xin Shu, You-dong Yang, and Jian Ma

Actual Projects for Carriers to Achieve Teaching Model Innovation for
Engineering Specialties   170
    Bin Chen, Yingchun Pan, and Yuqiang Wang

Design and Experiment of a New Synthesized Practical Training
Curriculum in College Education-Based on Real Engineering
Situations   175
    Bin Chen and Xiaodong Chen

Design and Implementation of an Attendance System for Engineering
Training Based on DSBA   181
    Wang Meilin, Fu Pinxin, Dai Qingyun, and Zhong Runyang

Discussion on Bilingual Teaching in Computer Experiment   189
    Zhaoyun Sun, Yuan Ma, and Linan Jiao

Software Process Measurement Based on Six Sigma   193
    Yu Lei, Li Zhibo, Hou Xuemei, and Du Zhuping

An Investigation on Applications of Cloud Computing in Scientific
Computing   201
    Huiying Chen, Feng Wang, and Hui Deng

A Study on Experiment Teaching of Logistics Engineering   207
    Liu Xu-yang and Liang Jing

The Discussion on Training Model of Vehicle Engineering Innovational
and Application-Oriented Talents   211
    Zhu Maotao, Chen Yazhou, and He Changyuan

The Development and Application of Electrochemical Biosensor   215
    Qian Xiang

The Research of Software Project Management Based on Software
Engineering Practice 221
   Li Li-ping and Wang Shuai

Instruction from Service Learning in America to Chinese Higher Education 226
   Yanli Guo and Shuli Gao

Reform of Quantum Mechanics in Information Specialty by
Computer-Aided Practice 234
   Chen Fengxiang, Wang Lisheng, and Tan Gaijuan

A Study of the Influence of Creative Thinking Instruction Implemented
in the Engineering Education "Mold Production Practice" Curriculum
on the Creativity of Vocational High School Students 239
   Kuang-Yao Li, Chuan-Shou Hau, Yu-Chun Huang, and De-Fa Huang

Teaching Reform and Practice on Fostering Engineering Capability for
the Undergraduate Student 246
   Shengbing Ren, Zhigang Hu, and Bin Wu

The Research of Automation Open Experiment Teaching Platform
under the Background of Large Engineering 252
   JiaLian Wang

Semantic Web Enabled Personalized Recommendation for Learning
Paths and Experiences 258
   Changqin Huang, Li Liu, Yong Tang, and Ling Lu

A Comprehensive Approch for Improving Chinese Computing
UndergraduatesŠ Entrepreneurial Spirits 268
   Jun Huang and Ling-li Hang

Designing of Virtual Experiment Platform of Engineering Graphic in
the Lab Based on VRML 275
   Hong Zhao and Linlin Wang

Cost Information Retrieval Model Based on Open Sources for Students
Learning of Construction Cost Management 281
   Wenfa Hu and Tingting Yu

Visualization and Collaboration of On-Site Environments Based on
Building Information Model for Construction Project Class 288
   Wenfa Hu and Shuting Guo

Research on Macro Instructional Design of Electronic Technology
Course for Different Major Vocational Students (HVAC Major as an
Example) 296
   Li Shidong

Some Consideration of Experiment Teaching and Practice of Biosystems
Engineering 304
  Ming Wei Shen, Fei Lin Hao, Yong He, and Lei Feng

A Performance Measurement System Based on BSC 309
  Yan Peng and Lijuan Zhou

Construction and Application of Simulation Experiment on
"Port, Waterway and Coastal Engineering" 316
  Wenbai Liu, Danda Shi, and Yibing Deng

Integrated Construction of Engineering Skills and Academic Literacies
for Undergraduates.. 321
  Li Cheng, Fan Shangchun, Qian Zheng, Wan Congmei, and Liu Zhao

The Practice Base Construction of Engineering Education Based on
TOPCARES-CDIO Model 328
  Dejun Tang, Haiyi Jin, Chen Wang, and Lixin Ma

Teaching Methods of the Introduction of Basic Engineering Course 334
  Zhou Huanhuai, Ying Huijuan, and Ai Ning

The Introduction of Oman Crude Oil Trading and Development 340
  Li Xiaosai and Dong Xiucheng

A Study of Engineering Students' Interaction Strategy in Oral English
Classes Based on Power Theory.................................. 346
  Xu Zhisuo and Wanq Li

Setting Up the Net Platform of Measuring and Drawing of Machinery
Based on PowerEasy 353
  Y.M. Lu and J. Miao

The Application of Auxiliary Plane in Illustrated Diagram on Space
Geometry Problems 359
  Y.M. Lu and Y.C. Wang

Study on Applying of Tax Planning in Enterprise 365
  Xiuju Gao, Maobao Du, and Liming Yang

Special Lecture for Graduates 370
  Cheng Qiaolian

Research and Practice System Architecture of Engineering Education
for Colleges of Finance and Economics 374
  Zhang Yuanyuan, Feng Hai-qi, and Wang Jian

Research on Entrepreneurship Education Based on E-Commerce 381
  Liu Zunfeng and Zhang Chunling

A Method to Query and Browse Mathematical Formulas 389
    Hong Liurong and Lu Zhuanghua

The Practice of Teaching Innovation in "Instrumental Analysis" Course
of Environmental Protection Program in Vocation College 399
    Ma Zhanqing

Research on Teaching Methods of Electromechanical Courses Oriented
to Innovation 404
    Xiuhong Zhang, Kai Zhang, Jie Wang, and Donghai Su

Trust-Based Privacy Authorization Model for Web Service
Composition 409
    Jun Zheng, Zhiqiu Huang, Jun Hu, Ou Wei, and Linyuan Liu

Research on Quality Management and Monitoring System of Post
Practice Process in Higher Vocational Colleges 416
    Wan Li, Yuan Ning, and Huiying Zhang

Training Students' Engineering Practice Innovation Capability through
Academic Competition 422
    JiaLian Wang

CDIO-Based Exploration and Practice of "Computer Network Design
and System Integration" Course 428
    Wei Guo and Hong Lu

Using Fishbone Diagrams in Inquiry-Based Teaching and Learning for
Engineering Education 435
    Wei Guo and Hong Lu

Professional Experiment Teaching Should Pay More Attention to the
Cultivation of Students' Creative Spirit 443
    Ying Li

The Cultivation of Research Capability for Undergraduate 449
    Ying Li and Ting Wang

Promoting the Formation of the Students' Learning Pattern
Effectively 455
    Ying Li and Ting Wang

Generalization and Application of Case Teaching in Marketing
Courses 461
    Zhang Cui-lin, Zhou Bo, and Wang Xing

ESaaS: A New Education Software Model in E-learning Systems 468
    Md. Anwar Hossain Masud and Xiaodi Huang

Design and Research of SOPC Embedded Digital Frequency Meter
Based on FPGA 476
    Hu Bing and Liu Xijun

Assessment of the Application of Wii Remote for the Design of
Interactive Teaching Materials 483
    Chien-Yu Lin, Yen-Huai Jen, Li-Chih Wang, Ho-Hsiu Lin, and
    Ling-Wei Chang

The Improved Genetic Algorithm Based on Fuzzy Controller with
Adaptive Parameter Adjustment 491
    Daohua Liu and Xin Liu

Smart Home System Network Architecture and Implementation 498
    GaoHua Liao and JieBin Zhu

Study of Numerical Control Machining Parameter Optimization 504
    GaoHua Liao and Jia Liu

Cooperative Learning Using Social Network Analysis 511
    Wei Hantian and Wang Furong

An Enhanced Recommendation Algorithm Based on the Count of
Common Rated Items 518
    Gao Jianxin, Huang Yongsheng, and Wang Huan

Design and Implementation of Security Reverse Data Proxy Server
Based on SSL 523
    Jiang Du and GuoXin Nie

A New Workforce Cross-Training Policy for a U-shaped Assembly
Line 529
    Jun Gong, Lijie Wang, and Sen Zhang

Author Index 537

Robust Exponential Stability Analysis for Uncertain Stochastic Neural Networks

Xinhuai Tang[1] and Li Xie[2]

[1] School of Software
Shanghai Jiaotong University
Shanghai, P.R. China
[2] Department of Information Science and Electronics Engineering,
Zhejiang University
Hangzhou, P.R. China
tangwang112@yeah.net

Abstract. The problem of robust exponential stability analysis for uncertain stochastic neural networks is investigated based on Lyapunov stability theory. The parametric uncertainties in the neural networks satisfy the Frobenius norm-bounded conditions. The exogenous disturbance and stochastic perturbation functions satisfy the Liptistz conditions. Based on linear matrix inequality approach, the sufficient exponential stable criteria and the asymptotical stability condition on uncertain stochastic neural networks are presented.

Keywords: robust exponential stability, uncertain stochastic neural networks, exgenous disturbance, stochastic perturbation, linear matrix inequalities.

1 Introduction

During the past decade, the problem of stability analysis of neural networks has received extensive consideration due to its theoretical importance and practical applications. The stability of neural network is regarded as one of the intrinsic character for the applications in optimization or pattern recognition. Therefore, there exist considerable research results which are presented about the stability analysis of neural network in recent past years.

In ref [1], some new stability conditions of recurrent neural network are derived by using a novel Lyapunov function, which provide milder constraints on the connection weights than the conventional results in the stability analysis. The ref [2], the celebrated matrix measure concept is introduced to the analysis for the stability of neural network. In ref [3], the absolute exponential stability analysis problem is investigated for a general class of neural networks by using of Lyapunov stability theory. In ref [4], the LaSalle method is used to give some extensions for the complete stability analysis of neural networks. Several LMI-based stable criteria have been presented for the problem of stability analysis for neural networks in recent years [5, 6, 7].

M. Zhu (Ed.): ICCIC 2011, Part V, CCIS 235, pp. 1–9, 2011.

In this paper, the problem of robust exponential stability analysis is investigated for uncertain stochastic neural network with exogenous disturbance and nonlinear stochastic perturbation. The sufficient conditions of robust exponential stability and robust asymptotical stability are presented in terms of linear matrix inequalities.

The structure of this paper is organized as follows: In section 2, the descriptions of the uncertain stochastic neural networks model are given. Some necessary assumptions and mathematical definitions are presented. In section 3, the robust exponential stable criteria and asymptotical stability conditions are developed. Finally, conclusions are given in section 4.

2   Problem Statements

Consider the uncertain stochastic neural networks described by the following form of a stochastic differential equation:

$$dx(t) = \{-[A + \Delta A(t)]x(t) + [B + \Delta B(t)]f[x(t)]$$

$$+[C + \Delta C(t)]g[x(t)]\}dt + \sigma[x(t)]dw \tag{1}$$

where $x = (x_1, \cdots, x_n) \in R^n$ is the state vector of the neural networks; $A = diag\{a_1, \cdots, a_n\}$ is a diagonal constant matrix with positive entries $a_i > 0$ $(i = 1, \cdots, n)$; $B = (b_{ij})_{n \times n}$ denotes the connection weight matrix among the neurons; $C = diag\{c_1, \cdots, c_n\}$ is the parameter matrix of exogenous disturbance; $\Delta A(t)$, $\Delta B(t)$, $\Delta C(t)$ are time-varying uncertain matrices with appropriate dimensions. $f[x(t)]$ denotes the neuron activation function; $g[x(t)]$ denotes the exogenous disturbance function; $\sigma[x(t)]$ is the noise intensity function denotes stochastic perturbation. $w = (w_1, \ldots, w_m)^T \in R^m$ is an m-dimensional Brownian motion defined on complete probability space $(\Omega, \mathcal{F}, P)$ with a natural filtration $\{\mathcal{F}\}_{t \geq 0}$, and satisfy the following conditions:

$$E\{dt^2\} = 0; \quad E\{dw_i \cdot dt\} = 0; \quad E\{dw_i^2\} = 0, \quad i = 1, \ldots, m;$$

$$E\{dw_i \cdot dw_j\} = 0, \quad i \neq j, \quad i, j = 1, \ldots, m \tag{2}$$

Throughout this paper, some assumptions are given as follows:

Assumption 1: The uncertain matrices $\Delta A(t)$, $\Delta B(t)$, $\Delta C(t)$ satisfy the following norm-bounded conditions:

$$[\Delta A(t), \Delta B(t), \Delta C(t)] = \sum_{i=1}^{s} \sum_{j=1}^{r} E_i \Xi_{ij}(t)[F_{Aj}, F_{Bj}, F_{Cj}] \tag{3}$$

Where E_i, F_{Aj}, F_{Bj}, F_{Cj}, $i = 1, \ldots, s$, $j = 1, \ldots, r$ are known real constant matrices of appropriate dimensions, and

$$\Xi(t) = \begin{bmatrix} \Xi_{11}(t) & \Xi_{12}(t) & \cdots & \Xi_{1s}(t) \\ \Xi_{21}(t) & \Xi_{22}(t) & \cdots & \Xi_{2s}(t) \\ \vdots & \vdots & \ddots & \vdots \\ \Xi_{r1}(t) & \Xi_{r2}(t) & \cdots & \Xi_{rs}(t) \end{bmatrix} \tag{4}$$

is an unknown real time-varying matrix satisfying the

$$\sum_{i=1}^{s}\sum_{j=1}^{r}\left\|\Xi_{ij}(t)\right\|^{2} \le 1 \tag{5}$$

Using the Frobenius norm, (5) can be denoted by $\left\|\Xi(t)\right\|_{F} \le 1$, where the matrix $\overline{\Xi}(t)$ is given as the following form:

$$\overline{\Xi}(t) = \begin{bmatrix} \left\|\Xi_{11}\right\| & \left\|\Xi_{12}\right\| & \cdots & \left\|\Xi_{1s}\right\| \\ \left\|\Xi_{21}\right\| & \left\|\Xi_{22}\right\| & \cdots & \left\|\Xi_{2s}\right\| \\ \vdots & \vdots & \ddots & \vdots \\ \left\|\Xi_{r1}\right\| & \left\|\Xi_{r2}\right\| & \cdots & \left\|\Xi_{rs}\right\| \end{bmatrix} \tag{6}$$

Assumption 2: The smooth functions $f(.)$, $g(.)$ satisfy the Lipschitz conditions. That is there exist the diagonal matrices L_1, L_2, such that

(a). $\left|f[x_1(t)] - f[x_2(t)]\right| \le L_1\left|x_1(t) - x_2(t)\right|$, $f(0) = 0$,

$$f[x(t)] = \{f_1[(x_1(t)], f_2[(x_2(t)], \ldots, f_n[(x_n(t)]\} \tag{7}$$

(b). $\left|g[x_1(t)] - g[x_2(t)]\right| \le L_2\left|x_1(t) - x_2(t)\right|$, $g(0) = 0$,

$$g[x(t)] = \{g_1[(x_1(t)], g_2[(x_2(t)], \ldots, g_n[(x_n(t)]\} \tag{8}$$

Assumption 3: There exists the constant matrix of appropriate dimension H, such that The stochastic perturbation function $\sigma(.)$ satisfies the following condition:

$$Trace\{\sigma[x(t)]\sigma[x(t)]\} \le \left\|Hx(t)\right\|^2 \tag{9}$$

In order to obtain our results, some definitions and lemmas are given, which will be used in the analysis procedure.

Definition 1: The considered stochastic neural network is said to be exponential stable in mean square, if there exist constants $\gamma \ge 1$ and $k > 0$ such that

$$E\{\left\|x(t)\right\|^2\} \le \gamma e^{-2kt} E\{\left\|x(0)\right\|^2\}, \qquad t > 0 \tag{10}$$

Lemma 1: For any real matrices X, Y and positive definite matrix Q with appropriate dimensions such that the following inequality holds:

$$X^T Y + Y^T X \le X^T Q^{-1} X + Y^T Q Y \tag{11}$$

Lemma 2 (Schur Complement lemma): For any positive definite matrices X, Y and symmetric matrix Q with appropriate dimensions such that the LMI

$$\begin{bmatrix} X & Q \\ Q^T & Y \end{bmatrix} > 0 \tag{12}$$

is equivalent to

$$X - QY^{-1}Q^T > 0 \tag{13}$$

3   Main Results

In this section, the sufficient conditions for robust exponential stability of uncertain stochastic neural networks with exogenous disturbance and stochastic perturbation are presented.

Theorem 1: The uncertain stochastic neural network (1) is robust exponential stable if there exist symmetric matrix $P > 0$, and positive constants k, ρ, ε_A, ε_B, ε_C, δ_{Bj}, δ_{Cj} ($j = 1, ..., r$), satisfying the LMIs

(a). $\begin{bmatrix} \delta_{Bj} I & \varepsilon_B F_{Bj}^T \\ \varepsilon_B F_{Bj} & \varepsilon_B I \end{bmatrix} \geq 0$, $j = 1, 2, ..., r$; $\tag{14}$

(b). $\begin{bmatrix} \delta_{Cj} I & \varepsilon_C F_{Cj}^T \\ \varepsilon_C F_{Cj} & \varepsilon_C I \end{bmatrix} \geq 0$, $j = 1, 2, ..., r$; $\tag{15}$

(c). $P \leq \rho I$; $\tag{16}$

(d). $\Omega = \begin{bmatrix} \Omega_{11} & \Omega_{12} & \Omega_{13} & \Omega_{14} & \Omega_{15} \\ \Omega_{21} & \Omega_{22} & 0 & 0 & 0 \\ \Omega_{31} & 0 & \Omega_{33} & 0 & 0 \\ \Omega_{41} & 0 & 0 & \Omega_{44} & 0 \\ \Omega_{51} & 0 & 0 & 0 & \Omega_{55} \end{bmatrix} < 0$ $\tag{17}$

where

$$\Omega_{11} = 2kP - A^T P - PA + L_1^T \Sigma_1 L_1 + L_2^T \Sigma_2 L_2 + \rho H^T H$$

$$+ \sum_{j=1}^{r} \delta_{Bj} L_1^T L_1 + \sum_{j=1}^{r} \delta_{Cj} L_2^T L_2 + \varepsilon_A \sum_{j=1}^{r} F_{Aj}^T F_{Aj},$$

$$\Omega_{12} = \Omega_{21}^T = [PB \quad PC],$$

$$\Omega_{22} = diag\{\Sigma_1, \Sigma_2\}$$

$$\Omega_{13} = \Omega_{31}^T = \left[PE_1^T, PE_2^T, ..., PE_s^T \right],$$

$$\Omega_{33} = diag\{\varepsilon_A I, \varepsilon_A I, ..., \varepsilon_A I\},$$

$$\Omega_{14} = \Omega_{41}^T = \left[PE_1^T, PE_2^T, ..., PE_s^T \right],$$

$$\Omega_{44} = diag\{\varepsilon_B I, \varepsilon_B I, ..., \varepsilon_B I\},$$

$$\Omega_{15} = \Omega_{51}^T = \left[PE_1^T, PE_2^T, ..., PE_s^T \right],$$

$$\Omega_{55} = diag\{\varepsilon_C I, \varepsilon_C I, ..., \varepsilon_C I\}.$$

Proof: Consider the following Lyapunov function

$$V(t) = e^{2kt} x^T(t)Px(t) \tag{18}$$

where P is positive definite matrix with appropriate dimension. By the Ito-differential rule, the derivative of the Lyapunov functional along the trajectory of system (1) is

$$
\begin{aligned}
\mathcal{L}V &= 2ke^{2kt} x^T(t)P\dot{x}(t) + e^{2kt} \dot{x}^T(t)Px(t) + e^{2kt} x^T(t)P\dot{x}(t) \\
&= e^{2kt} \{kx^T(t) - x^T(t)A^T + f^T[x(t)]B^T \\
&\quad + g^T[x(t)]C^T\}Px(t) + e^{2kt} x^T(t)P\{kx(t) \\
&\quad - Ax(t) + Bf[x(t)] + Cg[x(t)]\} \\
&\quad + 2e^{2kt} x^T(t)P\{-\Delta Ax(t) + \Delta Bf[x(t)] + \Delta Cg[x(t)]\} \\
&\quad + e^{2kt} Trace\{\sigma^T[x(t)]P\sigma[x(t)]\}
\end{aligned} \tag{19}
$$

It follows from the Assumption 2 and Lemma 1 that

$$
\begin{aligned}
x^T(t)PBf[x(t)] &+ f^T[x(t)]B^T Px(t) \\
&\leq x^T(t)PB\Sigma_1^{-1}B^T Px(t) + f^T[x(t)]\Sigma_1 f[x(t)] \\
&\leq x^T(t)PB\Sigma_1^{-1}B^T Px(t) + x^T(t)L_1^T\Sigma_1 L_1 x(t)
\end{aligned} \tag{20}
$$

$$
\begin{aligned}
x^T(t)PCg[x(t)] &+ g^T[x(t)]C^T Px(t) \\
&\leq x^T(t)PC\Sigma_2^{-1}C^T Px(t) + g^T[x(t)]\Sigma_2 g[x(t)] \\
&\leq x^T(t)PC\Sigma_2^{-1}C^T Px(t) + x^T(t)L_2^T\Sigma_2 L_2 x(t)
\end{aligned} \tag{21}
$$

$$
\begin{aligned}
-x^T(t)P\Delta Ax(t) &- x^T(t)\Delta A^T Px(t) \\
&\leq \varepsilon_A^{-1}\sum_{i=1}^s x^T(t)PE_i^T E_i Px(t) + \varepsilon_A \sum_{j=1}^r x^T(t)F_{Aj}^T F_{Aj} x(t)
\end{aligned} \tag{22}
$$

From the inequalities (14) and (15), we have

$$x^T(t)P\Delta Bf[x(t)] + f^T[x(t)]\Delta B^T Px(t)$$

$$\leq \varepsilon_B^{-1}\sum_{i=1}^{s} x^T(t)PE_i^T E_i Px(t) + \varepsilon_B \sum_{j=1}^{r} f^T[x(t)]F_{Bj}^T F_{Bj} f[x(t)] \tag{23}$$

$$\leq \varepsilon_B^{-1}\sum_{i=1}^{s} x^T(t)PE_i^T E_i Px(t) + \sum_{j=1}^{r} \delta_{Bj} x^T(t)L_1^T L_1 x(t)$$

$$x^T(t)P\Delta Cg[x(t)] + g^T[x(t)]\Delta C^T Px(t)$$

$$\leq \varepsilon_C^{-1}\sum_{i=1}^{s} x^T(t)PE_i^T E_i Px(t) + \varepsilon_C \sum_{j=1}^{r} g^T[x(t)]F_{Cj}^T F_{Cj} g[x(t)] \tag{24}$$

$$\leq \varepsilon_C^{-1}\sum_{i=1}^{s} x^T(t)PE_i^T E_i Px(t) + \sum_{j=1}^{r} \delta_{Cj} x^T(t)L_2^T L_2 x(t)$$

By Assumption 3 and the inequality (16), we have

$$Trace\{\sigma^T[x(t)]P\sigma[x(t)]\} \leq \rho x^T(t)H^T Hx(t) \tag{25}$$

Substituting (20)-(25) into (19), it can be derived that

$$\mathcal{L}V \leq e^{2kt}\{x^T(t)[2kP - A^T P - PA + PB\Sigma_1^{-1}B^T P + L_1^T\Sigma_1 L_1$$

$$+PC\Sigma_2^{-1}C^T P + L_2^T\Sigma_2 L_2 + \varepsilon_A^{-1}\sum_{i=1}^{s} PE_i^T E_i P + \varepsilon_A \sum_{j=1}^{r} F_{Aj}^T F_{Aj}$$

$$+\varepsilon_B^{-1}\sum_{i=1}^{s} PE_i^T E_i P + \sum_{j=1}^{r} \delta_{Bj} L_1^T L_1 + \varepsilon_C^{-1}\sum_{i=1}^{s} PE_i^T E_i P \tag{26}$$

$$+\sum_{j=1}^{r} \delta_{Cj} L_2^T L_2 + \rho H^T H]x(t)\}$$

$$\leq e^{2kt} x^T(t)\Pi x(t)$$

where

$$\Pi = 2kP - A^T P - PA + L_1^T\Sigma_1 L_1 + L_2^T\Sigma_2 L_2 + PB\Sigma_1^{-1}B^T P$$

$$+PC\Sigma_2^{-1}C^T P + \sum_{j=1}^{r} \delta_{Bj} L_1^T L_1 + \sum_{j=1}^{r} \delta_{Cj} L_2^T L_2 + \rho H^T H$$

$$+\varepsilon_A^{-1}\sum_{i=1}^{s} PE_i^T E_i P + \varepsilon_A \sum_{j=1}^{r} F_{Aj}^T F_{Aj}$$

$$+\varepsilon_B^{-1}\sum_{i=1}^{s} PE_i^T E_i P + \varepsilon_C^{-1}\sum_{i=1}^{s} PE_i^T E_i P$$

From the inequality (17) and Lemma 2, it can be obtained that

$$\Omega < 0 \Leftrightarrow \Pi < 0 \Rightarrow \mathcal{L}V \leq 0 \tag{27}$$

Take the expectation of the Ito differential operator of (18), we have

$$\frac{dE\{V\}}{dt} = E\{\mathscr{L}V\} \le 0 \tag{28}$$

which implies that

$$E\{V(t)\} \le E\{V(0)\} \tag{29}$$

where

$$E\{V(0)\} = E\{x^T(0)Px(0)\} \le \lambda_{Max}(P)E\{\|x(0)\|^2\} \tag{30}$$

On the other hand, from (18) it is easy to verify that

$$0 \le e^{2kt}\lambda_{Min}(P)E\{\|x(t)\|^2\} \le EV(x(t)) \tag{31}$$

Then, we have

$$E\{\|x(t)\|^2\} \le \gamma e^{-2kt}E\{\|x(0)\|^2\} \tag{32}$$

where $\gamma = \lambda_{Max}(P)/\lambda_{Min}(P)$.

From the Definition 1, we can obtain the result that the considered neural network (1) is exponential stable.

This completes the proof of Theorem.   □

Remark 1: In the proof of above theorem, we introduce the exponential factor e^{-2kt} in the Lyapunov function. The following theorem is presented the sufficient condition of the robust asymptotical stable of uncertain stochastic neural network (1), which can be regarded as the special form of theorem 1 in the case of $k = 0$.

Theorem 2: The uncertain stochastic neural network (1) is robust asymptotical stable if there exist symmetric matrix $P > 0$, and positive constants k, ρ, ε_A, ε_B, ε_C, δ_{Bj}, δ_{Cj} ($j = 1, \ldots, r$), satisfying the LMIs

(a). $\begin{bmatrix} \delta_{Bj}I & \varepsilon_B F_{Bj}^T \\ \varepsilon_B F_{Bj} & \varepsilon_B I \end{bmatrix} \ge 0$, $j = 1, 2, \ldots, r$; $\tag{33}$

(b). $\begin{bmatrix} \delta_{Cj}I & \varepsilon_C F_{Cj}^T \\ \varepsilon_C F_{Cj} & \varepsilon_C I \end{bmatrix} \ge 0$, $j = 1, 2, \ldots, r$; $\tag{34}$

(c). $P \le \rho I$; $\tag{35}$

$$(d). \quad \Omega = \begin{bmatrix} \Omega_{11} & \Omega_{12} & \Omega_{13} & \Omega_{14} & \Omega_{15} \\ \Omega_{21} & \Omega_{22} & 0 & 0 & 0 \\ \Omega_{31} & 0 & \Omega_{33} & 0 & 0 \\ \Omega_{41} & 0 & 0 & \Omega_{44} & 0 \\ \Omega_{51} & 0 & 0 & 0 & \Omega_{55} \end{bmatrix} < 0 \tag{36}$$

where

$$\Omega_{11} = -A^T P - PA + L_1^T \Sigma_1 L_1 + L_2^T \Sigma_2 L_2 + \rho H^T H$$

$$+ \sum_{j=1}^{r} \delta_{Bj} L_1^T L_1 + \sum_{j=1}^{r} \delta_{Cj} L_2^T L_2 + \varepsilon_A \sum_{j=1}^{r} F_{Aj}^T F_{Aj} ,$$

$$\Omega_{12} = \Omega_{21}^T = [PB \quad PC],$$

$$\Omega_{22} = diag\{\Sigma_1, \Sigma_2\}$$

$$\Omega_{13} = \Omega_{31}^T = \left[PE_1^T, PE_2^T, ..., PE_s^T \right],$$

$$\Omega_{33} = diag\{\varepsilon_A I, \varepsilon_A I, ..., \varepsilon_A I\},$$

$$\Omega_{14} = \Omega_{41}^T = \left[PE_1^T, PE_2^T, ..., PE_s^T \right],$$

$$\Omega_{44} = diag\{\varepsilon_B I, \varepsilon_B I, ..., \varepsilon_B I\},$$

$$\Omega_{15} = \Omega_{51}^T = \left[PE_1^T, PE_2^T, ..., PE_s^T \right],$$

$$\Omega_{55} = diag\{\varepsilon_C I, \varepsilon_C I, ..., \varepsilon_C I\}.$$

Remark 2: The theorem 1 and theorem 2 give the robust stable criteria of the uncertain stochastic neural network (1). If the consider neural network (1) is free of uncertainties $\Delta A(t)$, $\Delta B(t)$, $\Delta C(t)$, we have the following results.

Theorem 3: The stochastic neural network (1) is exponential stable if there exist symmetric matrix $P > 0$, and positive constants k, ρ, satisfying the LMIs

$$(a). \quad P \le \rho I ; \tag{37}$$

$$(b). \quad \Omega = \begin{bmatrix} \Omega_{11} & PB & PC \\ BP^T & \Sigma_1 & 0 \\ CP^T & 0 & \Sigma_2 \end{bmatrix} < 0 \tag{38}$$

where

$$\Omega_{11} = 2kP - A^T P - PA + L_1^T \Sigma_1 L_1 + L_2^T \Sigma_2 L_2 + \rho H^T H .$$

Theorem 4: The stochastic neural network (1) is asymptotical stable if there exist symmetric matrix $P > 0$, and positive constants k, ρ, satisfying the LMIs

$$(a). \quad P \le \rho I ; \tag{39}$$

$$(b). \quad \Omega = \begin{bmatrix} \Omega_{11} & PB & PC \\ BP^T & \Sigma_1 & 0 \\ CP^T & 0 & \Sigma_2 \end{bmatrix} < 0 \qquad (40)$$

where

$$\Omega_{11} = -A^T P - PA + L_1^T \Sigma_1 L_1 + L_2^T \Sigma_2 L_2 + \rho H^T H$$

4   Conculsions

In this paper, the issue of robust exponential stability analysis for uncertain neural networks with time delay and nonlinear perturbation is investigated. Based on Lyapunov stability theory, the robust stable criteria are given in terms of linear matrix inequality. The proposed approach is more flexible in computation by means of the Matlab-LMI toolbox.

References

[1] Matsuoka, K.: Stability conditions for nonlinear continuous neural networks with asymmetric connection weights. Neural Networks 5, 495–500 (1992)

[2] Qiao, H., Peng, J., Xu, Z.B.: Nonlinear measures: a new approach to exponential stability analysis for Hopfield-type neural networks. IEEE Transactions on NN 12, 360–370 (2001)

[3] Liang, X.B., Wang, J.: An additive diagonal - stability condition for absolute exponential stability of a general class of neural networks. IEEE Transactions CAS-I 48, 1308–1317 (2001)

[4] Forti, M.: Some extensions of a new method to analyze complete stability of neural networks. IEEE Transactions on NN 13, 1230–1238 (2002)

[5] Singh, V.: Global robust stability of delayed neural networks: An LMI approach. IEEE Trans. on CAS II 52, 33–36 (2005)

[6] Liao, X.F., Chen, G., Sanchez, E.N.: LMI-based approach for asymptotically stability analysis of delayed neural networks. IEEE Trans. CAS I 49, 1033–1039 (2002)

[7] Liao, X.F., Chen, G., Sanchez, E.N.: Delay-dependent exponential stability analysis of delayed neural networks: an LMI approach. Neural Networks 15, 855 866 (2002)

Low Computational Complexity Pitch Based VAD for Dynamic Environment in Hearing Aids

Yu-Jui Chen, Cheng-Wen Wei, Yi-Le Meng, and Shyh-Jye Jou

Department of Electronics Engineering & Institute of Electronics, National Chiao
Tung University
1001 University Road, Hsinchu, Taiwan, R.O.C.
chen_3341@163.com

Abstract. This paper presents a low computational complexity and high robust voice activity detection (VAD) algorithm. The algorithm is based on an efficient time-domain pitch detection and harmonic structure discrimination exploiting frequency decomposition by 1/3 octave filter bank defined in ANSI S1.11 standard. In addition, a simple yet efficient phoneme keeper (PK) is adopted for the detection of monosyllable languages, such as Mandarin. Simulation results reveal that the proposed VAD has very robust performance for Mandarin speeches in different environments, even for dynamic SNR (signal to noise ratio) and noise type. Furthermore, in white noise with 0dB SNR, the proposed VAD still has about 90 percent accuracy.

Keywords: Voice Activity Detection, Pitch, Dynamic Noise Environment, Hearing Aids, Mandarin Chinese.

1 Introduction

In hearing aids (HA) design, one of the most important problems is background noise disturbance, because the HA amplifies not only desire signal, but also background noise. The amplified noise will degrades speech quality, intelligibility; moreover, it may damage user's residual hearing. Thus the noise reduction algorithm is essential in hearing aids design.

Under low power and real-time hardware implementation considerations, noise reduction in HA usually adopts spectral subtraction type algorithms [1], i.e. Spectral Subtraction (SS) [2] and Multiband Spectral Subtraction (MBSS) [3]. These algorithms consist of spectral decomposition and noise reduction for noise cancellation and VAD for speech detection and aid of noise power estimation.

For spectral decomposition in HA, in order to reduce computational complexity and fit human hearing perception system (Non-uniform distribution in frequency domain, high resolution in low frequency and low resolution in high frequency,) a filter bank consisting of 18 filters (F22~F39) in 1/3 octave distribution [4] defined by ANSI S1.11 [5] is adopted. This filter bank offers non-uniform decomposition, hence efficiently processing acoustic signal, and being more suitable than FFT for compensation and NR.

VAD plays an important role of spectral subtraction, thereby greatly impacting the NR performance and computational complexity. A high performance VAD has

M. Zhu (Ed.): ICCIC 2011, Part V, CCIS 235, pp. 10–17, 2011.

following characteristics in general: (1) High accuracy- In order to improve the speech quality and intelligibility, (2) Low complexity- under limited battery storage in HAs, the VAD system must be low power to extend the life-time of hearing aids, (3) Robust to dynamic environment- the VAD system should be able to handle the dynamic environment because the background noise environment usually changes quickly in real world.

The traditional VAD usually detects voice based on energy [1], zero crossing rate [6] and entropy [7]. For energy-based method, voice activity is detected if input energy (or a parameter based on energy) is larger than a threshold (can be preset or adaptively updated.) However, this method is very sensitive to dynamic background SNR and noise type. For zero crossing method, which detects voice based on zero crossing rate of each frame, is relatively superior to energy-based method in dynamic SNR. However, it also has performance degradation in low SNR, such as 0dB. For entropy based method, which uses signal variation to discriminate speech, can immune SNR influence compared to the two formal methods. However, its performance still downgrades in non-white environments.

The threshold for voice detection should be adaptively updated to improve detection accuracy. For example, the energy based VAD can update its threshold with estimated noise energy during non-speech frames. However, the noise estimation greatly increases computational complexity (or power consumption,) since it requires a lot of multiplications and storages. In addition, the detection accuracy will also influence noise estimation, and vice versa. Hence, noise estimation in VAD will be a great issue, especially for low power applications.

In this paper we propose a VAD algorithm which detects speech depend on human speech characteristic, pitch and harmonic structure discrimination, instead of SNR or entropy parameters. Because pitch is a special characteristic of speech [8] and is basically independent of noise type and amplitude (assume there is only single speaker and noise is not speech-like,) the VAD can still detect pitch well even the noise spectrum is change drastically from the previous frame. And the noise reduction system can process speech and attenuation noise efficiently with this pitch based VAD. In addition, we also design a phoneme keeper for keeping the continuity of Mandarin Chinese characters and reducing power consumption in implementation.

This paper is organized as follows. Section 2 describes structure of filter bank based hearing aids system. Section 3 describes the structure and design of pitch based VAD algorithm. Section 4 shows the simulation results. Section 5 is the conclusion.

2 The Architecture of Filter Bank Based HAs

Fig 1 is the system architecture of our filter bank based CIC hearing aids. The noise speech is decomposed to 18 subbands by a 1/3 octave analysis filter bank (AFB) by ANSI S1.11 in order to improve design flexibility and match to resolution of human hearing system. Then subband signal is processed by VAD to decide whether the present signal is speech or not, and indicate noise reduction (NR) to provide appropriate process (attenuation for noise and spectral subtraction for speech). Then the enhanced signal is compressed and combined with neighbor subbands into 3 wide dynamic range compensation (WDRC) subbands for user's residual hearing ability protection. Finally, the compressed signal is synthesized synthesis filter bank (SFB) [4].

3   The Pitch Based VAD Algorithm

Fig 2 is the architecture of our pitch based VAD, we develop a pitch based VAD with low computational complexity to improve the efficiency of NR system and make our system robust to dynamic environment.

The VAD system firstly checks if the principle of phoneme keeper (PK) is satisfied. If it does, the VAD process will be skipped and the output of VAD will be set to 1 directly; otherwise, the VAD system will calculate the power of each subband in low frequency. Then uses nonlinear energy operator (NEO) and pitch detector (PD) blocks to decide if present signal is speech or not. These strategies are designed for pitch and harmonic structure discrimination. Finally the VAD uses majority vote (MV) block to filter out the short time peak noise disturbance. The PK block is designed especially for the character of Mandarin Chinese for higher performance.

The function of each subsystem is described as follow:

A.   Resoluble Frequency Subbands Power Calculator (RSPC)
The RSPC, as in (1), is used to calculate the average power , avg_power_Fj, in each subband of low frequency (123Hz~1620Hz) in time domain,

$$avg\_power\_F_j = \frac{1}{20}\sum_k power\_F_j(frame-k), \quad k = 1\sim19 \tag{1}$$

where the *power_Fj* is average power of each frame. The reason of only calculating low frequency subbands power is because the bandwidth of subband is narrow in low frequency but wide in high frequency in 1/3 octave filter bank, pitch and its harmonics are resoluble in low frequency (usually below 1 KHz) and is irresoluble in high frequency (usually above 2 KHz). Besides the sampling rate is much larger in high frequency subbands, so we can reduce huge computational complexity and power consumption if high frequency subbands power calculation is avoided.

B.   Nonliear Energy Operator (NEO) and Pitch Detector (PD)
NEO is a general method in neuron signal processing used to high light the peak of neuron spike for further separating it from noise and DC level. After NEO operation, the spike will be more sharp and higher, and the noise will be lower in time domain [9].

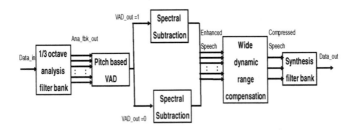

Fig. 1. Architecture of filter bank based digital hearing aid

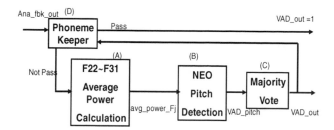

Fig. 2. Architecture and subfunction of the proposed VAD algorithm

In this paper, we apply NEO operator, as in (2), to process the decomposed signal of low frequency subbands (F22~F31) [5] simultaneously in filter bank domain to high light the pitch power in these subbands.

$$
\begin{cases}
SNRN\_F_j = \dfrac{avg\_power\_F_j{}^2}{avg\_power\_F_{j+1}{}^2} \quad , j = 22 \\[2ex]
SNRN\_F_j = \dfrac{avg\_power\_F_j{}^2}{\left(avg\_power\_F_{j-1}\right)\left(avg\_power\_F_{j+1}\right)} \quad , j = 23{\sim}31
\end{cases}
\tag{2}
$$

Because whenever pitch and its harmonics occur, the average power of corresponding subbands will increase quickly (e.g. if pitch occurs at subband F23, whose center frequency is 260Hz. Because the filter bank is 1/3 octave based, the second harmonic will locate at F26 and fourth harmonic will locate at F29. Therefore, the average power of these subbands will become larger than other noise dominated subbands.) Although in some situation, pitch may locate at the overlap range of two neighbor subbands or the third harmonic will locate at the neighbor subband of second or fourth harmonic, causing the power of these neighbor subbands to be close. Fortunately, the NEO is a bi-sides operation, which means it will consider the average power of both side subbands with target subband (e.g. when we calculate the *SNRN_Fj* of subband F22, then we will consider F21 and F23 together.) Therefore, with appropriate threshold value the NEO operator can still separate the pitch dominated subbands from noise dominated subbands in these situations.   So, after NEO operation, the *SNRN_Fj* of pitch dominated subbands will become huge.   And then if one of the PD functions, as in (3), is satisfied, the VAD_pitch will be set to 1; otherwise the VAD_pitch will be set to 0.

$$
\begin{cases}
1, \left(SNRN\_F_j > TH1\right) \cap \left(SNRN\_F_{j+3} > TH2\right) \cap \left(SNRN\_F_{j+6} > TH3\right) \\
\qquad , for \; j = 21 \; or \; 22 \; or \; 23 \\[2ex]
0, \qquad\qquad otherwise
\end{cases}
\tag{3}
$$

Based on the high discernment of NEO operator and the PD function, this pitch based VAD algorithm can provide high performance under dynamic environment. Because it can detect speech without noise spectrum estimation, meaning this algorithm basically has high accuracy independent of SNR value and can detect speech efficiently even in low SNR environment (assuming there is only single speaker.)

C. Majority Vote (MV)
The MV block is used to smooth the output of pitch based VAD to avoid short time peak noise disturbance situation.

D. Phoneme Keeper (PK)
Unlike English language has monosyllable and polysyllable, which means the length of time of each word is usually different, the length of time of each Mandarin Chinese word is almost the same for same speaker. Hence The PK block uses this character to keeper the continuality of Mandarin Chinese word and reduce computation complexity. Whenever the pitch is detected and stable, the output of VAD will be kept at 1 for a span of time which closes to the length of time of single Mandarin Chinese characters. This design can greatly reduce power consumption during speech present.

4   Simulation Result

MATLAB simulation is executed to evaluate the proposed VAD algorithm. The simulation results include the overall accuracy (overall accuracy), the miss rate (the ratio of the situation which speech is present but the output of VAD is 0) and false alarm (the ratio of the situation which speech is absent but the output of VAD is 1.) The three parameters are presented as percentage by comparing the pitch based VAD result with idea VAD result (speech interval is decided by person selection). And the simulation is performed under both stationary noise environment (white, car and factory) and dynamic environment (white change to car, white change to factory.) The simulation uses 27 Mandarin Chinese 2-characters concatenated into four sentences as speech signal and noise provided by NOISE-X 92 database [10] as disturbing noise signal.

A.Stationary Noise Environment Simulation
Table 1 shows the performance of pitch based VAD algorithm under several stationary SNR and three stationary noise environment. As we can see, in stationary white noise the pitch based VAD performs accuracy close to 90%. Because white noise is uniform distribution on the frequency axis, it does not disturb the NEO operator and PD too much. And the pitch also has high performance in stationary car noise, which is almost 87% in all SNR situations. Because car noise is dominated in very low frequency which does not impact the power of low frequency subbands (F22~F31) too much, the PD can detect speech precisely. However, the proposed VAD algorithm only performs 80% accuracy in stationary factory noise because the power of factory noise is mainly located in low frequency subbands which disturb NEO result significantly.

Besides we can observe first the performance of pitch based VAD seems to be uncorrelated to SNR, which means the NEO and PD operation are basically independent of noise power and can perform high accuracy in low SNR environment. Second, the performance of miss rate is usually worse than false alarm because the consonant of speech usually does not has pitch, so the proposed VAD will lost the consonant in the beginning of Mandarin Chinese easily.

B. Dynamic Environment Simulation

Table 2 shows the performance of the proposed VAD algorithm under dynamic environment. Because HA is a mobile device, VAD must be robust to dynamic environment. The dynamic noise means not only amplitude but type of noise of each subband will change suddenly during speech or anytime in test sound file. (e.g. Fig 3 is one of the test sound in dynamic environment. We can observe the noise type changes from white noise into car noise at 5.11 second and changes from car noise into white noise at 10.23 second suddenly.) As shown in Table 2, the proposed VAD algorithm still performs high accuracy in dynamic environment. The result is as good as in stationary noise environment, which means the performance of the proposed pitch based VAD is basically independent of the amplitude and type of non-speech like noise.

Table 1. The Performance of the Proposed VAD in Three Stationary Noise Environment (A) White Noise   (B) Car Noise (C) Factory Noise

Original Segmental SNR (dB)	(A) White Noise (%)		
	Overall Accuracy	Miss Rate	False Alarm
0	88.39	8.11	3.50
3	87.95	7.80	4.25
5	88.21	7.64	4.15
10	89.26	7.12	3.62

Original Segmental SNR (dB)	(B) Car Noise (%)		
	Overall Accuracy	Miss Rate	False Alarm
0	86.67	7.47	5.86
3	86.79	7.01	6.20
5	86.81	6.92	6.27
10	86.03	6.84	7.13

Original Segmental SNR (dB)	(A) Factory Noise (%)		
	Overall Accuracy	Miss Rate	False Alarm
0	77.30	15.14	7.56
3	83.10	9.30	7.60
5	84.24	7.82	7.94
10	85.50	7.20	7.30

Table 2. The Performance of the Proposed VAD in Two Dynamic Environment (A) White to Car Noise (B) Car to Factory Noise

Original Segmental SNR (dB)	(A) White to CAR Noise (%)		
	Overall Accuracy	*Miss Rate*	*False Alarm*
0	88.47	7.52	4.01
3	88.06	7.72	4.22
5	88.30	7.59	4.11
10	89.28	7.10	3.62

Original Segmental SNR (dB)	(B) Car to Factory Noise (%)		
	Overall Accuracy	*Miss Rate*	*False Alarm*
0	83.05	12.62	4.33
3	86.67	8.91	4.42
5	87.47	8.02	4.51
10	89.02	7.25	3.73

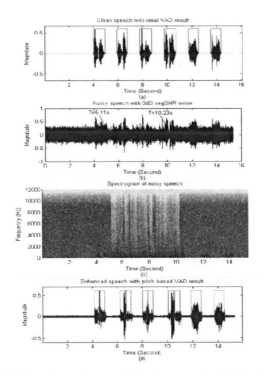

Fig. 3. VAD result in dynamic environment: (a) clean speech with ideal VAD result (b) noisy speech with 0dB segSNR noise (c) spectrogram of noisy speech(d) enhanced speech with pitch based VAD result

According to the simulation result, the proposed VAD algorithm performs high accuracy in both stationary and dynamic environment. The accuracy in stationary white and car noise is close to 90%. However the accuracy better in factory noise is only 80% because the power of factory noise is focus on low frequency subbands disturbing the result of NEO and PD operator. Also, the proposed VAD perform in dynamic environment as good as in stationary noise.

5   Conclusion

In this paper, we propose a time-domain pitch based VAD algorithm based on 1/3 octave filter bank in ANSI S1.11. The algorithm adopts low frequency subbands power calculator (RSPC), nonlinear energy operator (NEO) and majority vote (MV) for efficient pitch detection and harmonic discrimination. Furthermore, the proposed VAD also uses phoneme keeper (PK) for efficient Mandarin detection. The proposed VAD has low computational complexity and high robustness in dynamic background SNR or noise type. Simulations show that the proposed VAD can averagely reach 84.12 percent accuracy for 0dB SNR in three different stationary noise types. For dynamic noise type, the proposed VAD still performs 85.76 percent accuracy. The proposed VAD is well suit for low power and high variation requirements, such as noise reduction in hearing aids.

Acknowledgment. The authors would like to thank Prof. Tai - Shih Chi for the algorithm design suggestions. This work is supported by National Science Council, R. O. C. under Grant NSC98-2220-E-009-008.

References

1. Loizou, P.C.: Speech Enhancement: Theory and Practice. CRC, FL (2007)
2. Boll, S.F.: Suppression of acoustic noise in speech using spectal subtraction. IEEE Trans. Acoust. Speech Signal Process. (1979)
3. Kamath, S., Loizou, P.: A multi-band spectral subtraction method for enhancing speech corrupted by colored noise. In: Proc. IEEE Int. Conf. Acoust. Speech Signal Process. (2002)
4. Chang, J.H., Tsai, K.S., Li, P.C., Young, S.T.: Computer-aided simulation of multi-channel WDRC hearing aids. In: 17th Annual Convention & Expo. of the American Academy of Audiology (2005)
5. Specification for Octave-band and Fractional-octave-band Anolog and Digital Filters, ANSI S1.11-2004, Standards Secretariat Acoustical Society of America (February 2004)
6. Junqua, J.C., Reaves, B., Mak, B.: A study of endpoint detection algorithms in adverse conditions: Incidence on a DTW and HMM recognize. In: Proc. Eurospeech 1991 (1991)
7. Wu, B.F., Wang, K.C.: Robust endpoint detection based on the adaptive band partitioning spectral entropy in adverse environments. IEEE Trans. Speech Audio Process. (September 2005)
8. Wang, D., Brown, G.J.: Computational Auditory Scene Analysis: Principles, Algorithms, and Applications. Wiley/IEEE Press, NJ (2007)
9. Mukhopadhyay, S., Ray, G.C.: A new interpretation of nonlinear energy operator and its efficacy in spike detection. IEEE Trans. Biomed. Eng. 45, 180–187 (1998)
10. Varga, A., Steenneken, H.J.M., Tomlinson, M., Jones, D.: NOISEX-1992 (1992), http://spib.rice.edu/spib/select_noise.html

Design of a Programmable CCI Filter with Attenuation Compensation

YuJing Li[1], LinTao Liu[2], YouHua Wang[1], RuiTao Zhang[1], and RuZhang Li[2]

Sichuan Institute of Solid State Circuits, Chongqing, 400060, P.R. China
Science and Technology on Analog Integrated Circuit Laboratory Chongqing,
400060, P.R. China
Chongqing, China
li_yu22@126.com

Abstract. This paper presents a programmable CCI (Cascaded- integrator- comb) filter with attenuation compensation . A solution to the output attenuation is proposed. The CCI presented in this paper, whose interpolation rate R is 2 to 63, introduces gain according to the 6-bit scale values at the output of the CCI filter. It compensates for the insertion loss based on the value of R. The simulation results indicate that the CCI filter presented in this paper can control its output error within 0.25dB of its full scale.

Keywords: CCI, Error, Programmable.

1 Introduction

Cascaded-integrator-comb filters, also called CCI filters have a shorter delay, for they filter the signal, just where it is necessary, e.g., the notches of the filter are located at multiples of the revolution frequency of the proton beam [1-3]. Meanwhile, CCI filters can be implemented without multiply or divide oprations. As the result, the cascaded-integrator-comb(CCI) filters is one of best methods to implement interpolated operations, and often use to provide upsampling and image rejection in baseband signal chain.

2 Traditional Programmable Cci Filter

At present, in many CCI designs, the rate change R is programmable. The feature of programmable CCI is that it must be designed to handle both the largest and smallest rate changes. The largest rate change will dictate the total bit width of the stages, and the smallest rate change will determine how many bits need to be kept in the last stage. In many CCI designs, the output stage is followed by a shift register that selects the proper bits for transfer to the last output register. An example of such filter, Fig. 1 is a 4th Order filter and offers integer upsampling ratios that are programmable over the range $2 \leq R \leq 63$.

M. Zhu (Ed.): ICCIC 2011, Part V, CCIS 235, pp. 18–23, 2011.
© Springer-Verlag Berlin Heidelberg 2011

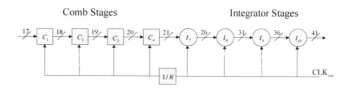

Fig. 1. Traditional CCI filter structure

Fig.1 shows the basic structure of the CIC interpolation filter. The comb section operates at the low sampling rate f_s / R, where R is the integer rate change factor. This section consists of 4 comb stages with a differential delay of one samples per stage. The system function for a single comb stage referenced to the high sampling rate is

$$H_C(Z) = 1 - Z^{-R} \tag{1}$$

The integrator section of CIC filters consists of 4 ideal digital integrator stages operating at the high sampling rate, f_s. Each stage is implemented as a one-pole filter with a unity feedback coefficient. The system function for a single integrator is

$$H_I(Z) = \frac{1}{1 - Z^{-1}} \tag{2}$$

The CCI filters shown in Fig.1 accept 17-bit wide data words as input to the comb stages. However, the output data word can grow to be as large 41 bits wide when an interpolation rate (R) of 63 (the maximum) is employed. This "growth" of the data path width is due to the integrator stages. The output data path width is variable and is a function of both the number of integrator stages in the CCI filter and the value of R chosen. We define that the output of the CCI filter is 14 bits wide. This is not a problem when R=63, because it is just a matter of using the 14 MSB's of the 41-bit output word. However, for lower values of R, fewer and fewer of the MSB's in the 41-bit output word actually carry data. This is because the data path width does not "grow" to a full 41-bits for values of R less than 63. In other words, for R<63 a certain number of the MSB's will carry nothing more than polarity information (a result of the internal sign extension logic).

The number of MSB's that contain only polarity information is completely dependent on the value of R chosen. This suggests the presence of a selector stage to select the appropriate group of 14-bits from the 41-bit output word based on the programmed value of R. Thus, the selector provides a constant 14-bit wide output data path, while still offering full 14-bit dynamic range. The system function together with a worst case input signal are used to evaluate the maximum register growth up to that point. And the growth together with the input register width is used to determine the minimum register width at the jth stage. As the result, the maximum register growth up to the jth stage can be shown to be

$$G_j = \begin{cases} 2^j, & j = 1, 2, ..., N \\ \dfrac{2^{2N-j}(RM)^{j-N}}{R}, & j = N+1, ..., 2N \end{cases} \tag{3}$$

Assuming that the input signal producing this register growth is at the low sampling rate f_s / R. The minimum register width based on this growth is

$$W_j = [B_{in} + \log_2 G_j] \tag{4}$$

As shown in equation(3) and (4) [2-3], the CCI filter architecture results in register growth. Thus, each internal stage of the filter must be designed to accommodate the appropriate growth for that stage. Based on the input word width requirement (17 bits) and the maximum range of upsampling (R=63), the growth requirements for each stage are shown in Fig.1.

3   Cci Filter with Loss

With regard to register growth, we can note that the number of bits at the output of each stage is a function of the largest R that the filter is designed to handle (63, in this case). When values of R less than 63 are chosen, the register growth is not complete. For example, when R = 63, a full 41 bits are used to carry the CCI output signal in the last stage. However, when $54 \leq R \leq 62$, the CCI output signal is carried by less than the full 41-bit range. Instead, the full scale CCI output signal spans less that 100%, but more than 50% of the full 41-bit word. The 14-bit output selector compensates for some of this register growth issue. When an R value is chosen that results in whole bits not being used at the upper end of the range, the 14-bit selector ignores those bits. However, the selector is constrained by the fact that it can only step by whole bit positions (fractional bits are a physical impossibility). Hence, for R values that are an integer power of 2, the signal at the output of the selector spans the full 14-bit range selected.   However, when R is not a power of 2, the signal at the output of the 14-bit selector spans 13+ bits, but not the full 14 bits. This poses a problem, because it represents an inherent loss through the CCI filter for non-power of 2 up-sampling ratios.

Equations(5) to (8) below relates the interpolation rate (R), and CCI attenuation (Loss):

$$W_1 = N\log_2(RM) + Bin \tag{5}$$

W_1 is actual bits of last stage in CCI filter before truncat. And

$$W_2 = W_1 - \lfloor W_1 \rfloor \tag{6}$$

W_2 is fraction part of W_1. And

$$W_3 = \begin{cases} W_2 + (B_{out} - 1) & \lfloor W_1 \rfloor \geq B_{out} - 1 \\ W_2 + \lfloor W_1 \rfloor & \lfloor W_1 \rfloor < B_{out} - 1 \end{cases} \tag{7}$$

W_3 is actual bits of output in CCI filter. So

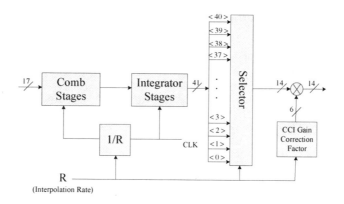

Fig. 2. Modified CCI filter Block Diagram

$$N_{loss} = \frac{2^{W_3}}{2^{B_{out}}} \tag{8}$$

In order to mitigate this insertion loss problem, the 14-bit output selector is followed by a 6 x 14-bit multiplier. Its purpose is to introduce gain at the output of the CCI filter that compensates for the insertion loss based on the value of R. The scalar uses a ROM lookup table that has a one-to-one correspondence with upsampling ratio, R. The structure of modified CCI filter is shown in Fig.2

The table below indicates the appropriate bit of the 41-bit output word (based on the value of R) that corresponds to the MSB of the selector.

Table 1. MSB of the selector

R	Relative MSB
2	20
3	23
4	24
5	26
6	27
7-8	28
9	29
10-11	30
12-13	31
14-16	32
17-19	33
20-22	34
23-26	35
27-32	36
33-38	37
39-45	38
46-53	39
54-63	40

We know that the hexadecimal numbers represent a 6-bit value with the least significant bit weighted as $2^{-5}(0.03125)$, which results in a scale factor between 0 and 1.96875. However, the minimum scale factor that is actually used is 1.00000, which corresponds to a gain of 0dB.

4   Simulation Results

The residual CCI attenuation before compensation and after compensation by the scalar is shown graphically in the following plot Fig3.

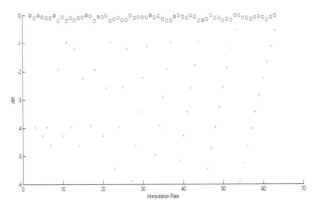

Fig. 3. CCI Scalar Error VS Interpolation Rate

The Cross plot is error of CCI output before compensation. The Circle plot is error of CCI output after compensation.

Fig.4 shows that Input and output of CCI filter for Interpolation Rate of 3, which gain correction factor is 32h.

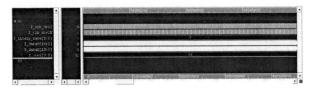

Fig. 4. Input and output of CCI filter at R=3

Fig.5 shows that Input and output of CCI filter for Interpolation Rate of 63, which gain correction factor is 22h.

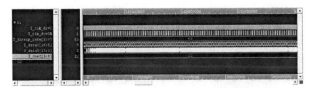

Fig. 5. Input and output of CCI filter at R=63

5 Conclusion

The programmable CCI filter in this paper introduces gain at output of the CCI filter that compensates for the insertion loss. The simulation results indicate that the 6-bit scale values offer sufficient resolution to maintain the CCI output level to within 0.25dB of its full scale potential regardless of the value of R chosen.This design can be applicated in the communication system which is high requirement in scale precision, and have a wide application foreground.

References

[1] Hogenauer, E.B.: An Economical Class of Digital Filters for Decimation and Interpolation. IEEE Transactions on Acoustics, Speech, and Signal Processing assp-29(2) (April 1981)
[2] Schnase, A., Nomura, M., Tamura, F., Yamamoto, M.: Cascaded integrator comb filters with smoothly varying coefficients for reduced delay in synchrotron feedback loops. Physical Review Special Topics - Accelerators and Beam 8, 122001 (2005)
[3] Kwentus, A.Y., Jiang, Z., Wilson Jr., A.N.: Application of filter sharpening to cascaded integrator-comb decimation filters. IEEE Transactions on Signal Processing 45(2) (1997)
[4] Wang, S.-H., Elliot, W.D., Meng, X.: Cascaded integrator comb filter with arbitrary integer decimation value and csaling for unity gain, United States patent US 7,102,548 B1 (September 5, 2006)
[5] GC4016 Multi-Standard Quad DDC Chip Data Sheet, Rev. 1.0, SLWS133A,Texas Instruments (August 27, 2001)
[6] Kwentus, A.Y., Jiang, Z., Wilson, A.N.: Application of filter sharpening to cascaded integrator-comb filters. IEEE Trans. on Signal Process. 45(2) (1997)
[7] Jang, Y.B., Yang, S.J.: Non-recursive cascaded integrator-comb decimation filters with multiple factors. In: Proc. 44th IEEE Midwest Sympo. on Circuits and Systems, Dayton, OH (2001)
[8] Janiszewski, I., Meuth, H., Hoppe, B.: In: Proceedings of SOCC 2004, Santa Clara, CA. IEEE, Piscataway (2004)
[9] Kaiser, J.F., Hamming, R.W.: Sharpening the response of a symmetric nonrecursive filter by multiple use of the same filter. IEEE Trans. on Acoust. Speech Signal Process. ASSP–25(5) (1977)

Application of Risk-Oriented Audit in the Process of Informatization in SMEs of Anhui Province

Li Xia and Liu Qingling

School of Accounting
Anhui University of Finance & Ecnomics
Bengbu, Anhui, 233030, China
li1212@yahoo.cn

Abstract. At present, the informatization construction of Small and Medium-sized Enterprises (SMEs) in Anhui province has embarked on the path of rapid and healthy development. The audit environment that the auditors are faced with is also changing along with it. This will inevitably affect the transition of audit objective, audit object and audit approach, and it also places greater demands on auditors. For this reason, innovations are required in risk-oriented audit of SMEs in order to adapt to the new situation.

Keywords: Risk-oriented Audit, SMEs, Informatization.

As a new audit method, yet an advanced audit concept, modern risk-oriented audit has become a heated topic in the circle of auditing profession. It represents the latest trend of modern audit approach and is an inevitable requirement of social economic development.

As an important force in the development of China's national economy, SMEs should choose modern risk-oriented audit methods emphasizing environmental elements when confronted with the fast-moving market environment. For informatization is a necessary tool of SMEs to accelerate their innovation and transition, SMEs in China are in the process of informatization, and so is Anhui province. Therefore, SMEs should constantly innovate to deal with the new circumstances which informatization brings when they adopt the risk-oriented audit method so as to give full play to its function.

1 Origin and Development of Risk-Oriented Audit

With the rapid progress of technology and constant changing of political and economic environment, contests between enterprises are increasingly intense and the uncertainty of business operation is on the increase which leads to more management's frauds. In order to reveal management's moral hazard behaviors, reduce audit risks and improve audit quality, traditional risk-oriented audit emerges as the times require. The emergence of traditional risk-oriented audit also meets the demand of reducing audit cost and improving audit efficiency. For many disadvantages of past high-risk audit projects in transaction-based auditing and system-based auditing, the cost is always high when analyzing risks, hence traditional risk-oriented audit based on risk

M. Zhu (Ed.): ICCIC 2011, Part V, CCIS 235, pp. 24–29, 2011.

assessment and analysis demonstrates its advantage. It makes great contributions from its first practical use in 1970s to its maturity in 1980s and then to its guidance on audit practices until the middle of 1990s.

However, the business activities continue to be increasingly complex, and the audit environment becomes complicated along with it which highlights the disadvantages of traditional risk-oriented audit. As a result, modern risk-oriented audit whose widespread adoption shows historical inevitability gradually enters the horizon.

Modern risk-oriented audit is a new audit basic approach theoretically based on strategic management theory and system theory. Staring from enterprise strategic analysis, through the basic idea of 'strategic analysis→ operating process analysis→ financial statement residual risk analysis', it closely relates financial statement error risk and enterprise strategic risk and puts forward the concept of analyzing and finding out financial report misstatement at source by the CPAs (Xie Rong, Wu Jianyou, 2004). Modern risk-oriented audit does not exclude basic approach like detailed audit and system-based audit, but rather further develops on that basis. Its emergence and development have certain theoretical foundation and reality condition.

Strategic management theory and system theory provide theoretical foundation to the emergence of modern management audit. The rampant practice of strategic management lays the foundation of modern risk-oriented audit. Strategic management theory argues that the competitive edge and core competence of an enterprise is the core of corporate performance in competitive market. Then, from the perspective of auditing financial statements, the financial risk will be higher if the enterprise is lack of competitive edge and core competence. Hence, auditors should improve the audit quality by studying the risk of the enterprise from a strategic perspective. According to the system theory, the enterprise is an element of the whole society system rather than an isolated subject, and it is influenced by various factors involving politics, economy and culture. The internal financial department belongs in the same system with other departments for there exists countless ties between them. Auditors should place the entity to be audited in the whole economic environment to fully understand its transactions, overall performance and financial position. For the various financial data of the entity to be audited, it's also necessary to find out audit trail with systematic point of view through the articulation between financial data and non-financial data. Modern risk-oriented audit is developed with such theoretical support.

A series of new audit standards released in February 15, 2006 make the development of modern risk-oriented audit in China possible. Included are <Chinese CPA Standards on Auditing No. 1121– understanding the entity to be audited and its environment and then evaluating important error risk>, <Chinese CPA Standards on Auditing No. 1231–procedures implemented in connection with important error risk evaluated>, <Chinese CPA Standards on Auditing No. 1141–consideration for frauds in financial statement auditing>, <Chinese CPA Standards on Auditing No. 1151–communication with management>, <Chinese CPA Standards on Auditing No. 1142–consideration for regulations and laws in financial statement auditing >, etc.

According to the auditing standards, all the audit firms should implement this since January 1, 2007. That is to say, all the audit firms should convert to the auditing pattern of risk-oriented audit. But questionnaire result shows that the implementation rate of small and medium-sized audit firms is incredibly low for they still apply the previous audit pattern. Even large and medium-sized audit firms including those with securities qualification only implement that in listed company auditing and larger clients. Only less than 20 percent of audit firms fully implement the risk-oriented audit (Hang Siyuan, 2008), which is caused by multiple factors such as relevant institutional environment, personnel quality and engineering level.

2 Current Situation of Informatization in SMEs of Anhui Province

The informatization in SMEs is an important means to promote China's economic growth and build a harmonious society, and it's also the inevitable course to the leaping development of industry. The central leading body of the Party and the State Council pay high attention to the informatization in small and medium-sized enterprises. On August 8, 2008, China initiated the 'Small and Medium-sized Enterprise Informatization Project' jointly organized and implemented by National Development and Reform Commission, Ministry of Information Technology and Telecommunications and State Council Informatization Office. The project aims to promote informatization of SMEs, enhance their application level of information technology and modern management level, accelerate technical progress, strengthen market competitive power and foster healthy and consistent development of SMEs. <National Informatization Development Strategy 2006-2020 > indicates that it's imperative to make and issue the guidelines for informatization in SMEs using differentiated guidance and preference support in order to build a public service information platform and promote flexible and diverse electronic commerce activities in SMEs.

The result of China's first SME informatization sample survey shows that 80.4% of China's SMEs have Internet access, 44.2% of which have already applied Internet to informatization. IResearch even predicts that the volume of e-commerce in SMEs can reach 697.5 billion (a comparative growth rate of 60%) and also predicts that the volume of e-commerce in SMEs will maintain a high growth rate at around 50%.

In order to study the informatization construction and its existing problems in SMEs of Anhui province, the former SME Development Authority of Anhui conducted an investigation into 81 SMEs(covering 17 industries) of 17 cities in the second half of year 2005. The designed questionnaire including 8 major terms and 102 minor terms looks into the hardware capacity of SMEs in Anhui, input and construction of informatization, network construction and application system construction. Result shows that the hardware capacity is enjoying rapid growth and the informatization construction has embarked on the path of rapid and healthy development. Questionnaire analysis indicates more than 78% of the SMEs have information functional departments, and the informatization affairs are in the charge of Deputy Manager or Assistant Plant Manager, some with Chief Information Officer (CIO). Additional 38% of the information functional departments are in the charge of department manager and the average fulltime information staff in each enterprise is 9.2.This represents that the operation of informatization falls to real point in respect of formulation and personnel. In addition, more than 80% of the SMEs have made informatization construction plans and three-quarters of them have stable capital investment. All of the enterprises have established informatization management regulations, from the collection; classification and sharing of information resources to the responsibilities of each department in informatization process with explicit and clear rules of awards and penalizations.

Specific to each city, it is somewhat different. As for Hefei City, data shows that the application of informatization technology in SMEs is relatively backward. The users with only several computers and no Local Area Network (LAN) take up 31.43% of the market share while enterprises with LANs that are still in the development phrase of IT infrastructure and simple implementation of ERP and OA account for 37.14% of the share. Enterprises in the initial stage and enterprises with better implementation of ERP respectively take up approximately 17.14% and 14.29%.

3 Implementation of Risk-Oriented Audit in the Process of Informatization in SMEs of Anhui Province

3.1 Coping with More Complicated Environment

Traditional and modern risk-oriented audit both came from the non-informational environment. Although they effectively solved various problems which auditing faced at that time but they are not able to meet the requirements raised by an informational environment. SMEs of Anhui province are developing rapidly on the informatization road with dramatic changes of environmental elements including supervisor mode and business process. For the openness and attack tendency of system and traceless attribute of Internet, audit objective is no longer single audit objective with more complicated environment and increasing uncertainties auditors face.

In this background, internal and external conditions must be taken into consideration when auditors audit the SMEs that are in the process of informatization. Attention should also be paid to the new problems arising from the introduction of software and hardware, information management and construction of Internet and application system. It's necessary to make a comprehensive investigation on all sorts of new factors so as to gradually reduce uncertainties and lower the risk level to the greatest extent. Auditors should make risk estimates through a comprehensive, systematic and associated perspective and accomplish adequate assessment about the risks of material misstatement.

3.2 Transforming the Audit Objective, Object and Scope at the Right Time

The general audit objective in the information environment is 'providing reasonable assurance that the entire business, financial system and the economic activities they carry are free of material misstatement' which is different from the traditional audit goal. For the changes of audit environment and objective, audit object and scope are extended to emphasize more on the impact of electronic commerce, information system, business process and management operating system on audit risks. Meanwhile, the adequate assessment of material misstatement risks becomes the core content of auditing in the informational environment witch is involved with many risks that non-financial factors bring about.

The informational environment has also made the audit object and scope more complicated when risk-oriented audit is conducted in SMEs. In the current environment, data is automatically generated by the computer. In this case, it's meaningless to make verification for the vouchers must agree with each other. Plenty of auditing work is completed out of book. The verification of whether the transaction is authentic should depend more on the specific audit procedures under risk assessment. If any abnormal business activity is found, it's required to expand evidence colleting and get more convincing evidence to certify the transaction is real. The risk-oriented way is comparatively complex.

3.3   Transition of Audit Approach

In the non-informational environment, auditors often start from financial reports and identify the important auditing points before trace the vouchers. But in the informational environment, as long as the auditors grasp the data of the entity to be audited, they can process it to regenerate new account book and reports and compare the new ones with the relative financial data of the enterprise. Through this way, they apply the detailed audit approach focusing on electronic data instead of the approach mainly based on audit sampling.

Moreover, the application of remote tech makes the remote auditing more convenient in the informational environment. Auditors can adopt the approach combining field auditing and remote auditing. According to the previous investigation, the Internet coverage rate in SMEs of Anhui has reached 85% with only 14.5% lack of website or domain name. This creates favorable conditions for remote auditing and improves the audit efficiency.

3.4   Strengthening Audit Personnel Training

Owing to the discrepancy of informatization construction in Anhui's SMEs and the various situations in different cities, it brings out the higher demand for auditors' quality. Auditors from different areas should adapt to the informatization environment in all levels and make high standard professional judgment to improve the audit quality. Auditors should not only be able to concretely analyze various kinds of inner and outer factors, possess abundant knowledge and skills of financial accounting and auditing and have an intimate knowledge of relevant policy, law basis and other basis, but also thoroughly understand computer knowledge and Internet application technology. They should also understand the operation of audit software and relevant theory and practice of information system to help them expertly derive, transform and process electronic data of the entity to be audited. For this reason, it is indispensable to carry out personnel training about informatization.

References

[1] Chen, L., Li, F.: Application of Risk-oriented Audit Judging from the Evolution of Audit Patterns. Contemporary Finance & Economics 6, 122–124 (2006)
[2] Hang, S.: Investigation and Analysis of Application of Risk-oriented Audit in China's Audit Firms, p. 28
[3] Jing, X.: Current Situation and Prospects Analysis of Informatization in China's SMEs, http://www.soft6.com/news/11/114476.html

[4] Liu, Q., Yong, Z.: Research and Analysis Report of Informatization in SMEs of Anhui Province. Anhui SME Online

[5] Li, Y., Jiang, Z., Qiao, S.: Risk-oriented Audit Pattern in The Informational Environment. Productivity Research 8, 143–145 (2008)

[6] Li, Y., Wang, C.: Study on Audit Orientation Pattern in the Informational Environment. Financial and Accounting Communication 5, 18–20 (2007)

[7] Xia, H.: Auditing in the Informatization Conditions. China Management Informationization 4, 67–70 (2006)

[8] Xie, R., Wu, J.: Theoretical Research and Practice of Modern Risk-oriented Audit. Accounting Research 4, 47–51 (2004)

[9] Zhao, J.: Study on Evolution and Application of Risk-oriented Audit. Research on Economics and Management 9, 82–85 (2008)

Design of DRM Middleware Player System in IPTV Based on JSE

Xie Weihua and Huang YaChao

College of computer science of Communication University of China
Beijing , China
xie_huang33@163.com

Abstract. This paper presents a design of DRM middleware player system in IPTV based on JSE. This design aims at the question of poor compatibility and unfriendly UI interface in DRM ,and presents the middleware interface method for IPTV DRM using JSE. This method has perfect extensibility, can be run in different platform, and can be used in different DRM agent terminal based on B/S architecture.

Keywords: DRM, Middleware, JSE , IPTV.

1 Introduction

At moment, the IPTV is applied in many places. The hotpot is the multimedia technology combination with the computer screen, tv screen and mobile screen. The key of this technology is to combine the media play function with the computer platform, tv SetTop box   platform and mobile platform. At the same time, the digital media right protection in three screens should be realized.

The present DRM technology has poor compatibility, and it can not be realized form one platform to another platform. Secondly, the user interface of DRM is not very good, and can not meet the habit to learn DRM and accept it.

On the other hand, middleware system has the good compatibility, and it is easy to be used in the different platform. Moreover it has the friendly interface to user. So user can accept it easily. It is easily developed to a final consolidated standard.

The architecture base on B/S(browser /server) mode and JSE(javascript extension) in IPTV application system is the most popular architecture. This paper aims to design a DRM middleware player system base on JSE in IPTV.

2 IPTV Digital Right Protection Technology

DRM(Digital Right Management) is also called to "content digital right encrypt protection technology ", is used the most broadly   at moment. The DRM technology contains three basic parts: the encrypt content, authentication, and content secret keys. DRM client only gets all of these things, and can normally decrypt stream and start to play. The main framework is as follow:

M. Zhu (Ed.): ICCIC 2011, Part V, CCIS 235, pp. 30–35, 2011.

The content provider sends the media content to the encrypting system, uses the assigned key to encrypt the media according to different algorithms. At the same time, the key also is saved by the corresponding secret managing system , and is visited by authorization system to provide the user authorization and key .

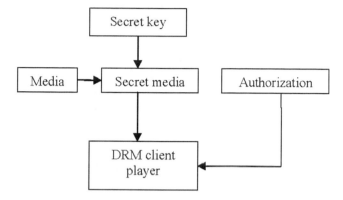

Fig. 1. Framework of DRM player

If the client with DRM ability should. play the encrypted media, it must be authorized. After being authorized, it get the key and use the key to decrypt the media and play it. This play is offline or online with using the stream media playing mode. The popular IPTV system almost use the DRM playing mode based on stream media.

3   Drm Middleware System and Module

A.   Middleware Conception
From the software technology, many application program must run at the different platform with the network situation. All of these pop out the new question to development of software running on the different platform. It mainly require the software system to have obvious compatibility.

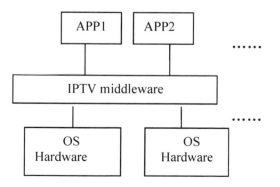

Fig. 2. IPTV middleware structure

In order to resolve the distributed and different system question, The middleware is presented. The middleware locates in the middle of OS software and user's application software and can shield the difference OS and network protocol and provide all kinds of communication method to meet the application program.

In IPTV middleware system, the middleware system combined with JSP(Java Server Pages) and JSE is applied very well. The JSE separates the part of browser core and low layer OS and hardware , and is very important.

B. JSE Application Method

In the IPTV middleware system based on JSP, all kinds of different function can be realized by the web page including the Javascript. The public document object structure including windows, documentation, location etc. structure in Javascript can not meet the function of client terminal and user needs. In order to expend the function of Javascript and improve the ability using the local function in client terminal, it use the JSE to do that in embedded browser.

This customized JSE is not the part of the standard of javascript, so it need for register in order to apply. After that, we can call them when the browser starts. The formation is in:

Object.function(var1,var2...);

The Object is the corresponding entity and aims to the target of special function.

Function is the function item of JSE, its parameter is transferred and translated by browser to do the its special function.

C. DRM Middleware System Module

The middleware system server framework based on stream media in IPTV system is :

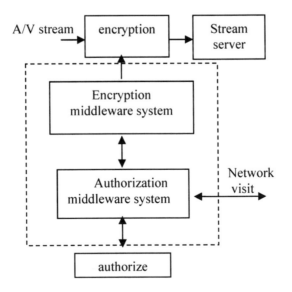

Fig. 3. DRM middleware player server system

A/V(audio/video)stream will be processed with the copyright information.If there are not middleware system, the encryption will be created with the different method in different system such as windows platform and linux platform, so the whole system will be one dependent system platform. When the middleware system join in, it decide how to call the corresponding system resources and is compatible with different platform. At the same time, since it use the architecture JSE with JSP and it can be used in different hardware platform.

So it use the JSE function to realize the request of client terminal and get necessary licence and the key used in the encrypted stream, and complete the authorization.

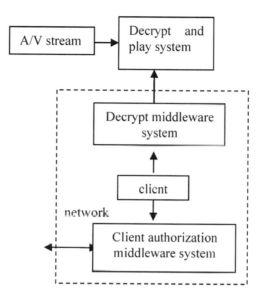

Fig. 4. DRM middleware client system

At receiving part, DRM client will call the authorization middleware functions, and through different system platform communicate with server, and get the licence and key of encrypted stream, then complete authorization work. After that, system call the corresponding decryption middleware system function through different parameters to realize application in different platform and different decryption types. Then it checks the system running state, and sends all of these sate to display terminal in order to realize the UI interface.

4   Design Method of Iptv Drm Middleware Base on Jse

A.   Functions of DRM Player Server Based on Middleware

The most functions are here:

Encryption middleware module.

Its main content is through DRM interaction to create the key of the encrypted stream. This module is called by DRM authorization system.

It contains the main middleware function interface.
- Encryption algorithm selection: encrypt.select()

This interface is to select the special encryption algorithm.
- Encryption algorithm start: encrypt.start()

This interface is to start the encrypting algorithm.
- Encryption key creature: encrypt.keycreate()

This module is to create the key randomly to encrypt the stream.
- Encryption state query: encrypt.getstate()

It get the state of encryption.

User authorization middleware module:
This module is to query the content authorization information and the user licence to decide whether user can be authorized and visit the key creature module to send the key to user.
It contains the main following interface:

- Encryption state query: encrypt.getstate()

It gets the state of encryption
- Authorization system selection: authorize.select()

It selects proper authorization system according different system platform and different encryption system.
- Authorization application: authorize.require()

It uses to receive the application of terminal, and completes the initial work.
- Authorization state query: authorize.getstate()

It gets the state of authorization.
- Licence of authorization get: authorize.requirelicense()

It is used to get the useful licencee,   its licence is used to check the validity of key and the right of user.
- State of licence: authorize.getstatelicense()

It is used to check the state of licence delivery and to judge the expiration of licence.
- Key request: authorize.getauthkey()

It gets the authorization key.

B.   Functions of DRM Client Based on Middleware
Decryption middleware system module:
This module is to receive the key of delivery and to decrypt the media stream.
The main function interface:

- Decryption algorithm selection: decrypt.selcet()

It selects the decryption algorithm with the current of stream and prepares to decrypt it.
- Decryption key getting: decrypt.getdecryptkey()

It get the useful key, and the key will be saved in local or from the network.
- Decryption algorithm start: decrypt.start()

It will start the decryption algorithm.
- Decryption algorithm state request: decrypt.getstate()

It will get the state of decryption algorithm in order to display
The client authorization middleware system.

The main function interface:
- Authorization mode selection: clientauth.select()
it selects the authorization mode, such as the local or network
- Authorization licence mode selected: clientauth.lincenseselect()
It selects the visiting mode of licence, such as local or remote server
- Key save and getting: clientauth.keysave()

It saves the key, it will save in local or remote server.

5   Conclusion

This paper presents a IPTV DRM middleware system based on use, this system uses the popular JSE middleware system method in IPTV system to resolve the question of poor compatibility, difficulty with different platform, unfriendly UI interface. This function interface can be easy to be translate into different client terminal and improve the DRM application.

References

[1] Buyens, K., Michiels, S., Joosen, W.: A Software Architecture to Facilitate the Creation of DRM Systems. In: Consumer Communications and Networking Conference (CCNC 2007), pp. 955–959 (May 10, 2007), doi:10.1109/CCNC.2007.193
[2] Campidoglio, M., Frattolillo, F., Landolfi, F.: The Copyright Protection Problem: Challenges and Suggestions. In: Internet and Web Applications and Services (ICIW 2009), May 24-28, pp. 522–526 (2009), doi:10.1109/ICIW.2009.84
[3] Xie, W., Wang, Y.: Realization of JSE Application Method of IPTV STB. In: Management and Service Science (MASS 2009), September 20-22, pp. 1–3 (2009), doi:10.1109/ICMSS.2009.5300804

A New Scheme for Detecting Faulty Sensor Nodes and Excluding Them from the Network

Shahram Babaei, HamidehJafarian, and AliHosseinalipour

Department of Engineering
Islamic Azad University-Tabriz Branch,Tabriz, Iran
tom.cat@sohu.com

Abstract. Development of wireless communications has provided the possibility of making small, low cost and low power sensors and caused the emerging of wireless sensor networks. Due to low cost sensor nodes and deployment of them in an uncontrolled environment, they are prone to have faults; so it is necessary to detect and locate faulty sensor nodes, and kept them out of the network; unless they can be used as communication nodes. In many cases, the range of failure occurred in the network is so wide and affect many sensor nodes and make common mode failures(CMFs); which multiple sensor nodes fail simultaneously in the same mode due to common reason. In this paper we consider CMF and represent a new fault detection algorithm for wireless sensor networks.

Keywords: component, common mode failure, fault detection, fault recovery, wireless sensor network.

1 Introduction

A wireless sensor network is made of a large number of small sensor nodes with low cost and low power consumption which consist of sensing, data processing, and communication components. Number of these sensor nodes can be very high and their distribution range can be very wide. Sensor nodes can be used in dangerous or inaccessible places. Due to Placement of sensor nodes in an uncontrolled environment, some of sensor nodes are prone to have faults; Fault is an incorrect state of hardware or software that results failure of a component [1]. Factures like environment, design shortage, operation and maintenance errors, phenomena and functional shortage can cause faults. In this paper we centralized on faults which occurred due to environment and phenomena. Sensor nodes even with failure have the ability to send, receive and process information [3]; this reduces the reliability in wireless sensor networks; so it is necessary to detect and locate the faulty sensor nodes, and kept them out of the network. Otherwise, these nodes can be used as communication nodes; which causes disturbance routing, false data gathering and incorrect decisions based on received information [1].

The goal of this paper is to locate the faulty sensor nodes in the wireless sensor networks and keep them out of the network. We propose and evaluate a fault detection algorithm to identify the faulty sensor nodes. Many of the algorithms

M. Zhu (Ed.): ICCIC 2011, Part V, CCIS 235, pp. 36–42, 2011.
© Springer-Verlag Berlin Heidelberg 2011

presented earlier allow the occurrence of common mode failure; this reduces the performance of wireless sensor networks. This paper aims to improve wireless sensor networks with detecting common mode failures.

The paper is organized as follows. We first briefly summarize the related work in Section 2. In section 3 we define the network model. In section 4 common mode failures described. The new algorithm for detecting faulty sensor nodes is proposed in Section 5. Simulation results are reported in Section 6. Finally we conclude our paper in Section 7.

2 Related Work

In this section, we briefly review the related works in the area of fault detection in wireless sensor networks.

In [11] an algorithm is presented for fault detection in wireless sensor networks. This algorithm is simple and has high accuracy to identifying faulty sensors. In this paper they use time redundancy to tolerate transient faults. But this algorithm can not recognize common mode failures.

In [3] Chen has introduced a fault detection algorithm in distributed wireless sensor network. Each sensor node makes a decision based on comparisons between its own sensed data and neighbors' data. Implementation complexity is low and the probability of correct diagnosis is very high. But this algorithm only detects permanent faults; and transient faults in communication that may occur for more nodes are ignored. Also this algorithm can not recognize common mode failures.

A faulty sensor identification algorithm is proposed in [4]. This algorithm is scalable and the computational overhead is low. To identify faulty sensor nodes each node compares its own data with neighbors' median data to determine its own status. If there was too much difference so the node is likely to be faulty. It also needs expensive GPS or other techniques to realize sensors' physical location.

In [7] a sensor fault detection scheme is proposed. In this work they used a record table, which records the history of all local decisions during the fusion process. Each node sends its local decision to the fusion center at every time step; the fusion center can identify a faulty sensor node by determining whether its behavior is very different from the others.

In [10], a failure detection scheme called MANNA is proposed for WSNs using management architecture. The manager has global view of the network and can perform complex tasks that would not be possible inside the network. However, this approach is too expensive because it requires an external manager to do tasks and communicates between nodes.

3 Network Model

We assume a square heterogeneous WSN witch has three kinds of sensor nodes named L, H and K; number of H and K sensors are less than L sensors and have larger transition range, better computational capabilities, high memory and higher energy than L sensor nodes.[2] All sensor nodes are randomly deployed in network. The sensor network is divided into several small cells, and neighbor cells are filled with different colors, white or black, as illustrated in Figure1.

■ L sensor Node   ■ H sensor Node   ■ K Sensor Nodes
■ Base Station

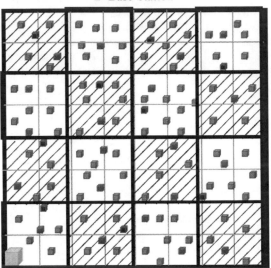

Fig. 1. A heterogeneous WSN

Each sensor node has the ability to identify its neighbors located within its transmission range; where each node S_i broadcasts a hello signal to its neighbors. All nodes which are located at the transmission range of the sensor and received hello signal, send back acknowledge signal. The main idea is that data sensed by a fault-free sensor node and its neighbors should be similar.

4 Common Mode Failure

Data sensed by two neighboring sensor nodes are similar when both of them are fault-free or both of them, because of a common reason, are faulty. In many cases, a failure domain is big enough to affect a lot of sensors and makes their data similar. This called common mode failure (CMF). Common mode failures are simultaneous failures due to a common cause in which multiple elements fail simultaneously in the same mode. In many fault detection algorithms of wireless sensor networks each sensor node S_i compares its sensed data with neighbors data, sensed at the same time. If at last half of the neighbors had the same data with node S_i, this node will be determined as fault-free; and broadcasts its status to neighbor nodes. In CMFs, faulty sensor nodes recognize as fault-free because of common mode of failures; this reduces the reliability in wireless sensor networks.

For example consider conditions that lightning in a part of wireless sensor network causes the electrical overhead on the electrical circuits and makes CMFs. Figure2 shows an example of wireless sensor network with CMF, where black and yellow sensor nodes are faulty and yellow nodes have CMF; Other nodes are fault-free. If we use fault detection algorithms presented in [2, 3], all of the yellow sensor nodes, because of CMF and similar sensed data at the same time, are going to detected as fault-free.

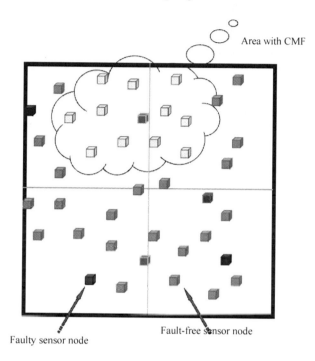

Area with CMF

Faulty sensor node

Fault-free sensor node

Fig. 2. wireless sensor network with CMF

5   The Chessboard Clustering Scheme for Detecting

In this section we introduce our fault detection scheme. We use Chessboard Clustering Scheme shown in figure1, for clustering our network. Transient faults could occur for most normal sensor nodes in sensor reading and internodes communication. So we use time redundancy to get over transient faults. Our algorithm has tow phases. The first phase starts after deployment sensor nodes in the area. Nodes have the ability to identify that if they are placed in black or white cells. At first only H-sensors in white cells and all L-sensors are active. All H-sensors in black cells turn themselves off. Clusters are formed around the H-sensors in white cells and each L-sensor selects the closest H-sensor as the cluster head. L-sensors close to these H-sensors become critical nodes. Then all active sensor nodes sense data and each H sensor located in white cells determines its likely status based on data comparison with one-hop member nodes after q different times comparison. After that all K sensors wake up, sense data, send data to all active H sensors placed in its transmission range and again sleep. According to data received from K sensors each active H sensor determines its deterministic status as GD or FT. In this step if H sensor's likely status and deterministic status be different from each other (it means

LG and FT or LF and GD) then critical H sensor wake all H sensors in black cells located in its transition range up; these H sensors wake up, sense data, send data to critical H sensor and again sleep. According to data received from H sensors critical H sensor determines its final status. Then all H sensors with deterministic status broadcast their status to members in parallel. The second phase starts when H-sensors in white cells determine as faulty or run out of energy. In these cases critical H sensor sends a request message to closest H sensor located in black cells and wakes it up. Then activated H sensor sends back a response message to critical node and this node turn itself and all faulty members off. Activated H sensor forms a different set of cluster in the network; so previous critical L-sensors become non-critical, and previous non-critical L-sensors become critical nodes. Because critical sensor nodes consume much more energy than other sensor nodes, switching CHs and making new clusters balances the energy consumption among L-sensors, and increases the network lifetime. However because faulty sensor nodes turn themselves off so these nodes can not be used as communication nodes again and this increases reliability of WSN. Because all K sensor nodes are sleep and only wake up for a very short time, the reliability of data sensed by these nodes are very high and data comparison between these nodes and H sensors determines CMFs occurred in network.

6 Simulation Results

We used MATLAB to perform our simulation. We used 1000 L-sensor nodes, 40 H-sensor and 20 K-sensor nodes in this simulation. All nodes are randomly deployed in a square region of size $100*100$ unit. Sensor nodes are randomly chosen to be faulty with probabilities of 0.05, 0.10, 0.15, 0.20, 0.25, and 0.30, respectively. We used the two metrics Detection Accuracy (DA) and False Alarm Rate (FAR) to evaluate our algorithm; where DA is defined as the ratio of the number of faulty
    sensor nodes detected to the total number of faulty sensors and FAR is the ratio of the number of fault-free sensor nodes diagnosed as faulty to the total number of fault-free sensor nodes. Figure3 and Figure4 shows DA and FAR for this simulation. Simulation results show that our fault detection algorithm achieves high detection accuracy and low false alarm rate even with a large set of faulty sensor nodes.

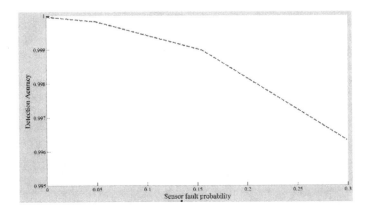

Fig. 3. DA with average 10 members for each CH

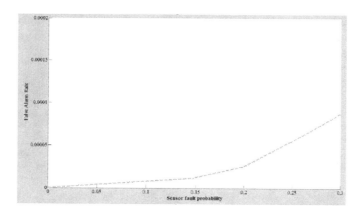

Fig. 4. FAR with average 10 members for each CH

7 Conclusion

In this paper we proposed a faulty sensor detection technique based on Chessboard Clustering Scheme where each CH identifies its own status to be either" good" or" faulty", after two or three times competition, and then broadcast its deterministic status to its members. Our proposed algorithm decreases power consumption and increases network life time. Because K-sensors are always slept and wake up only for a short time, so their sensed data are going to be correct with 99%. So the reliability of determined status bye these nodes are very high. We have simulated our proposed algorithm with MATLAB under different number of faulty sensor nodes in the same area. Our simulation results show that the DA is over 99% and FAR is as low as 0 when 30% sensor nodes are faulty. Simulation results support that our proposed algorithm can have a high detection accuracy and low false alarm rate with a large number of faulty sensor nodes existing in the network.

References

[1] Akyildiz, I.F., Su, W., Sankarasubramaniam, Y., Cyirci, E.: Wireless sensor networks: a survey. Computer Networks 38(4), 393–422 (2002)
[2] Yarvis, M., Kushalnagar, N., Singh, N., et al.: Exploiting heterogeneity in sensor networks. In: Proceedings of the IEEE INFOCOM 2005, Miami, FL (March 2005)
[3] Lee, M., Choi, Y.: Fault detection of wireless sensor networks. Computer Communications 31, 3469–3475 (2008)
[4] Ding, M., Chen, D., Xing, K., Cheng, X.: Localized fault-tolerant event boundary detection in sensor networks. In: IEEE Infocom, pp. 902–913 (2005)
[5] Koushanfar, F., Potkonjak, M., Sangiovanni-Vincentelli, A.: On-line Fault Detection of Sensor Measurements. Sensors. Proceedings of IEEE 2, 974–979 (2003)
[6] Ruiz, L.B., Siqueira, I.G., Oliveira, L.B., Wong, H.C., Nogueira, J.M.S., Loureiro, A.A.F.: Fault management in event-driven wireless sensor networks. In: MSWiM 2004, Venezia, Italy, October 4-6 (2004)

[7] Shrestha, A., Xing, L.D., Liu, H.: Modeling and evaluating the reliability of wireless sensor networks. In: Proceedings of Annual Reliability and Maintainability Symposium, Orlando, Florida, USA, January 22-25, pp. 186–191 (2007)

[8] Edwards, G.T., Watson, I.A.: A Study of Common Mode Failures, SRD-R-146, UK Atomic Energy Authority, Safety and Relia. Dir. (1979)

[9] Luo, X., Dong, M., Huang, Y.: On distributed fault-tolerant detection in wireless sensor networks. IEEE Transactions on Computers 55(1), 58–70 (2006)

[10] Yu, M., Mokhtar, H., Merabti, M.: Fault management in wireless sensor networks. IEEE Wireless Communications, 13–19 (2007)

[11] Chen, J., Kher, S., Somani, A.: Distributed fault detection of wireless sensor networks. In: Proceedings of 2006 Workshop DIWANS, pp. 65–72 (2006)

Integrated OLAP Architecture in Harbor Logistics

Xixu Fu, Xizhang Gong, Kaijun Wu, Shu Zhang, and Dongming Pan

Institute of Information and Education Technology
Shanghai Ocean University
Shanghai, China
XIN_WANG33@163.COM

Abstract. Information technology enhanced logistics in a great extent in today's environment. OLAP and decision support technologies can help enterprises improve their logistics chain greatly. However, enterprise level decision support can hardly provide enough supports in interenteprize affairs and large scale decisions. In harbor areas, collaborations of enterprises are important. An overall OLAP architecture can benefit the collaborations greatly as well as provide a better way to manage the enterprises. Such an overall architecture is advanced in this paper. Security and data warehousing is analyzed as well.

Keywords: Harbor Logistics, OLAP, Data Warehouse, Decision Support, Global Architecture.

1 Introduction

Information becomes more and more important in logistics industry today. Many information system have been designed for logistics management [1]. The whole logistics process can be adapted by related system seamlessly. These systems enhanced the whole logistic management both in efficiency and accuracy. It's hard to handle logistics without information systems.

Data warehouse and OLAP systems [4] become important when data is sufficient. OLAP systems can provide the global status and trends for management. With provided information, decision makers can design better strategies for the organize. OLAP systems needs great amount of data to provide accurate prediction. Data warehouse can extract and provide mass data for decision support process.

OLAP and data warehouse have been implemented for logistics in enterprise level in some [3]. Decision support systems also applied in logistics industry for better decision efficiency [4]. These system enhanced the management in logistics enterprises.

In a harbor city, logistics is one of the most important industries. Transportation is the main task of a harbor city in the logistic chain. Information technology have been implemented in every procedure in harbor logistics industry. From RFID [5] to ERP systems [6], mass data can be generated for analyze.

OLAP and decision support technologies can be applied in harbor logistics systems. However, as a center of transportation, enterprises may not have full logistic process from producing to sales. Focus on transportation can greatly improve the

M. Zhu (Ed.): ICCIC 2011, Part V, CCIS 235, pp. 43–49, 2011.
© Springer-Verlag Berlin Heidelberg 2011

efficiency and profit of enterprises. Collaborations become important for enterprises and global government decision. Since collaborations are important, enterprise level OLAP system can't be sufficient for such a region.

In this paper, global architecture is advanced for logistics industry in harbor cities and regions. First, related works about OLAP and logistic information systems reanalyzed. Then, a model of OLTP data flow in harbor region is set up. Based on the analysis of OLTP systems, data warehousing and OLAP model is designed. After that, distributed decision and hierarchical security is described. Finally, overall architecture is described and analyzed.

2 Related Works and Motivation

A. Devices and Systems for HarborLogistics

Many systems have been implemented in logistics industry [7]. RFID [5] system can provide identifications for goods. Transportation systems such as NAVIS and COSMOS have been applied to manage the transportation process. Computers and intelligent instruments have been implemented in most enterprises in logistics industry [8]. At enterprise level, ERP [1] systems have been implemented widely in logistic industry. These systems produced large amount of data for potential analysis.

B. Data Warehouse and OLAP

OLAP [2] methods analyze large amount data and provide statistical views and predictions for decision support. To find patterns from data, large amount of data is needed.

Data warehousing technology [2] provides a better way to store and search large amount of data than traditional database systems. Data warehouse provide large and integrated data source for online analytical process and enhance the efficiency of OLAP. Bell [9] also advanced some methods to update views in data warehouse over different schemas.

C. OLAP and Decision Support Systems in Logistics

Some OLAP systems [4] have been applied in logistics industry and improved the efficiency of management and logistics chain. Ho [3] advanced an infrastructure for logistics enterprise. The infrastructure can adapt for logistics work flow seamlessly. However, since transportation is the main task of a harbor city in the logistic chain, many enterprises don't implement full logistics work flow.

Cooperation become more and more important in harbor logistic industry [7]. Government also need a decision support system based on logistics data. A global OLAP can be important to provide such decision supports.

3 Data Flow in Harbor Logistics

A typical harbor logistics chain in an enterprise mainly include producing, warehousing, transportation and selling. Related management process including fiancé, device management, OA and so on. Typical data flow in a full logistics chain can be shown in Fig. 1.

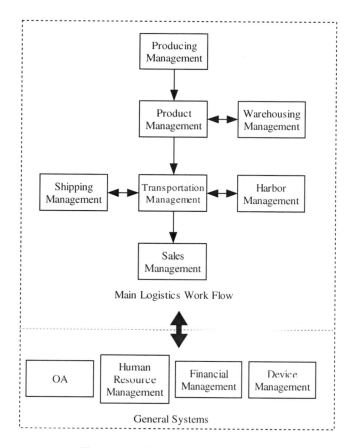

Fig. 1. Data Flow in Full Logistic Chain

As shown in Fig. 1, data flow from producing management system to sales management system and constitutes the main work flow of logistics chain. Management system of warehousing, shipping and harbor needs to exchange data with production management and transportation management systems. General systems such as OA and financial systems exchange data with all systems in the main work flow.

Information about entities such as products, staff and warehouses links the logistic chain management process together.

With the data flow of harbor logistics, OLAP systems and architecture can be designed for the whole logistics chain.

4   Global Olap Architecture

A.   Integrate Devices and Data Flow

There are many different devices and systems in logistics enterprises. These systems and devices should be integrated in the architecture as shown in Fig. 2.

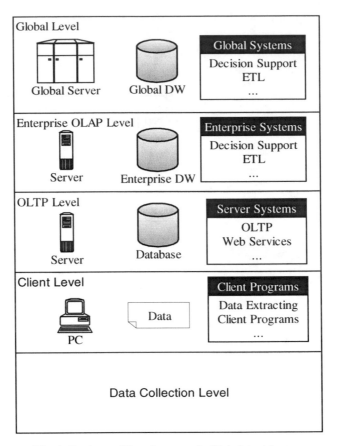

Fig. 2. Device and Data Integrate in Global Architecture

As shown in Fig. 2, devices and systems are divided into five layers in the architecture. The first level consists of data collection devices such as RFID cards and card readers. No system run on these devices, they only provide the function of raw data collection. The second is client level which run client programs. Data can be extracted from lower level by clients to OLTP database. The third level is the OLTP level which consists of Servers and databases. Server programs and web services are provided in this level. The fourth level is enterprise OLAP level. Enterprise OLAP and decision support systems run on this level. Data warehouses are needed for enterprises in this level. The top level is the global decision support level. In this level, government and decision makers can run global decision support functions with the global data warehouse.

Integration of systems needs uniqueness and integrity of data. To extract data from lower level to higher level, ETL systems must be setup to deal with heterogeneous data. Fortunately, RFID technology provides unique identification for products, which is the most important information in the logistics data flow. Other information can also be standardized or distinct by adding enterprise identification. Because the similarity and standard in logistics industry, data integrity can be well preserved in the whole global OLAP architecture.

B. Data Warehousing and OLAP

A typical architecture with OLAP is shown in Fig. 3. Many themes such as production and warehousing can be concerned in such OLAP system.

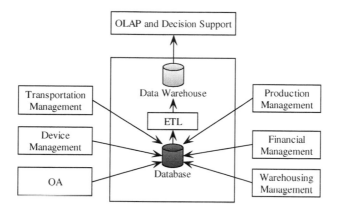

Fig. 3. Typical OLAP Architecture in Logistics Enterprise

As shown in Fig. 3, many fact tables should be created in correspond data warehouse. A galaxy schema should be applied in the design of data warehouse in enterprise.

To setup a global OLAP structure, themes can be selected from the union of all themes in enterprise OLAP systems. Fact tables should be created according themes. Data should be all data in the selected themes from all the enterprises. Let F_i be the set of fact tables in the ith enterprise, F be the set of fact tables in the global system. F can be shown as (1).

$$F = \bigcup_{i=1}^{n} F_i \qquad (1)$$

For this reason, global level data warehouse should be created using galaxy schema. Fact tables should be selected from fact tables in enterprise level data warehouses as needed. Data should be extracted from enterprise data warehouses.

C. Distributed Decision Support and Security

The whole global architecture and data exchange can be shown in Fig. 4. As shown in the figure, enterprises deal with daily transactions with OLTP systems. Transaction data can be extracted from OLTP database to enterprise data warehouse. Enterprise decision support systems create reports for decision makers to support decisions in enterprises. Global ETL programs extract needed transaction data directly from enterprise level data warehouses and provide precise global and enterprise level decision support information for government. Some information can be shared for enterprises to enhance collaboration though web services.

Global architecture demands higher in security both in system level and privilege level as well as providing better efficiency.

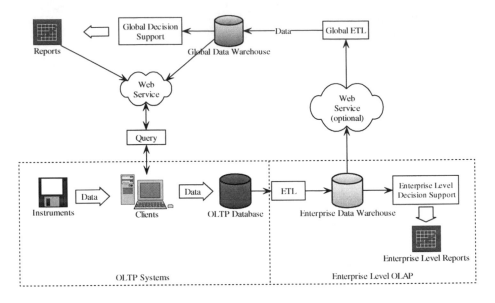

Fig. 4. Information Exchange Between .Enterprise Level and Globle Level

At system level, different systems can be implemented in enterprises. Enterprises need to set their own security policies. It's not wise enough to open the global writing privilege to enterprise users. Since transaction data can be converted to symbols, enterprises can convert data to XML format and provided them though web services. Some enterprise can also provide views for data extracting for convenience if policy of security permits.

At privilege level, security must be strictly set. Enterprise users can only get results within their privileges from web services. Government should keep their privilege in a secure way.

5   Results and Conclusion

Fig 5. shows the average time consuming in different affairs in a harbor region before and after the implementation of global OLAP architecture.

As shown in Fig. 5, time consuming in government and collaborate affairs dropped sharply after the implementation of global architecture. Efficiency within enterprises improved too with global decision support.

Implementation of global OLAP architecture in harbor logistics chain enhanced the collaboration among logistics enterprises and provided more decision support information for logistics enterprises. Government get global decision supports and global decisions can be carried out more efficiently. For the reason standardization of data format, information systems become more efficiency too. In a word, global OLAP architecture enhanced logistics industry in harbor regions in great extent.

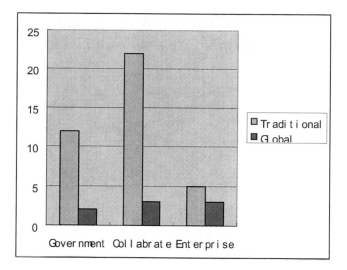

Fig. 5. Average Time Cosuming using traditional and global OLAP

Acknowledgment. This work is supported by social science project with contract numbered A-0211-09-0309, thanks for their supporting. Thank Xizhang Gong for the help given in project as the communication author.

References

[1] Barbosa, D.H., Musetti, M.A.: Logistics information systems adoption: an empirical investigation in Brazil. Industrial Management & Data Systems 110(5-6), 787–804 (2010)

[2] Inmon, W.H.: Building the Data Warehouse. John Wiley & Sons Incorporated, Hoboken (1993)

[3] Gts, H., et al.: An intelligent information infrastructure to support the streamlining of integrated logistics workflow. Expert Systems 21(3), 123–137 (2004)

[4] Ho, G.T.S., et al.: A hybrid intelligent system to enhance logistics workflow: an OLAP-based GA approach. International Journal of Computer Integrated Manufacturing 19(1), 69–78 (2006)

[5] Song, T., et al.: Design and Performance Analysis of Emulator for Standard Conformance Test of Active RFID. ETRI Journal 31(4), 376–386

[6] Glenn, P., Andrew, G.: The importance of knowledge management for ERP systems. International Journal of Logistics-Research and Applications 11(6), 427–441

[7] Klassen, R.D., Vachon, S.: Collaboration and evaluation in the supply chain: the impact on plant-level environmental investment. Production and Operations Management 12, 336–352 (2003)

[8] Ding, P., Lin, D.H., Sheng, H.Y.: Digital City Shanghai: Concepts, Foundations, and Current State. In: van den Besselaar, P., Koizumi, S. (eds.) Digital Cities 2003. LNCS, vol. 3081, pp. 141–165. Springer, Heidelberg (2005)

[9] Leung, C.K.-S., Lee, W.: Efficient Update of Data Warehouse Views with Generalised Referential Integrity Differential Files. In: Bell, D.A., Hong, J. (eds.) BNCOD 2006. LNCS, vol. 4042, pp. 199–211. Springer, Heidelberg (2006)

Innovative Education Practice of Heat Transfer Based on Constructivism Instructional Model

Li Xuemei and Ding Lixing[*]

Institute of Built Environment and Control,
Zhongkai University of Agriculture and Engineering, Guangzhou, China 510225
huangkai356@163.com

Abstract. Under the instruction of constructivism, this paper presents an innovative, interactive and independent instructional model based on innovative experiments. This advanced instructional model aims at cultivating students not only to grasp and use knowledge or skills but to discover problems and solve them in an active way, and to learn how to learn. Innovative experiment based on constructivism instructional model cultivates the students to become good adaptive learners. Innovative experiment helps students not only master knowledge or skills but also discover problems and solve them in an active way, and to learn how to learn. Innovative experiment is proved to be effective through students' feedbacks. Results show that innovative experiment creates an environment in which teachers enjoy teaching and students enjoy learning and thus makes happy education possible.

Keywords: innovative education practice, heat transfer, constructivism, model.

1 Introduction

With the rapid development of science and technology, better educational environment are provided for both learners and teachers. Innovative education attracts more and more interests. Learning theories and educational models also experience great changes in China. Much research has been done on this field. Modern educational technology enhances the education ability and efficiency, changes the traditional education model, students' study style and knowledge acquiring way. Modern educational technology plays an active role in increasing learning and teaching efficiency [1].

New demands of society for graduates have stimulated the development of education. Nowadays in China quality-oriented education and students' all-around development are advocated. To achieve this, the concept of education should be changed. Education should be oriented to: training specialized persons of educational technology at various levels for our country, carrying on the research and establishment of the theory of educational technological courses, exploring and applying various kinds of educational technology and having a try for the industrialization of new advanced educational technology [2-4].Researches show that even students who score well on tests are not competent in solving real-life or practical problems outside the classroom[2]. To solve this problem, one solution is to cultivate the students to become

---

[*] Corresponding author.

M. Zhu (Ed.): ICCIC 2011, Part V, CCIS 235, pp. 50–55, 2011.
© Springer-Verlag Berlin Heidelberg 2011

good adaptive learners. The traditional teacher-oriented, textbook guided educational model should be reformed. Based on advanced constructivism, a new instructional model is designed to stimulate students' learning interest and efficiency. In general, the instructional model is characterized by independence, innovation and interaction. The advanced instructional model aims at improving learner's capacity of independent learning, seeking information, choosing useful information, cooperating, and creating [4]. It is a challenge to the teachers' leading position in the education. Teachers' function transits to organizer and advisor instead of authority [4]. Transitioning a teacher from a leader role to more of a guidance position, would overall help the Chinese students gain the learning method.

Heat transfer is the science that deals with the energy transfer between material bodies as a result of temperature difference [5]. It is normally required in chemical and mechanical engineering and is recommended for electrical engineering students as well [5]. The innovative education of Heat Transfer is essential to stimulate students' learning enthusiasm, developing their creativity, collaboration, practicing skill, innate ability and personality. To achieve this, we design innovative experiments to cultivate the students to become good adaptive learners through collaborative learning. Innovative experiments are helpful to cultivate students not only to grasp and use knowledge or skills but to discover problems and solve them in an active way, to adapt to environment and to learn how to learn. [1]

Under the instruction of constructivism, this paper presents an innovative, interactive and independent instructional model based on innovative experiments. This advanced instructional model aims at cultivating students not only to grasp and use knowledge or skills but to discover problems and solve them in an active way, and to learn how to learn. Innovative education practice of Heat Transfer was performed for Thermal Energy and Power Engineering students at the Zhongkai University of Agriculture and Technology.

2 Constructivism Instructional Model

In the middle of the 20th century, the idea that knowledge is constructed through social collaboration shows up in the theories of Piaget, Bruner, and Vygotsky [6].Constructivism is in sharp contrast to behaviorism. Constructivism is a philosophy of learning founded on the premise that, by reflecting on our experiences, we construct our own understanding of the world we live in. Each of us generates our own "rules" and "mental models," which we use to make sense of our experiences. Learning, therefore, is simply the process of adjusting our mental models to accommodate new experiences. There are several guiding principles of constructivism: Learning is a search for meaning. Therefore, learning must start with the issues around which students are actively trying to construct meaning. Meaning requires understanding wholes as well as parts. And parts must be understood in the context of wholes. Therefore, the learning process focuses on primary concepts, not isolated facts. In order to teach well, we must understand the mental models that students use to perceive the world and the assumptions they make to support those models. The purpose of learning is for an individual to construct his or her own meaning, not just memorize the "right" answers and regurgitate someone else's meaning. Since education is inherently interdisciplinary, the only valuable way to measure learning is to make the assessment part of the learning process, ensuring it provides students with information on the quality of their learning.[6-7]

Curriculum--Constructivism calls for the elimination of a standardized curriculum. Instead, it promotes using curricula customized to the students' prior knowledge. Also, it emphasizes hands-on problem solving.

Instruction--Under the theory of constructivism, educators focus on making connections between facts and fostering new understanding in students. Instructors tailor their teaching strategies to student responses and encourage students to analyze, interpret, and predict information. Teachers also rely heavily on open-ended questions and promote extensive dialogue among students.

Assessment--Constructivism calls for the elimination of grades and standardized testing. Instead, assessment becomes part of the learning process so that students play a larger role in judging their own progress.

With the rapid development of computer science and popularization of internet, students have easy access to information and resources. The learning environment changes a lot. The key factors that influence the educational process include learner, teacher, task and environment. The influencing factors of learning process interact together. Teachers choose tasks suitable for learners. Learners interpret tasks in their individual way.

Task means anything that learners are given to do in the learning process. Teachers select or design tasks according to certain purpose. Learners attempt to implement the task through a series of cognitive activities. A good constructivist task should be both purposeful and meaningful. That is, it aims at training learners' skill as well as cultivating their self-learning ability.

Learning environment plays an important role in shaping the learning process. By providing learners with appropriate learning environment, learners learn how to learn and develop their all-around quality. Constructivism instructional model views that learning environment greatly affects the learning activity.

Constructivism instructional model presents that educational process is composed of the following six procedures: Create situation according to the learning/teaching target, seek and explore information independently, cooperation and communication with teachers, question creation, teacher instruction and conduction, student seeking solution independently, improvement of student capacity of practice and innovation, education evaluation[6-7]. Students learn learning method instead of knowledge from teachers. Education should not focus on teaching knowledge to students but to cultivate student's ability to further study, solving problem independently, creation, collaboration, personality. These abilities are required to be successful in career. What's more, the curriculum setting may be adaptable according to personal interest or strong suit. The curriculum setting should be suitable for cultivating graduates' competence in job-hunting. In a word, education technology should be career-oriented and aims at developing creativity, practicing skill, innate ability and personality instead of just imparting knowledge.

Constructivism instructional model views learning as a self-regulatory process of actively constructing new understanding from learner's learning experience and collaboration with others. One of the most important characteristics of constructivism instructional model is that the learner occupies the most central position.

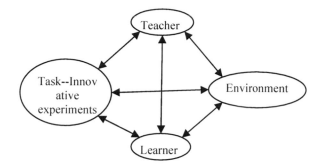

Fig. 1. Constructivism instructional model

3   Innovative Experiment of Heat Transfer

In Heat Transfer, heat exchangers if of great importance. Students learn that heat exchangers are devices that provide thermal energy between fluids at different temperatures through a wall. The primary modes of heat transfer are conduction and convection [4]. Different types of heat exchangers have different performances. The performances of heat exchangers are important in the field of heat transfer, especially in Thermal Energy and Power Engineering Major. For this reason, we present the Heat Exchanger Comprehensive Experiment based on constructivism instructional model.

Tasks are carried out through collaboration among teammates. The students search in the internet for the relative knowledge, design their experiment before then do it. During this process, engineering skills like creativity, teamwork, designing and problem solving are cultivated. Collaborative learning takes place in student groups through problem-based learning which stimulate students' learning interest. It can help students see the real nature of what they learn in the classroom.

During the task, the students have to implement different control functionalities in successive steps of increasing complexity. Innovative design process includes constructing different types of heat exchangers, including double-tube heat exchanger, shell & tube heat exchanger and spiral plate heat exchanger, by connecting the flow tube themselves in group. By changing the flow pass, parallel or counter flow is constructed for double-tube heat exchanger, shell & tube heat exchanger and spiral plate heat exchanger seperately. Then, the performances of heat exchangers are measured by experiments. After the experiment, students compare the performances of different types of heat exchangers. The comparison of performances of different types of heat exchangers helps students to master heat transfer knowledge and understand it furthermore.

This process can provide the students with all-around practice. Figure 2 and figure 3 shows the innovative experiment instrument---Heat Exchanger Comprehensive Experimental Platform, manufactured by Shanghai Lŭlan Limited Copomany.

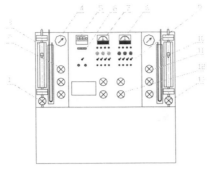

Fig. 2. Innovative Experiment Instrument (A)

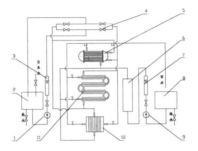

Fig. 3. Innovative Experiment Instrument (B)

4   Evaluation

A total of 126 students participated in the experiment. Students learn to provide creative solution to given problems in an interdisciplinary approach with emphasis on heat transfer. In general, groups of seven or eight members work best. Larger groups decrease each member's opportunity to participate actively. Smaller group makes students felt the task too heavy and difficult. During carrying out the group work task, group members communicate with teammates about what action has each member taken that was helpful for the group and what action could each member take to make the group even better. At the end of the project, students completed a brief evaluation form on the effectiveness of the group and its members. The form includes items about the group's overall accomplishments, the student's own role, and suggestions for changes in future group work. Students also filled in a questionnaire about their feelings and suggesting of the project. The group work was graded according to both the final group product and the individual contribution. Assessment becomes part of the learning process so that students play a larger role in judging their own progress.

Feedbacks from the questionnaire indicate students enjoy collaborative learning and thus make enjoyable education possible. Students not only grasp and use knowledge or skills but learn to discover problems and solve them in an active way, to adapt to environment. Results indicate that their creativity, collaboration, practicing skill, innate ability and personality increase a lot, which will contribute to their competence in job-hunting as well as success in future career.

5 Conclusion

New demands of society for graduates challenge tradition educational method. To achieve this, one effective way is to cultivate the students to become good adaptive learners through innovative experiment based on constructivism instructional model. Innovative experiment helps students not only master knowledge or skills but also discover problems and solve them in an active way, and to learn how to learn. Innovative experiment is proved to be effective through students' feedbacks. Results show that innovative experiment creates an environment in which teachers enjoy teaching and students enjoy learning and thus makes happy education possible.

References

1. Zou, X., Jiang, L.: On Development of Modern Educational Technology in China. Journal of Sichuan Teachers College (3), 59–62 (2005)
2. Liu, G.: Applying Modern Educational Technology Establish the Instructional Model of Independence, Interaction and Innovation. Modern Educational Technology 13(6), 55–59 (2003)
3. Qin, J., Shan, M., Tang, X.: Affect of Modern Education Technology on Teachers' Leading Position. Modern Educational Technology 16(4), 74–76 (2006)
4. Ding, L., Li, X., Lǔ, J.-h.: Construct Innovative Laboratory, Promote Quality-oriented Education. In: 2008 International Workshop on Education Technology and Training & 2008 International Workshop on Geoscience and Remote Sensing, pp. 115–118 (2008)
5. Holman, J.P.: Heat Transfer, 9th edn. China Machine Process, Beijing (2005)
6. Newby, et al.: Instructional Technology for Teaching and Learning. Prentice Hall, Englewood Cliffs (1996)
7. Bostock, S.: Constructivism in mass higher education: a case study. British Journal of Educational Technology 29(3), 225–245 (1998)

Research of Identity Metasystem Based Authentication Mechanism in SOA

Jun Hao Wen[1], Peng Li[1], Hai Jun Ren[2], and Fang Fang Tang[1]

[1] Department of Computer Science and Technology
Chongqing University, Chongqing, China
[2] School of Software Engineering
Chongqing University, Chongqing, China
tang6854@yeah.net

Abstract. To solve the confusion of the identity supply and management in the identity based authentication in SOA, we proposed a authentication mechanism based on identity metasystem which is suitable for SOA on the basic of some key technologies research on SOA and identity meta system. The authentication mechanism uses WCF to implement SOA and transmit identity and uses WCS-based identity supply mechanism to integrate different identifies between services of SOA. Compared with traditional authentication methods, the new proposed method based on modified identity metasystem can provide security, extensible and loosely-coupled authentication architecture for SOA.

Keywords: SOA, Identity metasystem, WCF, WCS, Authentication.

1   Introduction

With the development of information technology, SOA (Service-Oriented Architecture) is widely used as an architecture of enterprise application integration. In the SOA based system, authentication is the most important as the first checkpoint of security [1]. Current authentications: The method using password and username is so simple that can't ensure the security; Cookie share across domain method transfers identity through HTTP redirect but there is security problems of cookie itself[2]; Microsoft's Passport is a good solution but only rely on Microsoft identity[3]; PKI (Public Key Infrastructure) based method has powerful security but too complex and high cost[4]; Liberty Authentication requires federation account to mapping local accounts but can't support customer defined authentications[5]; The new method based on WS-Security supports authentication between web services but it can't suitable for the SOA based system[6]. In order to find a kind of uniform authentication mechanism, enterprises such as Microsoft, IBM, propose identity metasystem which can provide uniform identity provide mechanism [7]. In this paper, we propose authentication mechanism based on identity metasystem suitable for SOA which combine WS-Security based authentication mechanism.

M. Zhu (Ed.): ICCIC 2011, Part V, CCIS 235, pp. 56–63, 2011.

2 Research of Identity Metasystem Framework

2.1 Framework of Traditional Identity Metasystem.

Identity metasystem[8,9] defines the mechanism to make use different digital identity in different platform and applications, identity metasystem is a kind of abstract identity layer which is an indirection layer of all the other identity systems. The digital identity of a subject is represented by a set of claim which is provided by the identity provider through the safe and verifiable method. The statements are packaged in security tokens which can transmit breaking through the limits of processes and machinery. As shown in Fig. 1 there are three major roles in traditional identity metasystem.

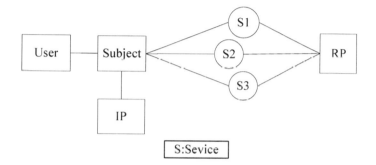

Fig. 1. Architecture of Identity Metasystem

① Subject: The object which makes statement.

Subject can be identified by the statement of the individual, can be a single user, it can be a company or organization. In authentication, subject is the object to be authenticated.

② Identity Provider (IP): Release a digital ID.

Identity provider can be provided with the identity of organizations or units of qualifications or it can be the user themselves (identity issued by a self-issued identity, the user of personal identity have all permissions).

③ Relying Party (RP): Some who needs identity.

3 Identity Metasystem Framework Base on WCF and WCS.

In order to meet the needs of authentication in SOA architecture we modify the traditional metasystem, propose identity metasystem based on WCF (Windows Communication Foundation)[10,11] and WCS (Windows CardSpace), Implement the identity metasystem clients and services of relying party (RP) using WCF; Using WCS as the Identity Selector and using the WCS provide a mechanism for identification, the architecture of identity metasystem based on WCF and WCS is shown in Fig. 2.

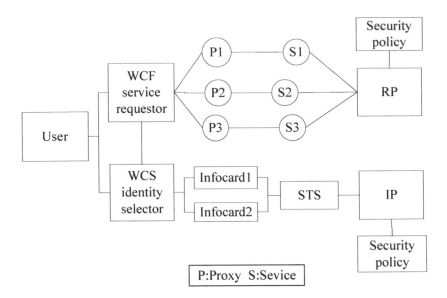

Fig. 2. Architecture of Identity Metasystem based on WCF and WCS

As Shown in Fig. 2, the identity metasystem architecture based on WCF and WCS, includes User, WCF service requestor and the proxy ,RP and security policy, WCS selector and information cards, IP and security token service component . Communication is finished through a proxy between the service requestor and the relying party service. WCF service requestor in the request as well as physical presence here, when the need for identity selectors need to call for information WCS identity card selection and the information card contains information about the identity provider. Their own identity provider has its own security policy, defines your own format and supported by a statement token type generated by a security token service entities and to request the security token is returned to the WCS identity selector.

4   Research of Identity Metasystem Based Authentication Mechanism in SOA

4.1   Authentication Process of Traditional Identity Metasystem.

In identity metasystem, user is the center of architecture. The transfer of security token from IP to RP needs the user's authorization. There are maybe other kinds of communication but the transfer of identity information must under the user's control which is the basic rule of identity metasystem.

Indeed, what the user should do is to get a security token from some IP and sending it to RP. The simple description is as follow:

① User A is asked to produce his identity.
② User A selects a IP.
③ IP sends the right security token to A.
④ User A sends the security token to RP

5   Research of Security Mechinasm base on WCF

The communication of traditional identity metasystem is based on web service which stands to SOAP and XML but the security is not enough for the open of XML and SOAP.WCF has some improve in security communication and the configuration of security is loosely coupled which is useful to the SOA architecture. The security transfer architecture of WCF is shown as Fig. 3.

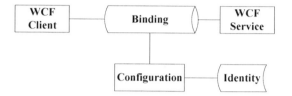

Fig. 3. Security Transfer of WCF Service

The format configuration and transfer type of security token is contracted by binding between WCF client and service. WCF decouple the business logic and the security configuration, the configuration XML files is shown as follow.

```
<wsFederationHttpBinding>
<binding name-"cardspaceFederatedBinding">
<security mode="Message">
<message algorithmSuite="Basic128"
issuedTokenType="
urn:oasis:names:tc:SAML:1.0:assertion"
issuedKeyType="SymmetricKey">
<add claimType=
"http://schemas.xmlsoap.org/ws/2005/05
/identity/claims/emailaddress" />
</claimTypeRequirements>...</wsFederationHttpBindi
ng>
```

Research of Authentication Mechanism in Identity Metasystem based on WCF and WCS.

The traditional identity metasystem provides a reference model which is as simple as possible; meanwhile the traditional identity metasystem is the abstract level identity provides architecture which can't meet all the needs of authentication in SOA based system. So, it is necessary to provide some new type of authentication method based on identity metasystem.

In the research, we propose WCF and WCS based identity matasystem which combine the traditional identity matasystem authentication process and WCF based communication method and WCS based identity selection mechanism, the detail of the process is shown as Fig. 4.

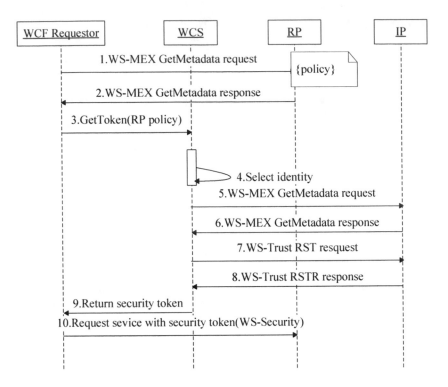

Fig. 4. Authentication Sequence of Identity Metasystem based on WCF and WCS

As shown in Fig. 4, in SOA architecture, when the WCF client makes a request to a service in RP, RP needs the client shows its identity. The messages are transferred between service requestor, identity selector, RP and IP by the time sequence.

The procedure of WCF and WCS based identity metasystem is shown as follow:

1.   When client requests a service using WCF, WCF needs request the policy of RP by a WS-MEX request.
2.   RP responses to the client and returns the policy.
3.   WCF calls for GetToken() method and start the WCS selector.
4.   User agrees the showing of the token and shows the "Choose a card" dialog when user choose a card, WCS can know the IP from the metadata of the selected card.
5.   WCS requests the security policy of IP by a WS-MEX request.
6.   IP sends the security policy to WCS by a WS-MEX response.
7.   WCS then sends a WS-Trust request to STS of IP to get the target RP security token.
8.   IP/STS validate the user certificate and send the security token to WCS.
9.   The security token of IP is sent to client.

10. WCF client then sends a request with security token to RP, RP then decrypts the token and if user is valid the requested web service will be accessed.

6 Anaysis of Trust Relationship

In this paper, we extend the 3-parts trust relationship to 4-parts which adds identity selector WCF between IP and Client. The 4-parts trust relationship is shown as Fig. 5.

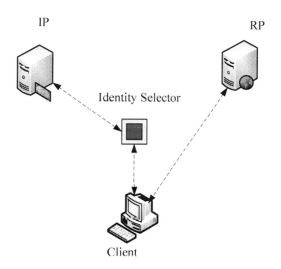

Fig. 5. Trust Relationship of Identity Metasystem

The traditional 3-parts relationship is easy to extend because the loose relationship between RP and IP. In identity metasystem the trust relationship of each other is mutual and is not only between IP and RP. The foundational protocols are simple and flexible; the whole architecture is manageable and extendible. All of mentioned above make the extension more easily. The modified architecture we proposed thanks to the flexible feature of identity metasystem.

7 Comparison

Comparing with traditional authentication method using username and password, the authentication using WCF and WCS based identity metasystem has great advantages on architecture and identity provide method and more suitable to the SOA based system application .The comparison detail is shown in Table 1.

From Table 1 we can analyze that the authentication method based on WCF and WCS based identity metasystem has the advantage on identity provide type, system architecture, service communication, compatibility, expandability and security.

Table 1. Comparison of the Authentication Types

Items	Username/Password	WCF and WCS based Identity Metasystem
Identity Provide	confusion	uniform
Archtecture	close coupled	loose coupled
Communication	SOAP	WCF
Compatibility	NO	YES
Security	password attack	WCF security binding
Expandability	HARD	EASY

8 Summary

In order to solve the confusion problem of identity provide and management, after the research of SOA related technology and identity metasystem, we proposed identity metasystem based authentication mechanism suitable for SOA. Through research and analysis the identity metasystem and authentication mechanism based on WCF and WCS, combined the security mechanism of WCF and identity selection mechanism of WCS, the new authentication method we proposed can meet the requirement of SOA application environment. Of course, SOA architecture is still in the development stage, we will pay more attention to the cross-domain authentication problem in SOA and make the authentication in SOA more robust.

Acknowledgment. This work is supported by the Fundamental Research Funds for the Central Universities Project No. CDJZR10090001 and Supported by the Fundamental Research Funds for the Central Universities Project No.CDJXS11181161 and Supported by Natural Science Foundation Project of CQ CSTC2010BB2244 and Supported by the Fundamental Research Funds for Central Universities Project No. CDJRC 10090002.

References

1. Yau, S.S.: Privacy, Security, Risk and Trust in Service-oriented Environments. In: 2009 International Conference on Computational Science and Engineering, CSE (2009)
2. Pujolle, G., Serhrouchni, A., Ayadi, I.: Secure session management with cookies. In: Communications and Signal Processing on Information (ICICS 2009), pp. 1–6 (2009)
3. Oppliger, R.: Microsoft. Net Passport: a security analysis. Computer 36(7), 29–35 (2003)
4. Zhang, X., Song, M., Song, J.: A Solution of Electronic Authentication Services Based on PKI for Enabling e-Business. In: IEEE International Conference on e-Business Engineering, pp. 431–436 (2009)
5. Krishnamurthi, G.: Using the Liberty Alliance Architecture to Secure IP-level Handovers. In: First International Conference on Communication System Software and Middleware, pp. 1–10 (2006)

6. Liu, W.-j., Pang, T., Qu, H.: The Research on the Application of WS-Security Signature Flow Middleware Based on SOA. In: International Conference on Management and Service Science, pp. 1–3 (2009)
7. Fumiko, S., Yumi, Y.: Generic Security Policy Transformation Framework for WS-Security. In: IEEE International Conference on Web Services (2009)
8. Hoang, L.N., Pekka Laitinen, N., Asokan: Secure roaming with identity metasystems. In: IDtrust 2008: Proceedings of the 7th Symposium on Identity and Trust on the Internet, vol. 283(1), pp. 36–47 (2008)
9. McLaughlin, L.: What Microsoft's identity metasystem means to developers. IEEE Software 23(1), 108–111 (2006)
10. McMurtry, C., Mercuri, M., Watling, N., Winkler, M.: Windows Communication Foundation Unleashed. Sams Publishing, New York (2009)
11. Lowy, J.: Programming WCF Services. O'Reilly Publishing, New York (2008)

Practice and Exploration of College-Enterprise Cooperation on Major Establishment

Guohong and Liuxiaoning

Department of Architectural Engineering, Henan Polytechnic Institute, Nanyang, China
ning7542@163.com

Abstract. College-enterprise cooperation and working-schooling combination are the only way to be taken for higher vocational colleges. Department of Architectural Engineering of Henan Polytechnic Institute has innovated upon the talents training mode "Expert + Enterprise, Employment + Entrepreneurship", which explores "2+0.5+0.5" flexible talents training mode and focuses on deep-level cooperation between college and enterprise through practices of college-enterprise cooperation in many years. Furthermore, the department has established a "Teaching, Learning and Practicing Integration" platform through the completion of actual production tasks assigned by the enterprise and the studio teaching mode. Teachers are able to realize production-teaching integration and work-study combination through technical service and combination of practical theory and practice.

Keywords: College-Enterprise Cooperation, Working-Schooling Alternation, Technical Service.

1 Reforming Talents Training Mode through College-Enterprise Cooperation

1.1 Practice of "Expert + Enterprise, Employment + Entrepreneurship" Talents Training Mode

The talents training mode "Expert+Enterprise, Employment+Entrepreneurship" is that formed through practice and exploration of college-university cooperation for about ten years by Architectural Decoration Engineering Technical Major of our department, featuring distinctive industrial feature and college characteristics. The core of this talents training mode lies in the deep integration and interaction of "Expert+Enterprise, Employment+Entrepreneurship" during the training process. It can be summarized as follows: to establish the major relying on enterprise; relying on the major to create enterprise; to promote employment by strengthening the major; joining the enterprise to establish business.

Relying on the enterprise to establish the major with order class as the platform. Cultivation should be implemented through the cooperation with Beijing Dongyi Risheng•Nanyang Harbor Decoration Company, while establishing "Harbor Design Class" to cultivate talents urgently required by the enterprises. Moreover, both college and enterprises should join the discussion about talents training plan, course system, and etc.. Experts and technical personnel from enterprises are employed to undertake

M. Zhu (Ed.): ICCIC 2011, Part V, CCIS 235, pp. 64–68, 2011.

the post of part-time teacher, take part in curriculum construction and undertake teaching tasks. In this way, a good effect has been achieved, and a talent sharing model has been formed based on mutual benefits and college-enterprise part-time employment. Meanwhile, teachers from the Institute are arranged to participate in production practice of the enterprises on schedule, so as to cultivate a teacher team specialized in both theoretic teaching ability and practical exercising capacity.

Relying on the major to create enterprise and construct the platform for business establishment. Based on specialized technical advantages of the Institute, college and teachers of the major jointly contributed to establish Nanyang Jianianhua Decoration Co., Ltd., which focuses on technological development and technical service according to the requirements of modern enterprise system. Professional teachers undertake the technical tasks of the enterprise. The experimental training room of the Institute serves as the support for technical support and development of the enterprise. The teaching forms of working-schooling combination such as practice on real topic, project drive and field teaching are implemented through the combination of specialized teaching and practice in enterprises. Students rely on the enterprises to conduct field training, work placement, and find a job. Excellent students rely on the brand, technology and capital of the enterprises to establish their own business. Jianianhua Decoration Co., Ltd. has constructed a favorable platform for students to establish business. Currently, there are already three students who have established their own branches.

The Institute and enterprises jointly developed "Three-in-One" course system. Relying on college-enterprise cooperation and joint development, a "Three Three in One" course system integrating working-schooling combination, accomplishment expansion and innovative incubation with occupational accomplishment cultivation as the core has been constructed in "Expert + Enterprise, Employment + Entrepreneurship" talents training mode. Based on college-enterprise cooperation, it is required to deeply analyzes the requirements of the post, make a conclusion on typical work tasks, implement learning area or project course development, and carry out teaching organization in semesters and stages; to bring accomplishment expansion education to talents training plan through the whole process of talents training; to systematize innovative incubation education and combine with talents training process to enhance the coherence and durability of business establishment education and improve business establishment level.

1.2 "2+0.5+0.5" Flexible Talents Training Mode Practice

According to actual production conditions of the enterprises, and the best practice experiences of other colleges and universities, a reform was intensified by the engineering surveying and mapping department of the Institute to implement the flexible talents training mode "2+0.5+0.5" in the form of "Working-Schooling Alteration", in which, "2" refers to two-phase professional study at school (the first academic year and the fourth and fifth semesters, or the first academic year and the third and fifth semester); the first "0.5" refers to the practices in enterprises sponsored by school; and the second "0.5" refers to the internship program sponsored by enterprises in the sixth semester. The flexible talents training mode "2+0.5+0.5" is characterized by the alteration of two-phase study at school and two-phase practices in enterprises, especially targeted at realizing the goal of strengthening the occupational ability and professional accomplishment of students through the "0.5+0.5", namely participation in social practices in enterprises and "Work-study Combination", and finally the goal of "Training by practice" by way of integrating practice and professional education would be achieved.

As considering enterprise and school, technology and skill, accomplishment and ability, a multi-dimensional curriculum system has been established for the major to integrate and develop modular program courses based on common surveying and mapping instruments, with focus on operation & maintenance of surveying instruments, as well as processing, analysis and application of surveying and mapping data. A curriculum system with theory and practice integration corresponding to modular courses has been established based on the three phases of basic skill training, construction of position competence and promotion of comprehensive abilities. Finally, the talent training mode is characterized by co-training between school and enterprise, co-development of quality education and occupational ability, as well as flexible combination of school education and enterprise practice.

2 Focusing on Deep Collage-Enterprise Cooperation, Building a Platform of "Teaching, Learning and Practicing Integration", and Strengthening the Training of Students' Professional Skills

2.1 Undertaking of Actual Production Tasks through College-Enterprise Cooperation

The surveying and mapping department of the Institute had paid more attention to the establishment of deep cooperation with enterprises at the beginning. The emphasis is placed on signing long-term agreements on instrument procurement, maintenance, operation, undertaking production tasks from those enterprises with more businesses and strong technology, and establishing economic interest community, in order to guarantee a smooth development of college-enterprise cooperation. For example, cooperation agreements on undertaking part of production tasks had been signed between the surveying and mapping department of the Institute and Nanyang Three-dimensional Surveying and Mapping Co., Ltd., and Nanyang Chunyang Surveying and Mapping Co., Ltd., and a platform of teaching, learning and practicing integration was also established. In 2008, a cadastral survey in Huangchuan, Xinyang City assigned by Nanyang Chunyang Surveying and Mapping Co., Ltd. was completed by students majored in surveying and mapping of the Institute as well as another cadastral survey in Zhenping, Nanyang City assigned by Nanyang Three-dimensional Surveying and Mapping Co., Ltd. in 2009. Through these two practices in several months, students were enabled to learn the production process and business standards of enterprises, and their practical operational abilities had also been greatly improved. More importantly, students were provided with opportunities to conduct independent operations, explore and learn to solve problems, and train students' abilities to identify, analyze and solve problems. Some of the tasks have not been learned by the students before, but through the process of "do first - then know - redo" and implementation of the cycle of "practice - learning - re-practice", "learning in practice" and "practice in learning" were truly realized, and students were trained to take the initiative to study rather than to passively study. Consequently, the self-construction of occupational ability and professional accomplishment of students were achieved and improved gradually [2].

2.2 Studio Teaching Mode

Student decoration design studio has been constructed jointly by the Institute, enterprise and students in the architectural decoration major of our department to launch working-schooling combination courses internally and undertake actual work tasks from enterprises externally. The studio is operated through the combination of teacher supervision and student independent management in order to construct a platform which combines class teaching and enterprise task, thus realizing the goal of "learning in practice" and "practice in learning". Taking the studio as the platform and project as the carrier, the production tasks are introduced from the enterprises in a proper timing to conduct project teaching as referring to the operation flow of the enterprises. Through the studio, students have successfully completed a batch of medium and large engineering projects including Yaoshan Hotel, Tanghe Electric Power Bureau and Tianquan Bathing Center, thus enormously improving the practical ability of the students and creating profits for enterprises, so as to realize college-enterprise win-win situation. The studio teaching mode changes the traditional practice of "Teacher Lecturing and Students Listening" and emphasizes working-schooling combination characterized by the integrated system of "Theory-Practice-Work".

3 Actively Launching Technical Services and Realizing Win-win Situation and Joint Development of College and Enterprise

In the Department of Agricultural Engineering, over 75% of teachers are specialized in both theoretic teaching ability and practical exercising capacity. Those with the titles of supervision engineer, construction cost engineer, architect and the work experience in enterprises accounts for over 50% of the total. Over the years, many teachers have gone to the forefront of production and actively launched technical and consulting services outside. They have successively completed Nanyang Dashiying Dushan First Port and Its Supporting Service Project, Landscape Planning and Design of Library and Administrative Building of Henan Polytechnic Institute, Decoration and Landscape Design of Yaoshan Resort Holiday of Pingdingshan, Bailixi Tianquan Bathing Center, Nanyang Night Scene Lighting Project, Shandong Rushan Maojiacun Residential Design, Western Tea Drinking Culture Experience Pavilion, Landscape Planning and Design of Xihui Coast • Lanhu Jingyuan in Rushan of Shandong, and other social production service projects.

Teachers have enhanced their ability for combining theory and practice through providing technical services to the society. Thus, a high-quality teacher team specialized in both theoretic teaching ability and practical exercising capacity has been established. Therefore, the service level of teachers has been improved as well as the teaching quality. Through offering technical services to the society, a real field training environment has been provided for the students, thus realizing the transformation from consumptive field training and productive field training and college-enterprise combination, production-teaching combination and working-schooling combination. The exquisite skills and warm and considerate services in society by the teachers and students have won extensive social appraisal and improved the familiarity of the Institute. Meanwhile, they have created economic benefits for the Institute and made contributions to the development of local economy.

4 Conclusions

As an inevitable development trend of higher vocational colleges, college-enterprise cooperation is not only an objective requirement raised based on economic development, but also the internal demand for existence and development of higher vocational colleges. However, the way of cooperation between higher vocational colleges and enterprises is still in the early stages or the initial stage of middle level cooperation as yet, far lagging behind the advanced stage of deep cooperation. Our department has only conducted preliminary exploration. Currently, we have preliminarily reached an agreement to run the school jointly with Beijing Dayi Shangyang Home Decoration Management and Consultation Company. It is expected that we can further practice and explore the deep economic relation between college and enterprise as well as construction of a long-term college-enterprise mechanism.

References

1. Zhu, J., Fan, G.: Practice and Exploration on the Talents Training Mode of "Expert+Enterprise, Employment+Entrepreneurship". Chinese Vocational and Technical Education (24), 84–85 (2010)
2. Wang, C., Muo, G.: Practice and Exploration of the Economics and Management College Students for Their Abilities to Start an Undertaking. Education & Voacation (1), 84–85 (2010)
3. Department of Higher Education, Ministry of Education of P.R. China. The CAHE's Affiliation of Combination of Production, Teaching and Research, "The Only Way". Higher Education Press (2004)

The Exploration of the Training Mode for Undergraduate Application-Oriented Engineering Creative Professionals

Hua Meng[1], Ran Zhen[1], Xue-li Wu[1,2,*], and Jianhua Zhang[1]

[1] Hebei University of Science and Technology, Shijiazhuang, China,
[2] Yanshan University , Qinhuangdao, China
meng7899@163.com

Abstract. According to the character of the application-oriented engineering undergraduates, the training of the creative professionals should be combined with local economic development has been proposed that fully consider of the regional economy on the demand for personnel training, and orientate their personnel training objectives scientific and rationally. the continuity and gradual practice, from easy to difficult, combining individual with synthesis and also combining curricular with extracurricular has been emphasized. It required strong financial protection, innovative environment, personnel training and cultural life on campus.

Keywords: application-oriented undergraduate, creative professional, training, development, practice.

" Enhancing the creating ability by oneself and building the innovated country" is a target of our country. The law about our higher education has clearly that the higher task is "train the senior special professionals who have the spirit of innovate and the ability of practice to promote the socialist modernization." therefore, the training of the creative professional is one of the important tasks which higher education is facing now. Since the reform for higher education, it has changed enormously, finishing an important across that from the elite education to mass education,. With the popularization of higher education, the underrated education attains more and more attention. a number of engineering colleges and the general undergraduate universities analyzed the needs of the society carefully, at the same time ,they raised the missions of engineering undergraduate education .For the engineering undergraduate school ,how to make the service emission for local economic, look for a new mode for train creative professionals and educate creative professionals with high moral according to the development of the native is the issue of application-oriented institutes must seriously study and hard practice.

1 First. Combined with Local Economic Development, Orientate Training Objectives Scientific and Rationally

Application-oriented institutes usually hosted by the provincial or industry, the basic orientation of their school to determine the "teaching-based, application-type" levels.

---

* Corresponding Author.

M. Zhu (Ed.): ICCIC 2011, Part V, CCIS 235, pp. 69–73, 2011.
© Springer-Verlag Berlin Heidelberg 2011

Therefore, for application-oriented, we need consider the native economic demand for personnel training carefully in the filed talent education and direction of major, knowing the trend of regional economic in time and setting major according with the development of the native economic, adjusting major direction the goal of training and training objectives in order to service for regional economic successfully, at the same time satisfy the market demand, it develop and improve faster.

Another feature of these schools is that as many former host for the provinces or industries, general engineering practice with emphasis on student ability and school-enterprise cooperation in the long run .And underrated students trained by these schools are famous for strong ability of practice, as a result, they attained community's and social's hearty welcome, It should be maintained as a school tradition in undergraduate engineering schools. However ,with combining of these schools, they pay more attention to subjects ,considering more academic and neglecting practice, as a result, engineering practice has not been properly considered and the practical ability of students is forward a downward trend. The "return project" campaign of American offers a good inspiration for these schools. The "return project" campaign contains both emphasis the system and background of the engineering and build the ability of engineering practice and the application of "integrated" thinking, rebuilding teaching content and structure, focusing on students' learning to learn and concept of lifelong education.. Application-oriented institutes should learn the spirit from The United States "return project" campaign. combined with their practice, innovating the theory of engineering education, building 'big project' concept of education, enhancing the companies and school's communication, increasing personnel training course and practice and innovation to enhance the students ability.

2   Second, Build Three-Dimensional Multi-level Platform to Training the Students Awareness of Innovation

Recently, schools enroll more students make the quantity increase sharply, however, the school's laboratory equipment and teachers haven't increase simultaneous, thus weaken many application-oriented institutes of the practice of teaching students in different degrees . Cultivating innovative talents, we must attach importance to engineering practical ability and improvement. Because innovative talents must has a new thought and the innovation though of engineering and technical personnel can not come out of nowhere, It's depend on the train and cultivate of engineering practical. Therefore, enhancing the ability of engineering practical is an important way for application-oriented institutes cultivate creative professionals. And teaching practice is also a main platform for cultivating the innovate ability .

The system design of teaching practice has its own internal rules and specific pattern. It should be emphasized the continuity and gradual practice, from easy to difficult, combining individual with synthesis and also combining curricular with extracurricular. so form the target space of the scattered cross-practice teaching with Continuity.

Full process in time: from the first year to the last year, putting the teaching practice as an important link into the system of teaching subject. Set the Experimental course alone and set the compulsory modules and elective modules to increase student's choice space so not only guarantee the experimental capabilities of all students, but also offer a larger space for the students who has spare capacity for learning and with interest for further development. Fully reflects the individualized training, so that each student in the university four years obtain the greatest development.

Series in depth: Facing different levels of students, setting basic technology training classes, training design capability, comprehensive ability, research ability to exercise various levels of experimental teaching project. The out-school science environment of students should be divided to three levels. For freshmen, they can choose to learn strong- practice courts to expansion basic knowledge to inspire learning interest and increase special knowledge. Students of Grade three and higher can apply for open innovation pilot projects and comprehensively participate in various competitions, taking part in senior's Graduation Project to strong the ability of integrated using of the knowledge they have learn. They can also involved in research students in the subject of further study to cultivate innovation.

Diverse in form: Setting all kinds of teaching practice in phases, for instance understanding study specializing in the production practice ,graduation practice, designing course, graduation design using the menu-style training (engineering, management, arts, science),and many levels setting(from the low to the high: major understanding training and comprehensive and innovative training) , all these combined and fully reflected the individualized training

Comprehension in content: strengthen the course of integration, combining with the various courses, setting lots of experiments, making the knowledge systemized.

3 Third, Strengthen the Teaching Management System to Garreteer the Training of Creative Professional

1. Perfect Practice Teaching Management System

To the manager, fields for science and technology activities and the center of engineering training should open to students all day. Management modes contain: Verify experiment unified for management, use detailed teaching methods. Teachers explain experiments in the class combine with the content of course explaining the main points for experiment. Experiments should finished by themselves according with the understanding in order to strength learning knowledge .Comprehensive, centralized management of the design experiment, should take the method of guiding open management for innovated experiments, and guided ways for teaching in order to fully develop student's personality, improve the ability of innovation and make a good circumstance for training creative professionals.

2. Evaluate and Incentive Scientific and Reasonably

For experiment course which teaching alone using experiment item bank to evaluate when the exam is on, students with different level choosing from the corresponding item bank in the pilot project take the exam to practice on the ability of students with higher demand, at the same time, credit points by way of conversion result and encourage students to choose experiment item with more difficult in order to develop the potential of everyone and maximize the development of individual students.

To improve students out-school activities, encourage the sense of innovation, improve students ability of science researching and promote students all kinds of capable .It should establishment technological innovation for university students, at the same time, for applying, the decision should be managed rigorously scientific, also, an effective quality monitoring system to ensure the results of innovation.

3. A good Guarantee with Money and Teachers

To promote practical teaching and improve the quality of practical teaching, a good guarantee with money and teachers is necessary. Schools committed to building a strong practice and good experienced teachers, at the same time, pay attention to training teachers with 'doubt-teacher'. Young teachers should have laboratory experience to improve the ability of practice. At the same time, pay attention to enroll talents from firms, teach students practice and encourage teachers to go to businesses to study, stretching the combine with school and firm to provide a good protection for promoting the innovated ability of students.

4   Fourth, to Rich Cultural Life on Campus and Make a Good Atmosphere for Training Creative Professional

The sense of innovation are not come out in one day, it's a long-term accumulation of advanced culture,. Universities should provide democratic, open and progressive cultural environment for students.

1. Make innovated culture: Universities should hold innovative report, innovation of academic lectures and academicians and famous teachers feathering and so on,. Teachers should learn the leading scientific research and advanced scientific techniques in nowadays to improve student's the ability of independent innovation, and to encourage the motivation of innovation.

2. Establish a team for student innovation

Organize a innovation team which the main members are students and the leaders are teachers, making innovated experiment which subjects can choice to training awareness of independent innovation, and improving the ability of independent innovation

3. Hosting more creative contests. through contests to improve training of racing, conduct practical skills competitions, mathematical modeling contest, English Competition, structural model design contest, "Challenge Cup" Technology innovation contests, while in the competitive mentality, and guide students to consciously improve practice and innovation.

4. To strengthen community building, especially the academic community, building academic community which main covered subjects the school have. Hosting all kinds of lectures and academic exchanges from time to time to form a good atmosphere which respect innovation and admire science and technology.

References

1. Chen, J., Zhu, L.: For Innovation-oriented Country, Promoting the Reform of Engineering Education in China. Research in Higher Education of Engineering 3, 47 (2006)
2. Zinser, R.: New Roles to Meet Industry Needs:A Look at Advanced Technological Education Program. The Journal of Vocational Education Research 29 (2004)
3. Zhang, Y.: Research on Higher Education for Bachelor of Engineering Application. Jiangsu Higher Education 2, 92–94 (2009)
4. Han, L.-q.: Research in Applied Orientation of Undergraduate Engineering Education. Research in Higher Education 10 (2007)

The Design and Implementation of Budget Management System Based on ExtJS and ASP.NET

Wu Bo and Peng Yan

Information Engineering College, Capital Normal University, Beijing, China
eaglebo@gmail.com, pengyanpy@163.com

Abstract. As the level of enterprise information technology continuing to rise, to achieve information management of budgeting is essential. This paper elaborates the critical steps and implementing key points in the implementation of the budget management system based on the combination of ExtJS and ASP.NET, and introduces the framework and technologies related. The budget management system further simplified the development process on the basis of the asynchronous communication of Ajax, and effectively implemented the separation between page express and business logic, which makes the implementation structure clearer thus improves the development efficiency as well as enhances the asynchronous communication between client and server. Moreover, the paper also briefly discusses the role of ExtJS in the system and the problems it posed.

Keywords: Budget Management System, ExtJS, asynchronous communication, RIA, ASP.NET.

0 Introduction

Budget has been taking a more and more important role as a financial planning tool in modern enterprises [1], however, there are some prevalent problems in current budget managements: 1. There is a lack of budget management awareness, the process of "editorial budget-budget implementation-budget adjustment-budget analysis" couldn't be strictly executed; 2. The foundation work of budgeting is not prepared, and the specific assessment indicator is not clear; 3. Monitoring and tracking of the budget implementation are not in place. All this shows that it is quite essential to achieve information management of budgeting.

The enterprise information management system experienced the evolution from C/S to B/S, between which the main difference is whether the client is fat or thin, while Rich Internet Application (RIA) obtains the advantages of both. RIA is a network application whose features and functions are similar to traditional desktop applications; its greatest feature is to handle most tasks which were transplanted from the server to the client, while the client interacts with the server only when some interactive data is necessary[2].

On the other side, with the advent of the internet age, building a B/S model platform system would be more practical [3]. At present China's digitalization of budget management system is still in the stage of development, many of the existing budget

M. Zhu (Ed.): ICCIC 2011, Part V, CCIS 235, pp. 74–81, 2011.
© Springer-Verlag Berlin Heidelberg 2011

management systems are based on general B/S mode [4,5]. General B/S mode ignored the interaction and communication capabilities between client and server, thus the user experience is not good. Yet this situation has been changed with the emergence of Ajax.Combining with the advantages of RIA and aiming at the popular AJAX technology, like many multinational corporations[6], we also have chosen ExtJS, a mature Ajax framework, to simplify the development.

This article will be divided into the following sections: the 1st section is an overview of the technology the system used; the 2nd section briefly describes the design of the system, including design of the structural function and the design of system architecture; the 3rd focuses on the system implementation and elaborate some of the key implementations. And based on the entire system, the 4th section summarizes ExtJS's impact on the system development process and the running performance. The last section is the conclusion.

1 System Technology Introduction

1.1 AJAX and ASP.NET

AJAX (Asynchronous JavaScript and XML) is a representative of RIA, it is a web development technology used to create interactive web applications. Its main purpose is to use client-side JavaScript scripts to exchange data with web server-side, thus users don't have to stop operation to wait for the sever data back, and the whole process is dynamically updated[7].

Generally there are several AJAX implementations in ASP.NET environment as below:

1) XMLHttp + WebForm: To make an asynchronous request on server-side WebForm through using JavaScript to operate the XML HttpRequest object.

2) XMLHttp+HttpHandler: It differs from the former approach by using HttpHandler instead of WebForm on the server side.

3) ASP.NET callback mode: Using ICallbackEventHandler interface and implementing RaiseCallbackEvent and GetCallbackResult to implement a callback, the client ultimately implements AJAX through calling ClientScript.GetCallbackEventReference.

1.2 ExtJS

Using AJAX frameworks will be more convenient and efficient compared to the ways of implementing AJAX in ASP.NET. Written with JavaScript, ExtJS is a new generation of AJAX framework platforms, it is mainly used to create a front-end user interface, and integrated with a number of commonly used and outstanding UI components; moreover, it has nothing to do with the background language[8].

On the other hand, ExtJS is scalable, it provided reusable objects and components, developers can design new components according to their own demand, which facilitates programming for developers who are object-oriented. At the same time ExtJS shields lots of differences among various browsers, thus there is no need for developers to operate DOM objects directly. Also it provides users a convenient solution to complex multi-table interaction queries such as page shows and tree displays by a perfect combination with JSON, XML and other data formats as well as a fast binding with the data of corresponding components.

Role and function of ExtJS in B/S system as shown below:

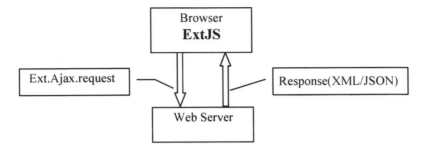

Fig. 1. Role and function of ExtJS in B/S system

Ext.Ajax.request responsible for sending http requests to the server, and after receiving the request, the server responses in the form of XML/JSON data format.

2 Design of the System

2.1 System Structural Framework

Budget Management System includes budget setting, budget preparation, budget execution, budget adjustments, etc., as shown below:

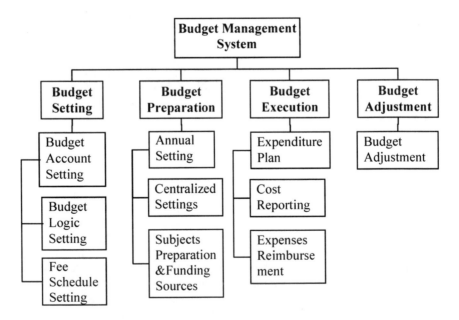

Fig. 2. Structural framework of the system

Functions of each part:

1) Budget Setting: this is an important function of the budget system; it is responsible for the initialization of the system, including budget accounts setting, fee schedule setting and budget logic settings.

2) Budget Preparation: make a preparation of the budget on an annual based expenditures and project expenditures, it can be divided into budget breakdown and budget summary according to the different requirements of budget. This part includes subfunctions such as annual setting, preparation of subjects and sources of funding, centralized settings and so on.

3) Budget Execution: A management process of working out an expenditure plan according to the contents of the budget preparation and reimbursing the actual expenses, also including making budget reporting management when needed, therefore this part consists of substructures such as expenditure plan, cost reporting and reimbursement of expenses.

4) Budget Adjustment: When there occurs off-budget costs or the cost overruns the budget during the execution of the budget, some of the subjects will bring accounts alarm or can't be reimbursed, in such cases budget adjustment is needed accordingly.

2.2 System Architecture

The hierarchical structure of the budget system is shown in Figure 3; from top to bottom are Presentation Layer, Business Logic Layer, and Data Access Layer.

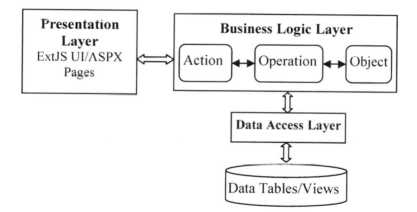

Fig. 3. Hierarchical structure of the system

1) Presentation Layer: Responsible for the display of client pages using ExtJS, including display of the input control, basic business processes, and data integrity control.

2) Business Logic Layer: This layer is the core of the processing of the systematic business function. It is divided into action, operation and object according to actual needs. Part of action format the data to JSON and make a simple process or transfer for the request of presentation layer through ASHX. Part of operation implement through static library function, responsible for business logic processing and making read and write operation on the database through operating the part of object.

3) Data Access Layer: Responsible for the CRUD operations on database. Designed with relational tables, database achieves list of queries through dataviews, and achieves complex business logic through stored procedures.

3   System Implementation

This section discusses the implementation in detail in respects of system communication, system access control, and system data acquisition.

3.1   System Communication

The core of client-server communication is the Ext.Ajax.request method, which can achieve asynchronous communication succinctly. Most browser pages' requests sending are achieved through Ext.Ajax in the implementation of this system. For example, to check the budget items in Ext grid, a getList request has to be sent to the database, the main code is as follows:

```
getList(){
    Ext.Ajax.request({
                url: '../Actions/BudgetData.ashx?act=show&d=' + new Date(),
                method: 'post',
                params: { ItemId: selectedRows.items[0].data.BudgetId },
                success: function(response, options){
                        var objJson = Ext.util.JSON.decode(response.responseText);
                        if (objJson.success){ // success operation
                        }
                        else showFailDialog('Failure info:' + objJson.error);
                },
                failure: function(response, options) { showExceptionDialog(); }
        });
}
```

First, the client sends a given field in the browse page as a params configuration item of Ext.Ajax.request to a server specified by url to process function, or to code a value, which needs to be sent, as JSON format through Ext.encode. Then the server returns the response results after dealing with the message request. Here since the response message is packaged into JSON format, the client needs to use Ext.decode to decode. Besides, when requesting data, a time stamp should be attached to the configure items of url in Ext.Ajax.request so as to get the up to date data.

3.2   System Access Control

The basic idea of Role-based Access Control (RBAC) is to classify access permissions into different categories according to different roles. In this system, the access permission is assigned by the positions of the users instead of the users themselves.

Particular way is, to create the database tables RoleInfo to represent role information and Privilege to represent permission of each role. The primary key id of table Privilege corresponds to the privilege fields in table RoleInfo, while the table Privilege stores the important information of level, name, and description of privilege. The levels of privilege are MOUDLE, PAGE, and FUNCTION, which respectively represent system function modules, system pages and page features. The name of privilege is the Chinese name of the corresponding privilege level, while the description of the privilege provides a specific description for the privilege level: It is the relative path of the page if the privilege level is PAGE, and it correspondingly is a specific function name of ExtJS when the privilege level is FUNCTION.

In actual implementation, the system will find the specified privilege according to the role which the user logs on as, then get the corresponding modules, pages and function settings from database to initialize. This method not only achieves RBAC well, but also improves the scalability of the system, i.e. if the functions of some roles changed, only to make some corresponding change to the Privilege table would be enough.

3.3 Data Paging: Paging in the Data Persistence Layer

The implementations of data paging are generally divided into paging with widgets in the front page, paging in the service layer and paging in the persistence layer. The third approach is comparatively the best implementing way in this system, as the database only need to search and return the data records in the page block that the user requests each time, thus improved the efficiency of database queries and reduced the data flow throughout the implementation process, and most importantly improved the overall performance of the system with the returned results being highly real-time. When page data change, instead of refreshing the entire page, only a refreshment of the parts where change occurs is needed, thus reduces the amount of data transmission. What's more, users can continue with other operations in the pages without waiting because the refreshing is asynchronous, hence enhances the user experience.

ExtJS has a good support on data paging; it can submit the paging parameters to the background program with only the configuration of a few properties, along with which includes whether remote sorting of data records is required. Since the method of paging in the persistence layer is adopted in this system, remote sorting is required when configuring data source STORE in the related components (e.g. gridPanel, treePanel) of ExtJS:

```
var store = new Ext.data.Store({
        proxy: new Ext.data.HttpProxy({ url: '../Actions/Data.ashx?act=list' }),
        reader: new Ext.data.JsonReader({
            // JsonReader config
        }),
        sortInfo: { field: 'DataId', direction: 'DESC' }, // sort mode
        remoteSort: true // remote sort is required
    });
```

Only setting the parameters is needed when sending data requests: store.load({params: { start: 0, limit: LINENUMBER}}), among which start provides the currently displayed page to the background program and limit provides the number of records per page to the background. Background processing function passes the two parameters to the appropriate function in the data persistence layer after receiving them, and then the function generates the corresponding SQL statements to operate the database.

4 System Performance

ExtJS framework brought a lot of convenience for system development, in the case of combining with the budget management system development, the convenience are mainly reflected as following:1) By providing a set of mature client component, ExtJS freed the developers from being distracted by CSS/HTML problems, thus saves the development time and improves the development efficiency. 2) ExtJS has a good implementation of Ajax, which strengthened the asynchronous communication between the browser and the server, and enhanced user experience by enabling users to proceed with other operations without waiting during the operations of remote data. 3) Has a good package of JavaScript, relatively overcame the problem of cross-browser display, besides, its components are with high reusability and also support object-oriented extensions. 4) The coupling between the pages and the background business logic is further reduced. The background implementation technology can be diversified on condition that there is no large change in the front page, while the background business logic changing doesn't require an adjustment of the front page either. This also benefits the division of work for developers.

With so many advantages, ExtJS also has some shortcomings, among which the most criticized is its problem of memory leak. The main cause of this problem is ExtJS's continuous and dynamic create, delete and query to the DOM. In general, there are several ways to alleviate this problem: delay loading widgets, dynamically load components and js files, use extend method to override or add destructor methods or events. Anyway, the upcoming ExtJS4 version made itself known that there will be a greater performance optimization in its components, form layout and some other respects, furthermore, it will also provide faster, easier and more stable applications[9].

5 Conclusion

The characteristics of the budget management system require high reliability and efficiency of information exchanging, at the same time need to meet good user experience, and the budget requirement changes accordingly when the users' budget environment has changed. Besides that pre-selection system also requests high scalability, and low coupling between business logic modules and other system modules. The introduction of ExtJS framework to the budget management system brought a great improvement in both system development process and system performance, and provided a good solution to the problems mentioned above.

As information technology and Web applications develop unceasingly, RIA, which has the advantages of both C/S and B/S, will be a trend in the development of software application, and ExtJS is getting more and more attention with its powerful performance in RIA implementations. It is believed that with the gradual popularization of ExtJS, there will be more new efficient software development models and the web applications will be further enriched.

Acknowledgments. This work was supported in part by Natural Science Foundation of China, under contract N0. 61070050.

References

[1] Chen, W.: Discussion on the Budget and Budget Method. Contemporary Manager (The Last Ten-Day of A Month), 40–42 (August 2006)
[2] Fei, W.: Implementation of Web System Using Framework Technic Based on Rich Internet Applications. Computer System & Applications, 77–80 (October 2008)
[3] Wu, D., Xiao, R.: Constrast Analysis on Information System of C/S and B/S Structure. Information Science 21(3), 313–315 (2003)
[4] Hu, W.-A., Ji, J.-C., Jiao, W.-B.: Design and Implementation of B/S Mode Budget Management System. Computer Systems & Applications 19(10), 158–162 (2010)
[5] Keyou, Z.: Design of B/S Mode Colleges Budget Management System. China Education Info., 37–38 (October 2009)
[6] Companiesusing Sencha [EB/OL] (December 4, 2010),
     http://www.sencha.com/company/customers.php
[7] Lv, L.-t., Wan, J.-h., Zhou, H.-f.: Research of Not Refurbishing and Updating Data Method in AJAX Web Application. Application Research of Computers, 199–220 (November 2006)
[8] Yang, Z.-j.: The Design and Implementation of Human Resources Management System Based on ExtJS and J2EE. Beijing Jiaotong University, Beijing (2010)
[9] EdSpencer. Ext JS 4 Preview: Faster, Easier, More Stable [EB/OL] (November 20, 2010),
     http://en.cnki.com.cn/Article_en/CJFDTotal-DNZS200918172.htm

Experimental Simulations of Flow Fields within Air-Conditioning Aircraft Cabin

Wang Jin, Pang Liping, Gong Mengmeng, Cui Yi, Xu Jie, and Wang Jun

School of Aeronautics Science and Engineering
Beihang University
Beijing, China
pang55677@163.com

Abstract. With the development of economic and the increasing of human comfortable requirements, it is important for the researchers to design cabin airflow in large passenger aircraft benefit for passengers 'health and comfort. According to the airflow and air quality problems in the cabin, some domestic experts and scholars had achieved initial results by simulating different forms of airflow circumstances in idealized aircraft cabin mockup. However, simulation results basing on simplifying original system model has many problems which are needed to do further experiment to verify the simulation results. This paper has studied two different air-supply flow fields with smoke-flow display technology by building Aircraft Cabin Environment Simulation Laboratory. Finally, through comprehensive evaluation and analysis, the best air-supply way is chose to supply a comfort and health cabin environment to the passengers.

Keywords: large passenger aircraft flow fields flow display technology.

1 Introduction

Flow field, temperature and air quality are of the main factors for the passenger comfort in the aircraft cabin. It is an important guarantee to design a fine flow field for a comfortable environment. At the same time, with the development of economic and the increasing of human comfortable requirements, IAQ has been drawn increasing attentions, not only in the ground, the plane too. Cabin Air Quality (CAQ) is related with the health, comfort and safety of the crew and passengers. Therefore, it is important for the researchers to design cabin airflow in large passenger aircraft benefit for passengers' health and comfort.

The typical cabin airflow is determined by the air parameters (temperature, humidity, flow) sent to the cabin, the cabin air-supply distribution form and location、 outlet form and location, the space geometry of the cabin and location of various heat sources (internal facilities and passenger). This shows that the factors affect cabin air distribution is too complex to design a fine airflow by the general theoretical calculations. Though some domestic experts and scholars have achieved initial results by simulating different forms of airflow circumstances in idealized aircraft cabin mockup, simulation results basing on simplifying original system model has many problems which are needed to do further experiment to verify the simulation results. The ideal simulation results deviate to the actual quality of the airflow due to the uneven flow distribution, the anisomerous installing location and the uneven air suction pressure of exhaust. Given the

M. Zhu (Ed.): ICCIC 2011, Part V, CCIS 235, pp. 82–88, 2011.

inadequacies of numerical simulation, it is necessary to do experimental simulations of flow fields within air-conditioning aircraft cabin.

Through building Aircraft Cabin Environment Simulation Laboratory, this paper has studied the two different air-supply flow fields by using flow display technology. Then through comprehensive evaluation and analysis, select the best air-supply way in the framework of the existing air-supply mode.

1   Experimental Environment and Method

1.1   Aircraft Cabin Environmental Simulation Laboratory

Fig.1 shows the picture of Environmental Simulation Laboratory, this platform simulated the full-size aircraft in the light of A320, including the cockpit and cabin. The internal layout of the cabin is single-aisle, cabin long is 37.57m, and the internal diameter is 3.70m. The cabin also equipped with a breathing, heat and moisture simulation human model of box shape.

The form of cabin air-conditioning system is up-supply and down-circle, with mixed air supplying from the upper of the cabin and returning from the grille down of the cabin.

Fig. 1. Environmental Simulation Laboratory

1.2 Experimental Method

This paper mainly study two different air-supply methods in the framework of the existing air-supply mode, respectively are air-supply from the central of the ceiling and the sidewall of the trunk.This Experimental study evaluated the airflow field in the cabin by smoke-flow display technology. Smoke flow display technology, for its visual characteristics of a high degree, is widely used in fluid experimental research.

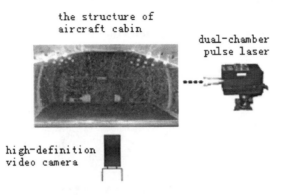

Fig. 2. The schematic image of environmental method

As the even layout of aircraft cabin seats, air inlet, air outlet and other along the horizontal layout, this experiment is mainly studied the airflow field around the single-row seats in the tail area of cabin. This area is isolated by transparent clapboard in order to avoid the influence of airflow in front of the environmental areas; And considering to get a clear airflow field display, this area is shaded darkly by various black blocking. In addition, the shade cloth is suspended around the area to avoid the impact of diffuse on the imaging results.

Fig.2 shows the schematic image of environmental method. The main experimental devices are the dual-chamber pulse laser, smoke generator and high-definition video camera. According to transient dynamic process of the gas-flow in the cabin, high-definition DV should be applied to capture the entire process of the smoke flow images, which can overcome the difficult of the common camera. In the experiment, firstly the experimenter should regulate the light intensity and angle of the light source to make the field angle of infrared ray can reach the ideal area of the cabin, and then spray smoke by starting the smoke generator. The smoke outlet should be putted in the middle of both sides of the inlet in the cabin in order to obtain even and accurate flow field display. When all preparation is ready, the high-definition DV was used to record single-row seat area airflow field which was displayed by smoke flow, finally analysis the experimental images to get the law of the different airflows.

2   Visualization of the Experimental Airflow Field

Although the cabin air distribution relates with many factors, the cabin airflow mainly depends on the type and location of the inlet according to the law of airflow. This paper mainly studies two different air-supply methods in the framework of the existing air-supply mode.

2.1 Air-Supply from the Sidewall of the Trunk

Gas pipe located in the sidewall of the trunk and the inlet arranged along the centerline of 45 outward. The air-supply from the sidewall of the trunk was the main air-supply pipe, with the auxiliary upper air-supply from the sidewall and down air-return to the sidewall.

Fig.3 shows the images of visual airflow field of air-supply from the sidewall of the trunk.

(a)Airflow field in the inlet

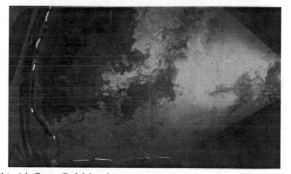

(b) Airflow field in the passenger and down returning area

Fig. 3. The images of visual airflow of air-supply from the sidewall of the trunk

In the inlet, the air flowing along the inclined 45 from both of sides collided in the symmetrical plane of aisle, and then the mainstream of air changed direction straight blowing down to the floor.

In the passenger area, the vortex forming in both sides of the aisle bring fresh air from the inside passenger areas along the inside wall to the outside passenger areas. The centers of the vortex were all on both sides of the central area of the passengers, which lead that the fresh air was all evenly mixed under the driving of vortex.

In the down returning area, part of the air was directly exhausted to the outside without exchanging with the inside air.

2.1.1 Air-Supply from the Central of the Ceiling

Refer to the air-supply way in civil buildings, this paper carried out experimental study about the way of air-supply from the central of the ceiling. Gas pipe located at the central of the ceiling and the inlet evenly arranged along the centerline of 45 outward. The air-supply from the central of the ceiling is the main air-supply pipe, with the auxiliary upper air-supply from the sidewall and down air-return to the sidewall. The location of inlet must make sure that the airflow flow from the inlet has a longer range to form a sufficient flow velocity satisfying the outside passages near the aisle.

Fig.4 shows the images of visual airflow in the situation of air-supply from the central of the ceiling

(a)Airflow field in the inlet the passenger area

(b) Airflow field in

(c)Airflow field in the down returning area

Fig. 4. The images of visual airflow in the situation of air-supply from the central of the ceiling

In the inlet, the mainstream flowed down to the floor along the ceiling and the cabin wall in the bottom of the trunk; meanwhile, the other air changed direction straightly blowing down to the floor after striking the surface of the trunk.

In the passenger area, some of the mainstream was directly discharged when reached the outlet and the rest continued to flow down to the cabin floor. After reaching the floor, the air changed direction flowing to the cabin aisle and mixed with the air straight blowing down to the floor to form the vortex of large area. The centers of the vortex were all on both sides of the central area of the passengers, which lead that the fresh air was all evenly mixed under the driving of vortex.

In the down returning area, the returning air was directly exhausted to the outside after finishing the exchanging process.

In the case that the cabin has certain internal structure, the direction of airflow plays a dominant role in determining the direction of airflow and fresh air distribution. Comparative analysis of visual experimental results of the two situations in Civil Airplane Cabin can get the following conclusions.

Air-supply from the sidewall of the trunk: the air from both of the side collided in the symmetrical plane of the aisle, and then the mainstream changed direction straight blowing down to the floor. This air-supply will cause the strong airflow near the aisle passenger; Furthermore, the vortex forming in both sides of the aisle bring fresh air from the inside passenger areas along the inside wall to the outside passenger areas.

Air-supply from the central of the ceiling: the mainstream flow down to the floor along the ceiling and the cabin wall in the bottom of the trunk which can increase the stability of the flow to satisfy the evenness of the airflow in the passenger area. Although the airflow will touch the ground in the flow process, it has been a degree of attenuation that will not make the velocity to drive the dirt in the ground; Furthermore, air vortex of this way is counterclockwise, which can drive the airflow from the outside passenger areas to the inside passenger to discharge the exhaled gases of passages.

The above analysis can be summarized that air-supply from the central of the ceiling is the best way of air-supply which can satisfy the evenness of the airflow and discharge the exhaled gases of passages quickly. However, it needs to be pay attention in the practical application: for single-aisle civil aircraft, air-supply from the central of the ceiling should coordinate with the ceiling decoration; for dual-aisles one, the air-supply from the sidewall of the trunk in the middle area is equivalent to the effect of air-supply from the central of the ceiling.

3 Conclusions

In order to solve the problem in the study of cabin airflow field, this paper has studied the two different air-supply flow fields with smoke-flow display technology by building Aircraft Cabin Environment Simulation Laboratory. Finally, through comprehensive evaluation and analysis, the best air-supply way is chose to supply a comfort and health cabin environment to the passengers.The display of the fresh airflow traces can be concluded that air quality of air-supply from the central of the ceiling is better than air-supply from the sidewall of the trunk and the waste of fresh air is less. Therefore, air-supply from the central of the ceiling is the best air-supply way which can supply a comfort and clean cabin environment to the passengers in large passenger aircraft.

References

1. Zhao, H.: Summary of research situation in micro-environment of air-conditioning train. Railway Locomotive & Rolling (2), 25(1), 44–48 (2005)
2. Zhang, T., Chen, Q.: Air distribution systems in commercial aircraft cabins. Building and Environment 42, 1675–1684 (2007)
3. Brindisi, A., Concilio, A.: Passengers' comfort modeling inside aircraft. Journal of Aircraft 45(6), 2001–2008 (2008)
4. Suo, Z., Wang, H.: Numerical simulations of different airflows in same room. Refrigeration and Air Conditioning (73) (2005)
5. Günther, G., Bosbach, J., Pennecot, J., Wagner, C.: Experimental and numerical simulations of idealized aircraft cabin flows. Aerospace Science and Technology 10, 563–573 (2006)

Reformation and Study on Practical Teaching in Mechanical Manufacturing Technology

G.H. Qin and H.C. Ye

School of Aeronautical Manufacturing Engineering,
Nanchang Hangkong University, Nanchang 330036, China
qin7689@126.com

Abstract. The Practical teaching can impart students to the practical skill and knowledge by the practice activities. It is used to verify the validation of the theoretical knowledge so that it can train students' practical ability, innovation ability, and ability of independency analyzing and solving problem. Mechanical manufacturing technology is a necessary and main professional fundamental course required for training modern senior mechanical manufacturing professions and management talents. The research of its practical teaching contents and methods can make students to understand course contents and accumulate professional knowledge. It is significant to train students' ability of analyzing and solving practical problem and to promote students' engineering capacity and innovation ability. Therefore, the corresponding practical teaching contents are firstly reformed for mechanical manufacturing technology. Secondly, the arrangement sequence of practical teaching contents is proposed to serve the acceptation of the theoretical knowledge. The reformed practical teaching can inspire students' interesting of learning mechanical manufacturing technology.

Keywords: Practical teaching, metalworking practice, production practice, course experiment, course design, mechanical manufacturing technology.

1 Introduction

Mechanical manufacturing technology is a processional course of mechanical design, manufacturing and their engineering specialty. The corresponding contents on the practical teaching in mechanical manufacturing technology are main tasks of students after working. It plays a very important role to reform the practical teaching of mechanical manufacturing technology in cultivating the practical talents.

The ministry of education of the people's republic of china announced a specialty catalogue of higher educational school in 1998. The specialty catalogue specified the incorporation of the old three narrow specialties (i.e., mechanical manufacturing technology and equipment, mechanical design and manufacturing, mechanical and electronic engineering) into a new wide caliber specialty being called as mechanical design manufacturing and automation. It is crucial for the successful realization of talent training to construct the reasonable course system. The course of mechanical manufacturing technology is established to accord with the specialty catalogue of higher education. This course was reformed from old four courses including

M. Zhu (Ed.): ICCIC 2011, Part V, CCIS 235, pp. 89–93, 2011.
© Springer-Verlag Berlin Heidelberg 2011

mechanical manufacturing engineering, jig and fixture design, metal cutting principle and cutting tool, and metal cutting machine tools.

Many higher schools have been carried out the reformations of teaching contents of mechanical manufacturing technology. The course reformation went though two reformation stages. The first reformation focused on the reduction of teaching times so that the same contents can be directly cancelled from old four courses in the manufacturing field [1]. Some higher schools combined metal cutting machine tools, mechanical manufacturing engineering and metal cutting principle and cutting tool to mechanical manufacturing technology [2,3]. Some higher schools mixed metal cutting principle and cutting tool, mechanical manufacturing engineering, and metal cutting machine tools with jig and fixture design to form mechanical manufacturing technology [4]. The first reformation can to a certain extent decrease teaching times. However, many independent contents can again occur in many multi-discipline courses of manufacturing fields. The second reformation was to organically integrate the teaching contents. Under the guidance of the important idea of taking the road of combining leaning with research and production, some higher schools integrated old four courses into mechanical manufacturing technology [5].

Different the teaching contents of mechanical manufacturing technology cause different practical teaching contents and their teaching times. Currently, our school reformed metal cutting principle and cutting tool, and mechanical manufacturing engineering into mechanical manufacturing technology [6]. There exist following shortcomings in the practical teaching process. Firstly, the imperfect adjustment of experimental equipments makes the arrangement of experiment contents. Secondly, the teaching content and teaching mode of course design are improper. Finally, the unreasonable arrangement sequence among metalworking practice, production practice and theoretical teaching affects the teaching quality. Therefore, the construction of mechanical manufacturing technology-oriented practical teaching system and teaching contents is discussed in detail. On the other hand, the teaching mode and teaching method are explored to meet the practical teaching of mechanical manufacturing technology.

2   Reformation Significance

Heighten students' ability to grasp and strengthen the theoretical knowledge. Teachers must instruct students to validate the theoretical knowledge during the practical course. It helps the training of students' operation ability and creative ability as well as the enhancement of students' intellect of knowledge points. Therefore, it is important for the practical teaching to improve the teaching quality. Mechanical manufacturing technology integrates multiple processional courses in which many knowledge points are difficult in being accepted. Obviously, it is significant for mechanical manufacturing technology to reform the practical teaching.

Train students' ability of applying theoretical knowledge to analyze and solve the practical problems. Recently, the society faces more and more the pressure of career. However, the supply of skilled workers falls short of demand. This phenomenon can show the society needs a great deal of skilled talents in addition to researched talent with high education. The metalworking practice aims at understanding perceptually basic machining methods about casting, forging, welding, heat treatment, turning, milling, planning, grinding, drilling and so forth. The emphasis of the metalworking practice is on students' ability training of basic skill and operation ability. In addition, the function of the production practice can strengthen students' grasp of the entire process from raw material, roughcast, machining, and assembly to sale. It focuses on the foster of students' specialized skill and engineering ability. The practical teaching will lay a solid foundation for students' future growth, because it can deep the realization of the unselfish labor, strict discipline and team spirit of workers and engineering technicians.

3   Reformation Strategy

The theoretical teaching can not only supply the practical teaching with the theoretical foundation but also accelerate the performance of the practical teaching. On the other hand, the practical teaching can validate the reliability of the theoretical teaching and in turn, serve the theoretical teaching. The following reformation strategies of the practical teaching are proposed to satisfy our theoretical teaching of mechanical manufacturing technology, as illustrated in Fig. 1.

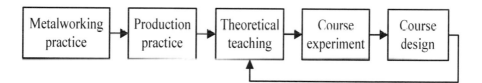

Fig. 1. The dialectical relationship between theory and practice

Without the consideration of their emphases, the aims of the metalworking practice and production practice are to resolve the lack of practical experience for students. Thus, they should be arranged before the theoretical teaching of mechanical manufacturing technology. The metalworking practice must be planned with a product machining process as the mainline. The combination of the metalworking practice with production process can make students know the characteristics of machining methods and the structures of machining equipments, realize the machining problems, formation causes and solution approaches, understand the corresponding theoretical knowledge.

The production practice can adopt production process practice as the primary strategy with the addition of visit. Main problems in recent production practice are listed as follows. Firstly, the practice mode is single. Current production practice used the observation and recordation as the primary method with the addition of instruction. Nevertheless, students are allocated to different positions in a large workshop, and a teacher is difficult in instructing all students. Secondly, the teacher team is unstable. The production practice is a practical course of tight combination with theory. A teacher must continuously learn the practice contents and the practice enterprise. It is well known that traditional classroom teaching has uniform teaching texts and clear teaching tasks. However, an enterprise is frequently updated its product and machining equipments. Simultaneously, the practical teaching text must be rewritten with the renovation of the corresponding practice enterprise. Thus a new instructor can neither know the practice contents in time, nor instruct students. Here, a novel method is presented to change the traditional single production practice into three stages, as shown in Fig. 2. The purpose of the investigation on web consists in knowing the practice contents in advance. It is preparing for practice in enterprise. A production practice specification must firstly be written to lay stress on the key points in the next practice stage. During the production practice, students must plan the machining process of a typical product. Moreover, students should visit the hot machining as well as other advance manufacturing technology and assembly process. After the practice in enterprise is over, students must be required to defense the practice results and write a practice report.

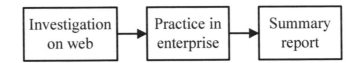

Fig. 2. The teaching mode of production practice

The experiment contents must be selected according to abstract knowledge points and existing experimental equipments. Four experiments, which include the cutting force measurement, the cutting temperature measurement, computer aided processing dimension analysis and the statistical analysis of machining error, are recently set for mechanical manufacturing technology in our school. However, some problems existed in our experimental course are as follow:

- Many experimental equipments have been not checked after new campus was moved. Thus, the cutting temperature experiment has not successfully been carried out.
- The enrollment expansion of our school causes the arrangement of all experimental courses behind the theoretical teaching.

Therefore, we will vary the irrelevant teaching mode of 'theory first and experiment second' into the mixed teaching mode of 'experiment with theory and theory with experiment'. Now, we reset the cutter angle measurement, the cutting force measurement, the statistical analysis of machining error and the eccentric machine assembly.

The process planning for workpiece machining has something to do with entire teaching course of mechanical manufacturing technology. It is an important part of mechanical manufacturing technology. So it is selected to be a teaching content of course design. At present, our course design has several disadvantageous factors:

- Students cannot know how to use the knowledge points. So they cannot know where to start the course design.
- The dispersive teaching mode cannot efficiently manage and instruct students. Thus, the instructor loses usually in touch with students. Students are not always earnest for the course design.

Our reformation strategy on the course design is suggested in this paper. It will separate the course design into three stages, as shown in Fig. 3. The detail thought is related as follow:

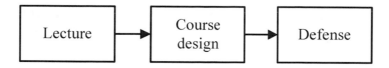

Fig. 3. Three stages of the course design

- Before students start to carry out the course design, we should arrange an instruction lecture with typical examples. The design method and design step must be clarified in the lecture. Simultaneously, some past excellent design cases are also demonstrated to students.
- Students should be arranged as concentrative as possible. The name school system must be stochastically implemented to strengthen the discipline management.
- A defense is arranged in the last stage of the course design so that students can clear every detail. Students can not only enjoy the interesting of solving problem, but also heighten their confidence of solving problem. Obviously, this stage can solidify the creative study and apply of theoretical knowledge.

4 Summary

Education and teaching formation is an important and arduous task in entire higher education. The theoretical teaching contents and methods have been reformed according to the course system of the wide caliber specialty. In order to satisfy the new course content and understand its difficult points, the reformation and study on practical teaching in mechanical manufacturing technology is both inevitable and necessary. The reformation strategy of practical teaching is suggested to attract students' attention to mechanical manufacturing technology. The proposed reformation strategies can help student to improve basic abilities of analyzing and solving problem.

References

1. Zuo, D.W., Li, J., Li, X.F.: J. Nanjing Univ. Aeronaut. Astronaut. (Soc. Sci.) 11(1), 87 (2009)
2. Zhang, S.C.: Fundamentals of Mechanical Manufacturing Technology. Tianjin Univ. Press, Beijing (2002)
3. Feng, Z.J.: Principle of Manufacturing Engineering and Technology. Tsinghua Univ. Press, Beijing (2004)
4. Yang, J.R., Zhang, Y.K.: Higher Educ. Forum (4), 86 (2010)
5. Hua, C.S., Liang, S., Hu, Y.N., Duan, M.Y., Wang, X.C., Chen, W.S.: Higher Educ. Forum 4, 58 (2004)
6. Qin, G.H., Ye, H.C., Jiao, Y.Q.: In: Zhou, X.L. (ed.) Proceedings of the 3rd International Conference on Education Technology and Training, vol. II. Institute of Electrical and Electronics Engineering, Inc., Los Alamitos (2010)

Reform and Exploration on Professional Personnel Training System of Geotechnical Engineering

Zheng Da

Chengdu university of technology, Chengdu, China
zheng5490@yeah.net

Abstract. In this paper, the undergraduate teaching problems of geotechnical engineering are analyzed at Chengdu University of Technology after studying teaching practice of this profession. New teaching idea is proposed that geology and structural design are the same important, and training of project quality and innovation need to be emphasized. Through the reform and research on personnel training program, further professional courses system and practice teaching system of geotechnical engineering, the undergraduate personnel training system of this profession is established in the university to meet the new personnel training requirements for Wenchuan earthquake disaster reconstruction and the national economy development.

Keywords: geotechnical engineering, training system, professional teaching, training idea.

1 Introduction

As a branch of civil engineering, geotechnical engineering is a discipline which adopts engineering geology, soil mechanics and rock mechanics to solve the technical problems related to rock and soil in different kinds of engineering. From the review of the development of geotechnical engineering in the recent fifty years, we can see that it has developed around the problems related to geotechnical engineering in civil engineering construction of our country. Since the implementation of China's policy of reform and opening up, with the utilization of high-rise building and city underground space and the development of expressway, the geotechnical engineers focus more attention on the problems related to geotechnical engineering in the construction of building, municipal and traffic engineering. Setting a foothold in southwestern region and facing to the whole country, the major of geotechnical engineering of Chengdu University of Technology plans to cultivate the inter-disciplinary technical talents who engage in the investigation, design, research and development, construction and management of geotechnical engineering. Facing the need of reconstruction and new situation of the development of national economy after the occurrence of Wenchuan earthquake, the teaching and management workers of this major analyze the mode of talent cultivation and method of professional education of the major of geotechnical engineering, abandon the teaching means which do not conform to the requirements of the times, and explores a new personnel training system [1,2].

M. Zhu (Ed.): ICCIC 2011, Part V, CCIS 235, pp. 94–99, 2011.
© Springer-Verlag Berlin Heidelberg 2011

2 Existing Problems of Professional Talent Cultivation

Compared with the undergraduate education of the major of geotechnical engineering in other key institutions of higher learning, the graduates of the major of geotechnical engineering from Chengdu University of Technology lack basic knowledge, fundamental skills, ability of practice and innovation, which mainly shows in the fact that the students feel that they have poor ability of using knowledge, few practical skills, weak ability of self development, and weak capacity of adapting to the work after they enter the society. Generally, the graduates reflect that the knowledge learnt in the school cannot be invested and used immediately, thus they have to spend more time to adapt to the work. However, many employing units hope that they can hire more university students with some practical skills instead of expending energy on the initial training of new graduates [3]. Through the analysis of the students' learning effect of the major of geotechnical engineering of the university in recent years, we find that the following problems exist in the study of the students: (1) The foundation of geology is weak, and the students have low learning initiative of the disciplines related to geology such as engineering geology, rock and soil engineering, and structural geology and lack the understanding of the importance of relevant knowledge of geology, which directly leads to their insufficient understanding of the engineering characteristics of rock and soil; (2) The knowledge of mechanics is not solid, and the students do not grasp the basic concepts and theories of the courses, including soil mechanics, rock mechanics, material mechanics and structural mechanics; (3) The design ability is poor, and the students do not form correct engineering concept is not formed or grasp the basic skills and methods taught in the classes of rock and soil anchoring and retaining, foundation engineering, foundation treatment and construction of underground engineering, etc which are closely related to the practical engineering; (4) The innovation capacity is insufficient, and the students lack the ability of deepening the theoretical knowledge and flexibly applying them to the design of rock engineering, namely, they only know how to imitate, but fail to gain a thorough understanding of the knowledge.

The occurrence of the above problems is inseparable from the disadvantages of the teaching modes and methods. Currently, the teaching mode is relatively single. The simple "cramming education" is taken as the main method in most courses, which obviously disconnects the teaching and learning, thus the teachers cannot communicate with the students in time. Moreover, the combination of theory and practice in the teaching process is insufficient; the class hours of the course plan related closely to the practice is few. Therefore, the students lack necessary opportunities to practice, which makes it difficult for them to understand the knowledge in the textbook or thoroughly master the knowledge and form new concept [4, 5].

It is evident that the traditional concept of personnel training shall be changed and broken through. Only through abandoning the rules and regulations, the method of cramming education and changing the disconnection between teaching and learning, the situation of laying emphasis on theories while neglecting practical teaching can we enhance the quality of undergraduate teaching.

3 Change of the Concept of Personnel Training

Facing the reconstruction of Wenchuan earthquake and new demand of the personnel training of geotechnical engineering by the development of national economy, the major of geotechnical engineering in our university needs to make efforts in the cultivation of the practical skills of the students, reform and exploration of the undergraduate personnel training system of the major on the basis of inheriting the tradition and maintaining the advantages and characteristics.

The major of geotechnical engineering possesses dual characteristics of geology and engineering, which requires both solid foundation of geology and good quality of engineering. Especially with the deepening of numerous large-scale engineering construction projects to complicated geologic environment in mountain area, a series of important engineering problems demand to be solved, which need a flood of high-quality professional talents who are able to solve the complicated engineering problems. In order to adapt to the new demand, through long-term teaching exploration and practice, we put forward the new concept of "attach equal importance to structural design and geology, strengthen engineering quality and cultivation of innovation capacity" to conduct the personnel training of the major of geotechnical engineering.

Relying on the State Key Laboratory of Prevention and Control of Geological Hazard and Protection of Geological Environment of Chengdu University of Technology, the major sets a foothold in Southwestern region and faces to the whole country, and it shall gradually forms the characteristic of "geotechnical engineering under the complicated geological environment in mountain area". The foundation of the discipline shall attach equal importance to the structural design and geology. The practice of geotechnical engineering lays emphasis on the theoretical direction of geology for the prospecting, design and construction of the geotechnical engineering. The personnel training requires the students to have relative strong capacity of understanding, analyzing and evaluating the problems of geotechnical engineering. Cultivate compound specialized talents who can uphold the Four Cardinal Principles and meet the requirements of socialist modernization, acquire profound and well-knit basic theories, knowledge and skills of civil engineering and geology, engage in geotechnical investigation and evaluation under comparatively complicated conditions in the fields such as municipal affairs, construction, highway, railway, airport, irritation, water electricity, mines, geological mines and environment protection as well as design, construct, manage, study, educate, invest and develop general geotechnical engineering projects. These lay foundation for students to develop into senior technical experts and management experts in geotechnical engineering. at the same time of possessing the basic capacity of designing geotechnical engineering.

4 Construct the Personnel Training System

Personnel training proposal and professional curriculum system. Take the concept of "attach equal importance to structural design and geology, strengthen engineering quality and cultivation of innovation capacity" as the guidance and uphold the policy of "lay emphasis on dual basic foundation, strengthen the studies of characteristic curriculum, improve the cultivation of practical ability" when formulating the personnel training proposal of geotechnical engineering so as to make the teaching content both conform to the requirements of the goal of cultivating inter-disciplinary talents and possess distinctive features[6].

Formulate a personnel training proposal with distinctive features: enhance the education of core curriculum of majors such as mechanics, geology and engineering, the relevant credits account for 22% of the total credits (170); the practical teaching link include the field practice of "four years running", indoor and outdoor experiment, curriculum design, graduation project, etc, the total credit hours reach up to 46 weeks, which account for 24% of the total credits, and the total time of practical training exceeds 8 months.

Strengthen the setting of characteristic curriculum: give full play to the traditional advantages of the geotechnical engineering of our university and carry out new concept of personnel training. On one hand, strengthen the setting of characteristic curriculum, and persist in the independent setting of three courses of rock and soil engineering, geotechnical engineering investigation and engineering geology; on the other hand, improve the setting of characteristic curriculum of engineering, and offer the courses such as rock and soil anchoring and retaining design, construction technology of geotechnical engineering. Besides, in order to widen the range of professional knowledge of the students, offer 45 individualized optional courses of 8 types, including foundation of geology, mechanics, foundation theory and method, design calculation, new technology and method, experiment, engineering budget and engineering construction, etc.

Enhance the construction of characteristic teaching materials: the college establishes a special fund for teaching materials. In order to support the construction of personnel training proposal and characteristic curriculum, the college makes a declaration and edits the "11th Five-Year" national planning teaching materials, and publishes a series of experimental teaching materials.

Implement the "Four-In" mode to promote teaching: famous teacher in class, result in teaching materials, project in practice, innovation in management.

Establish practical teaching system of "one focus, three levels and five experimental trainings".

One focus: focus on developing students' ability to practice and create in engaging in large-scale construction projects and prevention and control of geological disasters under complicated geological environment in mountains based on the characteristics of large-scale construction projects under complicated geological environment in mountains.

Three levels: organize teaching from the three levels of basic experiment, comprehensive designing style experiment and personalized innovative experiment. At present, the demonstration center of experiment teaching has developed 115 experimental items of the three levels. Among them, there are 44 basic and confirmatory experiments, which account for 38 percent of the total; there are 54 comprehensive designing style experiments, which account for 47 percent of the total; there are 17 innovative experiments, which account for 62 percent of the total.

Five experimental trainings: Through the establishment and practice of new practical teaching system based on five experimental trainings, namely, course experimental training, open experimental training, field experimental training, off-campus base experimental or practical training (establishing two stable long-term practice bases on Mount Emei and Majiao Dam as well as almost 20 practice bases by the college-enterprise cooperation) and pragmatic experimental training, we develop the four-combination experimental teaching mode which combines experimental teaching with theoretical teaching, experimental teaching with scientific researches, lab experiment with field experiment, geotechnical engineering basic experiment with project designing experiment. The experimental teaching mode can realize the goal of providing experiment, practice and innovation platforms for personnel training and of all-dimensional and multi-level practical training of students.

Establish the system of innovation capacity and individualized cultivation of university students.

Build the "research base of scientific and technical innovation of university students" to provide a platform for the individualized cultivation and innovation capacity of excellent university students. The base covers an area of 100 square meters with over 10 instructors, and more than 20 excellent students will be selected to be cultivated each year.

S&T projects establishment of university students: encourage the students to declare for the s& t projects establishment at province, university or college level. The state key laboratory will provide experimental conditions and fund support for the s& t projects establishment of university students. In recent five years, over 300 people have participated in the establishment of more than 60 s& t projects, which greatly enhance the innovation capacity of the students.

In recent years, the state key laboratory has undertaken more than a hundred scientific research and engineering projects with an annual fund of over 30 million Yuan, which provides substantial opportunities for the students of senior class and graduates of the major of geotechnical engineering to practice. All the graduates of the major accomplish the graduation field work and thesis with the support of the scientific research and engineering projects.

Form the teaching staff with high quality and reasonable structure.

In accordance with the requirements of "quality plus structure", implement "three major projects" (backbone project, elite project, famous teacher project), cultivate the teachers of this major according to the type and level, and gradually form a high-quality teaching and R&D team with proper scale, degree, profession and reasonable age structure with the help of academic leaders of the older generation and the demonstration of famous teacher.

5 Establish the Quality Assurance System of Personnel Training.

As the concept of higher education has transformed from "elite education" to "mass education", the teaching mode has transformed from "traditional mode" to "option system", and the student status management has transformed from "academic year system" to "credit system", the student status management becomes more difficult and the teaching quality gets out of control. In order to overcome the above problems and adapt to the new education mode, the college establishes four management mechanisms of tracking and forewarning system of student status management, monitoring system of teaching quality, feedback of employing unit, and process of graduation field work to construct the quality assurance system of personnel training.

6 Summary

With the development of national economy and change of demand of professional talents, the cultivation concept and mode of institutions of higher learning shall be transformed correspondingly. The reform of personnel training system of the major of geotechnical engineering is based on the change of the concept of personnel training and transformation of teaching idea and method. It is a long-term and arduous task, which requires not only the teaching staff but also the students to change concepts, and the teaching management and examination system must be changed correspondingly as well. Only through this way can the personnel training of geotechnical engineering keep in step with the times and satisfy the need of the society.

References

1. Joyce, B.: Teaching Mode. China Light Industry Publications, China (2009)
2. Zhou, H., Wu, X., Li, P.: Practice and Research of Project Management Professional Training. Science and Technology Innovation Herald 24, 205–206 (2008)
3. Huang, Y.: Discussion on Changes of Training Mode of Civil Engineering and Professional Teaching Methods. Science and Technology Innovation Herald 3, 165 (2008)
4. Li, X., Xia, T., Dong, H.: Teaching the Engineering Concept of Students in Courses. Henan Chemical Industry 3, 38–39 (2010)
5. Zhang, F., Gao, Z., Yuan, B.: Enterprising Talent Training Practice of Geological Engineering Speciality. Chinese Geological Education 3, 60–65 (2006)
6. Pang, L., Ou Yang, J., Yin, M.: Realization the Reform on Teaching Methods of Chinese Higher Education of Geological Engineering for Innovation. Chinese Geological Education 1, 57–60 (2004)

Discussion on Improving the Safety Training Effect of Three Categories of Staff

Zhong-qiang Sun[1], Wei-min Dai[2], Jing Wang[2], and Xu Han[2]

[1] School of environment science and engineering,
Hebei University of Science and Technology, Shijiazhuang, 050018, China
[2] Hebei Capital Construction Department of Communications Office,
Shijiazhuang, 050051, China
zhong7778@yeah.net

Abstract. The safety training is an important basic work in the field of safe production. It is also fundamental means of improving safety management level, and it is effective way to improve safety quality, safety skill and safety consciousness. Based on analysis of the main defects of training, the safety training content was perfection combined with the characteristics of highway and waterway construction, and the advanced training methods with various means was proposed that based on reform and innovation to speech method of traditional. The whole training process was formed a circulation system of continuous improvement, and the accreditation of the staff was obtained with good effects. The study has an important significance to improve the safety situation of highway and waterway construction in China.

Keywords: Safety training, safety production, effect.

1 Introduction

Construction industry is the high-risk industries in the world because of the characteristics of diversity of work activities and the shift of workforce. Safety is eternal theme for human life. Many accident investigation results in domestic and international revealed that employees' unsafe behavior accounted for more than 80% of the occupational accidents [1]. Therefore, it is an important issue how to improve safety quality, safety skill, and regulate safety behavior of employees.

The safety training is an important basic work in the field of safe production [2]. It is also fundamental means of improving safety management level, and it is effective way to improve safety quality, safety skill and safety consciousness. It is the concrete embodiment of implementing the principle of "safety first precaution crucial and comprehensive treatment" [3,4]. According to regulations of State Council that safety training was strengthened to achieve fundamental improvement in the safety situation. Therefore, the theory of safety training must be strengthened and the new training mode was introduction to improve the safety concept of employees. To improve the quality of training and achieve the ultimate goal of safety production, the content and method in safety training were reformed based on training practices of three categories of staff of highway and waterway construction in Hebei Province.

M. Zhu (Ed.): ICCIC 2011, Part V, CCIS 235, pp. 100–104, 2011.

2 Current Problems in Safety Training

According to "Production Safety Law" and the relevant regulations of the Ministry of Transport in China, three categories of staff of highway and waterway construction in Hebei Province have been training and achieved certain effects. But, it has a certain gap to the objectives, the reasons were as follows:

The Unsound Legal System in Safety Training. With advancement of technology and change of supervision system in government, there are some questions in current safety training such as legislative slow, some urgent need legislation vacancies but current laws have cross phenomenon and repetition that can not meet the current requirement in safety situation; administrative means was used rather than legal means to manage the safety training; The maneuverability of laws and regulations be different [5].

The Low Attention Degree of Enterprises. Some enterprises not pay attention to safety training and not brought into the development program of enterprise. Therefore, it is result that the scarcity of management talents and weak technology force; safety training was a mere formality that can not reach the targets because of deficient of the safety investment.

Poor of Pertinence of Content in Safety Training. The lack of pertinence of content in safety training, the hierarchy of curriculum is not strong and the content is overlap between the different courses. The main training content and form is single that it is the bulletin to the relevant laws, regulations, and safety document or written training to safety skills, which made the staffs to boring and uninteresting, then can not achieved the desired results.

Poor of Effect Evaluation and Quality Control. Safety training not treated as a cycle process by most training institutions, and it is poor effect evaluation and quality control. Even if the effect evaluation was carried out, which only arriving the reaction layer and the learning level but not the behavior of layers and effects layers, then can not achieved the desired results.

Irregularity of Structure Level in Stuffs. Age and educational background structure of "three categories of staff" are very different that the age from 30 to 60 years old and educational background structure is also from secondary school to master. Therefore, learning and acceptance ability of staffs was different that bring a certain influence to organize training, and can not achieved the desired results.

Poor of Modern Educational Means. At present, the speech method of traditional was used, which obsolete methods, single form of education and lack of flexibility [6,7]. Training content can not be keeping pace with the times, for example: the contents of training is not renewal for regulations and techniques that resulting in staffs can not grasp the latest national policy, and can not achieved the desired results.

3 The Ways to Improve the Quality of Safety Training

Design Reasonable Training System. (1)The principles of curriculum. It was based on national laws and regulations to improve the ability of staffs and to change the reality problems and future-oriented. (2) The curriculum model. The cluster mode of "broad base, active formwork and attention to practical" has been adopted to improve flexibility and adaptability of the curriculum. Such as a reasonable class size was set by restriction number and single treatment of the structure of three categories of staff to make the training has more purposiveness and pertinence. (3) Curriculum content. The knowledge, skills and attitudes were related to the choice of curriculum content, and succession, integrity, correlation would be pay attention to in the course of the scheduling. Therefore, the training Curriculum content of highway and waterway construction was constructed based on training experience and training content system of various industries: laws and regulations, safety management, safety technology, case analysis (Fig. 1). When explaining, it was according to Sequence of laws and regulations, safety management, safety technology.

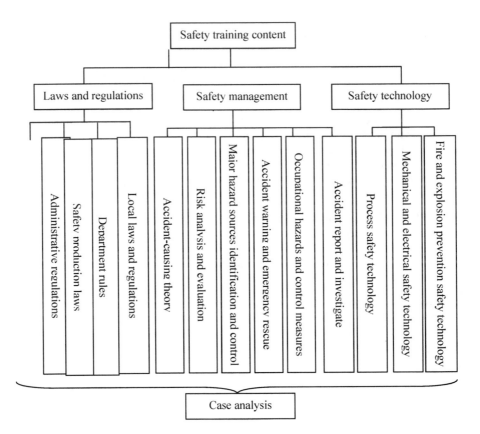

Fig. 1. The configuration frame diagram of safety training

Taking the content of laws and regulations construction as example, at present, it has cross phenomenon and repetition that a lot of safety laws and regulations in China, and therefore the relevant laws and regulations must be introduction. For example: "Production Safety Law", "Items of safe production Management of Constructive Project", "The Measure of Supervision and Management for safety production in highway and waterway construction " have regulations on the administrative organization setting and the full time manager equipment for safety in production, to avoid repetition and waste of time that the same contents be induction to one. The suitable training contents were selected base on different staffs in the training process, for example, it should be explained that safety regulations, safety management and so on for the person in charge; it should be explained that safety management methods, measures, procedures and so on for managers; it should be explained that safety operating rules, technical specification and labor discipline and so on for workers.

Construction of Teaching Staff. Construction of Teaching Staff was done well to ensure the quality of training according to the training requirements. The person who has safety production, theoretical knowledge and training experience was most suitable for the safety training. Therefore, the teacher resource database must gradually be established, which has characteristics of structural optimization, operational proficiency, and vigor. For example, the university professor of experiences as the training of teachers, benign development of training and research on construction would be effectively promoted and the various advanced teaching resources can make full used.

Archives Management. Establishing and perfecting the safety training archives, which was both the powerful guarantee to standardization of training and important means to sum up experience enlarge knowledge and increase theoretical level of specialty for training teachers. Therefore, the archives would be established according classify, collect, arrange and edit to training material, which would be rational used and updated. Training archives including all the laws, regulations, documentation and training programs of training; training organization responsibilities and requirements; training syllabus, curriculum standards, training materials; teaching plan, quality analysis results of training; registration forms attendance forms, examination results forms, test papers and so on.

Teaching Method. At present, speech method was used in training although the Variety of safety training methods. With the development of technology and the popularity of audio-visual equipment, the multimedia teaching was applied in training, which use of FLASH, video, pictures and sound. The quality of training can be improved by using both speech method and other methods. Therefore, the traditional training method combined with audio-visual method was used of "three categories of staff". This method is intuitive, usually no seen or negligible details could be seen by animation simulation of FLASH. Construction safety knowledge and skills were taught with systematic, scientific and comprehensive. In the teaching process, in order to arouse staffs' enthusiasm for studying, teachers should move around in the classroom not always stay platform, which can improve study effects. After training, the teachers styles integrating and teaching materials would gave staffs to communication and study in future.

Teachers need higher requirements on this method of training: firstly, teachers must collect the latest audio video data, the enthusiasm of staffs would be influenced training if data obsolete; secondly, they must pay more attention to the latest research developments to introduce the latest management experience and safety technology of domestic and international to staffs.

Case Analysis. Through analysis of the causes of the accident, the defects of management, technical and human behavior can found, and the preventive measures were proposed. Meanwhile, the bloody accident can make workers feel the precious of life, and strengthen their safety awareness, get rid of illegal. Thus, case analysis is important to teach in the course. For example, to explain the law of criminal punishment, " first sentenced for endangering public security of mine directors of Xinhua coal mine in China" as example, which can improved staff's safety awareness and understood the current state of punishment on illegal behaviors to avoid illegal phenomenon.

Idea Feedback. The practical effect of safety training was accurately obtained through the feedback mechanism, and the deviations of safety training was found and modified to improve the effect. Therefore, feedback form was designed to find the gaps in training and weaknesses, which include the content, teaching methods and organization management. It can provide the scientific advice and guidance for the next training, and to achieve continuous improvement in training design, teaching, management and evaluation.

4 Conclusions

As a basic of production, safety plays a important role in more complicated construction. To pursuit of economic benefit but neglect safety is wrong. Safety production is a reflection of the comprehensive level of enterprise management and an important part to achieve social stability and harmony, which is an investment for the future, and a guide and basic for lasting political stability. According to idea of "caring for life and human-oriented", the production and operation units should adhere to the policy of safe production and continuous learning, innovative training ideas, explore new ways and means of training. To ensure the healthy, sustainable and stable development of highway and waterway construction and improve the quality and effectiveness of safety training, safety training must be strengthened.

References

1. Zhou, G., Cheng, W.-m., Zhuge, F.-m., Nie, W.: China Safety Science Journal 18, 10 (2008)
2. Wang, Q.-y.: Journal of Safety Science and Technology 5, 193 (2009)
3. Liu, W.-h.: Journal of Safety Science and Technology 6, 169 (2010)
4. Duan, X.-h., Li, S.-z.: Journal of Safety Science and Technology 2, 95 (2006)
5. Zhao, D.-l., Hu, D.-t., Chen, Q.: Industrial Safety and Environmental Protection 34, 32 (2008)
6. Wang, L.: Journal of North China Institute of Science and Technology 1, 27 (2004)
7. Yu, M.-f.: Industrial Safety and Environmental Protection 34, 46 (2008)

XML Webpage Design Teaching Method Application: A Study

Li Yuxiang[1], Bi Danxia[2], Shao Lijun[3],Wang Shi[1], and Geng Qingjia[1]

[1] College of Mathematics and Information Science & Technology, Hebei Normal University of Science & Technology, Qinhuangdao, Hebei, China
[2] Trade Union of Hebei Normal University of Science & Technology, Qinhuangdao, Hebei, China
[3] College of Foreign Languages, Hebei Normal University of Science & Technology, Qinhuangdao, Hebei, China
bi6789@126.com

Abstract. Proceeding from arrangement of courses and choice of teaching methods (task-driven, divergent thinking, and analogism), this Article elaborates on how to arose students' interest and foster their innovative thinking and team spirit in the course of XML teaching, thus to raise the quality level of teaching of students.

Keywords: task-driven, divergent thinking, analogism.

1 Introduction

Along with the development in the Internet technologies, XML (eXtensible Markup Language), as a world language of the Internet, has received more and more regard from technicians for it has a good extensibility and a good structure, and is not subject to limitation by any platform; it is widely recognized within the industry in such aspects as data description, data exchange, data display, etc. But, in webpage design, it involves too many rules, codes and more (parser, browser, compiling software, format list, databank, programming language, web server receptacle), thus it is difficult both for many students to study and for teachers to teach. Through rounds of teaching and learning, we teachers and students have worked together and summed up some of our experience, and we'd like to present the experience in a hope to ease everybody's burden of study.

2 The Contents of the Course Should Be Able Arouse the Students' Interest, and Should Go from Simple to Abstract

Normally, the textbooks come in the following sequence: XML Introduction→ XML grammars→ XML File Structure: DTD Description →XML File Data: Schema Description → XSL(Extensible Stylesheet Language) →Application Programming Interface DOM, SAX →XML Data Island →examples of XML web application

In consideration of the fact that the students require what they learn is what they obtain, so let them lean the practicality of the course and fill them with a sense of contentment. DTD and Schema involve many grammars, DOM and SAX involve JAVA language, and the examples of application involve JSP built-in object; and the

M. Zhu (Ed.): ICCIC 2011, Part V, CCIS 235, pp. 105–110, 2011.

students have learnt HTML, VB, data architecture; so, with the students' interest considered, we go from shallow to deep, from simple to abstruse, by changing the sequence of the course to: XML Introduction→ XML grammars→ XSL (Extensible Stylesheet Language) →XML Data Island→ XML File Structure: DTD Description →XML File Data: Schema Description →Application Programming Interface DOM, SAX →examples of XML web application. Then, the students will feel the courses are practical, and are not abstruse either.

3 "Task-Driven Study" Method Is Applied in Teaching

"Task-driven study" method is a teaching method based on the structurist teaching method; it requires learning, both autonomously and interactively, from the learning resources, as driven by their strong question solving desire, by centering themselves closely around a common task, and under the guidance of the teacher. It requires creation of a "task" and a teaching environment to make students learn through exploration under a real task [1].

3.1 Task Description

The teachers should prepare examples of application before the lesson, and present the effect of examples to the students through multi-media classroom, thus to, through analysis of practical examples and creation of task, arouse the students' interest and initiatives in learning. The Figure 1 presents the example of the information retrieval module.

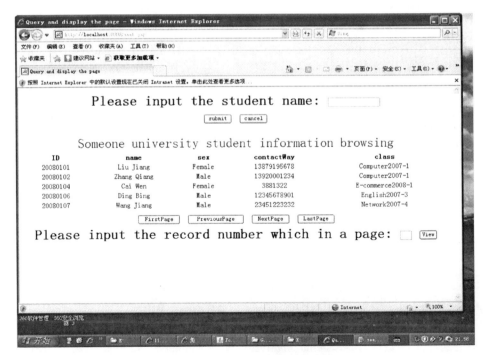

Fig. 1. Effect of the Example of Information Retrieval Module

3.2 Task Analysis

In the way of discussing, the teachers and students can make an analysis of the example in Fig. 1, find out the task to be fulfilled and the knowledge and techniques to be applied, and raise the question "what would the result be if "Submit Question" is single-clicked?".

3.3 Fulfill the Task

The teacher should, in the light of the contents being discussed, lead the students in designing and composing codes, place stress on the results of clicking "Submit the Question" button, submit the name to the server, specify in the "Form" JSP file to process the information submitted, and set the "Method", for example, <form action="seek1.jsp"; method="post">. When explaining on seek1.jsp, it should be stressed to retrieve, through the built-in object of request, the information for the request from the customer terminal, and give value to the related variable in preparation for processing by the system, such as String str=request.getParameter("name1").

The entire teaching activity is at all time driven by "task", the main thread running through our teaching and learning activity. Through example, the students are made to know what, how, and through what method, knowledge and technique we'll do, their interest and initiatives in learning is sparked, they are filled with a sense of fulfillment for their solving practical questions by using the knowledge and skills they have learnt.

4 Foster the Students' Divergent Thinking by Letting Them Fulfill One Task with Multiple Solutions

Divergent thinking is a thought process or method used to generate creative ideas by exploring many possible solutions; it involves multiple directions, angles, depth. It is characterized by bold hypothesis, is not limited by any existing knowledge or tradition; its information processing can be made in all directions; its results can be an unknown thing deduced from the known in which way to discover new information and new grounds. Guilford said: "It is in the divergent thinking that we see the clearest hallmark of creation". Without divergent thinking, people's thought will run barren. In this context, only divergent thinking, and only by raising multiple ways and methods can help solve creative questions [2].

Finding multiple solutions to one task is one of the training methods for fostering the multi-directional divergent thinking. Its objective is to let students give play to their respective intelligence and wisdom, to explore all reasonable solutions, to devise all feasible schemes, and, ultimately, to achievement the same result. When lecturing on creation of XML files, notepad can be used, XML editing software, such as XMLSpy can also be used; and the teacher can lead the students by raising this question: can we make use of the information in the databank, such as Access? If yes, we, in a big project, can divide the work and work interactively, where some enter the data with Access, and then convert it into XML file, some prefer interface design, some prefer programming. That raises the work efficiency, doesn't it? Then in what method can the tables in Access be concerted into XML file?

4.1 Using Access's Conversion Feature

The operating procedures are as follow:
Open the databank→ select the table →open → select the "File" menue → select "Export" →select "XML(*.xml)" in the "Export" dialogue box

4.2 Using XMLSpy's Conversion Feature

Operate in the following procedures:
Launch XMLSpy→ slect "Convert" menu→ select "Import the Databank" → select "Convert the Databank to XML" in the dialogue box→ single-click "Recognize" button → select Microsoft Access (ADO) (A) in the Source Databank dialogue box→ single-click "Next" button → single click "View" button → select databank → single-click "Open" button → single-click "Next" button → single-click "Select Databank Form" button → select databank form → select "Recognize" button → single-click "Import" button → single-click XMLSpy's "Save" to save the file.

4.3 Using Java for Conversion

Operating procedures run as follow:
Performing program devising → programming and generating ".java" file → compiling the programs and generating ".class" file → running ".class" file → generating XML file, where programming is a critical step, it falls into 2 parts: retrieving data from the databank; generating XML files out of the existing data.

To retrieve data from the databank, the first thing is to load the databank driver, then create databank connection object, create statement object, generate ResultSet object by activating the inquiry sentence, use re.next() to judge if the related record has been retrieved, save the data retrieved into the related character array.

Create XML file out of the data in the array, first obtain the object of parser, builde, and, on the basis of which, create a blank document node object, set the version of the node, document.createElement() to create a root node, add related Element node and Text file node, and lastly, save the created node tree into the XML file.

The above task is fulfilled with many a solution. It not only increases the students' interest in study, also fosters their divergent thinking. The teacher can give continuous guidance, let them observe the similarity and dissimilarity among the XML files generated by 3 methods, and then make an analysis of the environment of application for the 3 different methods. It can also be extended to analysis and choice of arithmetic, project-related decision, vocational planning, life planning, and realize the purpose of education.

5 Facilitating Understanding with Analogism

Analogism is a learning method of making comparison between the content of a course and those similar or identical to the content of the course, thus to establish a knowledge model to turn abstract to simple and help the students' understanding of new knowledge, promote their self-study, and foster their innovative thought[3].

5.1   A Comparison with HTML

Use IE browser to run HTML files and XML files respectively to let the students understand thatHTML's mark is fixed, predefined, and inextensible, while XML's mark is extensible, and are defined by itself. HTML marks indicate the information display format, XML marks indicate the logical structure of data; HTML is designed to display data, its focus is the appearance of data; XML is designed to describe data, its focus is the contents of data. HTML's data is difficult of reuse, XML's data is reusable. HTML's data is intermingled with typesetting and appearance of presentation, XML separates data from format displayed, which realize display of output in different modes, this provides basis for opening, share and exchange of data. It further stresses that XML is devised for saving, carrying and exchanging data; for display, use should be made of the extensible Singlesheet language (XML). The following is another example.

5.2   Comparison with C language

Through C language program design, the students acquires a basic knowledge of modularized program devising, who have grasped main function, subfunction, function call and more concepts. So, in explaining about XSL template, a comparison with modularized program design can reduce a complex task into a simple one, where the designers can do their design separately. In the C program, function is the unit for dividing the task; in XSL, template is the unit for dividing the task. C program has at least one main function, XSL file has at least one template; C program start executing from the main function, XSL starts conversion of XSL from root template. C language function is defined in the following form:

```
Type indication sign, function name (form parameter list)
{statement sentence}
The grammatical form of XSL definition template element is:
<xsl: template match="XPath express" language>
   <!—Output rule-->
</xsl: template>
The normal form C language function call is:
Function name (actual parameter list);
The grammatical format of XSLcall template is:
<xsl: apply-templates select="XPath expression">
   ......
</xsl:apply-templates>
```

Explanation in the light of given examples makes the students feel that the new knowledge is not unfamiliar any longer, and, at the same time, fosters a thinking methodology in students, thus make students can infer the whole from a single instance, and have a foundation for later study.

5.3 Comparison with English

XML has too many rules and codes, mostly in English. In the teaching and learning process, full use should be made of the English knowledge learnt to help the students understand new knowledge. For example, in getNodeName(), we have "get, Node and Name". If we learn them as 3 words, it would be much easier.

Through comparison with English, let the students understand that knowledge is not isolated, it is interconnected, and students should enrich them knowledge as much as possible. Thus knowledge is imparted and quality is enhanced also.

6 Conclusion

In XML teaching process, we applied multiple teaching methods, where the concept is all time observed of educating students, fostering their interest, raising their ability, optimizing the contents of course, teaching method and teaching process, as well as raising the efficiency. At the same time, students' team spirit should be fostered to lay a foundation for the later work and life.

Acknowledgement. The support from the Department of Science and Technology of Hebei Province is appreciated (Support Program No. 072135212). Hebei Department of Education Scientific Research Project(No. SZ090341).

References

1. Li, Y., Zhou, Y., Gu, C.: Foster Students' Innovating Ability by Task-Driven Study. Education and Occupation 15, 156–157 (2010)
2. Hezi, O.: Develop Divergent Thinking. Jiaxi Normal University (September 2009)
3. Preliminary Exploration into the Application of Analogism in Upper Secondary Middle School's Math Teaching [J], China Education Informationisation, by Yng, Z., December 2010: 38-40.
4. Cai, T., Liao, Z., Tang, W., Mo, J.: Practical Course in XML Webpage Design. People's Post & Telecom Press (2009)

Research on Applied Teaching Pattern of University Designing Lessons in the Major of Architecture

Bojia Liu[1] and Jianqing Wang[2]

[1] College of Civil Engineering & Mechanics, Yanshan University,
Qinhuangdao, Hebei, China, 066004
[2] Periodical Press, Yanshan University, Qinhuangdao, Hebei, China, 066004
liu906@126.com

Abstract. This article reseaches on characteristics and perspective of applied teching pattern in designing lessons in the major of architecture, as to contemporary situations of the society. It also discusses the strategies in making teaching targets, organizing teaching steps, etc., and proposes how to make students have more teaching techniques , and provide them chances of training in classes.

Keywords: designing lessons in the major of Architecture, applied teaching pattern, training of working techniques, teaching pattern.

1 Introduction

"learning to meet practical needs" is the most urgent desire of college students in their professional study, however, the idea of promoting all-round developments of human and guided by social demands of cultivating talents has gained widespread approval in the education field. The severe employment pressure highlights the general lack of work experience and insufficient ability of university graduates, thus, creating conditions to increase students' practical skills training is the key work of the college teaching reform. However, in terms of the existing teaching conditions, it cannot provide students the opportunities for comprehensive and systematic practice in a certain period. Thus, the urgent task and priority is the reform of teaching mode, combining the teaching content restructuring and diversified evaluation, making students acquire the necessary job skills training in the limited conventional courses, this might be a more practical and effective solution.

The working nature of architecture speciality possess both scientific and artistic qualities, various kinds of design courses as major professional ones, are responsible for cultivating students' comprehensive design abilities, and their teaching effects directly determine the success of professional training. However, in this kind of courses, the current teaching method over the years is still taking the traditional mode as major one,which previous is teachers' centralism teaching and arrangement and then students' accomplishment on their own. The malpractice of this teaching mode lies in the excessive separation of "teaching" and "learning"; due to the centralism teaching, and each design is a complex system containing lots of information and life experience, students don't have enough time to digest while listening, they even often do not understand the practical application of what they have learned, and thus they are lack of

M. Zhu (Ed.): ICCIC 2011, Part V, CCIS 235, pp. 111–116, 2011.
© Springer-Verlag Berlin Heidelberg 2011

abilities to organize their trivial knowledges into practical tools (design method). And in the process of working, teachers mainly help students to solve specific and concrete problems, and rarely involve the cultivation of working methods, causing students cannot grasp design essentials well in design courses learning which are closely involved with working situations, and missing valuable training opportunities.

Therefore, this type of courses, facing the request of social development, needs to change the thought, involve specialized training goals, apply scientific theories, carry out overall design for teaching and construct a teaching system with optimal structure and function, making students foster the ability of higher level thinking, learning to acquire new knowledge independently and solving the unknown problems on the basis of mastering the basic concept, theory and training skills, this is not only the ultimate goal of courses teaching mode reform, but also the original intention of the practical teaching patterns proposed in this paper.

2 Applied Teaching Pattern Overview

2.1 Brief Introduction

Applied teaching pattern mentioned in this article is different from the traditional one in which teaching and learning are separated, and also not to set practice separately in the teaching courses, but to advocate the integral strategies from practice to practice, which is oriented to cultivate the ability according to the general learning rule of design courses. The first practice refers to building a knowledge environment integrated with theory explaining by teachers, in this context, teachers don't have to rush into the segments of what it is and how to do it, but put knowledges into wider realistic backgrounds (e.g. related social and cultural backgrounds with design, demands, especially design experiences and feelings of teachers themselves), these vivid topics can always draw great interests from students, thus making them realize the use of knowledge, identify their study directions clearly and accumulate knowledges and skills that design requires at ordinary times, which plays a key role for them to understand theories, and thus students' thirst for knowledge can be more intense and sense of identity will be higher. The setting of this link can also promote the instructor to constantly update their knowledge system and keep aware of their professional dynamic.

The latter practice is still a process through doing design homework for students to master working method. What's new is that, practical teaching design changes the process which mainly relay on students' self-study (students often feel inadequate and confused) into a dynamic learning to solve problems gradually under the guidance of teachers through multiple links of control, and teachers and students control dynamic learning rhythm together. This teaching mode does not need extra investments like money and time, but depends on the control of process.

2.2 Characteristics

(1) Clear aim, which is benefit for teaching: creating situations builds a bridge between reality and theory, making students have the personal feeling that his education fits him for a certain job. Take the architectural design of kindergarten as an example,

on-the-spot visits or the memory of childhood experiences before the explanation of architectural design   method , can make students empathy to understand the particularity design elements of this architecture type in use modes, scale, structure, color and so on, this can help students capture the core ideas quickly and seize the teaching keys.

(2) Good interactivity, which can keep the teaching consistency: the effect of students' knowledge acceptance largely depends on whether the information exchange between both sides of teaching is flow or not. Due to the applical teaching mode increases the intermediate links of process control, and deals with the drawbacks of the past design courses which are that teachers talk through the whole class while later students finish their homework on their own, it can make students receive timely guidance from their teachers in different stages of doing their homework, teacher and students are in constant instructions and feedbacks, thus creating more communication opportunities, making students' thought to be more active, and is more propitious to form strong study atmosphere.

(3) Strong timeliness, more realistic significance: as a practical teaching method facing the reality and emphasizing the practice, in theory explanation and homework training, teachers and students will conscientiously and actively connect their knowledge with various phenomena of reality, and take knowledge accumulation and methods training required in work as part of the courses, thus narrowing the distance between theory and working abilities, and accelerating knowledge updating. Meanwhile, each stage of teaching is respectively done with corresponding actual work, teachers must require students learning from certain working standards, expound work background with different requests to students, and in a certain sense, doing homework is becoming reality-based training. Make students deeply feel their own needs to improve, and give them more power to study.

Today quality-oriented education and skills training are increasingly valued, practical teaching mode brings greater space for teachers and students. On the one hand, the materials introduced to teaching are more extensive and fit the realities, so students can easily resonates. Through the process control,taking independent thinking and responsibility consciousness and other quality raising as one of the contents of teaching and examination, can effectively motivate students consciously and comprehensively to study specialized knowledge. On the other hand, it puts forward higher requirments for teachers, demanding them to pay more attention to the new trends for their profession, and providing power for their scientific research.

Despite different courses have some difference in tactics , but they all can fundamentally cultivate students through courses learning to obtain necessary working skills like innovation consciousness, team cooperation spirit and ability of interdisciplinarity on the basis of mastering the fundamental principles, embodying the spirit of quality-oriented education.

3   Teaching Strategies of Applied Teaching Pattern in Architecture Design Courses

3.1   Positioning of Teaching Objectives

Various kinds of design courses are set throughout architecture education in order to mold students' knowledge structure and develop their professional ability. The precondition of the "application-orientated" teaching mode, including a clear teaching objective and reasonable positioning of it, are also the basis of the course teaching, based on which appropriate teaching acts should be taken.

(1) Development of sense of responsibility.In a world of increasing communication and fast-changing concept, students are inclined to be misled with access to more information, only to neglect the nature of design as well as responsibilities as a result of following the trend blindly. It is the primary task throughout to instruct the student, with all kinds of teaching methods, of their professional responsibilities to perceive the nature of design beyond complex surface and to exclude disturbance to achieve the realization of their own value, which include, for example, the cultural significance and contextuality in the design as well as the reflection of safety and low-carbon concept, etc.

(2) Willpower training.The work of architecture designing is integrated with interest and arduousness, which therefore requires not only interest into this major but also extreme patience as well as perseverance of pursuing perfection. However, this abilities is ignored in conventional teaching and causes that the student are not able to rapidly adapt themselves for the work in which they are involved. Teachers are supposed to help students establish correct working attitude according to their own characteristics.

(3) Development of working method.Students are supposed to master not only procedures of specific designs but also correct design method during learning in order to practice and comprehend by analogy during working. In this way, what they have learned is not just limited in the book but the skills to apply the knowledge, self-learning methods and awareness of mutual assistance.

3.2 Teaching Organization

3.2.1 Theory Teaching

Theory teaching in a design course, as design inspiration, is usually the lecture of design objective and the method introduction. "Application-orientated" teaching mode reorganizes the content of course with different emphases at different phases and guarantee of the consistency of teaching. Therefore, the teaching effect can be improved to a great extent.

(1) Stage of perceptual cognizance: Architecture is the product of the combination of both sense and rationality, the process of which is ignored by conventional teaching practices; additionally, it has flexible forms ranging from fieldwork, example appreciation to direct discussion. It requires little time while eliminating students' sense of strange toward new types of designs. If well-designed, it can impose a quite positive impact upon following teaching procedures.

(2) Stage of teaching design theory: When theoretical method is being taught, the theory teaching design is responsible for the elaboration of "how" and "why" on the basis of the "what" at the perceptual cognizance stage. The core of this stage is to instill concepts and methods to students and organize their ideas from top down.

3.2.2 Design Instruction

(1)Formation of overall design idea: Formation of design ideas is the most difficult part of the whole design, which requires students to establish a design framework through initial exploration. Teachers should, on one hand, inspire the imagination in the students without restraint as much as possible and, on the other hand, remind them to pay attention to all the factors related as well as the principles in relation to society, cultural background and corresponding subject; meanwhile, teachers should arrange the students to discuss their design plans and encourage them to introduce their other design as well as evaluate others' works. All these approaches contribute to grant the students the ability of rationale analysis, a better understanding of the nature of design and a conscious exert of scientific methods for the consideration of the relations between a design and all the factors comprehensively. Only in this way can their originality in their assignment be the Creating Work subject to reality.

(2) Process control: A design inception still requires a long process of repeated revision toward its completion. This process is the principal stage when teachers instruct the students with their design in order to help them develop their working skills and form right working methods. The completion of a design (in other words, real grasp of a design method) is a transition process described as "broad-narrow-broad". Given that the previous formation of deign inception and design ideas constitute the first "broad" part of the students' knowledge structures, the study afterwards is for the purpose of completion of the latter two parts of the whole system. Teacher should supervise the students during the revision of the design chart whether they manage to insist on the perfection of every single detail and whether the revision is conducted totally as required and in addition, summary should also be emphasized.

3.2.3 Construction of Feedback System for Assignment Evaluation

The submission of assignment is the finish of conventional teaching, leaving the students ignorant of evaluating methods and merit and demerit of their designs. The students feel at loss after completion of design, which brings the development of students' design abilities the low quality. "Application-orientated" is generated in a practical dilemma, of which the objective is to convey the students the knowledge itself as well as better application methods of the knowledge. Therefore, the design evaluation system is not only the measure to ensure teaching quality but also the conjunction as for the coherent system with following design courses. Teachers are supposed to first set an objective and scientific scoring system where related factor are involved according to their weighting; meanwhile the scoring system is more than simply the arithmetic addition and should clearly reflect the students' abilities of handling different situations. The time mode combined with stage summary and final evaluation is applied. The performance of students' assignment is divided into several "part", after which the method combined with student introduction and teacher evaluation is applied; therefore, students have the opportunities to show and learn from each other and they are also enabled correct errors occurred in their designs in time. After the completion of whole design, students' assignments can be scored systematically and comprehensively together with the advices for the students' future study. These should be fed back to the students in written materials and informal discussion can also be held by teachers as for direct talk students as well as solving their problems.

4 Summary

The core of "Application-orientated" teaching mode is to convert the conventional teaching mode with the ultimate objective of knowledge conveyance towards the omnibearing teaching mode with teaching in class orientating the students to self-directed learning, knowledge learning promoting performance ability and course exam trainings exercising professional qualities. Its advantages include not only the class atmosphere enlivened by cases quoted and students' enthusiasm stimulated but also the changes for students outside and inside class of access to self-discovery, self-performance and self-perfection and, furthermore, deeper understanding of knowledge learned and their major. Since problems to be solved in architecture design courses differ at different stages and the teaching requirements and features of every design course are various, different teaching strategies should be adopted correspondingly. Consequently, it still remains as a problem to be further explored how to combine the mode with conventional teaching methods and how to achieve results satisfied by both teachers and students with the most efficient use of teaching conditions current available. This paper is primarily a study on strategies and serves as accelerator for better ideas. Specific teaching methods and details still require specific analysis according to the situation.

References

1. Zhong, H.: Chinese University Teaching, vol. 1, p. 49 (2010)
2. Chen, X.: In: Proceedings of the 2008 International Conference on Industrial Design (2008)
3. Liu, B., Zhou, J., Tu, Y.: Research in Teaching, vol. 31, p. 68 (2008)

Design and Analysis of a New Undergraduate Curriculum for Information Technology Degree at Universities in West China

Xiaoying Wang[1], Weitong Huang[2], and Xiaojing Liu[1]

[1] Department of Computer Technology and Applications,
Qinghai University, Xining, Qinghai, China
[2] Department of Computer Science and Technology,
Tsinghua University, Beijing, China
wang6663@yeah.net

Abstract. As the information technology rapidly progresses, the cultivation of computer science undergraduates becomes more and more important, especially for the economic and society development in West China. In order to make the education to meet the current demands, a major shift of emphasis away from the traditional computer science curriculum is needed. In this paper, we would present and analyze the new undergraduate curriculum of information technology degrees we designed in Qinghai University. New concepts have been incorporated, which will help students to gain more laboratory experiences and practical skills. Effect evaluation shows that the new curriculum is appropriate and effective for educating students aiming at computer applications.

Keywords: information technology degree, curriculum design, West China universities.

1 Introduction

With the rapidly development of computer and information technologies (IT), more and more universities take the cultivation of students with solid practical abilities as a new important orientation. In fact, there is a significant demand for skilled graduates in the IT market, but still many undergraduates of computer science major cannot find suitable jobs in recent years [1]. Such phenomenon reflects that a great number of university graduates lack the basic professtional qualities and capabilities to meet the social needs. One of the important reasons is that the traditional curriculum for computer science degree usually put insights into basic theoretical knowledge education and thus doesn't catch up the speed of IT technology advancement. As a result, the capability of graduates couldn't meet the demand of most employers, and thus it becomes a contradictory situation that many employers cannot find qulified grandutes to employ and many graduates cannot obtain employment for themselves.

In order to cultivate students with better practical skills and abilities, a number of universities began to explore some new models of personnel training. With the concept of enhancing practical skills, the "3+1" cultivation model has been proposed as an innovative approach spreading domestically [2], which means students should

M. Zhu (Ed.): ICCIC 2011, Part V, CCIS 235, pp. 117–124, 2011.
© Springer-Verlag Berlin Heidelberg 2011

accomplish all of the courses in three years and then concentrate their effort on professional pratical training in the last year. Under such model, universities ought to cooperate with the enterprises to provide necessary practice bases for senior students, while the enterprises also can enlarge their social impact vice versa, leading to mutal benefits. Under such circumstance, new curriculums should be designed and carried out to fit the "3+1" cultivation model.

On the other hand, west regions in China are always relatively less developed, especially at the information technology area, which means that a lot more talents are needed. Hence, universities in West China should take the responsibility to educate qualifiable graduates filling the blanks of IT infrastructure construction and IT applications. According to such objectives, the Department of Computer Technology and Applications was established in Qinghai University with the great support of Qinghai Province and Tsinghua University in 2007. The main orientation of our department is to cultivate more students with high quality for local IT development. In 2009, we started the construction of "West China Oriented Innovative Experimental Zone for Training IT Talents with Pratical Abilities", which is a "Quality Engeering" Project approved by China's Ministry of Education. With the support of this project, we make further efforts on exploring a new paradigm for personnel training.

According to our personnel training objectives, this paper describes the design and implementation of the new Information Technology Bachelor's degree program. This curriculum took approximately three years to fully design and was implemented within the department of Computer Technology and Applications in the Fall of 2007, and produced its first four-year graduates in the Spring of 2010. We have referenced some key ideas of relevant researches in other universities both abroad [3,4,5,6,7,8] and inland [1,2,9] during the last decade. In this paper we will share some of the details of this new curriculum and an analysis of its implementation and impact.

2   Curriculum Design

Required Courses. The designed framework of main required courses and their dependencies across four years are as shown in Figure 1. As it can be observed, there are four kinds of courses in the hierarchy, as follows:

(1) Public Basic Courses
Some courses are publically required for all Engeering Major students, which we called public basic courses. For example, *English*, *History* and *Physics* are required in the first two years; *Document Searching* is required in the third year; and *Politics* and *Sports* are required during all semesters. Specially, *Physics* is important for information technology students, sicne it is the fundamental of learning electric-related courses.

(2) Specialized Basic Courses
This kind of courses mainly contains the ones that provide the theoritical basis for computer-related professional courses. *Electirc Circuit Theory* and *Fundementals of Electonic Technology* are essential for learning the internal hardware constitution principles of computers. *Advanced Mathematics* and *Probability Theory* are both essentials to gurantee the mathematics fundamental knowledges, which are very

important for further learning professional courses such as *Discrete Mathematics* and *Data Structure*.

(3) Professional Courses

From Figure 1 we can see that the all of the professional courses are arraged in the first three years, according to the "3+1" cultivation model.

In the first semester, freshmen are required to learn comprehensive IT knowledges by attending *Introduction to Information Technologies* classes. In the latter half of the semester, when students gets familiar with basic computer operations, *Fundametals of Programming* will be taught to let the students start to learn some C programming skills. This course will fruther be extended to the second semester involving C++ programming, which first introduces simple object-oriented concepts.

In the third semester, *Discrete Mathematics* will be taught to strengthen the training of logical thinking and reasoning, and to introduce Boolean knowledge which is the fundemental of modern computers. *VC++ Programming* is another programming course after C++, letting students to acquire skills of visualizable programming. In the fourth semeter, three courses of great significance will be taught, including *Java Programming*, *Computer System Platform* and *Data Structure*. A main principle of designing the curriculum is that programming skills should be emphasized and strengthened for our students, and thus they continue to learn programming relevant courses across each of the four semesters.

For junior students, there are various kinds of professional courses arranged in the third school year, covering many different areas. For example, *English Paper Reading* is taught with the objective to train the students to read English documents in order to obtain more advanced information about recent researches; *Object Oriented Methods* and *Software Engineering* help students learn to design, implement, and test individual software components from a holitics viewpoint; Professional knowlegdes about multimedia, graphics and images will be given in *Multimedia Technologies*, *Computer Graphics*, *Game and Animation Design* classses; Furthermore, *System Maintenance* helps train students to manage and maintain computer systems; *Web System Techniques* trains students to build up a complete dynamic website with three typical tiers; *Information Security* introduces some security issues and the approaches to prevent malicious attacks. In this way, junior students are offered with comprehensive professional knowledges by these courses, covering several different areas of computer applications.

(4) Comprehensive Practices

During the last year, there are no theoretical courses arranged but only comprehensive practices across the two semesters. After all the courses have been finished in the first three years, the undergraduates will be sent outside the school and go to enterprises for *Pratice and Training*. In the seventh semester, students must accomplish a small-to-medium software project in realist enviroments under the instructions of university teachers or engineers from enterprises. This process can greatly enhance the students' practical abilities, which is most important for them to get a job after graduation. Then, in the last semester, students have to finish the *Graduation Project* by conducting research and development under a specific topic to get their Bachelor degrees.

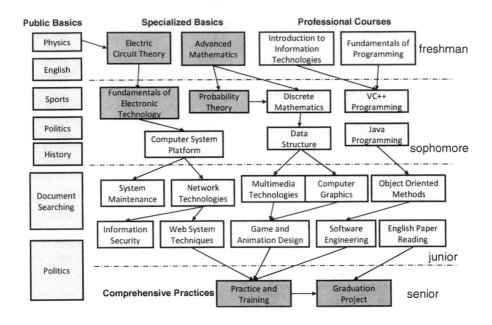

Fig. 1. Curriculum Design of Required Courses in Four Years

Elective Courses. As show in Table 1, a series of elective courses are available for students to select. Most elective courses are taken out in 4-6th semesters. For example, *Functions of Complex Variables and Integral Transformations* and *Computational Method* are regarded as mathematical courses following up with the *Advanced Mathematics* course, each taking 48 class hours to finish in the 4th semester. Besides, various types of courses exhibiting the computer technology progresses are set as elective courses for students to choose, involving the area of information storage, search engine, artificial intelligence and so on. In Table 1, "48(32+16)" means that it takes 48 hours to finish this course, wherein 32 hours are spent on theoretical classes and 16 hours are spent in laboratory for practical exercises.

Table 1. A List of Typical Elective Courses

Course Name	Credit	Total Class Hours	Semester
Functions of Complex Variables and Integral Transformations	3	48	Fourth
Computational Method	3	48	Fourth
Fundamentals of Search Engine Technology	2	32(16+16)	Fifth
Information Storage and Management	2	32(16+16)	Fifth
Software Analysis and Evaluation Technologies	2	32(16+16)	Sixth
Artificial Intelligence	3	48(32+16)	Sixth

Moreover, most elective courses will be taught by teachers we invite from top universities and well-known enterprises, with deep and solid foundation of knowledge and engineering experiences. This makes the elective courses valuable and attractive for more students. Through the cooperation with other universities and enterprises, the practical abilities of the students can be promoted to a higher level.

Practice Training. According to our objective of talent cultivating and the need of IT market, we have established a multi-stage, hierarchical, and progressive practice teaching system, as shown in Figure 2. The manner of practices contains two different kinds: practice inside classes and concentrative practices. As we can see from the above section, some of the practice processes are included into corresponding classes respectively. For example, the teacher of *Data Structure* course will lead the students to spend 32 hours in the computer laboratory doing programming work for practice. If some students could not finish their tasks in class time, they have to make efforts after class doing homework or other practices. Practices inside the classes ensure that the students can do exercises under full guidance and instructions of the teacher, who will help them to solve various kinds of problems.

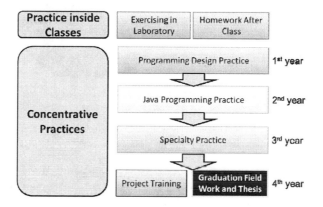

Fig. 2. Curriculum Design of the Practice Teaching System

Concentrative practices are arranged across the whole 4 years for undergraduate students, by setting up separate practice courses within or between different school years. In the summer after the first year finished, students have to attend the *Programming Design Practice* to solve small realistic problems by using basic programming skills by themselves. Then, in the second year, after the *Java Programming* course is finished, *Java Programming Practice* is required for all students to do Java practices further and more deeply. In the 3rd year, *Specialty Practice* will be conducted to train the students to do synthetic programming leveraging all kinds of specialty knowledge. Then, *Project Training* in the last year encourages students to learn real project development skills. Finally, after all these practices, students can spend a half year to design and implement an entire system for their *Graduation Field work and Thesis*.

Specially, most of the subjects and projects in the last year practices come from enterprise productions. Furthermore, a large number of senior students will be sent to different companies and organizations to work there as a practice process. In this way, not only the students can gain more practical skills by doing real-world projects, but also the enterprises can choose appropriate potentials to hire among the working students.

2.1 Curriculum Analysis

Proportion of Different Course Types. As we designed, the whole curriculum contains four different types of courses, including public basics, specialized basics, professional courses and concentrative practices. Here, the proportion allocation of the teaching hours of these courses is illustrated in Figure 3. It can be observed that professional courses occupy nearly the half of total. Besides, concentrative practices obviously take a remarkable ratio of 16% in the entire distribution.

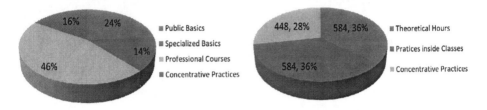

Fig. 3. Percentage of All Types of Courses   **Fig. 4.** Percentage of Teaching Hours of Professional Courses

Proportion of Theoretical and Practical Time. To gain deeper insights into the professional courses specifically, we compare the proportion of theoretical and practical time and illustrate it in Figure 4. As it can be observed, theoretical and practical hours are equivalent (both 584h), which means that in average each course takes a half time for students to do exercise by their own. Besides, 448 hours of concentrative practices are required outside ordinary lecture time, which makes the total practice time up to 64% of all the professional courses, exhibiting an obvious shift away from traditional computer science degree programs.

3   Implementation and Effects

This new curriculum has been designed and implemented firstly in the year 2007, and produces its first four-year graduates in this year. This section mainly introduces some distinguished aspects in the implementation.

Unique Courses. Different from other widely-used computer science curriculums, there are a number of unique courses in our implementation. For example, the *Computer System Platform* course is a newly brought point of view that incorporates computer composition principles, operating system, network platform, and computer infrastructures together, towards an integrated systematic perspective; the *System*

Maintenance course leads the students to know better about plenty of specific details when managing and maintaining different kinds of hardware, operating systems, network environments and database systems; the *Web System Techniques* course shows students how to establish a complex dynamic website by using mainstream technologies such as J2EE/.NET. It is notable that these unique courses have a common feature that they all provide significant practical applicability to fit potential hiring requirements of positions for IT construction.

Internship in Industries. To gain real-world design experience in industry, the concentrative practices in our program involves internship in industries. In order to function properly, it's important to have a number of companies and government organizations who are willing to participate in this program. With our persistent efforts, a variety of software companies and other organizations has involved in supporting internship. For instance, *ChinaSoft International* has donated a suite of developed enterprise cases and established a practice base in our department; Undergraduate students are dispatched to developed cities such as *Beijing*, *Shenzhen*, and *Wuxi*, etc. for internship in batches. Besides, during each summer and winter vacation, most of junior and senior students will be sent out to some departments in the local city such as Qinghai Information Center etc. for part-time work. From the internship reports submitted by the students and other kinds of survey, we found that they all feel that that it's more important to practice in reality than only reading and listening. As a result, students who have attended internship earlier usually progress quickly in following studies, exhibiting more enthusiasm than other students.

Performance and Effects. After a period of performing the new curriculum in out department, the first graduates are going to leave the university. Among these students, 14.3% of them will go on studying for a master's degree; 45.7% of them choose to join software companies inside and outside the province; others are going to some government departments or state-owned enterprises. Besides, 10% of current students are attending scientific and engineering researches by applying for national projects and joining the research work of faculties. We can see that the innovation of the curriculum has proposed a new paradigm of cultivating IT talents for undeveloped regions. The emphasis of practical abilities has exhibited actual effects during the personnel training process.

4   Conclusion

Since the technological advancement of computer engineering will continue at an ever-increasing pace, the education system should cope with it make the students stronger to enter into society. Most importantly, the students should learn the ability to learn by themselves. Considering the situation of universities in West China with less academic foundation of IT talents in need, this paper suggested a new degree program for the Information Technology degree. In this program, we emphasize that more time should be spent on students' practices and exercises by their own. The whole curriculum system is illustrated and described in details. From the following analysis, we can see that the new curriculum fulfill the thought of cultivating the practical abilities. As a result, the students could accumulate more industrial experiences by working on projects from enterprises or even working in the enterprises themselves. The implementation and performance of the new curriculum has been evaluated, which shows that the undergraduates could find suitable positions to work for the development of both economy and society in West China. Based on the current design, we plan to go on enrich the curriculum with more elective courses in variety to enlarge the breadth of students' major.

Acknowledgement. This paper is partially supported by 2009 Quality Engineering Project of China's Ministry of Education "West China Oriented Innovative Experimental Zone for Training IT Talents with Pratical Abilities at Qinghai University" and 2010 Course Construction Project (KC-10-3-16) in Qinghai University.

References

1. Lu, L.-n., Li, L.-n.: The Reform and Innovation of Teaching Model in Application-oriented Students' Training. Computer Education (13), 3–5 (2009) (in Chinese)
2. Wang, X.-y., Wu, D., Song, P., Jiang, J.-j.: Research and Exploring of "3+1" Talents Cultivation Approach, vol. (4), pp. 15–19 (2010) (in Chinese)
3. Director, S.W., Khosla, P.K., Rohrer, R.A., Rutenbar, R.A.: Reengineering the curriculum: Design and analysis of a new undergraduate Electrical and Computer Engineering degree at Carnegie Mellon University. Proceedings of the IEEE 83(9), 1246–1269 (1995)
4. Knight, J.C., Prey, J.C., Wulf, W.A.: A look back: undergraduate computer science education: a new curriculum philosophy and overview. In: Proceedings of the 27th Annual Conference on 'Teaching and Learning in an Era of Change', vol. 2, pp. 722–727 (1997)
5. Carley, L.R., Khosla, P., Unetich, R.: Teaching "Introduction to Electrical and Computer Engineering" in Context. Proceedings of the IEEE 88(1), 8–22 (2000)
6. Hissey, T.W.: Education and careers 2000, Enhanced skills for engineers. Proceedings of the IEEE 88(8), 1367–1370 (2000)
7. Farbrother, B.J.: A New Approach to Electrical & Computer Engineering Programs at Rose-Hulman Institute of Technology. In: Proc. 1997 ASEE Annual Conference & Exposition, Milwaukee, WI (June 1997)
8. Hughes, J.L.A.: Incorporating Project Engineering and Professional Practice into the Major Design Experience. In: Proc. 31st ASEE/IEEE Frontiers in Education Conf., pp. 16–21 (2001)
9. Yao, H.-s., Jiang, J.-j., Jiang, K.-q.: The Research and Experience of Undergraduate Education Plan and Curriculum System Reform of Normal College Computer Specialty by Lead of Employment. Computer Education (2), 43–46 (2009) (in Chinese)

The Study on Management Design Education Concept in Engineering Management Major

Guangshe Jia and Lingling Chen

School of Economics and Management, Tongji University, 1239 Siping Road,
Shanghai 200092, China
jia98067@163.com

Abstract. Based on the analysis of current status in engineering management education, this paper presents a new education concept in engineering management major. The role of this proposed design education could turn abstract capability cultivation into practical design activities in order to teach, learn and practice creative problem-solving skills. This paper expounds on the concept from three perspectives, namely, philosophy, quality and knowledge. Implementation and evaluation of management design education concept are discussed.

Keywords: Engineering Management; Management Design Education; Competition.

1 Introduction

In 2006, the report conducted by CAE (the Chinese Academy of Engineering) indicates the engineering managers have generally higher technical quality, but lower basic individual quality and comprehensive management quality [1]. At the same time, while numerous engineering management standards, endless stream of methodologies and tools are provided by professional associations or consulted organizations, projects are still fail at an astonishing rate. Yet the phenomenon puts up a question as management competencies of project managers outside of project management standards appear to be more relevant for their workplace performance than tools and techniques emphasized in the standards [2]. Jeffrey s. Russell holds that in order to meet the demands of future development in civil engineering management, the educators and students should have the ability to integrate key concepts, understand globalization, expand social awareness and use information technology to enhance learning [3]. David R. Riley thinks engineering management team are expected to provide key leadership functions, which involves decision making and judgment and requires a particular set of competencies and traits, such as communication, honesty, integrity, continuous learning ability, courage and so on [4]. Janice Thomas argues that a large number of agents call for new leadship approaches beyond the control-room. They think it's time to review our understanding of project management education and reflect about how to deal with the increasing level of complexity, chaos, and uncertainty in project environment[5]. As management is highlighted in the development of engineering management, the comprehensive management quality of employees in construction industry is becoming widely concerned. It's urgent to improve comprehensive management quality.

M. Zhu (Ed.): ICCIC 2011, Part V, CCIS 235, pp. 125–132, 2011.

This paper is in five sections. Section 1 analyzes the current status of management education in engineering management and points out the disadvantages of current educational approaches. Section 2 presents a review of design education in other disciplines and then illustrates management design education concept from three perspectives: philosophy, quality and knowledge. Section 3 discusses the implementation of management design concept and expounds on competition as a good approach and section 4 gives some suggestions to the evaluation. Section 5 is a summation.

2 Current Status of Management Education in Engineering Management

The generalized engineering management includes civil engineering construction, logistics, transportation, software engineering management. This paper discusses civil engineering management in narrow terms. Engineering management education abroad stemmed from 1920 when civil engineering profession was subdivided into CEM (civil engineering and management) and other majors. Chinese engineering management education began from Tongji university setting up construction economy and organization major (five-year education program) in 1956.

Table 1. Analysis of Different Management Education Approaches

Approaches	Description	Advantages	Disadvantages
"Learning by doing" (Practical teaching)	"Learning from practice" replaces the passive teaching method of "learning from others".	Students learn knowledge in the practice make it easier to improve the practical management capability.	It stresses on the accumulation of practical experience, but neglects knowledge which may produce the problem of binary opposition between theory and practice.
Problem-based teaching (Knowledge teaching)	Based on practical problems, students acquire the relevant knowledge through exploring, researching engineering problem.	Knowledge constructive process is supposed to be independent. Students grasp basic knowledge deeply and pay more attention to creativity.	Lack the concerns of strategic management concept. It's easy to take a part of management as for the whole.
Project-based teaching (Practical teaching)	Carry out teaching activity through a specific project.	It cultivates students' practical capability and builds bridges between theory and practice.	Project-based teaching has the instant feature while capability cultivation should be a long-term and sustainable process.
Case teaching (Knowledge teaching)	The necessary facts and materials for students to discuss who are supposed to be decision makers.	It fully exploits knowledge in the project cases and arouses students' interest for learning.	Case teaching which requires high for teachers' teaching level and students' theoretical base, doesn't achieve expected results in Chinese localization process

In the second half of 19th century, from pragmatic empiricism and functional psychology, Dewey proposed the basic educational concept-"education is life" and "school is society". Yet, the education approaches of "learning by doing" appeared. Influenced by Dewey's educational viewpoint, constructivist learning theory and situational learning theory, problem-based teaching and project-based teaching are implemented in engineering education from 1980s [6]. Case teaching originated from Harvard business school in 1920 and achieved good teaching results. From the 1980s, China applied these educational approaches to engineering management education and groped effective approach in practice [7]. *Table 1* shows the analysis of these teaching approaches.

All the teaching approaches above focus on students and motive learning atmosphere, and bilateral interaction between teachers and students. Some of them concern about management theory, while the others pay much attention to the management practices. It's hard to cultivate students' management ability systematically. In addition, scholars argue to improve management capability from expanding students' knowledge horizons [4][8], and develop informal project training to improve students' ability [9]. But the present system is fragmented and it's very difficult for students to understand how all the pieces of knowledge units and professional skills fit together to enable them become engineering managers.

Overall, management education should emphasize on both theory and practice. The proposed concept "management design" cultivates students' correct engineering view and educates innovative competence, problem-solving skills as well as engineering knowledge units to improve engineering capability systematically and comprehensively.

3 Definition of Management Design

Design education is the hot topic and main research direction of engineering education from 1980's, with increasing connotation. Harold Koontz holds that "management is a process of designing and maintaining a good working environment to reach fixed goal efficiently"[10]. He added design capability of problem-solving into three main management skills: professional skill, social skill and conceptual skill. Rittel asserts that design can be thought of as problem setting, locating, identifying and formulating the problem, its underlying causes, structure and operative dynamics- in such a way that an approach to solving the problem emerges [11]. Design process can also be defined as a process which involves all activities which can be performed by a designer from the beginning until locating the final solution. Hence, this design process is the dominating part of management planning, so this paper proposes management design education concept.

Kunz and Rittel addresses design problems by using argumentation structures to facilitate a discussion amongst the stakeholders about design issues, which allows the problem to be explored and framed [12]. Unlike problems of natural science, management design's goal is not clearly set and always changes according with project environment. As a result, management design often needs management foresight and enough cultural confidence to create and design new management mechanisms, modes, patterns, etc. Management design procedure is full of repeated actions of designing, implementing, assessing, redesigning. Students would benefit significantly by more exposure to engineering technical and managerial design process. It turns abstract ability cultivation into specific practical design activities in order to gain knowledge and experience.

Architectural curricula are composed of three general categories of academic work: 1) basic courses of liberal, arts; 2) professional courses dealing with important aspects of professional practice such as building structures, materials and construction or environmental control systems; 3)architectural studio [13]. Like architectural curricula and industrial design education, engineering management design education educates students from three perspectives, namely, philosophy level, quality level and knowledge level according with four categories of curricula, as shown in Figure 1.

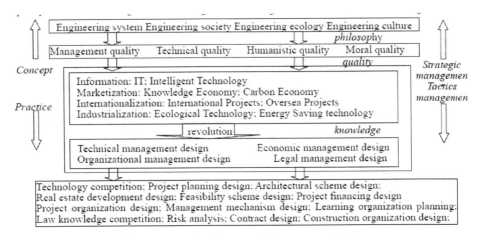

Fig. 1. Education Concept of Management Design

Philosophy Level. Engineering, by definition, is the application of science and mathematics to projects for the benefits of society [14]. The managerial targets of civil engineering are projects and projects activities which interact with economy, society and environment to create a very complex relationship. Management is a kind of systematic wisdom. The premise of management design education is the correct world view and engineering view. It should educates students deeply understanding engineering from four aspects: engineering system, engineering society, engineering ecology and engineering culture, which inquire into the nature of engineering and the original and inherent relationship in engineering, nature, society and human being development. Without the deep understanding of human world, instrumental rationality and natural law, we can't really understand projects and their social values, not to mention making right management decisions [10]. Therefore, management design education focuses on students' viewpoint about value orientation.

Quality Level. Knowledge is a set of principles, methods and methodology which exist independently while quality is the manner and inspiration of people to study, create and utilize knowledge and technologies. Swanson argues that due to the rapid development in technology, most of the jobs will no longer in 15 years [15]. The real difficulty for management design education is forming an engineering manager with adequate wide knowledge but also possesses the special adaptability which is need in complex environment we face today and in the more complex environment that we are likely to face in the future. Thus, during the design process of analysis, synthesis, interpretation, creation, assessment and criticism, universities should cultivate students' management quality, humanistic quality, technical quality, moral quality, etc. Students' ability to learn and adapt, able to lead the development of industry should be paid the much attention.

Knowledge Level. Engineers can't design without broad and wide professional knowledge. Engineering management has four knowledge platforms, namely, technology, economy, organization, law. The development of internationalization, industrialization and commercialization featured by knowledge economy endow management education with new contents.

Technical Management Design. The unprecedented development of technology brings extensive and profound innovation to engineering technical management. For example, IT technology can realize dynamic, comprehensive and tridimensional management in the projects' whole life cycle. Meanwhile, the application of intelligent technology and ecological technology can make construction industry change from a traditional "high energy consumption, high input, high pollution" industry to the one with sustainable development structure.

Construction projects are becoming more and more complex which requires higher technical management competence. Technical management design needs to cultivate students' technical competence and build broad knowledge structure of "T" type. On the basic professional technical-knowledge, the management design should pay attention to the integration with new technologies and managerial tools. Students are supposed to master modern information technology, utilize common project management software skillfully such as Microsoft Project and p3e/c and have independent learning skill to manage different technologies in the new technical platform and the capability to analyze, implement, develop and assess this technology.

Economic Management Design. The new economic environment requires for the matching economic management design skills to promote companies' economic management competence. The management problems appear as the elements of economic management vary, so the design should aim at the market with dynamic development. For example, with the urgency of climate problems and the global deep reflection of economic development way, low-carbon economy becomes the hot topic of economic development, bringing not only influences to construction industry's low-carbon energy saving technology, but also new challenges to economic management. One of the new missions is strengthening carbon-asset management in the construction industry. In the variable economic situation, students are supposed to have advantages of the related economic knowledge to analyze the macroscopic and microcosmic economic environment and forecast marketing changes. Moreover, they should have the adaptability to deal with changes, explore unknown areas positively and gain valuable experience in practice.

Organizational Management Design. Organizational management is through organizational structure and stipulation in responsibility and right to make the organizational members coordinate and cooperate to achieve organizational goals effectively and efficiently. The traditional organization types don't meet the needs of modern engineering projects. So it has developed into learning organization, virtual organization and portfolio-management organization or program-management organization. Modern engineering organization stresses more on information delivery mechanism, communication and coordination system, organizing learning skills. So, organizational management design requests students to have good learning ability, communication skills and teamwork and make full use of knowledge and resources outside the organization. They have professional skills to complete complex high-tech projects through the establishment of suited project organizations to realize the comprehensive utilization of resources [16].

Legal Management Design. As one of the four basic knowledge platforms, law is always not given enough attention. In engineering management, we use contract management more than legal management because the market follows the principle of "contract comes first". In contrast with the neglects of legal management in the universities, United States investigate the upper managers of 400 large-scale construction enterprises three times in 1978, 1982, 1984, the data shows engineering construction laws and regulations have always been considered as the most important course in the 28 courses of civil engineering graduates' curriculum [17].

Legal management design education should first focus on the cultivation of legal consciousness. Second, legal management should become strategic management from transactional management. Legal protection concept should be "active" rather than "passive". Finally, legal management should be international. With the development of internationalization, legal management education should broaden students' legal knowledge and international vision.

4   Implementation of Management Design

This new format will create a system that is a logical, workable, flexible, coherent, and focused engineering education process. It must be an integrated system for students to understand how all the pieces of knowledge and professional quality fit together to enable them to become an outstanding d engineering manager.

In revising the civil engineering curriculum to include engineering design as the central theme of the CE education process[12], we propose that a series of management design courses based on engineering projects be the core courses to improve students' management capability. It should be started with freshmen and each semester education is a prerequisite for each succeeding year. The comprehensive design education is taught in sequence which would be supported and surrounded by the relevant knowledge units and curricula. Management design is primarily an open-ended and recycled problem-solving process which needs broad and deep engineering courses such as relevant steel design, concrete design and irrelevant business, psychiatry courses.

Besides traditional teaching, competition is also an important supplement and promotion to class teaching and practical exercise, such as internships, field research, etc. In other areas, competition has become an important incentive mechanism to encourage innovation and invention earlier. It's a simulation approach which imitates real projects and organizes students into a team which would play a significant role to integrate knowledge, cultivate problem-solving capability, innovative awareness, coordination and cooperation skills and leadership skills. Management design competition from four aspects of technology, economy, organization and law can be conducted as shown in *Table 2*.

Table 2. Scheme of Management Design Competition

Technical management design competition	Economic management design competition	Organizational management design competition	Legal management design competition
1)Steel design competition;2)Concrete design;3)Project planning design;4) Architectural scheme design;	1)Project bidding scheme design;2)Real estate development scheme design;3) Project financing design;4)Feasibility scheme design;	1)Organization structure design;2) Learning organization Planning;3)Virtual organization design;4)Management mechanism design	1)Legal knowledge competition;2)Contract design;3)Risk analysis competition;4)legal mechanism design;

The management design education concept should organize well the input of multidiscipline theory and practical activities to teach and study various aspects of the engineering management. well implemented to educate students and cultivate engineers. The proposed concept would work in a completely integrated system with the present fragmented system. It focuses on students' systematic engineering view, solid professional knowledge, innovative spirit and practical capability.

5   Evaluation of Application of Management Design

The implementation effect is effected by three factors which interact with each other: First, whether the education concept of management design is feasible and rational; second, it's affected by students' learning attitude; third, to what degree the university supports management design education concept. As the complexity of individual development, it's hard to calculate the incremental effect of management design education.

This paper holds that collecting evaluation from employing company may be a more objective and effective way. We can compare the graduates who are trained with management design education with others who are not. Through the comparison, we can find out whether the management design can improve student management competence effectively and efficiently. Surveys are conducted in two ways. First, we can send questionnaires to graduates' grass-roots organizations and collect the assessment from grass-roots organizations such as colleagues, department heads. Second, we collect the information from company's human resource managers. At the same time, we can also obtain the evaluation from the perspective of students to find out problems in the implementation in order to adjust programs and continuously improve teaching methods. The questionnaires can includes questions about management design education concept, students' learning attitude (time and energy entrusted into learning), and the supportive level of school (teaching quality, interaction between teachers and students, good teaching atmosphere). From the perspective of students to investigate satisfaction of the management design is more targeted.

6   Summary

The most important thing in engineering education is to improve students' engineering capability, such as CDIO program conducted by MIT, so it can be said that the essence of engineering management is the management. The educational program of management design is based on the design procedure and education in architecture and manufacture, which focus on systematic managerial viewpoints, creative problem-solving skills, communication skills, adaptability to rapid changes, leadership skills and a much broader and deep understanding of engineering management design. W.P. Lewis and his partner investigated 66 professionals-designers and company executives from consultants and manufacturing and demonstrated that the usefulness of design education in organizing thinking about design [18]. While this paper presents the design education is feasible for managerial capability cultivation from theory, it still lacks of empirical research. Scholars who are interested in this topic can develop the further researches.

References

1. Chinese Academy of Engineering: Researches in Higher Education of Engineering 9, 3 (2010)
2. Crawford, L.: International Journal of Project Management 10, 1 (2005)
3. Russell, J.S., Hanna, A., Bank, L.C., Shapira, A.: Journal of Construction Engineering and Management 8, 662 (2007)
4. Riley David, R., Horman Michael, J., Messner John, I.: Journal of Professional Issues in Engineering Education and Practice 9, 143 (2008)
5. Thomas, J., Mengel, T.: International Journal of Project Management 12, 304 (2008)
6. Roberts, A.: Design Studies 15(27), 168
7. Xiong, H., Yue, A.: Researches in Higher Education of Engineering 3, 48 (2009)
8. Bergendahl, J.A.: Journal of Professional Issues in Engineering Education and Practice 5, 257 (2005)
9. Oglesby, C.H.: Journal of Construction Engineering and Management 14, 5 (1990)
10. Li, H., Wang, Z.: Science & Technology Progress and Policy 4, 52 (2010)
11. Rittel, H.W., Webber: Policy Sciences 5, 155 (1973)
12. Kunz, Rittel: Issues as Elements of Information Systems, Working Paper, vol. 8, p. 131 (1970)
13. Kurt, S.: Procedia Social and Behavioral Sciences 8, 402 (2009)
14. Kirschenman Merlin, D., Brian, B.: Leadship and Management in Engineering 3, 69 (2011)
15. Information on,
    http://www.humanities.curtin.edu.au/html/des/DesEd2000/preconference04.html
16. Yu, J., Qiu, K.: Management World 4, 9 (2006)
17. Xu, Y.: China Construction Education 3, 7 (2008)
18. Lewis, W.P., Bonollo, E.: Design Studies 22, 385 (2002)

Bilingual Teaching Mode Combined Top-Down with Down-Top Method

Wang Yun, Xu Zhenying, Dai Yachun, Zhang Kai, Jiang Yinfang, and Ren Naifei

School of Mechanical Engineering College, Jiangsu University, Zhenjiang, 212013, China
yun3987@163.com

Abstract. Bilingual teaching is very important for the internationalization of higher education and inter-disciplinary talent training. In this paper, we introduced the bilingual teaching development and pointed out the existing problems in bilingual teaching modes. Then, a novel bilingual teaching mode combined the Top-Down and Down-Top methods (BTMTDDT) is proposed. BTMTDDT is the combination of Top-Down management from the university authority and Down-Top communication between teacher and students. By BTMTDDT, the network and system of bilingual teaching mode can be implemented among manager, teachers, students, teaching, curriculum, textbooks, teaching quality and speciality. Therefore, the bilingual teaching "Student-centered and Teacher-Guided" can be developed with inspired teaching environment.

Keywords: Bilingual Teaching, Top-Down, Down-Top.

1 Introduction

Bilingual teaching is a kind of teaching mean of speciality courses which is conducted by the second language except the native language. The aim of bilingual teaching is to train talents with higher education and inter-disciplinary background, resulting in the promotion of higher education internationalization in our country. The bilingual teaching in some provinces such as Beijing, Guangdong, Shandong, Shanghai, Jiangsu, Tianjin, Zhejiang has been extended from the local "individual test" to the "group test".

China's entry into the WTO has accelerated the trend of internationalization and modernization. The inter-disciplinary talents that are proficient in bilingual and profession can be the backbones in the international competitive environment. Teaching mode reform with the aim of effectively cultivating bilingual talent is the inevitable trend for foreign language education to meet the social development, which is also the result of the quality education. It is necessary to carry out the research and practice of bilingual teaching to change the lapping situation in the language teaching in our country. The bilingual teaching practice is the laborious work to make the language acquisition throughout the management, education in school, subjects and the whole teachning process.

2 Recent Development of Bilingual Teaching

Bilingual teaching is not a newborn that dates back to 1960s. The Canadian French Immersion Program in Canada and Western European countries (such as Belgium,

M. Zhu (Ed.): ICCIC 2011, Part V, CCIS 235, pp. 133–136, 2011.
© Springer-Verlag Berlin Heidelberg 2011

Luxembourg, etc.) [1] that aimed at "language teaching" by "teaching language" with the actual emphasis on language education. In 1968, American issued the bilingual education law to protect the equal rights for the education of immigration students [2], the survey made by Aguire International showed that the bilingual teaching effect was determined by the class size and the teachers' language level. However, eventually America only apply bilingual teaching to the language teaching of limited English proficiency students and immigration students. Singapore began to implement the national bilingual teaching which is dominated by English [3], while India adopted the pyramidal bilingual teaching mode in the elementary schools, high schools and colleges. The other countries and regions such as Japan, South Korea, Hong Kong and Taiwan benefited from the long-term bilingual teaching [5]. Because the Situation-oriented Teaching Mode is stressed on the active participation of the learners, the strengthening awareness and response to the situation of the learners, it is widely used in the bilingual teaching and other education.

China hired the foreigners to teach scientific knowledge in the period of westernization movement, mainly including military school, scientific and technical school and church school of promoting the bilingual teaching [1]. However, it had not been conducted continuously. Up to now, bilingual teaching has been tried in primary and middle schools in the developed economic regions. For higher education, Ministry of Education, in 2001 urged to adopt foreign language teaching in proficient and specialized courses, especially in the urgent specialities of high-tech for the development. In three years afterit's the call, the courses with foreign language teaching would rise up to 5%~10% of all the courses. Furthermore, the original textbooks should be introduced and improved [6]. The advantages of bilingual teaching include the introduction of advanced foreign theories and skills, problems analyzing and solving abilities, two-way communication ability and proficiency of foreign language. According to the reaction of college bilingual teaching seminar held by senior education department and the group of bilingual teaching, three current modes of sinking, blending and bilingual thinking can be divided [7]. Only Tsinghua University, Zhejiang University, Shanghai Jiaotong University and Xiamen University has been in the rank of bilingual thinking mode. Most universities are still in the initial sinking and blending stages, which is far away from the aim of fostering the inter-disciplinary talents with foreign languages.

It is concluded that bilingual teaching started early abroad with long-term investment, and its pattern was relatively stable and effective [8]. Wang Xudong has analyzed the feasibility of bilingual teaching in China [3]. Lu Lianghuan has put forward "gradual infiltration method" aiming at the education of the level of the students' English comprehension [9], while Liangqing has developed and implemented this method [5]. Yan Yezhou proposed the suggestion of reforming to improve the bilingual teaching in advanced schools [6]. Houyin has discussed the application of Krashen's acquisitive theory to the bilingual teaching implementation [10]. Ying Kefu has introduced collaborative thoughts to cultivate talents whose major are MBA [11]. Current studies is mainly concentrated in the bilingual teaching mode, teaching method, curriculum construction measures and school management measures. The studies are relative scattered and not systematic. Many proposed teaching modes are not implemented in the practice. It is also lack of innovation in the teaching mode and theory. The main disadvantages of the existing bilingual teaching are inflexible model with ordinary teaching effect, the disjunction with major, lagging teaching means, the lackage of excellent bilingual textbooks, curriculum and teachers,little interested for students in the bilingual teaching, the lackage of quantization standard of bilingual teaching and the system of evaluation.

3   The Double-Line Bilingual Teaching Mode

The Concept of the Double-line Bilingual Teaching Mode. In order to achieve the actual effect of the bilingual teaching, Top-Down and Down-Top type of is applied, namely, to obtain the best input and output bilingual teaching effect as the goal, The double-line bilingual teaching mode is combined Top-Down management method of school to teachers and Down-Top management method of teachers to school.

Implementation of the Double-line Bilingual Teaching Mode. Top-Down mode means that management line begins from the university to dean, colleges, departments, teachers and students. The opinion of each stage should be consulted and unified. The relationship of the each stage should be comprehensively considered to formulate the measures, documents and policies which are suitable to the Situation-Oriented bilingual teaching,   such as the staff training, special allowance for bilingual teaching (Jiangsu University has formulated), bilingual teaching inspection mode and counterpart funds for textbooks, teaching aid, course resource digitalization and network, etc). Top-Down mode can improve the emphasis of bilingual teaching. This mode mainly embodies the principle of individual subjecting to the centralization.

Down-Top mode means that the operational line begins from individual teacher, in proper order to departments, colleges, dean and university. The collaborative relationship among university, teachers, students, classes, courses, materials, qualities, specialties, and individuals should be considered comprehensively by each stage of units. The detailed operational norm and resources of the collaborative Situation-Oriented bilingual teaching should be established and improved, such as the designing coursewares, constructing situations and the platform for learning. The association between knowledge of the main subjects and the coursewares will be dealt with by the departments and colleges. The implementation of teaching hardware and the teaching system of bilingual teaching can be provided by dean. The university president formulated the documents to ensure the stable implementation of bilingual teaching from the teachers and the subordinates without conflicts. Down-Top mode mainly reflects the principle of service from group to individual. Top-Down and Down-Top is implemented simultaneously with the ultimate goal of developing the three-dimensional network and system of the collaborative bilingual teaching. During the implementation of new teaching mode, the difficulty such as the link, synergy, conflict elimination and coordination between learn and teaching is desirable to be solved.

Besides the operation of the two principal line of Top-Down and Down-Top, the cooperation of individuals and team are still needed. The modern educational techniques and approaches, such as multimedia technology, network, teaching aids and GROUP discussing mode, can be applied to the bilingual teaching to construct "student-centered teachers-guided" teaching environment with the information increase of bilingual teaching and teaching effect improvement.

Actual didactical teaching practice and test must be carried out. Furthermore, pluralistic evaluation system and questionnaire (including investigating aim, contents, object, option designing, index designing and sampling method, etc.) for bilingual teaching can be developed to evaluate the student and teacher. The evaluation system of bilingual teaching can reflect the fairness, rationality, bidirectionality, guidance and incentive. Then bilingual teaching mode improves according to the feedback information to achieve the best effect of bilingual teaching.　Finally, through a small range trial and successful experiences, bilingual teaching will be broadened to the entire university.

4　Summary

It is inevitable to carry out bilingual teaching. However, most universities are still in the beginning stage, it is urgent for the reform of bilingual teaching mode. The paper has put forward the bilingual teaching mode of Top-Down and Down-top double-line. The reform of bilingual teaching mode can not only promote the breadth and depth of various disciplines and specialties when implementing the bilingual teaching, but also improve the teaching level of teachers and the comprehensive quality of students because of the higher request which is put forward for all aspects of schools, teachers, courses, teaching materials and students.

For the nature of bilingual teaching, it is important to create the language environment, strengthen "teaching language" and impel the development of the ability of language and professional skill by the bilingual teaching. Hereafter we will rely on the higher education to gradually extend to the bilingual teaching of all subjects. Additionly, we should reform the bilingual teaching on the aspects of teaching concept and theory, professional ethics cultivation, teaching environment, teaching management, teaching activities and practice.

Acknowledgement. This paper is supported by the Talent Foundation of Jiangsu Province under Grant (2008)30 Teaching Improvement Project of Jiangsu University under grant (JGZD2009016)

References

1. Yan, Q.X., Sheng, G.D.: Journal of Hangzhou Medical College 24, 119 (2003)
2. Terrence, G., Wright, W.E.: Education Policy 155, 155–158 (2004)
3. Information on, http://www.edu.cn/20020226/3021146.shtml
4. Information on, http://www.pep.com.cn/200212/ca8815.htm
5. Liang, Q.: Journal of Guangxi Traditional Chinese Medical University 7, 123–125 (2004)
6. Yan, Y.Z.: Journal of Jiangxi Vocational College of Finance 20, 131–133 (2007)
7. Wen, Y.H.: Research on National Education 3, 22–23 (1999)
8. Ellis, R.: Understanding Second Language Acquisition. Oxford University Press, England (1985)
9. Lu, L.H.: Prospect of Global Education 4, 66–68 (2001)
10. Hou, Y.: Journal of Shenyang Normal University 31, 155–157 (2007)
11. Ying, K.F., Shi, X.G., Zong, Y.Z.: China University Teaching 12, 42–44 (2004)
12. Li, H.J., Wu, G.L.: Journal of Jiangxi Agricultural University 2, 135–136 (2003)
13. Kan, C.M., Wang, L., Xu, D.S.: Nursing Research 21,171–172 (2007)

The Exploration of "Electro-Hydraulic Control Technology" Course Teaching

Jilin He, Shuibing Rao, and Song Jun

School of Mechanical and Electrical engineering,
Central South University, Changsha, Hunan Province , China
he8794@163.com

Abstract. "electro-hydraulic control technology" is an integrated curriculum. To achieve better teaching results, the exploration are made by the use of some teaching methods on the course of curriculum system, teaching methods, teaching means and other aspects. The use of multimedia technology to increase students' interests in learning and improve teaching effectiveness. During the course, analogy was applied to make the basic concepts and principle easy to be understood and accepted by students

Keywords: electro-hydraulic proportional control technology: Course teaching: Analogy Approach: Project Approach modern education technology.

1 Introduction

The advanced manufacturing technology, electronic technology combined with the hydraulic technology is the major feature of modern machinery .The various types of application of the combination represents an important mechanical direction and level. The "electro-hydraulic control technology" is a relatively new scientific technology and an integrated discipline which developed on the basis of the hydraulic drive technology and automation technology .It also is an important component of electromechanical integration technology .The "electro- hydraulic control technology" is an important course in mechanical engineering in college teaching profession, and an important technology to connect modern micro-Electronics and high power engineering machinery. As a basic course of engineering equipment major, the course of electro-hydraulic proportional control technology owns a series of features, such as rich content, wide range, large number students learning it, fast development and constant increase of content. In order to effectively transfer the important content of the course to the students and improve the teaching and learning quality at the limited course duration, the author made an investigate of how to receive better teaching results on "electro-hydraulic control technology" teaching.

2 Establish the "Student-Centred "Teaching Philosophy in the Teaching Process

In the teaching process, teachers should help, direct, and guide students. The aim of teaching activities is to cultivate students' awareness of thinking and guide students to

M. Zhu (Ed.): ICCIC 2011, Part V, CCIS 235, pp. 137–142, 2011.

continue to innovate through stimulating students' interest in learning and arousing the curiosity of students. Students are the main character of learning and teachers should pay attention to the learning process to enable them to be actively and proactively involved in the learning.

In the teaching process, teaching contents should be close to the students' coming professions. Through teaching, students learn not only theoretical knowledge but also gain practical skills and develop their generic skills.

In the teaching process, teaching methods should be flexible and varieties of teaching activities should be designed. In the teaching process, it is necessary for teachers to be active among the students, and teachers should stand behind the students to highlight the dominant position of students.

The process of teaching is the integration of teaching and learning. In this process, more attention should be paid to what students learn rather than what teachers teach.

3   Integration of Teaching Content, and Highlight the Practical Knowledge

Course content is the most important part of the training process. Selecting teaching content based on professional characteristics and training objectives and integrating organically so that it can receive more obvious results in the education reform.

3.1   System Analysis Course, and Make a Clear Distinction between Primary and Secondary Teaching Content

The main purpose of this course is to enable students to have a better understanding of the commonly used electro-hydraulic proportional control technology, after completing the course's learning, to know well electro-hydraulic proportional control valves, pumps, motors and other components of the structure and working principle, to be familiar with the basic knowledge of electro-hydraulic proportional control system and the theory analysis and design calculations of proportional hydraulic components and systems. The whole curriculum should focus on the theory analysis and design calculation of control systems. For the components it is need the students to make it clear of theoretical concepts and the main use of the formula.

3.2   The Connection and Review of Relevant Key Knowledge

The computer and network technology were widely used in preparation of the electro-hydraulic proportional control technology course. And a set of such course's teaching resource systems have been established, which is rich content, convenient to use and easy to update, to improve the efficiency of course preparing and increase the information content. Moreover, it is helpful to let students receive more knowledge what was learned before but is unfamiliar now.

For example, it is necessary for a student to have the basic knowledge of hydraulic like hydrostatics and fluid dynamic, especially be familiar with two classical laws: The Pascal's law and The Bernoulli equation, when teachers explain the basis of electro-hydraulic proportional control technology. Students have learned these two laws mentioned above, and especially were familiar with the first one at the beginning. But they almost forgot it after a few years. So through the learning of basic knowledge of electro-hydraulic proportional control technology and its specific application, students can connect these knowledge points together and deepen themselves' understanding about it. As a result, it is not easy for them to forget.

3.3 The Basic Theory of Knowledge Should Be Appropriate and Professional Expertise Should Highlight the Practical.

In the teaching process, we are bound to make it clear the basic concepts as the basic criteria. Basic concepts, formulas require students to master, but for some equations, as long as it is clear, we don't have to derive, and conclusions can be given directly. For some process, focusing on the concept, it is only need to understand the practical application of the basic concepts and formula. And to some content such as motion differential equations you don't need to explain.

In the teaching process, the function of the teaching must be emphasized. Teaching should combines professional knowledge with students' occupation, and makes clear the practical knowledge which closely related to the profession

4   Innovative teaching methods and students' ideas

4.1   The Reference of Analogy to Enhance Students' Interests in Learning

Analogy is a way of reasoning to compare an object or phenomenon with another, according to the class object or phenomenon with some property launches that another object or phenomenon has the same property, or a way of thinking by the law of an object or phenomenon introduced the law of another. Analogy in teaching can inspire the students and train creative ability by the means of compare unfamiliar problems with familiar things.

Analogy can be used to compare "electro-hydraulic control technology" to "Mechanical Design" and "electrical circuit" courses. It makes the basic concepts and principle is easy to be understood and accepted by students by analogy in "electro-hydraulic control technology" course. In addition, by analogy, comparison can be made between the "electro-hydraulic control technology" course's knowledge and syllabus knowledge, such as the analog summary of the performance of components of the servo valve, electro-hydraulic proportional valve and switching valves in the course. Analog approach highlights the importance and makes the students understand knowledge easily.

4.2   The Introduction of "Project Teaching"

"Project teaching" is an education activity that is oriented by practice and to complete project work by teachers and students. The essence is that it is based on project, and select engineering examples as a platform to create a learning situation for students and then students could learn and master the relevant theoretical knowledge through awareness, understanding and concrete action about the actual project.

In the teaching process, relevant typical engineering examples are used as a teaching content. The students are grouped, then, according to the layout of the task, students are allowed to find and gather information. Teachers conduct detail explanations of relevant knowledge points, and students work by engineering instances requirements of division of labor to complete project tasks, and then assess and summarize. In the teaching activities, students are always in the dominant position and teachers play the role of guidance and counseling. Project teaching methods can promote students' learning active and narrow the distance between theory and practice, so that students' unity and cooperation, independent thinking, innovation, creativity can be strengthened.

5   Improve Teaching Methods, and Strengthen the Practice Teaching

5.1   Improve Teaching Effectiveness by Multimedia Technology

A variety of charts, schematic diagrams and related forms are the prominent features of this course. In the teaching process, the use of wall charts, teaching models and other auxiliary teaching methods would greatly reduced the effect of their teaching. Instead, the multimedia technology applied to the teaching process will greatly improve the effectiveness of teaching. Compared with the traditional book, the multimedia edition teaching resource has many advantages. For example the teachers can modify teaching content according to the need at any time, high-definition pictures can improve video effects and animation designs which make the text and images working together can help the understanding of related knowledge points. All these greatly stimulate the students' enthusiasm of learning. And through the arrangement of hyperlinks, the animations, videos and other teaching resources can be also inserted in the explanation at any time to ensure the integrity of the whole teaching content.

Multimedia technology integrated by text, sound and image which makes teaching visualization and imagination. The curriculum components and control systems, etc. are made into CAI courseware and presented in class, so that students could learn more intuitive and impressive. Taking advantage of intuition, animation and fun of multimedia technologies to increase students' interests in learning and improve teaching effectiveness.

5.2   Improve Teaching Quality by Combine with Practical Teaching Methods

This course is an integrated curriculum, and practice teaching is an important part of the process. In the design process of teaching, we should tuck practice teaching programs into the teaching plan, and implement practice teaching according to phases and levels. In practice teaching, according to the actual situation of schools and students combined with project teaching methods ,we can create practical means of teaching for instance class exercise, course experiment, course design and production internships. Through the practice training, it can enhance the students' understanding of theoretical knowledge, mobilize the enthusiasm of study, stimulate their learning active, independent thinking and scientific analysis to solve problems.

6 Strengthen the Teaching Materials and Raise the Level of Teachers

Teaching materials should reflect the relevant changes in technology timely by organize relevant person to prepare realistic, content advanced and unique lectures which should be improved continuously after trial and modification. The book of < electro-hydraulic proportional control technology> whitened by our teachers, who are professional at this subject, has been adopted as the textbook, which is rich in content, structure reasonable and paying attention to the cultivation of students' abilities. What is more, it is good at processing the relationship between the basic, the systematic and the advanced. And it plays a very important role to ensure the quality of teaching.

In order to make the textbook more flexible and more easy to use, the textbook in the form of multimedia edition has been produced, which is based on the paper book. And it uses clear pictures, bright-colored colors and reasonable animations, so as to let students profoundly understand the principle and structure of the key hydraulic components and control circuits. Meanwhile, the multimedia edition teaching resources that has a strong retrieval function can be used to undertake searching for many contents of the book. It can be used to query related key points of knowledge promptly. So it is helpful to stimulate students' interests in learning and review related knowledge after-school effectively. In addition, it has been added with many pictures and other related resources in the form of the hyperlink that greatly enriched contents compared with the book. So it is quite useful for teachers' preparing and students' reviewing.

The key elements to achieve teaching objectives are teachers. Attentions should be paid to improve the professional level of teachers, the cultivation of ideological and moral qualities of teachers and continuous improvement and perfection of teaching methods and means. To continuously improve the quality of teachers, attentions should also be paid to the research capability of teachers, and practice ability.

7 Conclusions

Making full use of various modern education technologies, renewing education method and enriching the teaching content are the inevitable requirement of the further development of higher education reform. It need to note that there is no a simple causality between the adoption of kinds of modern education technologies and the improvement of teaching quality. In order to realize the goal of 'the quality education, ability cultivation and innovative spirit' in professional basal courses, teachers need to not only make full use of various modern methods, but research and explore the course's system, teaching content, teaching methods and teaching art comprehensively. Teachers should fully arouse students' enthusiasm and participation enthusiasm in the teaching, and help them become the subject in the teaching process. Only through this way, can we realize the combinations of teaching with learning, and scientific researching with teaching, and achieve the transformation from the traditional teaching mode to the modern teaching mode.

References

1. Dong, Q., et al.: Make our teaching more acceptable to students. Chemical Vocational and Technical Education (2006)
2. Guan, J.: Electro-hydraulic control technology. Tongji University Press, Shanghai (2003)
3. Jia, J.: Analogy in "hydraulic transmission" teaching application. Journal of Changzhou Information Vocational Technical College Journals 3 (2007)
4. Yang, Y., et al.: Broaden and develop electrical and mechanical compound talents. Higher Education Research 3 (2000)
5. Zhou, F.: The exploration and practice of curriculum in "Machine Electrical Control Technology". Anhui Vocational College of Electronics and Information 4 (2007)
6. Zhou, Y.: The retrospect and prospect of higher education reform and development in China. The Dynamic of Textbook Reform. 1(5), 1–10 (2001)
7. Wu, G., Qiu, M.: Practical electro-hydraulic proportional control technology. Mechanical industry press, Beijing (1999)
8. Lu, Y.: Electro-hydraulic proportional control technology. Mechanical industry press, Beijing (1988)
9. Zhang, H., Huang, Y.: Hydraulic transmission. Mechanical industry press, Beijing (1992)

Reform Practice in Experimental Contents and Methods of Plant Protection Specialty

Ming-wang Shi and Ju-huai Zhai

Henan Institute of Science and Technology, Xinxiang city, China, 453003
shi4673@163.com

Abstract. In this paper, according to the characteristics of modern plant protection experiments, the basic operations, basic skills and basic laboratory research training for the teaching content, Edited and changed the relevant supporting experimental teaching materials, laboratory equipped with the multimedia teaching environment, establishment, added teaching software related experiments. The Let has the scientific research item professor, the associate professor to teach the experiment to the student, scientific research to attract a group of young teachers in the experimental work of teaching, formed an excellent experimental class teacher to ensure the stability of the experimental teaching team, and promoted Experimental Teaching.

Keywords: Teaching reform, Plant Protection Specialty, experimental teaching.

1 Introduction

The experimental teaching is an important means to cultivate students' creativity, but there are many shortcomings of the creative education in traditional experimental teaching, which demands further reform of experimental teaching [1]. It is important to recognize and accommodate individual differences in establishing an inclusive community. Teachers should accept all students, identify their individual educational needs, and develop mutual understanding and acceptance among students [2]. To improve pharmacy education through integrating theory and practice, coherent constructively aligned course entities, and enhanced deep-level learning. The reform was conducted collaboratively with faculty and staff members, students, and stakeholders. According to the new curriculum reform , To achieve "deep foundation, wide caliber, high starting point" scenario. And "develop a solid foundation, wide knowledge, ability, and overall quality are high, can be entrepreneurial innovation and research and applied for plant protection personal" as personal training objectives. The whole training from the start, showed an experimental teaching demonstration centers to serve the school and practice of teaching undergraduate students the basic experimental task. At the same time, open to students, teachers and student's innovative pilot projects and provide a platform for research.

2 Experimental Teaching Idea

Competition in comprehensive national strength in the 21st century is talent competition, with the international competitiveness of the training; you must rely on

M. Zhu (Ed.): ICCIC 2011, Part V, CCIS 235, pp. 143–147, 2011.
© Springer-Verlag Berlin Heidelberg 2011

the quality of the higher education development. Undergraduate education is the subject and foundation of higher education, in undergraduate education, it plays an irreplaceable role. The highest level of competence was reported in relationships with students, while the lowest level was associated with teaching skills. Of the single requirements, the weakest skills were related to teach decision-making and encouraging students constantly to seek new knowledge [3, 4].

We have strengthened on practice-teaching that is to improve the overall quality and capacity of innovation and scientific thinking capacity of students' pragmatic ability and creativity as the center, teaching and research to promote experimental, experimental teaching and production practice. It is training students the basic experimental skills, comprehensive research skills and innovative experimental skills that construction of the basic experiment - comprehensive design experiment - three levels of an innovative experiment experimental teaching to Undergraduate general practice teaching [5].

Experimental teaching reform Accordance with the fundamental requirement of the "wide caliber, the solid foundation, strong ability, high-quality" to develop the "overall design, step by step, advantages, highlight the characteristics" of the reform program, it is subject to the plant protection system for teaching content and overall design and reform. Overall design is: ask students to improving the overall quality based on established a solid foundation and broad knowledge and innovation framework to adapt to social selection and self-conscious awareness. Graduates start their own business sense to change the pattern of employment statistics. Undergraduate training program of the main experiment (Figture. 1)

Program designed to follow the teaching content platform based on the curriculum of the subject, highlighting the basic experimental plant protection professional skills training principles [6].

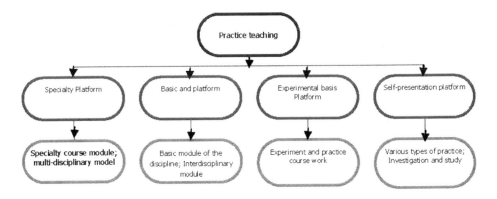

Fig. 1. Undergraduate training program of the main experiment

Experimental principle of combining teaching and research to promote the formation of students the scientific spirit. Experiment with the principle of combining the actual production, to develop student's practical ability, research ability, innovation and entrepreneur ship. Curricular and extracurricular, combining the principles of generality and individuality, to develop different levels of biological experiment for the undergraduate curriculum and teaching content. Experimental Courses break too much overlapping parts of the traditional biology teaching system, set up large integrated experimental biology, the ability to provide comprehensive practice for the student's development. Break the "routine" and "dependent" of experiment, according to the basic, comprehensive, innovative tertiary teaching, the integration of plant protection professional for the professional basis of experimental test, professional test, and plant protection technology experiment innovation to build some new plant protection experimental course Subject.

Enforcing reform and construction of laboratory, cultivating practice ability of students. To adapt to plant protection, agriculture, gardens, food, environmental science, agricultural red the environment of teaching and other professional requirements, general training, professional training needs of streaming, sharing resources, develop comprehensive and innovative abilities of students.

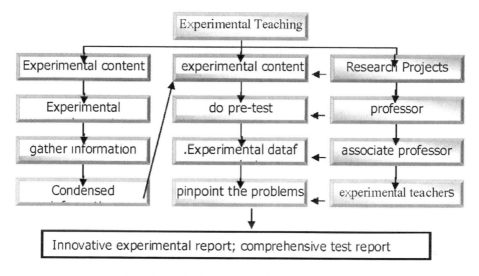

Fig. 2. Cultivating practice abilities of students

In light of cultivating practice abilities of students, enforce reform and construction of laboratory. The exploration methods and thoughts are presented, which created superior condition to train applicability talents who are useful to society (Figture2).Adhere to the "one center," perfect "combination of the two" builds "three levels" of the experimental teaching system. That adheres to train students in practical ability and creativity as the center, teaching and research to promote experimental, experimental teaching and production practice. The construction of the basic experiment-comprehensive design experiment - three levels of innovative experiment experimental teaching system, training students the basic experimental skills, comprehensive research skills and innovative experimental skills.

Establishing teaching - Experimental-Internships - Training course, increase the experiment, practice, weight training programs, and so experiment, practice, and practice hours over 38% of the total class hours. Enterprise product development, production in pilot projects, so the experiment content and scientific research, engineering, social application projects in close contact; Focus on comprehensive, broadening diameter, so entomology, plant pathology, pesticides, biotechnology, ecology and environmental disciplines, such as cross-penetration, strengthen the comprehensive abilities and innovative ability. According to the characteristics of modern plant protection experiments, the basic, basic skills and basic laboratory research training for the teaching content. Standardized experimental, students of modern experimental skills and expertise for future experiments, thesis design, laid the foundation for graduate study and employment. Combined with the principles of teaching reform to set up credit wants of tutorial and comprehensive student performance assessment, experimental teaching evaluation and experimental teaching quality recording. Building a foundation for an evidence-based approach to practice: teaching basic concepts to undergraduate freshman students [3- 7].

Teachers encourage students to engage in research [8]. Encourage students to learn to ask questions, find and develop their interests and expertise, training students to apply the knowledge gained, abilities and qualities to carry out independent research, students of innovation [9-14]; To strengthen cooperation and exchange, hire outside experts to undergraduate teaching in schools of advanced experimental theoretical and experimental skills to enable students to understand the frontiers of knowledge in related fields and technologies; set up a "Student Technology Innovation Fund", the organization and financing of students independently designed research project (thesis or Extracurricular), to carry out various scientific and technological innovation competitions to improve the quality of students, develop a practical and creative ability to create conditions for training to meet the needs of individual students, Comments on the place of general practice teaching in the curriculum are added [4, 15];

3   Summary

Implementation of the training base, the base under guiding technical director, production and management students first line to receive professional training, students of entrepreneurship and business management skills, improve their self-confidence, improve their entrepreneurial skills;

It edited and changed the relevant supporting experimental teaching materials, laboratory equipped with the multimedia teaching environment, establishment, and added teaching software related experiments. The ability of every student can be estimated by teachers in the course of experiment teaching, which the methods of quantification-orientated managements and target-assessing may be adopted. The attempt and accomplish nothing can be avoided after adopting the method. Student's ability of analyzing and solving problems are promoted. Set up and improve the experimental teaching demonstration center site, and strengthen the use of network information platform and multimedia teaching tools widely adopted, the sense of participation to mobilize the students for the experimental technique of learning, discussion free to explore space.

References

1. Katajavuori, N., Hakkarainen, K., Kuosa, T., et al.: Am. J. Pharm. Educ. 73(8), 151 (2009)
2. Truelson, S.D.: Bull. Med. Libr. Assoc. 49(4), 635–636 (1961)
3. Burns, H.K., Foley, S.M.: J. Prof. Nurs. 21(6), 351–357 (2005)
4. Donovan, C.F., Kuenssberg, E.V., Whitaker, A.J.: J. R. Coll. Gen. Pract. 20(suppl. 2), 68–71 (1970)
5. Dickinson, J.A.: Med. J. Aust. 2(13), 518–522 (1975)
6. Al-Jishi, E., Khalek, N.A., Hamdy, H.M.: Educ. Health (Abingdon) 22(2), 57 (2009)
7. Keller, L.O., Strohschein, S., Schaffer, M.A., et al.: Public Health Nurs. 21(5), 469–487 (2004)
8. Jaye, C.: Fam. Pract. 19(5), 557–562 (2002)
9. Allan, H.T., Smith, P.A., Lorentzon, M.: J. Nurs. Manag. 16(5), 545–555 (2008)
10. Mitchell, B.S., Xu, Q., Jin, L., et al.: Anat. Sci. Educ. 2(2), 49–60 (2009)
11. Kervyn, N., Yzerbyt, V.Y., Judd, C.M., et al.: J. Pers. Soc. Psychol. 96(4), 828–842 (2009)
12. Steinert, Y.: Med. Educ. 38(3), 286–293 (2004)
13. Whitbeck, C.: Sci. Eng. Ethics 7(4), 541–558 (2001)
14. McMillan, M.A., Dwyer, J.: Nurse Educ. Today 10(3), 186–192 (1990)
15. Irwin, W.G., Perrott, J.S.: J. R. Coll. Gen. Pract. 31(230), 557–560 (1981)

A Probe on Teaching Model of Course-Certificate Combination for Programmable Logic Controller Course in Institutions of Higher Education

Shi Xuhua

Institute of Information Science and Engineering, Ningbo University, Ningbo, China, 315211
hua4556@163.com

Abstract. The series of courses in Programmable Logic Controller are specialized courses with strong practicality for the major of automation. The courses improve the original teaching model and strengthen the important roles that practice teaching plays in the cultivation of students' professional and technical skills. The paper, aiming at the teaching status quo and existing problems of courses in Programmable Logic Controller in undergraduate colleges, probes on a teaching model of course-certificate combination, and provides countermeasures and suggestions based on the analysis of these problems.

Keywords: course-certificate combination, PLC course, undergraduate course teaching.

1   Introduction

At present, the undergraduate education of China has successfully transformed from elite education to mass education and has actually entered the mass education stage with a major purpose to cultivate ordinary labor for the country. The author believes that the promotion of the double-certificate education among undergraduate students is of great practical significance. On the stage of mass education, the academic certificate is not the only certificate proving the ability of professional talents and labors. With the rapid development of social economy, technology, and education, professional credentials play a more and more important role in improving the knowledge, ability, and development of professional talents and labors, and become a basic employment system in the modern society [1]. Professional credentials provide an evidence for undergraduates to prove their professional skills and are an important system for higher education to adapt to the demands of the market for talents and labor employment.

The Application of Electrical Equipment and Programmable Logic Controller is a main specialized course for the major of electrical automation, as well as a course that covers a wide range of knowledge, involves many relevant contents, updates a lot, emphasizes on theories and practical application. It is closely connected with practical production and engineering application and is specialized knowledge that can be directly applied in the work. The paper, with the teaching model of course-certificate combination in the programmable logic controller courses, probes on a teaching model for undergraduates.

M. Zhu (Ed.): ICCIC 2011, Part V, CCIS 235, pp. 148–152, 2011.

2   Existing Problems of and Countermeasures for Programmable Logic Controller Course Teaching

2.1   Problems in Teaching Contents

The syllabi and contents of teaching materials cannot adapt to the needs of practical production. In recent years, the requirements of the field of electrical control for computer and communication technology are promoted, while the contents of optional teaching materials have lagged behind the practical needs, and theoretical knowledge is seriously falling far behind the practice; the devices referred to in the teaching materials are made of old elements, some of which have become out of date, failing to highlight the key points of teaching in PLC technology application and only focusing on and strengthening teaching of aspects such as PLC orders and application, PLC programming methods, etc. The comprehensive course with a strong practicality is with too much "theorized" both in teaching contents and teaching models, and therefore, it is difficult to realize the teaching objective of the course. For example, the principle analysis of the electrical control circuit, design of basic control elements, and the narration for the predominant idea of principal design are generally very clear, but there are few contents involving technological design such as installation location diagrams, panel opening diagrams, electrical wiring diagrams, installation and adjustment. There is a gap between theoretical teaching and practical design as well as manufacturing requirements of the control system [2].

2.2   Problems in the Assessment Method

The sole assessment method is losing its gold content. At present, the close-book examination is usually adopted in the course, and the homework and experiment are taken into account in the total score at end of the semester. Due to insufficiency of teaching means, no scientific and diverse score assessment means is used. Therefore, the assessment system and method restricts students' knowledge innovation, and their scores cannot reflect the knowledge mastered and applied by the students in an overall and objective manner[3].

With the update and development in contents of the Application of Electrical Equipment and Programmable Logic Controller course, traditional teaching contents and methods cannot guarantee the requirements of cultivation objectives concerning the major, therefore, the idea must be updated and a set of all-around course teaching system including theoretical knowledge, teaching methods, and practical teaching is required to activate teachers and students' initiatives and to improve all-around teaching quality of the course through various teaching methods and means.

Besides, with respect to the employment prospect at present, the undergraduate education after entering the mass education stage is to cultivate ordinary labor for various industries, which requires that undergraduates should be equipped with not only solid theory basis, but also a high level of skills to be competent for the job. According to the employment situation of ordinary undergraduates in recent years, students with double certificates (certificate of graduation and professional qualification certificate) are popular among the employers and their employment rates are much higher than other students. Therefore, students cultivated by engineering colleges and universities should also be equipped with proficient operating skills. Teaching should be carried out according to the requirements for professional qualification certificate in the teaching scheme. To coordinate the organization of training and certification, training and certification of professional skills should be combined [4].

With the subsidies of the Provincial Department of Finance and municipal service-oriented professional construction, the Electrical Control and Programmable Logic Controller course is reformed, an assessment and training base for "PLC Programmable Logic Controller Designer" the Ministry of Labor of China is set up, and a teaching model of course-certificate combination for the programmable logic controller course is under exploration.

3   Model of Course-Certificate Combination for PLC Programmable Logic Controller

3.1   Platform Construction

In order to accomplish the course-certificate combination of the Application of Electrical Equipment and Programmable Logic Controller course, to enable students to complete the teaching contents required by the major as well as achieve medium or senior level of "CETTIC Programmable Logic Controller System Designer" specified by the Ministry of Labor of China within the specified teaching periods, to practice their practical ability, to train them to monitor automatic control with PLC and to inspire their learning interest, the college establishes a training and practicing base of programmable logic controller.

The programmable logic controller course is a theoretical and practical specialized course, therefore, the major pays much attention to the construction of the teaching team of the course[5]. In addition to the automation scientific research team, there are 3 associate professors and 2 lecturers in the first-line teaching team. The course teachers are all equipped with high theoretical level and certain engineering ability and scientific R&D ability. In order to enable the 5 major teachers to be assessed and appraised by the Ministry of Labor of China, they have received assessment training and obtained corresponding training certificates for qualified teachers.

3.2   Concerning Teaching of Course-Certificate Combination

In order to realize the combination of the programmable logic controller course and the course-certificate teaching and to strengthen the practicing link, a new technical knowledge system and a training system for practical ability are established and teaching contents as well as the syllabi are revised materially.

Adjustment of teaching contents, in addition to training, emphasizes on the systematicness and integrity of the theory of automation subject, strengthens the link of practical teaching, and gives prominence to practical engineering application. With innovative education as the objective, it gives prominence to contents of comprehensive and design experiments, and adds curriculum design and curriculum practice in combination with practical engineering subjects, so that teaching contents can not only adapt to practical production requirements, but can also practice and improve students' operating and innovative abilities. The course contents include the electrical control basis of traditional relay contactors, the principle of modern programmable logic controllers, PLC network communication, and software configuration technology. Based on the emphasis on basic theory of the course, the part of traditional relay contactor electrical control is reduced and prominence is given to the typical circuit, typical phase, and design thought; the key lies in the operating principle of PLC and the analysis as well as design of the control system comprising of PLC; emphasis is placed on the network technology application of PLC control system; the difficulty lies in the design and development concerning the monitoring software of principle computer. The first part, electrical control basis, takes up 12 class hours, the second part, principle of PLC, takes up 18 class hours, and the third part, network and software configuration technology, takes up 12 class hours. In order to strengthen students' practical ability, the experiment periods are added up to 34 class hours, amounting to 76 class hours. The experiment teaching mainly relies on students and is assisted by teachers; with respect to the contents, innovative experiments are the major part with verification experiments as the supplementary. The experiment contents include 4 class hours of verification experiments, 8 class hours of comprehensive experiments, and 16 class hours of design experiments. Design experiments, including "manipulator action stimulation", "temperature PID control", and communication experiment among PLCs, etc., are added with 6 class hours of certification teaching and stimulation experiment.

In order to make the assessment of PLC course-certificate combination more scientific and rational, and assessment results reflect students' knowledge, ability, and quality more authentically, close-book examination is adopted in the theory examination of the course. Theory assessment is combined with practice assessment, and multiple means are adopted to evaluate the course performance, namely that the weight of theory examination is 0.5, the theoretical examination covers all the knowledge, in which basic and application knowledge take up 55%, comprehensive knowledge and skills take up 30%, and difficult knowledge and design improvement of the course take up 15%; the weight of certificate takes up 0.25, 85% for the medium-level certificate, and 100% for the senior-level certificate; the weight of daily performance score is 0.25, which is evaluated in accordance with students' classroom performance, classroom discussion, extracurricular work, learning attitude, and self-discipline in study, and among all these performances, classroom performance, classroom discussion, and extracurricular work take up 30%, class experiment assessment takes up 50%, which is in combination of teacher-oriented tests and students' self-simulation tests with the field operation, operation specification and experimental skills as the objectives; others take up 20%.

4 Conclusions

The teaching reform of course-certificate combination of the programmable logic controller course plays an important role in reinforcing the course platform of the automation major[6]. The optimization of the teaching process has certain theoretical value and practical guiding significance for promoting the applied education and innovative education of the major as well as cultivating application-oriented engineering and technological talents with comprehensive quality and all-around development. The construction of the major in undergraduate courses should also be developed according to the objective of the major and the requirements for the "double-certificate" examination assessment and appraisal. The preparation of teaching materials and teaching contents should be arranged according to the class hours. The proportions of classroom teaching and practice hours should be determined first, and assessment and evaluation system should be established according to the objective of the major and the requirements for assessment and evaluation. There has been a relatively complete assessment and evaluation system for the professional skill appraisal and professional qualification certification facing ordinary workers and technicians. However, the specialized theoretical knowledge mastered by undergraduates has changed greatly, therefore, a new assessment and evaluation system [7] must be established to guarantee its guiding and promoting effects.

Acknowledgment. The paper is supported by Ningbo key construction service- oriented professionals (Sfwxzdzy200903).

References

1. Wan, Q.-l.: 2l century model of electrical engineering talents and teaching content and curriculum reform. Electrical & Electronic Education 21(4), 1–3 (1999)
2. Ties, C., Wang, Y.: The electric control and the programmable controller" the educational reform initially searches. Electricity Electron Teaching Journal 27(6), 25–27 (2005)
3. Xia, j.: The technical application undergraduate course colleges and universities school localization ponders. Higher Project Education Research (6), 80–83 (2006)
4. Shi, w., Xu, g.: Discussion current China development technology undergraduate course significance and strategy. Education Development Research (12), 57–60 (2003)
5. Lu, x., Zhang, h.: Constructs the high standard the programmable controller laboratory. Experiment Technology and Management 17(4), 18–21 (2000)
6. Xuewei, Wangdejin: Automation specialized educational reform discussion. In: China Automation Education Academic Annual Meeting Collection, pp. 342–345 (2007)
7. Duan, z., Hebo: Automated specialized practice educational reform one kind of solution. In: Chinese Automation Education Academic Annual Meeting Collection, pp. 539–543 (2007)

Discussion on Cultivating Model of Multimodal Innovation Capability for Students of Electric Automation Major

Shi Xuhua

Institute of Information Science and Engineering, Ningbo University, Ningbo, China, 315211
hua4556@163.com

Abstract. Aiming at cultivating electric automation professionals with innovative spirit and practical ability, this paper explores a multimodal cultivating model for innovative talents. The model mainly includes: setting up a directional teaching platform of modularization, implementing a project-driven teaching model, establishing a new experimental teaching idea, a zero adapting period and a double-certificate teaching model and the course design combining with technological competition, which will cultivate multimodal innovative talents from a plurality of angles. Teaching practice indicates that students cultivated by the cultivating model for innovative talents have stronger practical ability and employment competitiveness.

Keywords: multimodal innovation, talents cultivation, electric automation.

1 Introduction

In recent years, with the expansion of higher education, new graduates bear unprecedented employment pressure, so do students of automation major. According to statistics, the employment distribution of graduates from automation major presents a pyramid regularity [1] in different levels. About 95% of these graduates are working on control engineering in the middle and the bottom of the pyramid. Only about 5% of these graduates on top of the pyramid are engaged in academic research on control engineering theory. Therefore, students of automation major are required to have not only solid professional knowledge, but also a strong practical ability, based on which, they should also cultivate their own innovative thinking and innovative development ability. As far as the automation major is concerned, it has the following characteristics [2]: 1) it is a multi-disciplinary product, pooling the control technology, electrical technology, computer technology, information and communication technology, etc. Besides, some crossover branches of other disciplines are also included; 2) automation is a discipline which studies system characteristics and takes appropriate methods and measures to bring certain performance to a system; 3) it has the characteristic of system integration. The core of automation is control and system. The most fundamental problem of control is to exert control on the system to make it behave as scheduled. Therefore, according to characteristics of the automation, students should be cultivated by multimodal innovative cultivating model.

M. Zhu (Ed.): ICCIC 2011, Part V, CCIS 235, pp. 153–157, 2011.
© Springer-Verlag Berlin Heidelberg 2011

As the employment pressure increases gradually at present, students of automation major also suffer intense employment competition [3]. The college has readjusted the teaching model for the students of automation major, adopted a multimodal innovative cultivating model to perfect students' knowledge structure, strengthening their practical ability, expanding their employment direction, enhancing the employment competitiveness, and keeping the outstanding primary employment rate.

2   Construction of a Multimodal Teaching Platform

The construction of a directional teaching platform of modularization is the key to the cultivation of a multimodal innovation capability. As a local institution of higher education, the college is to cultivate high-level and application-oriented talents in order to meet the need of local economic development, to cultivate talents to adapt to the development of automation hi-tech industry, to meet social demand for professional production skills and application-oriented professionals, and to determine the connotation of application ability of the graduates of automation major by means of corporate survey, etc., with the connotation including knowledge structure and practical skills. Professional training scheme is to be revised and the modular direction course is to be set up based on it. The modular courses can not only solve the contradiction between a large quantity of contents and the limited class hours, but also solve the contradiction between the teaching contents and the graduates' difficulties of adapting to the rapid development of automation. It reflects a reform idea of a multimodal innovative model for practice and innovation capability. Based on the survey related to high and new technology enterprises and institutions of higher education, a directional teaching platform of modularization which includes contents of teaching, experiments and internships is set up. Different cultivation schemes are designed based on different types of students, different development needs and different major fields. At present, the electric automation of the college has three direction modules, which are electric engineering and the automation module, computer inspection and instrument module as well as industrial process automation module. Professional courses of modularization are also designed. The students choose major directions depending on their own wills and interests after teachers' introduction on the major.

3   Discussion on Cultivation Model of Multimodal Innovation Capacity

3.1   Major Courses Promote the Project-Driven Teaching Model

In view of the practical and applied nature of the automation courses, the project-driven teaching model is adopted in the major course teaching[4]. In the project-driven teaching, importance should be attached to the following links: 1) Project selection. Accurate project selection, content grasping and teaching objective highlighting are keys to the successful implementation of project-driven teaching; 2) Teaching contents. According to different teaching contents, the project is divided into learning type and training type. The project of learning type is in a smaller scale. After participating in the project, students can understand the key points and difficult points of the course. It is mainly applied in laboratories and practice process in classrooms; the project of training type is in a larger scale. Students are required to complete tasks of all links such as the project requirement analysis, system design, project implementation and testing under teachers' guidance. It is mainly adopted in course design and graduation design. 3) Project source. Introduced projects can be revised based on corporate projects. Generally speaking, projects come from three sources: projects derived from corporations that are real, in real time and balanced, and are applied mainly in the course design and the graduation design; projects derived from problems encountered in teachers' work, study and scientific researches that can be applied in teaching after being designed. These projects usually lead to unexpected effects; and projects derived from students' practice, e.g. extracurricular studio activities, etc., will easily stimulate students' thirst for knowledge and strengthen their self-teaching confidence; 4) Project members. Learners can be divided into several teams with three to four learners in each team. Multi-person cooperation will benefit the project implementation and cultivate their cooperative spirit.

In classroom teaching, the project-driven teaching model is adopted in major courses such as "computer control technology", "programmable control and PLC application" and practical application.

3.2 Zero Adapting Period and Double-Certificate Teaching Model

In order to improve the teaching quality of higher education effectively, the college adopts multiple approaches to cultivate students by the teaching model of "zero adapting period". Take the Zhou Ligong's 3+1 Innovative Education for example, the cultivation model of zero adapting period perfects and complements the "3+1" Innovative Education initiated by Mr. Zhou Ligong. "3+1" represents two parts of the four-year college learning: "3" represents the three years from freshman to junior; "1" represents the final year of the college learning. "Zero adapting period" refers that students can do technical design suitable for corresponding enterprises without any adapting period or optional practical training after graduation for they have completed the selected practical ability courses set up by the college and enterprises according to the industrial needs for talents so that their practical abilities are strengthened. Implementation of the teaching scheme for zero adapting period designed for application-oriented talents in embedded experimental classes provides the students with a good learning environment and a experimental platform, improves the status of the college in the information technology industry, and cultivates students of zero adapting period suitable for corresponding corporations with stronger technical development, application and promotion abilities. It takes the college two years to explore, adjust, and finally formulate the cultivation scheme. There are no less than 10 corresponding corporations of zero adapting period and no less than 3 bases for internship. During the construction period, students graduated normally from the two experimental classes can achieve the effect of the zero adapting period basically in corresponding corporations.

Meanwhile, in order to promote the students' employment competitiveness, the college also develops a double-certificate teaching model in relevant courses, such as the senior assessments in national SCM System Designer and Programmable Controller PLC System Designer that are designed in the courses of single chip microcomputer and PLC programmable logic controller. These courses combine classes and certificates to encourage students to take an examination and get double certificates successfully.

3.3   Combination of Course Design and Technological Competition

Course design is an innovative practical teaching link set up for senior students who have already finished their courses. Course design of this major includes "Comprehensive Design of DSP System", "PLC Control System Design", "Comprehensive Design of Embedded System", "Comprehensive Design of SCM System Application", etc. Students can make choices according to their own interests, and learn advanced and practical professional knowledge and skills as well as develop innovative thinking ability relying on modernized practical teaching platform of the college.

The end of the classroom teaching contents doesn't mean the end of the teaching process. The extracurricular technological activity is an effective method to stimulate students' devotion towards science and passion for innovation. The college launches technological competitions for college students through which we cultivated a minority of elite students. The college also makes every possible effort to stimulate students' innovation consciousness and expand their benefited range. For instance, the innovation base of the college organized many electronic design contests for college students on national and provincial levels and won a plurality of first and second prizes on the both levels. Teachers will introduce some innovative modes of thinking in contests into daily practical teaching, which brings a lot of new ideas and methods for experimental teaching reform. In order to cultivate students' innovation capability in a more effective way, the college established an innovative practice base which creates many opportunities for cultivation of students' practical ability. Students can exert their individual imagination and creativity to the maximum limit, improve their ability of logical thinking and innovation capability, transform knowledge into production, and create wealth by wisdom. Students can inspect knowledge that they have already learned through innovative practice so as to locate and make up the deficiencies and strengthen their understanding. Innovative practice is the sublimation of the central experimental teaching activities. Besides, it points out the direction for teaching reform and promotes the experimental teaching reform and innovation.

4   Conclusion

In short, innovative talents are the subject of independent innovation ability. Cultivation of innovative talents is a new mode for talent cultivation. Aiming at different requirements of different majors, only to make continuous exploration, practice and improvement combing the practices of the major and the college, can a large number of innovative talents who live up to the development of the modern society and the requirements of the times be cultivated. The major, through the construction of a directional teaching platform of modularization, cultivates multimodal innovative talents from perspectives such as implementing a project-driven teaching model, establishing a new experimental teaching idea, the zero adapting period and double-certificate teaching model, the combination between the course design and technological competition as well as the combination between teachers' scientific researches and students' innovative practice. The teaching reform during the past few years has already acquired primary achievements. The college will further summarize the experience and make unremitting exploration on the core teaching study problem of innovative talent cultivation.

Acknowledgment. The paper is supported by Ningbo key construction service-oriented professionals (Sfwxzdzy200903).

References

1. Tong, W., Duan, Z.T.E., Ji, K.C.: Automation Professional Practice Teaching and Creative Talent. In: Proceedings of the 2007 Annual Conference of Chinese Automation, pp. 203–205 (2007)
2. Zhou, N.: Automation of Higher Education Reform. Industry and Technology Forum 8(6), 182–183 (2009)
3. Zhou, N.: Automation of Higher Education Reform. Industry and Technology Forum 8(6), 182–183 (2009)
4. Li, G., Hu, l.: Experimental Teaching and Training Innovation Research and Practice. Laboratory Research and Exploration 27(9), 110–112 (2008)

Does the Missing of the Inflectional Morphology Imply the Impairment of Interlanguage Grammar?*
A Study Based on the Pro-drop Parameter

Tang Xuemei

Anhui Polytechnic University, Wuhu, Anhui Province, China
tang7654@yeah.net

Abstract. There are two major accounts of non-target-like use of L2 morphology, especially in oral English: the Impaired Representation Hypothesis (IRH) and the Missing Surface Inflection Hypothesis (MSIH). This article re-examines the impairment/unimpairment debate of interlanguage system in the light of empirical data from the author's investigations of Chinese learners who are learning English as a second language. A parameter of functional categories has been examined: pro-drop parameter. Through the analysis and discussion of the relevant data, evidences have been obtained to support the MSIH instead of the IRH.

Keywords: the impairment of interlanguage, the pro-drop parameter, functional categories.

1 Introduction

According to Selinker, about ninety-five percent of learners cannot eventually reach the level of a normal target language, that is to say, the majority of them cannot drive their interlanguage to the terminal of the continuum[1]. In the recent decades, researchers have been studying the possible reasons for the common failure in second language acquisition (SLA). Current researches on interlanguage in SLA have focused particularly on the failure of L2 learners to produce verbal inflectional morphology associated with functional categories.

It can be said that the nature of SLA is the resetting of parameters [2]. Chomsky's principle-and-parameter theory and the minimalist program provide us with a new perspective to study this issue. According to Universal Grammar (UG) every speaker has grasped a set of principles and parameters. Within the framework of the minimalist program, the computational system is 'given' by UG and is invariant. What vary are properties of the items that enter into the computation (for example, their feature composition and feature strength). So, the acquisition of a language is just the application of the principles of UG into a certain language.

---

* This work was supported by a grant from the Social Science Foundation of Anhui Province (2009sk384).

M. Zhu (Ed.): ICCIC 2011, Part V, CCIS 235, pp. 158–163, 2011.

Functional categories and their features are regarded as the basic divergence among languages. In this article, in order to have a better understanding of the nature of interlanguage, a qualitative investigation has been done on the pro-drop parameter, one of the features of functional categories, through which the two accounts of the impairment of interlanguage grammar are reexamined.

2   The Impairment of Interlanguage Grammar

Within the framework of the minimalist program, although there are different hypotheses concerning the possible reasons for the common failure in SLA, researchers come to an agreement that the impairment of interlanguage grammar lies mainly in the functional categories and their properties. There are two major accounts for non-target-like use of the second language (L2) morphology: the Impaired Representation Hypothesis (IRH) and the Missing Surface Inflection Hypothesis (MSIH). The question is whether the frequent omission of verbal inflection means that functional categories are impaired in L2 grammars.

2.1   Impaired Representation Hypothesis (IRH)

Hawkins and Chan argue for the 'failed features hypothesis' whereby the interlanguage representation is restricted to those features and feature values available in the first language (L1) [3]. Beck and Eubank propose that interlanguage feature strength is permanently 'inert' or unspecified (the 'local impairment hypothesis') [4,5]. They have suggested, accordingly, that L2 knowledge of functional categories associated with feature strength is permanently impaired even if learners eventually acquire overt agreement morphology. In some of these studies, in particular, the absence of target-like inflectional suffixes has been taken as the primary evidence for concluding that L2 learners do not project associated functional features or categories.

2.2   Missing Surface Inflection Hypothesis (MSIH)

Haznedar and Schwartz first put forward this term, Missing Surface Inflection Hypothesis, to make it clear, it is at the surface morphological level that inflection is assumed to be absent, rather than at the abstract featural level [6]. There is not a relationship between the use of inflectional morphology and overt subjects. Similarly, Prévost and White also argue for a mapping problem between abstract features and surface morphological forms [7]. It is possible for a lexical item to be inserted into the hosting node, even though some of its features may be missing or partially specified. In the light of this analysis then, there is no syntactic deficit in interlanguage grammars. All the accounts of missing L2 inflection described above suggest that the absence of target-like inflectional suffixes doesn't imply the failure for L2 learners to acquire the corresponding functional categories and their properties.

3   Pro-Drop Parameter

The parameter examined in the current investigation is the pro-drop parameter. Lydia White used the pro-drop parameter to indicate the presence or absence of a subject in the sentence [8]. The pro-drop parameter variation has effects on the grammars of all languages; each of them is either pro-drop or non-pro-drop, that is to say, a pro-drop parameter has two settings: pro-drop in which pro is permitted as subject, and non-pro-drop, in which pro is not allowed.

Chomsky develops a theory of feature-checking [9]. Within the framework of minimal program, sentences are the projections of functional phrases (IP), on which there are kinds of features including nominal features (Φ features, D features). [+strong] D feature means that the nominal features on the functional category I are [+strong], which requires the overt movement of the subject in a sentence from its original position in the verb phrase (VP) to the specifier of IP to check its Φfeature. In other words, in languages that have [+strong] D feature, like English, their [+finite] sentences must have overt subjects with nominative case. In languages which have [-strong] D feature, the nominal features on functional category I is [-strong], which does not require the overt movement of the subject in a sentence from its original position in VP to the specifier of IP to check its Φ feature and the Φ feature is checked only in the logical form not in the phonetic form. In other words, in languages with [-strong] D feature, like Chinese, their [+finite] sentences permit covert subjects (pro). So, Chinese is a pro-drop language or null-subject language. In pro-drop languages, the 'empty category' pro fills the appropriate part of deep structure but does not appear in the surface of the sentence. For example, [pro] 停电了 (ting dian le).

4 Investigation

4.1 Hypotheses

In the current investigation, the feature on pro-drop parameter which has been studied is [±strong] D feature. This feature results in two variations between English and Chinese. One is that in English declarative sentences there must be overt subjects with nominative case, while Chinese allows the 'empty category' pro to fill the appropriate part of subject in deep structure but does not appear in the surface of the sentence. The other is that [+strong] D feature requires the dummy subjects "there" or "it" to fill the subject position in certain English 'existential' sentences and 'weather' sentences; Chinese with [-strong] D feature does not require them.

Hypothesis 1: According to IRH, features of English on pro-drop parameter cannot be reset in Chinese learners' interlanguage system because they are not available in L1 and are permanently impaired. It is predicted that most Chinese students will not use overt subjects in English declarative sentences and expletive subjects in English existential or weather sentences. Or they will show a random alternate between presence and absence of those necessary subjects.

Hypothesis 2: According to MSIH, features of English on pro-drop parameter can be reset in Chinese learners' interlanguage system although features of Chinese on pro-drop parameter are different. Mistakes only indicate a mapping problem between abstract features and surface morphological forms. It is predicated that in students' interlangauge system [+strong] D feature on pro-drop parameter is accessible, which means most Chinese students can use the overt subjects in English declarative sentences and the dummy subjects "there" or "it" in 'existential' and 'weather' sentences correctly.

4.2 Subjects

The subjects for this study are 90 sophomores from Anhui Polytechnic University, who have been divided into three different groups: (i) 30 Chinese-speaking art majors as L2 learners of English, (ii) 30 Chinese-speaking science majors as L2 learners of English, and (iii) 30 Chinese-speaking English majors as L2 learners of English. Generally speaking, data from subjects of different English levels are more reliable. All of the data are from verbal interaction between the teacher and students.

4.3 Methodology

In the present investigation, the subjects were asked to orally describe a simple landscape painting in English, during which many declarative sentences would be definitely used. Furthermore, the description of the positions of different objects in the painting, such as houses, trees, mountains, would also definitely involve English 'existential' sentences. All the descriptions were done within 15 minutes and were recorded by computers or recording pens. The aim is to test whether English [+strong] D feature is accessible in the interlanguage system of Chinese learners whose native language has [-strong] D feature by observing how well Chinese learners with different English levels acquired [+finite] features of English.

In this investigation, one-way analysis of variance (ANOV) and SPSS are used as tools in order to process the data more reasonably.

4.4 Results

In order to test whether English [+strong] D feature is accessible in Chinese learners' interlanguage system, that is to say, whether overt subjects could be used in their declarative sentences and whether they could use expletives if necessary, their recording materials were processed and analyzed. The results are as follows:

Item 1: The obligatory presence of subjects in English declarative sentences

Table 1. Descriptive data of *item 1*

	N	Mean	Std. Deviation	Minimum	Maximum
1.00	30	.8667	.34575	.00	1.00
2.00	30	.9333	.25371	.00	1.00
3.00	30	1.0000	.00000	1.00	1.00
Total	90	.9333	.25084	.00	1.00

Table 1, presenting a summary of the number of tokens of correct usage of item 1, clearly displays a fact that vast majority Chinese students (86.7% art majors, 93.3%

science majors, 100% English majors) have a good command over the overt subjects in English declarative sentences. On average, only about 6.7% students made mistakes. For example, some of them didn't put the obligatory subject 'It' before the verb 'rain'.

Table 2. ANOVA of *item 1*

	df	F	Sig.
Between (Combined)	2	2.175	.120
Deviation	87		
Within Groups	89		
Total			

From table 2, we can see F=2.175< F0.05=3.15, P=.120>.05. Hypothesis 2 is supported and there is no significant difference among the three groups of students. Therefore, [+strong] D feature is accessible in Chinese students' interlanguage when D feature is [-strong] in their native language, Chinese.

Item 2: The obligatory presence of subjects in existential sentences

Table 3. Descriptive data of *item 2*

	N	Mean	Std. Deviation	Minimum	Maximum
1.00	30	.8667	.34575	.00	1.00
2.00	30	.9667	.18257	.00	1.00
3.00	30	1.0000	.00000	1.00	1.00
Total	90	.9444	.23034	.00	1.00

From table 3, it is clearly shown that most Chinese students (86.7% art majors, 96.7% science majors, 100% English-majors) could use expletive subject "There" in English existential sentences correctly.

Table 4. ANOVA of *item 2*

	df	F	Sig.
Between (Combined)	2	2.017	.132
Deviation	87		
Within Groups	89		
Total			

From table 4, we can see F=2.071< F0.05=3.15, P=.132>.05. Hypothesis 2 is supported and there is no significant difference among the three groups of students. It also proves the accessibility of [+strong] D feature in Chinese students' interlanguage when D feature is [-strong] in their native language, Chinese.

5   Conclusion

This article has presented evidences for Missing Surface Inflection Hypothesis from the investigation of pro-drop parameter of functional categories. As is shown from the results, the syntactic system and the feature-checking mechanism in interlanguage system are not impaired. The missing of the inflectional affixes of verbs is caused by some external reasons out of the syntactic system. However, interlanguage is a dynamic transitional continuum from the initial knowledge of a language to native proficiency, and is often regarded as an unstable set of language characteristics produced by learners. It is far from easy to get clear picture of its true nature, so the debate on the impairment of its syntactic system will continue. The key for this debate is to answer the following two questions. How is morphological system related to syntactic system? And what are the crucial reasons for the missing inflectional affixes in interlanguage grammar? The first one is the root for the divergence between "impaired hypothesis" and "unimpaired hypothesis", while the second one is concerned with the different accounts on the missing surface inflection hypothesis. Interlanguage is a road approaching the target language. It is also the mirror of the nature of all human-specific languages. The profound understanding of this special language phenomenon will definitely do a lot of benefits to SLA.

References

1. Selinker, L.: Interlanguage: International Review of Applied Linguistics 1, 209–231 (1972)
2. Changhui.: Missing Inflections and Impairment of Interlanguage Grammar. Modern Foreign Languages 1 (2005)
3. Hawkins, R., Chan, Y.-C.: The partial availability of Universal Grammar in second language acquisition: the 'failed features' hypothesis. Second Language Research 3, 187–226 (1997)
4. Beck, M.: L2 acquisition and obligatory head movement: English-speaking learners of German and the local impairment hypothesis. Studies in Second Language Acquisition 20, 311–348 (1998)
5. Eubank, et al.: 'Tom eats slowly cooked eggs': thematic verb raising in L2 knowledge. Language Acquisition 6, 171–199 (1997)
6. Haznedar, B., Schwartz, B.D.: Are there Optional Infinitives in child L2 acquisition. Cascadilla Press (1997)
7. Prévost, P., White, L.: Missing surface inflection or impairment in second language? Evidence from Tense and Agreement. Second Language Research 16 (2000)
8. White, L.: Implications of parametric variation for adult second language acquisition: an investigation of the pro-drop parameter. In: Cook, V.J. (ed.) Experimental Approaches to Second Language Acquisition. Pergamon, Oxford (1986)
9. Chomsky, N.: The Minimalist Program. MIT press, Cambridge (1995)

Innovation on Practical Teaching of Graphics Mapping for Comprehensive Ability Cultivation

Xin Shu, You-dong Yang, and Jian Ma

Zhijiang College of Zhejiang University of Technology, Hangzhou,
Zhejiang Prov 310024, China
shu8886@yeah.net

Abstract. To cultivate students' comprehensive abilities in graphics mapping curriculum design, the novel teaching methods are presented, such as project-teaching method and research-teaching method, according to the requirements and characteristics of the experimental teaching. The new architecture of graphics mapping is constructed and the practical teaching requirements of relative curriculums are fused. It raises the students' project qualities and the teachers' teaching quality in the engineering drawing.

Keywords: graphics mapping, project-teaching methodology, comprehensive abilities.

1 Introduction

Social development requires engineering and technical personnel to have not only high mechanical product design capability and product innovation, but also innovation capability and good engineering quality. Graphic mapping course is designed for Mechanical Engineering students who contact with the practical application of large-scale design training for the first time, which combines engineering graphics, two-dimensional and three-dimensional CAD design, engineering materials, Interchangeability and Technical Measurement and Mechanical Manufacturing Mechanical Technology and other fundamental courses. It can not only conduct the comprehensive training of what the student has learned, but also lay a good foundation for the following courses and practical aspects, so it plays a connecting role in developing comprehensive ability of students.

Graphic mapping program is designed to train students graphic skills, spatial imagination and practical ability. Meanwhile, it should also focus on training students in computer graphics, three-dimensional shapes and innovative design of comprehensive ability. To achieve this requirement, we need to readjust the content and depth of the entire system, reform the methods and means of practice and reasonably arrange the process of teaching.

2 Drawing Practice Teaching System Mapping and Timing

The determination of the mapping object is the key of building a new curriculum system. To meet the requirements of the integrated practical teaching, we've found a

M. Zhu (Ed.): ICCIC 2011, Part V, CCIS 235, pp. 164–169, 2011.

excellent part for the training, namely first-grade gear reducer. It not only includes common parts (shafts, disc cover classes and boxes) and standard parts, but also reflects the assemblage relationship between different parts. The training covers a wide scope and requires the students have a good knowledge of the course, which can help teachers learn about the students' comprehensive training and their capacity of the course. In addition, it has a direct relationship to the further courses such as "Theory of Machines and Mechanisms" and "Design of Machinery". The first-grade gear reducer is the most appropriate mapping part for the course. The details about the requirements and objects of the mapping traning are shown   bellow(All the work are done by teams):

➢   Complete the assemblage diagrammatic sketch of the gear reducer;

➢   Survey all of the non-standard parts and complete their sketches;

➢   Complete the three-dimensional modeling of different parts and the assemblage sketch;

➢   Complete the assembly sketch drawing;

➢   Complete the two-dimensional assemblage drawings and important part of the engineering drawings;

These trainings help students develop their ability of applying the learned knowledge, analyzing issues and solving problems, mastering the whole process of mapping and cartographic CAD software to draw engineering drawings by the basic methods and skills. It also enables them learn about the measurement, data access, hand drawing, CAD graphic design and other skills at the same time.

However, the Mapping practice teaching plan, which is originally arranged for a week after Engineering Drawing is finished, cannot carry out as expected. Lack of the professional knowledge and the understanding of any machinery emotionally, it is difficult for students to understand and master the knowledge such rational dimensioning, dimensional tolerances and fits, surface roughness, metal material and heat treatment, design and manufacturing in the absence of any mechanical processing of perceptual knowledge of the situation. A week is too short for the students to know well about the course and the knowledge they can obtain is limited. It is also a challenging task for the teachers. After discussions, we change the training plan. The time is still a week while the mapping practice time is reset late in the second grade. For the first and second grade students, we'll arrange some related courses so that they can have an initial knowledge about the design of machinery.

As to the shortage of time, our solution is to divide the mapping into several parts and combine some parts of the mapping with the relevant courses during the first two years. To complete the parts of the mapping and stretche the practice time, we can make an arrangement like this: during the fourth semester late in the three-dimensional course, the students are divided into groups of 5-6 and a gear reducer layout mapping exercise is assigned as a extra-curricular work. It demands every student to draw the assembly diagram, mapping each non-standard pieces of drawings, dimensioning, and technical requirements, and then sketches three-dimensional modeling and assembling parts to complete the important parts drawings. Having enough time, students may find themselves mistaken during the process of modeling and they can return to modifying, meanwhile teachers can give a good guidance for the students one by one. For some students who's creative, they can innovate a new design on the original one. By this way, during the final week focused on surveying and mapping, we can do better in completing the mapping with meeting all the requirements of the training successfully, including the shortage of time and the richness of the knowledge.

3   The Methods to Train Students' Comprehensive and Practical Ability

The new system and process of teaching call for a new teaching method. We combine the   students' weakness with the problems unfolded during the mapping week, find the connection between them and solve the problems together with the students. It will help them form a better understanding of the course and obtain more skills than before. Here we list some common problems that students may easily run into during the mapping week:

➢   Students are always confused when it comes to choosing appropriate views to express the parts and marking the parts of dimensions and technical requirements and so on;

➢   The lack of the carefulness in study makes the students fear of difficulties and troubles that they come across during the training and still remain in the same wrong situation. They are not use to referring to the interrelated references and looking up the standard manuals.

➢   The lack of the abilities to show a creative personality to fulfill a complex design and express it appropriately.

Thus, we've come up some revolutions in the way of teaching.

Disperse the knowledge, apply the project—teaching methodology. Let's have a look of the Figure 3-1. It shows the procedure of the practical teaching.

Scattering the points of the course and realizing the project-teaching methodology means dividing the practical training into several separate and interrelated parts. Set up unique requirements to meet the needs of the emphasized parts. It allows teachers help the students in the self-study learning and master the course step by step. In the practical teaching, we can help students form an initial understanding of the knowledge involved in "Design of Machinery" and lay the foundation for the further courses.

Value the training of students' sketch.Sketch is a convenient expression of design to show creative ideas and the way of thinking for a technical personneland. A designer must obtain the ability of drawing freehand sketches, for it is not only the basis of computer graphics, but also the foundation for creative design [2]. The combination of sketches and computer reflects the path of the modern design, and meets the needs of the future practical engineering design [3]. Besides, it is a disadvantage for students to form a holistic concept in mind and to gain the ability of spatial thinking and image thinking when using the two-dimensional computer graphics, especially in reading and checking the drawings. Thus, in the practical training, it is important for students to obtain the ability of drawing drafts and pay more attention to the standards and the requirements of the mapping. Most importantly, the lack of assembly sketch will cause

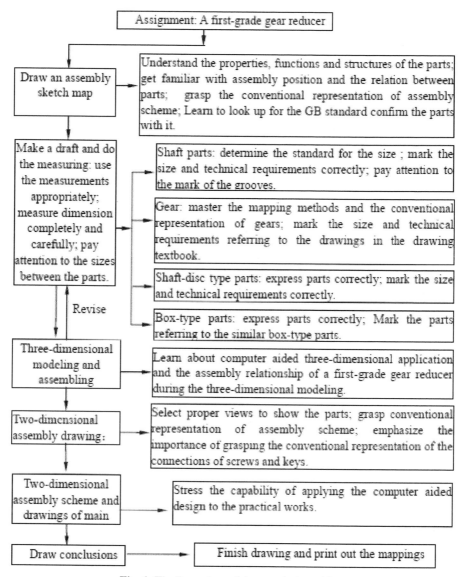

Fig. 1. The Procedure of the practical teaching

a lot of problems and cost more time to complete the drawing. Before mapping on the computer, teachers should help students check and give some comments on the sketch to realize the fitness of the assembly sketch.

Students access to information and rigorous, careful style of work. Some survey showed that the first priority of modern enterprise in hiring a staff is MQ (manner quotient), and then IQ (intelligence quotient)[4]. As an engineering and technical personnel, he must be in a strict, serious work style. Therefore, in the mapping training, it requires students to solve the problems, which come across during the mapping, by the means of the Internet, textbooks, design manuals and other methods and to respect national standards firmly during the mapping and to learn independent thinking and problem-solving approach. Meanwhile, teachers play an active role in guiding, organizing and inspiring the students to obtain all the required skills in the whole way. Emphasize the spirit of exploration and inspire them to forma strong interest to learn. Meanwhile, teachers are both strict to students and themselves. It is important for teachers to learn the progress of students' work and have them explain the purpose of the design.

With the mapping work going further and further, students can personally feel the rigor of the design. The rigor and carefulness help the students obtain a good personality and prepare them for the future work.

In practice, teaching research teaching methods. During the graphic mapping curriculum design, applying the research-teaching methods notonly requires the interaction between teachers and students, but also calls for the interactive learning among students. Students have become the protagonist, removing the model, measuring the size, determining the expression of the program, sketching, drawing graph and they all complete the work all by themselves; while teachers have become the supporting roles, playing a more counseling, guiding, checking, helping and suggesting role[5]. Divide students into groups and cooperate the program together. As for the program, teachers can set a number of questions for the groups to think, discuss and explore. Meanwhile, teachers should strengthen the real-time counseling visits of during the mapping, point out some representative problems and give timely comments. Thus, it helps students learn, summarize and get to the knowledge all together. Using such teaching mode can not only make students identify and solve problems themselves, but also train them about self-learning and the ability of innovation. In addition, it also help them learn spirit of teamwork. Those all contribute to students personality development.

Strengthen the innovation and creative ability. Jiang Zemin says: "Innovation is the soul of a nation's progress and the inexhaustible motivation for national prosperity." Thus, in mapping training, it is important to tell students that they should not stick the the problems to traditional way and they can find access to problem by considering conventional methods, breaking the stereotypes, the traditional thinking and thinking habits, reverse thinking, divergent thinking, novelty thinking. For example, during the three-dimensional modeling and three-dimensional parts assembly model, we encourage students innovate a new design on the original one by modifying the original mechanical parts, adjusting to construct new institutions and systems. Then teachers and students can discuss the feasibility of the new structure and do more further work. Innovative experiments training enables students personally experience the innovative design of the initial process and allows them form the engineering quality, innovation, hands-on training and exercise capacity.

4   Extrude the Check Mode of Mapping Process and Teaching Effect

Examinations is aimed to estimate students' mastering of knowledge and the techniques and it also reflect the teaching effects. As for a practice class like mapping, the marks that students recieve should not be confirmed only by the drawing quality of assembly sketch and the drawings of parts. It also should considere the following aspects:

> Stress the check and inspection of the process;
> The rationality of the design of assembled structure and the eligible choose of parts;
> Learn about their ability of using materials and knowledge, find out their real circumstance by oral response;
> find out their sense about teamwork and gain by writing mapping summary.

In a word, according to their drawings, make sure the circumstance of their mastering of assemble structure design, the functions of the parts and the eligible choose of parts. Reading their summary and obtain their learning situations. Therefore, we can give them a fair mark with every aspect taken into consideration. During the improved mapping exploration, three-dimensional concrete sculpt help students improve their ability of interspace conceivability and do good to their innovations. The mapping week make a great teaching effect , not only enhance and deepen the use of learned knowledge and improve their ability of analyse and solve the problem by themselves, realize the connection of knowledge and practice, nurture engineering consciousness and design ability, but also nurture themselves individual obligation, corporate and interpersonal ability by teamwork.

5 Summary

The improvement of the complex abilities and engineering personalities has a direct relationship with the development of modern constructing. It should run along with the students' process of study, even through his all life, for ut can't be realized in the practice tache of drawing and mapping at once. The establishment of new teaching system of drawing and mapping inplants more meaning to the mapping design, which enhance the connection of interrelated courses and the the students' cognition to their major. However, the new teaching system of drawing and mapping still have some problems remain to be solved ,such as the big span of the time, high standards to the teachers and so on. It calls for much more further work.

References

1. Ye, X., Hu, X.: How to Strengthen the Teaching in Mechanical Mapping Practice and Raise Student's Project Quality. Journal of Lishui University 31(5), 108–111 (2008)
2. Li, Y., He, P.: The Reform and Practice of Mapping Teaching in Mechanical Parts. China Education of Light Industry, 67–68 (January 2007)
3. Du, L., Li, L., et al.: Study of Teaching Practice on Surveying and Mapping of Engineering Graphics Based on Three Dimensional Modelling. Journal of Chongqing Technology and Business (Natural Sciences Edition), 407–410 (April 2009)
4. Xu, G., Jiang, L., Liang, Y.: Quality Education of Engineering Drawing Course. Journal of China University of Mining & Technology, 4–7 (August 2003)
5. Hong, Z.: The Teaching Practice and Exploration of Drawing Mapping Week. Channel Science, 54–55 (September 2007)

Actual Projects for Carriers to Achieve Teaching Model Innovation for Engineering Specialties

Bin Chen, Yingchun Pan, and Yuqiang Wang

Zhejiang Water Conservancy and Hydropower College, Hangzhou 310018, China
{chenbin,panych,Wangyq}@zjwchc.com

Abstract. A teaching reform and innovation with actual projects for carriers has been carried out during last years, and the experiences have been summarized in this paper. Quite a few actual projects which are not only correlated to the curriculum closely, but also all already finished have been well-chosen, with part of them used by one or several lessons, others must be used throughout the curriculum. The concrete design of curriculum frameworks, teaching methods, and teaching effects have all been discussed, for a deeply explaining for the work. Several minds and proposals have also been put forward for the further study.

Keywords: actual projects for carriers, teaching model innovation, engineering specialities.

1   Introduction

The Harvardcasemethod are famous for US MBA class[1], but has rarely been adopted by engineering major. In recent years, along with the rapid development of college education in china, many studies have been conducted in the higher education area, and the "Harvardcasemethod", here has another name with "actual projects for carriers"   or CDIO teaching pattern is attracting increasing interest in engineering universities[2-5].

In this study, a teaching model reform has been carried out, full use of   the "actual projects for carriers" method. A experiment invoved 184 students has been carried out, in order to gather experience for further pedagogical reforms.

2   General Ideal of Teaching Reform

The primary goal of teaching reform is to raise students' enthusiasm to learn. The teachers tell students not only what is the desk, but also how to make the desk. Students are sure to put their heart into the work and thus the learning initiative will be excitated. Furthermor, because the knowledge is learned during the students' conduct themselves, it will be no doubt better remembered usually.

The following points may be attentioned on, to get good results.

(1) The targets of projects should have a certain charm for students, and the conquest of problems should give students successful delight.
(2) Knowledge and technique out of the textbook may be necessary, since the first point has been accepted.

M. Zhu (Ed.): ICCIC 2011, Part V, CCIS 235, pp. 170–174, 2011.

(3) One or several projects throughout the curriculum arc also indispensable, to form a integrated knowledge system for students. But the projects can be divided into several modules, used in defferent learning stages.

3 Optimization of Class Structures

The units teaching activities have been organized and carried out according to a philosophy of three-dimensions-unification, here, the "three dimensions" are (i) forming process of knowledge; (ii) active process of thought; and (iii) process of emotional development respectively. The favourable teacher-student interaction will give a well condition for the class teaching, since all the learning activities are finished by the cooperating between teachers and students. The optimized class structures are shown in Fig.1.

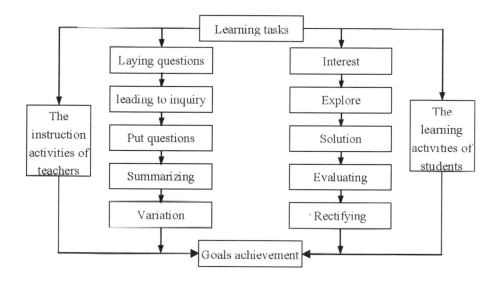

Fig. 1. Optimized class structures

Through a partnership in which   educate and support each other, the class teaching could be spread by a macro program with "identifying the target→creating interest→guiding   and   exploring→continuous   working→summarizing   and evaluating→feedback and rectifying→aiming to the new target". Incentives have been given continually, and the knowledge has been learned simultaneously.

3 Specific Approachs

3.1 Enriched the Curriculum by Actual Engineering Projects, Building the Curriculum Frame and Dividing Knowledge Units

During the preparing for the lessons, typical engineering projects should be selected and dissected, then the typical engineering problems could be extacted from them. By summarizing the problems and their resolution processes, a integrated system of cases could be established, as a result the process of learning could be carried out under entire practical engineering circumstance. It has proved by that students' enthusiasm for study is improved.

3.2 By the Integrate of Teaching Contents and Engineering Projects, Stimulating the Initiative and Creativeness of the Students

The teachers give full respect to the autonomous thinking of students, and replaced the one-way transmission with bi-directional exchange activities. A research-based teaching has been adopted based on the typical actual projects, to impove students' capacities of finding, analyzing and solving problems. A lot of times, the teachers can also be enlightened by students.

3.3 Based on the Actual Projects, Abundant Teaching Materials can be Found, Which are Useful for the Reform and Innovation of Teaching Method

Audio-visual animation is an effective means of teaching in multimedia-assisted engineering teaching. The modern educational technology depending on computers and other facilities would be adopted and improved, since large amount of photographs, blueprints and videoes can be offered by actual projects. That means, the actual projects can not only enrich the substantive knowledge, but also provide large amount of materials for the multimedia courseware, which can make the classes vivid and interesting.

3.4 Several Projects Throughout the Curriculum are Indispensable

The actual engineering projects can be fitted for defferent knowledge units, but must have one or several projects throughout the curriculum, to give students a holistic engineering conception.

3.5 In the Practice Teaching Stages, The Method are Also Effective

It has been demanded that all the selected materials in pratice teaching stages come from actual projects, and the virtual projects are unacceptable.

4 An Example: The Curriculum Reform and Innovation of Water Conservancy Construction

The curriculum of water conservancy construction is a main basic course of water conservancy and hydropower engineering subject. The course contents include the construction of: (i) water diversion; (ii) earthwork and stonework; (iii) concrete work; (iv) blasting engineering; (v) foundation and anti-seepage engineering; (vi) lifting, hoisting, and installation work; and (vii) construction organization and planning. In this study, three typical engineering project have been selected throughout the curriculum, which are an earth-rock dam, a concrete dam, and a sluice respectively. The curriculum framework is shown in Fig.2.

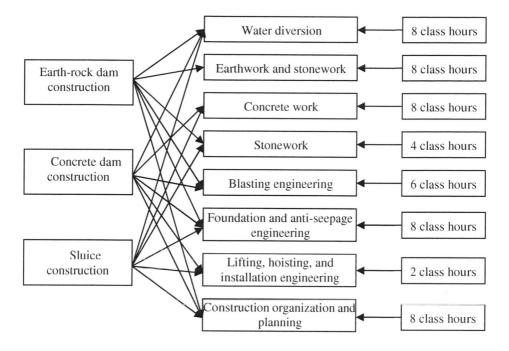

Fig. 2. The curriculum framework of water conservancy

Yet other work such as river regulation work, irrigation projects should be teaching, with the total class hour to 64. Some other needful engineering projects should be selected for the special sections.

5 Teaching Effect

The activities of curriculum reform and innovation have carried out for three years, and the effect is generally pretty. Existing problems may be short of the typical projects mainly, since quite a few engineering data have been kept secret. A complete range of engineering is difficult to collect, which involve in the owner, the surveyer, the disigner, and the builder.

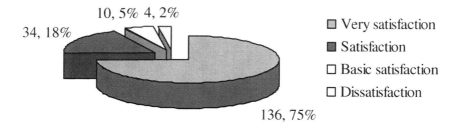

Fig. 3. Statistical result of the general degree of satisfaction

After the curriculum finished, a questionnaire survey has been carried out in order to understand the teaching effect further. Total 184 students(coming from 2 majors, total 4 classes) have been questioned, with the results showed in fig.3.

The reasons for dissatisfaction, according to the questionnaire, are mainly too quickly teaching and too large quantity of assignments, that should be impoved later.

6 Conclusions

Different from the science education, the engineering education is relatively technical, and the actual projects have been used more or less in the past. In this study the method of case teaching has been raised a level, and the curriculum has been organized by taking the actual engineering projects as index. One or several projects throughout the curriculum are indispensable, to form a integrated knowledge system for students. Result of questionnaire survey and performance compare before and after teaching innovation have indicated that the reform is successful, and can provide reference for colleagues.

Acknowledgements. This work was financially supported by the special funds of 2010 Zhejiang enhance local colleges and universities' academic level.

References

1. Information on, http://www.hbs.edu/learning/
2. Lu, Y.: Journal of Hunan University of Science and Engineering 31(8), 24 (2010)
3. Wang, H.B., Li, C.M.: Journal of Guangxi University for Nationalities (Philosophy and Social Science Edition) 6, 190 (2009)
4. Crawley, E., Malmgvist, J., Ostlund, S., Brodeur, D.: Rethinking Engineering Education-The CDIO Approach. Springer, German (2007)
5. Hu, Z.G., Ren, S.B., Wu, B.: China Higher Education 22, 44 (2010)

Design and Experiment of a New Synthesized Practical Training Curriculum in College Education-Based on Real Engineering Situations

Bin Chen and Xiaodong Chen

Zhejiang Water Conservancy and Hydropower College, Hangzhou 310018, China
dong5623@163.com

Abstract. A new synthesized practical training curriculum has been designed in the paper, in which all the learning activities of students are placed in real engineering situations. The curriculum framework, organizational forms, teaching management, and the exam of teaching are all discussed in the paper. A teaching experiment involved 133 students, who are all hydraulic engineering special field, has been carried out with groups of 3 or 4 students formed. The teaching effect has proved that the model is successful, and students' abilities of integrating knowledge and flexible application are both apparently enhanced. A questionnaire has also been done, with several concerns has been surveyed and summarized.

Keywords: college education, practical training, curriculum, real engineering situations.

1 Introduction

In higher vocational education, practical training of students is usually of key importance. Many studies have been conducted during the last years in china, and different teaching methods have been presented [1,2], among them the "working-process-oriented curriculum" being most accepted [3,4]. But for the agriculture, forestry and irrigation majors, the method above mentioned is not very suitable for use, so another model must be explored [5].

In this study, a new synthesized practical training course has been designed which is especially suitabe for the students of irrigation and hydraulic engieering major. A experiment invoved 133 students has been carried out, in order to gather experience for further pedagogical reforms.

2 Curriculum Framework

The designed course is a synthesized appliaction for all the former lessons, and a simple review is necessary since the former lessons are usually learned for years. A complete design process of certain typical hydraulic structure should be required for every students. The typical hydraulic structures can be the dams, sluices, pump stations and so on. The curriculum framework is as shown in Fig.1.

M. Zhu (Ed.): ICCIC 2011, Part V, CCIS 235, pp. 175–180, 2011.
© Springer-Verlag Berlin Heidelberg 2011

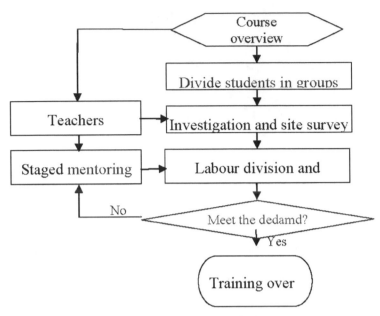

Fig. 1. The designed curriculum

3   Organizational Forms

3.1   Investigation and Site Survey

In this curriculum, 40 small reservoirs with earth or stone masonry gravity dams in Linan county, east china have been selected. Before the operation, a detailed investigation and site survey are necessary, including the work of data collection and site survey for a 1/10000 topographic map. A professional teacher should guided the work, and fig.2 was working situations.

Fig. 2. Students just in site surveying

Fig. 2. *(Continued)*

The work of investigation and site survey would provide reliable basic materials, which are indispensable for the next engeering design.

3.2 Decomposition of Curriculum

The entire curriculum has down into several small stages, and each stages contained a relatively independent task and function. The main stages include(i) study of technical specifications and model texts. Several binding specifications are collected and a seasoned engineer has been invited for a nichetargeting explaining; (ii) hydrologic calculation and safety assessment of flood control system, to verdict whether the current dam height and spillway width can meet demand of the flood control; (iii) constructional design, mainly including the design of dam, spillway, and water conveyance structure. The impervious structure is usually critical and must be doubling alertlyattentive; (iv) mechanical and environment design, such as dam slope protection, dam crest rigidification, and so on; (v)   draw the construction papers; (vi) construction organization design; and (vii) budgetary estimate of design.

The total time of the course is 10 weeks, which is usually enough for a rich experienced engineer. But the students are the first time to do this, so masses of modification are unavoidable, which means, the whole work above mentioned may be relatively large.

4   Teaching Management

Although a open teaching process has been adopted, before each stages, the teacher should given students   some advises. A computer house connecting with it is necessary, since large of work must be done depending on the computer. Division of labour is also important, or part of students may do everything, while others do nothing. The teachers must have a overall grasp. After each stages ended, the students' fruits must be checked and graded, as part of the grades at ordinary times.

The joint checkup of drawings is also adopted, in order to simulate the actual engineering process as realistic as possible, and decreasing the design faults. Different viewpoint and scheme should be put forward and compared, which could not only improve the design results, but also wide students' horizon.

The exam of teaching is easy since the fruit will be used in pratical engineering, but has not a concrete standard. Several aspects can be taken into account including periodic performances, the amount of work, ultima users' feedback, and so on.

5   Existing Problems

4.1.The Responsibilities of Students Should be Further Strengthen. Although the teachers have explained the importance of work, some students draw the blueprints roughly, and not just a few mistakes have been found. A final checking and modifying are allimportant to guarantee the project quality.

4.2. Plenty of Teachers with Lavish Engineering Experiences are Necessary A fairly large number of teachers are come from colleges and universities, who are often lacking practical experiences. So it is necessary that the teachers undergo a on-the-job placement in the engineering units.

4.3. The traditional teaching environment may not be able to meet requirements of the new curriculum, so a reform of classroom may be necessary. Especially a large of work of drawing must depending on the computers discontinuously, while the total computers are usually infinte.

6   Teaching Effect

6.1   Fruits of the Curriculum

The projects are already fininshed and showed as in Fig.3. As a whole the curriculum is successful.

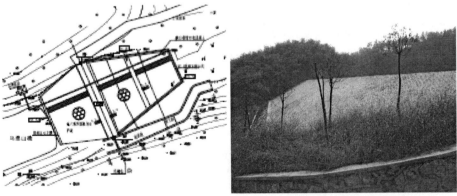

a. Blueprint of students   b. Photo of project live-action

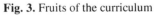

Fig. 3. Fruits of the curriculum

6.2. A Questionnaire Survey and its Statistical Result

After the curriculum finished, a questionnaire survey has been carried out in order to understand the teaching effect. Total 10 questions have been designed and 130 students have return the questionnaires. The results have been counted as follows.

(1) About the curriculum format. Total 83 students has answered the question and 59%(49 students) among them approved this reform. Others advised adopted the format of redesigning finished projects, or go out to engineering units for practical training.

(2) About the building of groups. Three ways can be selected, namely(A) work individually; (B) designated group leaders by teachers, then the leaders organize members themselves; and (C) grouping by teachers, considering the previous performance sorting. 35%, 41.8%, and 22.4% of students have selected (A), (B), and (C) respectively.

(3) About the the size of the group. number of people selected one, two, three, or four are roughly equivalent.

(4) About the learning initiative. The statistical result is shown as Fig. 4,a.

(5) About the division of labor. The statistical result is shown as Fig. 4,b.

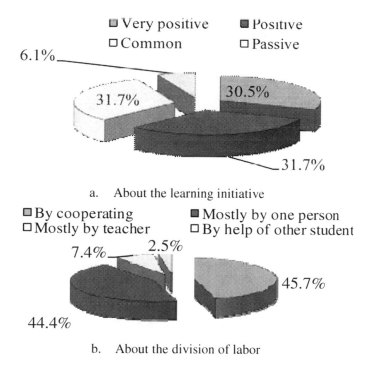

a.   About the learning initiative

b.   About the division of labor

Fig. 4. Statistical results for question 4 and 5

(6) About the problems for teachers, 90.1% of students reflected that the main problems include two aspects, means, (A) often cannot find teacher; (B) teachers are lack of practical experience, part of teachers are even will not operate.

(7) About the qualities of fruits, 13.4% of students thought that the qualities of fruits are good and can be used in construction, 68.3% of students thought that the fruits are ordinary and have to be improved by teachers. Yet 12.1% of students indicated that the work is done at random.

(8) Four options have been given for learning difficulty, with (A) cannot obtain guidance; (B) lack of hardware, especially the computer; (C) no special classroom; and (D) cannot find reference materials. 22.4%, 34.1%, 25.9%, 17.6% of students have selected for the options respectively.

(9) About the principal acquisition, four options including (A) strengthened the understanding for knowledge; (B) raised the hands-on capabilities; (C) strengthened the understanding for major; and (D) improved organization, coordination and communication skills have been given, and 30.0%, 30.8%, 31.5%, and 7.7% of students have selected.

(10) About the general degree of satisfaction. The statistical result is shown as Fig. 5.

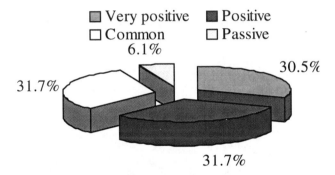

Fig. 5. Statistical result of the general degree of satisfaction

Acknowledgements. This work was financially supported by the special funds of 2010 Zhejiang enhance local colleges and universities' academic level.

References

1. Jing, M., Wu, A.H.: International Handbook of Education for the Changing World of Work, Part III, Section 4, p. 649 (2009)
2. Information on, http://www.geneva.edu/object/iso_curricular
3. Jiang, Q.B., Xu, G.Q.: Vocational and Technical Education 26(22), 46 (2005)
4. Zheng, X.M.: Vocational and Technical Education 31(28), 49 (2005)
5. Xu, H.: Vocational and Technical Education 28(34), 5 (2007)

Design and Implementation of an Attendance System for Engineering Training Based on DSBA

Wang Meilin[1], Fu Pinxin[1], Dai Qingyun[1], and Zhong Runyang[2]

[1] Faculty of Information Engineering, Guangdong University of Technology, Guangzhou
510006, Guangdong, China
[2] Department of Industrial and Manufacturing Systems Engineering,
The University of Hong Kong, Pokfulam Road, Hong Kong
wang33440@yeah.net

Abstract. The algorithm of Double-signature Based Attendance (DSBA) was proposed so as to meet the requirements in terms of accuracy, real-time operation and traceability in engineering training center of high educational institutions. Under these considerations, this paper provides a model that is so-named DSBA-0. According to the real-world problem in engineering training center of China Jiliang University (CJU), we established the DSBA-1 model that is intended to overcome the disadvantages of DSBA-0. The DSBA-1 model was successfully applied to an attendant system CJU. Since the system is significant, this paper concentrates on demonstrating the system design and implementation, aiming at providing useful references to the practitioners and academics.

Keywords: DSBA Algorithm, RFID, Attendance System, Engineering Training.

0 Introduction

Since 2003, our team has implemented MES(Manufacturing Execution System) based on RFID in several leading manufacturing enterprises located in Guangdong, China, such as KEDA Ltd., Greatoo Molds Inc., Hitachi Elevator (Guangzhou, China) Co.,Ltd and so on. On the basis of the successful implementations of MES, we introduced MES and its management model into engineering training center of China Jiliang University (CJU). In 2010, the teaching course of engineering education has been put into operation in a better way as enterprises' MES do. During this project, we discovered that the attendance of teachers and students caused troubles, much time was wasted in recording, calculating and query. Therefore, the problem of attendance has become a bottleneck of the center.

Due to the requirement of the attendance problem from enterprises, many kinds of attendance production have been invented. Usually, they applied B/S model [2] or a mixed model of B/S with C/S [3] and their attendance identification technique is

M. Zhu (Ed.): ICCIC 2011, Part V, CCIS 235, pp. 181–188, 2011.

fingerprint identification technique [4,5] or RFID [6,7,8]. However, most attendance systems are built on their own requirements and have their own methods. Study on attendance algorithm is rare and there is no general algorithm. Based on the model of check-in and check-out signature in reality, the author brought up a Double-signature Based Attendance (DSBA) algorithm which could be used universally and is of great practicality. It can not only solve the problem of workers' attendance in enterprises, but also students' attendance in engineering training center of high educational institutions.

1   Double-Signature Based Attendance (DSBA)

1.1   Introduction of DSBA

In order to describe DSBA, some definitions are provided as follows. StartTime: the time when attendance begins to check in. Only people come at that moment or before is called punctual. After that time one's attendance can be counted as late. EndTime: the time when time is up and it begins to check out. Anyone who checks out before that time is leaving early. LogInTime: the time of arriving and checking in. LogOutTime: the time of checking out and leaving.

Generally, when the attendance check is required, one is asked to sign on their checking in and also on their checking out when time is up. The checking-in signature will tell whether this one comes or not. If he comes, his signature time of checking-in will tell whether he is late or not and his signature time of checking-out will tell whether he leaves early or not. Based on the double signatures model, Double-signature Based Attendance (DSBA) was put forward.

According to DSBA, whether there is LogInTime tells whether the someone's attendance or not. If there is LogInTime and it is later than StartTime, then this one is late and their difference is his/her delay time. If LogOutTime is earlier than EndTime, then this one leaves early and their difference is his/her time span of leaving early from duty. Otherwise, one's attendance is normal.

1.2   DSBA-0 Attendance Model

DSBA-0 attendance model is the one based directly on DSBA, irrespective of other accidental factors. The model is demonstrated as Figure 1:

Attendance status in this model include absence, come late, leave early (the time span of coming late and leaving early can be counted) and normal. DABA-0 model is a fundamental model. In reality, all the personnel may not comply with it totally. For example, they leave without signing to check out, therefore, their LogOutTime is unavailable and whether they leave early or not can not be identified. Also, they sign many times during StartTime and EndTime, how to deal with their signature is also a problem deserved to be discussed.

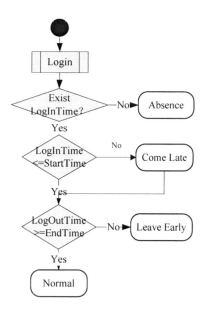

Fig. 1. DSBS-0 Model

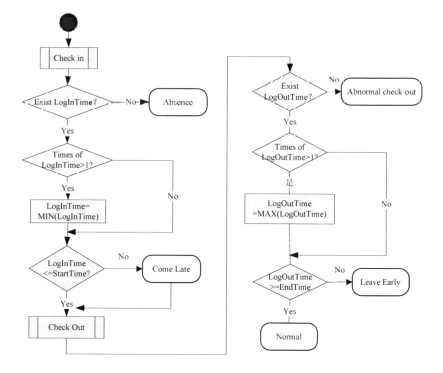

Fig. 2. DSBA-1 Model

1.3   DABA-1 Attendance Model

In light of the problems of DABA-0, we proposed the modified DABA-1model which aims to solve the problems above and enhance its practical value. When one intends to leave without signing, DABA-1 model will remind him/her that he/she doesn't sign yet. When one signs several times during StartTime and EndTime, the model will choose his/her first signing time as LogInTime, last time as LogOutTime to identify whether he/she comes late or leave early. The model is displayed as Figure 2:

2   Application of DSBA-1

The engineering training center of China Jiliang University (CJU) has the advantages of large area and variety training items. And with the expanding enrollment of higher education institutions, each instructing teacher has to instruct more and more students. CJU attaches great importance to the attendance of students, they   count students' attendance into their usual performance, and deduct their scores when students commit being absent from class, being late and leaving early. And the deduced scores is directly proportional to the times of students' offences. This requires instructors at the training center to check students' attendance both before and after class. It's difficult for instructors to check students' attendance and the exact minutes of each student's being-late and leaving-early all by themselves. This causes inconveniences to the assessment of students' usual performance.

To solve the problem of students' attendance in the engineering training center of CJU, we applied RFID-based technology in the center and established an attendance system on the basis of the DSBA-1 attendance model.

2.1   System Introduction

The attendance system is made up of two parts, namely the web management subsystem and the workshop management subsystem (Figure 3). Workshop management subsystem is made up of workstations in workshops, wireless bus, intelligent terminals (Figure 4).

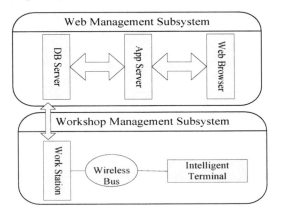

Fig. 3. System Architecture

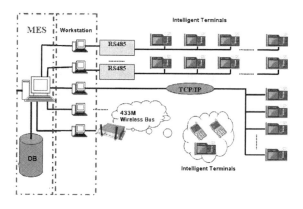

Fig. 4. Deployment of Workshop Subsystem

Each student has their own unique student card (RFID tagged), and students are required to punch their cards on the intelligent terminal before beginning their training (recorded as checking-in). The intelligent terminal collects IDs of student card and their punch-card time. Similarly, students punch their cards when their training ends (recorded as checking-out). Through workshop management subsystem the card information and checking in/out time will be saved to the database server. Web management subsystem does the attendance check according to the DSBA-1 model. Results of the attendance are stored in the database server, and can be queried on the web page and the intelligent terminal.

2.2   Attendance in the Workshop Management Subsystem

Workshop management subsystem uses intelligent terminals to check the attendance. There are two kinds of intelligent terminals. One is bound to the equipments, which not only checks students' attendance but also checks attendance of devices. The other does not bind to the equipments, it only check the attendance of students, known as attendance terminal. Whether to bind to the equipments or not should be determined according to characteristics of varied types of training items. No matter which type of intelligent terminal is used, attendance of students can be checked and the way of checking is the same.

After arriving at the engineering training center, students will be assigned to equipments by their instructors and they need to punch their student cards on the intelligent terminal binding with the training equipments, then check out at the end of their training. Instructors can view students' attendance information that they are in charge of. Attendance information includes who hasn't check in till this moment, who has left early, who has been late, and who attend as required.

2.3   Attendance Check in Web Subsystem

Attendance functions of Web management subsystem includes checking attendance of students in training, tracing historical attendance, summarizing attendance results, and real-time attendance and attendance summary of equipment. Web management subsystem is develpoed for the management staff, they can view attendance information offered by the attendance system through any computer with Internet access in the office.

2.3.1 Real-time Attendance Check on Students

When do real-time attendance check, teachers can choose a workshop to monitor its attendance. This real-time attendance check of a workshop is done in accordance with the DSBA-1 model.   Function fun_PeopleAttendance in Microsoft SQL Server 2000 is used to realize this. In real-time attendance check, the page will display student ID, name, class, training items, instructors and attendance information of all students in a workshop. And it can also display the minutes of students' being late or leaving early.

2.3.2 Attendance Summary

In student's attendance summary, one can query students' name, class and training attendance status for all classes. This helps teachers at the center to have a general understanding of the attendance. And thus facilitates their accessment on students' usual performance.

The attendance summary of equipments is calculated based on a required period of time (one month or one semester). And it altermately guides the accessment on teacher's bonuses.

3   Performance Analysis on Attendance System

Coordinate of Performance Analysis of Attendance is drawn based on actual information from engineering training in CJU. A real case is about 300 students' card data statistics and analysis on one morning(See Figure 5).

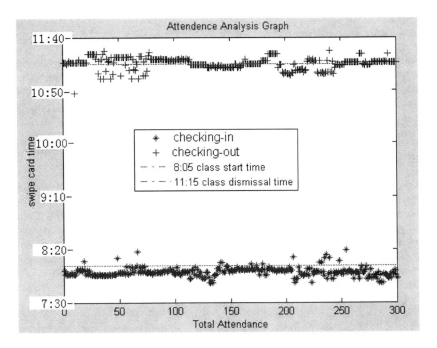

Fig. 5. Coordinate of Performance Analysis of Attendance

In this figure, students check in after the start time of class(8:05) are recorded late on attendance status; students check out before the end-time of class(11:15) are recorded leaving early on attendance status. Card-punching at other times are recorded normal on attendance status. Put statistics of attendance of these 300 students into a table, we can get Table 1:

Table 1. Attendance Results Tables

Attendace Status	Number
Normal	180
Come late only	6
Leave early only	105
Come late & Leave early	9
Total	300

From statistics in the above table, we can see that the DSBA attendance algorithm can solve the problem of staff attendance. And it has solved the problem of attendance on engineering training in higher education institutes. It provides a basis for the usual performance assessment on students and teachers and saved a lot of time for management staff, instructors and students.

4   Conclusion

This paper bases on the actual needs of students' attendance problems of engineering education in higher education institutions and proposed DSBA algorithms to meet the requirements as accuracy, timeliness and traceability, and then applied the algorithms to solve the actual attendance counting. DSBA-1 model is established catering for the requirement of engineering training attendance of CJU after analyzing the shortcomings of DSBA-0 model. DSBA-1 model has great application value since it has been successfully implemented in universities as well as manufacturing execution system of leading enterprises. It has successfully solved difficulties of attendance checking in these organizations proved its practicality and universal application. Data analysis on the practical application can not only provide accurate data and statistics, but also provides supporting data for educational officials to make better decisions.

The improved attendance model DSBA-1 established on the DSBA algorithm can be further developed on the timing choice and diversity. It can be used on the enmployee attendance check   catering to enterprises' actual conditions. It also can be adjusted to production workshops where staff mobility is high and production conditions are adverse. So this model has certain application prospect.

Acknowledgements. The authors are most grateful to the case company for providing technical and financial supports, and grateful to all the project team members for their hard works. The authors would also like to thank 2010 National Natural Science Fundation of China grant (61074146), Education Department of Guangdong Province grant (CGZHZD0608), 2008 special funds to information service industry of Guangdong grant (GDIID2008IS005) and 2008 Guangdong and Hong Kong Bidding

Project grant (2008A011400008) for providing partial financial supports.   The authors are grateful to HKU Small Project Funding (200907176106), HKSAR ITF (GHP/042/07LP) and HKSAR RGC GRF (HKU 712508E).

References

1. Zhong, R., Dai, Q., Zhou, K.: Design and Implementation of DMES based on RFID. In: Proceeding of 2nd International Conference on Anti-Counterfeiting, Security and Identification. IEEE, Guiyang (2008)
2. Jiang, Z.: Design and Implement of Student Attendance Management System Based on ASP.NET. Journal of Shanxi Polytechnic Institute 5(1), 35–37 (2010)
3. Sun, T., Li, S., Li, Y., Zheng, J.: Research on Attendance Management System Based on Integration Model of B/S and C/S. Computer Engineering 29(8), 170–172 (2003)
4. Jian, X.-c.: Management of Checking on Work Attendance Using Finger Mark Identify. Journal of Inner Mongolia Agricultural University (Natural Science Edition) 27(1), 108–110 (2006)
5. Duan, S., Tian, J., Li, H.: Research on an Efficient System of Work Attendance Using Fingerprint Identification. Computer Engineering 29(9), 37–38 (2003)
6. Lim, T.S., Sim, S.C., Mansor, M.M.: RFID Based Attendance System. In: 2009 IEEE Symposium on Industrial Electronics and Applications (ISIEA 2009), Kuala Lumpur, Malaysia, October 4-6, pp. 778–782 (2009)
7. Wahab, M.H.A., Mutalib, A.A., Kadir, H.A., Mohsin, M.F.M.: Design and Development of Portable RFID for Attendance System, 173–178 (2010) 978-1-4244-5651-2/10/$26.00 ©2010 IEEE
8. Wang, Z., Mu, P., Dai, S., Shi, H.: The Application of RF Card Reader in Terminal of Checking on Work Attendance. Chinese Journal of Scientific Instrument 25(S2), 584–586 (2004)
9. Liu, J.-q., Zhao, D.-f., Ding, H.-w.: Automatic check on times of city bus circular running by wireless technique. Journal of Yunnan University (Natural Sciences Edition) 28(2), 113–118 (2006)

Discussion on Bilingual Teaching in Computer Experiment

Zhaoyun Sun, Yuan Ma, and Linan Jiao

School of Information Engineering, Chang'an University, Xi'an, 710064 China
sun80901@163.com

Abstract. This paper analyzes the important meaning of bilingual teaching in experiment courses, especially in the field of Computer Science. Considering the practice of bilingual education in Chang' an University, this paper lists several problems faced in bilingual teaching in experiment courses, and brings forward some efficient measures to improve the bilingual education.

Keywords: Bilingual education, Bilingual teaching in experiment course, International talents.

1 Introduction

Under the new situation of joining into WTO, China needs a large number of senior technical talents with global outlook and professional knowledge. Chinese Ministry of Education clearly required that capable universities should actively recruit foreign scholars and experts to engage in the bilingual teaching in specialized courses [1].

"Bilingual Teaching" refers to that teachers use a foreign language for the teaching of content subjects in different disciplines [2]. Nationally speaking, the word "Bilingual" mainly refers to "Chinese" and "English". The main difference between "Bilingual Teaching" and "College English Teaching" is that the former uses English as a language tool to teach in specialized courses, which is good for students to understand and master the advanced international and professional knowledge.

According to the actual situation of China's universities, it is unrealistic to widely promote bilingual teaching in all the courses at present. However, as a universal field, computer science should be developed with the international standards as soon as possible in order that students can use English with ease for communicating and thinking in specialized fields.

In our case, many computer courses have been included in bilingual education programs in Institution of Information Engineering in Chang'an University, especially the course of "Delphi: Advanced Computer Programming Techniques" which was supported by the Construction Project of National Bilingual Education Model Course. Moreover, as a supplement to the theory course, the experiment course with bilingual teaching mode can not only help students to master the international and professional computer skills, but also exercise their thinking ability in English.

Firstly, we have mentioned that computer science is a universal field. For instance, the programming language used in the experiment course of "Delphi" is developed

M. Zhu (Ed.): ICCIC 2011, Part V, CCIS 235, pp. 189–192, 2011.

based on English, and its latest reference books mostly come from abroad. If teachers use the traditional Chinese teaching pattern, students will not afford to grasp the essence of the course. Secondly, it is impossible for some deep contents such as code or object properties to have their completely Chinese version. If teachers do not use the bilingual pattern in experiment courses, students will encounter language barriers. Finally, in terms of the feedbacks, the graduates working in the computer field generally said that they use English in a high frequency during their work. Therefore, in order to enable graduates to adapt to their work, it is important to use bilingual teaching mode in computer experiment courses.

2   The Key Factors to Bilingual Teaching in Computer Experiment

Through the practice of bilingual teaching in computer experiment courses, we find some main factors affecting the quality of bilingual education.

The emphasis on bilingual teaching in experiment courses. There is a common phenomenon in China that universities often pay more emphasis on theory teaching than on experiment teaching. The experiment class hours usually not more than 20% of the total class hours. As an important part of experiment education, bilingual teaching in experiment courses will surely be affected under the poor situation.

The English proficiency of students. Students' English level directly affects the implementation of bilingual education. It is reported that nearly 50% of the students spent almost twice as much time as any other courses for rehearsal and preparation, and about 13% of the students have great difficulties [3]. The bilingual teaching in experiment courses put forward a high demand to the students that they should have enough vocabulary and good skills to communicate and think in English. However, since the English level is not balanced among the students, the promotion of bilingual teaching in experiment courses is restricted to some extent.

The ability of bilingual teachers. Bilingual teachers should have wealthy teaching experiences, solid academic knowledge, and rich researching capabilities; meanwhile, bilingual teachers should also possess a high level of English, which means that teachers can switch skillfully between English and Chinese to communicate accurately with students. On the one hand, the majority of the bilingual teachers are lack of specialized English training; On the other hand, bilingual teachers should also improve their teaching methods to meet the needs of modern bilingual education. Therefore, the overall level of bilingual teachers is not optimistic.

The materials used in bilingual teaching in experiment courses. Bilingual teaching made a high demand to the teaching materials [4]. Many bilingual teachers prefer to choose the outstanding original theory materials from abroad, but it is hard to find the original experiment materials. Moreover, even if there are some original experiment materials, how to choose them to meet the teaching requirements is worth considering.

The improvement of the bilingual teaching methods in experiment courses. Because carrying out the bilingual teaching in experiment courses aims to cultivate "international" and "skilled" personnel, it is not wise to continue the old teaching methods, such as "teacher demonstrate and students follow". This kind of method is so out of date that it leads to a lack of independent thinking. If students just blindly copy and mechanically repeat, it is impossible to increase their enthusiasm and creativity.

The management in bilingual teaching in experiment courses. Bilingual education started late in China so that it has not formed an effective management mechanism, which further restricted the smooth development of bilingual education. The evaluation of bilingual teaching in experiment courses is also different from general courses. These not only increase the difficulties in teaching quality monitoring, but also increase teachers' workloads [5]. Therefore, what kind of security mechanism of bilingual teaching in experiment courses we should design is a key point that whether the bilingual education can be carried out smoothly or not.

3   The Effective Measures to Improve the Bilingual Teaching Quality of Computer Experiment

Strengthen the emphasis on bilingual teaching in experiment courses to stimulate students' participation. Universities should increase the investment on the experiment education to supply the bilingual teaching in experiment courses with a favorable environment. Meanwhile, teachers should find ways to stimulate students' enthusiasm and initiative, produce a relaxed experiment environment, create a rigorous academic atmosphere, and establish an active interaction mechanism.

Enhance students' English language abilities to lay a solid foundation for the expansion of bilingual education. In addition to strengthen the general English education and professional English education, universities should also gradually carry out bilingual teaching in some basic subject from the lower grades. Only in this way can students gradually adapt to the bilingual teaching methods and pave the way for the bilingual education in specialized courses in the higher grades [6].

Carry out English training and international exchanges to improve the quality of teachers. Universities should build a bilingual teacher organization with reasonable specialty structure and appropriate age gradient. On the one hand, universities should introduce academic leaders of bilingual education to teach and help the other teachers to improve their English teaching skill; on the other hand, we must also encourage the bilingual teachers to actively participate in various forms of continuing education to improve their English proficiency.

Carefully design the contents of bilingual teaching in experiment courses. We should select the advanced, innovative and practical original materials for bilingual teaching in experiment courses, and these materials must meet the needs of the requirement mentioned in training plans; Furthermore, if the original materials are difficult to understand, universities need to organize some bilingual teachers who are professional in specialty, proficient in English, and rich in experience to compile the experiment materials after doing in-depth research on the actual needs of students.

Innovate bilingual teaching pattern in experiment courses to enhance the teaching quality. In order to solve the problems faced in the experiments, students can access to English reference books, English system help files, or they can discuss with their classmates, but teachers should not answer students' every question. If students can use English to think and communicate all along, and they ultimately solve the specialty problems by their own efforts, their initiative and self-confidence will be greatly excited.

Establish a management mechanism. Universities should give bilingual teachers policy and funding support, and create more training opportunities for teachers to study abroad. Besides, universities should also put forward the explicit requirement on the teaching outline, teaching materials, and teaching assessments, which will avoid the randomness and blindness in bilingual teaching in experiment courses. In addition, universities should organize the work of identifying the qualifications of bilingual teachers. Only the teachers who pass the bilingual proficiency tests can get on the podium of the bilingual teaching classrooms.

4   Conclusion

Bilingual education in experiment plays a positive and effective role in enhancing the overall competitiveness of students. Through practice and exploration in recent years, bilingual education in computer experiment has received much recognition. However, improving the quality of bilingual education in experiment courses is still a gradual process and an arduous task. Therefore, in order to develop students' English ability and consolidate students' specialty skills, universities should solve the practical problems encountered in the process of bilingual teaching. In addition, universities should also further strengthen the exploring and researching in bilingual teaching methods, so that the level of bilingual education in computer experiment can be greatly improved.

References

1. Yang, Z.: Strengthen Practice Training and Enhance Innovation Capability. Research On Cultivating the Innovation in Laboratory (2005)
2. Zhao, H., Tuo, X.: On How To Solve the Problem Of Bilingual Teaching. Education and Vocational 2 (2006)
3. Chen, Y.: Discussion On Cultivation International Talents. Economist 5 (2006)
4. Yang, L.: Practice in Bilingual Teaching of "C Programming Language". University Education 1 (2003)
5. Man, J., Xiao, X.: Practice In Bilingual Teaching of "Java Programming Language". Fujian PC 11 (2010)
6. Xu, X.: Problem and Strategy On the Bilingual Teaching. Frontier Teaching Quality 8 (2010)

Software Process Measurement Based on Six Sigma

Yu Lei, Li Zhibo, Hou Xuemei, and Du Zhuping

National Digital Switch System Engineering & Technological R&D Center
Zhengzhou, Henan, China
yumessenger@hotmail.com

Abstract. The objective of software process measurement is to find the abnormal conditions, such as incompliance and instable, in the real executing process of software process by measurement, so we can supply quantity proof for software process control and management. However, there are gaps between customer satisfaction degree measurement and software product quality degree measurement in mostly software process measurement approach and practice currently, cause the problems like ambiguity of measurement aims, and difficult to evaluate the effect of measurement etc. This paper put forward a new software process measurement approach based on Six Sigma theory, which combines customer satisfaction degree, software quality, software process altogether. The approach is based on ISO9126's software internal-external-user quality model, uses QFD(quality function deployment) to confirm the aim of software process measurement and measurement technique factors, using SPC(statistics process control) method to do trend analysis and stability analysis for measurement items, to find and remove abnormal instances, constructs performance baseline for measured process performance, improves and justifies software process according to measurement results, and provides focus for software test and maintain, finally insure the implementation of the target of customer satisfaction degree and software quality.

Keywords: Software Process Measurement, Six Sigma, SPC, Customer Satisfactory Degree.

1   Introduction

Measurement is the process by which numbers or symbols are assigned to attributes of entities in the real world in such a way as to characterize the attributes by clearly defined rules [1] [2]. Software process management is about successfully managing the work processes associated with developing, maintaining, and supporting software products and software intensive systems. By successful management, we mean that the products and services produced by the processes conform fully to both internal and external customer requirements and those they meet the business objectives of the organization responsible for producing the products [3].

Controlled processes are stable processes, and stable processes enable you to predict results. This in turn enables you to prepare achievable plans, meet cost estimates and

M. Zhu (Ed.): ICCIC 2011, Part V, CCIS 235, pp. 193–200, 2011.
© Springer-Verlag Berlin Heidelberg 2011

scheduling commitments, and deliver required product functionality and quality with acceptable and reasonable consistency. The objective of software process management is to ensure that the processes you operate or supervise are predictable, meet customer needs, and (where appropriate) are continually being improved. Measurements are the basis for detecting deviations from acceptable performance. They are also the basis for identifying opportunities for process improvement.

Six Sigma is a best-in-class change strategy for accelerating improvements in processes, products, and services. Six Sigma is enterprise wide. Six Sigma focuses on "critical to quality" factors [4]. DMAIC model is the basic process management model in Six Sigma, means the cycle of process define, process measure, process analyze, process improve and process control. In Six Sigma architecture, SPC can be applied to individual software processes, such as test process and review process [5][6][7]. A process has one or more outputs. These outputs, in turn, have measurable attributes. SPC is based on the idea that these attributes have two sources of variation: natural (also known as common) and assignable (also known as special) causes. If the observed variability of the attributes of a process is within the range of variability from natural causes, the process is said to be under statistical control. The practitioner of SPC tracks the variability of the process to be controlled. When that variability exceeds the range to be expected from natural causes, one then identifies and corrects assignable causes.

ISO/IEC 9126-2002 is the unique international standard about software quality measurement. In ISO/IEC 9126-1, a software quality model is provided showed in fig 1.

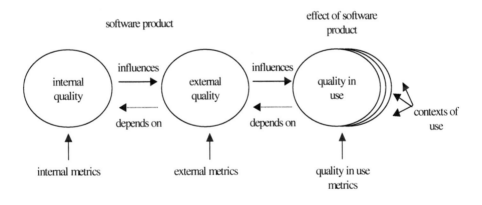

Fig. 1. ISO 9126 quality model

The internal metrics may be applied to a non-executable software product during its development stages. This allows the user to identify quality issues and initiate corrective action as early as possible in the development life cycle. The external metrics may be used to measure the quality of the software product by measuring the behavior of the system of which it is a part. The external metrics can only be used during the testing stages of the life cycle process and during any operational stages. The quality in use metrics measure whether a product meets the needs of specified users to achieve specified goals with effectiveness, productivity, safety and satisfaction in a specified context of use.

It is recommended to use internal metrics having a relationship as strong as possible with the target external metrics so that they can be used to predict the values of external metrics. However, it is often difficult to design a rigorous theoretical model that provides a strong relationship between internal metrics and external metrics. Software process measurement's current problems as followed [8][9]: process measurement(internal quality) is divorced from software quality and customer satisfactory(quality in use), which leads to the in-notable effect of software process measurement on software quality.

2   Software Process Measurement Approach Based on Six Sigma

In Fig.2, a new software process measurement approach is put forward based on Six Sigma theory, which combines plan phase, track phase and summary phase.

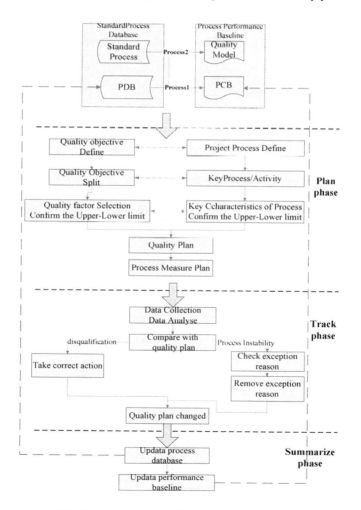

Fig. 2. Process and Quality Measurement Model

1. Plan Phase

In the plan phase, the project defines the performance objective and the upper-lower limits of key sub-process, according to PCB of organize standard process. Quantitatively-manage object should be sub-process or activities because the process performance is usually the result of combined and overlapped by sub-process performance, so it is difficult to exactly understand the change-trend of process performance.

2. Track Phase

In the track phase, measure group will apply measure data collection, validation and analyze data, and feedback the measurement result timely to related persons. When the analysis showed process is instable, measure group need combine with project team; find out the special reason caused process exception (or called assignable factor), correct it and control the process. The correct actions include enforcing the tools training, advancing the peoples capability and enhance the process review, etc. The project process or the performance goals of process need to be changed if necessary.

3. Summary Phase

In the summary phase, measure group and SEPG need to complete the measurement analysis report and update the result into PDB (Process Database) and PCB (Process Capability Baseline).

3   Measurement Technology

1. Define Measurement Goal

The high-level manager of the organization defines the high administrative level business objectivity. According to the content of business goals, SEPG defines the quality and process capability goal for the organization, such as the delivery quality, productivity, schedule, defect rate etc. It analyses the priority levels between the objectivities and defines the objectivity priority. This paper applies QFD to analyze objectivities and sorts the priority levels. The detailed steps are as follows:

Establish customer requirement expanded chart: splitting the determinate performance objectivity into the different idiographic indexes, and organizing the sub-goals (refers to indicator level) in terms of category (refers to rule level).

Table 1. The Customer Requirement Expanded Table

Customer Requirement (Performance Objectivity)	Rules level	Indicator Level (Sub goal)
Satisfaction	Maintenance	Reliability
		Response Capability
		Expansibility
	Delivery	Postponed Time

Table 2. The Key Customer Requirement Confirmation Table

Customer Requirement		Impor tance	Contender Analysis		Improvemen t Goal	The key-customer requirement		
Goal	Sub-Goal		Own PCB	Industry Ahead		Characteristi c	Absolute	%
Maintenan ce	Reliability	5	3	5	5/3=1.67	1.5very important	12.5	29.1%
	Response Capability	5	4	5	5/4=1.25	1.2 important	7.5	17.4%
	Expansibility	5	2	5	5/2=2.5	1.2 important	15	34.9%
Delivery	Postponed Time	4	2	4	4/2=2	1 general	8	18.6%

Establish the key-customer requirement confirmation chart: aimed at every sub-goal, confirm its factor such as importance, comparativeness in the industry, status in existence, improvement objectivity and so on. Then, calculating its weight and sorting by it. In Contender Analysis Col, 5 means very good, 4 good, 3 general, 2poor, and 1 very poor.

4   Measure Indicator Definition and Weight Deployment

- Refer to the organizational objectives, measure group analyze the OSPA and identify the critical sub-processes which will affect the organizational objectives mostly;

- farther, make sure the critical output variable Y and all the input variables X's;

- Based on QFD method, map the critical process variables to the process performance objectives, as follows the steps:

  - Aim at all the critical customer requirements, abstract the corresponding technical quality factor (sub-process variables), cluster the process class using KJ method.

Table 3. Quality table

Technical demands Customer Requirement	Design review	Test	Train	Maintain	Plan	Track
Reliability	Strong	Strong	Well	Well	None	None
Response	None	None	Well	Strong	Well	None
Expansibility	Strong	None	Well	Well	None	None
Delay Time	None	None	Well	None	Strong	Strong

-   Define quality table. Quality table define the relationship between the customer requirements and the technical demands (sub-process variables), including four levels: Strong, Well, Week and None. Quality table transform the customer world requirement to the technical world demand.
-   Define the critical quality factor table; transform the critical customer's requirements to the critical quality factors, which are the output variables of sub-process need to be quantitatively controlled.

Table 4. Critical quality factors table

Technical demands / Customer Requirement			Design review	Test	Train	Maintain	Plan	Track
Reliability(29.1%)			Strong	Strong	Well	Well	None	None
Response(17.4%)			None	None	Well	Strong	Well	None
Expansibility(34.9%)			Strong	None	Well	Well	None	None
Delay Time(18.6%)			None	None	Well	None	Strong	Strong
Critical Quality Factors		Weight %	23.8%	10.8%	24.8%	22.4%	11.2%	11%
	Contrast analyze	Contender	Strong	Week	Strong	Week	Week	Week
		Difficulty	4 Difficult	5 very difficult	3 general	2 easy	3 general	2 easy
		Relevance	Positive	positive	positive	negativ	positive	positive
	Quality factors	Goal	Bigger Better	Bigger Better	Bigger Better	Smaller Better	Closer Better	Closer Better
		Confirm	Yes	Yes	Yes	Yes	Yes	Yes

For the importance of quality factor i,

$$\text{Weight}[i] = \text{Sum} (Q_{ij} * A_{ij}) \tag{1}$$

Q_{ij} means the customer[j]'s weight value, the A_{ij} means the relationship between the quality factor[i] and the customer[j]. Finally the Weight[i] need to be unitary in percent form.

5   Measurement Analysis Technique

To establish the quantity understand of software process, we should model or analysis the process performance by using related statistics analysis method, confirm the process ability baseline and the improvement opportunity field. The examples of measurement data analyzing method include process ability exponent, relativity analysis, regression analysis, control diagram, and so on.

Basing on the statistic analysis method and supporting tools defined in PCB measurement plan, measure group statistic and analysis the project measurement data Y and X's, to find the key process input variables X's that impacts Y. If possible, try to confirm the function relationship between Y and X's, that is Y = f (X). The common method of recognize key input variables X's are:

- Using trend diagram helps understanding the process variable's movement direction, providing possible checkpoints for farther statistics analysis.

- Statistic methods such as relativity analysis and standard deviation analysis can help in understanding the impact of input X's to output Y. Regression analysis, which models the relationship between process out Y and process input X's by function expression, so that we can predict and control the process variables more effectively.

6 Measurement Performance Baseline

For key output Y and some key input X's, measure group gather the form of control diagram, group and plot the measurement data, remove abnormal conditions by analysis, construct or update the PCB.

1) For decided process output Y and some key input X's, the process team gather the value of process variables, grouping and plot the control diagram.

2) Through analysis the trend of process variables, find and remove the abnormal factors that cause the process instable.

3) Remove abnormal data points, repots control diagram.

4) Repeat step 2 and 3, until the control process runs in a stable condition. Recognize the effective change range of process performance variables, such as CL, UCL and LCL.

The Basic instable process testing methods are the four instable process testing measures proposed by Western Electric in [10], showed as Fig3.

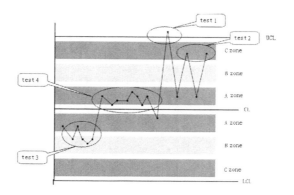

Fig. 3. Four instable process testing measures

7 Summary

According the current problems of software process measurement, i.e. process measurement is divorced from software quality and customer satisfactory, which leads to the in-notable effect of software process measurement on software quality, a new software process measurement approach is put forward in this paper based on Six Sigma theory. The approach try to combine customer satisfaction degree, software quality and software process altogether. QFD tool is used to combine the process measure and the software internal and external quality cited from ISO9126 reference model, to confirm the aim of software process measurement technique factors. SPC method is used to do stability analysis for measurement indicator, to find and remove abnormal instances, and finally insure the implementation of the target of customer satisfaction degree and software quality.

References

1. Fenton, N.E., Whitty, R.: Introduction. In: Fenton, N., Whitty, R., Iizuka, Y. (eds.) Software Quality Assurance and Measurement, A Worldwide Perspective, pp. 1–19. International Thomson Computer Press, London (1995)
2. Technical Report CMU/SEI-92-TR-25 ESD-TR-92-25 (September 1992)
3. Florac, W.A.: Measuring the Software Process — Statistical Process Control for Software Process Improvement (1999)
4. Tangxiaofen: Six sigma hard-core tutorial. Chinese Standards publisher (2002)
5. Bertolino, A., Marchetti, E., Mirandola, R., Lombardi, G., Peciola, E.: Experience of Applying Statistical Control Techniques to the Function Test Phase of a Large Telecommunications System. IEEE Proceedings – Software 149(4), 93–101 (2002)
6. Jacob, A.L., Pillai, S.K.: Statistical Process Control to Improve Coding and Code Review. IEEE Software 20(3), 50–55 (2003)
7. Cangussu, J.W., DeCarlo, R.A., Mathur, A.P.: Monitoring the Software Test Process Using Statistical Process Control: A Logarithmic Approach ESEC/FSE 2003, Helsinki, Finland, September 1-5, pp. 158–167 (2003)
8. Komuro, M.: Experiences of Applying SPC Techniques to Software Development Processes. In: ICSE 2006, Shanghai, China, May 20-28, pp. 557–584 (2006)
9. Caivano, D.: Continuous Software Improvement through Statistical Process Control. In: Proc. of the 9th European Conference on Maintenance and Reengineering 2005, pp. 288–293 (2005)
10. Western Electric, Co., Inc.: Statistical Quality Control Handbook. AT&T Technologies, Indianapolis (1958)

An Investigation on Applications of Cloud Computing in Scientific Computing

Huiying Chen, Feng Wang*, and Hui Deng

Yunnan Computer Technology Application Key Lab
Kunming University of Science and Technology
Kunming, China, 650500
wf@cnlab.net, chenhhabc@yahoo.cn

Abstract. In recent years, "cloud computing" is one of the most popular terminologies in computer society. Many IT providers and enterprises are eager to move closer to "cloud" in order to solve the current bottlenecks encountered in various fields such as scientific computing. In common, scientific computing needs a huge number of computers available to perform large-scale experiments. These should not only require enormous money to construct, but also need a lot of follow-up time and manpower to maintain and operate. Cloud computing provides a new computing pattern for scientific computing, which could make scientists dynamically access to computing infrastructure on demand, such as computing, storage resources and applications. The emergence of this new computing pattern has brought new opportunities and challenges for computational science. This thesis starts with the introduction of cloud computing, and then probes into the application prospect and results of cloud computing in scientific computing.

Keywords: Cloud computing, scientific computing, computational science, virtualization.

1 Introduction

Scientific computing is a kind of numerical calculation, and it is mathematical calculation in computer processing of scientific research and engineering[1]. Scientific computing involves the construction of mathematical models and numerical solution techniques to solve scientific, social scientific and engineering problems. These models often require a huge number of computing resources to perform large scale experiments and meet with a great quantity of complex mathematical calculations. Along with the rapid development of computer hardware technology, these needs have been initially addressed with dedicated high-performance computing (HPC) infrastructures such as clusters or supercomputers. However, the cost of construction and maintenance is tremendous. With the advent of Grid computing, new opportunities became available to scientists[2]. The use of computing Grids in scientific computing has become so

---

* Corresponding Author.

M. Zhu (Ed.): ICCIC 2011, Part V, CCIS 235, pp. 201–206, 2011.
© Springer-Verlag Berlin Heidelberg 2011

successful that many international projects led to the establishment of world-wide infrastructures available for computational science.

Even though the widespread use of Grid technologies in scientific computing, the procedure cannot always carry through as you wish. There exist some problems, especially technical hurdles. In most cases scientific Grids feature a pre-packaged environment in which applications will be executed, sometimes specific tools and APIs have to be used and there could be limitations on the hosting operating systems or on the services offered by the runtime environment. In practice a limited set of options are available for scientists, and they could not be elastic enough to cover their needs. This problem could constitute a fundamental obstacle for scientific computing.

Cloud computing can solve these problems. By means of virtualization technologies, cloud computing offers to end users a variety of services covering the entire computing stack, from the hardware to the application level, by charging them on a pay per use basis. By using cloud based technologies scientists can have easy access to large distributed infrastructures and completely customize their execution environment, thus providing the perfect setup for their experiments. There are enough options available to scientists to cover any specific need for their research. In the meantime, leasing infrastructure from the third party can largely reduce costs for scientific research organizations.

The rest of the paper is organized as follows: first, we provide an overview of cloud computing by summarizing the key technologies applied to cloud computing. Then, we will introduce several solutions that are pertinent to scientific applications and provide a rough discussion of their features by highlighting how it can support computational science. Final thoughts and key observations about the future directions of cloud computing, as a valid support for scientific computing, are discussed at the end.

2   The Key Technologies of Cloud Computing

Cloud computing is a new computing mode with data-centric data-intensive supercomputing. So inevitable it has its own unique technology in data storage, data management, programming mode, concurrency control and so on.

Data storage technology. To ensure the high reliability, high availability and economy, cloud computing uses distributed data storage and redundant storage mechanism to store information, i.e. same multiple copies. In addition, cloud systems often need to satisfy multiple users' request and deal with multiple parallel applications, so data storage technology must have high throughput rate and high transfer rate. At present, GFS (Google File System)[3] and HDFS (Hadoop Distributed File System) are the widely used date storage technology. Many IT providers, including Yahoo and Intel, use HDFS in their cloud schemes[4-5].

Virtualization technology. Virtualization[6] is a technology to realize the partial or complete machine simulation and time sharing by cutting the rock-bottom computing resources into multiple or merging them into one running environment. After using virtualization technology, the movement way of system is logical, so virtualization technology could shield the complexity of physical movement, and then the system shows to users is the simple logic state of movement. As shown in Figure 1.

Fig. 1. The operating of virtualization technology

Data management technology. The management of cloud data is read optimization. And in the database we usually adopt column storage methods to improve reading efficiency, so we can store cloud data after dividing tables by column. At present, there are some relatively mature cloud data management systems, such as BigTable (Google)[7], HBase (Hadoop), Sector/Sphere, etc.

Parallel programming model. Programming model must be simple for unprofessional users in cloud computing system. Actually the complex data calculation and task scheduling in the background of system are executed in parallel, only transparent to users and programmers. So far Google's Map Reduce[8] is the main programming model for cloud computing systems.

3 The Application Prospect of Cloud Computing in Scientific Computing

Since Google has proposed the concept of cloud computing[9], the major business organizations have invested in constructing cloud platform. Now, let us explore the specific application of the cloud computing for scientific computing, and you'll have a preliminary understanding from table 1.

Table 1. Cloud Computing Application Fields

Application Fields	Application Scenarios	Application Fields	Application Scenarios
Scientific Research	Meteorological Data Processing	Graphic Image Processing	Animation Material Storage and Analysis
	Seismic Survey		
	Ocean Information Monitoring		High Simulation Animation
	Astronomical Information Processing		Mass Image Retrieval
Medical Science	DNA Information Analysis	Internet	E-mail Services
	Mass Patient Cases Storage and Analysis		Online Real-time Translation
	Medical Image Processing		Network Information Retrieval
Internet Security	Virus Database Storage and Matching	Social Security	Citizen Information File Storage
			Criminal Record Storage
	Spam Shielding		Suspect Fingerprint/DNA Matching

All scenarios listed in the table 1 have features like large data storage or finding information in large data sets, and actually they are the instances of scientific computing. In addition, cloud computing can store and manage large data sets, and also achieve massive data search. So cloud computing can be used in scientific computation like grid computing, or even better.

At present, the use of cloud computing in computational science is still limited, but the first steps towards this goal have been already done. In 2009, the Department of Energy (DOE) National Laboratories started exploring the use of cloud services for scientific computing. On April 2009, Yahoo Inc. announced that it has extended its partnership with the major top universities in United States of America to advance cloud computing research and applications to computational science and engineering[10]. Next we'll describe the results of cloud computing so far achieved in the scientific computing.

Science Clouds. Science Clouds[11-12], one of the first cloud-based infrastructures for computational science, was initiated by the University of Chicago (UC) and the University of Florida (UFL) with two objectives: Make it easy for scientific and educational projects to experiment with EC2-style cloud computing, and Better understand the potential and challenges that cloud computing poses for these communities and what can be done to overcome them. The first cloud, at the University of Chicago, became available on March 3, 2008, and was named "nimbus"[13]. The University of Florida cloud[14], made available on May 13, 2008.

The "nimbus cloud model" has proved popular among resource providers. In fact, the GridFTP and container scalability tests at UC proved so popular that two new private clouds were configured on newly purchased infrastructure to support this mode of usage for internal UC projects.

AzureBlast. AzureBlast[15] is a parallel BLAST engine running on the Windows Azure that can marshal the compute power of thousands of Azure instances. BLAST(Basic Local Alignment Search Tool)[16] is one of the most widely used bioinformatics algorithms in life science applications. It is not only relevant to a large number of research communities; it represents a large-number of science applications. These applications are usually computation intensive, data intensive and can be parallelized by a simple coarse-grained data-parallel computational pattern. While high performance is often considered desirable, scalability and reliability are usually more important for this class of applications. The experience presented in literature [15] demonstrates that Windows Azure can support the BLAST and associated class of applications very well due to its scalable and fault-tolerant computation and storage services. Moreover the pay-as-you-go model, together with elasticity scalability of cloud computing greatly facilitates the democratization of research. Research services in the cloud such as AzureBlast can make any research group competitive with the best funded research organizations in the world.

SciCloud. The Scientific Computing Cloud (SciCloud)[17-18] is a project established at the University of Tartu. The main goal of this project is to study the scope of establishing private clouds at universities. With these clouds, students and researchers can efficiently use the already existing resources of university computer networks, in solving computationally intensive scientific, mathematical, and academic problems. Traditionally such computationally intensive problems were targeted by batch-oriented models of the Grid computing domain, where as current project tries to achieve this with the more interactive and service oriented models of cloud computing that fits a larger class of applications. The established interoperable private clouds also provide better platforms for collaboration among interesting groups of universities and in testing internal pilots, innovations and social networks. The project mainly targets the development of a framework, including models and methods for establishment, proper selection, state management (managing running state and data) and interoperability of the private clouds. Once such clouds are feasible, the networks can also be leased to commercial enterprises or governmental institutions for such diverse applications as drug discovery, seismic analysis, and back-office data processing in support of e-commerce and Web services[19].

Aneka. Aneka[20] is a platform and a framework for developing distributed applications on the cloud. It is based on the .NET framework and this is what makes it unique from a technology point of view as opposed to the widely available Java based solutions. Aneka, which is an interesting solution for different types of applications in educational, academic, and commercial environments, has been used to provide support for distributed execution of evolutionary optimizers and learning classifiers. In these cases a significant speed up has been obtained compared to the execution on a single local machine. The preliminary results presented in literature [21] have shown that the use of Aneka has contributed to reduce the execution time of the learning process to the twenty percent of the execution on a single machine.

4 Conclusions and Future Work

This paper presented the background, key technologies and scientific application prospect of cloud computing, a new on-demand and service-oriented computing model. Cloud computing can completely overturn the original calculation mode of scientific fields, and provide scientists completely customizable and flexible services. It adopts virtualization technology to share resources worldwide transparently, so as to achieve maximum utilization of resources naturally. The adoption of cloud computing as a technology and a paradigm for the new era of computing has definitely become popular and appealing within the enterprise and service providers. It also has widely spread among end users, which more and more host their personal data to the cloud. Nevertheless, this trend for scientific computing is still at an early stage. What could make cloud computing attractive for scientific institutions is the possibility of having a fully customizable runtime environment for their experiments. The active interest of government bodies such as the Department of Energy (DOE) in cloud computing will probably open pathways to the establishment of more science clouds.

According to the survey results, the platforms based on cloud computing can provide a very good operating environment for scientific experiments, increase the performance of applications and reduce the execution time of scientific experiments. Nevertheless, the practical application is still limited, so our next job is to do more research to expand the applications of computing clouds in computing science areas, and also to improve the restrictive conditions of clouds such as the necessity of lasting of high-speed network connection and the insecurity of cloud data.

Acknowledgment. This work is primarily supported by Yunnan Computer Technology Application Key Lab in Kunming University of Science and Technology. We appreciate the support from Natural Science Foundation of China (10878009), and also gratefully acknowledge the helpful comments and suggestions of the anonymous reviewers.

References

1. Scientific computing, http://baike.baidu.com/view/605662.htm
2. Chin, J., et al.: Scientific grid computing: the first generation. Computing in Science & Engineering 7, 24–32 (2005)
3. Ghemawat, S., et al.: The Google file system. ACM SIGOPS Operating Systems Review 37, 29–43 (2003)
4. Gillam, N.A.L.: Cloud Computing Principles, Systems and Applications (2010)
5. Vecchiola, C., et al.: High-performance cloud computing: A view of scientific applications, pp. 4–16 (2009)
6. Armbrust, M., et al.: A view of cloud computing. Communications of the ACM 53, 50–58 (2010)
7. Chang, F., et al.: Bigtable: A distributed storage system for structured data. ACM Transactions on Computer Systems (TOCS) 26, 1–26 (2008)
8. Dean, J., Ghemawat, S.: MapReduce: Simplified data processing on large clusters. Communications of the ACM 51, 107–113 (2008)
9. Cloud Computing, http://baike.baidu.com/view/1316082.htm
10. HP, Intel and Yahoo! Create Global Cloud Computing Research Test Bed, http://www.businesswire.com/portal/site/google/?ndmViewId=news_view&newsId=20080729005585&newsLang=en
11. Keahey, K., et al.: Science clouds: Early experiences in cloud computing for scientific applications. Cloud Computing and Applications 2008 (2008)
12. Science Clouds, http://scienceclouds.org/
13. The Nimbus Cloud, http://www.nimbusproject.org/nimbus_cloud
14. Ludascher, B., et al.: Scientific workflow management and the Kepler system. Concurrency and Computation 18, 1039 (2006)
15. Lu, W., et al.: AzureBlast: a case study of developing science applications on the cloud. Presented at the Proceedings of the 19th ACM International Symposium on High Performance Distributed Computing, Chicago, Illinois (2010)
16. Altschul, S.F., et al.: Basic local alignment search tool. Journal of Molecular Biology 215, 403–410 (1990)
17. Scientific Computing on the Cloud (SciCloud), http://ds.cs.ut.ee/research/scicloud
18. SciCloud, http://dougdevel.org/scicloud/trac/wiki/SciCloud
19. Srirama, S., et al.: SciCloud: Scientific Computing on the Cloud. Presented at the Proceedings of the 2010 10th IEEE/ACM International Conference on Cluster, Cloud and Grid Computing (2010)
20. Vecchiola, C., et al.: Aneka: a software platform for.NET-based Cloud computing. In: High Performance & Large Scale Computing. Advances in Parallel Computing. IOS Press, Amsterdam (2009)
21. Chu, X., et al.: Aneka: Next-generation enterprise grid platform for e-science and e-business applications, pp. 151–159 (2008)

A Study on Experiment Teaching of Logistics Engineering

Liu Xu-yang [1] and Liang Jing [2]

[1] Department of Technical Support Engineering,
Academy of Armored Force Engineering, China
[2] Department of Equipment Command,
Academy of Equipment Command & Technique
liuengineering@TOM.COM

Abstract. Based on the characteristics and requirement of experiment teaching of logistics engineering, the article not only analyzes several aspects of experiment teaching of logistics engineering such as content, method and support, but also expounds the idea of construction of its development.

Keywords: logistics engineering, experiment teaching.

Integrated developmental students who own firm basic knowledge and all-around ability of engineering practice and bringing forth new ideas are demanded by the training target, the course system and contents of logistics engineering. They are required to apply compound technique of three subjects including mechanics engineering, management science and engineering and business administration. They also should be able to program, design, manage, maintain and again- develop logistics equipment from several aspects such as technique, economy, organization, etc, and deal with work in field of logistics engineering, such as program and design, plant supervision operation, and so on.

To reaching these targets, relevant experiment teaching environment must be constructed, and the ability of experiment teaching must be strengthened. Experiment teaching is the effective method of bringing up vocational capability of students' and the important part of bringing up practical operation capability of those. Compared to theory teaching, experiment teaching is more direct, practical, integrative and creative. The action to strengthen education for all-round development and capability of innovation is vital and irreplaceable. We should pay attention to theory teaching. At the same time, we should put emphasize to organization and implement of practice subject. In other words, we should pay more attention to bringing up students' capability of actual operation, integrated management, organization and planning by experiment teaching of logistics engineering. By this way, the knowledge and skill learned from the training is possible and available to be used by students. By this way, the way for competence for their job can be paved. Based on practical requirement of future job of students specializing logistics engineering, the article brought experiment teaching into teaching course system, preliminarily constructed several aspects of experiment teaching of logistics engineering such as content of teaching, method of teaching and support of teaching.

M. Zhu (Ed.): ICCIC 2011, Part V, CCIS 235, pp. 207–210, 2011.
© Springer-Verlag Berlin Heidelberg 2011

1 Basing upon Practical Requirement, Setting Up Content of Experiment Teaching

Aiming at the actual business requirement of logistics engineering, basing on principles of basic, representative, design and integration, following experimental content are designed:

1. Experiments of Operation

These experiments involve a lot of operations, such as maintaining and packing, handling equipment to load, unload and convey, managing material, and so on. These experiments help students to bring up their capability of practical operation.

2. Experiments of Business Disposal

These experiments require students to deal with business as application, accommodate, check and account, in and out, conveyance, etc. For example, we can invest a model system of three-dimensional storage, pipelining and management information system, and ask students to train for handling all kinds of business basing on the flow of equipment serving and distribution of all levels of managers. These experiments help students to bring up their capability of combining of their systematical thinking and practical operation.

3. Experiments of Simulation and Emulation

1) Developing modeling and simulation modules which can analyze the organizational and functional requirements of logistics enterprises by using logistics simulation software. For that students can build up on computer logistics business organization structure and departments business process diagram, and complete all procedures of BPR analysis of logistics enterprises.

2) Using logistics emulation software for process modeling and cost programming analysis of the various activities in logistics engineering project. During the process of program activities, various economic and trade index of the program can be calculated, the investment return of grogram activities can be analyzed by real-time manner.

3) Constructing the operation model of supply chain by using logistics simulation software, examining and verifying the logicality and rationality of the design of supply chain system.

2 Enriching Teaching Artifice, Changing Teaching Means

Basing on characteristic and content of the course, we innovated and reformed ways and means actively and deeply, tried our best to mobilize initiative and enthusiasm of students', illuminated their thinking sufficiently during the experiment teaching.

1) Taking experiment teaching method of case when teaching subject basic experiment and theory configuration. Paying attention to presentation the real examples in design and optimization of logistics flow and program and planning of logistics center in informationization condition. letting the students experience, analyse, and

design in the established scene. Developing their capability of independent thinking and problem solving. The difficult of case experiment teaching is choose of the case. Only improve the quality of the case, can teachers and students interact well.

2) Taking experiment teaching method of professional experience during subject experiment. The teachers set the environment of experiment teaching into activity scene of logistics management according to the teaching implement scheme drawn in advance, endure students with duty of their posts, organise them to manage logistics task basing on restriction condition and action rules established, and to improve the students' capability of organise and management and capability of central duty-fulfillment.

3) Taking experiment teaching method of distributed simulation training during comprehensive, innovative and developmentativ subjects development experiment teaching. We combine the dispersible information technology lab, storage training warehouse and key technology lab of logistics by using of computer network and communication technique, issue instructions of experiment teaching unitivly, construct the environment of logistics operation and management simulation in the condition of informationization, carry out simulation training, discuss logistics implement projects, improve the students' capability of post-changing, decision-making and organization.

3 Relying on information Technique, Improving Experiment Teaching Support

The essential of experiment teaching support is the design of software and the configuration of hardware. The design of software mainly reflects information characteristics. We design and development software of equipment support, integerate management teaching, experiment teaching information databases and technique equipment databases by using of informational technique of database, communications, network, simulation, artificial intelligence, virtual reality, etc. The configuration of hardware consists with the laboratory equipment and experiment equipment. We constructed the information technology labs with all kinds of information technology such as network technology, videotex technology, virtual technology and a.i technology. We also constructed key technologe labs of logistics engineering configurated with all kinds of information management equipment.

1) The lab of mechanical engineering. The laboratory provide service for basic courses and introductory courses such as engineering drawings, engineering machinery, machinery basis, equipment design basis of the logistics, fluid transmission and control, traffic engineering, etc.

2) The lab of logistics management science and engineering. We constructed the logistics enterprises simulation lab, teached with softwares of logistics simulation and logistics center management simulation. The experiment softwares of logistics simulation teaching system are based on the internet, including a simulation system of FLEXSIM, ARENA and logistics management process simulation, logistics information system, logistic equipment command systems, etc.

3) The lab of professional logistics. The laborotry provides service to courses of design and management of automated three-dimensional storehouse, logistics automation technology, technology and application o identification code, packaging

engineering and technology, etc. Typical experiments can be done in the lab such as design simulation of automatic three-dimensional storehouse, logistics automatical identification, operation of logistics equipment, packing experiment, equipment malfunction diagnosis, etc.

4 Some Ideas of Experiment Teaching Development

The students's capability of issues identification and problems solving was greatly improved and teaching effect was reformed by experiment teaching of logistics engineering. Nevertheless, the experiment teaching needs further improvement in the future. We should make efforts as following:

1) The teaching content should be more precursory, interesting and comprehensive. We should increase experiments closer to reality to improve students's capability of operation.

2) Increasing input and maintaining the progressiveness of experiment equipment, especially new equipment.

3) Improving integrated quality of experiment teachers. The practical education qulity greatly dependents on teachers' capability of practice application. Teachers must have the actual operational experience of logistics management, otherwise, it is difficult to cultivate high-quality people.

4) Opening the laborotry in time and letting students chose experiments. We should let students do experiments according to their own needs and time to strengthen their proficiency of actual operations and skills.

References

1. Hu, X.-l., Qin, J.: Cases in Teaching for Invigorating Education, on: PLA Newspaper (March 8, 2007)
2. Hu, H.-g., Zhang, Y.-s.: Logistics comprehensive experiments. Journal of Academy of Jiaxing 17(1), 82–84 (2008)
3. Gan, H.-y., Li, Z.: Experiment Teaching Reform of the course of modern logistics management. Journal of Education Research 29(4) (2007)
4. Chen, X.-l.: Oractice of Class Teaching of Logistics Professional Theory. Journal of Vocational Education (8) (2006)

The Discussion on Training Model of Vehicle Engineering Innovational and Application-Oriented Talents[*]

Zhu Maotao[1], Chen Yazhou[2], and He Changyuan[3]

[1, 2, 3]School of Automotive and Traffic Engineering, Jiangsu University
Zhenjiang, Jiangsu, P.R. China
zhu_20044@sina.cn

Abstract. Vehicle engineering major includes mechanical engineering, structural engineering, transportation engineering, etc. This paper introduces problems of traditional vehicle engineering teaching. We should strengthen the base of discipline construction to increase students' learning interest. At last, a method of training vehicle engineering innovative application talents is introduced.

Keywords: vehicle engineering, innovative application talent, discussion.

1 Introduction

The automobile industry is one of our pillar industries, but our automobile industry is still in the lower position compared to the global [1]. With the rapid development of China's automobile industry and the increasing application of new technologies, the society put forward new requirements of vehicle engineering professionals, which is urgent to be more innovational and more application-oriented talent.

Currently vehicle engineering discipline is the main transportation of China's automobile talents. Cultivating the high-quality innovational talents is not only an urgent requirement which the times put forward to colleges and universities, but also the basic purpose of modern education [2].

2 Innovation and Creative Talents

The core of innovation is the process of creating a new thing, which is a change from the thought to practice. Innovational talents are these people who have innovation consciousness, who have innovation spirit, who can think innovative and can obtain innovative achievements. Innovational talents have much relation with theory talents, application-oriented talents, who are divided according to different standard. Practical ability is one of the points on creative talents. If we want to cultivate innovational talents, we must first have a practice teaching system [3].

[*] This paper is funded by the teaching reform project from School of Jingjiang, Jiangsu University.

3   The Problems of Traditional Vehicle Engineering Teaching

At present, in the aspect of talents cultivation, most colleges and universities with vehicle engineering profession have the common problems which are mainly such as the rigidity of teaching ; class textbook update slowly ; theory and practice out of line ; the deficiency of the base of the discipline at depth.

Teaching method is rigid. Teachers regard students as knowledge receiver, adopting mechanical rigid teaching methods, which can cause students emotional confrontation. So there is no resonance. As a result, enthusiasm of students participating in activities is not high. Students just passively accept the content taught in class

The teaching material contents update slowly. The contents of books can't keep up with the pace of practical science and technology development. Laboratory equipments fall behind. Experimental condition is poor. Student lacks the independent design and innovation ability.

Theory and practice are disjoined. The practical ability of students is poor. Faults exist between the contents and actual production.

As a supporting basic discipline, teaching content of vehicle engineering is not enough, which many closely subjects are artificially separated. Some teachers lack of cross-interdisciplinary teaching. The ability of training cross-interdisciplinary is weak [4].

4   Strengthen the Base of Discipline Construction

In the aspect of general education courses, students should not only have solid natural science foundation, social science foundation, but also should have the good humanities, artistic accomplishment, and correct application in their mother language, writing ability. In the first two years, basic knowledge and self-study ability should be emphasized to improve their professional interest.

In the aspect of mechanical engineering courses, students should have wider and solider knowledge and skills of mechanics, mechanical principle, mechanical design, electrical and electronic technology, hydraulic and hydraulic transmission theory.

In the aspect of major professional courses, students should have much more practical capability about automobile structure, automobile theory, engine principle, automobile manufacture process, and so on.

At the same time, we should strengthen the students' ability of applying foreign language by Bilingual Teaching.

5   Method of Training Vehicle Engineering Innovative Application Talents

Develop Innovative Teachers. At first, teachers should have ability of inspiring students to think and broadening their thought, because they are leaders in student learning. The update of education thought and transformation of education concept are crucial [5]. Teachers aren't only transmitters of knowledge, but also the guiders who inspire students to learn, to stimulate the students' enthusiasm. And students become the subjects in learning.

Before cultivating vehicle engineering innovative application talents, we must cultivate teachers who have the ability of innovation. This ability can be constantly improved through various ways, by which teachers can gradually enhance the consciousness and the ability of developing innovation education. At the same time teachers can build up the concept of innovation education.

Integrate Theory with Practice. The key to solve the problem of disjoined connection between theory and practice is to strengthen practical training, the extra-curricular science and technology and social practice.

Consolidate the theoretical knowledge through experimental teaching. Base on open experiments and rely on innovation laboratories. Learn and use various experimental instruments to train students' ability of integrating the theoretical knowledge and experimental instruments. Guide students to form teamwork spirit through experiments and practical exercises.

Experiment plays an important role in improving students' perceptual understanding, enhancing the spatial concepts and understanding of the principles. Therefore, classroom teaching and experimental teaching must be combined together. Guide students to know more and guide students pay more attention to practice so that they can find and solve problems by themselves, improve their skills and achieve the purpose of innovation. At last students enrich their knowledge.

Both students and teachers should emphasis on training practical skills. According to students' professional requirements, teachers should take advantage of two weeks skills training every semester, and arrange for some professional skills operation, such as mechanical mapping, metalworking, automotive structural experiments, engine disassembly and other practical training. Through these training and operation, students can master a variety of expertise and skills. And students learn to analyze and solve problems from base training and operation of engineers.

The extra-curricular technology practice is the best way to test the students' theoretical knowledge and their practical abilities. Advocating and organizing students to participate in various extra-curricular science and technology practices, such as the project group, the business competition and the modeling competition using software like AutoCAD ,which can train the students the sense of competition and innovation, and the ability of technology innovation and entrepreneurship training employability. Students get more professional skills in the extra-curricular science and technology practice. Students can have better understanding of the theoretical knowledge, and they promote the transformation from knowledge to ability.

Change Teaching Method, Enhance Class Efficiency. With the rapid development of automobile technology, textbook knowledge has failed to meet students' desire of understanding of auto technology, so traditional teaching method must also be adjusted accordingly.

For example, in the course of automobile structure, teachers can combine some supplementary materials such as currently popular models, the future development tendency with basic structure and principle teaching. Teachers can adopt homework method to make students learn by themselves. And teachers should help students solve their learning problems for inspiring creative thought. At the same time, teachers can use multimedia teaching way to increase their learning interest. By the way, teachers also should strengthen the communication between teachers and students.

Cultivate Students' Learning Interest, Build the Environment of Innovation. Most students are interested in joining the subject project, and want improve their capacity through the project. Therefore, teachers regard it as an opportunity, and guide students autonomously learning. In the projects students not only learn how to search information and use the related experimental instruments, but also can learn the spirit of teamwork, to regulate the academic thesis, improve the academic accomplishment.

For example, Guide students to attend the National Student Energy-saving Car Competition. Through this competition, students' innovative ability and autonomous learning interest are increased. There should be students' BBS, where students can communicate conveniently, exchange research results so that they can raise the goal of inspiring each other and improving together.

Strengthen Academic Exchange. Many experienced engineers should be invited for lecture in order to compensate for shortcomings of book knowledge updating slowly. Schools should make students know what kind of talents the enterprise needs. Even, inviting foreign experts to lecture make students know the forefront of automobile technology.

6   Conclusion

Training of applied talents of vehicle engineering is a system. Only continuing to explore and improve the vehicle engineering professional training programs can there be more high-quality applied and innovative talent.

Firstly, strengthen disciplines of basic education, and implement interdisciplinary education.

Secondly, change teaching methods to raise students' interests.

At last, integrate theory with practice, focusing on academic exchanges.

References

1. 2006 China Automobile Industry Yearbook, pp. 340–342. China's Automotive Industry Yearbook Department, Tianjin (2006)
2. Chen, A.: Innovative Thinking and Teaching. China Light Industry Press, Beijing (1999)
3. Hu, S.: Cultivating Students' Innovative Ability of Effective Ways. Wuxi Commercial Vocational Technical College Journals, 65–67 (2007)
4. Ying, L.: American Higher Automotive Engineering Talents Training Method and the Enlightenment. Higher Engineering Education Investigate Press (2004)
5. Xia, S.: Reform Experiment Teaching Mode of Training Students' Innovation Abilities. BBS of Vocational Education (2007)

The Development and Application of Electrochemical Biosensor

Qian Xiang

School of Science, Changchun Institute of Technology
Changchun, China
qianppdd@163.COM

Abstract. This paper introduces the basic principles of electrochemical biosensor and its advantages of functional diversity, miniaturization, intelligence, integration, low cost, high sensitivity and so on. Its application, present situation and development trend were reviewed.

Keywords: biosensor, electrochemical techniques, applications, development trend.

1 Introduction

In 1962, Clark [1] proposed the idea of biology and sensor, from which generates a new analysis system device "enzyme electrode" as a new entrance to the field of life sciences. Bio-sensing technology is a combination of chemistry, biology, physics, electronics and many other interdisciplinary as well as the biotechnology, information technology and pharmaceutical industries with widely use in food testing, environmental protection and many other areas. Among them, electrochemical biosensor is the most widely used with the characteristic of its high selectivity, high sensitivity, high detection speed, easy miniaturization, easy online monitoring and so on.

Table 1. Development stage of electrochemical biosensors

Main stage	Features
First generation of electrochemical sensors	Natural substances (such as O_2) are as the electronic transmission media, by detecting changes in the concentration of H_2O_2 or oxygen consumption.
Second generation of electrochemical biosensor	A man-made electronics (small form) is a transmission medium between media and the electrodes living center, rather than O_2. The current in the mediator will change with the concentration of reflecting substrate.
Third generation biosensor (third-generation medialess bio-sensors) media	Redox proteins and direct electrochemical behavior of enzymes is the theoretical basis. It is a novel biosensor with character of transferring between enzymes and direct electron without media introduction, O_2 independence and other electron acceptors. So simple immobilized without additional toxic substances.

M. Zhu (Ed.): ICCIC 2011, Part V, CCIS 235, pp. 215–220, 2011.
© Springer-Verlag Berlin Heidelberg 2011

Electrochemical biosensor is one combining biologically active material with electrochemical sensing element transducer (electrochemical electrode combination). Its development has gone through three stages, as shown in Table 1:

2 The Basic Principle of Electrochemical Biosensors

At the beginning 60 years of the 20th century, biological sensors came into the research stage. With the development of bioelectronics, biotechnology, semiconductor technology, sensor technology and micro machining technology, the biosensor research is mature increasingly and various types of biosensors published one after another. It has been a new information technology with the development of electronics, engineering and biomedical mutual penetration in recent years. The International Association of Theoretical and Applied Chemistry have recommended a very strict definition of biosensors. It is an independent and complete unit with the transducer through the space using to maintain direct contact biological recognition element (biochemical receptor), which provides specific information on quantitative and semi-quantitative analysis [2].

Molecular recognition and conversion compose the biosensors. Molecular recognition is the basis for selective detection of biological sensors. Organisms' enzymes, antibodies, tissues, cells and other substances can make selectively differentiate among specific substances.

The basic principle of biosensor is that receptors containing living matter and the mainly unit is in its sensitive primitive nucleic acids, cells, antibodies, enzymes and biological activity. Capture the target reaction between base elements and sensitive through a variety of physical or chemical transducers. Then the extent of the reaction conditions captured expresses by the number of discrete or continuous signals that obtain the basic information of analysis. The sensor principle is in Figure 1:

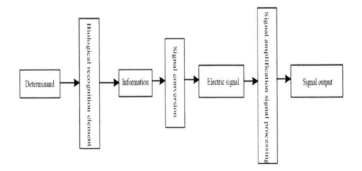

Fig. 1. Schematic sensing biosensor

Electrochemical sensor composes with the sensitive film and electrochemical converter, while the sensitive film is to identify the analytes and the electrochemical converter is to convert biomass to electrical signals.

3 The Application of Electrochemical Biosensors

Biosensor has been widely applied such as biomedical, chemical, clinical testing, pharmaceutical, environmental monitoring and food. Nano-materials, bacteriological diagnosis of infections diseases [3], the fermentation industry, genetic diagnosis[4,5], drug analysis [6], ATP testing soil samples, DNA damage [7], D-luciferin, ATP and other kits have widely researching.

3.1 Biomedical

Electrochemical sensors have become an important biomedical research tool due to the simple operation, high sensitivity and selectivity. Currently, DNA sensors most commonly used for quickly and directly identify a specific sequence of DNA with biological specificity in vivo affinity. The advantages are not only the good selectivity, wide varieties and low cost, but also the simple, rapid and sensitive electrochemical analysis [8]. The biggest advantage of DNA sensor is the diagnosis of clinical disease, which can help doctors' diagnosis and treatment of disease timely from the DNA, RNA, proteins, their understanding of the role of diseases and its development. Biosensor electrochemical analysis has become a hot spot in DNA sequences. At the same time, DNA sensors can also do the drug testing.

DNA electrochemical sensor can divide into five types with their own advantages and disadvantages, as shown in Table 2, which Drummond discussed in detail [9].

Table 2. DNA comparison of the electrochemical sensing method

Sensor type	Advantages	Disadvantages
Direct DNA electrochemical	High sensitivity, no mark, a wide range of electrodes application	High background signal, simple, casily damage the samples
Indirect DNA electrochemical	High sensitivity, without standard procedure, multiple targets detected by an electrode	Difficult preparation of the probe layer , damaged specimen
DNA-specific instructions detection of redox	Medium sensitivity, used to detect multiple targets, same samples	Possible of sequence changes
Electrochemical nano-particles enlarge	Particularly sensitive , applied to different nanoparticles for the detection of multiple targets	More detection step and uncertain of surface structure reliability and strength, often damage the samples
DNA-mediated electron transform	High sensitivity, no mark, only for mismatch detection with independent sequence , appropriate for DNA-protein	Biochemical treatment for target sample

3.2 Food

Starch determination
Starch is the most commonly used raw material in the fermentation. The traditional method is very troublesome to turn starch hydrolysis (acid solution) into glucose and then do a set of sugar experiment. However, the enzyme electrode biosensor can quickly detect the starch. Determination of an internal hydrolysis needs to join the pool of quantitative determination of glucoamylase to the enzyme electrode output after adding starch samples. It takes 1min to show the stability readings of starch hydrolysis into glucose. Another method is external hydrolysis. It needs to add α-amylase and glucoamylase. The purpose of a glucose concentration determination is to calculate the starch content. Rennerberg [10] developed a method with more subtle and economical that glucose oxidase and glucoamylase will immobilized, and the electrodes measured hydrogen peroxide biosensor electrode amylase. This method has been widely used.

Food composition analysis
In the food industry the number of glucose can be used as an important indicator in the storage life of fruit maturity. The enzyme electrode-based biosensor can measure the glucose content among the honey, apple juice, jam and wine. And for other sugars, like beer, sugar and maltose, there are already more mature measurement sensors.

An amperometric biosensor developed by Niculescu [11] can be used to detect ethanol content in beverages. This is a biosensor with alcohol dehydrogenase protein buried in the polyethylene while the proportion of different enzymes and polymers can affect the performance of the biosensor.

Detection of food freshness
In food industry, freshness evaluation of food quality testing is a key indicator especially of freshness of food, fish and meat. Volpe [12] raised biological sensitive material as xanthine oxidase. By combination with hydrogen peroxide electrode, the degradation process can determine the fish produced in the two substances: the concentration of hypoxanthine (HX) and inosine mono phosphate (IMP) inosine xanthine riboside (IIXR) which can evaluate the freshness of the fish with a linear range of 5×10^{-10} - 2×10^{-4} mol / L.

3.3 Environmental Monitoring

The problem of environmental pollution is a very important issue for a long time. Many researchers hope to have fast, online, continuous monitoring equipment. The successful development of electrochemical biosensor solves this problem. Environmental bio-sensing products can be used to monitor air, soil and water.

BOD (biochemical oxygen demand) is an index to characterize the degree of organic pollution in comprehensive, such as sewage water treatment, plant monitoring and operation control process. The biochemical oxygen demand is the most important and commonly used indicator. The concentration of glucose and glutamate can accurately measure BOD biosensor. In addition, NO_3^- is one of the major water pollutants. Moreover, will harmful human body health when added to food.

Biosensor is not only for the water industry itself, but also to meet the demand for government law enforcement agencies, government departments, monitoring of sea water, sewage, rivers, reservoirs and other water pollutants, chemical residues, pesticides, herbicides, poisons and the species of microbial biomass.

With the development of sensing principles and identify mechanisms, all countries have conducted research and development with integrated analysis of relevant biological sensor system. On the one hand, it can further improve environmental field that combined with monitoring experiments biosensor technology. On the other hand, it also can promote the environmental monitoring instruments development [14].

3.4 Military

High-tech weapons would be a serious threat to national security, such as biological weapons in modern warfare, nuclear weapons, chemical weapons and other advanced technologies for high-tech war under the threat of biological warfare agents. Therefore, it is a very important defense to do biological germ warfare agents. National defense research focuses on the development of simple, rapid biological warfare agent sensor suitable for field work. The important three proofing of medicine are the detection, identification and monitoring. However, the present study was only experimental phase. But it will come true in the near future with its rapid growth trend, the experimental results and the stage of practical application. In 1981, Taylor [12] successfully developed the nicotinic acetylcholine receptor biosensor and a biosensor anesthetic receptor, which two receptors can detect 10^{-9} chemical and biological warfare agents within 10s, which include influenza virus, Bacillus anthracis, Venezuelan equine encephalitis virus, yellow fever virus. Common germ warfare agents have the plague bacillus, salmonella, anthrax, botulinum, etc. Due to self-reproduce, it can cause enemy personnel, sick animals and plants live micro-organisms. It has been reported monitoring Vibrio cholera and Salmonella piezoelectric immunosensor [15]. Therefore, it is very broad application for the biological sensor in the military.

4 Biosensor Development Trends

The electrochemical biosensor as one of the key support of biotechnology will certainly be a great development with the promotion of materials science, biology and computer science in recent years.

In the near future, electrochemical biosensor will be further involved in disease diagnosis, environmental monitoring, medicine, food industry, fermentation industry and other fields. Meanwhile, the sensor chip technology will also enter the application then into the integration of the detection system. With nano-technology and the gradual development of micro-processing technology, a variety of small biological sensors will easy to carry and have emerged in the market that makes it possible directly detect the food. At the same time, it also will become a reality of disease diagnosis at home for people. With the continuous development of bio-sensor technology, the commercialization of electrochemical biosensor will further accelerate. Electrochemical biosensor is bound to bring great change into people's lives, and has a very broad application prospects.

References

1. Clack, L.C., et al.: Electrode systems for continuous monitoring in cardiovascular surgery. Ann. N. Y Acad. Sci. 102, 29–45 (1962)
2. She, L., Zhang, R., Xu, Z., Chung, Q.: Biosensors Overview 14 (2007)
3. Wu, S., Chen, Y.H., Liu, J., et al.: Hepatitis B virus DNA probe A preliminary study of piezoelectric crystal sensors. China's Public Health 16, 429–430 (2000)
4. Zhou, L., Liu, Y., Liu, M., Zhong, et al.: With a quartz crystal sensor detects DNA single-stranded DNA of exploration. Biotechnology Bulletin 1, 38–41 (2002)
5. Wang, J., Cai, X., Rivas, G., et al.: DNA electrochemical biosensor for the detection of short DNA sequences related to the human immunodeficiency virus. Anal. Chem. 68(15), 2629–2634 (1996)
6. Brett, A.M.O., Serrano, S.H.P., Macedo, T.A., et al.: Electrochemical determination of carboplatin in serum using a DNA modified glassy carbon electrode. Electroanalysis 8, 992 (1996)
7. Wang, J., Nielsen, P.E., Jiang, M., et al.: Mismatch sensitive hybridization detection by peptide nucleic acids immobilized on a quartz crystal microbalance. Anal. Chem. 69, 5200–5202 (1997)
8. Xie, L.Z., Yang, T., Bao, X.: DNA electrochemical biosensor research and application. Sichuan Ordnance Journal, 30–39, 119 (2009)
9. Drummond, T.G., Hill, M.G., Barton, J.K.: Electrochemical DNA sensor. Nature Biotechnology 21(10), 1192–1199 (2003)
10. Renneberg, R., et al.: Appl. Microbiol. Biotechnol. 28, 1 (1998)
11. Niculescu, M., Erichsen, T., Sukharev, V., Kerenyi, Z., Csregi, E., Schuhmann, W.: Anal. Chim. Acta 463(1), 39–51 (2002)
12. Piermarini, S., Volpe, G., Ricci, F., Micheli, L., Moscone, D., Palleschi, G., Fuhrer, M., Krska, R., Baumgartner, S.: Recent Developments in Biological Toxins Analysis. Analytical Letters 40(7), 1333–1346 (2007)
13. Sara, R.m., Lopez de Aldaa, M.J., et al.: Biosensors for environmental monitoring: A global perspective. Talanta 65, 291–297 (2005)
14. Taylor, C.J., Bain, L.A., Richardson, D.J., et al.: Construction of a whole cell gene reporter for the fluorescent bioassay of nitrate. Anal. Biochem. 328(1), 60–66 (2004)
15. Zhu, N.N., Zhang, A.P., Wang, Q.J., et al.: Electrochemical detection of DNA hybridization using methylene blue and electro-deposited zirconia thin films on gold electrodes. Anal. Chim. Acta. 510(2), 163–168 (2004)

The Research of Software Project Management Based on Software Engineering Practice

Li Li-ping and Wang Shuai

Computer and Information Institute,
Shanghai Second Polytechnic University, Shanghai, 201209, China
li_li2626@yeah.net

Abstract. This paper aimed at the feature of software engineering and software project management, applying the idea of project management to the teaching of software engineering practice. Theory contacts with practice, let students understand the principles and methods of these two courses through project-driven software development and cultivate the spirit of team work. Results showed that this approach increase the teaching effect of project management and software engineering at the same time.

Keywords: Software project management, Software engineering, Software engineering practice, Project-driven.

1 Introduction

Software engineering is a comprehensive, high practical course, which is one of the core compulsory courses for the software engineering undergraduate in ordinary colleges and universities. Because strong theoretical and lacking enterprise application environment and poor actual teaching cases in most schools, the teaching of software engineering is very abstract and hard to understand [1]. Software engineering practice is an important part of software engineering curriculum. It is an important practical course to train students to master the software development process, methods and capability. It is a subsequence course of software engineering and connects closely with software engineering course. The objective of software engineering practice is to understand the methods and techniques of software engineering better through designing and implementing a comprehensive project using software engineering method.

Software project management is also one of the important specialized courses of software engineering. Through this course, hope students understand the various basic theories, methods and techniques of large software project management. For the same reason with software engineering course, the teaching of this course is to stay on the books, abstract and difficult to understand.

In this paper, we apply the software project management principles and methods to software engineering practice teaching, through the use of project management to guide the software development, focusing on the mandate to project manager, role division, tasks division, document review and the results assessment. We explore some useful attempt in the teaching content, teaching methods, assessment and other aspects of the

M. Zhu (Ed.): ICCIC 2011, Part V, CCIS 235, pp. 221–225, 2011.
© Springer-Verlag Berlin Heidelberg 2011

two courses. Results showed that this attempt can improve synchronously the teaching effect of software project management and software engineering practice course. This method also can foster student's innovative ability and team coordination in software development.

2 Important Idea of Project Management

Project management is the application of knowledge, skills, tools and techniques to project activities to meet project requirements [2]. Software project management is a series of activities for analyzing and managing people, products, processes and projects in order to make software project complete successfully in accordance with a predetermined cost, schedule and quality. Software project management is an important part for software engineering majors; the teaching objective is developing team skills and let students understand the means of 'management by project'. Software project management include nine knowledge areas of the PMBOK (software project management body of knowledge): project integration management, scope management, time management, cost management, quality management, human resource management, communications management, risk management and procurement management.

Software project management is a course which has certain degrees of difficulty and span. It has five standardization processes: Initiating Processes, Planning Processes, Executing Processes, Monitoring and Controlling Processes, and Closing Processes [2]. The Initiating Processes defines and authorizes the project or a project phase; The Planning Processes defines and refines objectives, and plans the course of action required to attain the objectives and scope that the project was undertaken to address; The Executing Processes integrates people and other resources to carry out the project management plan for the project; The Monitoring and Controlling Processes regularly measures and monitors progress to identify variances from the project management plan so that corrective action can be taken when necessary to meet project objectives. The Closing Processes formalizes acceptance of the product, service or result and brings the project or a project phase to an orderly end.

However, most of the current textbook of the software project management is too theoretical. The abstract and theoretical knowledge of the content make students can not understand the course deeply, so learning motivation is not strong. In order to grasp the principles of software project management, a lot of practical experience is required associate with theoretical knowledge in the textbook. But most students have not chance to do the practical projects, so there is no concept of project management. The traditional teaching approach is inclined to make students lose interest for the project management courses which focus on a lot of practice experience. Therefore, how to keep software project management courses vivid, let students shift from passive learning to active learning, from no interest to rapture to the class, increase the practical teaching of the course, theory contact with practice is the focus of education reformation.

2.1 The Teaching of Project Management Based on Software Engineering Practice

Software engineering practice is an important practical course to train students the capability of software development. Software project management is a new course in many school, how to make the course achieve better results, we are in the exploratory stage. The teaching of software engineering practice based on project management is project-driven and team collaboration. The teaching has not only pay attention to the final result, but also pay attention to the project implementation process. The whole development process is provided a real scenario for specific project from the Initiating Processes to the Closing Processes, include requirement analysis, system design, coding and testing, to equip students the ability of managing, analyzing and solving problems in practical projects. The whole process is completed through the guidance of teacher and collaboration between students. The teaching focus is on developing the team skills by elaborating a partly given software project in a group of five [3].

In our school, in order to cultivate software engineering undergraduate a high quality and practical ability, we set up two practice courses for software engineering: software engineering practice I and software engineering practice II. Software engineering practice I opened in the sixth semester which accomplished by simulating a complete textbook project for every student to master the entire software development process from requirements analysis, modeling, system design, database design, coding and testing. In software engineering practice I, we require students to master corresponding documentation writing and can use the appropriate development tools such as Rational rose, Microsoft Visio and Power designer etc.

Software engineering practice II is the direct successor course of software engineering practice I. It is a comprehensive practical course on the basis of a specific project by way of team work. The students can compose the teams on their own authority. Software engineering practice II covering five topics: business modeling, system design, database design, coding, testing and corresponding document writing. In the development process of the project, each student has a role, assign the corresponding task. The objective is on one hand let students further understand the whole process of software engineering methods and techniques, on the other hand by members' collaboration to enable students to understand the software project management principles and methods. Finally, can improve students' software development skills and cultivate engineering creative design capability.

In order to achieve all these objectives, the courses for software project management and software engineering practice II were opened in the seventh semester, and the class time of the two courses have a difference. Software project management is the first week class and software engineering practices II starting around the fourth week. This is very beneficial to us to introduce the basic idea of project management to software engineering practice teaching activities. It is essential for the course that every student understands the theories of project management before entering the team phase.

First of all, students should understand some basic concepts, principles and methods of project management, then through a series of project in software engineering practice II to carry out these theories effectively. Teaching theory before practice, which is conducive to students first had the concept of project management, and then apply the theory to the practice. In the late, after each theory class there are project exercises corresponding to the class. The detailed approach is as following:

- By the project-driven thought, software engineering practice II will be assigned to teams of five to develop a common software project with given cursory requirement and a technical foundation. Each team chooses a specific project, such as "student management system". They can free association, everyone share different roles such as project manage, requirement analysis, design, coding and testing. The project manager is the person responsible for accomplishing the project objectives. One student can serve as more than two different roles, assign tasks and responsible according to different roles. Let students familiar with the basic pattern of team development and collaborative development.

- The project proposals must be submitted at the beginning of the course. The course supervisor (teacher) reviews the proposals and approves or rejects the respective proposals [4]. Project manager tracks the project plan and manage the whole process. The project team must complete technical documentation such as project charter, project development plan, requirement specification, design specification, database design specification, and testing report.
- The management process simulates software company with hierarchical management. Project manager of each team is responsible for completion and manage of the project, and each member of the group responsible for their own role to the project manager. This can enable students understand the software company's management style, experience a sense of teamwork, increase management awareness.
- Given the right to project manager, team members are assessed by the project manager. The final grades submitted to the teacher, the teacher reviewed the grades according to submitted documentations and competitive examination. Project manager is assessed by teacher based on the completion of project documentation, the management of project process and the completion of the system, generally team scores ± 5%. The grade is composed by four parts, documentations complete, scientific and reasonable (30%) + competitive examination (40%) + team collaboration (20%) + discipline in class (10%).
- Competitive examination: At the end of the class, project team must demonstrate the management process and the implement system. Everyone needs to explain their responsible tasks. The detailed method is shown as follows:

1) Prepare a speech file (a PPT file) to introduce the project initiating, project planning, project executing, project monitoring and controlling, and project closing processes.
2) The live demo of the implement system. The project team should describe the function of the system, encountered problems and solutions of problems in the development process.

In summary, we can see the teaching of software project management based on software engineering practice is project-driven, emphasize not only the result of the project, but also on project development process. Our project teams simulate software development company's project teams. Scores of students simulate the bonus of company employees.

All the submitted documentation, the project charter is to identify existing project, including confirmation of the project, mandate of the project manager and an overview of project goals, etc. [1]; project development plan, including task decomposition, staffing, schedule, cost plan, quality assurance and configuration management plans; other documents are submitted in accordance with the various stages of software engineering. All the documents must submit in accordance with the standard document templates.

With these constraints, in order to make the project complete successfully, get high grades, students must complete the assigned tasks, because the report is ongoing according to roles. Currently, the teaching has achieved initial success, after a semester of practice, software project management and software engineering practice courses have achieved good results, students generally respond better.

3 Summary

Software Engineering and software project management are the important courses for software engineering curriculum. The complexity inherent to the software project management makes the course design an equal complex task. In this paper, we have presented some research for software engineering and software project management from teaching experiences in the last years. The software project management principles and methods are applied to software engineering practice teaching, focus on task identifying, task partitioning, staff organizing and results assessing. After a semester experience, the students' representation and achievement showed this research have achieved good results. It is much better if there are real commercial environment to realize a project rather than in the simulative environment. Teaching in the future, we will continue to explore ways to improve software engineering teaching according to our school and student's characteristics.

References

1. Bourque, P., Dupuis, R.: Guide to the Software Engineering Body of Knowledge. IEEE Computer Society, Los Alamitos (2004)
2. PMI, A Guide to the Project Management Body of Knowledge (PMBOK Guide), 3rd edn (2004)
3. Shaw, M.: Software engineering education: a roadmap. In: ICSE - Future of SE Track, pp. 371–380 (2000)
4. Bernhart, M., Grechenig, T., Hetzl, J., Zuser, W.: Dimensions of software engineering course design. In: ICSE 2006, Shanghai, China, May 20-28, pp. 667–672 (2006)

Instruction from Service Learning in America to Chinese Higher Education

Yanli Guo[1,2] and Shuli Gao[1]

[1] Business College of Beijing Union University, Beijing, China 100025
[2] Business School of Nankai University, Tianjin, Chian 300071
GUOTEACH@tom.com

Abstract. With American higher education, this paper research the theory and the mode of service learning, and discuss three factors influencing the effect of service learning on improving of student's professional ability. And then explore the enlighten and significance of American service learning to the reform of higher education in China.

Keywords: Service Learning, Higher Education, A Taxonomy of Significant Learning, America.

There are many differences between American and Chinese higher education in teaching conception, which lead to the huge difference in the whole teaching system and teaching design. In China, higher education emphasis on the process that teachers give lecture and students learn as well as result control, the core of teaching is the imparting of knowledge. While in the U.S., experience is the core of teaching. Then based on this teaching conception, students taking part in and experiencing always go deeply into the whole teaching process, just like Junior Professional Officer (JPO) program praised highly about "Tell me and I forget it, teach me and I remember it, involve me and I learn it." Therefore, in American higher education, people develop various forms of experiential teaching methods, in which service learning has become an indispensable method of experiential teaching.

Service learning came into being at 60s of the 20th century and has been gradually developed into the movement of education reform from the mid 90s. In 1993, the organization of Service Action defined service learning [1] is an innovative approach in education, in which school cooperate with communities, and curriculums designing are connected with social services, and students participate in organized service activities to meet the needs of communities in order to foster their social responsibility, at the same time they can acquire knowledge and learn to cooperate with other members and improve abilities in analysis, evaluation and problem-solving in the process of servicing.

1 Definition of Service Learning

1.1 The Concept of Service Learning

Service learning is a teaching, learning and reflection method. Specifically speaking, students or trainees participate actively in well-organized service projects to meet the

M. Zhu (Ed.): ICCIC 2011, Part V, CCIS 235, pp. 226–233, 2011.

needs of communities, meanwhile they finish their academic curriculums and improve themselves in the learning process. Service learning can be performed in the primary schools, secondary schools, universities, institutions or community service plans to involve students into communities and foster their sense of social responsibility. It is an experiential teaching and learning method. In most cases, social service programs recruit participants and need to provide structured time and planning, learning outcome is reflected in the improvement of trainees' service experience. As a teaching method, service learning belongs to experiential education conception. More specifically, it integrates meaningful community services into teachings that enrich trainees' learning experience, promote their social responsibility, encourage them to participate in life-long education, and strengthen services for the common interests of communities.

1.2 Service Learning and Community Service

Generally, service learning and community service are different. Community service focuses on service and public welfare. U.S. Department of Education consider community service as student volunteers participating in voluntary activities organized by non-school organizations which have no a direct formal connection with courses. Its main objective is to meet communities' needs. While service learning is not only a kind of public service activities [2], but also an particularly integral part of school curriculums. It is linked closely with school curriculums and its service activities include application and reflection on the content of courses, students can earn credits through participation in service activities. Service learning's core is the combination of curriculum services and reflection. With clearly learning objectives, service learning projects focus on both service-oriented process and learning process, which can meet actual needs of the communities, improve students' practical abilities, and promote knowledge innovation and applications, in addition, students who get involved in service activities can obtain experiential learning experience and enhance their sense of social responsibility and civic awareness.

1.3 The Characteristics of Service Learning

(1) Service
As the name suggests, there are two objectives in the project of service learning: service and learning. In service learning, studying is integrated into servicing. Therefore, the major goals of service learning projects are providing service learning activities which are well-organized and high quality to meet the actual needs of communities and resolve hot issues, and realize promotion in physical and human environment, etc.

(2) Sociality
Service learning integrates communities service into curriculums and applies course content into service process, providing opportunities for students to broadly understand and contact with society. Students learn to cooperate and communicate with others through personal involvement in social activities and then improve their abilities of discovering   problems   and   solving problems in   real situations. In   addition, service learning is also targeted to promote community development and increase

social responsibility of students. It is focus on improving students' social communication and social responsibility, then enable them can adapt to society easily.

(3) Reflection

Reflection is an important part and a basic feature of service learning. It is a kind of behavior that students exert critical thinking at different service stages by connecting service experience with course content. In the United States, whether primary education and secondary education or higher education, they all put exceptional emphasis on inspiring students to think critically. Service learning projects stress students' communication and reflection after participating in service activities, and development of students' independent thinking. It helps students avoid participating blindly in services and helps them internalize experience of service learning into their own abilities.

Reflection on service learning have the characteristics of 5C [3]: Connection, Continuity, Context, Challenge, and Coaching. It is means that reflection should combine school with community, combine experience with application, and continuously provide students with the opportunities to do reflection, which should be meaningful, challenging, and can give students the necessary support and supervision.

(4) Openness

In service learning study is extended from school to social spaces and classroom is made as an open society, which is conducive to the socialization of students. The time for service learning is flexible, that's to say, service requesters can negotiate with service providers about what time and how long will be last. Interestingly, students in the U.S. have a great diversity of sources, staff involved in service learning also have diversity, which including different races, countries, grades, gender, learning directions, learning capabilities, and different backgrounds. Therefore, Students can contact with groups of different cultural backgrounds and learn how to get along and resolve problems together with different peoples. Openness of service learning also refers to let different students make multiple choices, such as different service contents, methods and arrangements to meet different needs of students.

2   Service Learning Model in American Higher Education

2.1   The Role of Service Learning in Course Education of America Higher Education

According to Fink's model of curriculum design - A Taxonomy of Significant Learning (Figure 1), course teaching can be designed from "foundational knowledge", "application", "integration", "human dimension", "caring and learning how to learn" in order to help students construct meaningful learning experiences. "Foundational knowledge" mainly help students understand and remember course information, basic knowledge and ideas, as well as change existing misconceptions. "Application" focus on improving students' professional skills, encouraging them to form critical, creative and practical thinking habits, and developing ability of managing projects independently. "Integration" help students to link knowledge and theory what they learn from course with realms of life, so as to make knowledge internalization and sublimation. "Human dimension" emphasize that students should learn to understand themselves and others. In addition, students should cultivate the sense of responsibility and compassion, forming right feelings, interests, and values, knowing how to care for and respect for others. Finally, in addition to teach students knowledge, skills, and how to form self-awareness, how to care about others and society, the most important thing of college education is to make students know how to learn and how to be a good self-directing learners.

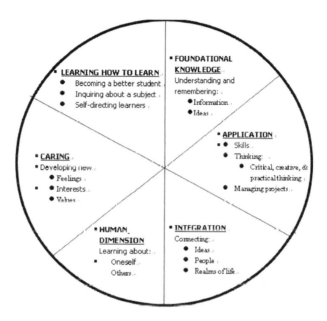

Fig. 1. A Taxonomy of Significant Learning [4]

Service learning plays an important role in the taxonomy of significant learning. Classroom teaching can help students understand basic knowledge and master practical skills and learning methods, but this method will take long time for students to master other aspects, while experiential teaching is the best way in these areas. Therefore, service learning has become the important method to improve students' professional and comprehensive abilities. Through organizing some service activities, students will learn how to apply theoretical knowledge and professional skills to reality, learn to care for others and social issues, and learn to get along with others and understand them and respect others. Through continuous reflection and communication after service, service learning can improve students' ideology level so as to guide their thinking, including critical and creative thinking to combine human dimension with the realm of life, thus students can think deeply and reach ultimate goal of realizing knowledge internalization and purification of the mind.

2.2 The Basic Mode of Service Learning

Nowadays service Learning in American education system has become a universal teaching method. Many universities provide students with a variety of opportunities about service learning and provide funds. The basic mode includes: one-time and short-time service learning, continuous extra-curricular service learning, curricular service learning, massed service learning, etc. [5].

(1) One-time and short-term service learning mainly refers to the whole school learning activities which period is only one day or a weekend. This kind of activity highlights the collaboration between the university and the community. In order to provide students with real life experience in accomplishing assignments and group projects and enhance students' understanding on social issues, economic issues, urban problems and other issues, many universities develop one-time or short-term service learning activities that associated with the course content.

(2) Consecutive extra-curricular service learning is mainly developed in the form of projects, such as leadership development projects, religious organizations service learning activities, service-oriented activities that organized by students, dormitory service activities and university sports service activities etc.

(3) Service learning in course primarily refers to introducing service learning into courses and help students apply the knowledge into real context, think deeply about the purpose and function of knowledge, then understand the multi-levels of knowledge meaning, form different opinions about social issues and improve their abilities of independent thinking and problem-solving. There are many forms in the implementation.

First, to establish curriculum cluster generally including 2-3 courses. Curriculum cluster is composed of common themes, assignments, classroom activities and other special projects to help students think from different perspectives when they explore same problem and topic. In a curriculum cluster, service learning can be introduced into one course, such as application-based courses, or introduced into all cluster courses at different levels.

Second, to establish an independent service learning modules. Students who elect independent service learning module usually do 44-55 hours of community services in each semester. They should keep diary in the service process and write a reflective paper or complete a reflective project by associating service experience with course content. It can obtain a credit that called 4th credits in American universities.

Third, to make peak experience curriculum. Experience curriculum can be a separate course or a set of courses. There are different forms of teaching methods, including lecture, team-based study, project reporting, case study, discussions, field trips, practice exercises, visiting professor lecture and group reporting etc. Integrated curriculum objectives and flexibility of teaching methods make it easy for the peek experience to combine with service learning.

(4) Massed service learning

Massed service learning means that students take more than 10 hours per week in servicing experience in a considerable part of the time such as a semester or a summer vacation. Massed service learning can use course mode or extra-curricular mode. In specific implementation, there are various forms such as summer internships, independent study, action research, national or international services etc.

3   Service Learning's Effectiveness at Improving Student's Professor Skills

Yi Lu and Kristina T. Lambright[6] has researched factors influencing service learning's effectiveness at Improving Graduate Students' Professional Skills. They found three key factors: the amount of time, group dynamics, and age, influencing the effectiveness of service learning projects at improving graduate students' professional skills. Teachers and students are time sensitive when they are participating in service learning[7,8]. It is indicated that the effect of long-term project at improving the student's professor skills is better than short-term project. The student reported that more time they spend on working for a service learning project, more helpful at improving their professional skills. Similarly, Conrad and Hedin[9] had found in 1982, practical educational project can improve students' achievement with the increase of time sensitive. Therefore, we should create more opportunities for students to be involved into projects outside of the classroom.

Yi Lu and Kristina T. Lambright thought group dynamics in service learning projects are also important. They demonstrated that among the students in our sample who worked in groups, those who believed their groups worked more like teams felt service learning was more helpful in improving their professional skills than students in less cohesive groups. Instructors should devote to training students being stronger team consciousness and encourage students agree the rule of team working and obey it. Through training, students should learn to make decision about how to assign a responsibility to every team member and learn to resole the problems. Instructors can enlighten students when they are facing conflicts inside a team which is helpful to make the team function perfect.

Age is another key factors on improving the students' professional skills(Yi Lu and Kristina T. Lambright,2006). Their research revealed younger students appear to benefit more from service learning project than older students. The authors explained the results that younger students believed service learning improved their professional skills more than older students, because older students likely have had more opportunities to develop their professional skills in other contexts.

4   Enlighten and Significance

4.1   International Education

As one of the experiential teaching methods, service learning embodies the learner-centered teaching theory. "Tell me and I forget it, teach me and I remember it, involve me and I learn it." This is very important for the reform of international education idea.

Introducing such experiential teaching methods as service learning to replace the traditional teacher-centered education in classroom, and combining the study of theory in classroom with the services out of classroom, would help students grasp all contents of A Taxonomy of Significant Learning, so as to merge knowledge and techniques, procedure and method, feeling, attitudes and values[10]. The students who participating in social activities related to the course can improve learning effects, increase knowledge and techniques, obtain reflective practice and cooperative consciousness, enhance the consciousness of citizenship and sense of social responsibilities, and improve self-respect and self-worth.

In the developed countries such as the United States, the service learning has pervades virtually every aspect from primary schools, high schools and universities to communities. The internationalization of Chinese higher education should adopt the teaching conception of service learning. It will be good for catering the needs of international students and teaching domestic students, and keep in harmony with foreign universities.

4.2 Teaching System and Course Construction

The service learning integrate vocational and academic course and realize the mixture of teaching, research and social demands. Though participating in the service activities with elaborate design, students apply the course knowledge and enhance the professional skills when satisfying social demand. It is very important to construct application-oriented teaching system because it pay more attention to improve the ability of practice, independently thinking, analyzing and solving problems on one's own. And it can strengthen their sense of social responsibilities so as to resolve the problem that is the one-child generation lacking sense of social responsibilities in China. We can construct the application oriented teaching system by using the basic model of service learning of USA higher college for reference.

(1)Replace the traditional practice with service learning
The study of Yi Lu & Kristina T. Lambright[6] indicates that the service learning, as an alternative to traditional practice, would improve the professional skills of students. Now the general problems in practice phase are the disjoint of practice and course, the formalization of check, the lacking of improving professional ability of students and helping to obtain employment. If replacing the traditional practice with service learning, we could resolve all of the problems.

(2)designing an independent service-learning modules in the teaching system
Service-Learning should be designed as a crucial part of teaching plans. We should develop independent service-learning modules in the practical training and other practical courses to encourage students take "the forth credits" and participate into reflective project and finish reflective paper.

(3)Establishing curriculum clusters and applying service-learning modules into practical curriculum
Based on the major, a curriculum cluster including 2 or 3 courses should be developed. And we can design two different types of cluster: the one is opening and the other is closed. In the former, students can choose some part of cluster, but in the latter, students have to participate into all of courses in the cluster they have chosen. Not only in a curriculum cluster, we can put service learning and learning by doing into practice, but also in the traditional practical courses, this new teaching method can make the change.

References

1. Zhou, J.: The Summary of Service Learning in America. Studies in Foreign Education 31-4, 14–18 (2004)
2. Hao, Y., Rao, C.: Theoretical Models of Service Learning in American Higher Education Institutions. Comparative Education Review 11 (2009)
3. Cui, S.: Service-Learning in America: Characteristics, Principles and Operational Procedures. Studies in Foreign Education 35-10, 14–19 (2008)
4. Fink, D.: Creating Significant Learning Experiences: an Integrated Approach to Designing College Courses (2003),
   http://www.finkconsulting.info/publications.html
5. Liu, B.: Basic Models of Service-Learning in American Research Universities. Fudan Education Forum 3-2, 76–79 (2005)
6. Yi, L., Lambright, K.T.: Looking Beyond the Undergraduate Classroom: Factors Influencing Service Learning's Effectiveness at Improving Graduate Students' Professional Skills. College Teaching 58-4, 118 (2010)
7. Banerjee, M., Hausafus, C.O.: Faculty use of service-learning: Perceptions, motivations, and impediments for the human sciences. Michigan Journal of Community Service Learning 14, 32–45 (2007)
8. Kendrick, J.R.: Outcomes of service-learning in an introduction to sociology course. Michigan Journal of Community Service Learning 3, 72–81 (1996)
9. Conrad, D., Hedin, D.: The impact of experiential education on adolescent development. Child & Youth Services 4, 57–76 (1982)
10. You, z., Hu, y.: Educational meaning and instruction from American service learning courses. Heilongjiang Researches on Higher Education 07 (2010)

Reform of Quantum Mechanics in Information Specialty by Computer-Aided Practice

Chen Fengxiang*, Wang Lisheng, and Tan Gaijuan

Department of physics science and technology, Wuhan University of
Technology, Wuhan, China
chenpaths@126.com

Abstract. Quantum Mechanics is an important compulsory and basic course for students who study in information science specialty, and it also the theoretical basis of modern physics and modern engineering technology. Because many basic concepts of quantum mechanics are different with those in classical physics, these bring difficulties in understanding for students. In the traditional teaching pattern, theory teaching is over-emphasis while practice teaching is less. So there is necessary to reform the quantum mechanics teaching pattern. With the introduction of computer-assisted practice, it will deepen the students understanding on nonobjective conception and comprehensive theory. In this paper, the tunneling effect in quantum mechanics is used as an example. All students were required to demonstrate the tunneling process by using Matlab software, this practice process increases the understanding of the theoretical knowledge in Quantum Mechanics.

Keywords: Engineering education, information science specialty, quantum mechanics, reform and practice.

1 Introduction

Higher engineering training plays a very important role in industrialization and modernization process in China and makes important contributions for economic and social development. Till now our college engineering education has achieved great progress, but there are still some problems as listed: ①The research on engineering training is not sufficient and the theoretical guidance for engineering training is still lack. ②There exist the problem of insufficient investment in engineering education both for the government and the college. For the equipment, knowledge, and technology involved in engineering training update quickly, these demand higher standard teaching and practice requirement. More investment is needed. ③The content and methods of engineering education is too obsolete, which unable to meet needs of the developing technology. ④ Fewer practice opportunities. The theory and practice teaching are separating from each other, and the theory teaching has an absolute majority proportion. The multidisciplinary training course is rare [1].

---

* This work is supported by the teaching reform project 'The virtual platform construction in Quantum Mechanics" of Hubei province.

M. Zhu (Ed.): ICCIC 2011, Part V, CCIS 235, pp. 234–238, 2011.
© Springer-Verlag Berlin Heidelberg 2011

In information specialty in School of Science, Wuhan University of Technology, two directions--named the optical information science and technology and the electronic information science and technology were set up. The purpose of the whole training system aims to cultivate the people who will master the basic theory, knowledge and skills in Optical Information Science and Technology, Electronic Information Science and Technology. These people will work in optical communication, optical information processing and the related electronic information field. In the future they can do the jobs such as scientific researcher, R&D personnel and managers in such industries. Accordance with the training mode "deep foundation, wide caliber", the quantum mechanics course was selected as a basic core course for students. We consider that this course, on the one hand, will lay the important physical basis for students; on the other hand, it will train students with scientific way of thinking and research method. But in real teaching processes, we found that most students can hardly understand and accept the contents of quantum mechanics. This is partly due to the research objects of quantum mechanics focuses on the microscopic particles. The relevant theory is too abstract and difficult to understand; in the other hand, now the students are more interested in practical training. But the physical process of micro-particle and physics theory in quantum mechanics can not be directly observed. And the relevant practical teaching is lack, which affect initiative learning of students.

With the rapid development of computer technology, it is possible to introduce practical teaching into the teaching process of quantum mechanics. Combining computational physics methods and the powerful function of the computer graphics software, we will encourage students to design demonstration experiments related with quantum mechanics by themselves [2]. By this method, it will increase dynamic and visual representation form in this course, making the nonobjective theory into practical one. In addition, this method will consolidate learning effect and train the practical skills and innovative spirit of students. In the following, the tunneling effect in quantum mechanics was used as one example.

The introduction of tunneling effect. Tunneling effect is one specific physical phenomenon in quantum mechanics. According to classical mechanics, if a particles with energy E is shooting toward a square potential barrier, when E is lower than V_0 (the height of the barrier), the particle can't penetrate the barrier and it will rebound back; when E is higher than V_0, the particle will pass through the barrier. But in quantum mechanics, particle is usually considered equivalent to wave. Considering the wave character of the particle, particle often has some chance of penetrating the barrier and certain chance of being bounced back, no matter how high the barrier height. The phenomenon that any particle can penetrate the barrier with higher energy than its kinetic energy is tunneling effect. This phenomenon is attributed to the wave character of the particle.

For one-dimensional square potential barrier as shown in Fig.1, a particle with energy E is shooting towards the square barrier along the x-axis direction. The parameters for the barrier are:

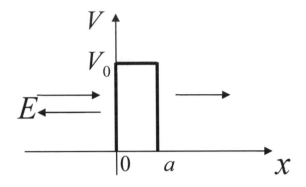

Fig. 1. The one-dimensional square potential barrier

$$V(x) = \begin{cases} V_0, & 0 < x < a \\ 0. & x < 0, x > a \end{cases} \qquad (1)$$

After solved the Schrodinger equation inside and outside the barrier, combined with the continuity conditions for wave function and the one-order derivative of wave function in the boundary, the transmission and reflection coefficients are [3]:

$$T = \frac{4k^2\kappa^2}{(k^2 - \kappa^2)sh^2\kappa a + 4k^2\kappa^2 ch^2\kappa a}$$

$$R = \frac{(k^2 + \kappa^2)sh^2\kappa a}{(k^2 + \kappa^2)sh^2\kappa a + 4k^2\kappa^2} \qquad (2)$$

Where $k = \sqrt{2mE}/\hbar$, $\kappa = \sqrt{2m(V_0 - E)}/\hbar$, m is the particle mass, $\hbar = h/2\pi$, h is the Planck constant. It can be found that $T + R = 1$, where R represents the probability of bounce back and T represents the probability of particles penetrating through the barrier. The sum of transmission coefficient and reflection coefficient equals to 1, which represents the probability conservation. Whenever a particle encountered a barrier, it will transmit or to be reflected. It can be seen from Eq.(2), even though $E < V_0$, the transmission coefficient is not equals to zero. This is the unique tunneling effect in quantum mechanics.

Supposed that $\kappa a \gg 1$, by using $sh\,\kappa a \approx \frac{1}{2}e^{\kappa a} \gg 1$, the expression of T in eq.(2) can be turned to :

$$T \approx \frac{16k^2\kappa^2}{(k^2 + \kappa^2)^2}e^{-2\kappa a} = \frac{16E(V_0 - E)}{V_0^2}\exp\left[-\frac{2a}{\hbar}\sqrt{2m(V_0 - E)}\right] \qquad (3)$$

It can be seen from Eq.(3) that the transmission coefficient T depends on the mass m of the particle, the width a of the barrier and the difference $(V_0 - E)$. For example, for a electron with energy E=1eV, the barrier parameters are $V_0 = 2eV, a = 2\overset{\circ}{A}$, the corresponding transmission coefficient is $T = 0.51$; while for $a = 5\overset{\circ}{A}$, the transmission coefficient drops to $T = 0.024$. So in macroscopic surroundings, the value T is very small, which results in the tunneling effect is not easily observed.

The Matlab demo in practice teaching. In practice teaching process, students were required to use the Matlab software as a basic tool, combined with the GUI interface and commanding functions in this software, the tunneling phenomenon should be demonstrated vividly. As the wave character of the particles is the inherent character of microscopic particles, this character is not the nature of the large number of particles. This wave-particle duality character for micro-particle results in tunneling effect as a random phenomenon. Most practice demo was achieved by the Monte Carlo method [4-6]. The basic procedures are listed as following: firstly, when the barrier height, barrier width and incident electron energy are given, the corresponding transmission and reflection coefficients were calculated, and then a random number r with uniform distribution between (0,1) was produced randomly. Secondly, the random number and transmission coefficient were compared. If $r < T$ is satisfied, then the tunneling procedure is shown; and if $T < r < 1$ is satisfied, then the reflected procedure is shown. After these, the presentation interface finished by students was shown in Figure 2.

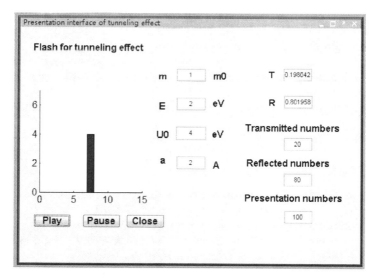

Fig. 2. The tunneling phenomenon interface made by Matlab

In Fig. 2, the quantum tunneling effect interface was realized by the GUI tool in Matlab software. Just enter the particle mass m, energy E, the barrier height V_0, the width of the barrier a and the presentation number of particles, then click the Play button, the transmitted and reflected probability of the particles will be shown in the text boxes for the transmission coefficient T and the reflection coefficient R. During this process, when a particle is reflected back by the barrier, the statistics number of the reflected particles will add 1 automatically (the initial value is 0); when a particle penetrates and reaches the right region of the barrier, the statistics number of the transmitted particles will add 1 automatically (the initial value is also 0). If the Pause button is clicked, the particles will stop. After all the incident particles completed their motion, the transmission and reflection number of particles will be shown in the corresponding statistics text box. After this demo, modify the parameters and click the Play button, the dynamic presentations of particles will carry out again.

In Fig. 2, the presentation numbers were selected as 100, the particle mass is 1 times the electron mass, and the energy is 2eV, the barrier height is 4eV, the barrier width is 2 angstroms. According to the Eq.(2), the calculation results show that T is 0.198 at this time and R is 0.802; while the statistics results show that the transmitted numbers are 20 and the reflected numbers are 80, which means that the transmission probability is 20% and the reflecting rate is 80%. The theoretical calculation coincides with the statistical results very well. After students experienced such practice trainings, they generally feel they learn better than they only experienced theoretical teaching. When in theoretical teaching process, they just listened and learned passively, while practical process requires individual initiative and creative learning.

2 Summary

Engineering training is a kind of teaching mode featured with explicit project, strong practice, comprehensive synthesis and distinctive innovation. This training is an open teaching pattern which is student-centered and the issue focused on the practical application in curricular and extracurricular teaching. In our early exploration in quantum mechanics teaching, with the introduction of computer-assisted innovation, the ability and creativity of students were greatly improved, which further excites the students' interest in learning. Further work includes introducing similar practice reform to other theoretical physics courses, so students can feel the regular and wonderful aspects of physics.

References

1. Chen, Q.-l., Zou, W.-x.: Research and Exploration in Laboratory 28(6), 94–95 (2009)
2. Lu, Y., Liu, Y., Deng, L.: Physics and Engineering 19(5), 8–10 (2009)
3. Zeng, J.: Quantum Mechanics, pp. 38–41. Science Press, Beijing (2005)
4. Luo, L.-j.: Journal of Shenyang Normal University (Natural Science) 24(3), 296–299 (2006)
5. Deng, L.-l., Zhang, Y.-n.: College Physics 29(1), 16–18 (2010)
6. Zhao, l., Fu, W., Wang, X., et al.: Journal of Beijing Normal University (Natural Science) 37(3), 369–372 (2001)

A Study of the Influence of Creative Thinking Instruction Implemented in the Engineering Education "Mold Production Practice" Curriculum on the Creativity of Vocational High School Students

Kuang-Yao Li, Chuan-Shou Hau, Yu-Chun Huang, and De-Fa Huang

P.O.BOX 7-304 Taipei, Taipei City 10699, Taiwan
huangyyll@163.com

Abstract. The purpose of this study is to explore the influence of creative thinking instruction implemented in the engineering education "mold production practice" curriculum on the creativity of vocational high school students. Of the selected objects, 37 in the experimental group and 33 in the control group underwent experimental teaching for a period of twelve weeks.

In regards to data processing, "the "Torrance Tests of Creative Thinking" was adopted as the quantitative evaluation instrument. The data obtained then underwent statistical processing using one-way Analysis of Covariance, ANCOVA and t-test. In addition, with the researcher's self- compiled "creative learning worksheets," "student interview outline," and "student learning feedback questionnaire survey" as the quantitative data, the effectiveness of the study implementation has been found. The research results indicate that:1. the experimental teaching can enhance the students' performance in creative thinking; 2. The students were fascinated by the creative instruction activities.

Keywords: mold making practice, creative thinking instruction, creativity.

1 Introduction

In the diverse and challenging society of today, people should not only have professional knowledge, but also cultivate the problem-solving ability [1]. Therefore, the Ministry of Education [2,3] has implemented the vocational high school new syllabus since 2006 to engage in the core curriculum planning, internship planning and strengthen industry-academia integration as well as the active cultivation of students' creative thinking ability. The mold production practice is the core curriculum for internship courses, mechanical engineering group. The course is intended for students to design and produce one mold using a variety of equipment and cultivate various skills.

Sternberg believes that one must have considerable expertise to talk about creation." [4] In other words, it is only through the background knowledge as support that the foundation and resources for creation can be laid. Yeh Yu-Chu [5] also proposed that although creativity is related to personal traits, cultural literacy, and learning environments, individuals' motivation to create depends on their solid domain knowledge. The students' display of creativity depends on three elements: the prior knowledge of

M. Zhu (Ed.): ICCIC 2011, Part V, CCIS 235, pp. 239–245, 2011.

creativity, creativity intention, and creativity related skills and capacity [6]. Therefore, the effective application of the creative thinking instruction related professional knowledge and strategies shall help enhance the students' prior knowledge of creativity.

In this study, the purposes are as to explore the influence of creative thinking instruction implemented during the mold production internship course on students' creativity thinking ability.

2 Literature References

The Meaning of Creativity: Rhodes [7] has studied a variety of creative definitions, from which the 4P of creation have been summarized, including: "the creator's personality traits," "the creation process," "the created products," and "the created environment." Mao Lien-Wen [8] also believes that creativity is nothing more than studying the correlations among the "creator," "creation behavior," "created products," and "created environment." In this section, the researcher's analysis of the meaning of creativity shall be explored based on the summary within the scope of the four items.

The Creative Thinking Instruction Model: The "teaching model" refers to a systematic project that forms curriculums and guide teaching under teaching scenarios, which is a systematic teaching process [9]. Maker [10] believes that teaching should have the following characteristics:1.To have a clear purpose and central area; 2.To make basic assumptions on the learners' characteristics and learning programs; 3. To serve as indicators for the development of daily learning activities; and 4. To provide specified learning activity models and requirements [11].

The teaching models proposed by the researchers are quoted as follows: 1.The Creative Problem-solving (CPS) Teaching Model: This model system which has been developed by Parnes [12] solves problems through systematic approaches, which gives special emphasis to the problem solver's formulation of a variety of solution plans before selecting or implementing them. 2."Asking, Thinking, Doing, Evaluating" (ATDE) Creative thinking instruction Model: Chen Lung-An [13] integrated the opinions of the researchers and proposed the ATDE which includes four elements, asking, thinking, doing, and evaluation. The ATDE model gives a special emphasis to the students' knowledge and experience-based creative thinking, which is "make out of nothing and create new from the existing." On the basis of the students' original basics, opportunities for the spread of thinking are provided, thereby allowing students to give full play to their potentials.

In summary, creativity can be summarized into four steps: 1. To explore from all perspectives and entertain all possibilities; 2.To produce a variety of creative ideas; 3.To rate the strengths and weaknesses of the variety of creative ideas to select the best ideas; and 4. To implement the ideas and assess the results [14].

The Internship Courses at Vocational High Schools: The expertise curriculums of Dept. of Mold and Die Engineering consist of two parts: the professional courses and internship courses. "Mold production practice" is a required internship course. Prior to the implementation of the course (allotted for the second year), the students are required to take up "die basics practice." The syllabus is as follows: 1.To familiarize with engraving machines, EDM machines, and other processing machinery; 2.To familiarize with the structures of the various molds and the overall function of the mold components in the molds; 3.To develop mold processing capabilities; 4.To develop "care of materials, machinery, and equipment" habit and cultivate correct work methods and attitudes; 5.To comply with plant safety and health practices; 6.To establish correct values that help individuals engage in skill development and understand their responsibility in nation-building.

3 Research Methods

The experimental group is 37 students enrolled in the Third Grade Class Chung at Dept. of Mold and Die Engineering, Nangkang Vocational High School in 2009; the control group is 33 students enrolled in the Third Grade Class Hsiao at the said school.

The Experimental Design: In this study, the quasi experimental design "nonequivalent pretest and posttest control group design" has been adopted. With the school classes as the basic units, the experimental group "Class Chung" engaged in the "import-type creative thinking instruction" while the control group (Class Hsiao) engaged in the "traditional teaching." (Table 1).

Table 1. The nonequivalent pretest and posttest control group experimental design

Group	Pretest	Experimental processing	Posttest
Experimental group	Y1	X1	Y3
Control group	Y2	X2	Y4

Note:

＊.Y1, Y2, Y3, Y4 have adopted creative thinking tests.

＊.X1 is the experimental group which has undergone creative thinking processing for a period of 12 weeks.

＊.X2 is the control group which has undergone traditional teaching processing for a period of 12 weeks.

The Research Design: According to the above-mentioned study design, the independent variables in this study have been adopted as the teaching methods while the independent variables of creative thinking ability have been tested, as shown in Fig. 1.

The Research Tools: 1. Torrance Test of Creative Thinking (TTCT) and interview. TTCT consists of two parts: the graphics and languages. **Reliability analysis:** The raters have achieved consistent reliability; the graphics aspect, the raters' reliability has shown high correlation, and the language aspect, the inexperienced and experienced raters have shown high reliability. the retest reliability aspect, the test has been implemented twice. After two years of testing, most of the retests have reached significant levels. **Validity analysis:** includes four types, namely, content validity, concurrent validity, predictive validity, and construct validity. The factor analysis results are considered satisfactory. 2. Two groups of students were randomly selected for interviews in order to gain an insight into the students' learning conditions and the students' ideas and thoughts after the creative thinking instruction, thereby indirectly gaining an insight into the internship course conduction conditions and facilitating the analysis and comparison of the research results.

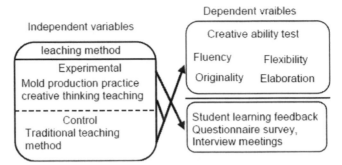

Fig. 1. The research design

4   Results and Discussion

The data analysis results and discussion are as below:

The Influence of the Creative Thinking Instruction Implemented during Creative Thinking Instruction on Students' Creative Thinking Ability: As for the students that have received creative thinking instruction, based on the group regression coefficient homogeneity test summary table of the creative thinking test conducted for the experimental group and control group, the F values have not reached significance. This result finding coincides with the group regression coefficient homogeneity assumptions. Therefore, the adjustment results caused by the covariates signify consistent actions within the groups and that the group differences under the different covariate values are consistent, thus the analysis of covariance continued to be carried out (Table 2).

Table 2. The group regression coefficient homogeneity test summary table of the creative thinking test conducted for the experimental group and control group

Type		Source	SS	df	MS	F
Graphic	Fluency	Teaching method *Pre-test	1.042	1	1.042	.014
		error	4139.983	56	73.928	---
	Flexibility	Teaching method *Pre-test	14.557	1	14.557	.493
		error	1623.511	56	29.518	---
	Originality	Teaching method *Pre-test	27.149	1	27.149	2.179
		error	685.315	56	12.460	---
	Elaboration	Teaching method *Pre-test	48.739	1	48.739	2.691
		error	995.998	56	18.109	---

Table 2. (*continued*)

Type		Source	SS	df	MS	F
Language	Fluency	Teaching method *Pre-test	.826	1	.826	.008
		error	6099.900	56	108.927	---
	Flexibility	Teaching method *Pre-test	5.601	1	5.601	.137
		error	2288.254	56	40.862	---
	Originality	Teaching method *Pre-test	138.600	1	138.600	1.746
		error	4446.360	56	79.399	---

The analysis of the effectiveness of the experimental processing on the vocational high school students' graphics creativity sub-items is as shown in Table 3. After excluding the effects of the pretest on the students in the two groups, the students in the experimental group had significant higher scores in "fluency" and "elaboration" of graphics and "originality" in languages under the "Torrance Test of Creative Thinking" than the scores of the students in the control group (Table 3).

Table 3. The analysis of the effectiveness of the experimental processing on the vocational high school students' graphics creativity sub-items

Type		Source	SS	df	MS	F
Graphic	Fluency	Pre-test	5.069	1	5.069	.070
		Teaching method	1228.559	1	1228.559	16.911***
		error	4141.025	56	72.650	---
	Flexibility	Pre-test	107.531	1	107.531	3.676
		Teaching method	65.312	1	65.312	2.233
		error	1638.068	56	29.251	---
	Originality	Pre-test	65.606	1	65.606	5.157
		Teaching method	47.419	1	47.419	3.727
		error	712.465	56	12.723	---
	Elaboration	Pre-test	9.223	1	9.223	.494
		Teaching method	492.758	1	492.758	26.413***
		error	1044.737	56	18.656	---
Language	Fluency	Pre-test	196.985	1	196.985	1.840
		Teaching method	815.255	1	815.255	7.617**
		error	6100.726	56	107.030	---
	Flexibility	Pre-test	346.327	1	346.327	8.606
		Teaching method	5.451	1	5.451	.135
		error	2293.855	56	40.243	---
	Originality	Pre-test	261.586	1	261.586	3.252
		Teaching method	1127.826	1	1127.826	14.021***
		error	4584.959	56	80.438	---

The responses of the students in the experimental group regarding the mold production practice imported in creative instruction learning

In order to gain a deeper understanding of the changes in creativity during the creative thinking teaching material implementation process, the learning response questionnaire surveys and interview outlines have undergone quantitative analysis in this study to obtain more detailed results.

Based on the research results, the experimental group's learning response questionnaire survey statistical table and mean scores show that after excluding question 7 and 14 with negative-intention options, the experimental group's mean scores in the items were 3 points higher after the experimental teaching for a period of 12 weeks, indicating the positive learning results and responses of creative thinking instruction on the students in the experimental group.

5 Summary

During the research process, the students in the experimental group and control group received creative thinking instruction also received the pretest and posttest. The results are as follows:

The Experimental Teaching Activities can Partially Improve the Students' Creative Thinking Ability Performances: After excluding the previous ability differences observed in the students in the two groups through analysis of covariance, the students in the experimental group had significantly higher scores than the students in the control group in terms of "fluency," and "elaboration" in the graphics under the "creative thinking test activities", indicating the implementation of creative thinking instruction in the   mold production practice curriculum has significantly improved the creativity results.

The Teachers' Reflection of the Creative Thinking Instruction Implemented in the Mold Production Practice Curriculum: The senior teachers that have participated in this research agree with the importance of this plan and are willing to provide internship curriculum instruction in the future in order to offer more versatile and useful contents and teach students courses that allow them to apply their knowledge. In terms of professional course instruction, the curriculums and instructions should strive to link with real-life applications in order to establish the basis for future research and development and lifelong learning, and should cite more relevant examples, which shall be of considerable help in inducing and stimulating student creativity.

References

1. Li, C.-C., Wang, C.-C.: Creative Problem Solving Topic Production of Teaching. Technical and Vocational Education Bimonthly 45, 39–44 (1998)
2. The Machinery Group Mold Production Practice Curriculum Standards Promulgated by the Ministry of Education (2005)
3. The Ministry of Education, The Description of the Vocational School Group Curriculum Provisional Outline, Equipment Standards, and Supporting Measures. Technological and Vocational Education, Taipei (2005)

4. Hung, L.: Utilizing Wisdom (1999); Translated from Robert, Sternberg, J.: Original Intelligence applied. Ylib, Taipei City (1999)
5. Yeh, Y.-C.: The Scale Development of the Factors Affecting Elementary School Children's Technological Creativity Development Journal of National Taiwan Normal University. Science of Education 50(2), 29–54 (2005)
6. Yeh, Y.-C.: Creativity Instruction-The Past, Present, and Future. Psychological Publishing Co., Ltd., Taipei (2006)
7. Rhodes, M.A.: An analysis of creativity. Phi Delta Kappa 42(7), 305–310 (1961)
8. Mao, L.-W.: The Reference Framework of the Implementation of Creative Thinking Education. Creative Thinking Education 1, 2–9 (1989)
9. Wei, H.-T.: A Study of Creativity Problem-solving Teaching Implemented by Junior High School Technological Education. Master Thesis, Department of Industrial Education, National Taiwan Normal University, Taipei (2001)
10. Maker, C.J.: Curriculum development for the gifted. PRO-ED, Austin (1982)
11. Lai, M.-J.: The Influence of Creative English Teaching Strategies on Elementary School Gifted Students' Creativity and Academic Performance. Master Thesis, Graduate Institute of Special Education, National Changhua University of Education, Changhua (1991) (unpublished)
12. Parnes, S.J.: Creative behavior guidebook. Scribner's, NY (1967)
13. Chen, L.-A.: The Creative Thinking Instruction in Theory and Practice. Psychological Publishing Co., Ltd., Taipei (2007)
14. Li, F.-M., Chuang, Y.-H.: Creative Thinking. Wun Ching Publishing Group, Taipei (2008)

Teaching Reform and Practice on Fostering Engineering Capability for the Undergraduate Student

Shengbing Ren[1], Zhigang Hu[1], and Bin Wu[2]

[1] School of Software, Central South University, Changsha 410075, China
[2] Undergraduate School, Central South University, Changsha 410083, China
FINEREN@TOM.COM

Abstract. In university engineering education, there is a widespread lack of fostering engineering capability, which makes it difficult for students to transform their knowledge into capability after graduate, and leads to an embarrassing situation in which the graduate can not easily get a job and the enterprise can not easily find an appropriate graduate. This paper proposes a teaching reform approach based on CDIO-CMM model according to the latest achievement from CDIO engineering education reform, and constructs the four-stage teaching pattern centered on fostering engineering capability including teaching conceiving, teaching designing, teaching implementing and teaching operating. For the student engineering capability evaluation, a capability maturity evaluation method is described. The practice shows that the teaching reform can activate the initiative of students in learning and helps personalization on fostering engineering capability.

Keywords: engineering capability, capability maturity, teaching pattern, evaluation method.

1 Introduction

The development and competition of the global economic in integration, comprehensiveness, and industrialization puts forward higher requirements on the training of engineering talents. However, for a long period, the engineering education in university generally pays more attention to the professional knowledge learning and lacks the cultivation on students' engineering capability, which makes it difficult for engineering graduates to transfer their knowledge into their capability.

Absence of the cultivation on engineering capability in the course teaching is mainly manifested in the following aspects: (1) Theoretical course teaching almost does not consider the demand of engineering application, and the organic combination and transformation between the knowledge and the engineering capability is also omitted; (2) The absence of intimate connection between the practical course teaching and the industrial community keeps students from contacting the real environment related to the modern engineering and lacks the cultivation on capability to solve actual problems; (3) The relationships between the theoretical course teaching and the practical course teaching is not handled from the viewpoint of the industrial community, thus the independent practical course teaching system is not established.

M. Zhu (Ed.): ICCIC 2011, Part V, CCIS 235, pp. 246–251, 2011.
© Springer-Verlag Berlin Heidelberg 2011

According to the industrial community demand for engineering talents and the country strategic layout to industry development, the engineering education in university needs to deepen the course teaching reform.

On the basis of the studying on the international advanced engineering education pattern, such as CDIO [1] etc, School of Software of Central South University brings the concepts of CDIO engineering capability maturity and builds CDIO Capability Maturity Model(abbreviation CDIO-CMM) [2] with referring to the thoughts of Capability Maturity Model (CMM) [3] in software. This paper mainly studies the course teaching reform on fostering students' engineering capabilities based on the CDIO-CMM model, which includes teaching pattern and evaluation method.

2   The CDIO-CMM Model

The CDIO engineering education pattern is the latest achievement of the international engineering education reform in recent years, and the core concept is keeping the whole process as carriers, in which modern industry products or system lives from research, development, to run, improvement ,even expiry and discard. Students can learn engineering in an active, practical, and course related way in order to cultivate their modern engineering capability. Although the CDIO engineering education pattern puts forward clear definition on fostering engineering talents with one vision, twelve judgement standards on teaching philosophy, four ability requirement levels and five guidelines, it does not take further description about how to progressively cultivate and systematically evaluate engineering capability for students, and also does not define the growth process for students' engineering capability. With introducing the concepts of capability maturity, CDIO-CMM model divides students' engineering capability into four capability maturity levels [3]: initial level, fundamental level, professional level, and application research level. Characteristics of each capability maturity level reflect the improving direction or status on students' engineering capability, and this makes students' engineering capability increase orderly, and thus gradually become mature.

In CDIO-CMM model, each capability maturity level stipulates some key course fields except initial level. Students basically take the course as the studying unit in the learning process, and therefore the course teaching is the most basic practical activity in the CDIO learning process. Every key course field contains a series of key practical teaching activities which are organized according to the type of teaching activities, and their implementation affects the formation of the students' CDIO engineering capability. When all key practical teaching activities in one key course field are implemented according to the requirements, the CDIO learning goals, which are required to achieve in this key course field, will be realized. So the students' CDIO engineering capability is cultivated incrementally and iteratively by implementing the key course teaching.

CDIO-CMM model not only organically combines capability, knowledge system, and quality cultivation together, but also paies more attention to the CDIO engineering capability fostering incrementally and iteratively with dividing the capability maturity into different levels. But the implementation of the key course teaching has an important influence on achieving the learning goals of each key course field, thus each key course teaching within the same key course field should be processed cooperatively during the course teaching process. Obviously, CDIO-CMM model puts forward higher requirements for the course teaching implementation, so the current course teaching should be reformed, which contains two aspects such as the teaching pattern and the evaluation method on the students' capability.

3   CDIO-CMM Based Course Teaching Reform

3.1   Four-Stage Teaching Pattern Based on the Key Course Field

The effective method meeting the CDIO-CMM model requirements for the course teaching is building a teaching team by taking the key course field as the unit. An uniform and effective guiding teams for the course teaching is formed with integrating CDIO teaching process, to guide and coordinate students to learn in an active and experiential way. On the one hand, the teaching content can be arranged appropriately to reduce the burden of students. On the other hand, the advantages of teachers can be integrated effectively, and the team teaching also provides reference for the cultivation of the students' cooperation spirit. In order to better facilitate the integration of the course teaching, the teaching process is divided into four stages based on the key course field: teaching conceiving, teaching designing, teaching implementing, and teaching operating.

During the course teaching conceiving stage, a key course field is taken as a unit, and a teaching team is built according to the teaching requirements for capability integration and course content synthesis. A team leader is also designated, who is responsible for the key course field teaching activities such as   planning, communication, supervision and coordination, and organizes the teaching team members to investigate the existing teaching infrastructure and the status of students' engineering capability. According to the existing teaching infrastructure and the status of students' engineering capability, integrating with the concept of CDIO engineering education and CDIO-CMM model, we need confirm the teaching contents and the corresponding learning effects, and distribute the teaching tasks among members based on the characteristics of each member.

During the teaching designing stage, the teaching team member should discuss the teaching schedule and the required cooperation with each other. Each member should jointly study and discuss on every course, such as contents, period distribution, teaching methods, teaching means, and cooperation, etc. They should jointly design the teaching case and the course project for each course, and confirm the method and the mean for the teaching performance assessment, and define the teaching risk and management strategies. They also should furtherly design the teaching process, and ensure that corresponding learning effects are reflected and are feasible. When studying on teaching methods and teaching means, we should focus on diversity and integrating the characteristics of students and teachers to avoid uniformity and mere formality. The analysis of teaching risk is one of important tasks at the teaching designing stage. Considering the teaching risk before teaching implementation and teaching operation, it helps not only to strengthen teaching management and supervision, and to take preventive measures, but also to effectively deal with the risk when it occurs, and to avoid affecting teaching effects.

Within the teaching implementation stage, every team member collects teaching resources and writes lecture notes. The team member should make teaching media and teaching tools, and construct teaching cases, and check the effectiveness of teaching facilities, and implement the prototype of the course project in a cooperative way. At the same time, all team members need to discuss and modify the problems and the difficulties which they encounter during the teaching implementation.

At the course teaching operation stage, each team member should carry out teaching in a cooperative manner according to the designed teaching process, and guide and coordinate students to make active learning and experiential learning. The team also should discuss and evaluate students' learning effect and learning situation, and discover the learning process problems, and start the management strategies for teaching risk in time. The key of the course teaching operation stage is the successful collaboration among members, so the team leader need to seriously organize members to carry out various forms of cooperation including mutual lecture listen, teaching coordination meeting, guiding students to complete course projects, etc.

According to the teaching process based on the key course field, it can not only foster the teaching team with cooperation spirit, which makes every member utilize the advantages and avoid the weakness and systematically integrates teaching resources, and flexibly diversify teaching to realize the teaching objective for capability integration and course content synthesis, but also reduce the learning burden of students. This is also helpful to form the learning culture with open, shared and diverse characteristics.

3.2   Key Course Field Based Evaluation Method on Capability Maturity

In order to understand the present situation of students' engineering capability, according to the CDIO-CMM model, we evaluate the capability maturity separately by the grade. The capability maturity level indicates the direction to improve the students' engineering capability.

In order to implement the evaluation of engineering capability maturity, an evaluation team should be set up, which includes one team leader, one vice team leader, 5-9 team members, and when necessary one secretary can be added. All members of the evaluation group should meet some conditions as followings: mastering CDIO-CMM model; be familiar with CDIO engineering education pattern; understanding the major's requirement for students' knowledge, ability and quality; be good at discovering problems and solving problems; fairness, justness and working hard and uncomplainingly.

Once the evaluation team is set up, the evaluation conceiving should be completed firstly, in which the learning effect of the evaluated key course field is confirmed with integrating teaching environment and resources. Secondly, the corresponding evaluation method according to different types of expected learning effect is also determined including contents, methods, means and steps to collect information and information sources. Thirdly, it is completed to sample the assessed students from the perspective of the engineering capability evaluation, while the samples should be representative, and the information contents and related problems in information collection should be able to reflect students' engineering capability. After collecting students' information, the evaluation team can make statistical analysis for the collected information, and determine the next investigating area and working emphasis related to the key course field in CDIO-CMM model.

Furthermore, the students' learning process environment is accessed. According to the result of information analysis, the actual status is mastered, which shows the implementation of the key course teaching practice related to CDIO-CMM model. It is investigated to determine whether the implementation of the key course field meets the requirements of CDIO-CMM model. At the same time, the differences between the key course teaching practice and the actual investigation's are recorded. After the actual investigation, the evaluation team should submit the investigation report, which clearly states the strong point and weakness on students' engineering capability. At last, the evaluation team analyzes the object and draws a profile for the key course field, and writes the analysis report on students' engineering capability maturity.

4   Teaching Reform Practice

This paper takes software engineering major as an example to show our practice on fostering students' engineering capability. According to CDIO-CMM model, with deeply investigating and researching the knowledge system on software engineering major in combination with the demand from the domestic and international enterprises, we divide all software engineering major courses into thirteen key course fields. The fundamental level contains seven key course fields: foreign language, humanistic quality, mathematics, computing theory, computing system, software development tool, and basic practice. The professional level contains three key course fields on the basis of the basic level: software engineering technology, software engineering management, and professional design. The application research level also contains three key course fields based on the professional level, such as innovation and pioneering, engineering training, and scientific research.

In order to implement the key course field based teaching pattern, company engineer is invited to join the teaching team in our school. Teaching seminars is regularly held to exchange teaching experience and to discuss problems happened in the teaching process. At the same time, younger teachers without engineering background are required to enter enterprise to carry out a half year engineering practice. The case-based teaching method is generally utilized, which reflects the principle of learning-by-doing. The student centered pedagogical thought is considered to improve student learning initiative and innovation through heuristic teaching etc. Meanwhile, advanced and practical teaching platform is built by using the existing network conditions.

In order to understand students' capability status before course learning, each key course field based teaching team drafts the course-questionnaire and investigates the students existing knowledge, ability, and quality according to learning needs from the key course field.

The score of the key course field is calculated by the following rules:

1) the key course field score=the key course field questionnaire score*50% +($\sum$(the ith key course score)/the numbers of key courses)*50%;

2) the ith key course score=(the course questionnaire score *50% + the examination score*50%)*60% +the score of spot investigation or practice *40%;

3) the course questionnaire score=$\sum$(the kth student questionnaire score)/numbers of students;

4) the examination score=$\sum$(the kth student score)/numbers of the evaluated students.

The 2006's evaluation results show that two key course fields, which are "humanistic quality" and "professional knowledge", obtain lower score, and are the weakness among all grades. While the scores are higher on three key course fields, which are "foreign language", "mathematics" and "computation theory", and those are strong items among all grades. The scores of "engineering training" and "innovation and pioneering" are poor in graduating class. Therefore, we improve the cultivation scheme by the following rule:1) adding professional introduction course in the cultivation scheme, adjusting the "humanistic quality" key course field with increasing the elective courses, and extending the engineering training from three weeks to five weeks; 2) encouraging students to do extra practice, and holding more lectures on innovation and pioneering; 3)designating teachers to take part in engineering practice, and learning CDIO engineering education philosophy; 4) improving the organization and the management system according to the requirements of CDIO engineering education and CDIO-CMM model. The 2008's evaluation results show that the sophomore student has met the demand of the fundamental level and the junior student has met the demand of the professional level.

5   Conclusions

With the continuous development of the national economic construction, the cultivation of engineering talents increasingly draws the society's great attention. Based on CDIO-CMM model, this paper proposes the reform on course teaching, which keeps the engineering capability fostering as its core, and fully describes the four-stage teaching pattern and the corresponding evaluation method on the capability maturity which based on the key course field in CDIO-CMM model. This offers an important reference function to improve the quality of engineering education at present.

References

1. Crawley, E.F., Malmqvist, J., Ostlund, S., et al.: Rethinking Engineering Education: The CDIO Approach. Springer, New York (2007)
2. Software Engineering Institute in Carnegie Mellon University: The Capability Maturity Model (CMM): Guidelines for Improving the Software Process. Publishing House of Electronics Industry (2001) (in Chinese)
3. Chen, Q.Y., Ren, S.B., Hu, Z.G., et al.: CDIO Capability Maturity Evaluation and Improving Architecture for the Undergraduate Student in Engineering. Journal of Research in Higher Education of Engineering 6, 31 (2009) (in Chinese)

The Research of Automation Open Experiment Teaching Platform under the Background of Large Engineering

JiaLian Wang

School of Automation, Hangzhou Dianzi University,
Hangzhou Zhejiang 310018, China
wangbb33@126.com

Abstract. This paper analyzes the main problems of automation in experimental teaching under the background of large engineering, and proposes to build an open experimental teaching platform in general engineering colleges. According to overall framework in three-dimensional and hierarchical, training the ability of engineering innovation is the center, the open experimental teaching platform is constructed from the basic experiment, experiment, technological innovation and college-enterprise cooperation. It strengthened the ability of students in engineering experiments and received the initial good results.

Keywords: engineering education, experiment teaching, platform.

1 Introduction

Engineering is activities that people general use scientific theories (including natural, technology and social sciences) and techniques to transform the objective world [1]. The engineering education is a special education that based on technical sciences and fosters the engineers who can transform science and technology into productive forces [2]. In recent years, the employment of students shows diversified trends, employer requires student whose awareness of engineering, infrastructure of engineering and the overall quality are increasinged. Howerve, the traditional engineering education is difficult to solve current problems.

In 1993, MIT dean of Engineering Joel Moses first proposed the "large Engineering" educational philosophy and pointed out that this is the new development of engineering education in the future, which is widely recognized in engineering education. The report that the engineering education delegation of the State Education Commission visited to the USA in 1996 is the first mentioned the concept of education about the large engineering in China.The educational philosophy of the large engineering is an modern engineering education that engineering talent is the training target, engineering background is the main line,which focused on the engineering awareness, engineering quality and engineering practice of students and integrate engineering education, natural science education, the humanities and social science education [3]. It emphasizes the relationship between knowledge and integrity, and reflects the uniform width and professional in knowledge structure. It also requires students have complex and diversity ability to make them have good abilitis to adapt in a wide area. It is the

M. Zhu (Ed.): ICCIC 2011, Part V, CCIS 235, pp. 252–257, 2011.

nature of the large engineering that is a system of teaching philosophy "engineering model" with practical, integrated, innovative and integrated the science, technology, non-technical, engineering practice [4].

In this note, we consider the problem how to build the opening experiment teaching platform under the background of large engineering. The purpose of this paper is to obtain platform which can strengthen the engineering ability's of students, improve their social satisfaction, enable students to quickly qualified the requirement of enterprises. Firstly, we analyzed the existing main problems of automation in experimental teaching, and propose a construction approach, which is based on the integration of existing resources, use existing laboratory and build from hardware and software aspects.Then, based on this, efficient operation for mechanism are obtained.

2 Problem Formulation

In recent years, with the rapid development of modern information, automation technology and information technology is cross-cutting deeper, At the same time, automation involves the wide and systematic knowledge, all students have the difficulty in mastering the knowledge. Thus students must accepted comprehensive training in order to have the ability to solve practical engineering problems. However, most of the enterprises currently don't have the training conditions of students in engineering practice, and there are more uncontrollable factors in the practice of outside school. It is necessary to solve the problems how to strengthen the ability of Engineering for School students.

For instance, Hangzhou dianzi University have been built 12 automated laboratory, although some laboratories have been opened, which still cann't meet the training needs of students. There are the following problems:

1. Although the number of laboratories meet the requirements, but most experimental content is only the supplement and extension of classroom teaching. Experiment focus on teaching the theory without innovation; the contents of experiment delay, the method of experiment is dated and inflexible not to stimulate enthusiasm in practical learning. This traditional mode of experiment teaching no longer meet the demand for engineering training.

2. There are many resources in some laboratory that hardware resources are relatively abundant, however, the opening hours of laboratory is not enough, even more very few students take part in the opening laboratory, or with lack guidance of teachers, students still do nothing to. There is existing some extent problem of waste and duplication i the use of performance, which benefit students very narrow from the openness of the laboratory.

3. The management system of experiment and person have been established, but the fund and incentive still aren't in place. In particular, school has introduced   high level teachers , but there are quite a number of highly educated teachers in engineering capacity is weak, fewer engineers and technicians, teachers structure is irrational, it is difficult to adapt the requirements of engineering education.

In order to solve the above problems, it's important in developing a good student how to integrate existing resources and build a suitable platform whic enhance their ability in engineering practice and system design capabilities.

3 Main Result

The construction of the opening experiment-teaching platform includes three direction aspects. It is used three-dimensional network management in laboratory management, on the other hand, the main experimental teaching system is multi-level approach, in addition, operating mechanism is safeguard to ensure the opening experimental teaching platform runing smoothly.

1. Three-Dimensional Network Management

According to the above building plan, it is decided to set up the center of platform network management, and a remote virtual laboratory system is established, A three-dimensional network management system is show in Figure 1.

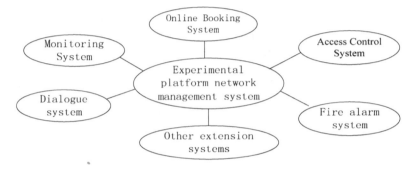

Fig. 1. Network management system of teaching experimental platform

Online booking system can control the time of teachers and students who also can choose appropriate time. Access control systems can strictly control the the time of student accessing lab, timely view each student's situation what's time in or out. Monitoring system is constantly monitoring, which teachers can check the use of laboratories each time, reducing student's game time. Teacher and student can free to contact by dialogue system, that reduce their time in back and forth. Other extesion systems are reserved for future development.

This experimental network management model requires students to advance preparation and prepare for the best work, exercise professional skills in hands-on activities. Meanwhile, this puts forward higher requirements for teachers, students are well prepared, will propose a variety of problem.

2. Multi-level Platform Model

The multi-level platform model of platform that open through experimental content ,experimental time and space take a different open mode to meet the actual needs of students at different levels. We proceed from the overall training system, building innovative engineering education as the goal of multi-experimental teaching system such as in Figure 2.

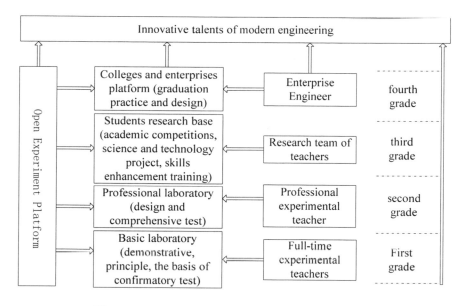

Fig. 2. Automation open experiment-teaching platform

Basic laboratory emphasis on basic and systemic knowledge and skills. In the basic experimental technique, it put emphasis on basic experimental principles, methods, and skills training, and training.the initial spirit of innovation and overall quality.

Professional laboratory is based on basic or college-enterprise cooperation laboratory.In hardware design, software development and automation systems and so on, it stress to strengthen skills in practice, and improve the overall proficiency. Evenmore, it focus on training basic skills of engineers, developing practical and creative engineering capability.

Students research base carry out the activities with the technology project academic contests and academic competition through technological innovation platform, it establish the innovation and expansion of experiment, training students the spirit of cooperation, challenge awareness, learning and innovation. Students take part in the research activities, which form a specific project characteristics and achieve the basic goals of personnel training.

College and enterprise cooperately build a platform which based on the open experimental platform, according to the features of petrochemicals, steel, electric power industries and integrated automation system, that combined with scientific research, and created multi-level, platform or device of engineering practice, an effective solution is obtained to achieve the   question for the actual instrument engineering practice. A comprehensive approach is teams or individual students directly to receive engineering training and complete the pre-service pre-employment training.

3. Operating Mechanism

The operating mechanism of the open experiment-teaching platform is considered from learning mechanism, protection mechanism and students in engineering practice system.the whole framework is showed in Figure.3.

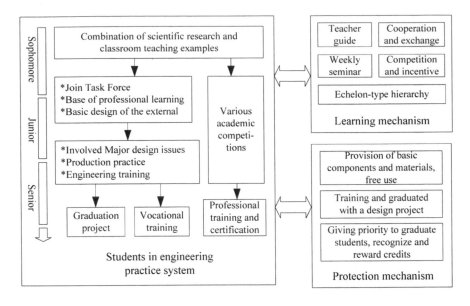

Fig. 3. The operating mechanism of the open experiment-teaching platform

In order to increase the open efforts of laboratory, platform provide students more practice opportunity, operating mechanism can make sure system operating normally.

4   Conclusion

In this paper, we have analyzes the main problems of automation in experimental teaching under the background of large engineering, and developed a reasonable simple platform, which need not teachers and students run back and forth,and used easy, to enhance the engineering ability of students. Efficient mechanisms have been obtained to guarante platform operating smoothly. With the initial operation, all parties show good results. In other words, it strengthened the ability of students in engineering experiments and received the initial good results.

Acknowledgements. This work was supported by the Education of Zhejiang Province under grant Y200804975, Y200907366, Higher Education of Zhejiang Province under grant Y201008. New Century Education Reform of Zhejiang Province under grant YB09025.

References

1. Zhu, G.F.: Higher Engineering Education in China Problems and Solutions. Research in Higher Education of Engineering 4, 1–6 (1998)
2. Yao, Y., Zheng, G.Z., Liao, L.Q.: Reform in the Mechanical Engineering Experiment Teaching System in Higher Engineering Education. Journal of Chongqing Institute of Technology 21(9), 174–176 (2007)

3. Zhao, X.J.: The Teaching method exploration of Engineering Survey major against a background of big Project. Engineering of Surveying and Mapping 17(2), 74–76 (2008)
4. Xie, X.Z.: An Exploration of the Connotation and Essential Features of "Large scale Engineering". Research in Higher Education of Engineering 3, 35–38 (2008)
5. Moses, J.: My Life, pp. 284–285, 344 (2007)
6. Zhang, Y.J., Zhou, Y., Han, Y., et al.: Cultivating student's innovative spirit and pratical ability based on laboratory openning platform. Experimental Technology and Management 25(2), 23–25 (2008)

Semantic Web Enabled Personalized Recommendation for Learning Paths and Experiences

Changqin Huang[1,2], Li Liu[2], Yong Tang[1], and Ling Lu[2]

[1] Department of Computer Science, Sun Yat-Sen University, Guangzhou, 510275, China
[2] School of Educational Information Technology, South China Normal University,
Guangzhou, 510631, China
chunchun474@yeah.com

Abstract. To enhance the efficiency and effectiveness of e-learning in on-line course system, a semantic web-based learning system is proposed to support personalized recommendation for learning paths and experiences, where three ontologies are put forward to construct the knowledge of learners, course and learning objects. The learning paths can be established by similarity matching of the course ontology and learner ontology, or adopt the predecessor's learning experiences. Then personalized learning contents are recommended by matching between learner's features and learning object ontology. And personalized learning experiences are formed by evaluating the learning paths, and can be reused by recommendation based on the similar compare. Experimental results suggest that the proposed system can improve the learning performance.

Keywords: E-learning, Personalized learning, Learning path, Experience.

1 Introduction

With the rapid development of computer and internet, e-learning has become an indispensable learning way in the field of education. However, the traditional "one curriculum for all" learning way is no longer enough to meet the needs of learners due to the differences from requirements [1]. And then more and more personalized recommendation systems have been developed and are trying to find a solution to realize personalization in the learning process. Semantic web is a new technology to achieve artificial intelligence, which can make the web more useful, more user-centered, and more responsive to human interaction [2]. In semantic web-based learning system, the learning information is well-defined, and the machine can understand and deal with the semantics of the learning contents to provide adaptable learning services with the support of ontologies. In this paper, we develop a semantic web-based personalized learning system to recommend the learning resources and learning paths based on learner profiles, learning objects and learning experience.

The rest of the paper is organized as follows. Related work is summarized in Section 2. Section 3 presents the system architecture and its workflow. In Section 4, the ontology models are constructed to express the knowledge. The implementation strategy of personalization is depicted in Section 5. Section 6 represents the experiments and results. Finally, the paper concludes with Section 7.

M. Zhu (Ed.): ICCIC 2011, Part V, CCIS 235, pp. 258–267, 2011.
© Springer-Verlag Berlin Heidelberg 2011

2   Related Work

Over the past decades, personalization is still a focus of research. C.M. Chen et al [3] propose a Personalized E-Learning system based on Item Response Theory (PEL-IRT) in which both the course material difficulty and the learner ability are considered to provide individual learning paths for the certain learner; and their follow-up work [4] improves and perfects the system by providing personalized learning path guidance based on genetic algorithm, but it neglects the construction and representation of knowledge, and resources can not be shared and reused in this system. The advent of semantic web brings new chances to solve the problem. Cisco [5] has developed a system for reusable learning objects, in which each learning object can be mixed with each other and match a specific explanation of the curriculum and activities. Some Practices demonstrate that some intelligent and personalization services in e-learning can be achieved by using ontology and semantic web technology [6]. Jovanovi et al [7] have developed TANGRAM which applies an ontology-based approach to automatic decomposition of learning objects into reusable content units for personalized learning. This is similar to C.M. Chen's work[3], but TANGRAM can not generate a learning sequence for learners. The follow-up researches make it up. Z.W. Yu et al [1] present a semantic recommendation approach oriented to learning contents, in which learning paths can be generated to guide learners. However, these researchers have not taken the reuse of learner experiences into account. R. H. M'tir et al [8] make a study to solve this problem, they introduce a method to capitalize and reuse learning experience. Nevertheless, it can not compare learners' many personalization parameters with many learning objects' characteristics in detail. According to the analysis of the aforementioned researches, deep personalization in learning systems should be further studied.

3   A Semantic Web-Based Personalized Learning System

To narrow the gap between current personalization requirements and related research achievements, a semantic web-based personalized learning system is proposed based on learning paths, learning contents and learning experiences recommendation.

As illustrated in Fig. 1, the proposed system consists of five modules and four databases. The five modules are the learner management module, course resource management module, learning path generation module, personalized recommendation module and evaluation module. The four databases are the learner profile database, course ontology database, learning object database and learning experience database. The learner management module is responsible for the learner modeling. And the learner model information is stored in the learner profile database. The course resource management module is charge of the course's knowledge structure and the related learning objects. The course information and learning object information are stored in the course ontology database and learning object database, respectively. The semantic relations of the two databases are established via semantic annotation based on course ontology and learning object ontology. The learning path generation module can tailor a learning path for each learner according to the course structure and the learners' learning status. Meanwhile, the learning paths can also directly come from the learning experience database based on the similarities of learners' learning status and learning preference. After the learners select the knowledge point to learn, the personalized recommendation module will generate a learning object recommendation list according to the learners' learning preference and learning level. While the learner finishes his study, the evaluation module is triggered to assess his learning effects by a test. If this test indicates that the learner has reached his learning goal, the system can assess the current learner's learning processes, and then the reasonable learning paths with excellent learning effects can be stored in the learning experience database.

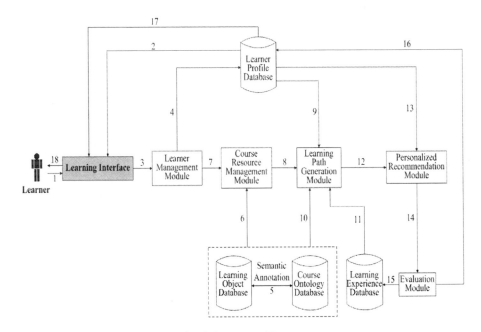

Fig. 1. System architecture

4   Knowledge Model Based on Ontology

To get the semantic support in this learning system, three ontologies are constructed according to their semantics, which are learner ontology, course ontology, learning object ontology, respectively. The ontology based model consists of two parts: learner model and course resource model.

4.1   Learner Model

Learner modeling is the basis of any personalization learning systems. In this system, learner modeling process is implemented in the learner management modules, which is mainly in charge of collecting the learners' personal information to model the learner profiles and update them during the learning process. There are many educational standards for modeling the learner profile. The most typical standards are IEEE PAPI and IMS LIP. In this system, we adopt the IMS LIP parameters and extend its specification.

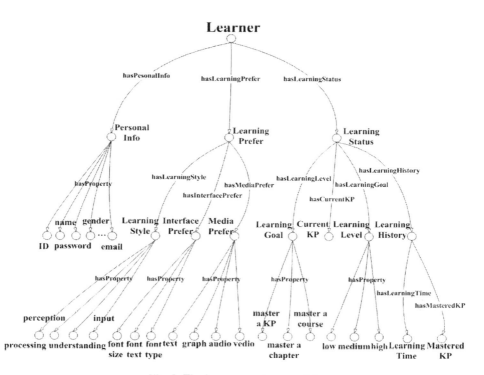

Fig. 2. The learner ontology model

The learner ontology embodies the knowledge of a learner, and it consists of: (1) personal general information, such as name, age, gender and so on, it usually keeps static throughout; (2) personal preference information. It mainly refers to the learning style. This system constructs the learner ontology based on FSLSM [9]. When a beginner logs into the system, the Index of Learning Styles (ILSs) is used to test his learning style and then fill his style information in the associated record, otherwise the system will try to automatically fill the possible information by analyzing his log files; (3) personal learning status information, it is presented by learning level, learning goal, current learning knowledge point, mastered knowledge points and so on. This kind of information will be updated constantly during the learning.   The learner ontology can be represented as Fig. 2.

4.2 Course Resource Model

This model includes course ontology and learning object ontology.

Course materials generally consist of several chapters. Each chapter has one or more knowledge points. And a knowledge point comprises a set of learning objects. Each chapter can be future divided into several knowledge points. Each knowledge point has a set of related learning objects. So the entities (Course, Chapter, Knowledge Points, Learning Object) and their relations(depending on the concrete course) compose a course ontology. Learning object ontology is classified into six subontologies to indicate the resource semantics, and these subontologies are MediaType, AppliedKnowledgePiont,

FileZie, AccessRate, DifficultyLevel, ApliedLearningStyle. One of the important relations is the belongsToKP, which makes the learning object link with a certain knowledge point of course ontology model. To realize the semantic description of course resource, the learning resources are annotated with the learning object ontology, and are linked with the relations of belongsToKP, and the annotated entities can serve as the instances of the learning object ontology. They have been described in our previous work[10].

5   Personalized Learning

5.1   Personalized Learning Path Generation

Two approaches are adopted to generate the personalized learning paths. One is obtained by semantic inference in the course ontology. The inference will be carried out in two directions: vertical inference and horizontal inference. We use two-dimension arrays to store the learning paths. In vertical inference, inference is conducted up and down based on the hasPrevious relation and hasNext relation in the course ontology model. In horizontal inference, inference is done left and right via the hasSibling relation. The other method is conducted by making the learner's personal features, learning style and learning goal match with the ones of the former learners, whose learning paths has been stored in the learning experience database. The system will recommend the first three matching paths to the learner as described in Section 5.3.

5.2   Personalized Learning Content Recommendation

Actually, the aforementioned learning path is a link list of knowledge points. After the learner selects a knowledge point from the learning path, a series of learning objects related semantically to this knowledge point can be formed via automatic inference. Meanwhile, a refined strategy is applied to tailor personalized learning content according to the learner's learning level and learning style. In fact, the refine process is complemented by matching with the corresponding parameters in the two ontologies. The two relations, "hasLearningLevel" and "hasLearningStyle" in the learner ontology, are corresponding to these relations :"hasDifficultyLevel" and "hasAppliedLearningStyle" in the learning object ontology, respectively. The learning level and the difficult degree are represented as {low, middle, high}, which is quantified as {-1, 0, 1}. The learning style information is recorded as {perception, input, processing, understanding}. Each dimension has two values, which can be quantified respectively as-1 and 1.

Definition 1: Level Similarity (LevelSim) describes the similarity between the learner's learning level (LL) and the learning object's difficulty (OD). It can be calculated as follows:

$$LevelSim(LL,OD) = \begin{cases} 1, T = 0 \\ 0.5, T = 1 \\ 0, T = 2 \end{cases} (T = |LL - OD|). \qquad (1)$$

Definition 2: Style similarity (StyleSim) depicts similarities of the learning styles between the learner's and the learning object's.

$$SS(LL,LO) = LStyle \times OStyle = \begin{pmatrix} ls_1 \\ ls_2 \\ ls_3 \\ ls_4 \end{pmatrix} \times (os_1 \quad os_2 \quad os_3 \quad os_4)$$

$$= \begin{pmatrix} ss[1,1] & ss[1,2] & ss[1,3] & ss[1,4] \\ ss[2,1] & ss[2,2] & ss[2,3] & ss[2,4] \\ ss[3,1] & ss[3,2] & ss[3,3] & ss[3,4] \\ ss[4,1] & ss[4,2] & ss[4,3] & ss[4,4] \end{pmatrix}$$ (2)

A $4*1$ column matrix and a $1*4$ row matrix are used to describe the learning styles of the learner and the learning object. For example, [-1;1;-1;1] denotes the learner has the learning style of "Intuitive, Verbal, Active, Sequential". These matrixes are calculated according to Equation (2).

SS is the product of the column matrix and the row matrix. LStyle denotes the style of the learner, and OStyle describes the style of the learning object. The number of the digit 1 in the leading diagonal represents similarities of the styles. Let the number be n (obviously, $0 \le n \le 4$), the style similarity (StyleSim) can be formalized as Equation (3).

$$StyleSim(LS,OS) = n$$ (3)

Finally, the similarities are described between the learner and the learning object as below, and Where α_1 and α_2 ($0 \le \alpha_1, \alpha_2 \le 1$) are regulatory factors to adjust the weight of each item.

$$LOSimilarity = \alpha_1 \times LevelSim(LL,OD) + \alpha_2 \times StyleSim(LS,OS)$$ (4)

5.3 Personalized Learning Experience Reuse

In this system, the item "learning experience" is represented by successful learning paths achieved by predecessors in the learning system. When a learner learns the selected knowledge points and passes the associated tests, the system thinks his learning path is constructed, and will evaluate the learning path according to the learner's learning outcomes and learning time spent in the learning process. The first three learning paths with higher outcomes and less time are regarded as excellent paths by ranking, and they are stored in the learning experience database. Thereby the latter learners can refer to the learning experiences if they are at the similar learning status with the predecessors.

When a learner achieved the selected knowledge points and passed the tests related with the knowledge points, we can think his/her learning path is accomplished. The system will evaluate the learning path according to the learner's learning performance and learning time spent in the learning process. In this system, we consider learning paths with higher performance and less time as excellent paths. These paths will be stored in the learning experience database. The latter learners can refer to the learning experiences if they are at the similar learning status with the predecessors.

Definition 3: Learning Status (LS) describes the learning situation. It is represented below:

LS={L_1, L_2, L_3, L_4}, where L_1 denotes current learning knowledge point, L_2 learning level, L_3 learning goal, and L_4 learning style.

Definition 4: Learning Status Similarity (LSS) describes the similarity of learning situation between two learners. The formula is described as follows:

$$LSS(LearnerA, LernerB) = \sum_{i=1}^{3} SL_i + \frac{1}{4} SL_4 \qquad (5)$$

Where LearnerA and LearnerB represent two different learners, and SL_i is the ith item of the learners' learning status similarity. SL_1, SL_2 and SL_3 are depicted as Boolean values. When LearnerA and LearnerB have the same properties, the value will be 1; otherwise, the value will be 0. For example, SL_1 stands for the similarity of current knowledge points. Suppose that LearnerA and LearnerB have the same current knowledge points, then, $SL_1=1$. Otherwise, $SL_1=0$.

As mentioned before, the result of SL_4 is a real value between 0 to 4. To balance the weights among SL_i (i=1,2,3) and SL_4, it is divided by 4. Thereby, $0 \leq LSS \leq 4$.

Definition 5: Learning Path Suitability (LPS) is used to describe the suitability of the learning paths. It is represented as follows:

$$LPS = \{LSS, LO, LE\} ,$$ where, LSS denotes learner's learning status similarity, LO learner's outcome, and LT learning time. The calculation of LPS can be described as follows:

$$LPS(LearnerA, LernerB) = \beta_1 \times LSS(LearnerA, LernerB) + \beta_2 \times LP + \beta_3 \times LT$$

$$= \beta_1 \times (\sum_{i=1}^{3} SL_i + SL_4) + \beta_2 \times LP + \beta_3 \times LT \qquad (6)$$

Where β_1, β_2, β_3 ($-1 \leq \beta_1, \beta_2, \beta_3 \leq 1$) are regulatory factors to adjust the weight of each item.

6 System Implementation and Experiments

The before-mentioned proposition is designed and developed based on the implementation described in the existing research [10], and the current system can get learner model and guide the learner for better personalized learning. When the learner comes to the course interface, he can choose a knowledge point to learn. The system will generate a learning path for him according to his learning goal and learning status. If the learner is unsatisfied with the recommended learning path, he can refer to the predecessor's learning paths by clicking "Recommend the other learning paths" in the main interface. After the learner selects a knowledge point(s) from the learning path, a list of personalized learning objects will be recommended to the learner on the basis of the semantic matching between his learning level & learning style, and learning objects.

   To verify the performance, a series of experiments is designed and implemented. During studying the course of "C Programming", sixty students, who participate in the study of the chapter of "Data Types" and "Operators and Expressions", are selected and investigated. Their study period lasts two weeks. According to whether they register themselves, these students are naturally divided into two groups: the general group and the registered group, and only these students in the registered group are asked to offer their personal information at the beginning of the studies. This information can contribute to personalized services provided by the system. At the same time, the system can only provide limited personalized services to the general group. After each student finishes the study, the system makes this student take a test to assess his learning effect, and meanwhile, the learning time of each knowledge point is limited within 30 minutes. The system will force each student to take an associated test when the required time ends. Certainly, the learners can also actively have the tests in advance when they finish learning of some certain knowledge point. Learning outcomes and learning time are selected as two indicators to measure the students' learning efficiency and learning effectiveness as shown in Fig.3 and Fig.4.

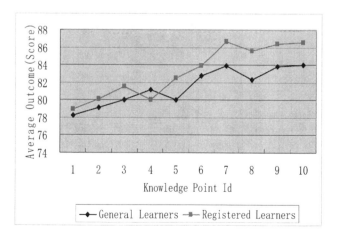

Fig. 3. Comparison of average outcomes

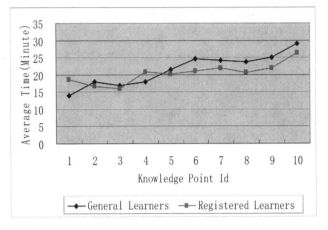

Fig. 4. Comparison of average time

As illustrated in the figures, the facts can be presented:(1) At the beginning, the registered learners spent much more time than the general learners, but with low scores; (2) Along with the learning progress, the registered can get higher score than the general ones with less time at the third knowledge point; (3) At the fourth one, the output of the general group is better than that of the registered group;(4) After the fifth one, both of the two groups perform steadily. Although the scores of the general learners gradually become increased for the limited personalized services, the registered learners can normally achieve higher score with less time than the general learners.

As these figures suggest, staring with the fourth knowledge point, the registered group's score is lower and the time is much more than the general one. As the learning is forwarding, whether the registered group or the other, the learner models become more perfect for the adjustment based on analyzing behaviors, thus they both bring these learners better learning effects, and make it to become steady. Obviously, the registered learners can get more personalized services and perform better than the general learners due to the relatively accurate learner model. On the whole, this personalized learning support can better improve the efficiency and effectiveness of individual learners.

7   Conclusions

This study applies semantic web in implementing personalized learning recommendations for learning paths, learning contents and learning experiences. A semantic web-based learning system is proposed to support semantic descriptions and applications, in which knowledge model is constructed on the basis of learner ontology, course ontology, learning object ontology, meanwhile. The learning paths can be acquired by using the similarity matching based on the course ontology and learner ontology, or adopting the predecessor's learning experiences after the learning paths are evaluated. Personalized learning contents are recommended by matching learner's features with learning object ontology. The experiment results reveal that the system can improve the learning performance.

Acknowledgement. The work is supported by the National Natural Science Foundation of China (Grant No. 60940033), the National Key Technology R&D Program (Grant No.2008BAH24B03), the Research Fund for Youth Scholars of Ministry of Education of China (Grant No. ECA080286), the China Postdoctoral Science Foundation (Grant No. 20080440121, 201003374), the key University Student Research Project of SCNU (Grant No. 09JXKC02), and the National & Guangdong Province Innovation Experiment Program for University Students (Grant No. C1025320, C1019919).

References

1. Yu, Z.W., Nakamura, Y.C., et al.: Ontology-Based Semantic Recommendation for Context-Aware E-Learning. In: Indulska, J., Ma, J., Yang, L.T., Ungerer, T., Cao, J. (eds.) UIC 2007. LNCS, vol. 4611, pp. 898–907. Springer, Heidelberg (2007)
2. Devedzic, V.: Semantic Web and Education. Springer Press, Heidelberg (2006)
3. Chen, C.M., Lee, H.M., Chen, Y.H.: Personalized E-learning System Using Item Response Theory. Computers & Education 44(2), 237–255 (2005)
4. Cisco: Reusable learning object strategy: designing and developing learning objects for multiple learning approaches, information on, http://business.cisco.com/
5. Chen, C.M.: Intelligent Web-based Learning System with Personalized Learning Path Guidance. Computers & Education 51(2), 787–814 (2008)
6. Zhu, X.J., Li, X.F.: Ontology Based Sharing and Services in E-Learning Repository. In: Proc. of IFIP Int'l Conf. on Network and Parallel Computing Workshops 2007, pp. 18–21 (2007)
7. Jovanović, J., Gašević, D., Devedžić, V.: Dynamic Assembly of Personalized Learning Content on the Semantic Web. In: Sure, Y., Domingue, J. (eds.) ESWC 2006. LNCS, vol. 4011, pp. 545–559. Springer, Heidelberg (2006)
8. M'tir, R.H.j., Jeribi, L., Rumpler, B., et al.: Learners Experiences Reuse to Improve Personalized E-Learning. Proc. of 3rd International Conf. on Information and Communication Technologies, pp. 335–340 (2008)
9. Felder, R., Silverman, L.: Learning and Teaching Styles in Engineering Education. Journal of Engineering Education 78(7), 674–681 (1988)
10. Huang, C.Q., Ji, Y., et al.: A Semantic Web-based Personalized Learning Service Supported by On-line Course Resources. In: Proc. of the 6th Int'l Conf. on Networked Computing, pp. 1–7 (2010)

A Comprehensive Approch for Improving Chinese Computing Undergraduates' Entrepreneurial Spirits

Jun Huang and Ling-li Hang

College of Computer Engineering, China Jiliang University
Hangzhou, Zhejiang, China
huangyyll@163.com

Abstract. According current education statues in Chinese computing undergraduates' education, we carry out an "entrepreneurship education" program that instill entrepreneurial spirit, activities and knowledge in Computer Engineering students by integrating entrepreneurial education in our discipline-related education. The paper describe our experimenting approch based on the computer project-based active learning combined with an interactive entrepreneurial atmosphere and team work abilities, and discuss some exiting problems in developing computing entrepreneurship education at China's universities. Results from our first 3 years indicate the program enable students to be more proactive in improving their performance and retention, attitudes toward engineering as a curriculum and career, and levels of self-confidence. The critical factor for success in this approch are practice teaching and Second Classes, project-based learning and team work, etc.

Keywords: computing entrepreneurship education, practice teaching, Teamwork skill, China.

1 Introduction

In China, the field of computer science and technology plays a pivotal role in the rapid growth of China's economy through the training of a talented pool of scientists, engineers, and IT professionals. By the end of 2010, there were 600 universities that had departments of computer science running 900 computing related specialty programs, with total enrollment of over 450,000 undergraduates. In addition to these Computer Science and Technology programs, there were more than 10 computing related disciplines and nearly 2,010 related specialty programs with nearly 1,010,000 undergraduates [1]. However, the increasing enrollments also had brought adverse effects on the quality of education. Despite government statistics that show that there is a big shortage of IT professionals in China, the unemployment problem for the graduates from university grew significantly after 2008. Several reasons can be explained:

• Current computing curricula in China putted a strong emphasis on science and technology disciplines in theory. This is an essential requirement to prepare computing professionals with the analytical skills that a computing engineer must have. However this preparation on specific subject matters of computer field

M. Zhu (Ed.): ICCIC 2011, Part V, CCIS 235, pp. 268–274, 2011.

frequently is not accompanied by an effort to prepare students about equally important non-computing technical aspects of their profession. These shortcomings are particularly felt in relation to skills such as planning, organization and inter-personal communication. All this is further aggravated when they have to work within a team [2].

• Frequently, during their courses, students develop very little awareness about the outside world and the markets where they will be looking for a job or fighting to keep it, witch can jeopardize their future employability.

In addition, even though some students are employed, when starting his career, these graduates have to face serious behavioral mismatches and very limited knowledge about the activity sectors and businesses where they become involved.

Therefore, in order to remain competitive in the future for our computing students, there is a clear need for making some changes in computing education. The research presented in this paper describes our experiment that has been active for the last 3 years that attempts to address these shortcomings.

2 Our Experimenting Approch

According to Richard Felder [3], active and cooperative learning methods facilitate learning and skills development. Active learning means students do something in class "beyond simply listening and watching". Through discussion, questioning, arguing and brainstorming, students engage in active experimentation and reflective observation, key aspects of effective learning [4].

China Jiliang University is a regional university of regular undergraduate education for quality supervision, inspection and quarantine in China, located in Hangzhou, Zhejiang. The department of Computer Science and Technology (CST) at the University has one of the highest student enrolments in undergraduate courses in the university. In order to heighten innovation and entrepreneurship in computing to undergraduate students as part of their learning environment, we have carry out "entrepreneurship education" program that instill entrepreneurial spirit, activities and knowledge in Computer Science and Technology students by integrating entrepreneurial education in our discipline-related education. Our basic approach is based on the following components:

• Team-based projects that focus on real-world problems;
• Definition of project ideas made with the contributions of practicing computing engineers from several companies that are invited to present some of their IT real-work challenges.
• Projects designed around a situation where teams play the role of competing companies in a market place.
• Faced with a specific challenge (as will be outlined ahead in the paper) each team tries to identify possible solutions and must make its evaluation, both in technical and economical terms.
• Chosen solutions must be converted into a business case, with different teams playing the roles of competing companies in a marketplace.

The key factors for success in this program are project-based active learning combined with an interactive entrepreneurial atmosphere and team work abilities. Results from our last 3 years indicate the program is effective for increasing students' interest in entrepreneurial intentions, which enable students to be more proactive in improving their performance and retention, attitudes toward engineering as a curriculum and career, and levels of self-confidence.

3   Practice Teaching and Second Classes

Practice teaching (including experiments, graduation practice and graduation thesis or design) is one important teaching aspect in the entrepreneurial education for our Computer Science and Technology students, which can improve students' talents, experience, and ways of learning and encourage their interaction and collaboration with their faculty and students. In the experimental teaching, we have reduced the verification experiments, increased the design experiment, to develop students entrepreneurial qualities and abilities. Specialized courses designed experiments is to require students divide into several groups, each student of group are required to construct solutions to designing problems. The role of the teacher is to act as a guide and facilitator of learning by directing the students' thinking in the right direction. Learning programming is an iterative process with continuous refinements, revisions, modifications, and reuse of previous solutions and examples that was constructed before. Normally, students spend a considerable amount of time performing designing activities. In addition, they have to explain, reflect on, and summarize the solution process to the teacher.

In the Database System designing course, for example, teacher first introduce several enterprises for the object oriented conceptual modeling that are used throughout the course to illustrate various concepts, then illustrate the modeling of the data relationships and constraints by Side-by-side EER and UML diagrams of these enterprises and provided mappings of these enterprises in the various implementation data models. In order to give the students the opportunity to fully explore the use of such technology for the development of database applications, students are required to divide into several team groups and implement a simple Databases-Web project. The only requirement for choosing the appropriate Web technology and database is that the students must chooses an enterprise and provides a real-time demonstration of their interface in class. In the first phase, the students work in groups to design and implement the enterprise in the relational database of their choice. Students are required to have both an EER and UML conceptual design of their enterprise. In the second phase, students work in groups to choose the Web technology that the group will use and to design a common look and feel for the Web forms. In the last, students are required to implement a Web form that illustrates select, insert, update, and delete access to the underlying database. This experimental model of education can not only guide students to think independently and take the initiative, but also can encourage them to dare to explore and innovate.

Another example is the Software Engineering designing course which requires students develop simple game software. The designing course was divided into three phases [5]. The first phases are design. In the design phase, students were provided with an opportunity to formulate their game ideas and learn about game design and able to develop the game concept prior to writing any of the actual code. The second is software development. The Integrated Development Environment is Microsoft Visual Studio. As with some other programs, we utilized cross-platform, non-proprietary APIs. Open Graphics Library (OpenGL) 3D graphics API was used for rendering and Open Audio Library (OpenAL) audio API was used for audio. The scripting language Lua was used for setting state variables. C and C++ were used for the programming languages. In the process of project development, Students were encouraged to use simple OpenGL primitives to represent their virtual worlds. The aim was for students to concentrate on the programmatic elements of building a game and not spend excessive time learning a specific modeling program. Students were discouraged to utilize modeling programs such as Maya, 3D Studio Max. During development, students were provided with several iterations of developing their game and receiving feedback on their game and were expected to use their prior knowledge of design and programming in to implement their designs. To foster a connection to the broader community and give students an opportunity to observe their game played by users, the users took a field trip. After receiving the feedback from the other users, the students are required to make change and submit the second prototype. Along with new version, a document detailing how the feedback was used in the updated prototype was needed. The last phase is product release which required students complete all documentation and present game demonstration. We dedicate 2 sessions to students to refine and release the games. A pre-release was submitted at the beginning to enable instructors to assess the progress of each group. The last session was our show and tell day. Each student presented his game to the class and was then allowed to play and critique each other's games. In lieu of a final exam, students were given 3 additional days to submit the final version of the game in DVD form, from which the game can be implemented and run automatically.

While giving much attention to the design experiment in classroom teaching, we also focus on a large number of second classes [6] through the entrepreneurial activities to increase student practical skills. The second class refers to the learning and life outside the classroom, practices, etc., mainly including participation in social practice, social work, participation in community organizations and so on. In order to enhance the second class effect, we have initiated the Undergraduate Vocation Social practicing Program every summer vacation. Besides our department often organizes students to form social practice teams, visit and participate in different IT enterprises, the students with entrepreneurial intentions are also encouraged to work in IT company, participate in company operating process and understand the enterprises research topics, their IT products, company managing process and the mode of financing. In order to enable these students to participate fully in enterprise without having to hold additional class learning, we provide significant advantages over doing social practice as part of the practicing course or project practicum course in summer period under the supervision of a computer science faculty member. Students who take part in social practice are required to have contract with the supervisor, specifying the practicing content and the means by which it will be assessed, and ensuring the least working time students participate in practicing activity besides.

4   Developing Teamwork and Communication Abilitiesas

Developing teamwork and communication skills is vital to personal and business success. The best approach to achieve teamwork ability is project-based learning, which places greater emphasis on targeting the learning of complex experiences, geared to an enterprise goal or objective. By adapting project-based learning methodology [7], the students can be guided to work on long-term challenges that involve enterprise problems. This helps students see the complexity and interdisciplinary aspects of enterprise in a more realistic fashion, helping them prepare more effectively for the real challenges ahead.

In the project-based learning, we focused on the technical and team-working aspects of entrepreneurship. In particular, we expect the students to be able to assess technical feasibility of business ideas, to make a simple budget plan based on complexity analysis, to make design decisions given business requirements through team discussion, and to experience different roles in a virtual enterprise environment. First, students are required to conduct a brief market research of computing industry and result in a business plan. They select their own teams based upon one another's interests and the type of project each student wanted to develop and form virtual start-up companies. Each virtual company adopts a simple company structure, consisting of CEO, project leader, and programmers. The CEO is responsible for keeping track of the company financial data. The project leader is responsible for defining the project tasks. Programmers bid for programming tasks. The team members are required to agree on what needs to be done and by whom. Each student then determines what he or she needs to do and takes responsibility to complete the tasks. They can be held accountable for their tasks, and they hold others accountable for theirs. During the project, students can switch roles in each stage, witch permit one student have opportunity to experience all the roles. During the project, a series of nine stages are used to cover topics such as: business idea assessment, virtual company organization, software engineering for start-ups, and business plan development. At the end of the project, all virtual companies manage to finish a prototype of the project.

In order to follow up and support to the teams, the professor met with the teams frequently, mainly to be informed about the individual and group performance, to promote reflexive thinking about their actions and decisions, and to analyze the technical and operational aspects of their ideas. During the meetings students also defined new tasks and goals, received orientation, materials and information, and fixed the goals and date for the following meeting. The way applied by the professor was fundamental to achieve real progresses at this stage. In addition, during the project, we often invite local entrepreneurs, venture capitalists and patent lawyers present talk to the students. These talks range from personal entrepreneurial experiences, to lectures on intellectual property. They expose all students to entrepreneurial activities, insight and knowledge.

In addition, in order to motivate student to committee to working together actively in project developing, in the evaluation on the students of project team learning achievements and grades on how well the he or she met the design requirements, not only the quantity and quality of individual work are required to assess, but the assessment would also include student individual teamwork skills and interacting ability.

5   Summary

Creativity and innovativeness are among the most essential attributes of computer graduates and also of successful IT entrepreneurs. Entrepreneurship, or the process of starting a new venture, is one of the main roads to new technological innovations. In past 3 years, our department developed entrepreneurship add-on modules for existing disciplines and implement the entrepreneurship education program, which have obtained the great effect in students self-confidence in entrepreneurship and entrepreneurial intentions. In addition, this module and program also foster creativity and innovative thinking of our students and significantly enhance students' lifelong ability and desire to innovate.

Conclusions expressed by students in their final reports revealed the following most frequent statements: a) Pride and satisfaction for the work done in the program; b) Self and group confidence to start up an small company after graduate from college; c) Development of deep friendship among members of team and teamwork skills; d) autonomous learning and creativity to find solutions; e) overcoming of their own limits and improvement of self-esteem and planning and organization of business.

Entrepreneurship education involves with multidisciplinary, many skills and strong technical factors. Besides, that the teachers' knowledge and experience about entrepreneurship education largely effect on our entrepreneurship education and that the contradiction between higher requirements for teachers' comprehensive quality and weaker faculty force is the main factor [8]. However, we must admit that College entrepreneurship education relatively lags behind in china at present, and the major reason is lack of the qualified teachers. First, our teachers have not yet sufficiently recognize about the importance of entrepreneurship education and unwilling to change their mind and adapt the new IT knowledge structure to cultivate students' basic quality about the professional knowledge revenue. Secondly, most of teachers who all along engaged with theory teach, have little entrepreneurship experience and entrepreneurial training and cannot guide student's entreprencurial practice, which also greatly restrict development of college entrepreneurship education. The last problems is that college entrepreneurship education is not formed the relatively mature theoretical entrepreneurial system and the frame in China, which cannot explain entreprencurial activity from the height of the theory, explore the emergence and development of entrepreneurship, or sketch out the general significance of successful experience. Base on the above problems, many literatures put forward many beneficial improvements and get initial results. We hope our practice in college entrepreneurship education can shed light on things and can do to minimize the likelihood of problematic entrepreneurship education in China.

References

1. Zhang, M., Lo, V.M.: Undergraduate Computer Science Education in China. In: SIGCSE 2010, Wisconsin, USA, March 10-13, pp. 396–400 (2010)
2. Smith, A.J., Collins, L.A., Hannon, P.D.: Embedding new entrepreneurship programmes in UK higher education institutions: challenges and considerations. Education+Training 46(8/9), 555–567 (2006)

3. Felder, R.M.: A longitudinal study of engineering student performance and retention. IV. Instructional methods and student responde to them. Journal of Engineering Education 84(4), 361–367 (1995)
4. de Oliveira, M.: Entrepreneurship Training: a case study in Engineering Students. In: International Conference on Engineering Education ICEE-2010, Gliwice, Poland, July 18-22, pp. 1–7 (2010)
5. Huang, J.: Improving Undergraduates' Teamwork Skills By Adapting Project-based Learning Methodology. In: The 5th International Conference on Computer Science & Education Hefei, China, August 24-27, pp. 652–655 (2010)
6. Gao, M.: Research of University Second Class Construction. Journal of Tangshan College 23(6), 90–94 (2010)
7. Thomas, J.W.: A review of research on project-based learning. Autodesk, San Rafael (2000), http://web.archive.org/web/20030812124529/www.k12reform.org/foundation/pbl/research/*
8. Wei, Y., Guo, W.: Construction of the Entrepreneurship Education Teachers Based on the Characteristics of Business Education Level. International Education Studies 3(2), 91–96 (2010)

Designing of Virtual Experiment Platform of Engineering Graphic in the Lab Based on VRML

Hong Zhao and Linlin Wang

School of Mechatronic Engineering,
China Jiliang University, Hangzhou, China
zhaoqiansun1213@163.com

Abstract. This paper analyzes the reasons why VRML is suitable for the designing of virtual experiment labs of Engineering Graphic and discusses about the scene of Virtual Experiment of Engineering Graphic and its designing process. Besides, the designing procedures of the virtual assembly experiments and the compiling VRML assembly programs are also illustrated by giving concrete examples. It shows that three-dimensional designed soft wares and VRML techniques used in the virtual assembly experiments will surely improve the authentic sense and the interaction of the models which is very valuable.

Keywords: virtual experiment in the lab, virtual assembly, VRML, engineering graphic.

1 Introduction

The method of experimental teaching has always been an important way of improving students' map interpretation ability in the teaching process of engineering graphics. In recent years, with the rapid development of software and hardware technology of computer and network as well as the emergence of VRML, it becomes possible to establish a virtual laboratory through networks. To simulate experiment process by adopting virtual reality, it enables students to complete experimental teaching through networks. It provides great convenience in cultivating students' spatial imagination ability, spatial thinking ability, practical ability, innovative ability and engineering consciousness.

2 The Features of VRML Applicable in Designing Engineering Graphics Online Virtual Laboratory

In accordance with the definition of Web 3D, VRML (Virtual Reality Modeling Language) is a kind of layout and content used for defining three-dimensional world. It is the only international standard of open language in building 3D multimedia and sharing virtual world up to now and we have no option but to choose VRML if we want to design a online three-dimensional virtual laboratory that complied with international standard. The reason why VRML is applicable to the design of online three-dimensional virtual laboratory also lies in the following features.

M. Zhu (Ed.): ICCIC 2011, Part V, CCIS 235, pp. 275–280, 2011.
© Springer-Verlag Berlin Heidelberg 2011

1. The establishment of VRML is based on the virtual world of internet. The application purpose of VRML is to realize three-dimensional effect in web page and the users interaction based on three-dimensional objects, to share 3D entity and scene through internet and to establish an interactive three-dimensional virtual laboratory [2].

2. Real dynamic interaction: The characteristics of graphic rendering of VRML is "real-time", it is also the biggest distinction between it and animation software. The object in the scene of VRML is not only "dynamic" but also "interactive".

3. The required page view of system configuration for lower client: The VRML file does not need too high system configuration. With only one Pentium II and a better 3D graphic accelerated card, it will meet the requirements of enjoying VRML world.

4. The technology applicable to the current status of networks: VRML faces to networks and develops with it. Its ingenuity lies in the fact that it only transmits VRML file (with a filename extension of ".wrl") with limited capacity, which means that it delivers only the model that describes scene and localizes the generation of animation frame.

5. Open international standard: The latest international standard of VRML is ISO/IEC-14772-1; 1997. As a matter of fat, VRML has now become the standard of data sharing and data publishing in fields of CAD, animation, 3D modeling software. Moreover, ISO has taken it as an important model of the development of future standard to develop and research it.

6. The function of script: Add programming language into Script node and set object behavior. Programming language is inclined to use Java; it may also use any other programming language that is supported by VRML explorer. And this lay a foundation for the interaction of complicated virtual experiments.

3   The Overall Design of Engineering Graphic Online Virtual Laboratory

The virtual laboratory mentioned in this chapter refers to laboratory facilities needed in the establishment of a distance learning system through network. It needs to build a site, which is the carrier of virtual laboratory space. I will make it clear through the example of building a simple website system as follows.

The Method and Needed Software Tools of Building Virtual Space: There are two methods of building virtual reality by VRML. The first one is to program a source code and generates into text file, and then convert to website file with a filename extension of ".wrl"; the second is to apply three-dimensional modeling software, we can build a three-dimensional object first and then assemble it in virtual world to form a verified and colorful virtual world. I will put emphasis on research of the second method, that is, to build all kinds of three-dimensional model in 3DStudio Max.

We can use VRML, 3D Studio MAX 3.0, Photo-shop6.0, FrontPage 2000, etc. as authoring tools in the system. Please pay special attention in reducing the occupying space of files as much as possible when modeling; first of all, guarantee to use modeling software applicable to the operation of network.

4 The Structural Design of Website

Website is composed of numerous HTML page and VRML node, it all depend on the actual needs. The home page will be linked with other pages through hyperlink button and hypertext link. Each experiment is a combination of virtual space and HTML content [3].Its structural relationship is shown in Figure 1

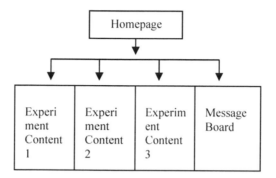

Fig. 1. The Structure of the System

5 Design the Scene of Virtual Experiment by VRML

Generally speaking, the virtual scene in the experiment includes real experiment backdrop and virtual model. For the making of virtual model, we consider the exterior appearance it shows to the experimenter, to be specific, its exterior geometrical features (length, width, height, color, etc.).

The method of modeling in virtual reality can be concluded into two categories: ① the method on the basis of 3D image; ② the method on the basis of ordinary image. The first method is to conduct the modeling and rendering of virtual environment by making full use of computer graphic technology; the second method is to produce virtual environment by application of image in multi-angle view, panoramic view and any other directions. For the virtual model in virtual experiment that needs an interactive object with experimenter, we can adopt the modeling method based on graphics.

There are two methods of building virtual reality by VRML: The first one is to program a source code and generates into text file, and then convert to website file with a filename extension of ".wrl", it can be done by text editor such as WordPad, Word etc,; the second one is to adopt assist modeling software, for example, 3DS MAX. We can build a three-dimensional object and assemble it in virtual world.

6 Build Virtual Experiment by VRML

Virtual experiment includes two categories: one is "demonstrative" experiment that only makes demonstration on experimental phenomena and the experimenter; the other is "operative" experiment, in which the experimenter participates in experiment and act as a leader. Nevertheless, the operative experiment can adopt many methods, for example, shoot real experiment with a camera and convert it into avoid other formats that is available for download and play. It can also demonstrated by flash or other multimedia software such as 3D animation [4].

The making of operative experiment is more complicated and mainly involves in two problems:

The Demonstration of Experimental Phenomenon. It means how to page-out a corresponding incidents, how the animation is activated and realized when any specific incident happens. In other way, it means the realization of animation. Virtual experimental phenomenon is mainly generated by interpolation animation, viewpoint animation and frame animation. Their application environment also differs according to their different operating principles. Viewpoint animation changes the location of surrounding landscape through changing the location of embodiment. Therefore, it is applicable to the case when there are many dimensional landscapes in the animation. Interpolation animation does not change the location of embodiment, but it changes the location of physical object. Therefore, it is applicable to the case when there are little dimensional landscapes in the animation.

The Realization of Virtual Model Operation. It means how to realize the interaction between users and virtual model.In order to make virtual experiment interactive, we can add that similar sensor node to ordinary shape node. Sensor node refers to the node that can feel all the operations of the user. Sensor reacts relying on the input device of the observer, and the most common input device is mouse. When the mouse of the observer moves to the virtual object equipped with sensor, the sensor will feel the mouse. Generally speaking, there are three types of actions that make sensor works, which are move, click and drag. These three types of actions will make the virtual object equipped with sensor change according to the actions of the observer, it is in this sense that interactive virtual reality realizes.

The Realization of Engineering Graphic Networks Virtual Assembly Experiment

Preparation of Virtual Assembly Experiment: The teacher can alternate three-dimension software teaching such as Pro/ENGINEER during the teaching of engineering drawing in the second semester to students of mechanical majors and enable the students to complete simple assembly of work under the assistance of teachers after about one course of VRML program explanation.

In the following comprehensive perfective course of engineering graphics, the teacher will ask the students to do three-dimensional →two-dimensional designing to most of the parts of gear box by adopting three-dimensional designing software, and to make corresponding virtual design and virtual assembly experiment.

Besides, the teacher can also adopt VRML virtual assembly demonstration in a large scale in the design of teaching courseware, through which it will improve teaching effectiveness, activate project atmosphere and strengthen the students' learning interest.

Design of Virtual Model: With the rapid development of network technology, the three-dimensional entity we designed is required to have a good adaptability to INTERNET and be able to communicate about three-dimension information on the

INTERNET. The design of virtual model, on the one hand, is required to express the inner and exterior structure shape of complicated models; on the other hand, it is required to express the components and assembly relationship of the mode. Consequently, we are required to take the following into consideration when making virtual models [5]:

The component of virtual model. For simple form, we can make an all-in-one three-dimensional model directly; for cut table entity, we should take cutting plane as boundary and make two treatments; for assembly form and complicated assemble form, we should build component parts respectively.

Steps of making virtual model. With the aid of three-dimensional design software, we can accurately build each parts of virtual model. If there are several graphics files are stored separately, they should bear the same coordinate system in order to make an accurate positioning. However, the graphics file generated in this way can not be opened directly by network browser and need to convert the format into VRML file with a filename extension of ".wrl", in order to transmit and browse on INTERNET conveniently.

How to endow virtual mode with dynamic composition, dynamic separation and other virtual reality? In accordance with the international standard of VRML, we should make full use of the diverse function of VRML and edit the above-mentioned *.wrl file in text editing tool

Design of Reducer Virtual Assembly: Let's take reducer (see figure 2) as an example to expound the making of VRML virtual assembly model.

Fig. 2. Three-dimensioned Virtual Assembly Model for the Decelerator

Three-dimensional Modeling: Apply three-dimension designing software such as Solid works, Pro/ENGINEER and etc. to build structuring model for each part of reducer. Apply VRML output interface and generate VRML file with a filename extension of ".wrl". Modify *.wrl file to make a dynamic effect and control flow. In case that the output of three-dimensional software shows the VRML file of this reducer structure occupies too much space, we should reedit it. We should find the Shape {...} corresponding to case and gear, and then add animation, sound, optical properties, sensor function and etc. into the corresponding locations according to detailed design requirements.

Assembly of Virtual Scene: We can set 6 viewpoints in scene, namely "front view", "overhead view", "right view", "left view", "rear view", and "bottom view", of which "front view" is the default value in scene. When entering laboratory, it can realize the interaction of sound. By press "VIEW" button unceasingly of the browser, the scene will swift to different viewpoint. Finally, we can still apply "INLINE" node and page-out different models that have been finished and the hyperlink object to return homepage.By applying this system, the environment showed in front of the user is "touchable" and "walk able" just like in the real world and this is the rudiment of virtual laboratory. It is also possible to add into virtual space any experimental content as required.

7 Summary

There are several features of designing virtual engineering graphics laboratory by three-dimensional designing software and VRML: (1) it can create a best visual effect with low cost; (2) it is easy to learn the operation process; (3) the generated file is very small and it is convenient to make quick browse and transmission on the INTERNET. With the further combination of VRML with Java, HTML, virtual player and network database system, the method of virtual assembly laboratory will be widely used and rapidly developed. In one word, it is possible to crest an experimental environment of virtual reality based on VRML, and make modern distance learning based on network environment develop into a higher level.

References

1. Feng, k., Zuo, z.: Key Technology in Developing Web-Based Engineering Drawing CAI Software. In: CADDM, vol. 10(2), pp. 89–95 (December 2000)
2. Zhao, H., Wang, L.-l., Zheng, S.-y.: The analyzing and designing of virtual experiment of Engineering Graphic based on VRML. Journal of Science of Teachers' College and University 28, 33–38 (2008) (in Chinese)
3. Ge, W.-q., Wu, X., Xv, J.-c.: Study on parameter control realization of virtual experiment system for engineering graphics model. Journal of Shandong University of Technology (Science and Technology) 6, 43–48 (2006)
4. Xu, M.-f., Li, A.-j., Xiao, X.-m.: Study of experimental platform for engineering graphics model based on virtual reality. Machinery Design & Manufacture 8, 56–59 (2006) (in Chinese)
5. Qiu, L.-h., Ye, L., Huang, X.-f.: Design Method of Virtual Experiment of Engineering Graphics. Journal of Qingdao University of Science and Technology (Natural Science Edition) 5, 76–80 (2006) (in Chinese)

Cost Information Retrieval Model Based on Open Sources for Students Learning of Construction Cost Management

Wenfa Hu and Tingting Yu

1School of Economics and Management, Tongji University,
1239 Siping Road, Shanghai 200092, China
hu_yeahe@126.com

Abstract. Construction cost management course is currently one of the core courses in construction colleges. Since any construction project is so unique and complex that it is difficult for students to find out the right price in a short time during their learning of construction cost management course. This paper presents a cost information retrieval model based on distributed database which would search all kinds of construction cost and price data based on open online resources. By converting information from distributed database to data warehouse and data mining technique, the useful cost information from massive data is collected automatically and the trend of future prices and rates of construction can be predicted. This retrieval model can provide students more construction cost and price information than ever, and students can eventually estimate construction cost rapidly and correctly that is the core of construction cost management course.

Keywords: construction cost management, information retrieval, open sources, learning.

1 Introduction

The process of construction projects is essence in construction management. No matter the project owner or contractors, both of them hope to achieve the expected economic benefits in this deal. Most attention of project participants, however, will be focused on entire construction cost management. The purpose of the curriculum of construction cost management is to help students seek further professional and basic skills, familiar with the basic principle and method of the whole process of construction cost, master the use of labor, materials, machines consumption quota and the procedure of estimating construction budget.

The basic process of construction cost can be described as follows. Firstly complete the Bill of Quantities for the construction project. According to the construction on-site drawings, calculate the amount of each list items. Then verify accurately the final project cost based on the cost estimation information that obtains from all practical resources. Among them, it is the most important to estimate the unit price correctly, the construction cost is combined with the selection of labor, materials, machines unit price. Unreasonable cost information is overwhelmingly likely to reduce the accuracy of project costs.

M. Zhu (Ed.): ICCIC 2011, Part V, CCIS 235, pp. 281–287, 2011.
© Springer-Verlag Berlin Heidelberg 2011

The main characteristics of current project cost information are market-oriented and special. There are two main reasons. Under the pattern of pricing through Bill of Quantities, the project cost information is mainly from the enterprise internal economic measure, settlement material and the master of the market. Because of variety of work procedure and productivity, the cost control system and risk-bearing capacity in different construction enterprise changes and different companies would suggest various price to clients based on themselves estimation and information. In addition, the innovation of modern construction technology promotes the construction productivity and management process optimization that accelerates the development of new construction materials. This dynamic cost information is an obstacle for students to learn construction cost management course.

Current open web resources have created a good learning platform for students. Through this platform, a large amount of construction cost information including price information issued by local cost management departments, quotes of building materials manufactures online, other information from market research and so on, could be searched. To face numerous and jumbled cost information, students feel it hard to make their decisions. In fact, construction cost changes with the market, and it is not fixed set of data, so the cost information demands for dynamic management. Therefore, it is possible for students to find reasonable information in the course of learning process through applying computer information technology to manage the construction cost information.

2   The Construction Cost Information Distributed Database Model

Database is a warehouse which is used to organize, store and manage data according to its structure. The construction cost information distributed database is a process of collecting, processing, analyzing and releasing construction cost data. The establishment of this database can be mainly divided into three parts: data requirement analysis, conceptual model of distributed database design and the logical model of distributed database design.

Data Requirement Analysis. The main task of data requirement analysis is to explicit type, range, quantity and practical application of all kinds of cost information required in the valuation course according to the actual use demand.

The construction cost information distributed database is established for the purpose of providing students with cost information required in the construction cost management course and solving the problem of inquiry difficult. Data stored in the database should first reflect price information comprehensively and then must be constantly updated and supplemented in order to ensure the timeliness of information. Cost information of built construction has great value of reference, so it also should be included in the database.

In summary, the data in need basically has the following three categories: market cost information promulgated by the departments of each district project cost management; price information issued on construction related website and collection of historical data.

The Conceptual Model of Distributed Database Design. Based on the classification, collection and generalization of various construction cost information, the database conceptual model design is the process of establishing the abstract concept of data model. This conceptual model reflects structure of actual construction cost information, cost information flow and the relationship between cost information from different sources etc. The key point of the conceptual model design is not specific implementation details on the computer, but a kind of abstract form. According to this concept, the paper presents a conceptual model shown in figure 1.

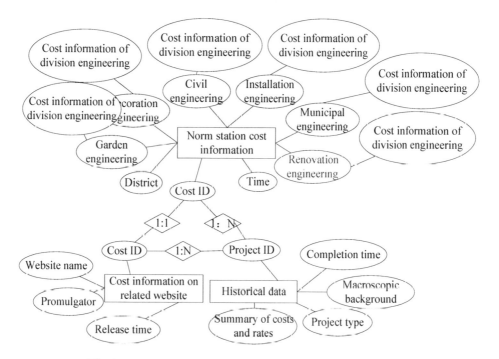

Fig. 1. Conceptual model of construction cost distributed database

Among them, the cost ID and project ID is three entities foreign key. Since built projects contain multiple cost information, it is in a one-to-many relationship with other entities. At the same time, we define a one-to-one relationship between Norm station cost information and Cost information on related website.

The Logical Model of Distributed Database Design. The main job of logical model design is to design the database conceptual model into a kind of logic mode, namely adaption to a sort of logical data model supported by a particular database management system.

Based on designed conceptual model, the task of logical model is to realize users' needs by utilizing DBMS and further convert concept structure for the corresponding data model. The specific practices are as follows. An entity is converted to a relationship model. Attributes of entities are attributes of relationships, code of entities are code of relationships. A contact is converted to a relationship model. The code of each entity which connected with a contact and the attributes of the contact both convert to the attributes of the relationship.

Relationship Model of Cost Information on Related Website Entities. Cost information on related website entity mainly provides cost information of all kinds of construction on the website. In order to reflect detailed background of the information, we have designed three branch tables: Website name; Promulgator; Release time. It is convenient for users to understand the sources of data and evaluate reliability. The relationship model between different cost tables is shown in figure 2.

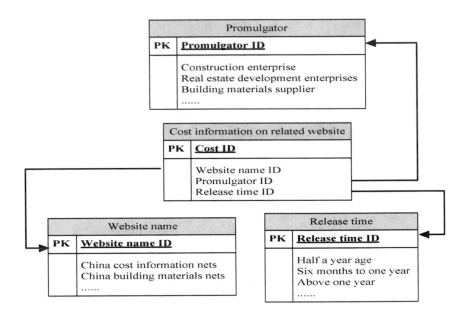

Fig. 2. Relationship model of each table in cost information on related website entity

Relationship Model of Quota Cost Information Entities. First, design a norm station cost information table to record construction cost information released by the station. Then design eight branch tables to reflect specific information contents. They are civil construction cost information table, installation construction cost information table, decoration construction cost information table, municipal construction cost information table, garden construction cost information table, renovation construction cost information table, timetable and district table. At last, design division construction cost information targeting the first six tables. So, quota cost information will be classified orderly.

Parts of quota information are listed as example in figure 3.

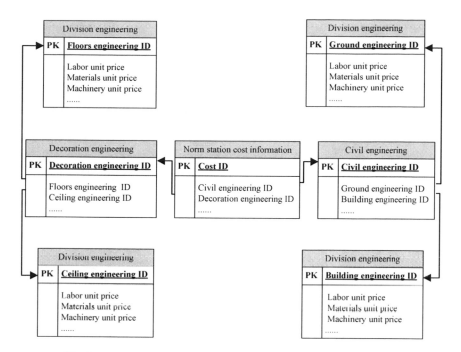

Fig. 3. Relationship model of quota cost information between entities

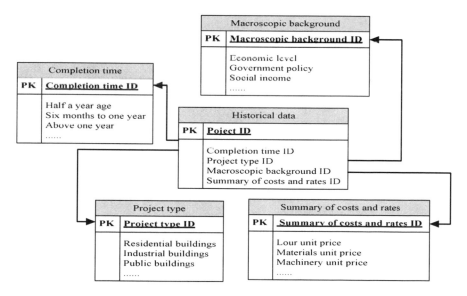

Fig. 4. Relationship model of historical data between entities

Relationship Model of Historical Data Entities. Historical data entity consists of one piece of base table and four pieces of branch tables, respectively records completion time, macroscopic background, project type and summary of costs and rates. The objective of this design aims at making full use of historical data and accumulating construction experience, laying the foundation of data mining, shown in figure 4.

3   The Construction Cost Information Data Mining System

The establishment of construction cost information database has an important meaning for students leaning of construction cost management. On the basis of this database, we can still further establish data warehouse and data mining to get more knowledge.

Data mining is the non-trivial process of obtaining effective, novel, potentially useful and ultimately comprehensible pattern from a large amount of data stored in database, data warehouse or other information database. It can further power the function of database and find existing various useful information. The data mining system is suggested in figure 5. Cooperation of data mining and data warehouse, on the one hand, can simplify the process of data mining and improve the efficiency of data mining and ability. On the other hand, the data mining technology has become a very important and relatively independent aspects and tool in the data warehouse application.

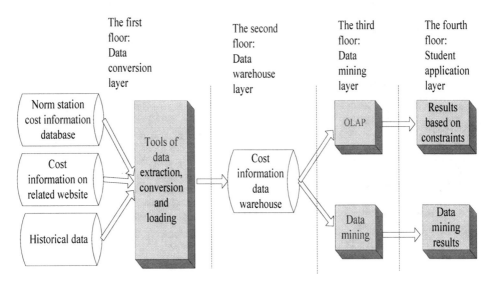

Fig. 5. Data mining system

The methods of data mining analysis are: classification, valuation, forecasting, gathering, description and visualization, etc. These methods have certain value for construction cost dynamic management, avoiding the situation of "data mass, information scarce".

4   Conclusion

Along with the popularization and application of the quantities-bill-based pricing mode, we propose setting up the construction cost information database as an effective solution to the problems students faced with during their learning construction cost management. Through classification and summary of the data, we can find out internal relations. Thus, the combination of open network resources and historical data could improve the efficiency of searching information. It helps students quickly grasp the entire process of construction quotation and lay a solid foundation of major study.

References

1. Kiziltas, S., Akinci, B.: Automated generation of customized field data collection templates to support information needs of cost estimators. Journal of Computing in Civil Engineering 24(129), 129–139 (2010)
2. Terzis, V.: The acceptance and use of computer based assessment. Computers and Education 56(4), 1032–1044 (2010)
3. Lu, G., Lu, P., Liu, C.: Studying on construction programs of the platform of primary products marketing. IFIP Advances in Information and Communication Technology 346, 8–13 (2011)
4. Moon, S.W., Kim, J.S., Kwon, K.N.: Effectiveness of OLAP-based cost data management in construction cost estimate. Automation in Construction 16(3), 336–344 (2007)
5. Wright, M.G., William, T.P.: Using bidding statistics to predict completed construction cost. Engineering Economist 46, 114–128 (2001)
6. Fujii, K., Yoshida, K., Okuyama, N., Kawakami, S., Hayashi, H., Ishiro, Y.: Study on construction cost evaluation method of fuel cycle facilities. Transactions of the American Nuclear Society 91, 514–515 (2004)
7. Valerdi, R.: Heuristics for Systems Engineering Cost Estimation. IEEE Systems Journal 5(1), 91–98 (2011)
8. Sabiquero, A., Baice, A., Viho, C.: Automatic CoDec generation to reduce test engineering cost. International Journal on Software Tools for Technology Transfer 10(4), 337–346 (2008)
9. Zeng, Q., Wan, L., Xiong, G., Zhou, J., He, S.: Product cost evaluation system in concurrent engineering. Journal of Tsinghua University (Science and Technology) 43, 406–409 (2003)
10. Frank, F., Randolph, K., Richard, R.: Process cost modeling: Strategic engineering and economic evaluation of Materials technologies. JOM 59(10), 21–32 (2007)
11. Lane, J.A., Boehm, B.: System-of-systems cost estimation:analysis of lead system integrator engineering activities. Information Resourse Management Journal 20(2), 23–32 (2007)
12. Leunq, M.-Y., Skitmore, M., Chan, Y.S.: Subjective and objective stress in construction cost estimation. Construction Management and Economics 25(10), 1063–1075 (2007)

Visualization and Collaboration of On-Site Environments Based on Building Information Model for Construction Project Class

Wenfa Hu and Shuting Guo

School of Economics and Management, Tongji University,
1239 Siping Road, Shanghai 200092, China
hu_yeahe@126.com

Abstract. Construction project course is a highly integrated and practical curriculum in construction management program of Civil Engineering department, in which students should understand comprehensive knowledge relevant to construction sites. However, in the traditional learning process, students are always lack of intuitive awareness and understanding of the practical engineering knowledge for lack of effective experiments or internship opportunities. It is difficult for students to grasp the knowledge learnt from the class. This paper presents a model that can offer the students a visual construction site environment based on Building Information Model (BIM) by use of computer technology, which provides students with a practical platform and collaborative learning environment. By studying and practicing on this platform, students can comprehensively grasp the knowledge learning from the class and enhance their professionalism.

Keywords: Construction project course, Building Information Model (BIM), simulation construction site, collaborative learning.

1 Introduction

Construction Project course is a highly integrated and applied curriculum. Its main task is to train students to master the ability to plan, organize, command and control the whole construction project and the ability to coordinate with the others during the whole process. Students had better combine the knowledge they learn from this class with specific construction projects and directly participate in the whole project management activities in order to truly develop their practice skills, collaboration skills, adaptability and innovation.

Construction project has the characteristics of one-time and long production cycle time, which require students to have a long and specific internship period on the construction site. However, students' practice time and free time is limited, which makes students always miss the effective experimental / internship opportunities. So after they finish the construction project course, most of them are only armchair strategists who can't take advantage of the theoretical knowledge learning from the class to solve real problems and lack the capabilities to communicate and collaborate with the parties involved with the construction project.

M. Zhu (Ed.): ICCIC 2011, Part V, CCIS 235, pp. 288–295, 2011.

Based on the problem, this paper establishes a model that can offer the students visual construction project site environment based on Building Information Model (BIM), which provides a practical platform for studying this course. This model can easily build three-dimensional structures that can enhance students' awareness and understanding of the real construction project. Students can also effectively participate in the activities of construction project in this model. By practicing on this platform, students can develop their capacity to analyze and solve problems and their skills to communicate and collaborate with the others. Therefore, they can master the knowledge learning from the class more effectively.

2 Principles of Building Information Model (BIM)

Definition of BIM. Building Information Modeling (BIM) represents the process of development and use of a computer generated model to simulate the planning, design, construction and operation of a construction project. The resulting model is a data-rich, object-oriented, intelligent and parametric digital representation of the construction project, from which views and data appropriate to various users' needs can be extracted and analyzed to generate information that can be used to make decisions and to improve the process of delivering the construction project. As a new computer technology, Building Information Modeling (BIM) brings the construction industry more intelligence software that extends from CAD to project cost software, schedule software, service equipment management software etc, based on which the efficiency of information transmission can be highly improved.

The Advantages of BIM. There are several advantages of BIM technique: (1) Visualization of the construction project. The key benefit of BIM is its accurate geometrical representation of the parts of a building in an integrated data environment.

(2) Improvement of coordination efficiency. BIM makes information sharing and exchange become smooth, timely and accurate and free from time and place restrictions.

(3) Simulation characteristics. BIM can not only simulate 3D building models, 4D schedule and 5D cost estimate but also simulate operation that isn't able to be operated in the real world, such as emergency evacuation simulation, simulated sunlight, heat transfer simulation, etc.

(4) Integrated management. BIM can integrate objective design, feasibility studies, decision-making, design and planning, supply, implementation of the control and operation management into an integrated management process..

(5) Full life-cycle management. BIM provides a platform for the parties involved in the construction to consider the process of project life-cycle, based on which, the participants manage to achieve the win-win situation and make the overall goal optimal.

The Disadvantages of BIM. There are many disadvantages in BIM: (1) It's difficult to determine the ownership of the BIM data and protect it through copyright and other laws for the lake of the related laws.

(2) It's difficult to determine who will control the entry of the data into the model and be responsible for any inaccuracies.

(3) BIM views the whole process of the construction project as the research object, which makes the construction industry require more professionals who have comprehensive ability and quality about construction projects. However, in the reality some professionals' ability and quality can not meet this new situation.

(4) The existing BIM software is so precise that the architects' design capabilities is limited in the early stages of building design, which hampers the creativity of architects to a certain extent.

3   Model of Visual Construction On-Site Environments Based on BIM

Introduction of Model of Visual Construction On-site Environments Based on BIM. The model of visual construction on-site environments can be built by using the technology of BIM. We can input the relevant information about the virtual construction project into this model and this model will show us the basic situation and characteristics about the construction project, such as 3D building models, environment around the buildings, the main construction site, main structure, temporary facilities, machinery and equipment, etc. The database of this model includes the information of design, materials and equipment, contract, quality, investment, schedule, operation and evaluation, based on which, the parties involved in the project (students group) is able to manage the virtual construction project on the computer. The participants should finish their work on time and input their work information into this model timely so that they can communicate and exchange information with each other at any time and make plan for themselves. This simulated system realizes real-time information sharing and exchange and highly improves the efficiency of collaboration. The model of construction on-site environments based on BIM is shown in Fig.1.

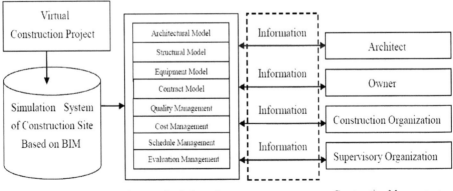

Fig. 1. Model of construction on-site environments based on BIM

The specific operation of model of visual construction on-site environments based on BIM during the construction project life the operation is as follows:

(1) The early stage and planning stage of the project. At this stage, the simulated system can form 3D building models, on which, pre-parties (students groups) involved in the construction project can carry out all aspects of simulation test and then make judgments about the feasibility of the project and determine the design amendments. The participants are able to acquire a series of excellent results ultimately such as ideal project design, accurate 3D models, pre-documentation, etc.

(2) Project bidding phase. Students can write bidding documents and contract documents based on the information provided by the simulation system. And they should become familiar with the bidding process and different groups play different bidders. Then based on a number of open network operation, bidders (students groups) can simulate the process of bidding.

(3) Project construction phase. At this stage, construction organizations can carry out virtual construction in this simulation system. Firstly the construction project should be divided into small unites that are independent and easy to check by the software provided by the system. The WBS (Work Breakdown Structure) of the construction of the main structure is shown in Fig. 2. Secondly, the owner and the general contractor can communicate on-line to determine how to distribute the work to subcontractors (students groups). Thirdly, the contractors can carry out virtual construction. In the process of the virtual construction, the model would show the information about progress, cost requirements of the qualities simultaneously. So the owner, the contractor and the architect can communicate timely and make decisions together in order to optimize the construction program.

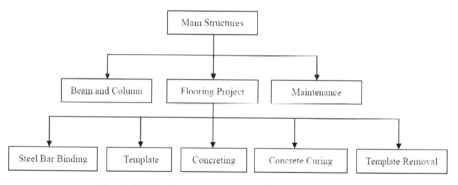

Fig. 2. WBS of the construction of the main structure

(4) The operational phase of the project. After the completion of the project, the model can simulate the operation of the project, which helps students to understand the operations of the building.

The Development of the Model of Visual Construction On-site Environments Based on BIM. (1) Establishment of the construction database. The database is consisted of four parts, namely, construction resource information, construction equipment information, construction materials information and project cost information, which can be updated in real time.

(2) Extraction of the proposed construction project. Users can inquiry and obtain the latest information from the construction database. Then they can extract the related information about the proposed construction project.

(3) Establishment of the model. Users can input the information into the BIM and the information can be integrated by BIM. The model of visual construction on-site environments can be built in the platform of BIM by professional software.

The process of the development of the model of visual construction on-site environments based on BIM is shown in Fig. 3.

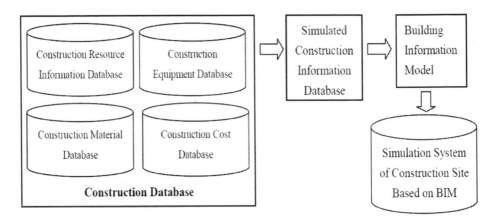

Fig. 3. Process of the development of the model based on BIM

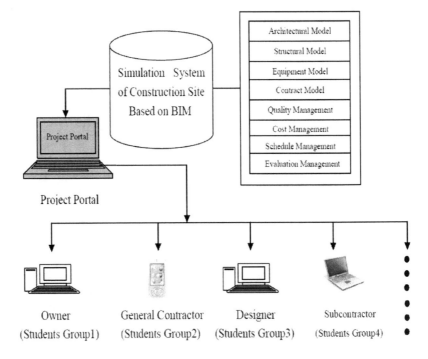

Fig. 4. Application of the model based on BIM

Application of the Model. The user sends the query request, information changes and other operation to the system server through the LAN (and even within the entire Internet). According to the definition of all the permissions of the user, the simulation system of construction site based on BIM integrate the information required by the user and send the information to the user. According to the operational processes and user rights the model can provide the information of the construction project from pre-project to the search point, based on which the user can operate on the computer interface. Therefore, students can participate in the construction project activities based on the model. The application of the model is shown in Fig. 4.

4 Simulation Teaching Based on the Model of Visual Construction On-site Environments

Distribution of Student's Role. The teacher divides the students into different groups according to the participants in the construction project and designates a leader for each group. Each leader is responsible for information management and coordinating the relationship among members in the group, and participates in the decision-makings of construction activities on behalf of the whole group. Each simulation group represents a participant involved in the construction projects. The following table is about the distribution of 30 students.

Table 1. Distribution of 30 students

Students Group	Construction Project Participants	Group Size
Students Group 1	Owner	3
Students Group 2	Architect	3
Students Group 3	General Contractor	3
Students Group 4	Subcontractor 1	6
Students Group 5	Subcontractor 2	6
Students Group 6	Subcontractor 3	6
Students Group 7	Supervisory Organization	3

Information Sharing and Communication. In the simulation system, students can feel like that they are working at the construction site. They are able to manage the whole process of the project dynamically by online bidding, online enquiries, online procurement, web conferencing, virtual construction, etc. The main work of each role is as follows.

(1) Students on behalf of the owners can make preparations for project proposals, feasibility report of the project, construction bidding documents and contract documents. The owners are able to get the information about the project schedule and the problems occurred in the process at any time. And they make decisions by communicating with the other participants through the network meetings.

(2) Students who represent the contractors can make constructions in the virtual system. And they can have discussions and communications with owners, designers and material suppliers at any time. And the contractors should import virtual simulation results into the modal at the same time.

(3) Students who represent the architects may provide owners with suggestions about the design after the discussions on whether the construction plans meet the requirements of construction processes and construction technology, so that the coordination between design and constructions can be realized.

(4) Students on behalf of the supervision organization help the owner examine the design drawings. During the construction process, they should supervise the contractor and report the information of construction progress and construction quality to the owner.

Information sharing and communication is as shown in Figure 5.

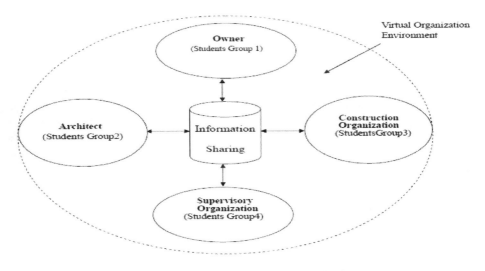

Fig. 5. Information sharing and communication

Meaning of the Usage of the Model of Construction On-site Environments Based On BIM in Construction Project Course. Project systems simulated by the model will show the entire process of construction dynamically and vividly. Students involved in the project system will play a role in the construction, so that they can immerse themselves in the project site environment, in which way can the process of teaching be interactive heuristic, collaborative and situated. And the students will have a good knowledge of what they have learned in class and improve themselves.

5   Conclusion

BIM has five characteristics, including visualization, coordination, simulation, optimization and easy to plot graphic design drawings. Based on BIM, this paper puts forward the model of construction on-site environments which can be applied to construction project education to make up for the shortage of students' internship experience and provide a effective practice platform and collaborative learning environment for the study of construction project course. By participating in the virtual construction activities, students not only improve their comprehensive ability but also acquire abilities of practical skills, collaboration skills, adaptability and innovation. Therefore, students can master the knowledge learning from the class more effectively.

References

1. Guo, Q.-j., Liu, H.-p.: Educational reform and practice in the course of engineering project management. Journal of Architectural Education in Institutions of Higher Learning 16(1), 85–89 (2007)
2. Feng, L., Lu, H.-m.: Blueprint of construction project management information system based on BIM. Construction Management Modernization (4), 362–366 (2009)
3. Han, S.H., Chin, K.H., Chae, M.J.: Evaluation of CITIS as a collaborative virtual organization for construction project management. Automation in Construction 16(2), 199–211 (2007)
4. Sacks, R., Radosavljevic, M., Barak, R.: Requirements for building information modeling based lean production management systems for construction. Automation Construction 19(5), 641–655 (2010)
5. Chau, K., Anson, M., Jhang, Z.: 4D dynamic construction management and visualization software. Automation in Construction 14, 512–524 (2005)
6. Sriprasert, E., Dawood, N.: Multi-constraint information management and visualisation for collaborative planning and control in construction. ITcon - IT in Construction 8, 341–366 (2003)
7. Zhang, J., Han, B., Li, J., Lu, W.: 4D visualization management of construction site. Construction Technology 35(10), 36–38 (2006)
8. Zhang, J., Wang, H.. A 4D~(++) site model and 4D management system for construction projects. China Civil Engineering Journal 36(3), 70–78 (2003)

Research on Macro Instructional Design of Electronic Technology Course for Different Major Vocational Students

(HVAC Major as an Example)

Li Shidong

Building Equipment Engineering Department,
School of Mechanical & Electrical Engineering,
Shenzhen Polytechnic, XiLi Lake, Nanshan District,
Shenzhen, China 518055
liwangmy@163.com

Abstract. Taking the teaching of electronic technology course for vocational students major in HVAC (Heating Ventilation and Air-Conditioning) as an example, this paper discussed the existing situation and its defect in macro instructional design, and illustrated a new macro instructional strategy which restructured the syllabus and pedagogy to solve the conflict between the students' limited leaning ability and the electronic skills required as a qualified HVAC professional.

Keywords: Macro Instructional Design, Electronics Course, HVAC, Vocational High Education.

1 The Existing Situation of Macro Instructional Design of the Electronic Course

In China it is well known that the learning ability of the vocational students enrolled in recent years declines swiftly due to the expansion of higher education enrollment, and their learning ability varies vastly with their majors and colleges. This situation causes a series of problems in the teaching of electronics course. Here we make a comparison to show what the problems are.

In brief the existing situation of macro instructional design of the electronic course for tree year vocational students is actually the 'compressed' version of the relevant electronics major undergraduate courses. In China it is called a 'Fortified Biscuits Version'.

M. Zhu (Ed.): ICCIC 2011, Part V, CCIS 235, pp. 296–303, 2011.
© Springer-Verlag Berlin Heidelberg 2011

Table 1. The comparisons of existing situation of the electronic course's macro instructional design

	undergraduate students & vocational students major in electronic	non-electronic major vocational college students ('compressed version of the left one')
Scope and depth of the course	Emphasize the integration of the deductive procedure of electronic theory as a branch of science, with full and profound course content.	Theoretical analysis is simplified in all chapters and conclusions are usually given directly, but most of the chapters are still retained to maintain the integrity as a branch of science.
Difference in practical learning class hours	Usually with several independent leading or follow-up practice courses such as "Production of Electronic Products" or "Electronic Production Technique" etc.	All experiments, mainly confirmatory ones, are retained in class hours, as students are non-electronic major, no additional leading or follow-up practice course is offered, so practical class hours are severely insufficient.
Difference in theory learning class hours	Usually the analog and digital electronics course are separate, with leading or follow-up laboratory courses, total learning hours up to 150~240 hrs.	The analog and digital electronics course are merged into one course, without leading or follow-up laboratory courses, total learning hours (including laboratory experiments) are less than 90 hrs.
Students' learning ability	Electronic major is a hot major; the university admission criterion is higher, so students usually have better learning ability and initiative.	Vocational college is a type of popularized high education; its students usually are less initiative in learning attitude with weaker manipulative and abstracting thinking ability.
The difficulty of learning	The content of course is wide and profound and difficult to learn, however the students have sufficient learning ability and class hours to tackle the difficulties they face.	Although the content of course is less profound and difficult to learn, the students lack sufficient initiative and learning ability to tackle the problem, what's worse, the class hours are by far less than the relevant undergraduate ones.

2 Why the Existing Teaching Situation of Electronics Can't Meet the Practical Needs

Although the 'compressed version' of macro instruction design for the electronics course does keep the most of the chapters to maintain the course's integrity as a science theory, it becomes an obstacle to teachers who want to individualize the syllabus and pedagogy in accordance with the students' learning ability and vocational demand, so the teaching quality still cannot be guaranteed.

Firstly, the inferior the students' learning ability, the less class hours they have. The 'compressed' macro instruction design of the electronic course claims to opposite the "jerry-built" teaching by insisting on keeping the most of the chapters to maintain the structure integrity of electronic course. But the practice shows that the students just cannot digest the knowledge the teachers try to feed them within the reduced class hours.

Secondly, the 'compressed' syllabus of the course can't individualize the teaching in accordance with the students' vocational demand as a non-electronic major. We find that the circuits for electronic major application focus on the high frequency signal processing, while the circuits for non-electronic major application focus on low frequency signal measurement and motor control. These two kinds of application differ so much in their circuits that this difference should have been reflected in the syllabus and pedagogy of the macro teaching design but actually it is not.

Thirdly, the 'compressed' or 'fortified biscuit' like electronics courses fail to meet the practical skill training demand for vocational students. As the theory teaching and experiment teaching hours are merged in one course, all the experiments are nothing but confirmatory experiments which are just designed to make the students believe the theories the teachers want to feed them. These experiments only require the student to connect discrete devices that are already fixed on a breadboard with circuit lines, and after that, to observe or record what will happen on oscilloscope. For those electronic major students, such confirmatory experiments might be sufficient for them as they will have some leading or follow-up practical courses such as Production of Electronics, etc. But for non-electronic major students, such confirmatory experiments obviously cannot offer the students adequate operative skills training which a skilled technician needs.

3   The Solution Is to Restructure the Macro Instruction Design (HVAC Major as an Example)

What is macro instruction design? It means what to teach and how to teach. Macro instruction design is the key factor for teaching quality. With optimized macro instruction design, even if several classes are not so satisfied, the course as a whole must be high quality. On the contrary, with an inferior macro instruction design even if every class is well organized, the course is nothing but a waste of time and efforts as a whole. We believe that this electronics course for non-electronic major vocational students needs an innovative macro instruction design, we take the HVAC major as an example to illustrate how the new macro teaching strategy should be.

4   Set a Proper Aim and Chose Most Useful Content for the Course

A Proper Teaching Aim. A proper teaching aim does not simply mean to lower the course standard, it means to individualize and optimize the course to fit the students and to adapt to their vocational requirements. We can't pretend that the vocational students have the same initiative and learning skill with their undergraduate peers, what we should do is to face it and to tackle the problem. We found that in many HVAC positions, the employers just want his people to judge the state of circuits or debug the circuits embedded in HVAC devices. So we adjust the aim of the course from obtaining the ability of circuit calculation and design to obtaining the ability of understanding and debugging the circuit.

The Scope of the Course. That scope should be carefully defined to meet the HVAC vocational requirements. Remember that we break free from the 'compressed' macro instruction design version does not mean we can eliminate the scope or content of course as we wish. On the contrary the scope and content should reflect the newest trend of corresponding industry (such as HVAC industry) and its commonly used techniques.

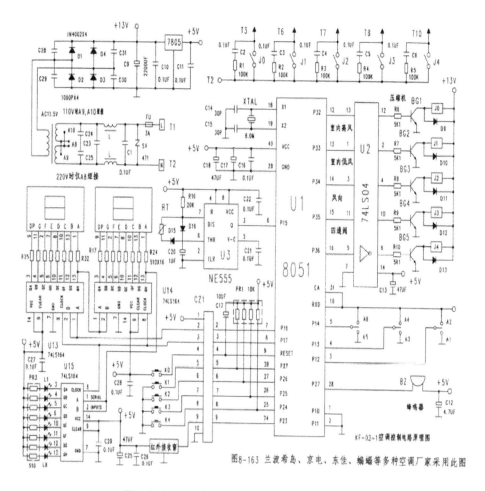

Fig. 1. A example of circuit for air conditioner [4]

Different vocations have different stresses on electronic application. Originally the electronics are use to process the audio video signals, later it is used mainly on digital AV devices, so the traditional electronic course are focused on how to detect, amplify, and transfer the analog or digital signals within an as wide as possible transmission band. But in HVAC industry the application is quite different, usually people are interested in how to detect a low frequency signal (such as temperature), the timer or counter, the logic or microprocessor control, alarming, AC-DC power, and most importantly the motor drive, etc [1][2][4]. So the content of the electric circuit are quite different from the traditional ones, it is mainly based on IC chips rather than discrete device, digital or MPU control circuit rather than analog circuit, with typical AD-DC power and motor driver units. Even if there are some analog circuit elements, they are limited to several applications like AC-DC power and Operational amplifier based low frequency signal processing.(refer to figure 1[4]) .

Table 2. The macro instruction design of electronics for HVAC major (contents to be cut or to be retained)

contents	Macro instructional design of the course for undergraduate students or vocational electronics major students	Macro instructional design of electronics course for HVAC major vocational students we prefer.	The basis or reason of our choice (application background of electronics in HVAC industry)
Focal points of Analog electronics	1) Physics of Semiconductor Devices	1) for the semiconductor devices, we only focus on its external features。	We believe the students are most likely to be a technician or engineer rather than a scientist.
	2) Amplifier circuit Teaching. The basic amplifier circuit including discrete devices (including the common emitter, common base, common collector), multi-stage amplifier, power amplifier, negative feedback circuit, and differential amplifier circuit, oscillator circuit.	2)Amplifier circuit Teaching: Simplify the teaching of discrete device circuits, only include the basic common emitter amplifier, multi-stage amplifier circuit, and differential amplifier, focus on the external characteristics of an amplifier, simplify or cut the teaching of the feedback circuit, power amplifier, and oscillation circuit.	The power amplifier, negative feedback circuit analysis, oscillation circuit and other discrete devices units, are mainly used to detect and amplify the AV signal in an as wide as possible transmission band-width with lest distortion, and these are difficult to the students. But, in HVAC applications, such circuits are not commonly used circuit.
	3) circuit based on OP amplifier ICs.	3)this is one of the focal points of our course. Many examples are given and discussed.	The circuits based on OP amp ICs are widely used in HVAC facilities for temperature s.
	4) voltage regulator and power supply circuits。	4) we are only interested in the application of IC based power circuits.	The power circuits based on regulator ICs are widely used in HVAC facilities.
Focal points of digital electronics	Number system and codes, logic algebra and function, logic gates, combinational logic and sequential logic circuit, bi-stable trigger, semiconductor memory	All contents are retained except the semiconductor memory. But teaching is more focused on case studies of typical application circuit, rather than design.	In the HVAC industry, digital circuits are more widely used than analog circuits. And it is lucky that digital circuits are easier to learn for the students, and they are more interesting.
Power electronics for motor drive	Usually they are not included in electronics course, for some majors there will be a leading or follow-up course to deal with it.	Simply introduce some practical motor control circuits based on SCR, FET, GTO, IGBT, or solid-state relay device.	In the HVAC industry, motor drive electronic circuit is essential. But such an important part is usually ignored in existing teaching plans.

But the 'compressed' version syllabuses still focus on the discrete devices including the circuit theory and calculation. They claim to feed the student a full spectrum of theoretical knowledge, but actually such knowledge will most likely never be used in their future career. What is worse, learning such theoretical knowledge occupied the precious class hours which should have been used to enhance the most needed practical ability of understanding, assembling, debugging and maintenance of the circuits in HVAC facilities.

Our practice shows that, after restructuring the macro instruction design, the student can bypass the difficult contents such as power amplifier, negative feedback circuit, oscillator circuit, differential amplifier and focus on the most commonly used circuit elements such as power supply, op amp application, digital circuits and motor drive circuits. That means less difficult to learn with better learning quality and more adequate scope of knowledge they need in their future career.

5 Restructure the In-Class Practical Teaching

We classify the experiments into three breakdowns by purpose and teach in different way: the confirmatory experiments, skill proficiency enhancement experiments, and project coursework.

Table 3. The macro instruction design of electronics for HVAC major (experiments and practical teaching)

Practical teaching	Macro instructional design of electronics course for undergraduate students or vocational students major in electronics	Restructured macro instructional design of electronics course for HVAC major vocational students
Focal points of practical teaching	Focuses on training students in scientific experiments, engineering design capabilities, and the ability to design experiments to test hypotheses, or to complete complex product design.	Focuses on raising the ability to understand, implementation, and check an existing circuit design, focusing on product manufacturing, testing, commissioning, service, debugging or tests on existing design or products.
Confirmatory experiments	Confirmatory experiment teaching is carried out in laboratory. Confirmatory experiment teaching is separate from the theory teaching. As its teaching hours are not integrated into theory teaching hours.	Confirmatory experiment teaching is fulfilled with computer CAI simulation software (such as EWB), these experiments are interspersed throughout the theory teaching to greatly help the students understand the electronics theory.

Table 3. (*continued*)

Skill proficiency enhancement experiments	No skill proficiency enhancement oriented experiments, but each chapter has its own confirmatory experiment, usually up to 10 or more in whole course, such as the basic amplifier, multi-stage amplifier, the differential amplifier, the negative feedback circuit, the power amplifier, OP amp IC based circuit, power supply, the combinational logic (encoder and Decoder), counter (synchronous, asynchronous), 555 applications, ADDA conversion, etc.	Fewer experiments with more intensive basic skill training: 2~3 for analog electronics (basic amplifier circuit, OP amp IC application circuit, power supply), and 2~3 for digital electronics (combinational logic, counter and display, 555 applications, AD conversion). With fewer items, more time are allocated to each experiment to focus more on skill training, for example the skill of circuit production, use of instruments , circuit debugging, etc.
Projects Coursework	No project coursework in this course, but usually is included in follow-up courses.	An individualized project is assigned as after class coursework. Some circuit units can be directly from parts of real HVAC facilities.

The Confirmatory Experiments. They are designed to verify the theories students learned and give them a perceptual understanding. We integrate these experiments into theoretical class hours but only by CAI software simulation in PCs.

The skill proficiency enhancement experiments. They are designed to enhance the widely used electronics production skills. These skills include the ability to use instruments and tools, the ability of welding a circuit and circuit debugging. These skill proficiency enhancement laboratory experiments should be fewer but more efficient (refer to Table 3), emphasizing the proficient and standardized basic skills training.

The Projects Coursework. This is designed to integrate the knowledge and skills of the course as a whole to enhance their ability. There is only one project throughout the course, but what is essential is that the project should start from the beginning of the course step by step from design to production and commissioning. These self-driven projects are directed by teachers after class. These projects are individualized according to students' interest and ability.

Our class practice shows that interspersing the EWB simulation experiments into theory class hours helps the students a lot to understand the theories that are usually 'boring' to them. And the skill proficiency enhancement experiments are fewer but better organized, so the students can focus their limited time on fewer experiment items and more skill training. Thus they experience more success and less failure. That helps to solve the conflict between fewer class hours and too many experiments. And the project coursework is individualized to fit different students, many successful small and smart products are completed, that will help to boost their confidence.

6 Summary

We can conclude that the restructured macro instructional design of electronics course does help a lot to the HVAC major vocational students with diversity of learning ability. It solves the dilemma of limited class hours and high vocational requirement especially in practical skills.

References

1. Liu, S.: Maintenance of Refrigeration and Air Conditioning Equipment and Its Digital Circuit Technology. Xidian University Press (November 2003)
2. The Vocational Skills Certification Courses Textbook Editorial Committee "Refrigeration Equipment Maintenance Workers". China Labor Press (September 1996)
3. Chang, W.-p.: Research on teaching reform and practice in the course of electronic technology. Journal of Henan Mechanical and Electrical Engineering College (January 2004)
4. Yang, G., Yang, Y.: The Air-conditioner Maintenance and Its Microcomputer Circuits, p. 364. Xidian University Press (November 2000)

Some Consideration of Experiment Teaching and Practice of Biosystems Engineering

Ming Wei Shen[1], Fei Lin Hao[2,*], Yong He[1], and Lei Feng[1]

[1] College of Biosystems Engineering and Food Science,
Zhejiang University, 310029 Hangzhou, China
[2] College of Biology and Environment Engineering,
Zhejiang Shuren University, Hangzhou 310015, China

Abstract. Bio-systems engineering specialty is developed from traditional agricultural engineering science, and was first set up in Zhejiang University in 2002. The course and experimental system are gradually established and matured in recent years. To meet the requirement of practice ability improvement and analyze current status of experiment and practice system, three possible ways to extend the experimental and practice system are explored: (1) sharing the research lab facilities to extend the scope and depth of experimental teaching; (2) integrating design in course teaching; (3) co-operating with the company to participate in project implementation process, and engaging experienced technician as experimental and practice tutor. The possible measures are discussed and analyzed.

Keywords: Experiment teaching; practice; Biosystems engineering.

Introduction

Biosystems engineering specialty is first set up in China after incorporating four specialties of Agricultural Mechanical Engineering, Agricultural Electrization and Automation, Agricultural Water & Soil Engineering, Agricultural Bio-Environment and Energy Engineering, which are pertained to Agricultural Engineering Science. The Biosystems engineering specialty engages in area of biosystems and related environment, equipment and establishment, etc., and arms to resolve the engineering and technical problem that related to biosystems.

With the establishment of Biosystems engineering specialty, the subject is changed accordingly and further extended in scope and depth, the research area includes not only original Agricultural Engineering, but also stretches to Environment Engineering, Bio-medical Engineering, Aquiculture Engineering, etc., the education in Biosystems Engineering science aims to bring up the excellent personal with both biological knowledge background and engineering & technology theory and application ability. The Biosystems Engineering is application based specialty and stresses strongly on practice ability, so it has a high demand to practice-based teaching and experiment. In

---

* Corresponding author.

M. Zhu (Ed.): ICCIC 2011, Part V, CCIS 235, pp. 304–308, 2011.
© Springer-Verlag Berlin Heidelberg 2011

recent years, various subject based laboratory and experimental base are setup, and which are open to all teachers and students to encourage free research exploration of students. In the same time, the depth and scope of experiment teaching are further and consequently explored to enrich the subject content. Until now, experimental teaching system run smoothly and has gotten relatively good result. While comparing with counterparts in developed country and area such as in USA, Europe, Biosystems Engineering Science education in Zhejiang University is still lag behind both in experimental teaching and practice, the students still have difficult to adapt social work initially when graduating from University. Based on this, the cultivation mode related to experiment and practice teaching is discussed and investigated.

1 The Situation and Problem of Experimental Teaching and Practice Mode

At present, measures in experimental teaching and practice include: (1) a series of subject based labs are set up, such as "biological sensor and testing technique lab", "precision agriculture and 3S technology lab", "bio-production robot lab", "physical property of bio-material lab", etc., (2) practice bases inside and outside campus have been established, such as "protected agriculture production practice base", etc. These labs and practice bases have been established to meet the requirement of experiment teaching of corresponding subject, which are managed in open way and encourage free research of the undergraduate and graduate student, a team of full time technician are in charge of lab and practice base.

In an effort to rich the experiment teaching content, the experiment content are gradually developed to synthesized and exploration type of experiment teaching. The process is slow due to lack the equipment and facilities. Investment in experiment teaching is very much limited and have difficult to satisfy the need of further exploration of experiment teaching. Furth more, the time that allotted to experiment teaching and practice are low comparing with theoretical teaching in classroom, and is even lower in comparing with counterparts in other universities in developed country such as University of California, Davis of U.S.A, etc., they have assigned nearly equal time in theoretical and experiment teaching & practice, moreover, they arrange project design and discussion course for improvement of practice ability.

In practice bases inside of campus in Zhejiang University, it includes protected agriculture facilities, such as greenhouse, and it also has an agricultural mechanism display hall. The coverage of practice teaching mainly consists of Agricultural Bio-environment engineering, environment monitor and control, agricultural machinery, etc.. For practice base outside of campus, it main function is to provide a place for visiting and in-situ introduction for students, the cooperative project based practice teaching is rare and not arranged in subject system of Biosystems engineering.

2 The Construction and Expansion of the Experiment and Practice System

The training of bio-systems engineer begin with acquiring knowledge of mathematics, physics, chemistry, biology, etc., then learns and develops engineering analytical and comprehensive methodology, finally leads to application of knowledge and method to practice. In the process of experiment teaching and practice, the main objective is to improve analytical and design capabilities of the students. So, it is especially important to improve practice based teaching and which requires further extending experiment and practice spectrum. In consideration of current condition, the following proposals are proposed.

2.1 Share the Equipment and Facilities Resource of Research Lab to Expand the Experiment Teaching Scope

One of reason that limit experiment teaching expansion is the restricted investment both in equipment and facilities, most equipment of experiment teaching lab are old fashioned and function inadequately, which has difficult to meet the innovation experiment teaching requirement and free exploration need. Comparing with the limited investment in experiment teaching lab, the research lab has been developing fast in recent years with the abundance and multi-channel money support from research project, such as 211 projects, 985 projects and construction fund from government, provincial government, university and various enterprises. Some research labs have reached the first-rate establishment in China. It would be beneficial if the resource of the research lab could be shared in experiment teaching.

An attempt is taken in lab of "precision agriculture and 3S technology", the undergraduate students are led into the lab to do experiment. The result is rewarding and encouraging, on the one hand, the content of experiment teaching is widely expanded due to abundance and first rate equipment, it also provides chance for free and further exploration. On the other hand, the utilization ratio of equipment is improved, more students could have a chance to do experiments with high level and precise equipment, and get much deep understanding on the research frontier of biosystems engineering science, which could inspire interest in further study and research.

In utilization of research laboratory, it concerns not only in sharing the equipment and facilities, but also that content of the experiment teaching should be modulated correspondingly. So, in the subject arrangement concerning with experiment teaching, the technician in lab management (both from research lab and experiment teaching lab) should be included in discussion of experiment arrangement and give technical advice. There is another problem of management system, mechanism should be set up and optimized to encourage the manager of research lab to share the equipment and facilities.

There is another benefit in opening the research lab to undergraduate in experiment teaching, it is always have a lot graduate students in research lab, with the graduate student assistance in experimental teaching, the undergraduate could gradually lead to research work and foster interest of scientific research, which would further open view of students of Biosystems engineering science. The lab of "precision agriculture and 3S technology" has got excellent result both in content enrichment and interest cultivation in subsequent 3 years of operation.

2.2 Example Design and Discussion Are Systematically Included in Subject Teaching Practice

The expanding of experimental content largely depends on equipment and facility, sharing with research resource is one option to improve and extend experiment teaching. Another important aspect is to set up an application related design and discussion course, the objective is through introduction and analysis of practical example in Biosystems engineering field, the student gradually grasp basic idea and method in project design and implementation.

Nowadays, the teacher often employ unconsciously this practice in classroom teaching, and not regarding as an independent way of subject teaching, the degree it could be carried depends on interest, knowledge and experience of the teacher. So, in practice, some teacher may omit this aspect of content due to various reasons, such as lack of experience in real practice and knowledge, etc., which is even more that nowadays most teachers seldom have experience in real practice outside the campus and lack necessary technique to cope with student in example design and discussion.

Example design and discussion is a very important way as to give students the basic idea of project, and could enhance the understanding of the Biosystems engineering specialty, it also gives the students some basic notion of subject related project. So, for the application based specialty as Biosystems engineering, it should independently set up subjects that aim in example design and discussion of real project, and should not act in option way that depends on the teacher willingness. Once this kind of subject is established, it has different requirement of teacher in real practice experience. So, in addition to sending teacher to be trained in enterprise, some experiential technicians could be invited to assist in example design and discussion course.

2.3 Cooperative with Enterprises to Enhance Practice Teaching

Until now, there is no arrangement in sending student to enterprise to practice, it remains and limits on visiting the related enterprises for many years. The disadvantage is obvious, the students lack necessary knowledge in entering job market and have a comparative long period to adopt work because of absence of experience and training, especially most enterprises would prefer to recruit new staff with work experience. If some practice teaching is carried on in enterprise, it would be an advantage for job haunting of application based science as Biosystems engineering.

The problem lies in how to undertake cooperative working relation with enterprises; it could be through application of scientific research project in enterprise, and some experience technicians are invited as tutor in practice. In this way, the student could have a deep understanding of the real practice and gain experience and knowledge, the mechanism could be set up accordingly to ensure smooth operation in practice.

The practice could enhance subject learning and get a deep understanding of the Biosystems engineering science, and let the students has some knowledge of related work in future job market. In the process of carrying the project, the students could gradually learn skill of group cooperation, exchange and project management, etc., which are precise experience in their future work career.

3 Conclusion

Experiment teaching and practice is one of important aspect in subject learning, so, how to improve effect of experiment teaching and practice are worth studying especially for application based subject as Biosystems engineering.

The Biosystems engineering specialty in Zhejiang University is set up in 2002 after incorporating with four second grade science of agricultural engineering. Considering the development trend in developed country and to meet civil need in professional cultivation in field of Biosystems engineering science, the possible ways to extend experiment teaching and practice is discussed. (1) Share the equipment and facilities resource of research lab to expand the experiment teaching scope, (2) Example design and discussion are systematically included in subject teaching practice, (3) cooperative with enterprise to enhance practice teaching. Advices and consideration are presented in an attempt to construct and further perfect experiment teaching and practice, and to improve the quality of student cultivation of Biosystems engineering specialty.

References

1. Tu, C., Shen, M., Guo, Y.: The construction of experiment teaching and practice system of Biosystems engineering science, pp. 473–477. Undergraduate teaching reform and practice system construction of Zhejiang University (August 2007)
2. Hao, F., Shen, M.: Investigation of teaching problem of research oriented university. Chian Education Innovation Herald 594, 3 (2011)

A Performance Measurement System Based on BSC

Yan Peng[1] and Lijuan Zhou[2]

[1] School of Management, Capital Normal University Beijing 100089, China
[2] College of Information Engineering, Capital Normal University, Beijing, China 100048
liliode@sina.cn

Abstract. Balanced scorecard (BSC) provides an integrated view of overall organizational performance and strategic objectives. Using financial and non-financial measures, the Balanced Scorecard (BSC) approach appraises four dimensions of firm performance: customers, financial (or shareholders), learning and growth, and internal business processes. This research first summarized the evaluation indexes synthesized from the literature relating to HR(Human Resource) performance measurement. Then, indexes fit for Performance Evaluation can be selected from the system easily base on API indicator. Finally, BSC map is created to explore a new kind of performance management model.

Keywords: Strategic, Performance Measurement, Bayesian Networks.

1 Introduction

Measuring organizational success and implementing effective strategies for success represent continuous challenges for managers, researchers and consultants[1]. The wide varieties of industries rethinking their performance management and performance measurement systems, and the many performance measurement frameworks, theories and models that have emerged serve as testimony to the importance attached to developing comprehensive and effective measurement systems.

Many different theories and methods of performance for conducting an evaluation have been applied in various organizations for many years. These approaches include ratio analysis, total production analysis, regression analysis, Delphi analysis, Balanced Scorecard, Key Performance Indicator (KPI), Data Envelopment Analysis (DEA) and others[2]. However, empirical studies showed poor results on it's holistic claim; e.g. too many financial indicators, lack of systematically measured process results etc.[3]. The BSC is a comprehensive performance measurement framework[4]. Its comprehensive nature derives from the four interlinking perspectives that it encompasses: (1) financial perspective, (2) customer perspective, (3) internal perspective, and (4) learning and growth [5].

This study explores the extent to which the balanced scorecard (BSC) is understood and utilized by human resource (HR) managers within the IT company and, more specifically, the extent to which the scorecard's 'learning and growth' performance measures that are applied in the company. This research tries to establish a link between management theory and information management system. Finally, a Performance Measurement System based on BSC was established.

M. Zhu (Ed.): ICCIC 2011, Part V, CCIS 235, pp. 309–315, 2011.
© Springer-Verlag Berlin Heidelberg 2011

2 Related Work

In 1987, Johnson and Kaplan pointed out that the broad use of mainly financial performance measures did no longer support the requirements in changing competitive circum-stances to predict future performances relying on non-financial measures. In order to address these shortcomings, researchers and practitioners developed a couple of approaches. Balanced Scorecard is one of the most important and widely adopted performance measurement methods. But organizations with implemented scorecards face serious problems to model causalities due to tedious data extraction and maintenance of reliability problems. To overcome these issues, a software information management system can be used to establish cause-and-effect relationship map easily.

This section briefly reviews the underlying concepts adopted by this research, such as the definitions of performance evaluate index and Balanced Scorecard (BSC).

2.1 KPI

Performance measurement can be defined as a system by which a company monitors its daily operations and evaluates whether the company is attaining its objectives. Key performance indicator is a number or value which can be compared against an internal target, or an external target to give an indication of performance. That value can relate to data collected or calculated from any process or activity.[6] To fully utilize the function of performance measurement, it is suggested to set up a series of indexes which properly reflect the performance of a company. [7] Key Performance Indicators will differ depending on the organization. A business may have as one of its Key Performance Indicators the percentage of its income that comes from return customers. A school may focus its Key Performance Indicators on graduation rates of its students. A Customer Service Department may have as one of its Key Performance Indicators, in line with overall company KPIs, percentage of customer calls answered in the first minute. A Key Performance Indicator for a social service organization might be number of clients assisted during the year.[8] In order to be evaluated, KPIs are linked to target values, so that the value of the measure can be assessed as meeting expectations or not.[9] In selecting Key Performance Indicators, it is critical to limit them to those factors that are essential to the organization reaching its goals. It is also important to keep the number of Key Performance Indicators small just to keep everyone's attention focused on achieving the same KPIs.

2.2 The Balanced Scorecard

The BSC frame is based on four processes that bind the short-term activities to long-term objectives. The balanced scorecard is that employs performance metrics from financial, customer, business process, and technology perspectives. By combining these different perspectives, the balanced scorecard helps managers understand the interrelationships and tradeoffs between alternative performance dimensions and leads to improved decision making and problem solving.[10] It defines perspectives to measure these indicators: 'Financial', 'Client/ Beneficiary', 'Internal Processes', and 'Learning and Evolution' [11]. The basic concept is that good vision and strategy are absolutely necessary to reach the strategic success in the organization. These two elements must be modeled by the management team and have to be clearly transmitted to all factors in the organization, then to be continuously monitored. With BSC as the core of effective management system, the 4 angles are dependent. They are linked by a chain of relation between cause and effect that describes the strategy of enterprise. The adjustment of each single aspect may lead the improvement and adjustment of strategic goal. By 2004 about 57% of global companies were working with the balanced scorecard.[12] To construct and implement a Balanced Scorecard, managers should articulate the business's vision and strategy; Identify the performance categories that best link the business's vision and strategy to its results ; Establish objectives that support the business's vision and strategy;   Develop effective measures and meaningful standards, establishing both short-term milestones and long-term targets. Collect and analyze performance data and compare actual results with desired performance, etc.[13]

3   HR Performance Management System Based on BSC

Strategic appraisement and management are a relatively complex process, which concerned with the factors of each aspect, in strategic management system, it is very important to establish effective model. BSC technology is taking strategy as core. BSC extend Financial', 'Client/ Beneficiary', 'Internal Processes', and 'Learning and Evolution' 4 aspects sequentially to the local goal of relation between cause and effect, and then develop corresponding appraise index. However, for diversity, huge scale and complex structural organization, it is very difficult to comprehensive and explains strategy and the index of entire system clearly. This paper that uses systematic theory and information system technology to establishment 'decompose-mass' multilayer BSC map. Thus the system may meet each kind of diversity and large-scale organization, according with reality more, decision accuracy is higher, and forms dynamic strategic appraisement and management process.

The research goal of this project is taking computer technology and the method of BSC as foundation, create a convenient software system for the user, thus performance indexes can be easily be selected and BSC map would be built automatically. New strategic appraisement and management system can used to dissolve decidedly scheme, offer practical model, method and technology, serve for strategic decision. Project research from establishment strategic control model leaves, put forward and establish a kind of strategic control model based on BSC.

3.1   Establish BSC Map

The performance was divided into four dimensions: social dimension, supply chain dimension, organization performance dimension and subordinate dimension. Each dimension also divided into more detailed index. HRPMS have quoted the partition way of index in this model and made some adjustment for a part index. Fig.1 shows the Seller performance measurement model frame, and then derived the strategy map of their performance measurement (show as Fig 2(a)).

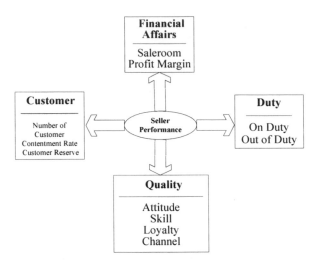

Fig. 1. Seller Performance Evaluation Model

The strategic and strategic map made clear with BSC establishment; Designing balance to tally the 3 crucial variables of card: Measure index (measures), measure standard (targets) and action plan (programs); Receiving establishment is multilayer to alter-granularity Bayesian network, implementing the analysis of cause-result and carry out feedback and mid-term adjustment and correction.

3.2 Performance Evaluation Index

After BSC established, users may select a long-term or short-term target, choose a key factor form main menu easily. When strategic picture is chosen, then the window will show as Fig.9(a). After related operation, the system would pop the HR Key Performance Indicators frame automatically, shown as Fig.9(b).

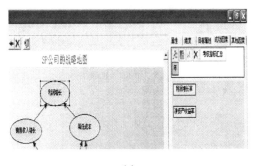

(a)

Fig. 2. KPI Function of System

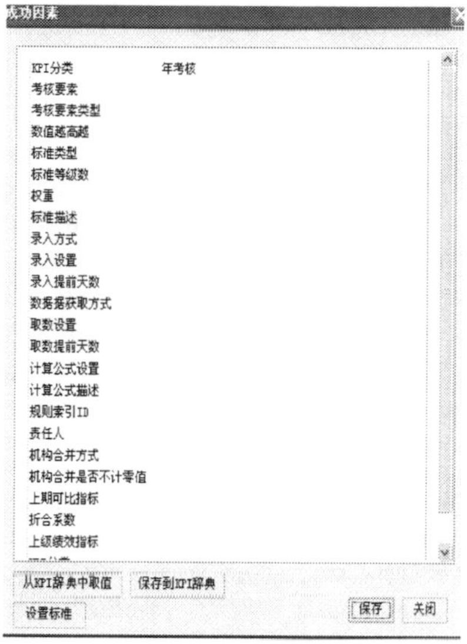

成功因素

KPI分类	年考核

考核要素
考核要素类型
数值越高越
标准类型
标准等级数
权重
标准描述
录入方式
录入设置
录入提前天数
数据是获取方式
取数设置
取数提前天数
计算公式设置
计算公式描述
规则索引ID
责任人
机构合并方式
机构合并是否不计零值
上期可比指标
折合系数
上级绩效指标

从KPI辞典中取值　保存到KPI辞典
设置标准　　　　　　　　　保存　关闭

(b)

Fig. 2. (*continued*)

System can not only complete and analyze the strategic goal of a enterprise / department, but also may decompose strategy into subt-target, then convert it into measureable Performance Measurement goal and action plan. And it can also do the effective enforcement management: System offers the functions include Performance plan check, Performance data collection and handling the data automatically. Then realize all-sided HR Performance Management.

3.3 BSC Performance Management System

The HR Performance Management System created based on the real practice of domestic enterprise Performance Management, with both qualitative analysis and quantitative check approaches. Users may set their crucial parameter of the enterprise internal process, then install a all-around performance measure process in which covered sampling, calculation and analysis, divided enterprise human resource performance measure goal into following indexes:

(1) System may realize various measurements: Month check, season check, year check, regular check and switch to a full member check.

(2) Constitute HR performance measurement plan in the system: multi-departments and multi- HR performance can be accomplished in one plan. Users may set the employee who you want to measure, and set up the content of measure notice in advance, issue timetable, issue performance measurement automatically. For the convenience arrangement on time and progress, system may generate performance measurement schedule automatically.

(3)   System issue measurement message to every employee according to the KPI or data access rules and issue timetable. The measure comment handled automatically by the system.

In a word, strategic decision is a relatively complex process, is concerned with each aspect of an enterprise. This software system program the comprehensive integrated models of quantitative calculation, expert qualitative analysis and intelligent technology, it can effectively avoid making decision only at one's will or misplay because lake of decision-making information. The use of the system would rising appraise, accuracy and scientific of performance management.

4 Conclusions

In this paper, we explore and establish a new kind of strategic control software system based on BSC. In this strategic management system, users may control the BSC strategic model in a convenient way. It is very convenient that with the aid of IT technology to control strategic management. In this special application, users can establish the balanced scorecard map automatically according to KPI which established by enterprise's decision-maker. The system with stronger self-study ability and self-adapt ability, model express and inference is more vertical, definite, thus make the entire systematic more flexible.

Acknowledgements. This work was supported in part by Natural Science Foundation of China, under contract N0. 61070050.

References

1. McPhaila, R., Heringtonb, C., Guildingc, C.: Human resource managers'perceptions of the applications and merit of the balanced scorecard in hotels. International Journal of Hospitality Management 27, 623–631 (2008)
2. Wu, H.-Y., et al.: A fuzzy MCDM approach for evaluating banking performance based on... Expert Systems with Applications (2009), doi:10.1016/j.eswa, 01.005
3. Kueng, P., Wettstein, T., List, B.: A Holistic Process Performance Analysis Through a Performance Data Warehouse. In: Proceedings of the Seventh Americas Conference on Information Systems (2001)
4. Kaplan, R.S., Norton, D.: The balanced scorecard measures that drive performance. Harvard Business Review 70(1), 71–79 (1992)
5. Kaplan, R.S., Norton, D.P.: Using the Balanced Scorecard as a Strategic Management System. Harvard Business Review 74(1), 75–85 (1996)
6. Munir Ahmada, M., Dhafrb, N.: Establishing and improving manufacturing performance measures. Robotics and Computer Integrated Manufacturing 18, 171–176 (2002)
7. Alemanni, M., Alessia, G.: Key performance indicators for PLM benefits evaluation: The Alcatel Alenia Space case study. Computers in Industry 59, 833–841 (2008)
8. John Reh, F.: How an organization defines and measures progress toward its goals, http://management.about.com/cs/generalmanagement/a/keyperfin dic.htm

9. Parmenter, D.: Key Performance Indicators. John Wiley & Sons, West Sussex (2007) ISBN 0-470-09588-1
10. Banker, R.D., Chang, H.: A balanced scorecard analysis of performance metrics. European Journal of Operational Research 154, 423–436 (2004)
11. Kaplan, R.S., Norton, D.P.: The Strategy Focused Organization. Strategy and Leadership 29, 41–42 (2001)
12. Ahn, H.: Applying the Balanced Scorecard Concept: A n Experience Report. Long Range Planning 34(34), 441–446 (2001)
13. Kaplan, R.S., Norto, D.P.: The Balanced Scorecard: Measures That Drive Performance. Harvard Business Review, 71–79 (July 2005)
14. Kaplan, R.S., Norton, D.P.: Strategy Maps: Converting Intangible Assets into Tangible Outcomes. Harvard Business School Press, Boston (2004)

Construction and Application of Simulation Experiment on "Port, Waterway and Coastal Engineering "

Wenbai Liu, Danda Shi, and Yibing Deng

College of Ocean Environment & Engineering,
Shanghai Maritime University,
1550 Haigang Av., Shanghai, 201306, P.R. China
Wen_33@yeah.net

Abstract. Construction and innovation of the platform of simulation experiment on "Port, Waterway and Coastal Engineering" is conducted to meet the requirements for constructing key disciplines, construction education highlands in Shanghai and training professionals for Shanghai international shipping center. The application of simulation experiment alters the traditional experimental education and leads to the revolution of the mode of teaching and learning. The framework of the platform consists of several sub-modules: display and analysis of the platform, software design and construction of a new platform of digital research. The specific discussion is given about the simulation experiments on soil mechanics and hydraulics. Simulation experiment is formed as integration by the simulation of the earlier stage, investigation, design, supervision and management of engineering, providing students with professional experiments and trainings of difference and improving the reform of experimental education system.

Keywords: Port, Waterway and Coastal Engineering, Simulation experiment, Framework, integration.

1   Introduction

Under the guidance of the project on constructing key disciplines and building education highlands, construction and innovation of the platform of simulation experiment on "Port, Waterway and Coastal Engineering" is conducted, including construction of simulation laboratory and training of senior laboratory personnel, to meet the demand for establishing subject groups in Shanghai Maritime University and training professionals for Shanghai international shipping center, the platform will become an important base to develop talents for building international shipping center in Shanghai including construction and design of ports and waterways. Also it meets the demand for developing teaching staff and doing scientific researches in support of declaring provincial and national projects basically. Construction of high-level simulation laboratory requires continuous study and practice in respect of knowledge, notion, framework, execution and supervision.

M. Zhu (Ed.): ICCIC 2011, Part V, CCIS 235, pp. 316–320, 2011.
© Springer-Verlag Berlin Heidelberg 2011

2 Construction of High-Level Laboratory

Recognition of the Status and Role of Laboratory

The laboratory in a university can be an important base for developing students' higher sense of innovation and creativity, doing scientific researches and developing science and technology, and one of the basic conditions for the university. The working level of laboratory can be regarded as an important sign which indicates the level of higher education, scientific research and management in the university. It can be said the level of laboratory is the level of university.

Important Base for Developing High-Quality and Innovative Talents

Developing talents is a fundamental task of building a high-level university. Teaching in the laboratory to carry out experiments and scientific experiments, is an important part of training creative talents. Experimental teaching enables students to consolidate and deepen their theoretical knowledge and develop their practical skills and ability to solve and analyze problems, training their rigorous, realistic and innovative style of work and scientific spirit.

Important Base to Carry Out Scientific Research

University laboratory building is an important part of discipline construction. For engineering disciplines, the level of the laboratory means the level of the discipline. While a laboratory with advanced facilities is interpreted as a condition necessary for opening up new areas of disciplines, developing frontier disciplines and training high-level talents.

3 Application of Simulation Technology to Experimental Teaching

With the development of computer virtual technology, the technology of simulation is applied by modern education to experimental teaching, called simulation experiment. The application of simulation experiment changes the traditional education mode, revolutionizing the way of teaching and learning[1]. The technology of simulation is applied to teaching experiment as a key to simulation experimental education.

The technology of simulation promote the reform of experimental teaching. Simulation experiment makes use of computer and the program of corresponding courses to complete the experiment. The experiment in simulation technology means from design to commissioning of pilot projects everything is realized in the computer's virtual environment, which reflects the flexibility of space and time and makes design and comprehensiveness experiment easy and feasible. Simulation experiment enables the laboratory to open and expand the scope of experiment, giving students more opportunities for experiments. In order to truly promote the use of the technology of simulation, technical and environmental conditions are no problem, the key problem is to change the concept, first of all is the change of teachers' concept. That requires training a team of high-quality laboratory personnel, continuous updating knowledge and promoting the collection, processing and application of experimental information. The construction of simulation experiment improves students' initiative and enthusiasm for experiments and injects new life and vitality into experimental teaching.

4 Thinking of Construction for Virtual Reality Laboratory

The Guidance of Construction of Simulation Experiment on "Port, Waterway and Coastal Engineering"

First of all is advancement. The starting point for port-waterway engineering lab should be high and be based on the latest developments in engineering technologies and experimental teaching methods, focusing on the integrated application of simulation technology and other new technologies. Secondly is economic principles. Port-waterway engineering is a huge system that laboratory configuration should follow basic and unique requirements and adhere to the principle of "quality be first with economic rationality". Thirdly is principle of comprehensiveness. A fairly complete simulation system of port-waterway engineering should be formed to provide undergraduate and postgraduate students with an advanced and innovative experimental environment, as well as practical teaching methods with integrated characteristics of fun and competitiveness. The teaching function of laboratory can be applied to many courses of engineering majors, like port-waterway engineering, traffic engineering and environmental engineering, which makes itself a base as the integration of scientific research, experiment, academic exchange, training for talents and discipline construction. Lastly is principle of practicality. Construction of research-based numerical simulation software of laboratory leads to the formation of experimental software series. It should be encouraged that to promote construction and reform of curriculum and raise the level of teachers so that construction of teaching staff could be improved.

Goal of the Construction of Port-Waterway Engineering Simulation Laboratory

The construction of port-waterway engineering simulation laboratory is conducted to build a bridge between practice and theory, to provide students with practical training platform, to deepen students' understanding of port-waterway engineering and to improve their operational capacity. The port-waterway engineering simulation lab in our university should be built into a multi-type structured teaching platform which includes a number of professions but is with port engineering at the core. Also it can be the platform of numerical simulation software and other simulation software for doing scientific research and carrying out experimental teaching. It can be used to carry out basic, comprehensive, design and innovative experiments, as well as experiments for scientific research.

5 Construction of Port-Waterway Engineering Simulation Experiment

The innovation of simulation experimental teaching and practical study, based on the construction of simulation experiment on "Port, Waterway and Coastal Engineering", is supported by the combination of the construction of key disciplines, teaching staff and educational highlands. The construction of simulation experiment on "Port, Waterway and Coastal Engineering" includes the formation of framework, the creation of each sub-module and display and analysis capabilities of simulation platform, the design of software, the construction of digital research platform and the realization of port-waterway engineering experimental integration.

Construction of Simulation Platform

Computer simulation technology is applied to experimental teaching, changing the traditional teaching mode and revolutionizing the way of teaching and learning[1]. Computer simulation technology is a brand-new experimental aids and an effective experimental tool which helps to develop comprehensive capability for innovation.

The port-waterway engineering simulation platform is made up of network, computer room, touch screen, display screen(including main screen and auxiliary screen), sand table, display cabinets, software, database and material collections. According to technology type, the sub-modules of simulation platform can be classified as follows, marine area demonstration, environmental assessment, natural disaster assessment, seismic hazard assessment, site selection(reconnaissance), project bidding, port project planning, preliminary investigation, preliminary design, detailed investigation, construction design, construction inspection, construction supervision, project management, project reported procedures, supervision and inspection of safety and quality, construction, completion and acceptance, operation and put to service, etc [2]. By structure type the sub-modules can be classified into wharf(long-pile, sheet-pile and gravity type), yard, coastal protection, etc. By cargo type the sub-modules can be classified into container terminal, bulk cargo terminal, general cargo terminal, dedicated wharf, etc.

The display and analysis function of simulation platform is classified into four levels. The first is display. The 3D-display of process of port-waterway engineering construction. The display of process, details, exterior, interior and operation. Each section can be displayed either one by one or individually. The second is display and analysis. Classified display and analysis is carried out by industry, profession and work type, or by professional course, internship and design. The third is analysis and study. This level has engineering investigation, project planning, structure calculation and analysis, flow field analysis, deformation field analysis, microscopic analysis, integration of analysis results and engineering design. The fourth is deepening of analysis and research which has structural analysis, fluid (water)-solid (structure) coupling analysis, fluid (gas)-stream (water)-solid (structure) coupling analysis, fluid (water)-solid (structure)-solid (rock and soil) coupling analysis, structural vibration analysis, geotechnical dynamic analysis and seismic response analysis.

Hardware configuration includes network equipment, display screen(main screen and auxiliary screen), touch screen, sand table, display cabinets, etc. Software program includes managing software supported by touch-screen, managing software of simulation platform and integration software(ABQUAS, FULENT, PFC2D, SWS-3, GEDOG, wharf structure design, slope design, Vinent). Port-waterway engineering simulation experiment platform includes functions of teaching experiment and scientific research while each function has a certain number of sub-modules.

Application of Computer Simulation to Soil Mechanics Experimental Teaching

Conception of Soil Mechanics Experiment Simulation System. The purpose of soil mechanics experiment is to figure out how to precisely determine various mechanical parameters of soil by experiments. Design of Soil Mechanics Experiment Simulation System must follow the law of experimental teaching which requires vividness, visibility, easy to operate and real time. By the mean of simulation with an effort, mechanical behavior of soil can be revealed. Soil Mechanics Experiment Simulation System is divided into two parts: First, multimedia presentation systems, and second, simulation program.

Virtual Teaching of Hydraulics Experiment

Hydraulics is a basic technical course in the study of port-waterway engineering. Strong visualization and practicality is characteristic of hydraulics laboratory equipment and apparatus. Take it for example that the basic principles and the experimental devices of head loss experiment, as well as the function of simulation apparatus and how to fulfill the function. In the process of the experiment, according to the design, data can be input either manually or automatically. The former is to input data into computer manually after getting the readings. The latter is to make use of corresponding sensors to collect data and transfer it to computer by the virtual instrument's A/D card.

6 Summary

Port-waterway engineering simulation experiment is formed as integration by the simulation of the earlier stage, investigation, design, supervision and management of engineering, providing students with professional experiments and trainings of difference, supporting science and technology services and technical trainings as well. Port-waterway engineering simulation lab, which will level up practice teaching on "Port, Waterway and Coastal Engineering", is highly professional. It intensifies the construction of comprehensive experiment platform and promotes the reform of experimental teaching system.

Acknowledgments. This material is based upon work supported by National Natural Science Foundation of China (Nos. 51078228 and 50909057) , Shanghai Municipal Education Commission of China through research project 07ZZ99, and Shanghai Maritime university of China through key discipline construction project A290209002. Shanghai 4th undergraduate education highlands construction project B210008G, Shanghai Maritime university Science Foundation(No. 20110000), Shanghai Maritime University teaching reform & management reform project in 2010.

References

1. Wei, W., Tao, W., Yan, Q.: Exploratory discussion on virtual laboratory teaching information platform system based on visual simulation technique. Experimental Technology and Management 27(3), 78–81 (2010)
2. Hong, C.: Port and Waterway Engineering Undergraduate Curriculum Reform. Higher Educational Research in Areas of Communications 1, 44–45, 94 (1998)

Integrated Construction of Engineering Skills and Academic Literacies for Undergraduates

Li Cheng, Fan Shangchun, Qian Zheng, Wan Congmei, and Liu Zhao

School of Instrument Science & Opto-electronics Engineering,
Beihang University, Beijing, 100191, China
Package_1@126.com

Abstract. The current development trends of international higher engineering education and related disadvantages in China are described. According to the medium and long-term educational reform and development program as well as outstanding engineer training program, an integrated construction of engineering skills and academic literacies is implemented. Its aim is to establish high-level teaching platforms and train high-quality innovative engineering personnel. Based on the core curriculum system of measurement and control technology and instrumentation in Beihang University, the multi-cultivation links are adopted, including national excellent course, hierarchical experiment, designing experiment and engineering practice. The accumulations of academic literacy and the developments of practical ability run through the whole education process. Then the effective combinations of classroom teaching, multi-hierarchical experiment and technological practice are achieved. These experiences will help to establish the training system for prospective high-level engineering innovative personnel.

Keywords: higher engineering education, engineering skill, academic literacy, undergraduate education.

1 Introduction

Since 90's of 20 centuries, the developed countries in the world have focused on the technical developments and talent qualities by adopting the characteristic talent training programs, such as K-12 educational programs including "Project Lead the Way", "Science for All Americans", "Benchmarks 2061" in USA, "Developing Russia Program" in Russia, "Center of Excellence (COE) Program" in Japan, "Brain Korea 21 (BK21) Program" in Korea, "Top University Program" in Singapore and etc [1-5]. This movement is so influential that it has acquired a global dimension. The impetus comes from industry needs and national sustainable developments. How does this apply to China? We have witnessed to dramatic changes in higher engineering education. Universities have had to adjust to a new training system for undergraduates and graduates. They have searched for new sources of funding and enterprises and involved professors and students into engineering practical activities. However, this phenomenon is not encouraging. On the one hand, China has the largest engineering

M. Zhu (Ed.): ICCIC 2011, Part V, CCIS 235, pp. 321–327, 2011.

educational scale in the world; on the other hand, many university graduates cannot be adapted to the enterprises. Moreover, the very qualities and attributes necessary for enhancing, educating and mentoring a creative spirit are in decline in important areas. There is also a recognition of a lack of engineering, critical thinking and problem solving skills in our education systems and a trend toward trying to enhance those skills. Thus, a medium and long-term educational reform and development program is issued in 2010 in China. According to the issued program, China will build several internationally known universities and construct successfully to become a creative country until 2020. It's essential to develop high-level creative personnel for a creative country. These personnel in engineering field should feature the prominent original innovation ability, outstanding engineering practice ability and prominent international communication and cooperation competence [6]. Owing to the lack of innovative engineers and technicians in China, a professional training plan of outstanding engineers has also been performed in 2010. In this case, it's urgent to advance the engineering education reform, foster the engineering technical personnel and promote the whole innovative ability for universities, institutions and enterprises [7].

What qualities the innovative talents cultivated by universities? How to enable them to meet the qualifications required by China's innovative construction and the development of globalization? This has given rise to a new historic subject for higher educational activities. As one of 61 universities implementing the program firstly appointed by Chinese Education Department, Beihang University explores the engineering educational reform with respect to cultivation purposes, cultivation contents, cultivation methods and cultivation standards. Taking an example, Higher Engineering Education 2010 Forum was held in Beihang University. For the only undergraduate major in the field of test and measurement, measurement and control technology and instrumentation has become an important branch of current information scientific field, featuring wide range, abundant theoretical knowledge and strong engineering application. In this paper, the distinguishing educational explorations and practices are demonstrated to facilitate the integrated innovative development of undergraduates and graduates. The present discipline construction advances are analyzed from the view of the engineering-oriented teaching and practical links.

2 Engineering Needs and Development Architecture for Undergraduates

Under the guidance of regression engineering views, a viewpoint on higher engineering education is presented to develop the engineering scientific research personnel, engineering technical personnel or other personnel with engineering technical background [8]. For example, setting up the funding to support the reform of engineering research center, where more than 1/10 undergraduates are required to join the engineering projects and the cooperations between universities and enterprises are applied, such as MIT, Michigan University and etc. However, more attentions are paid to theoretical knowledge than practical disciplinary links in China.

The major of measurement and control technology and instrumentation in Beihang University regards the critical component development as training basis and the system implementation as training main thread, respectively. The focus on the basic research, interdisciplinary studies and system integration is highlighted to encourage undergraduates to enter the laboratory to participate in engineering projects. The characteristics of cultivation mode are shown as following:

(1) With regard to the curriculum setup, Table 1 lists the newly revised core courses for undergraduates to lay a basis for general education and professional education;

(2) With regard to the team development, a team, fulfilling discipline construction, scientific research, course teaching and management, is built with a liability professor as the leader;

(3) With regard to the cultivation content, the cultivation of experimental and practical ability runs consistently through the higher education process as shown in Table 2;

(4) With regard to the practical conditions, the major is provided with the specialized laboratories related with the advanced test technology, advanced sensor technology, precision opto-mechatronics technology, process monitoring technology and etc. These software and hardware resources can offer the engineering issue-oriented disciplinary subjects and practicing platforms to improve their innovative and practical abilities.

Table 1. Curriculum Development Architecture

Category	Curriculum	Credit	Teaching hours
core curriculum for undergraduates	Automation test basic	3	48+6
	Signal analysis and processing	3.5	56+8
	Sensor technology and application	2.5	42+6
	Aerospace test system	3.5	42+6
	Error theory and data processing	2.5	44+4
	Sensor system and network	3	44+4
	Introduction to speciality	1	14

Table 2. Practice Links for Undergraduates

Category	Curriculum	Credit	Teaching hours
required	General society practice	1	80
required	Professional society practice	1	160
required	Electronic engineering practice	2	2 weeks
required	Electrionic circuit design practice	2	2 weeks
required	Mechanical engineering practice	2	2 weeks
required	Test system course design	2	2 weeks
required	Production practice	3	3 weeks
required	Graduation project	8	576

3 Development of Engineering Skills and Academic Literacies

1. Course Teaching Integrating Engineering Practice and Academic Skill

The course teaching is the basis of training undergraduates, which produces necessary specialized knowledge accumulations, analysis methods and practical experiences. Since it simply uses teacher as main role and students as auxiliary role, the traditional teaching mode of imparting knowledge is no longer adapted to the current education training system for innovative engineers [9]. According to the internal relations between each knowledge point, we summarize the systematic approaches by strengthening bases, highlighting practices, emphasizing qualities and catering innovations. By using "*sensor → signal processing → test system*" as main thread and "*knowledge application → knowledge innovation*" as auxiliary thread respectively, the knowledge points related with measurement and control technology are determined. Then, the teaching team is formed with perfect practical ability and with different structures of knowledge, education, title and age. To some extent, this type of team is more reasonable, stable and united. Compared with single teaching mode, it's more beneficial for undergraduates to make them study from different viewpoints.

Since they supplement each other, the engineering property and academic property should not be separated from course teaching. Based on the reform of national excellent course "sensor technology and application", we perform the following operations to enhance the scientific, applicative and academic performances:

(1) With regard to the curriculum architecture, sensor technologies are geared to national critical requirements and defense constructions;

(2) With regard to the curriculum content, engineering problems and hot phenomena in sensor technology are introduced, such as the giant magnetoresistance (GMR) effect awarded the 2007 Nobel Prize in Physics and the graphene material awarded the 2010 Nobel Prize in Physics;

(3) With regard to the curriculum purpose, case reports on sensor's practical application are added to further illustrate the design and application characteristics of sensors;

(4) With regard to the curriculum organization, heuristic teaching and exploratory teaching are advocated during courses. For instance, a number of student-dominated lectures and discussions are arranged by dividing them into several groups and assigning each group an instructing teacher. In accordance with the engineering problem solving, the undergraduates are required to submit an academic paper as one of their performance evaluations.

2. Multi-hierarchical and Integrated Experiments

As a main approach to carry out modern higher engineering education, the practical link is explored and improved all the time by using comprehensively all of research project groups, experimental platform resources and curriculum development architectures. With aid of experimental and research advantages of both *National Key Laboratory of Inertial Technology* and *Key Laboratory of Opto-Mechatronics (Beihang University), Ministry of Education*, an advanced test integrative experimental platform is established to implement the teaching transfer of research findings. The integrative experimental platform has the functions of *"signal generation → information acquisition → information transmission (local and remote) → information processing (local and remote)"*. It is composed of advanced sensor technology sub-platform, intelligent instrument sub-platform, dynamic test and signal processing sub-platform, test object and physical signal generation sub-platform, integrative experimental environment sub-platform and photoelectric detection sub-platform, wherein the advanced sensor technology sub-platform is the basis and core link. Figure 2 shows the corresponding basic, advanced and integrated experiments by means of the established integrative experimental platform. The multi-hierarchical experimental arrangements tend to meet different teaching requirements for undergraduates with differentiation levels. Under the circumstances, on the one hand, the undergraduates can select experimental subjects depending on their interests or technical levels; on the other hand, this type of flexible subjects can foster specific technical personnel with keen interested in engineering technology. The training system contributes to the selection and follow-up development of engineering candidates.

The designing experiment in experimental links emphasizes the independent analytical, exploring, designing and practicing abilities. For the *National Excellent Course "Sensor Technology and Application"*, we develop a sensor designing experimental platform. The structure diagram of platform is demonstrated in Fig.2. The undergraduates are divided into groups and required to independently use electronic components to design, build and debug the sensor circuit system presented by themselves in the sensor experimental platform. This link can make them experience the sensors, scientific instruments and debugging tools, which supplies the necessary foundation for follow-up technical exploitations and innovation practice activities.

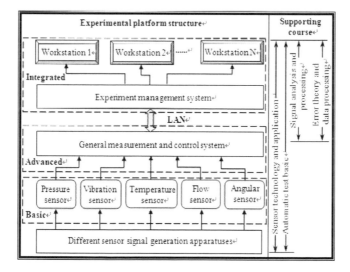

Fig. 1. Diagram of multi-hierarchical experimental platform

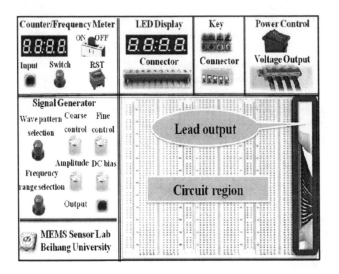

Fig. 2. Diagrm of sensor designing experimetnal platform

3. Engineering Technical Practice

The course teachings and experiments are used to provide undergraduates theoretical and practical foundations. Only through multiple engineering practice processes, the innovative and practical abilities can be increased furtherly and effectively. Consequently, we build the transfer bridge between theoretical knowledge and engineering problems as well as between ideas and actions by making full use of course, laboratory and technological activities. As shown in Table 2, the practical training links involve the abundant disciplinary courses from sophomore class to senior class. Meanwhile, an idea that *nothing is more important than participation* is imparted to stimulate their creative thinking through scientific and technological activities during the classroom instructions, such as "*Instrument and Optoelectronic Cup Technological Competition*", "*Student Research Training Program (SRTP)*", "*Fengru Cup Technological Competition*", "*National Undergraduate Innovative Test Program (ITP)*" and etc. With the focus set on completion, in addition to results, they can complete a stage in their studies and careers.

Another important training approach is to guide them to participate in the laboratory and enterprise researches. For example, at the graduation project stage, a ladder-shaped training system composed of Duty professor, young teacher, graduate and undergraduate is formed. The training mode results in an exploratory, interactive and engineering team atmosphere. The undergraduates can understand the research interests, learn the research method and master the engineering techniques step by step in the positive atmosphere. Besides, in cooperation with more than 20 off-campus practice bases, they are arranged to enter the research institutions and enterprises. In this manner, they may contact with frontline technical staff and apply known theories and methodologies in this real, practical enterprise projects. Such joint training mode is called "dual tutorial system", the emphasis of which lies in making use of the enterprise resources outside school.

In general, the purpose of higher engineering education is to comprehensively exercise the exploratory capacity of undergraduates, and then further inspire them to independently practice new ideas or new methods in practical issues. Following the purpose above, the measures are put into effect to allow them comprehend the practical process of *"groping repeatedly → exploring disciplines → examining methods → proving ideas"*. This enables to form the research style of diligently practice and independent critical thinking, which the prospective high-level engineering technical candidates should possesses.

4 Summary

The importance of higher engineering education reform is emphasized to improve the practical abilities for undergraduates and meet the needs of high-level creative engineers. Based on the teaching characteristics of measurement and control technology and instrumentation in Beihang University, the integrated construction of combining engineering skills with academic literacies is implemented by establishing the teaching and scientific research team and catering to the national significant needs and engineering projects. The adopted methods consist of introducing scientific research results into course teaching, and strengthening engineering case teaching and hierarchical practices. The practical advances help to develop the literal, academic, engineering and creative abilities with which high-level engineering technical personnel are provided.

Acknowledgement. We thank the National Excellent Course "Sensor Technology and Application", the Beijing higher education teaching reform, the "11th Five-Year Plan" key project of in Beijing Association of Higher Education and the education teaching reform in Beihang University for supporting this research.

References

1. Camarda, C.J.: In: Proceedings of the 29th International Thermal Conductivity Conference, pp. 3–42 (2008)
2. Zhurakovskiy, V., Nesterov, A.: In: 114th Annual ASEE Conference and Exposition (2007)
3. Sekimoto, H.: Progress in Nuclear Energy 50(2-6), 71–74 (2008)
4. So, Y.S., Hyoung, K.S., Tae, H.M.: Expert Systems with Applications 36(3), 5087–5093 (2009)
5. Zaharim, A., Yusoff, Y.M., Omar, M.Z., et al.: WSEAS Transactions on Advances in Engineering Education 6(9), 306–320 (2009)
6. Fang, J.C., Wan, J.W., Meng, X.F., et al.: Journal of Beijing University of Aeronautics and Astronautics (Social Sciences Edition) S(22), 24–26, 31 (2009)
7. Cong, Y.Q., Sun, P.D., Zhang, Y., et al.: In: International Conference on Optics, Photonics and Energy Engineering, vol. 2, pp. 501–504 (2010)
8. Alkhairy, A., Blank, L., Boning, D., et al.: In: ASEE Annual Conference and Exposition (2009)
9. Zheng, J.M., Pan, X.H.: China University Teaching (12), 4–7 (2008)

The Practice Base Construction of Engineering Education Based on TOPCARES-CDIO Model

Dejun Tang, Haiyi Jin, Chen Wang, and Lixin Ma

Dalian Neusoft Institute of Information, P.R. China
dulalalala@yeah.net

Abstract. TOPCARES-CDIO is based on the CDIO engineering education concept and with characteristics of Dalian Neusoft Institute of Information (Dalian Neusoft II) application-oriented personnel training mode, which attaches great importance to enhance the ability of students. College Students Entrepreneurial Center (Student Office & Venture Office, hereinafter referred to as SOVO) is Dalian Neusoft II has created a groundbreaking IT Talents Cultivation Base in China's colleges, which combined with a new educational philosophy and engineering education mode. Compared with some foreign countries, Chinese students' entrepreneurship education is still relatively backward. This paper combines the opportunities and status of Chinese college students' entrepreneurship education and career guidance, corresponding to Dalian Neusoft II the actual characteristics, developed a suitable college student and effective new model, which is the construction of engineering education business practice base based on TOPCARES-CDIO. For the reform of SOVO practice teaching base, it conducted in-depth study and research, highlighting introduces SOVO based on TOPCARES-CDIO engineering education philosophy, working to enhance the ability of students carried out important reforms.

Keywords: Practice Base, Engineering Education, TOPCARES-CDIO, SOVO.

1 Introduction

CDIO engineering education model is the latest achievements of an international engineering education reform in recent years, founded in the Massachusetts Institute of Technology, where four letters of CDIO represent Conceive, Design, Implement and Operate. CDIO reform vision is for students to provide a systems and products with conceive-design-implement-operate under the context of emphasizing project-based engineering education so that students can master the deep technical base of knowledge, lead new products and new systems development and operation, and understanding of engineering technology research and development for social importance and strategic impact. TOPCARES-CDIO is based on the CDIO engineering education concept and with characteristics of Dalian Neusoft II training model and methods [1]. TOPCARES is Neusoft educational philosophy "education creates the

M. Zhu (Ed.): ICCIC 2011, Part V, CCIS 235, pp. 328–333, 2011.
© Springer-Verlag Berlin Heidelberg 2011

values of students" the highest interest of the first letters of the eight ability acronym in English, shown in Fig. 1. Design and implementation of TOPCARES-CDIO training mode and methods will be the fundamental guarantee for Neusoft to achieve "education students to create value, students create social value" educational philosophy, for the Institute applied talents of engineering education reform pointed out the way forward.

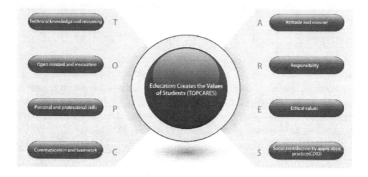

Fig. 1. TOPCARES-CDIO philosophy of engineering education

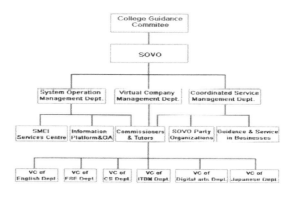

Fig. 2. SOVO Organization Chart

Entrepreneurship education has been called "the third of the education passport". The first target of the United States the best students is their own business. Compared with some foreign countries, Chinese students' entrepreneurship education is still relatively backward. "Innovation and entrepreneurship education to the needs of all students, combined with professional education and personnel training into the entire process." This paper combines the opportunities and status of Chinese college students' entrepreneurship education and career guidance, corresponding to Dalian Neusoft II the actual characteristics, developed a suitable college student and effective new model, the construction of engineering education business practice base based on TOPCARES-CDIO. As for the weak links and bottlenecks of students in the entrepreneurial process, Dalian Neusoft II has set up an independent functional department College Students Entrepreneurial Center (SOVO), as shown in Fig. 2. It established nearly 6800 square space students practice entrepreneurial base, using "virtual company" business model, so that students learn professional knowledge at the same time gain experience the true reality, comprehensive understand the mode of operation of modern business and work flow, training students in business practices and enhance the core competitiveness of employment.

2   Development Status of SOVO Practice Base

SOVO is Dalian Neusoft II has created a groundbreaking Entrepreneurial Practice Base in China's colleges, which combined with a new educational philosophy and engineering education mode. SOVO founded in 2002, after years of practice and exploration, has become a feature of the brand of Dalian Neusoft II. SOVO now has 38 virtual companies, 6800 square office space, 1,000 regular employees and 2,000 interns. With TOPCARES-CDIO educational philosophy, companies are matched by a team of professional education of department and a professional society, and with professional instructors and business mentor.

SOVO core objective is to train students in the entrepreneurial spirit, teamwork, practice ability and self-management capabilities. It adopted a "virtual company" business model, experience the true reality comprehensive understanding of the mode of operation of modern enterprises and work processes. Students in school apply to set up own virtual company, through competition for the respondent, as the company manager, assistant manager and market, technical, financial and other positions. Management of the virtual company's operations is equivalent to the entity, the project development process strictly in accordance with ISO quality assurance system and the CMM-related specifications.

SOVO is a platform based on positions in the engineering practice. Through enterprise operation and management mode, students can engage in researching and developing of real business projects in SOVO, participate in professional competitions above the provincial level, listen to management consulting class lectures, enjoy the GSP entrepreneurship training, docking Government business support policies and declare incubation entities, experience the company's operations related processes, such as staff recruitment, beginning education, company operating plan defense, annual performance commitments, branding and the foreign cooperation and so on. Base on First-class office environment and real project experience, SOVO is a practical base of Neusoft elite students and the cradle of future entrepreneurs.

3   Construction Guidelines of SOVO Practice Base

Around the needs of Dalian Neusoft II TOPCARES-CDIO professionals building and professional core abilities as the goal, SOVO will be built to the domestic first-class with Neusoft characteristics job and entrepreneurship education practice base and incubator base, formed entrepreneurial training, entrepreneurial (employment) trainees and entrepreneurship (employment) services trinity "SOVO- entrepreneurial practice base" model, that is, "Neusoft model", and successfully declared a university science park in Liaoning province, to promote employment and entrepreneurship education in universities of the all provinces and the country healthy development model serve as model, radiation and leading role, as the entrepreneurial city of Dalian economic development make due contributions.

Entrepreneurial practice bases the overall objective of the next five years are: 1, to make the Institute accepted SOVO engineering practical platform training undergraduates that are not less than 50%, each year SOVO graduate employment rate is 100% , which the employment rate of high-quality professional counterparts in more than 60%; 2, SOVO will be built to the domestic first-class job and entrepreneurship education practice base and incubator base, the cradle of school-run enterprises of Dalian Neusoft II.

4   SOVO Practice Base Construction Characteristics Model

Attaching great importance to the practical activities of students, SOVO is the personnel training process the primary practice base and link, run a unique set of entrepreneurship education and entrepreneurship guiding of the new model, including:

1. Corporatization Operation Management Model: SOVO adopts the "virtual company" system, which was established by the students into SOVO different professional direction of virtual companies. In addition to the virtual company is not a registered legal entity, the various operations management system in accordance with an entity operating system. SOVO is managed by college and departments of Dalian Neusoft II, the college level has SOVO management platform, which consists of Virtual Company Management, Operations Management and Integrated Business Management. SOVO manages macroeconomic virtual companies and services them. As shown in Fig. 3 and Fig. 4, each department manages directly its virtual companies, organized students to set up virtual companies in different professional direction, technical support and guide the virtual company operations, while professional education team, student mass organizations and SOVO organic integration, by a professional as a unit, give full play to the party organizations, students, community organizations in SOVO the role of construction and development to enhance the quality of more students in professional.

Fig. 3. SOVO operating mode

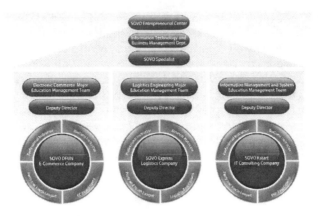

Fig. 4. Department of SOVO operations architecture

2. Company Professional Matching Model: to establish professional virtual company, simulate business processes, and emphasize the overall quality of training of students. Each department readjusts SOVO management structure, professional as a unit, each professional match at least one more SOVO company closely associated with the professional. Each SOVO company at least match more than one the professional societies, the company's internship staff are arranged in the professional community to meet SOVO the company continued development of human resources reserves.

3. PM System for Project Development Model: in order to better complete students capacity of conceive, design and implementation, SOVO relying on Neusoft Group to make students participate in the project development process in full accordance with ISO9001 quality assurance system and the CMM related specifications. R&D projects were implemented PM system. Strict, scientific and standardized project management processes it make students participate and complete a project to connect directly to the field of learning experience to current latest standardized IT project development and management experience.

4. Multiple Training Model: for truly technical, knowledge, enhance the comprehensive capacity of the core competitiveness of the employment of students, SOVO train students include the IT expertise, project management and business management, human resources management, marketing and finance and so on. After training, the students should conduct a comprehensive feedback system to ensure that each training to achieve the desired results.

5. Dual-mentoring Model: on the one hand, each SOVO company with professional mentors and business mentors, professional instructors from the various departments serve as the backbone of professional teachers, business mentor who is cultural liaison teachers of each department. On the other hand, a full-time SOVO staff responsible directed two low-grade SOVO trainees. Regular employees worked in the SOVO office, implemented company management and attendance, work 15 hours per week. SOVO staff must firstly take exercise in each department of professional practice societies, in principle, has not been the experience of professional societies, can not be SOVO employee.

6. Professional Incubator Model: SOVO create business environment, build specialized incubators, venture service centers and University Science Park. SOVO built a complete information platform, and had online reservation system for booking conference rooms and training rooms, which is for the smooth functioning of SOVO business model to provide effective protection. Over the years, hatching success entities have more than 60.

7. Student Employed Patterns: in order to better improve and enhance students responsibility, professional attitudes and habits, SOVO management carry out in full accordance enterprise procedures, the students enter SOVO implement recruitment and employment system, the virtual company's recruitment process in accordance with corporate recruitment "employees". Employees need to sign a confidentiality agreement, half-yearly performance evaluation, if performance appraisal who failed would be fired.

8. Competition Driven Model: technology competition as the starting point to develop students awareness of technological and entrepreneurship innovation, and in performance appraisal every year SOVO companies sponsored or organized at least one school professional skills competitions, or participating in college level expertise competition and winning.

5 Summary

SOVO is a bridge between the campus and the enterprise, the starting point for business and employment. SOVO run in practice more than 9 years, and there are more than 5,000 students applied for SOVO company positions, total of 35 entities hatching success. In the meantime, SOVO praised by Li Changchun, Li Keqiang, Wang Qishan, Liu Yandong and other party and state leaders and employing enterprises, domestic and foreign visitors. TOPCARES CDIO Training Mode is Dalian Neusoft II reference CDIO engineering education, the latest achievements of educational reform. Of course, this reform can not be reached the aim in one move, although some success has been achieved, but still needed in the implementation process of all stakeholders through the Institute for further confirmation and testing, and make timely revision.

References

1. Wen, T.: Exploration and practice of the integrated training model based on TOPCARES-CDIO. Computer Education 11, 5–8 (2010)
2. Hernández, J.T., Ramírez, M.C., Carvajal, J.A.: In: Teamwork Assessment in Order to Promote Engineering Students Innovative Attitude. edited by Active Learning for Engineering Education (2009)
3. Wang, G.: CDIO engineering education reading and thinking. China Higher Education Research 5, 86–87 (2009)
4. Lin, Y.: Exploration of CDIO engineering education. Journal of Harbin University 4, 137–140 (2008)
5. Campbell, D., Dawes, L., Beck, H.: An extended CDIO syllabus framework with preparatory engineering proficiencies. In: 5th International CDIO Conference (2009)

Teaching Methods of the Introduction of Basic Engineering Course

Zhou Huanhuai[1], Ying Huijuan[2], and Ai Ning[3]

[1] City College, Wenzhou University, Wenzhou 325000, P.R. China
[2] College of Chemical Engineering and Materials Science,
Zhejiang University of Technology, Hangzhou 310032, P.R. China
[3] College of Chemical Engineering and Materials Science,
Zhejiang University of Technology, Hangzhou 310032, P.R. China
yiyalazihei@163.com

Abstract. Taking "Unit Operation" as an example, this paper describes the essentiality and instructional objectives of the introduction of basic engineering course. Teaching methods of the introduction course and its application are also deeply discussed.

Keywords: Basic engineering course, Introduction, Teaching Methods.

Introduction

Introduction means something that leads up to a pain part. The first step of learning a course is usually to learn its introduction. However, some teachers and students do not attach great importance to the introduction, for they believe it is abstract and insipid so that there is no point spending too much time and effort on it. Some teachers even skip these tedious knowledge directly, leaving students learn by themselves. Actually, introduction plays an important role in teaching, because it usually summarizes the instructional task, category, development history and learning skills of the course in a rigorous scientific and highly ideological way. The main target is to enable students to know the content, understand the orientation and master the study method, so students can be stimulated to learn the course enthusiastically. Therefore, good teaching methods of introduction can make students really know "what to learn, why to learn and how to learn".

"Unit Operation" is not only a compulsory course, but also the first basic engineering course for students of chemical engineering, environmental engineering, pharmaceutical engineering, chemical machinery and automation majors, etc. It describes the principle and equipments of every unit operation in all kinds of chemical process. Therefore, it is significant to introduce these contents properly because it is not only the beginning of this course but also the total overture of other engineering courses. And a proper delivering of the Introduction is of great importance for students to complete all courses successfully.

M. Zhu (Ed.): ICCIC 2011, Part V, CCIS 235, pp. 334–339, 2011.

"Unit Operation" in Zhejiang University of Technology is a paradigmatic course at the provincial level. A set of better teaching methods and systems has formed after ten years' unremitting efforts. Taking "Unit Operation" as an example, this paper discusses the teaching methods of the engineering introduction course..

1 Instructional Objectives of the Introduction

1.1 Understanding Learning Objectives

Nowadays, higher education is in a transitional period, from elite education to mass education. In the context of popular education, universities enroll increasingly diverse students. And the degree of the knowledge they master, the level of their leaning ability, their leaning willingness and their value orientation have significant difference and diversity. With the development adjustment of China's economic and social structure, the graduates have increasingly diverse options in the job market. Thus, teachers should help students set up their individual learning goals, rather than giving them all high requirements. For instance, all the students should be required to master the basic principle of unit operation, but only a part who have spare capacity to grasp the development of a new process, the diagnosis of technical process and the operation of strengthening method. And those students who want to become elites of this field should work toward the objective of mastering the innovative design method. Individual learning goals are shown in the pyramid diagram in figure 1:

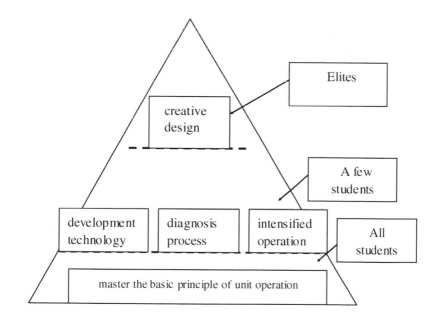

Fig. 1. Individual learning objectives for different students

1.2 Enhancing Motivation of Learning

Teaching is students' cognitive activity under teachers' guidance. Interest is human beings' psychological tendency to understand things and the motivation to learn things. Confucius said: "People who know it learn not so quickly as those who love it; those who love it learn not so quickly as those who enjoy it." Dense interest may drive you to study hard without feeling tired and bored. Experienced directors always clip the most splendid parts of the movie together as beginning in order to attract the audiences' attention. Introduction to a course is like the title and preamble to a wonderful movie. Thus, in the introduction teaching, teachers should combine the text with production and real life and arouse students' interest according to their different mental characteristics.

Affected by the social and economic focus, students of the traditional majors, such as chemical engineering, always don't love their majors. This requires teachers publicize aggressively themselves and their cutting-edge research in the introduction class in order to attract students to take a keen interest in their majors.

Praise and encouragement is important means of inspiring students' emotion. Teachers should be passionate enough to encourage students to set up their confidence to overcome learning difficulties.

Besides aspects mentioned above, teachers can also introduce the development of the subject and the appealing stories of famous scientists to form their outlook on life and world, stimulate their learning interest, and finally make them love it.

1.3 Connecting "Basic Course " with "Specialized Course"

"Unit Operation" is the development and extension of the practical engineering application from the basic courses, such as mathematics, physics and chemistry. It links "basic course " and "specialized course".

"Unit Operation" plays an irreplaceable role in forming students' engineering concept, developing their creative ability of thinking, and training them to work independently.

Most parts of unit operations in this course have rigorous theoretical foundation, some of which have high generality and abstraction, and also have flexible forms in specific chemical process and equipment. So it is difficult for the student to master these parts.

Learning begins with thinking, and thinking begins with doubting. In the class of the instruction of "Unit Operation", teachers may extend the previous knowledge to new one rather than opening a new course. Learning from the familiar knowledge can make students to think more positively, and they can find the laws on their own so that they can understand what they have learnt clearly and have a deeper impression. This always has a multiplier effect.

1.4 Teaching the Study Methods

There is an old saying: "Give a man a fish; you have fed him for today. Teach a man to fish, and you have fed him for a lifetime." As to a certain subject, teachers are the knower, but as a teacher, he can not just be satisfied with job of changing the fresh students to veterans. He should enable students to master the learning skills and become a "good learner" by combining "teaching" with "learning".

Instruction is the beginning of the instructional course. Teachers should make student understand "what to learn" and "how to learn"; teach students not only to collect, but also to sort out knowledge, just like the busy bees, who can finally turn all kinds of flowers into sweet honey. Therefore, teachers should pay more attention to develop students' learning ability and study methods, to guide students to master the correct way to learn. For instance, in the class of the instruction of the "Unit Operation", teachers can use the metaphor of "building block" to explain the significance of "unit operations" for the chemical production and chemical engineering research; they also should state clearly the difference and connection between the two methods of chemical processes: "experimental research", "and " mathematical model method ", which are the two main lines of "Unit Operation".

1.5 Establishing Harmonious Relationships between Teachers and Students

Teaching is a multi-directional interpersonal activity, which requires teachers to be emotional and enthusiastic in class, because teachers and students are both co-participants, they influence and interact with each other. Firstly, teachers must cultivate their own knowledge, artistic talent, attractive language and other aspects of personal charm to infect students in teaching practice. Just like the old saying "Love me, love my dog", teachers could turn students' admiration for them to their love for the subject. Secondly, teachers should be good at creating teaching and learning environment to let students enjoy the process of learning; what's more, to take good care of the students and respect them is a good way to win their respect and trust, which can eliminate the "generation gap" and make students be fond of asking questions and be willing to transfer information to teachers so that teachers can solve the problems more easily.

To establish harmonious relationships between teachers and students is the premise and source of arousing students' interest. Teachers should make full use of "introduction course" from the psychology effect and win the students' "first impression" of teachers and this course by enriched content and humorous expressions.

2 Teaching Methods and Techniques of Introduction Course

To achieve the above purpose of teaching, appropriate teaching methods and techniques are also needed.

2.1 "Situational" Approach, Leading Students into "Simulation " Chemical Plant

Higher engineering education has technology science as its main subject, the technique application as the main professional content and cultivating students to become engineers who can turn technology into production as the main target. So it has the typical characteristics of application, practice, and comprehensiveness. In the process of engineering education, we should always take the engineering practice and training as the core work of teaching, and pay much attention to develop the students' innovative spirit and practical abilities.

Since the 90's of the twentieth century, "situational" approach plays a significance role in teaching. Greebo and Moore both think that "situational" awareness is fundamental in all cognition activities, which makes learning far beyond knowledge acquisition. Study contains establishing a world in which they use tools and develop an increasingly rich understanding of tools itself. And this comprehension will be promoted by gradually learning and application in "situational" way. As we all know, "situational" approach is the most effective way in learning. For example, the best way to learn a foreign language is to live in that country, and the best way to learn to swim is to practice in the water. Similarly, in teaching "Unit Operation", teachers should start the introduction lessons by building a chemical production of specific situations with videos and images, so that the students may begin to learn this course in a pleasant situation.

2.2   Example Teaching, Giving Full Play of the Instruction Course

In the increasingly opening social environment, college students' psychological characteristics have changed a lot. Now they are simply fond of accepting new knowledge, at the same time they easily hate boring things. Consequently, students will feel bored with the insipid language in instruction course; but if teachers always use some examples while teaching the new knowledge, it will develop students' interest and inspire them to learn and discover the secret of the subject. To cite the daily activity of drying clothes in the sun to analyze the mechanism of the three heat transfer phenomena is really a good example.

Introduction is foreword, and also is an unfinished speech. Instruction course is the beginning of a subject. With limited time, it is impossible and unnecessary to analyze every instance. The function of example teaching is to make instruction course give full play to guide the students and pave the way for the main content.

2.3   Question Teaching, Giving Mutual Effect of Instruction Course

In question teaching, teachers raise the questions and guide the students to find the answers themselves in order to promote their enthusiasm. It is proposed by Soviet teaching expert M • A • Danilov in the 70's of the twentieth century.

Thinking begins with questions, and develops by solving questions. Hence, to create questions can enhance students' ability of thinking. It is the core of intelligence and its development can arouse students' curiosity. In the instruction course of "Unit Operation", teachers can ask several questions(for example, how to turn turbid water into clean drinking water? What do people do from ancient times? What is the principle of the treatment? How to make the process become more reasonable and more effective?) to guide students to think. In this case, students can learn the relevant sections of the rest contents with the questions.

2.4   Correlation and Application of the above Methods

Any teaching methods and means serve for teaching purposes and can not be isolated. The correlation of the methods is shown in figure 2: first of all, chemical engineering atmosphere is created by "situational" approach; then in such atmosphere, some examples related to the production and real life are given; finally, some questions are given to stimulate students to think deeply.

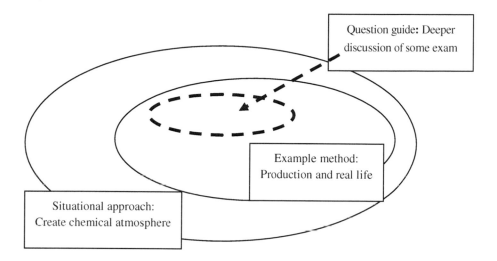

Fig. 2. Correlation and application of the several teaching methods

3   Conclusion

"Everything is difficult at the beginning", "Well begun is half done". Good teaching methods of instruction courses can make a good start of learning "Unit Operation".

The famous educator of the former Soviet Union Suhomlinski said: "Only when teachers have the unparalleled wider knowledge than they books, they can be true experts, artists and poets in teaching." Teachers must focus on developing their knowledge widely, continue to enrich and improve themselves in order to become a real expert.

References

1. Kong, C.-q., Yuan, Q., Chen, X.: On Constructing School-based Model for Cultural Quality Education in University of Science and Engineering. Journal of Nanjing University of Aeronautics and Astronautics (Social Sciences) 10(3), 84–87 (2008)
2. Wang, Z.-s.: On teaching modes of the introduction lesson. Journal of Wuhan Institute of Technology 29(5), 86–87 (2007)
3. Wang, B., Men, Y.: Investigation and Analysis on Employment Present Situation of Engineering Graduates. Research in Higher Education of Engineering 3, 45–59 (2010)
4. Bie, D., Zheng, Z.: On the Educational Ideas of World-class Universities. Research in Higher Education of Engineering 4, 82–92 (2010)

The Introduction of Oman Crude Oil Trading and Development

Li Xiaosai and Dong Xiucheng

China University of Petroleum, Beijing
18 Fuxue Road, Changping, Beijing China 102249
jane.doe@sohu.com

Abstract. As the most active trading grade of crude oil, Oman has a special position in the Middle East crude oil market. Authors are willing to introduce oman crude oil and his trading ,and to share their knowledge and understanding for his market in this article.

Keywords: Oman, Oman crude oil, PG market.

1 Basic Introduction of Oman and Oman Crude Oil Industry

As the oldest independent state in the Arab world, Oman has a wealth of archaeological and historical marvels, including ancient walled cities, forts and mosques. Crude oil has become the wealth resource for modern Oman now. The Oman is the third largest country in the Arabian Peninsular who has 309 thousand square meter country Area. The population is 2.84 million and about the 60% citizen is Arab. Muscat is the capital and also the biggest city of Oman. As the hometown of famous Sailor Sinbad in stories of 1001 Arabian Night, Oman is well known by whole world peoples.

Although as an important PG crude oil supplier, Oman is not an OPEC member country. Benefit from the Enhanced Oil Recovery (EOR) project, the Oman oil production has some improvement from 2008. The current oil production is around 670kb/d. This number improved most 100kb/d in last 5 years. Occidental Petroleum and UAE's Mubadala enhance their E&P operation in Mukhaizna oil field. This area's production will reach 150kb/d in 2012. Therefore, the Oman's production will keep a stable increasing in next few years. About 80% crude oil production is handled by Petroleum Development Oman(PDO) which owned by the Government of Oman. The percentage of POD's equity holders will be listed as follow: Mog: 60%, Shell: 34%, Total: 4%, Partex 2%.

2 The Importance of Oman Trading

Oman is the PG market benchmark for many grades such as Saudi, Iran, Kuwait and Qatar. Not like WFA area, most PG crude oil cannot be traded freely. About 80%-85%

M. Zhu (Ed.): ICCIC 2011, Part V, CCIS 235, pp. 340–345, 2011.
© Springer-Verlag Berlin Heidelberg 2011

Middle East crude oil have the destination limited, and most major PG supplier sell their crude oil only base on the term contract. As the result, the trading volume of PG spot market is very limited. Compared with other grade, the spot market of Oman is most active and complex.

China is the biggest buyer for Oman crude oil. The following figure can show the Oman import figure in recent years.((Refrence to Figure 1 as below.)

Since we have known the importance of Oman crude oil, we need to learn the Oman market well both in Physical and Paper market.

3 The Introduction of Oman Physical Market

It mentioned at the early part that the current Oman production is around 670kbd. According to the normal PG spot cargo size is 500kb, there should have over 40 cargos available in the market monthly. Base on the equity holder and their share ratio, the Oman cargo will be assigned to the following producers:(Refrence to Figure 2 as below)

MOG: 26 cargos each month, including at least 16 cargoes to sell.

Shell: 15 cargos each month, including 10-12 cargoes to sell.

TOTSA: 2 cargos each month.

PATTEX: 0.8 cargos each month.

Occidental hold the largest rest market share, they have 4 cargos per month.

BP, CNPC, IPC, Itochu, Japex, ConocoPhillips is other producers; their cargo number is influenced by the Oman production.

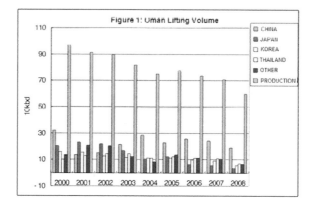

Except above companies, many end user, trading companies and bank join the Oman spot market which consist a very active and complex trading market.

Since we have known the trading volume, play and trading period of Oman physical market, we need to find out what factors may affect the Oman trading price.

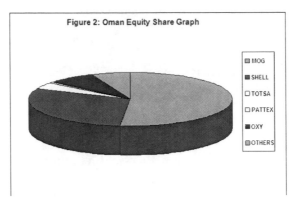

Figure 2: Oman Equity Share Graph

● Dated Brent/Dubai Spread
Compared with other area, PG grade have quantity and logistical advantage for Asian refiners. Expect above reason, the price benchmark should be one important reason for buyer's choice. Urals arbitrage chance may give Oman sellers a lot of pressure. In order to cover the differential between DTD Brent and Dubai, the premium or discount will be used as the compensation in the spot market. Therefore, the DTD Brent/Dubai Spread is an important figure to indicate the Oman spot market level.

● ANS market and Oman arbitrage to US market
Same as Urals arbitrage chance, Oman also have chance to flow to US market if Dubai/WTI differential is very wide.

● Other PG crude oil OSP
Because of the similar quality, Oman crude oil can be replaced by other PG grade. Base on our system refinery's value, AM, KEC, Barsrah Light and Upper Zakum can be the substitute grade for Oman. Most of this grade are traded base on term contact and cannot be trading freely. Their OSP should be important figure to decide which grade have better economic. That is also one reason that the Oman spot market became to be active after other PG crude oil OSP announced.

● The ESPO market level
As the new Far East export grade, because of similar quality with Oman and also the potential boost production. The ESPO market became a focus point of Asian crude oil trading market. The production of ESPO will increase to 700kbd in the near future. The shorter transportation distance to Asian refineries and same trading benchmark (Dubai link price) are other two advantage of ESPO. These factors may have big impact to Oman spot market level.

There also have other reasons may affect the Oman spot trading market level. As I mention early, Oman spot market is a very complex and flexible market. In order to know this market well, we also need to fully analysis and understand Oman future trading market as well.

4 The Introduction of Oman Future Trading

There are two major Oman future trading market exit. One is Platts Oman trading and another one is DME Oman trading. The compare and contrast between two trading market will help us to understand them well.

Table 1. The compare and contrast between two trading market

	DME	PLATTS
Exchange Type	Fully electronic exchange	Fully electronic exchange
Purpose	Set up a new Middle East Crude oil trading Benchmark and make Oman crude oil trading level more transparent.	Make Oman crude oil trading more transparent.
Launch Time	2007 June 1st	2005
Membership	Floor Members, Off-Floor Members, Clearing Members, Market Makers	
Trading Merchandise	DME Oman Crude Oil Futures Contract WTI Oman financial Spread (have closed) Brent Oman financial Spread (have closed) DME Oman Crude Oil Financial Contract (started from 2008 Jun 2nd) DME Brent Crude Oil Financial Contract (started from 2008 Jun 2nd)	Platts Oman Partials
Standard Contract Volume	1,000 U.S. barrels (42,000 gallons).	One partial equal to 25kb
Trading Time	DME Trading Hours (All times are New York time): Electronic trading is conducted from 6:00 PM until 5:15 PM New York Time via the DME Direct® trading platform, Sunday through Friday. There is a 45-minute break each day between 5:15PM NEW YORK TIME (current trade date) and 6:00 PM NEW YORK TIME (next trade date).	From 4:00 to 4:30 PM of Singapore time. Players can revise their bid and offer at any time from 4:00 to 4:28 PM, the bid and offer price is fixed in last one minutes.
Daily Price Assessment	Daily Settlement Price: The DME will publish a daily Final Settlement Price (NYMEX Intraday Price) at 4:30 p.m. Singapore time (4:30 a.m. New York Time). This can be used by traders of Middle East Sour Crude as a reference Daily Post Price: Daily Settlement is at 2:30 p.m.(New York Time),the Post Close Price	Platts assessments take into consideration bids and offers made up to no later than 16:00:00:59 hours Singapore time. Platts will take into account changes in price, but not changes to volume/date/terms & conditions, made to bids and offers up to16:29 hours Singapore time.

Table 1. (*continued*)

Settlement	For DME Oman Crude Oil Futures Contract: Only Physical For DME Oman Crude oil Financial Contract: Only Cash	Cash settlement: Any position amounting to less than 475,000 bbl by the calendar month's end is understood to be cash settled, unless both counterparties mutually agree to deliver/take delivery of a smaller top-up cargo. Partial contracts will be settled based on Platts assessments published on the last working day of each calendar month.
Delivery	The Minimize delivery volume is 1000BBLS.	Convergence of partials to a full cargo: Once a principal acquires nineteen 25,000 bbl parcels of the same grade (Dubai or Oman) from a single seller within the calendar month, the partials automatically converge into a physical cargo of 475,000 bbl. This is equivalent to a full cargo of 500,000 bbl with commercial tolerance of minus 5%.
Operational tolerance	+/- 1,000 barrels tolerance, subject to terminal performance for cargoes delivered FOB terminal.	+/- 1,000 barrels tolerance, subject to terminal performance for cargoes delivered FOB terminal.

Until now, both two Oman future markets have a lot of players. The reason to support and run these markets is that both market assessments are used as the PG grade OSP benchmark. Actually, both Platts and DME are trying to get the support for the major PG producers' support. Oman and Dubai have started to use DME assessment as Oman and Dubai's benchmark, other PG country such as Saudi, Iran, Kuwait and Iraq still use Platts Oman and Dubai as OPS benchmark. Therefore, the support from the PG producers should be the energy to support these markets or be the limitation of these two markets development.

5   Achievement and Suggestion for Oman Trading

The big buyer will benefit all PG grade buyers, many of them also join the Platts future trading market and become the partners to fight for their comment interest. For example, due to their Dubai physical cargo position, one of player may has more bullets to sell into the Platts Dubai market. Therefore, they cover the Platts Dubai market trading and we cover on Platts Oman market trading.

Although Oman production will have a further improvement in following years, compared with DME and Platts future market volume, the physical cargo is still limited. At the mean time, more and more trading companies want to attend Oman trading to expand their business, the Oman physical cargo will more and more hard to gain. On the other side, since more new crude oil market will be explored and developed, it will be easy to find the substitute grade for Oman in the future. Expect Isthmus, Urals, AM and even Basrsah light can be the replace grade for Oman.

Except the physical resource, diversification of trading method is another key issue. For Oman market, the linkage between the physical and future market is very tight, therefore, setting a monthly trading plan for whole Oman position is very necessary. Although flexibility may bring us more opportunity, but the careful planning will help trader to add the value of physical cargo and reduce the trading risk.

Hope this article can help some joiner traders to understand the basic information of Oman market well.

References

1. http://www.argusmediagroup.com/
2. http://cn.reuters.com
3. China Is the Biggest Importer of Crude Oil of Oman (Source: The Economic and Commercial Counsellor's Office of China in the United Arab Emirates)
4. Oil Market Outlook in Oman (2010), Source http://www.okokok.com.cn

A Study of Engineering Students' Interaction Strategy in Oral English Classes Based on Power Theory

Xu Zhisuo and Wang Li

School of Foreign Languages, Wuhan University of Technology
xu96965@126.com

Abstract. In oral English classes given by foreign teachers and native teachers, for engineering students and English majors, there are considerable differences in the interaction between teachers and students, which is caused by the different power relations among them. By adopting quantitative and qualitative analysis, this research compares different power relations between classes given by foreign teachers and native teachers, and between classes for engineering students and English majors. Results show that power relation in native teachers' class is stronger than that in foreign teachers'; power relation in engineering students' class is stronger than that in English majors'. The paper further explores the reasons for the differences and put forwards strategies to enhance interaction in engineering education.

Keywords: engineering education, oral English class, power theory, interaction strategy.

1 Introduction

For most Chinese students, classroom learning is the main way to study English and classroom teaching is vital to students' English learning. This is also true for oral English learning. Yang Xueyan believes that in oral English class, "the language is not only the teaching means but also the course contents".[1] In consideration of the special qualities of language class, interaction provides a good opportunity for students to practice language. Therefore, smooth classroom interaction can help the students have a better command of language by which he can transform language knowledge to communicative competence easily.[1]

The concepts "power" and "solidarity" were first proposed by Brown and Gilman in their research on the second personal pronoun T and V. According to ZhuWanjin, if a person can control another person's behavior, he has the power over the latter. The differences in cultural tradition, social position, ideology, religious belief, social stratum, race, age, sex, profession, and even in the amount of some specialized knowledge or the life experience constitute the concept of "power" and "solidarity" in the abstract sense.[2] The power relation negates the possibility of the absolute equality between language users and reflects asymmetrical social relations. British sociolinguist Spenser Oatey divided power into five kinds:①reward power: the speakers have the positive control over the hearer. For instance, the speaker can give the hearer high

M. Zhu (Ed.): ICCIC 2011, Part V, CCIS 235, pp. 346–352, 2011.

scores, positive recommendations and so on;②coercive power: the speaker has the negative control over the hearer. For instance, the speaker can decry or punish the speaker; ③expert power: the speaker has the special support or technique of which the hearer is in need ; ④legitimate power: owing to his or her superiority in some aspects such as age or social status, the speaker is authorized to instruct or request the hearer to do something. For example, the speaker is a police or the hearer's teacher and so on; ⑤ reference power: the hearer admires the speaker and wants to be the same with him/her in some way , because the speaker is a sports star, a pop star, a national hero and so on.

The solidarity relation suggests there are some commonness and intimacy between people in certain extent. To build solidarity relations, people should have some common experiences and social features, such as the same interest, age, religion, occupation. Also, the solidarity relations can be established and enhanced by the subjective endeavor of interaction participants other than the objective commonness.

The power relation in class has an immediate effect to the development of the interaction between teachers and students in classroom. Thus, to reduce the power and strengthen the solidarity in class is of great importance to for classroom interaction.

Research Design

Hypothesis: The paper makes research and discussion concerning the following questions:

1) Is the power relation in Chinese teacher's oral English class different from that in foreign teacher's?

2) Is the power relation in oral English class(or audio-visual English class) given to the engineering majors different from that to the English majors?

3) What strategies can be taken to reduce the teacher's power in the oral English class for the engineering majors so as to improve the classroom interaction?

Investigation. This research adopts the questionnaire and the classroom observation as measuring methods. Considering the freshmen have just entered the university and may not have adapted to the English study in university and for the juniors and seniors, English is not a compulsory course, this research select three groups of sophomores as the subjects, each consisting of 100 students:

Group A: sophomores majoring in English

Group B: sophomores majoring in engineering (including automotive engineering, electrical and electronic engineering and communication engineering) from the International Communication Institute

Group C: sophomores majoring in engineering (also including automotive engineering, electrical and electronic engineering and communication engineering)

Table 1. Characteristics of the subjects

	Group A	Group B	Group C
Major	English	Engineering	Engineering
Teacher	Foreign teachers	Foreign teachers	Chinese teachers

A trial survey is carried on among 30 students and their feedbacks to the questions are collected. Based on these feedbacks, we revised the questionnaire and sent it to the subjects. We sent each group 100 questionnaires and get 100, 98 and 99 back respectively from Group A, Group B and Group C.

Results Analysis and Discussion

We carry on the statistics of questionnaire results from the three groups, and make the contrastive analysis combined with classroom observation. Therefore we make a comparison between Group B and Group C, to analyze the factors contributing to the power relation from the perspective of teachers. Also we make a comparison Group A and Group B, to analyze the factors contributing to the power relation from the perspective of students.

Comparison of Power Relation. Various forms of address are most widely and frequently employed in verbal communication with distinct social identity.[2] Different ways of addressing others (for example, by the position, the full name, the first name or the nickname, etc.) directly shows the different power relation and social distance between the interaction parties. To put it specifically, different ways used by teachers and students to address each other reflect the different power relation between them. Generally these address forms are used by teachers for students: English FN (first name), full Chinese name and student number. The teacher who uses FN has relatively the weakest power over the class. And students generally address their teachers with the following three forms: FN; "Mr. \ Miss \ Mrs. + surname" (for example Mr. Zhang); "surname + 'LaoShi'" (for example "Zhang LaoShi"). The teacher's power manifested by the first form is relatively weaker then those manifested by the latter two. Therefore, it's possible to judge the size of teacher's power by the address forms used between teachers and students.

Comparison of Power Size between Group B and Group C. According to the results of the questionnaire, the use of address forms between teachers and students in class given to Group B and Group C can be represented by the following diagram:

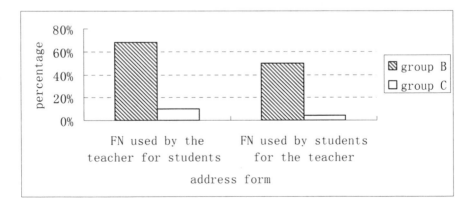

Fig. 1. The comparison of the use of FN between Group B and Group C

68% students in Group B are called by FN while only 10% in Group C. Moreover, 50% students in Group B address their teacher directly by FN, compared with 4% in Group C. Obviously the teacher's power in Group B is weaker than that in Group C. It can be concluded that for the oral English class given to engineering majors, foreign teacher has weaker power over the students than Chinese teacher do.

Comparison of Power Size between Group A and Group B. Both teachers and students influence the extent of power relation of the class.

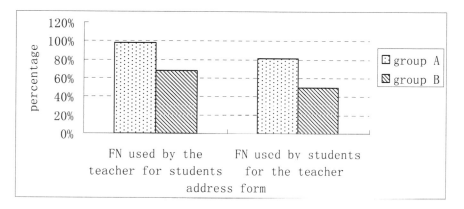

Fig. 2. The comparison of the use of FN between Group A and Group B

The diagram shows that in the oral English class for English majors, FN is the most frequently used address form between the teacher and students. The teacher almost always call the students by FN (the percentage is as high as 98%) and 81% students call their teacher by FN. It indicates the intimate relationship, which is in accordance with the results of our class observation. For engineering majors, the figures are 68% and 50%. These figures indicate that the foreign teacher's power over non-English majors is stronger than that over English majors.

2 Causal Analysis

Teacher's Influence. 1) Teacher Talk. Teacher talk plays a key role in the classroom. Teacher talk controls the content and progress of class, and implements power by interrupting students, changing the topic, and questioning continuously. Successful dialogue requires equality between both sides of the conversation based on a common apperception. From the record of classroom observation of group B and group C (totally six classes with three classes in each group), we find that native teachers account for 53% to 67% of the total amount of teacher talk, and the number for foreign teachers is 48% to 54%. The results show that students have a greater say in foreign teachers' class, which indicates smaller classroom power.

2) Questioning Method. Brock, Nunan and others have raised the concept of display question and referential question. The former indicates that the asker already know the answer, while the latter refers to questions which the asker does not know the answer. [3] Brock believed that the referential question increased language learners' output in the classroom and thus promoted their language acquisition. Thornbury suggested that more referential questions should be used in the classroom, which was more close to the true and natural conversation pattern. [4]

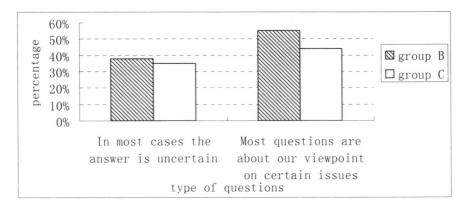

Fig. 3. Comparison of questioning method in group B and group C

The figure shows that there are more referential questions in foreign teachers' questions. This is consistent with our classroom observation. This indicates that the conversations in classes given by foreign teachers are more close to the true and natural conversation pattern and there is less power in classes given by foreign teachers if compared with classes given by native teachers.

3) Feedback Mode. Cullen divided teacher's feedback into the evaluative feedback and discoursal feedback.[7] The former is the feedback that teachers tell the students whether the response was acceptable or not. This kind of feedback is rare in real communication. In the latter, teachers care more about the contents which is similar to or close to natural verbal communication. Results of the questionnaire revealed that: 35% of the students in foreign teachers' classes thought that the evaluation were often about the content, 22% of the students thought that the evaluation were about grammar and the form of language; for native teachers, they were 26% and 39% respectively. As for the question on correcting students' mistakes: 24% of students in group B chose "The teacher points it out directly and gets it corrected", 60% of students in group B chose "The teacher guides our correction"; while the data for group C were 33% and 51%.

Through comparative analysis of the above four aspects, this conclusion can be drawn: for engineering students, power in classes given by foreign teachers is less than that of native teachers, the power difference is mainly caused by the teachers.

Students' Influence. 1) Professional Knowledge. Knowledge about the topic affects the power of the two sides of the conversation. The difference of their language skills easily leads to the power phenomenon that the more fluent speaker gain the upper hand of the conversation. And the bigger the difference, the greater the power difference will be. This power relationship leads the high power party to occupy the speaker's status, and the weak side could only stay in a passive position of the listener. Thus, the normal turn-taking would be blocked, adequate communication would be difficult to achieve. For English majors, their differences in professional knowledge and language skills with teachers are apparently less than that of engineering students. So given that the teachers are all foreigners, classes for English majors in group A show less power than classes for engineering students in group B.

2) Preparation Before Class. The amount of information that the speakers know about the topic also produces power. The one with more information is easier to be in the power position; the party with less information is more likely to be in the weak position. For students, this power difference could be weakened by preparation before classes. Investigation on English majors and engineering students shows: 32% of English majors often do preparations, 49% "sometimes" prepare for the class, only 19% "rarely or never" do preparations. But for engineering students, the figures are 17%, 41% and 51% respectively. This makes the same teacher possess smaller power for English majors than engineering students.

3) Communication After Class. Through the investigation we found that the English majors do more after-class communication with teachers than engineering students.

Table 2. Communication Between Teachers and Students

How and about what do you communicate with your oral teacher besides class? (more than one can be chosen)	Group A	Group B
A、 Hardly any communication	8%	12%
B、 face to face; about problems on learning	28%	32%
C、 face to face; about problems on learning and others	41%	32%
D、 through Email or Internet; on any issue	52%	9%

In general, the English majors spend more time communicating with teachers, and the conversation are wide-ranging. Engineering students tend to communicate face to face with teachers about their problems on learning during the break or after class. English majors are not limited to face-to-face communication, and the topics are not just about study, they try to communicate on all kinds of issues in all possible ways. This also led to more harmonious relations between the English majors and teachers, teachers' power is even smaller.

Suggestions and Strategies. In engineering students' oral English class, strategies should be taken by the participants----the teacher and the students, to reduce power and achieve high solidarity between the teacher and the students, thus to promote classroom interaction and to improve teaching efficiency.

Teacher's Strategies. Foreign teachers have advantages in oral English teaching partly due to their western culture which laid stress on democracy and equality. While

Chinese teachers, influenced by traditional Chinese concept of "showing respect to teacher and his teaching", can adopt the following strategies. To begin with, address forms with short social distance, FN, should be used in class. Then, teacher talk should be reduced to a proper quantity to give students a greater say. In addition, referential questions and discoursal feedback should be used in class. And the active atmosphere of foreign teachers' class can be attributed to novel and diversified teaching methods and forms which encourage more students to take part in classroom interaction. According to the result of our investigation, over 50% of the subjects choose "role playing" and "group discussion" as their favorite interaction activities and most students suggest teachers to adopt various activities.

Students' Strategies. The following strategies can be adopted by engineering students The first and foremost thing they should do is to improve their English, especially oral English, to narrow the gap between the teacher and themselves. Then, students can do some preview and preparation so as to have more information related to the lesson. Last yet importantly, students may communicate with teachers as much as possible, which can promote class interaction.

To put it in a nutshell, it is indispensable for both engineering students and English majors to improve oral English and to accumulate cultural knowledge. Self-confidence, correct view of language learning and less sense of anxiety can also help to reduce power relationship and promote classroom interaction.

3 Summary

Power relation in class has considerable influence on classroom interaction. By adopting quantitative and qualitative analysis, this research compares different power relations between classes given by foreign teachers and native teachers, and between classes for engineering students and English majors. We found: power relation in native teachers' class is stronger than that in foreign teachers'; power relation in engineering students' class is stronger than that in English majors'. To reduce the power relation teachers can adopt address form with high solidarity, control the quantity of teacher talk and the adopt referential questions and discoursal feedback; students should improve their English level, do preparation communicate actively with teachers.

References

1. Yang, X.: Classroom Strategies for Foreign Language Teaching: Situation and Significance. Foreign Language Teaching and Research (2003)
2. Zhu, W.: Conspectus of Sociolinguistics. Hunan Educational Press, Changsha (1992)
3. Brock, C.: The effects of referential question on ESL classroom discourse. TESOL Quarterly (1986)
4. Thornbury, S.: Teacher research teacher talk. ELT Journal (1996)

Setting Up the Net Platform of Measuring and Drawing of Machinery Based on PowerEasy

Y.M. Lu and J. Miao

School of Aeronautical Manufacturing Engineering,
Nanchang Hangkong University,
Nanchang 330036, China
y_m5564@126.com

Abstract. "measuring and drawing of machinery" is a practice teaching step in engineering drawing. The character and the current states about it are analyzed in this paper. So the net platform is built based on PowerEasy. It creates a teaching model which has interesting and opening. The platform provides examples of parts and various kind of literature. Many problems can be settled, such as limited parts, absence of guided learning, lack of date, and so on. By this platform, a teacher can stimulate fully the motive of study. It helps to exploit potential ability of innovation, to train abilities of analyzing and solving problem. Not only engineering consciousness is strengthened, but also teaching effect is improved.

Keywords: Teaching platform, measuring and drawing, PowerEasy, 3D-models building.

1 Introduction

"Measuring and drawing of machinery" is a necessary practice teaching step in "engineering drawing". By this step, students can review and consolidate contents on engineering drawing, as well as apply various kind of knowledge on measuring and drawing of machinery to enhance the ability of practice and analyzing. Consequently it lays a foundation for curriculum-design and graduate project in future.

In current, machine parts generally used to adopt a gear pump and primary gear reducer. In additional, in the classroom teacher gives simply instruction in knowledge of course and method of drawing, meanwhile Students make engineering drawings. The period of time is one week. Therefore there are a number of deficiencies. It is as follow:

    a. Because parts are fewer, it is unfavorable to students in the cognitive process.
    b. The teacher can't be in classroom at anytime. So it is unfavorable to solve problems that students encounter.
    c. The relevant information is limited in hand for students. It is unfavorable to train the ability on solving problems.

M. Zhu (Ed.): ICCIC 2011, Part V, CCIS 235, pp. 353–358, 2011.

Although there are some literatures about measuring and drawing of machinery are on net from college, this does not facilitate to update content and parts still are fewer. Future more, we only show the process of assembling parts and can't take part in it. Therefore in order to improve teaching quality and effect, according to teaching content and means, a net platform is built by PowerEasy server and Vrml-3D. This platform which is interesting and opening, gives an instruction means which is flexible to students. In the platform, students complete the process of assembling by mouse clicking parts.

2 PowerEasy server

PowerEasy server is background manage system that is advanced, flexible and convenient characteristic. For people who don't possess specialized knowledge, they easily can build a net platform on it by learning it in short time. It consists of the channel, columns, the foreground and background, templates, style, CCS, label, etc.

  d. Design of template completely separate from program in the system. Users can apply different template on the channel, columns, and edit modify web surface at any time.
  e. Special function and the same content can be of a number of special columns in all sites. It provides enrich categorization means of Web information.
  f. Web interface is managed by innovative use of a bookmark, so managers and readers can switch surface and save times. This background can be managed for convenience; easy to use and humanized operate.
  g. It can create static web-page, also support to visit in ASP and create HTML file. In addition, it provides interface function that is integrated DVbbs by member.
  h. It provides two functions which are collection and creation data timely. They are independent each other.

3 Setting Up the Net Platform of Course

Designing Concept and Platform Framework. For building "net platform on measuring and drawing in Nanchang Hangkong University", we aim at two aspects: the one is to give a platform for students learning knowledge about machine measuring and drawing. Another is to enrich the teacher's teaching and promote activity of students learning. As for these two aspects, the structure of the web site is designed as showed in Fig. 1.

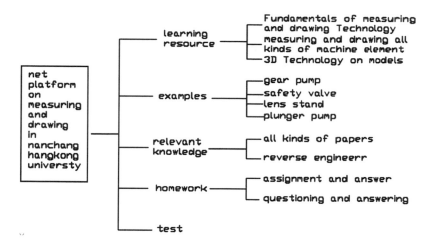

Fig. 1. Platform framework

Material Preparing. Materials include the text, picture, animation, etc. The animation of them is an important material on the teaching platform. As for measuring and drawing, it is common and effective methods, during teaching, which is the explanation example. Usually, when example is explanation, the teacher shows the process of assembling parts and construct of mechanical parts to make students have impressive. Therefore, 3D design of machinery parts can be accomplished in the circumstance of Solidworks. Next, Virtual Assembly is complete by VRML-3DX. We build web-based virtual assembly interactive environment, to browse and operate the assemblies (Fig.2). Users watch shape of object from different by mouse dragging object and operating assembling and demount a part by mouse clicking. As for the machinery part exhibition, videos are adopted to play it in rotating.

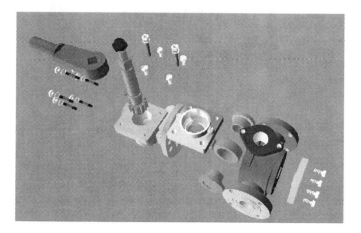

Fig. 2. Assembly of part

Construct Platform Based on PowerEasy. Based on PowerEasy, the teaching platform is set up. The homepage combined dynamic photos with static picture frame. The top of homepage involves all channel of the teaching platform, like as examples, learning sources, relevant knowledge, homework, testing (Fig.3). There are the hot photo slides at the middle of homepage on the left. Students view the photo center with mouse clicking. At the middle of homepage, the newest and hottest sources column, which can be found conveniently and timely to students, is designed. In the middle of homepage on the right, there is a log window. At the bottom, there are copy right and linking way.

Fig. 3. The top of homepage

The channel on example provides a system to view 3D-models (Fig.4). Under this channel draws drawn and various videos of parts made with Solidworks and Autocad can be watch and download for students. If the student sign up a membership, he publishes himself draws and videos under webmaster admitted, even if download web-site sources.

Fig. 4. The channel on examples

The channel on learning sources provides a lot of information about course on measuring and drawing, such as lesson plan and courseware, etc (Fig.5). After class, students find information they want from it.

The channel on relevant knowledge provides some literatures, new technology and method, and the up-to-date information about technique on measuring and drawing. They are published with the release system by webmaster, so students could read and download in any time.

Fig. 5. The channel on learning resource

Through the channel on homework, the teacher gives students assignments of the course. In additional, some questions and answers on Solidworks and "measuring and drawing" are provided by web-site. Moreover message-function is set on it. When they have problems, the student gives messages for the teacher, and then the teacher could answer questions on net.

The channel on test only provides exam papers (include answers) on "measuring and drawing" and "solidworks" to make students self-testing when reviewing their lessons.

4   Conclusion

The online teaching platform is a dynamic website. Supported by PowerEasy background, it cans liveupdate the newest information. With full background functions and simple operation, any a teacher or student can master the routing maintenance and become a supervisor of the website.

Constructed the platform, according to their learning means and capability, the student studies course contents before class or after class. It fully embodies the teaching notion of student-center. To some extent, the lacking of instruction is solved, and then students enhance their interests and initiatives on measuring and drawing of machinery. Therefore, the teaching effect is improved. It plays an important role to develop creative spirit.

Acknowledgment. This work is supported by the Teaching Transformation Research Project of Jiangxi Province (Grant No. JXJG-08-7-51).

References

1. Zeng, H., Liu, S.F., Liu, X.Y.: Lab. Sci. (2), 120 (2008)
2. Hao, M.J., Song, D.C.: Modern Mach. (5), 58 (2007)
3. M W W. Mach. 6, 34 (2007)
4. <PwerEasy Web Site Management System>,
   http://baike.baidu.com/view/28735.htm#1

The Application of Auxiliary Plane in Illustrated Diagram on Space Geometry Problems

Y.M. Lu and Y.C. Wang

School of Aeronautical Manufacturing Engineering,
Nanchang Hangkong University, Nanchang 330036, China
y_m5564@126.com

Abstract. In the engineering project, the illustrated diagram on space geometry can be utilized to solve two problems including the point of intersection of lines and the line of intersection of planes. This paper analyzes the application of auxiliary plane to the intersection problems comprehensively. Firstly, the auxiliary plane is introduced to simplify the intersection. Secondly, the objects appear as true size in the auxiliary plane view.

Keywords: Descriptive geometry, auxiliary plane, point of intersection, line of intersection.

1 Introduction

In the engineering project, many space geometry problems can be solved by the way of illustrated diagram. It is a useful for auxiliary plane to illustrate space geometry problems. By analyzing the auxiliary plane applied to illustrate space geometry problems, this paper introduces the considerations and method of choosing auxiliary planes.

Because the conformal projection for representing the shape of space objects is much better than the other ways, it is extensively applied to engineering drawings. In this projection system, the relative position of planes is indicated as the following three cases: the vertical plane of projection plane, the parallel plane of projection plane and the slant plane of projection plane. The projection characteristic of different locating plane is listed as Table 1.

Table 1. The projection characteristic

The vertical plane	The projection of a plane is focused into a line in the vertical projection plane Plane appears as foreshortened surface in the other projection planes
The parallel plane	The projection of a plane appears as true size in the parallel projection plane The projection of a plane is focused into a line in the other projection planes, and the projection appears as edges parallel to axis respectively
The slant plane	Plane appears as foreshortened surface in all the projection planes

M. Zhu (Ed.): ICCIC 2011, Part V, CCIS 235, pp. 359–364, 2011.
© Springer-Verlag Berlin Heidelberg 2011

Application Analysis of Auxiliary Plane. Space geometry problem in the engineering project mainly contains estimate, localizing, track, etc. The solution to the problem concerns the following basic construction method, which contains vertical, parallel and intersection between geometric elements, the auxiliary plane is often used in the intersection drawings.

The solution of a Line and a Plane Intersection. If a line and a plane intersect, one of which is at particular position, the projection of intersection point can be obtained according to the focus projection. The intersection point of a line and a plane at general position is obtained by the way of constructing auxiliary plane.

According to space analysis, the solution to intersection point is as follows (Fig. 1):

(1) Draw auxiliary plane P including the given line DE.
(2) Solving the intersection line MN of auxiliary plane P and given plane ABC.
(3) The intersection of line MN and line DE is the point required.

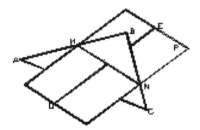

Fig. 1. Space analysis of intersection point

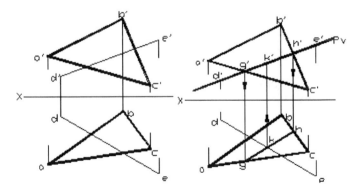

Fig. 2. Intersection point of line and plane

Example 1: Solving the intersection point of line DE and plane ABC (Fig. 2);

The intersection point of a line and a plane at general position is obtained by the way of constructing auxiliary plane on the line, auxiliary plane should locate on special position to draw simply, thus the intersection line of plane and plane can be obtained according to the focus, so a plane perpendicular to plane V is as follows in Fig. 2.

The Solution of Plane and Plane Intersection. If a plane and a plane intersect, one of which is at particular position, the projection of intersection point can be obtained according to the focus projection; the intersection point of two planes at general position can be obtained by the way of constructing auxiliary plane.

According to space analysis, the solution is as follows (Fig. 3):

(1) Draw a plane S1 to intersect P and Q at line L1 and L2.

(2) The point A is intersection of plane P, Q, S1, yet at P, Q.

(3) Continue to draw plane S2, and repeat steps 1 and 2. And then, point B can be obtained.

Line AB is the intersection of plane P and Q.

Example 2: Solving the intersection line of plane ABC and DEF (Fig 4)

Two plane is at general position, the way of auxiliary plane can be adopted; drawing the vertical plane and parallel plane simpler, So the parallel plane is selected; Draw the horizontal plane S1, S2, and obtain K1、K2 (k2, and k2′), K1K2 is the line required.

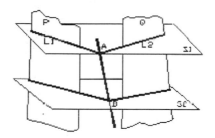

Fig. 3. Space analysis of intersection line

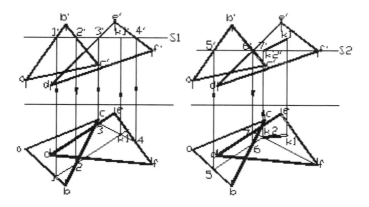

Fig. 4. Intersection line of plane and plane

The solution of Plane and Object Intersection. The intersection point of line and object is named as penetration point, which is the common point, Generally auxiliary plane method is an efficient and useful method.

When solving above-mentioned penetration point, penetration point can be obtained according to the focus projection if one of two elements is focus, on the contrary, auxiliary plane must be used. The method is as follows:

(1) Draw auxiliary plane including the line.
(2) Solving the intersection of auxiliary plane and curved solid;
(3) Solving the intersection point of line and intersection line which is the penetration point.

Example 3: Solving penetration point of line AB and oblique elliptic cylinder (Fig. 5)

Line and axis of cylinder is at general position, auxiliary plane must be adopted to solve penetration point. If drawing the vertical plane including AB, the intersection is the ellipse, which is disadvantageous for drawing. But if drawing the plane parallel to axis cylinder on the line AB, the intersection is two Straight Line parallel to axis of cylinder, which is advantageous for drawing. Therefore, through a point G on line AB, draw line GH parallel to axis of cylinder, and plane ABGH is parallel to axis of cylinder. The intersection point of M1, M2 and cylinder bottom is two points on the auxiliary Intersection, from two points, draw the line parallel to axis of cylinder, which is the intersection, finally, solve penetration point K, L, as shown in Fig. 5.

Above-mentioned auxiliary plane is a general position plane, but the plane for solving the intersection point and line is especial locating plane.

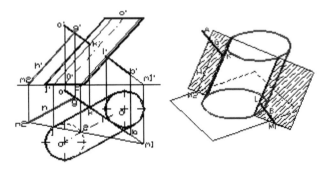

Fig. 5. Penetration point

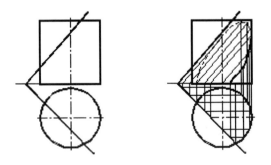

Fig. 6. Solving the intersections

Solving the Intersections. The intersection is the line common to the cutting-plane and the cut object. In fact, to make intersections is to find the intersection of planes; If the cutting-plane at especial position intersects curved solid, the views of intersection can be found by making points on the revolutionary surfaces. On the contrary, auxiliary plane must be used. The method is as follows:

(1) Draw an auxiliary plane, when the cutting-Plane intersects two revolutionary surfaces, the intersection must be either a straight line or a circle.

(2) Solving the intersection L1.

(3) Solving the intersection L2.

(4) The intersection of L1 and L2 is the point on the intersection; Draw a series of points, then connect these points smoothly to form the views of the intersections.

Example 4: Solving the intersection of cylinder and the slant plane (Fig. 6)

In Fig. 6, the axis of cylinder is perpendicular to plane H, cutting-plane is at general position, so the intersection is an ellipse in the space, Because cylinder bottom is on the plane H, cylinder is cut by both cutting-plane and plane H, the intersection is incomplete ellipse curve. And the views P of cutting-plane is no focus, the views of the intersection can be obtained according to constructing auxiliary plane, so the frontal plane is taken as auxiliary plane. The intersection of frontal plane and cylinder is two parallel lines while the intersection of frontal plane and cutting-plane P is a frontal line, these intersections intersect mutually at points, which are common points on the intersection of the cylinder and P. In the same way, a series of common points may be obtained. These common points are connected smoothly to form the views of intersection.

Solving the Intersections. Intersection is actually intersections of two objects surfaces. Which is divided into three categories, they are intersections of polyhedral and polyhedral, curved solid and polyhedron, curved solid and curved solid, the previous two intersections can be solved by completing intersection of plane and polyhedron, intersection of plane and polyhedron. But intersections of curved solid and curved solid can be obtained according to the focus projection if one of two elements is focus. On the contrary, auxiliary plane must be used. The method is as follows (Fig. 7):

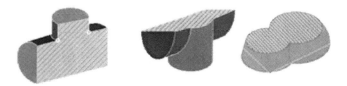

Fig. 7. The intersection line of two cylinders

(1) Draw auxiliary plane which intersects two curved solids, and the intersection must be simple.

(2) Respectively solve intersections of auxiliary plane and two curved solids.

(3)The intersections of two intersections are common points on the intersections. In the same way, a series of common points may be obtained. These common points are connected smoothly to form the views of intersection.

Example 5: Solving the intersection of cone and sphere (Fig. 8)

As shown in Fig 8, the axis of cone and sphere is perpendicular to plane H, the views of which is no focus, so the views of the intersection can be obtained according to constructing auxiliary plane, the horizontal plane is taken as auxiliary plane for this problem. The intersection of cone and sphere appears as true size of circle in the top view. In the same way, a series of common points may be obtained.

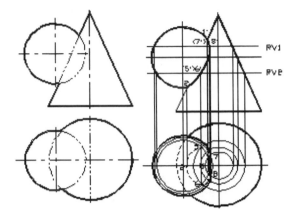

Fig. 8. The intersection of cone and sphere

2   Summary

From above-mentioned examples, auxiliary plane is either at general position or at special position, such as example of penetration point. In short, the method of auxiliary plane is based on the theory of common points, the intersections of line and plane is the common points of two planes and a line, the intersections of plane and plane is the common points of three planes. From geometry theory, the position of auxiliary plane is no limit, one of which is the vertical plane of projection plane, the parallel plane of projection plane and the slant plane of projection plane. As all above-mention examples, the principle to select auxiliary plane is as follows. First, the intersection is simple, such as line and circle etc. secondly, the objects appears as true size in the auxiliary plane view.

Acknowledgment. This work is supported by the Teaching Transformation Research Project of Jiangxi Province (Grant No. JXJG-08-7-51).

References

1. Textile University of China. Descriptive geometry and engineering drawing. Shanghai Scientific and Technical Education Publishing House (1997)
2. Zhao, Y.X.: Vertical Assistant Surface Method Extract Interfingering Lines. Journal of Anhui Agricultural University 27(3), 291 (2000)
3. Qu, S.P., Jia, Q., Liang, J.J.: Solving intersection line of slope in engineering based on Auxiliary Plan. Heilongjiang Science and Technology of Water Conservancy (1), 53 (2002)
4. Li, C.G.: Discussion about Application of Auxiliary Plan. Journal of Chongqin Petroleum College 1(9), 20 (1999)

Study on Applying of Tax Planning in Enterprises*

Xiuju Gao, Maobao Du, and Liming Yang

Hebei University of Science & Technology Qin Huangdao China
xiu23265@126.com

Abstract. Tax planning for enterprise is a kind of financial management activities to obtain economic interest by using current taxation policy, and it can take positive effect in improving business profit level and competitiveness. This paper mainly discusses the method of taxes and tax planning during the founding period, evolution period and mature period in order to make it run through the whole life cycle of the enterprise. It can play the genuine role of tax planning and satisfy the after-tax profit maximization adjusting the related tax planning key according to different cycle stages.

Keywords: Tax planning, Tax benefits, Tax preference.

Under the market economy condition, the enterprise as a independent economic benefit main body, its behavior goal is to pursue after-tax profit maximization. Therefore studying tax planning has extensive and profound significance for consummating modern enterprise financial management in consideration of the the influence of tax planning in the economic development of the enterprise .

1 Tax Planning in Founding Period

The company in founding period can rely on the national tax preferential policies made tax revenue in adverse conditions, such as it just keeping its foothold on the market, its product not being widely recognized by the market, and in short of funds maintaining operating and enterprise competitiveness.

Endeavour to Procure Government Funding. Science and technology innovation fund is one kind of subsidizing style by the national government in order to solve enterprise financing difficulty.The emphasis of the innovative fund is for small and medium size enterprises which is founded initially, have high-tech content, have good market prospect, and with high risk, and are in great need of government support. It greatly alleviates the financing difficulties of small and medium size enterprises. And the country needs to be the key support of high-tech enterprises, is reduced to 15% (25%) other enterprise tax rate of enterprise income tax. Enterprises shall strive to

* Science and Technology research and development program of Hebei No: 10457285 Small and Medium-sized enterprise development challenges and policy support research No: 200901A302.

M. Zhu (Ed.): ICCIC 2011, Part V, CCIS 235, pp. 365–369, 2011.

become science and technology enterprises at the beginning in order to get the government supportting funds and obtain tax benefits considering the subsizing policy.

Eendeavour to Procure the Loan from Financial Institution. Enterprise will raise funds through various channels in order to meet their own capital demand of development.Borrowing money from external is the most common way. According to relevant provision of the tax law of our country, the enterprise's loan interest will be fully deducted before taxes if they loan from financial institutions. However the loan interest expense from non-financial, institution ,if it is not higher than the same period loan interest calculation amount portion within, will be deducted, its loan interest may not be fully deducted. Thus, different financing channels, will lead to different tax burden. And this kind of difference, just for enterprises' financing of tax planning provides space. The lending rate of non-financial institutions is generally higher than that of financial institutions. Therefore, it is advisable for the enterprise loans from financial institutions.

2   Tax Planning of Development Period

Enterprises obtain certain space of living after founding period, and begin to enter into the development period. Along with enterprise's growing, enterprise's business scope is expanding accordingly, non-dutiable labor services are more and more concurrently. Therefore advertising expense and non-dutiable labor services concurrently become the emphasis of tax planning in this period.

Tax Planning of Advertising Expense. The advertising expenses are getting bigger and bigger proportion of operating cost with advertising's remarkable role in the modern enterprise.It is not ignorable for the enterprises to get the revenue interest by the tax duty of tax planning.

The Relevant Regulations on Deduction Pre-tax of Enterprise Advertising. Current enterprise income tax law stipulates: advertisement expense of taxpayer each tax year is permitted to be deducted if it does not exceed 15% of sales revenue that year; The exceeding part is permitted to be deducted when it is carried-over in later taxation year.

Tax Planning Idea of Advertisement. The advertisement expense distribution is not balanced in each period and even fluctuates intensely because enterprises have different marketing solutions in different period. According to this characteristic, the basic idea of tax planning in enterprise advertising expense is: reasonable distributing advertising expenses each year, allowable proportion of deduction as far as possible in order to get the time value of money.Of course, tax planning can be implemented under the premise that it can ensur the sales income level.

Engaged in the Taxable Services of Tax Planning. Engaged in the taxable services is to show taxpayer engaging in taxable sale of goods or services at the same time, also engaged in the taxable services, and engaged in the taxable services with a certain goods or providing taxable services and no direct link and affiliate relationship.

The Planning Ideas of Taxable Labor Services Concurrently. For VAT taxpayers, engaged in the taxable labor services means that taxpayer in sell the cargoes mixed with the labor service which belong to business tax. According to the PRC provisional regulations on VAT regulations, taxpayers who engaged in the taxable labor services shall account the sales of selling cargoes or taxable labor services and the taxable labor services respectively. If they don't account respectively, its non taxable labor services shall be imposed with VAT, together with goods or taxable labor services. It is clear that different accounting method lead to different tax burden, which actually also provides a certain place of tax planning for taxpayers. Comparing these two kinds of accounting method, the difference of the tax burden lies in the sales of taxable labor service. If it is counted respectively , this part of the sales should pay business tax, If not, it shall pay VAT. For VAT and business tax ,different calculation basis and the applicable tax rate lead to different discrepancy of money payment. Accordingly, introducing ratio of deductible VAT on purchase and business tax, use reference from the management accounting, this paper provide theoretical and methodological guidance for tax planning of enterprises which have mixed non taxable labor service by discussing the break-even point analysis method in the taxable services with the business tax burden balance VAT concurrently.

The Plan Analysis of Non Taxable Labor Services Concurrently. Taxpayers engaged in the non taxable labor service concurrently do not account respectively or can't account accurately shall be imposed VAT, its sales include sale of the taxable labor service and that of cargoes, the total sales of the taxable labor service shall be deemed sales with tax treatment; the amount of tax to be paid from non taxable labor service for buying cargoes permitted to be deducted from output tax if it is in accordance with the stipulation.

The amount of tax to be paid of VAT of non payable taxable labor service

= output tax - deductible VAT on purchase.

= the sale of non taxable labor services /(1 + VAT rate) × VAT rate - deductible VAT on purchase   (1)

The business tax of non taxable labor services sales= the sales of non taxable labor services ×tax rate

Therefore, the tax bearing balanced formula of non taxable labor service tax is:

The non taxable labor services sales /(1 + VAT rate) × VAT rate - deductible VAT on purchase

= the taxable services sales × tax rate   (2)

Deductible VAT on purchase = the taxable services sales earning ratio / (1 + VAT rate) x VAT rate - the taxable services sales x tax rate   (3)

If the equation is divided by the non taxable labor services on both sides, then we get balance ratio of sales, namely:

Balance ratio (deductible VAT on purchase/the taxable services with P says) sales

= VAT ratio /(1 + VAT ratio) - the business tax ratio   (4)

Counting 17% VAT ratio with 5%, 3% the tax ratio of business tax deductible VAT on purchase calculation of the taxable services sales ratio respectively, balance ratio generally exists in two forms, as shown below:

Tax burden equilibrium point ratio of the non taxable labor services concurrently

VAT ratio (%)	Business tax ratio (%)	Equilibrium point ratio (%)
17	5	9.53
	3	11.53

For example,the taxpayers who apply to the 17% VAT rate and 3% tax rate, the left sum of the equation is larger than the right sum,which illustrates that the tax burden of VAT is heavier than that of business tax   when   P is less than equilibrium point ratio[17%/(1+17%)×100%-3%=11.53%], the venture to the sales of the taxable services shall be accounted for separately and the enterprise should pay business tax in order to reduce the tax burden; when   P is higher than equilibrium point ratio[17%/(1+17%)×100%-3%=11.53%], the left sum of the equation is smaller than the right sum,which illustrates that the tax burden of VAT is heavier than that of business tax ,taxpayers should cope with the sales of goods with the non taxable labor services, and unify accounting in order to reduce the tax burden by paying together.

Tax Planning of Mature Period. The enterprises of mature period have entered a rapid expansion stage. The hardware construction of enterprises have incline to be mature, development speed can still be very quick, but will not develop increase by degree generally. Enterprises of this period may merger in many ways, integrate the existing resources in order to improve competitiveness from the scale economy on one hand; On the other hand, Enterprises should improve competitiveness through the research and development of new technology in order to control the commanding heights of technology innovation. Therefore, method of payment of the enterprise merger and hi-tech research and development become the emphasis of tax planning at this period.

Tax Planning on Method of Payment of Merger. Merger in enterprise's expansion behavior is very important. During the merger process, effects of different methods of payment should not be ignored. Therefore, it is necessary to choose the most advantageous method of payment and start a further analysis according to China's current tax law.

In the purchase sum which the consolidated enterprise pay to the acquired enterprise or its shareholders, if non-stock rights payments are not higher than 20 percent of the stock rights face value, the previous year deficit of acquired enterprise should be compensated by the consolidated enterprise through relevant gains (pre-tax profit offset of five consecutive years). In the purchase sum which the consolidated enterprise pay to the acquired enterprise or its shareholders, if non-stock rights payments are higher than 20% of the face value of stock rights, the previous year deficit of acquired enterprise can't be compensated by the consolidated enterprise. Because in both cases, deficit of the acquired enterprise in previous years are dealt with by different means, it will influence income tax burden of the merger enterprise. Generally speaking, it is beneficial to both of the enterprises that the ratio of non-stock rights payments with stock rights face value can be controlled under 20 percent.

Tax Planning on High-tech Research and Development of Enterprise. According to the current enterprise income tax law: the costs of enterprise in high-tech research and development can be numbered into enterprise administration costs, and they will be fully deducted pre-tax according to the fact. At the same time, in order to encourage enterprise technology development, and enhance the enterprise the technical level, the state administration of taxation stipulates that the research and development expenses in new technology ,new products and new crafts which have not form intangible assets yet will be deducted 50% in accordance with the provisions on the basis of occupied solid deduction ;But if the research and development expenses in new technologies, new products and new crafts have formed intangible assets ,they will be amortized 150% according to costs of intangible assets.

The usualness, high investment and the encouraging tax policy of enterprises in research and development technology activities provide a broad space for its tax planning . The adding and deduction of high-tech development expenses should obey a prerequisite: enterprises that have profit that very year. The profits here are the income money taxable without adding and deduction. Therefore ,it is of great importance to estimate the annual expenditures in high-tech research and development. So the enterprise should conform the general expenditure in research and development on condition that it will not affect progress of technology development expenses in order to get the purpose of achieving most tax benefits and enjoy the tax privilege adequately by adjusting expenses of developing technology in year properly.

Tax planning goal is determined by the maximization of enterprise value of the enterprise .Tax planning must plan synthetically centre on the overall objective which should be taken into the general investment and managing strategy of the enterprises. The optimal solution is the one that can satisfy the highest interests if there are diverse options available. Enterprises should consider it generally , measure it widely, and also pay attention to the consistence between objective of tax planning and the entire enterprise development target. But the enterprise cannot violate the enterprise's management goal in order to obtain the tax planning goal. Only in this way, the enterprise can grasp the nature and soul of tax planning, and can change it the sharp tool that is beneficial to its own development.

References

1. Zhang, L.: Theory on enterprise income tax planning. The Northern Economy, vol. 9, pp. 78–79 (2007)
2. Yu, J.: Tax planning of financing investment on high-tech enterprise behavior (Jinqing Yu). Small and Medium-Sized Enterprise Technology, vol. 7, pp. 33–35 (2007)
3. Zhang, X.: Explore the tax planning on business practice of enterprise. Law and Social, vol. 5, pp. 446–447 (2008)
4. Xia, C.: Case analysis on tax planning of new technology. Accounting Communication Financial Version, vol. 11, pp. 101–102 (2008)

Special Lecture for Graduates

Cheng Qiaolian

School of Management, Harbin Institute of Technology, Harbin, China, 150001
cheng23269@126.com

Abstract. Specialty, depth, novelty, and flexibility are characteristics of special lecture. The lecture for graduates may be the complement of general course and lay the foundation for students' work experience and thesis. The contents of the lecture can be frontier knowledge, classical theory, the deepening and expansion of basic theory, relevant disciplines, practical training, or innovative thinking. In order to make a good lecture, colleges should pay much attention to lectures, arrange for the contents of lectures reasonably, and use a variety of teaching methods to mobilize the enthusiasm of the students, while higher demands on teachers.

Keywords: graduates, special lecture, general course.

1 Introduction

Special lecture is different from general course. The certain content of general course can be departed from the whole course because it is the part of a larger system. Its purpose is to make basic principles clear for students, focusing on the "linear or plane" of knowledge, while special lecture, on the contrary, focusing on one or a number of issues, that is "point".

Special lecture has the character of specialty depth, novelty, and flexibility. "Specialty" refers to essential teaching about a topic. "Depth" means that teachers talk about a certain question deeply and thoroughly from many angles, multi-lateral, multi-level [1]. "Novelty" refers to the current information provided. "Flexibility" means that teachers, with more autonomy and flexibility, can change teaching content and methods according to the requirements of students and times.

2 Purposes of Special Lectures

To Extend and Supplement General Course. The general course can not cover all the knowledge in a discipline. The knowledge needed by students, not concluded into the general curriculum, may be taken into special lectures to compensate for the lack of general courses. Students can learn a lot with this way.

To Update Knowledge and to Adapt to the Times. Because science and technology has the rapid development today, the knowledge need adjusted to adapt to the times. However, the contents of textbooks can not been updated synchronously. In the lecture,

M. Zhu (Ed.): ICCIC 2011, Part V, CCIS 235, pp. 370–373, 2011.

teachers can introduce timely the latest achievements or research trends at home and abroad, to make students to learn new theories, new technologies and new methods, so that students can adapt to the times of knowledge development.

To Implement of Quality Education. Lectures can help students learn knowledge of related fields, to increase their information, adjust their knowledge structure, so that they work and study more easily in the future.

To Prepare for Practice. Teachers can combine theoretical and practical issues about a particular area by the design of lectures to help students grasp the capability of solving practical problems, so that they can quickly adapt to the environment and be familiar with the business.

To Lay the Foundation for the Thesis. In the lectures, teachers can sort out the basic theory and point out the frontier and trends of the discipline in order to help students clarify and choose their own interesting research questions for the thesis.

3   The Content of the Special Lecture

The contents of special lectures may have many optional issues.

The Frontier of Knowledge. In the lecture, teachers may introduce the latest research information to the students and strengthen the student's sense of innovation. Teachers may also take this opportunity to present appropriately some new ideas of their own research results. By the discussion, students will understand of relevant content better and arouse the research desire.

The Classical Theory. In the lecture, teachers may introduce all kinds of esoteric classical theory in layman's language to the student, in order to enable students to better understand the development of the discipline and the theoretical essence. Through learning and reading classic literature, students can broaden their own views, thus they can stand in a high point to understand professional knowledge and writing their thesis easily.

Deepening and Expansion of General Courses. Special topics in lectures may be the expansion and deepening of a unit of general courses. Teachers may integrate or expand the contents of general courses according the students' needs of thesis and practice [2].

The Knowledge of the Relevant Disciplines. In lectures, the information of related disciplines is taught to students, such as the basis theory or representative results of certain discipline, to broaden their knowledge structure and to inspire them to think from multi-angle or multi-lateral.

Practical Issues. According to the social hot spots, teachers may let students do practice investigation or organize some internships in companies. Also, teachers may invite some experts or business personnel with practical experience to take appropriate seminars. These ways can improve students the skills of analyzing and solving practice problem.

Innovative Thinking Training. In lectures, teachers may train students using the basic innovative methods, approaches and techniques, such as the level thinking, reverse thinking to improve the students' ability to innovate.

Content of all the above can be used alone in lectures, also comprehensively, to enrich the course content and to broaden students' understanding of knowledge.

4 Suggestions

To Pay Much Attention To Lecture. Colleges should (1) change the old thinking that lectures are not courses. Many famous universities abroad put the lecture in an important position, and regard it as an important way to cultivate talents. Therefore, colleges should pay much attention to the significance of lecture and take it into teaching plans.

(2) encourage teachers to offer lectures. Because the content of lecture is current, highly professional, covering a wide range of accessible information, it's difficult for teachers to prepare lectures. They often spend a long time and do more mental work. Therefore, hours of lectures should be considered as 1.5 times than the normal courses' hours [3]. (3) select teachers reasonably. Colleges should change the structure of teachers through inviting guest professor from the companies. In order to get to the best teaching results, lectures may be undertaken by several teachers in case that one teacher has the restrictions on the structure of knowledge.

To Arrange the Content of Lectures. Teachers should be required to (1) select suited topics. Due to time limitation, a lecture does not include all information about theory and practice. Teachers should select suited topics are according to the students' needs and professional nature. It is necessary to pay attention to the convergence between lectures and courses. (2) update the contents of lectures. According to the actual development of theory and practice, teachers should adjust the contents of lectures and adapt the trend of social development.

To Combine Kinds of Teaching Methods. If a lecture is boring, the students would not have a high Interest to listen it [4]. Therefore, in lectures, teachers should use a variety of teaching methods, such as the case studies, class discussion, role-playing, sand table drill, to fully mobilize the enthusiasm and initiative of students.

Lectures can be many models. One is that teachers give all information to students. The other is that teachers put forward a topic firstly and then students read relevant literatures. The latter approach will have advantages over traditional learning methods of students' acquiring knowledge. It is possible to enable students to develop the habit from the "learning" to "study" [5].

More Requirements for Teachers. To implement lectures, the teachers should not only be very knowledgeable on the basic theory and professional issues, but also research them deeply so that teachers can grasp the key issues [6]. Therefore, teachers who must combined teaching with scientific research regard the issues in lectures as their own research topics, to enrich and deepen the curriculum. To update teaching content, teachers should firstly keep up the pace of the times and understand and track the frontier research of contemporary natural science and social science in order to enrich the teaching content continually. Secondly, teachers should collect new information and new problems about practice. Thirdly, the students' demand for knowledge must be observed so that teachers can design the content and the process of lecture pertinently.

References

1. Shao, L.: Special Lecture of Political Lesson. Anhui Education (6), 41 (2001)
2. Zhao, Y.: Teaching Quality of Special Lectures. Journal of Tonghua Normal College (4), 29–33 (1999)
3. Zhang, Y.: University Graduating Class should Give Special Lecture. Jilin Education Science. Higher Education Research (4), 89 (1994)
4. Hu, L.: Special Lectures Combined with Professional Characteristics. Health Professional Education (12), 41–42 (2003)
5. Jia, S.: Giving Lectures - Contacting Modern Technology and Cultivating Innovation Spirit. Mechanics and Practice (20), 48–49 (1998)
6. Yuan, J.: Factors and Processes of Increasing the Attractiveness of Special Lectures. Journal of Communist Party School in Urumqi (3), 70–73 (2005)

Research and Practice System Architecture of Engineering Education for Colleges of Finance and Economics

Zhang Yuanyuan[1], Feng Hai-qi[2], and Wang Jian[2]

Central University of Finance and Economics 39 South College Road, Beijing, 100081
zhang26589@126.com

Abstract. The chance and challenge in engineering education was faced by the colleges of finance and economics. The system of engineering education should be made which is suitable for the colleges of finance and economics. The system of engineering education is dynamic, open and integrated, according to the self characteristics, we produce a cross and multi-dimensional architecture. The goal of education can be realized, cultivating engineers with skills in researching, designing and developing all kinds of informational system and software system which is covered areas of education, technology, economics and management.

Keywords: engineering education system architecture cross & multi- dimensional.

1 Introduction

In our country, we have already had a lot of key universities, which were based on the situation of expanding enrollment, uniting between colleges and the implementing of project '211' or '985'. The developed orientation of the universities is integration and application. Their goal is to be the top university in country, even in the world. Now, the major of computer science and technology has already been set up in 851 colleges including general colleges, technical colleges, financial&economic colleges, teacher-training colleges, medical colleges, agricultural colleges and others. The university of finance and economics also had this major, for example, Shanghai university of finance and economics, Northeast university of finance and economics, Zhongnan university of finance and economics, etc. As known, engineering education plays an important part in technology major. Computer science and technology as a technology major can support and assist the subject development in university of finance and economics, in these reasons, the system of engineering education should be made which is suitable for the colleges of finance and economics, the goal of education can be realized, educating engineers with skills in researching, designing and developing all kinds of informational system and software system.

2 Chance and Challenge

Our country's economic development being upgrade stage, which means new technology, innovation and international competition, and what makes the big amount

M. Zhu (Ed.): ICCIC 2011, Part V, CCIS 235, pp. 374–380, 2011.

of excellent engineer is quite needed for training and fostering. For carrying out the <National long-term education reform and development plan for next decade (2010-2020)>, Ministry of education has decided to perform the "Plan of Educating and Culturing Excellent Engineer". This decision is the important innovation of high education reformation, also is the effective way of researching engineering education in Chinese mode, it has times meaning [1].

In global times, so many problems cannot be resolved by single subject, whatever the people face to the important problem of economics, environment, resource, security and continued development, or the technical problem of design, manufacture and maintenance. The major of computer science and technology in college of finance and economics has already been set up for more than 5 years. Every college has accumulated experience in building up interdisciplinary construction, and the direction and emphasis of research is characteristics. However, the poor basis of research, lacking for research team and team leader is ubiquitous in constructing the subject.

3   System Architecture

Engineering education is a social process which can educate engineers according to the demand of society, it is different with general education and special education. High engineering education process is like a process of producing products, it should be constructed and analyzed as a integrated system, as shown in figure 1.

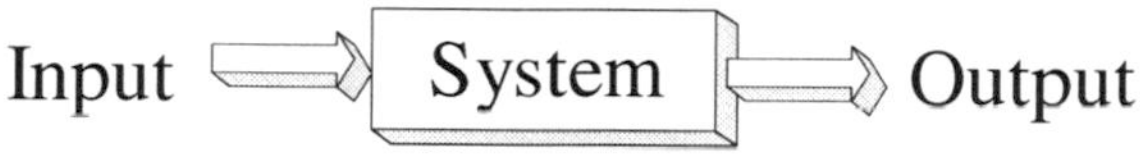

$$\text{Input} \implies \boxed{\text{System}} \implies \text{Output}$$

Fig. 1. System Architecture

Input includes student, fund, equipment, object of school, etc. Output mainly includes excellent graduate student every year and the honor of school. The architecture of the system is dynamic and open. The dynamic system is adjusting with the feedback. The open system is reforming with the requirement. The adjustment and reform is happened every now and then.

3.1   Demand Analysis

The architecture of engineering education is a system, what makes the first considered is the system's demand. Now, "Plan of Educating and Culturing Excellent Engineer" has been advocated, the future trend of country's education is emphasized on technology education, not the general education in undergraduate's study, and paying more attention to characteristic and innovation.

The target of engineering education is cultivating innovative engineers and developing the modern engineering practice education. Reforming the content, mode and management of practice education, and strengthening the student's comprehensive quality and ability of engineering practice, can service the engineering and be adapt for the demand of modern engineering practice [2,9,10]. The goal of engineering education is fostering the qualified engineers according with the economic social's demand. The student with major in computer science and technology in university of finance and economics occupied the work almost in bank and enterprise. Engineer with skills in researching, designing and developing all kinds of informational system and software system which is covered area of education, technology, economics and management is needed.

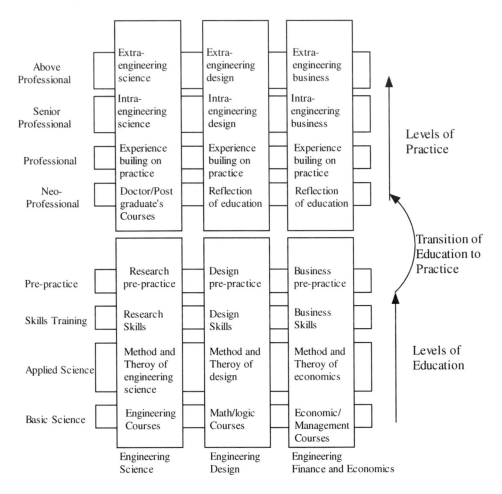

Fig. 2. Architecture of cross & multi-dimensional engineering education system

3.2 Implement

<National long-term education reform and development plan for next decade (2010-2020)> has been published, in the plan, it has affirmed the important status of interdisciplinary science. "The chief character of modern science development is

unifying micro and macro, combining reductionism and holism, crossing with subjects, penetrating with every area with basic science like math, and managing advanced technology & means. All of the characters can foster the important breakthrough in science and exceed the knowledge of objective world", "Between basic science and applicable science, science and technology, nature science and social science, the interdisciplinary sciences produce discovery of important science and product of new subject, is the most active part of science research, it should be emphasized and disposed mostly". It can be concluded the highlight of developing interdisciplinary science is national long-term development plan [3,7,8]. The characteristic subject is economics and management in university of finance and economics, the major of computer science and technology is as support and development. For accomplishing development with interdisciplinary sciences, we produced a multi-dimensional & cross innovative engineering education architecture, as shown in Fig2.

Engineering education has stable basic in scientific principle and engineering method, if the system can combine the social need and self characteristics, form the disciplinary engineering training, will acquire the applied future and show the value.

3.3 The System of Quality Evaluation

From 2000, MIT, Swedish National Agency for Higher Education and other two universities produce the CDIO Education Model, it is an abbreviation of Conceive-Design-Implement-Operate, is the latest achievements of the international engineering education reform in recent years, the research is last for four years and supported by 2000 million dollars. The graduate student's ability which is defined in curriculum of CDIO is basic knowledge of engineering education, ability of oneself, teamwork and ability of engineering system. Many CDIO standards have been used all over the world, in China, the standards should be completed in our situation.

According with the character of practice education and rule of teaching, a dynamic and overall evaluation system has been designed in our school. Dynamic means timing and random of evaluating, supervising the sample of the system randomly. Overall means the evaluation system contains the process of college's management, teacher's instruction and student's practice.

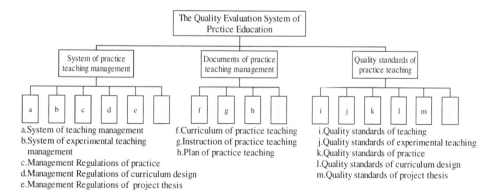

Fig. 3. Evaluation System

3.4 Perform and Practice

Practice is the core of engineering education and the guarantee of engineering education system. In our school, with the spreading concept of engineering education, we construct the triune engineering practice model, use the resource and explore the effective way of engineering education system has been performed in our school. In daily teaching, for breaking through the limited of equipment and environment in software and hardware, we have the virtual experimental teaching. In the process of teaching to practice, we have introduced the actual training practice and the school -enterprise cooperation project. What make the student be a qualified engineer in future.

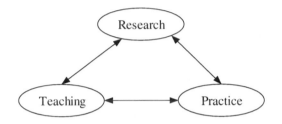

Fig. 4. Triune engineering practice model

3.5 Virtual Experimental Platform

Considering the education scheme, the particularity of engineering experiment, the setting of experiment, the object of construction and the need of function, our college has been constructed the virtual experimental platform of electronic technology, security information and network training.

The virtual experimental platform of security information is provided the functions including by editor of equipments renewal, supporting all kinds of experiment of the security information, making use of the platform to run effective experiment online, and supporting for security information teaching requirement.

The virtual experimental platform of network is consisted of exchange equipment, routing equipment, safety equipment, management software and server. Students can experiment the network according to the requirement of teaching, the experimental content is combined with project of typical application in market. The typical application of network environment can be simulated by the platform.

3.6 Actual Training and School-Enterprise Collaboration

The important and special part of engineering education mode is actual training and school-enterprise collaboration. In Combination with the engineering practice, the basic operation skills training as the foundation, the design as the main part, in order to improve the student's ability of study, engineering practice, system thinking & researching, teamwork and communication, develop the practice in researching, designing and innovation, help student to find the interest, potential and speciality of oneself. The practice courses is set up in junior, for strengthening student's grasp of the society's value and understanding of engineering chain or the culture of enterprise. In senior grade, we set up course of design and practice, which is accomplished in enterprise. The training time which is out of school is 10-12 months accumulated by four years. The graduation design is also link with the practice training. One part is used the time of winter and summer vacation, and the other maybe use the whole semester. At the same time our school is expanding the international collaboration actively. Now more than 10 enterprises are collaborated with our school, such as agricultural bank, commercial bank, stockjobber, etc.

4 Summary

After more than 5 years of practice, the implement of engineering education system in our college has been accomplished satisfactory result. On the one hand, it support the system of experimental teaching, advance the teacher's scientific level, renew the content of teaching, reform the method and mode of teaching. The achievement is included: 20 excellent teaching results in school, 27 experimental instructions published, 16 teaching research projects, 200 papers been published, etc. On the other hand, it plays more and mort important part on student's ability of engineering practice, teamwork and innovation. Since 2004, our students have been organized for kinds of subject competition, like international math competition, national math model competition, national ITAT competition, etc. 75 students own the award. In addition, undergraduates have accomplished some social practice project, 136 students own the prize, and accomplished the research of electronic commerce organized by the ministry of education and business in 2006. What we have the result is encouraged. In the "125" national plan, for supporting the rapid, healthy development of economic, still need lots of excellent engineers, and engineering education development in colleges of finance and economics is still on the road.

Acknowledgement. The paper is supported by "Public Project on Beijing Municipal Commission of Education".

References

1. Li, F.T.: Research and Practice of Engineering Education Mode. University Education Scientific 3, 173–178 (2010)
2. Wang, Z.H., Chen, Z.G.: Engineering Education Idea and Characteristics of Technology University. China's High Education (2006)
3. Liu, Z.R., Nie, R.H., Wu, L.G.: Reform of Practice Teaching System. Laboratory Research and Exploration 4, 22(2), 4–7 (2003)
4. Esendal, T., Rogerson, S.: A Framework to Bring Engineering Students' Work-based Experiences into Their Education. IEEE REGION 8 SIBIRCON, 89–95 (2008)
5. Yi, C., Liao, H., Zhou, W., Chen, T.: Re-engineering of Computer Engineering Education Based on CDIO Education Model. In: The 5th International Conference on Computer Science & Education, pp. 746–750

6. Berggren, K.R., Brodeur, D., Crawley, E.R., et al.: CDIO: An international initiative for reforming engineering education. World Transactions on Engineering and Technology Education (2), 49–52 (2003)
7. Zhang, H.: Adapt to the Social Development of Chinese Engineering Education. Reform Engineering Education 4, 5–10 (2005)
8. Liu, H.Z., Kong, H.B., Zou, X.D.: Comprehension is Innovation. Research of Higher Engineering Education 6, 13–18 (2008)
9. Liu, J.P., Zhang, F.: Exploration of Strengthening Practice Teaching in Higher Engineering Education. Teaching Jinwei 5, 54–56 (2010)
10. Fan, Z.H.: Comparation and Revelation Training Mode of Engineering Education. Journal of Nanjing University of Aeronautics (Social Science Edition) 1, 67–73 (2006)

Research on Entrepreneurship Education Based on E-Commerce

Liu Zunfeng[1] and Zhang Chunling[2]

[1] Student Affairs Department, Hebei United University, Tangshan, Hebei, China
liuo2525@126.com
[2] College of Management, Hebei United University, Tangshan, Hebei, China

Abstract. To develop entrepreneurship education and to cultivate entrepreneurial talents can help alleviate the current severe employment situation for college students and improve the overall quality of them. By analyzing the difficulties facing the college students and combining entrepreneurship education with courses of e-commerce, this paper holds that e-commerce is an effective way of self-business initiation and that it is a key point to realize the transition from entrepreneurship awareness to entrepreneurial actions. In the end this paper puts forward a framework of entrepreneurship education system.

Keywords: entrepreneurship education, e-commerce, entrepreneurship awareness, entrepreneurial actions.

1 Introduction

Entrepreneurship education is a new education concept put forward by western countries in the nineteen eighties. It is about cultivating people's comprehensive entrepreneurial qualities, such as entrepreneurship awareness, entrepreneurship thinking, entrepreneurial skills, etc, and making sure that they would have some kind of entrepreneurial abilities. Regarded by UNESCO as the "third passport" of education, entrepreneurship education is given the same important position with academic education and vocational education. Along with the coming of popularization stage of higher education in China, our country also actively puts much attention to researches of developing entrepreneurship education. Cultivating entrepreneurial talents is of highly practical significance for alleviating the employment pressure for graduates and cultivating compound talents' surviving ability and competition ability and entrepreneurial ability.

I . E-commerce: An Effective Way of College Students' Entrepreneurship

A. *The Severe Employment Pressure Facing the College Graduates Is Calling For Entrepreneurship Education*

Along with the coming of popularization stage of higher education, more and more college graduates will walk out of colleges into our society, making it much more

M. Zhu (Ed.): ICCIC 2011, Part V, CCIS 235, pp. 381–388, 2011.

difficult to find a job. When it comes to solving college students' employment problem, entrepreneurship education inevitably attracts much attention. Encouraging college students' entrepreneurship is undoubtedly an effective measure to alleviate the current severe employment situation. By vigorously developing entrepreneurship education to change the traditional talents training targets, we can train the students to master not only professional knowledge and skills, but also entrepreneurial knowledge and skills and improve their entrepreneurial qualities and abilities, making college graduates become creators of new jobs as well as high-quality applicants.

B. College Students Grown up in The Information Age are more Likely to Accept Entrepreneurship Education Based on E-Commerce

Nowadays college students are originally raised up in network environment and they have more advantages than any other social classes to set up their own business with the help of the Internet. What's more, it is definitely feasible for college students to set up their own business with the help of the Internet, because they will live and work in such an environment, form new communication modes and thinking modes. From the perspective of university student's entrepreneurial abilities, almost every colleges and universities regard it as one of the professional training objectives. The college students have full capacity to start their own business on the Internet with their creativity, wisdom and passion. For the college graduates who have just walked out of school and who have little economic strength, to set up their own business with the help of Internet is undoubtedly the first choice. Through this they can manage their time freely, know many friends while making their own money and continuously improving their capability of operating business.

C. The Advantages Of E-Commerce Make College Students' Entrepreneurship Possible.

E-commerce has advantages like virtualization, openness, accessibility, cheapness. For instance C2C (Consumer To Consumer) in e-commerce serves as a kind of network virtual shop which is favored by thousands of college graduates, giving them little economic pressure with its relatively low entry threshold. Therefore, e-commerce business activities with the Internet's help in China have achieved unprecedented rapid development during the past few years, and knowledge economy has provided those with higher education with resource superiority. At the same time the popularization of the Internet also provides college students with information superiority. Contemporary college students are gradually becoming a vigorous force in this boom of entrepreneurship.

II. The Difficulties Facing Entrepreneurship Based On E-Commerce

A.   The Ratio of Transition from Entrepreneurship Awareness to Entrepreneurial Actions is Low

Entrepreneurship entails two aspects: forming independent entrepreneurship awareness and conducting entrepreneurial actions. Those students who have the entrepreneurship awareness of using e-commerce to set up their own business account for a big of the undergraduate students, but those who have taken actual entrepreneurial actions account for only a small proportion, and the number of students who have realized self-employment is even smaller. According to a survey by Hebei Youth Corps Committee, only 52% of the university students who will graduate soon have an entrepreneurial desire, but as far as the rate of success is concerned, Zhejiang province has the highest rate, which is only 4% and Hebei province only 0.3% while the global average entrepreneurial success rate is about 20%. This illustrates that how to transform the entrepreneurship awareness to entrepreneurial actions is an issue of great importance.

B.   The Lack of Practices of Both Entrepreneurship Education and E-commerce

Universities and colleges define entrepreneurship education as a kind of education to enhance the students' self employment ability, to make graduates became the creator of more professional posts; as a kind of education to develop and improve college students' basic entrepreneurial qualities, to cultivate the creative spirit and creative ability of high-quality builders of socialist modernization. But the current development of entrepreneurial education faces many problems: in the first place, the development of entrepreneurship education has a short history, resulting in there being not enough qualified teachers and the low education quality; in the second place, at present the entrepreneurship education in our country is only well carried out in a few key universities where the economic development is relatively good and there are also a lot of colleges which did not pay attention to the entrepreneurship education, thus causing many difficulties for the popularization of entrepreneurship education, the enhancement of its influence and the training of more entrepreneurial talents; in the third place, at present the entrepreneurship education in some universities is not included into the professional education. They only appear in some other forms (such as seminars, clubs, practices, competitions, etc), making it more difficult to have enough effects.

In many colleges and universities the practical e-commerce teaching can not meet the needs of entrepreneurship education: because of reasons like lack of money and equipments, many schools can not arrange enough courses for practical e-commerce teaching. Without experimentally virtual environment, those colleges and universities can only let the students browse some web sites or do some online shopping when conducting e-commerce experiments. In this way, students can only see the superficial processes of e-commerce. They would neither know the background processing of e-commerce nor the operating procedures. In some universities the experiments of e-commerce are only about programming and website building. The students are only asked to write programs and make web pages or to build e-commerce sites by imagination. Although doing so can cultivate students' website built ability, this is not all what e-commerce experiment is about. E-commerce is not about cultivating students' programming ability, which deviates from the training goal of the course. Many students in some colleges and universities came for this course with full interest but they left with disappointment. Modern college students are active thinkers and they have a strong sense of participation for new things. E-commerce is a course which focuses on practical actions. At first the students have every interest to learn it but the interest declines in the middle and last stage of the course because there are not enough practices and too much theories. It can be concluded that education without enough practices can not achieve the goals of entrepreneurship education.

C. The Lack of "Two-qualification Teachers"

Entrepreneurship education, as an education combining practical experience and personal practice, is different from traditional imparting of summarizing knowledge or the theories in the colleges. Therefore it is improper for the traditional college teachers to teach e-commerce, otherwise many problems would arise. This is because that they are academic experts who lack entrepreneurial experience and the practical ability. Apart from being unable to arouse student's interest, they don't have effective entrepreneurial methods and their entrepreneurial plans tend to fail in real business situations. Therefore colleges and universities need to introduce advanced teachers with entrepreneurial experience to improve the quality of the entrepreneurship education.

"Two-qualification teachers" mean teachers who can not only teach professional knowledge, but also carry out professional practices. E-commerce is a discipline which needs many practical actions. If the teachers don not have any practical experience or can not keep close contact with actual e-commerce, what they teach in class will not be in line with the real situations in e-commerce. Therefore having enough professional teachers is of fundamental significance for successful entrepreneurship education based on e-commerce.

Compared with other types of entrepreneurship, e-commerce is a method featuring low threshold, low risk, and easy accessibility. Especially for the modern college students grown up in Internet environment, it is much easier for people in this Information Age to use the Internet to set up their own business because they are so familiar with the network. Many people think that entrepreneurship is only about having a brilliant idea. In fact it is far more complicated than that: there are various problems in areas of finance, law and technology. In our country e-commerce industry is far from mature. There are many things which are not properly regulated in this new industry and they may pose many problems for the college students when they are trying to set up their own business with the help of the Internet. So the colleges and universities should strengthen the training of "two-qualification teachers".

III Measures and Suggestions

A. Effective Guide from Entrepreneurship Awareness to Entrepreneurial Actions

Ma Yun, China's e-commerce master, once pointed out: with thousands of methods in mind, one would wake up in the morning and still deal with his work with the old method. In the first place many people would like to venture out, but they are often stopped by themselves: they just can not turn their thoughts into real actions. Although the transition of entrepreneurial actions from entrepreneurship awareness can be influenced by the entrepreneurial team, technology, families and societies, the initial capital and entrepreneurship education, it is also determined by some subjective factors. The students are not confident and pessimistic about setting up their own business because they do not have enough knowledge and experience about entrepreneurship. In the second place, the young entrepreneurs are not confidant about their own qualities. They can learn to make up for the lack of knowledge, but the entrepreneurs' qualities are not easy to make up for. They have a low level of acceptance for risks and unknown factors and lack mental continuity. Many college students have no confidence when facing risks and variable factors, especially when it comes to taking economic risks and opportunity risks. What's more, lack of mental continuity along with other subjective factors poses great difficulties for the transition of entrepreneurial actions from entrepreneurial awareness.

Colleges and universities should actively guide the students to transform their entrepreneurial awareness into effective entrepreneurial actions. Entrepreneurship education should be included into various professional talents cultivation plans and professional curriculum system as well as setting up related courses about entrepreneurship. Nowadays the education in many colleges and universities puts much more emphasis than necessary on book knowledge learning, and ignores the arrangements and guide of practical training. It is proved that only through real and practical training can the students really learn something useful. It is an effective way to transform the entrepreneurship awareness to entrepreneurial actions by real practices and at the same time the indispensable customer relations, commercial network and other social resources also increase along with practical entrepreneurial actions.

B. Creating Entrepreneurial Atmosphere by Changing Education Concepts

Teachers should change the evaluation standards of students: those with good academic results are good students as well as those who have good entrepreneurial performance. Colleges and universities should strengthen the promotion of self-business initiation by selecting "campus entrepreneurial star", conducting business plan contest, and exchanging entrepreneurial experience to build a comfortable and harmonious environment for their entrepreneurship. It is also of highly importance to promote the training of entrepreneurial talents by the school radio, newspapers, promoting windows. What's more it is necessary to create an atmosphere of promoting and supporting entrepreneurship and tolerating failures.

C. Strong Support from Colleges, Society and the Government

The entrepreneurship of college students needs strong support from colleges, society and the government. Therefore a systematic supporting and guaranteeing platform must be created to promote the entrepreneurship education.

Those qualified colleges can found an entrepreneurship center, organize an entrepreneurship guiding team by two-qualification teachers to give the students systematic and specific directions. Especially it is also highly recommended to regularly invite successful alumnus entrepreneurs to give lectures about their own entrepreneurial experience to the students, to give the students more perceptual information about entrepreneurship. With the same learning background, the students would find it very easy to identify with their alumnus entrepreneurs and this will greatly boost the entrepreneurial confidence of the students. Sometimes students would find that their entrepreneurial actions would have conflicts with their classes in colleges because of the time arrangements. It is suggested that elastic management should be carried out to solve this problem. The entrepreneurial behavior itself is a kind of exploration, as well as a kind of learning, a kind of active, positive way of learning. It is recommended to combine our country's traditional education style "more learning, less thinking" with that of the United States "more thinking, less learning" and to implement elastic management of class arrangement and length of schooling, allowing entrepreneurial students to study related courses by ways of mass learning, distance learning or turning in assignments. The students should also be given 3 to 6 years to finish their undergraduate courses and the method that entrepreneurial practice can account for credits of related courses, which is invented by Industrial and Commercial College of Yiwu.

D. The Construction of the Entrepreneurship Education System Based on E-Commerce

Based on the advanced entrepreneurship education experience the courses arrangements in the colleges of our country should include the following four aspects: entrepreneurial awareness, entrepreneurial expertise, entrepreneurial abilities, and entrepreneurial psychological quality. The entrepreneurial awareness mainly includes entrepreneurial needs, motivation, interest, ideals, beliefs, the formation and development of the outlook of the world. We should not only cultivate students' entrepreneurial self-awareness, but also cultivate the students' entrepreneurial social consciousness. Entrepreneurship expertise mainly includes the imparting of the professional knowledge, management knowledge and comprehensive knowledge. While imparting professional knowledge we should focus on cultivating the effective learning methods of the college students. They are supposed to have the idea of studying actively for a life time and to have the ability to use the knowledge effectively and to open new horizons of the vision of the knowledge. Entrepreneurial abilities mainly include professional abilities, management abilities, the ability to work alone, and the comprehensive ability of technology, social net-working and management expertise. Entrepreneurial psychological qualities mainly include formation and development of independence, courage to take risks, tenacity, self-discipline, adaptability, collaboration, meticulousness, and extroversion.

How to design practical teaching links is of fundamental significance in combining entrepreneurship education with e-commerce. It is suggested the course be divided into three stages: e-commerce recognition, virtual training with the help of Deyitong e-commerce laboratory, conducting real comprehensive application with the help of Alibaba on Taobao (famous e-commerce websites in China). All these can be clearly seen in the following tree view:

(Deyitong means Deyitong e-commerce laboratory system)

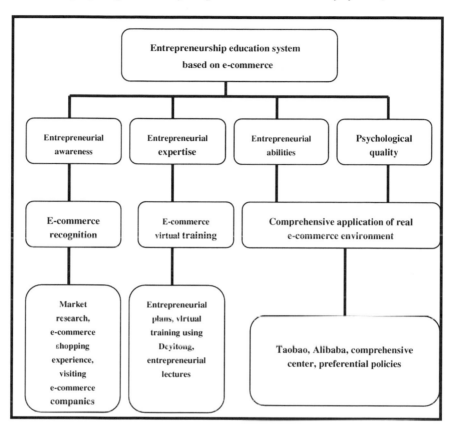

Fig. 1. Entrepreneurship Education System Based on E-Commerce

In this system, this idea guides the transition of the students' entrepreneurial actions from entrepreneurial desires: with entrepreneurial actions certain achievements students could have the privilege not to sit for the examination of the e-commerce course and different credits would be awarded to them according to their entrepreneurial performance. The reason why we chose Taobao is that it is the largest and the most formal e-commerce trade platform in China: in the year of 2009 Taobao realized daily turnover target of 100 million RMB with individual trading day turnover even realizes 400 million RMB. This has created about a million jobs and many college students are online shopkeepers. In addition, the controlling corporation of Taobao, Alibaba Group Corporation has held many national competitions like "future inline businessman challenging competition" which were based on Taobao. Therefore we finally decided to choose Taobao as designated platform for transactions.

In a semester if the credit score of a student's online shop reaches above 200 points with 95% positive comments, the student would earn the credits of the e-commerce course without taking the examination. There being no cheatings in this matter is very important, because there are people who specialize in creating positive comments and high credit score by false trades. We can avoid this by regularly checking detailed lists of the students' accounts. Zhang Mingye from Hebei Financial Institute puts forward an idea, "outsourcing e-commerce services ", which means to organize the students to help small businesses get trade orders with the help of alibaba.com e-commerce. This is also an effective e-commerce model which can be adopted.

2 Summary

In a word, college students' independent entrepreneurship is an effective way to alleviate the current severe employment situation, of which using e-commerce is an effective method, how to combine e-commerce courses with entrepreneurial education to guide the transition of entrepreneurial actions from entrepreneurial awareness is of great importance. And all of these could not be successfully carried out without the support of colleges, government at all levels and the society.

References

1. He, X., Zang, Y.: Analysis on the gap between college students' entrepreneurial actions and entrepreneurial awareness. Modern Business (April 2010)
2. Jia, S.: Research on the development modes of entrepreneurial college students. Higher Engineering Education Researches (February 2009)
3. Tu, D.: On the curriculum system of college students' entrepreneurship education. Higher Education Researches in Heilongjiang Province (October 2009)

A Method to Query and Browse Mathematical Formulas

Hong Liurong and Lu Zhuanghua

Shangqiu normal college, Henan, China
hong_11234@126.com

Abstract. Mobile learning is becoming a new way of learning with popular concern. WML, as a major technical support for mobile learning, does not support the expression of mathematical formulas so that the mathematical formulas is difficult to be transferred and reused. This paper studied the structural characteristics of mathematical formulas and proposed a structure model for mathematical formula. According to this model, markup language of a universal mathematical formula was designed. This markup language may be used to transport and express mathematical formula in mobile learning environment. Its structure is simple and is easy to browse.

Keywords: mathematical formula, markup language, Mobile learning, WAP.

1 Introduction

As more and more theoretical and practical researches about mobile learning, mobile learning, as a new way of learning, has become more and more popular in practical application, among which the mobile learning which is based on WAP technique is a major manner [1-3]. Wireless Markup Language, as the standard language of WAP technical application, provided useful support for mobile learning. However, the typical problem of it is the browse of mathematical formulas. At present, in order to display mathematical formulas, the formulas have to be browsed in the form of pictures. Thus, two problems appear: one is that pictures occupy too much memory of mobile equipment; the other is that the formulas are difficult to reuse. The way to solve them is to use a markup language to describe and display mathematical formulas. The major markup language nowadays is MathML. But this language is very complex, difficult to browse and not suitable for mobile equipment. Based on this problem, the paper proposed a markup language in order to describe mathematical formulas with a simple text. This description occupies little memory, uses few plug-in units and can be used in mobile learning equipment.

2 Mathematical Formula Model

Mathematical formula is a recursive and natural language [4], which expresses its meaning with a two-dimensional structure. Through analysis, the structure in

M. Zhu (Ed.): ICCIC 2011, Part V, CCIS 235, pp. 389–398, 2011.
© Springer-Verlag Berlin Heidelberg 2011

mathematical formula was divided into three kinds of structure model and based on this; a universal model for mathematical formula was established.

2.1 Forms of Mathematical Formula

(1) Basic Form

The structure of basic type is as shown in Figure 1 including 11 types and their names are as shown in Figure 1-1 to Figure 1-5 respectively and A is defined as the body.

(2) Compound Form

In the mathematical formula, binomial expression, matrix, determinant and conditional formula are a special entirety. The paper called this type of structure as compound type, which took the constituents of this special formula such as large brace, medium brace, small brace and determinant symbol as the body part. Compound type can be divided into three parts:

1) Formula element

As a component of the compound type, formula element only occupies a rank position. In addition, it can be connected to the other components in eight directions.

2) Block symbol

Occupying several rank positions of the compound form, block symbol has only one character. In the mean time, its boundary is free. The characters of block symbol usually include ""O"、 "o"、 "0"、 "1"和"*". And the shape of block symbol usually is triangle or rectangle, as shown in Figure 2.

3) Replicator

Replicator, occupying one or more rank positions, is characters that demonstrate the continuous permutation in the directions of →↓↘↙. Replicator is composed of at least three dots in the same line, as shown in Figure 2. Replicator has three connection types: the first type is both ends of replicator are connected to formula elements; the second type is one end of replicator is connected to a formula element with the other end pointing to the beginning part or end part of a row or column, as shown in Figure 2(c); the third type is neither end of replicator is connected to formula element, they directly occupy a row or column, indicating the repetition of the row or column, as shown in the third line of Figure 2(d).

As for the compound type, it can be classified into two categorizes:

1). Regular compound form

The compound form that has neither block symbol nor replicator is called regular compound type. Figure 3 is its geometric sketch map.

2). Irregular compound form

The compound form that has block symbol and replicator is called irregular compound type. This kind of compound type often appears in conditional formula, determinant and matrix.

The structure of compound type is very complex. According to its characteristics, their representation methods are given as follows:

1) The formula element of the compound form can be represented directly through the mark number of row or column.

2) Irregular compound form is much more complex. The formula element is still represented by the mark number of row and column, while the three functions can be defined as the representation of block symbol and replicator.

Function $Tri(x_1, y_1, x_2, y_2, x_3, y_3, p)$ is used to represent triangular block symbol. The first six parameters represent the mark number of row and column of triangular block symbol's three vertexes. The last parameter represents the character type of block symbol. To ensure the consistency of the representation, it is stipulated that the parameters with low mark number of row and column are at the fore, while the parameters with high mark number of row and column are in the rear. In addition, they are ranked with row at front and column at the end.

Function $\mathrm{Re}\,c(x_1, y_1, x_2, y_2, p)$ is used to represent the rectangular block symbol. The first four parameters represent the mark number of row and column of the rectangle's upper left vertex and lower right vertex. The last parameter represents the character type of the block symbol.

Function $\mathrm{Re}\,p(x_1, y_1, x_2, y_2)$ is representation of replicator. The four parameters represent the mark numbers of row and column of replicator's two ends. A replicator may occupy more than one mark number of row and column. As long as the mark numbers of row and column of the replicator's two ends are known, it would be much easier to infer the mark numbers of row and column occupied by the replicator. It is stipulated that: $X_1 \le X_2, Y_1 \le Y_2$, as shown in Figure 2(b). Table 1 can be referred to for the representation of irregular compound form.

(3) Mixed Connection

In some fractals, e.g., the fraction $\dfrac{x^2 + 1}{x + y}$, the top of the numerator cannot be expressed clearly by the above fractals. So the mixed connection is introduced to solve this problem. By interconnecting the above two forms right and left, the right line of the left form and the left line of the right form are on the same vertical line. The centers of all fractals are on the same level line. The entirety that is constructed in this way is called a mixed connection. For instance, the numerator of the above fraction is a mixed connection.

Table 1. The presentation of irregular compound form

type	formula element						Block symbol	replicator
	a_{11}	a_{12}	a_{22}	a_{1n}	a_{2n}	a_{nn}		
Representation	(1,1)	(1,2)	(2,2)	(1,4)	(2,4)	(4,4)	Tri(1,2,1,4,3,4,*)	Rep(1,3,1,3) Rep(2,3,2,3) Rep(3,3,3,3)

Fig. 1. 1(a) top-right form

Fig. 1. 1(b) bottom-right form

Fig. 1. 1(c) Top- bottom-right form

Fig. 1. 2(a) Top form

Fig. 1. 2(b) bottom form

Fig. 1.-2(c) top-bottom form

Fig. 1.-3 embed form

Fig. 1. 4(a) top-left form

Fig. 1. 4(b) bottom-left form

Fig. 1. 4(c) Top-bottom- left form

Fig. 1. 5 mixed form

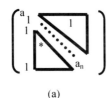

(a)

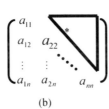

(b)

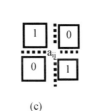

(c)

$$\begin{bmatrix} a_{11}x_1 + ... + a_{1n}x_1 \\ a_{21}x_1 + ... + a_{2n}x_2 \\ .... \\ a_{m1}x_1 + ... + a_{mn}x_n \end{bmatrix}$$

(d)

Fig. 2. 4 examples of Irregular compound form

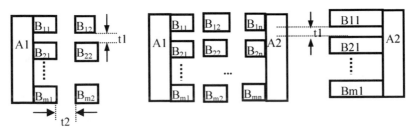

Fig. 3. Regular compound form

2.2 Models of Mathematical Formulas

A universal mathematical formula is composed of the above fractals and the mixed connection whereas each fractal consists of fractals and the missed connection. Based on the above analysis, a universal mathema- tical formula can be divided into basic form, replicators and block symbols. Hence, as seen in Fig4, the logic structural model of the mathematical formulas can be constructed. The significance of this type of model lies in analyzing the logic structure of universal mathematical formulas and building the markup language of mathematical formulas. Text-based storage and description of the mathematical formulas can be achieved.

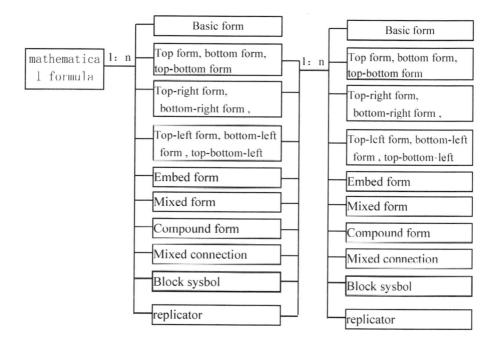

Fig. 4. The logic structure of mathematical formulas

3 Mathematical Formula Markup Language

By applying XML technique, a universal mathematical formula markup language (UMFML) can be designed on the of above mathematical formula models.

3.1 Elements of Mathematical Formulas and Their Markup

According to the definition of mixed connection, the relationship between upper left form, left inferior form, left upper-lower form, upper form, lower form, upper-lower form, right upper form, right lower form, right upper-lower form and mixed forms is containing and being contained. In order to clarify the complexity of the markup language, all the referred forms are marked by one element; others are marked by an element respectively; mixed connections and basic forms are used in irregular compound forms as an element. Rectangular block symbol, triangle block symbol, replicator and elements of formulas are marked by respective element. It begins with the root element <Eq></Eq> marking all formulas. Table 2 presents the elements of all formulas.

3.2 Defining the Properties of the Elements

Properties link the name values and elements together. Attribute list declaration is used to limit the attribute set of preset element types, build the limit of the property types and provide default values. Elements can define the types of forms but cannot define the concrete structure of the formulas. The concrete structure of the formulas can be defined by the properties of elements in UMFML.

Table 2. UMFML elements and its marked sign

Elements type	marked sign	Elements type	marked sign
Basic form element	<Str></Str>	Embed form element	<Embed></Embed>
Mixed form element	<Mix></Mix>	Mixed connectiong element	<Mxl></Mxl>
Compound form element	<Comp></Comp>	Triangle block element	<Tri></Tri>
rectangular block element	<Tec></Tec>	Formula element	<FE></FE>
Replicator element	<Rep></Rep>	Root element	<Eq></Eq>

(1) Properties of Mixed Forms
As seen in Fig 5(a,b), besides the main part, a mixed form can express clearly the numbers of its related forms and their location relation. These two formulas are mixed in structure and consists of two forms., so the property value should be set respectively.

Firstly, the location variables of top, upper right, lower right, bottom, lower left, upper left are defined as R1、 R2、 R3、 R4、 R5、 R6. The value is correspondingly 1, default is 0.

(2) Properties of Embedded Forms Elements
The property of embedded forms elements is defined as position, and its value is enumeration type. It shows whether upper left location is contained in embedded structure or not. If the value is 1, the upper left location is contained; if the value is 0, the upper left location is not contained. For example, position=0 in fig 6(a); position=1 in fig 6(b).

$$\sum_{i=1}^{1000}$$

(a)

$$P_1{}^{\text{sec}}$$

(b)

$$\sqrt{x}$$

(a)

$$\sqrt[3]{x}$$

(b)

(3) Properties of Compound Forms Elements

Compound form is a complicated structure, and its main part and the number of the main parts should be defined firstly. It is distinguished by the property BodyClass and the value of the property is necessary. As the main parts applied in compound forms are limited, the value range of properties is zero or one among '(','[','{ ', '|', '||' or is zero or one among '}',']',')','|','||'.

(4) Properties of Rectangular Block Symbol Elements

The elements of rectangular block symbol mark the block symbols of a compound form. In the second part, it is defined that a function is used to express a block symbol. Four parameters of the function are used to express the location of upper left point and lower right point of the rectangular block symbol; the last parameter expresses the type of the block symbol. So there are five properties of the block symbol: Lrow, Lcol, Rrow, Rcol, CharName, and they represent respectively the location of the upper left point, the location of lower right point and characters of block symbols. Until now, the characters of block symbol: "0""1""O""o""*" have been defined, so the value of CharName must be one of these five. Properties of rectangular block symbol elements are necessary.

(5) Similar to the properties of rectangular block symbol elements, in view of seven parameters in triangle block symbols, so seven properties are defined to express the location of vertexes and the symbol type. They are : Row1, Col1, Row2, Col2, Row3, Col3, CharName. The value of CharName can only be one of the block symbol types. The order of the first six properties expressing the vertexes is from row to column, and from big to small.

(6) Properties of Replicator Elements

Replicator is expressed by the location of its three endpoints, so it is defined that there are four properties of replicator elements. They are : Row1, Col1, Row2, Col2. The order of expressing the vertexes is from row to column, and from big to small.

(7) Properties of Formula Elements

In the formula elements, two properties Row and Col are defined, so the line number and column number can be expressed.

3.3 Define DTD Text of UMFML

A XML text not only needs to be good in form, but also effective. The validity of XML text is assured by DTD text(Document Type Definition). According to the logic structural model of mathematical formulas, characters of mathematical formulas and the correspondent operational symbols are regarded as the form of characters. For instance, a+b is expressed directly in the form of string, written as "a+b", but not in the form of plus in MathML. The following is the DTD text in UMFML:

```
<?xml version="1.0"
encoding="gb2312"?>
<!DOCTYPE eq[
<!ELEMENT
eq (Mix*,Str*,Embed*,Comp*,Mxl*)>
<!ELEMENT Str (#PCDATA)>
<!ELEMENT Embed (Mix*,Str*,
                 Embed*,Comp*,
Mxl*)>
<!ELEMENT Mix
(Mix*,Str*,Embed*,Comp*)>
<!ELEMENT Comp
(Tec*,Tri*,Rep*,FE*)>
<!ELEMENT Tri EMPTY>
<!ELEMENT Rec EMPTY>
<!ELEMENT Rep EMPTY>
<!ELEMENT FE (Mix*,Str*,
Embed*,Comp*,Mxl*)>
<!ATTLIST Embed position (0|1)
#REQUIRED>
        <!ATTLIST Mix
        R1 (0|1) #REQUIRED
        R2 (0|1) #REQUIRED
        R3 (0|1) #REQUIRED
        R4 (0|1) #REQUIRED
        R5 (0|1) #REQUIRED
      R6 (0|1) #REQUIRED
          >
<!ATTLIST Comp
        BodyClass CDATA
#REQUIRED>
          <!ATTLIST Tri
          Row1 CDATA
#REQUIRED
        Col1 CDATA #REQUIRED
        Row2 CDATA
#REQUIRED
        Col2 CDATA #REQUIRED
        Row3 CDATA
#REQUIRED
        Col3 CDATA #REQUIRED
        CharName (1 | 0 | O|o)
#REQUIRED >

<!ATTLIST Rec
        Row1 CDATA
#REQUIRED
        Col1 CDATA #REQUIRED
        Row2 CDATA
#REQUIRED
        Col2 CDATA #REQUIRED
        CharName (1 | 0 | O|o)
#REQUIRED >
<!ATTLIST Rep
        x1 CDATA #REQUIRED
        y1 CDATA #REQUIRED
        x2 CDATA #REQUIRED
        y2 CDATA #REQUIRED>
        ]>
<eq>
```

The following is the document of formulas (1) described by UMFML:

$$f(x) = \frac{\begin{vmatrix} 2 & 3 \\ 5 & 4 \end{vmatrix}}{\sqrt[7]{x^2}} + \overrightarrow{AB} + \int \sin(x)dx \tag{1}$$

```
<eq>
    <Str>f(x)=</Str>
        <Mix R1="1" R4="1" R5="0" >
    <Str>-</Str>
    <Comp BodyClass="|,|">
        <FE Row="1" Col="1">2</FE>
        <FE Row="1" Col="2">3</FE>
        <FE Row="2" Col="1">5</FE>
        <FE Row="2" Col="2">4</FE>
    </Comp>
    <Embed position="1">
        <Mix R2="1" >
            <Str>x</Str>
            <Str>2</Str>
        </Mix>
        <Su>7</Str>
    </Embed>
    </Mix>
        <Str>+</Str>
        <Mix R1="1" >
            <Str>AB</Str>
            <Str>→</Str>
        </Mix>
        <Str>+∫sin(x)dx</Str>
</eq>
```

4 Conclusion

Based on the structural characteristics of mathematical formulas, this paper proposes a new mathematical formula structure model. Further, a universal mathematical formula markup language: UMFML, is designed according to this new model. UMFML is easy in structure and convenient to browse. The users of an open WAP browser can design their own formula browser plug-ins easily by using this markup language. Besides, it is practical as it provides an effective transmission mode to any learning content concerning mathematical formulas. Due to its text-based characteristic and the display mode isn't described, it's easy to achieve the inquiry and multiplexing of the formulas.

Acknowledgement. This research was sponsored by National Natural Science Foundation of Henan Education Department(No. 2009B520024).

References

1. Ye, C., Xu, F., Xu, J.: Review of Mobile Learning. e-Education Research (03), 12–19 (2004)
2. Jiang, L., Yu, L.: Application of Mobile Learning Based on 3G in Adult Education. The Variety of Mass Media and School Education (03), 67–68 (2007)
3. Li, S., Wu, X.: Application of Mobile Learning Based on WAP in High School English Study. E-China Education (14), 52–54 (2009)
4. Chan, K.F., Yeung, D.Y.: Recognizing online handwritten alphanumeric characters through flexible structural matching. Pattern Recognition 32(7), 1099–1114 (1999)

The Practice of Teaching Innovation in "Instrumental Analysis" Course of Environmental Protection Program in Vocation College

Ma Zhanqing

Hangzhou Vocation and technical college Hangzhou China 310018
ma25603@126.com

Abstract. According to the characteristics of vocational education, taking the work of professional positions in the typical task-oriented as direction, we reformed the"instrumental analysis"course of the environmental protection program from several aspects such as teaching content, teaching methods, assessment mechanism, etc. This will strengthen the professional ability of students in teaching process; combine the traditional teaching theory and practical operating to achieve the integration of knowledge and practicing teaching so that we can enhance our students' hands-on skills and the ability to solve practical problems. Students will greatly increasing the interests in learning through information access, self design in accordance with national standards for training, preparing training materials and a series of other learning processes. The principles of instrumental analysis are no longer a burden but a positive initiative study based on training mission which is searching and mastering of useful technical knowledge, so as to achieve a solid technical grasp of theoretical knowledge, strengthened hands-on operational capability. These steps would lay a solid foundation for students to the next step of the specialized courses study, graduation and continue learning in future employment.

Keywords: Vocation Education, Instrumental Analysis, Teaching Content, Professional Ability.

1 Introduction

"Instrumental Analysis"is a required course for students in environmental protection program in Vocation College for instrumental analysis methods play an important role in environmental monitoring industry. With the advances in modern science and technology, new equipment and new technologies emerging [1,2]. In the teaching process of "Instrument Analysis", the teaching contents are getting more and more, materials for students are getting thicker and thicker. Teachers compete for giving more speeches in class while students think about just passing off the class. Traditional "Instruments Analysis"teaching method is based on taking instrumental methods as teaching unit, training operations practice always comes after the theoretical study [3]. This brings out that the theory classes are boring and the practice operating practice is blinded. "Instrumental Analysis"courses involving the contents of physics, chemistry and mathematics, etc. [4,5]. Due to the weak knowledge foundation of vocational

M. Zhu (Ed.): ICCIC 2011, Part V, CCIS 235, pp. 399–403, 2011.
© Springer-Verlag Berlin Heidelberg 2011

college students, learning theories are more difficult for them. With the social development, environmental protection enterprises' demand for talent is more pragmatic, more emphasis on the practical application ability of vocation college students. According to the return visit results of graduates, students cannot apply their"Instrumental Analysis" knowledge well in their work. The characteristics of intellectual thinking of vocation college students are mainly images based. Therefore, the teaching innovation of"Instrumental Analysis"course in teaching content, teaching methods and evaluation system of vocational education and training should in accordance with objectives of environmental protection education, combined with the current knowledge level of vocation college students and the actual learning situation to further enhance the the teaching quality and teaching effectiveness of "Instrument Analysis" course. To training high skilled person who can meet the requirements of monitoring and analyzing in environmental protection industry to is imminent.

2   Reconstruction Program Based on Occupational Status

2.1   Conform Course Contents in Accordance with the Professional Post Tasks

Instrumental analysis methods contain many sections. Because of the limited academic hour of "instrument analysis" course, the teaching contents are not all-inclusive; otherwise it will be less effective. Based on research and a return of graduates, we found that most graduates who working in environmental industries and enterprises monitoring small or medium equipment, only a small number of them engaged in large-scale monitoring and analysis instruments. According to the situation above, the "Instrumental Analysis" course content need to be reconstruction to meet the requirements of personnel in environmental protection industries and enterprises in the actual job. The reconstruction process of course contents is shown in Figure 1. Thus, the selected teaching contents are potential analysis method, UV-visible spectrophotometry, gas chromatography, atomic absorption spectrometry and High Performance Liquid Chromatography as five commonly used methods of analysis.

In addition, we will include a brief introduction of infrared spectroscopy, mass spectrometry, NMR and fluorescence analysis to improve students' interests in learning; and guide them learning by themselves. Those contents would not be the examined.

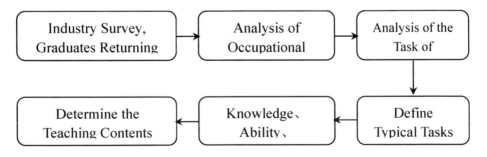

Fig. 1. The Process and Methods of Reconstructing the Course

2.2   Integration of Teaching Based on Typical Tasks

Taking the analysis of environmental indicators in real professional environmental monitoring post as typical job tasks(Table1),and the national standards as the basis,we stimulate students' learning enthusiasm and interest in learning through the completion of practical tasks. Considering hands-on training to teaching as a guide, do first and teach, learning by doing, we let the theoretical knowledge of task completion infiltrate in practical training process. In accordance with the recognition sequence, from shallow to deep, outside to inside, easy to difficult, we design the sub-unit of learning in typical working tasks. After students have mastered the practical skills, we would further summarize and expand theoretical knowledge of technology. Students master theoretical knowledge and technology of basic operating skills when they complete the tasks to achieve integration teaching skills. Moreover, students can complete the sample collection and pretreatment, qualitative and quantitative analysis, data processing and the whole process of preparing the report through the course. Through the integration of teaching in typical tasks, the enthusiasm of students' independent study is growing, so that they actively participate as the main study. In the past, students completed the training in accordance with the steps on the books; nowadays, students take the initiative to access to relevant information, take the initiative to design training programs and procedures, analyze problems, their problem-solving ability has been improved.

Table 1. Design of Typical Task in Teaching

No	Typical Task	International standards	Knowledge and skills unit
1	Determination of pH value of surface water	GB 6920—86	Potential Analysis
2	Determination of fluorine content in surface water	GB 7484—87	
3	Surface water content of anionic detergent	GB 13199—91	
4	Determination of surface water TN	GB 11894—89	UV-visible spectrophotometry
5	Determination of phenol content in surface water	GB 7490—87	
6	Cu content in surface water	GB 7474—87	Atomic absorption spectrometry
7	Ca and Mg in surface water content	GB 11905—89	
8	Determination of DDT in surface water	GB 7492—87	Gas chromatography
9	Organic phosphorus in surface water content	GB 13192—91	
10	Surface water benzo (b) fluoranthene content	GB 13198—91	High Performance Liquid Chromatography
11	Surface water benzo (a) pyrene content	GB 13198—91	

2.3   Assessment Mechanism to Reform the Course

The traditional assessment method basically based on final exams, and even final exams would determine the final course grades. There is a large part in the test involves memorize of the contents so that the students memory would directly affects their test results.

Restructured curriculum assessment will be: 30% from final examination skills and knowledge assessment, 40% from training skills assessment, 30% from the overall quality of assessment. This new assessment mainly focuses on testing the ability that the examination cannot test, and help to stimulate students' potential the motivation. Final exam would exclude delete those rote contents, and focus on assessment the skills and knowledge. Students can just understand the basic principles. The assessment of training skills is to evaluating the training action,the task implement results which contains performance of the core competencies and key professional capacity in process of completing typical tasks. Usually the assessment of overall quality is mainly to evaluating practical and realistic and meticulous work style, team spirit and sense of competition, safety and environmental awareness and so on.

Rigorous and scientific evaluation system will help to strengthen the students' motivation to learn, inspire and enthusiasm for independent learning, culture and enterprising positive spirit, and promote students to master the instrument of a solid basic skills to enhance the students learning ability.

3   Conclusions

Taking the typical task in environmental protection post as the direction, and to developing professional competence as the goal, we reformed the content, teaching methods and assessment mechanism of environment protection program course "Instrumental Analysis" and combined the traditional teaching of theory and practical operation to achieve the integration of teaching. At the same time create a good learning environment for students, improve the quality of teaching and improve students' hands-on skills and the ability to solve practical problems. Through information access, self-design in accordance with national standards for training, preparing training materials and a series of learning process, students greatly increasing their interest in learning. The instrumental analysis principles are no longer a burden but a positive initiative based on training mission. They search and master useful technical knowledge, so as to achieve a solid technical grasp of theoretical knowledge. The hands-on operational capability has been strengthened also. These steps would lay a solid foundation for students to the next step of the specialized courses study, graduation and continue learning in future employment.

References

1. Bao, C.-l., Jia, Q., Chen, B., et al.: Discussion on Experimental Teaching Reformation for Instrumental Analysis. Research and Exploration in Laboratory 28(10), 123–125 (2009)
2. Luan, C.-l.: Discllssion on Theoretical Teaching of Instrument Analysis of Higher Career Education. Guangdong Chemical Industry (10), 71–73 (2005)

3. Shi, Q.-z.: Discussion onReform of Teaching method of Instrumental Analysis in Higher Vocational Colleges. Journal of Zhenjiang College 21(2), 106–108 (2008)
4. Zhou, B.: Reform and Practice of Instrumental Analysis Curriculum in Higher Vocational College. Journal of Yangling Vocational & Technical College 9(4), 75–77 (2010)
5. Ma, Q.-z., Yang, X.-f.: Ideas on Teaching of Instrumental Analysis Experiment Based on Constructivist Theory at Higher Vocational College. Science & Technology Information (5), 620–621 (2010)

Research on Teaching Methods of Electromechanical Courses Oriented to Innovation

Xiuhong Zhang, Kai Zhang, Jie Wang, and Donghai Su

School of Mechanical Engineering, Shenyang University of Technology,
Shenyang 110870, China
xiu99562@126.com

Abstract. Based on the current state that the teaching methods of electromechanical courses can not meet the requirements of rapid development of economy, this paper describes the necessity, scheme and method of teaching reform, and proposes the deepening reform requirements on teaching methods and practical operation. This educational reform can provide the strong protection for the cultivation of innovative mechanical engineering technological talents.

Keywords: Electromechanical course, Educational reform, Teaching method, Innovative talent, Mechatronics.

1 Introduction

With the development of modern industrial production, the mechatronics, combined with the pneumatic, hydraumatic, sensor, PLC, network and communication technology, has become the key component of modern industrial science and technology [1-2]. For a long time, the electromechanical courses organize the education mainly according to the traditional theoretical system, and treat discipline as the core. Furthermore, it takes the imparted theoretical knowledge as the starting point of organizing education, the primary clue of educational process and the main criteria of quality assessment. This traditional course arrangement is beneficial for students to systematically master the theoretical knowledge and develop the design product. However, some defects exist in the traditional electromechanical courses, such as the irrational class periods and the obsolete educational methods, etc [3-4]. As a result, the students can not firmly grasp the theoretical knowledge and lack the necessary social practice and operation ability, so that they could only understand the theoretical knowledge of textbook, and lack the engineering practical ability, especially the technical innovation ability. Nevertheless, in order to revitalize the northeastern old industrial bases and develop the equipment manufacturing industry, it is necessary to cultivate large quantities of high-quality engineering technological talents with the pioneering spirit, cooperation awareness and innovation ability. For a long time, the Shenyang University of Technology is dedicated to cultivate applied high-quality talents for local economic construction and equipment manufacturing industry all the time, and always puts the promotion of educational and teaching quality first. By successively deepening educational and teaching reform and enhancing infrastructure,

M. Zhu (Ed.): ICCIC 2011, Part V, CCIS 235, pp. 404–408, 2011.

the quality of talent cultivation has been continuously improved, and the achievements of educational and teaching reform emerge now and then. The exploration of the cultivation of creative talents in general undergraduate colleges and universities has become the key point of educational and teaching reform with the advent of a new century.

2 Problems of Existence

There primarily exist several problems in current education

(1) The class periods are very few. With the teaching reform in depth, the teaching class periods of electromechanical courses have been obviously reduced as other specialized courses, so the contradiction between many teaching content and few class periods appears. How to promote the teaching quality to greatest extent in shorter time is a puzzle with regard to education.

(2) The teaching mode is singular. Generally, the traditional teaching mode only pays attention to theoretical education, and does not stimulate the awareness of students for active learning. In modern information age, how to absorb the students in studying professional knowledge and resist the temptation is worth thinking for the educators.

(3) The theory does not match the practice. The practical section of education should emphasize the instantiation of object model and the dynamic demonstration of control flow. However, the controlled objects are ordinarily difficult to be abundantly assembled in laboratory due to the huge volume, high price and complex maintenance. The students can not feel the interest and knowledge during the practical process and the achievability after this process, thus considerably frustrating the learning enthusiasm of students.

(4) The quality of the enrolled students decreases on the whole. Due to the expand enrollment, the receptivity and learning activity of present students have declined in comparison with previous ones. They do not grasp the basic courses firmly, thus bringing the great difficulty in teaching such courses.

With the development of economy, the requirements of society on the talents also increase. As a result, the society proposes the new requirements on the knowledge structure of talents, especially the technical personnel of the electromechanical major. The requirements are that not only do the technical personnel of the electromechanical major possess the engineering competence, but also contain the strong creative consciousness. The traditional school-running mode was substantially constrained with the method and way of talent cultivation. The cultivating specification of talents, the setting of curriculum system, and the arrangement of practical teaching system do not break away from the traditional education mode thoroughly. Since there are the irrational arrangements of class periods and the obsolete teaching methods in some specialized courses, the students can not master the theoretical knowledge proficiently, and lack the necessary social practice and operation ability. Consequently, until the course is over, the students only understand some theoretical knowledge of textbook and lack the engineering practical ability, especially the technical innovation ability.

3   Reform Implementation Plans

The features of electromechanical courses are comprehensive and difficult. In order to solve this problem, the course arrangement should be positively improved and timely rectified. Furthermore, the unique courses should be constructed according to the features of each major. The course reform should keep on with the engineering education as the main clue, the combination of theoretical education and practical guidance, and the integration of school cultivation with social economy. Besides, the practical engineering ability of students should be comprehensively trained from multilevel and multiple target on the basis of educational base.

(1) The course arrangement should meet the requirements of enterprises, and keep up with the social development trend. According to the investigation into the talent demand conditions in enterprises and the employment situation of recent graduates, and the job qualifications of employment position groups, treating the working process as the guidance and the working task or product as the carrier, referred to the related vocational qualification standards, the courses could be arranged and the syllabus of electromechanical courses would be rewritten by discussing with the enterprise personnel.

(2) The confirmation of course content is intimately related to the tasks of every stage in the process of working. During the deep coupling with enterprises, the working tasks of different stages in working process of vocational positions are confirmed by the investigation into the employed persons and the relative personnel of vocational position groups and the experts, through the description of students working in the vocational positions, and via the analysis, induction, collection and integration, so that the working tasks and content both transform into the course content of leaning field. By analyzing the frequency of utilization and accessibility of various tasks in every stage of the working process, the content and class period arrangement of the professional core curriculum suitable for different levels would be ascertained. Especially, the comprehensive ability of students should be improved, and the major setting should highlight the cultivation of the integrative competence. The electromechanical courses are interdisciplinary, but the textbooks including mechanics, electronics and hydraulics are relatively deficient. One target of this research is to write a new textbook named "Mechatronics" based on the necessity for cultivating the electromechanical comprehensive competence at present. This textbook should highlight the necessity for innovation, integrity and practice.

(3) The educational competence and innovative consciousness of teachers should be improved to build the elaborate courses. In order to grasp the every educational section of theory, practice and examination of courses during the education, not only should the innovation spirit of students be adequately developed, but also the enthusiasm in education and reform of teachers should be fully motivated. Only propelled by the activity of teaching and learning the educational can be quality greatly enhanced. Consequently, the university could cultivate more excellent talents for the socialist modernization construction, and create a batch of elaborate and excellent course.

4   Reform Implementation Methods

The educational methods of this research are mainly improved as follows.

(1) Utilizing the network education speeds up the construction of network teaching platform. The network teaching platform of Shenyang University of Technology provides the network teaching service for the whole school. The network teaching platform includes the public teaching platform, multimedia courseware making system and network realtime interactive answering system. The network public teaching platform consists of the student work area, the teacher work area and the management work area. The primary functional modules include bulletin board, answering, discussion broad, online self-test, online operations, download area and resource. Accordingly, an important task of this research is to accelerate the construction of network teaching platform, and improve the interaction between teaching and learning by employing this platform to contact teachers and students.

(2) Enlighten the innovative thinking and independent learning capability of students by contacting the engineering practical problems. The students should be induced to initiate innovation group, and positively take part in all levels of mechanical innovation competition. Consequently, the innovative consciousness and practical operation ability of students could be fostered during the practice, thus increasing the interest of study. Our school has participated in the mechanical design contest belonging to the city, province or country many times, and achieves the excellent performance. However, there are few entries combining the mechanics with the electronics. The main reason is that such entries have the higher requirements on the comprehensive application capability and the greater difficulty. In contrast, due to the great difficulty and more innovative ideas, the entries combining mechanics with electronics could become the developing direction of modern mechanical products. As a result, such combined entries could be easier to embody innovation, practice and advancement.

(3) Keep pace with the times and stimulate the appetite for knowledge of students. The teachers should keep up with the times, understand the latest technology trends of the courses, and impart them to students. Integrated with the significant success of contemporary science and technology development in our country, the teachers could illuminate the roles of the course in this success, thus stimulating the thirst for knowledge and improving the interest, curiosity and motivation of the study of students.

(4) Reform and optimize the practical section. The practical education is the critical section for forming the technical application capability. In order to cultivate the professional technology ability, the traditional practical education mode must be reformed. The simple experimental courses already can not meet the requirements of students on the expertise study. The cultivation of innovative capability and engineering competence must be emphasized in the process of course and graduation design. During the practical education section, starting from the actual demand and actively participating in practice study should be highlighted. During the practical study, the innovative capability of students should be fully performed, and the innovative consciousness of them should be cultivated. Especially, the business/school partnership should be strengthened. Consequently, our education can be directly faced

to the enterprises, and the enterprises can directly take part in the cultivation process of engineering technician.

(5) Found the innovation education base. The educational resource is the important guarantee for the educational quality. The present educational practice resource of school should be continuously optimized so as to realize the open and share of resource and impel the suitable and efficient utilization of experimental equipment. On this basis, the innovation education base could be founded, the innovation education should be institutionalized and normalized, and the cultivation of research and innovation capabilities of students should be highlighted.

5 Summary

The electromechanical courses must insist on the development guideline "orientation to modernization, the world and the future". Starting from the practice, the educational reform thinking and cultivation object should be confirmed, the course system, teaching methods and content should be deeply reformed, and the educational quality should be improved. By cultivating the comprehensive application ability, practical operation ability, engineering design and innovation ability of students, the train of professional engineering technician could be suitable for the requirement of future social development. At the same time, their teamwork spirit should be strengthened in the process of experiments and designs. In order to grasp the every educational section of theory, practice and examination of courses during the education, not only should the innovation spirit of students be adequately developed, but also the enthusiasm in education and reform of teachers should be fully motivated. Only propelled by the activity of teaching and learning the educational can be quality greatly enhanced. Consequently, the university could cultivate more excellent talents for the socialist modernization construction.

References

1. Li, Y.Q., Han, Y.Y.: Reform and Exploration on the Innovative Education Mode of Mechatronical New Technical Courses. China Electric Power Education (22), 57–58 (2010)
2. Wang, D.: Exploration on Teaching Reform of Comprehensive Innovation Design Course of Mechatronical System. Journal of Technical Supervision Education (2), 56–59 (2008)
3. Pei, X.M., Feng, Z.W.: Deepen the Educational and Practical Reform on Electromechanical Courses Promote the Cultivation for High-Quality Innovation Talents. China Education of Light Industry (4), 62–63 (2008)
4. Lu, B.Y.: Reform in the Teaching of the Electromechanical Engineering and Cultivation of Innovative-typed Talents. Journal of Baicheng Normal College 20(6), 95–97 (2006)

Trust-Based Privacy Authorization Model for Web Service Composition

Jun Zheng[1], Zhiqiu Huang[2], Jun Hu[2], Ou Wei[2], and Linyuan Liu[2]

[1] Quality Engineering Technology Center,
China Aeronautics Polytechnology Establishment, Beijing, China
[2] College of Computer Science and Technology,
Nanjing University of Aeronautics and
Astronautics, Nanjing, China
ajun23201@126.com

Abstract. The rapid growth of web applications has prompted increasing interest in the area of composite web services that involve several service providers. This increased use of composite services has meant that more and more personal information of consumers is being shared with web service providers, leading to the need to guarantee the privacy of consumers. This paper proposes a trust-based privacy authorization model for service composition, it uses privacy authorization policies to specify the privacy privileges of services. Then it utilizes the trust relationships among services to make privacy authorization decisions. Comparing to the traditional privacy access control approaches, this model can make the fine-grained authorization decision, thus efficiently protecting consumers' privacy.

Keywords: Privacy, Access control, Web Service composition, Trust.

1 Introduction

The past decade has witnessed a phenomenal growth in the number of users who routinely use the web to obtain information, conduct research, or carry out financial transactions [9]. While the ability of the web to provide customized information and financial services has boosted personal and business productivity, it has raised significant concerns regarding consumer information privacy. Once personal information is disclosed online, it may be abused or accessed without authorization, thus increasing the risk of illegal collection, usage and disclosure of personal sensitive data [5]. Hence, the issue of protecting the data privacy of consumers has become of crucial.

Privacy is the right of individuals to determine for themselves when, how, and to what extent private information is communicated to others [3,6]. Privacy concerns are fueled by an ever increasing list of privacy violations, ranging from privacy accidents to illegal actions [4,10]. In order to accomplish the business goals, a service consumer has to release some private data to support the collaborative work; on the other hand, in

M. Zhu (Ed.): ICCIC 2011, Part V, CCIS 235, pp. 409–415, 2011.
© Springer-Verlag Berlin Heidelberg 2011

order to meet the needs of security, a strict control mechanism is required to protect these private data [11].

Currently, there are many researches about the privacy access control approaches in service composition. However, most of them use the method of "all-or-nothing" to make privacy authorization decision, namely, it authorizes either all privileges or none. But, in fact, due to the untrustworthy nature of the Web service, a set of services with the same functions may have different privacy disclosure risks because of their different trust degrees. Take the shopping scenario for example, the seller with the higher trust degree is more trustworthy in protecting the privacy of customers, on the contrary, the seller with the lower trust degree may disclose the privacy information to the other unauthorized party for their own interests.

To overcome the above drawbacks, this paper presents a trust-based privacy authorization model for Web service composition, this model utilizes authorization policies to specify the privacy privileges of services, introduces trust relationships among services into composition design. The composition makes the decision on privacy authorization according to the trust degree of the services.

The remainder of this paper is arranged as follows. Section 2 gives the method of computing the trust degree of services. Section 3 proposes a trust-based Web service privacy authorization model. Section 4 analyzes the privacy authorization process. Closely related work and comparison are reported in Section 5. Section 6 concludes the paper with proposals for future work.

2   The Computation of the Services' Trust Degree

The participants of the services composition are a set of strange services from different organizations, so they lack the necessary trust between each other. Therefore, when the consumers disclose the private data to the providers, it requires that the providers have a certain trust degree. The consumers release privacy privileges according the trust degree of providers, the higher the trust degree is, the more the privacy privileges will be released.

Definition 1: Trust Degree. Trust degree is a measure indicating the trustworthy degree of the services. Let S be a set of finite services of a service composition. For any a service $s \in S$, funtion $ftd(s)$ is used to obtain its trust degree, where $ftd(s) \in [0,1]$, 0 indicates that it is untrustworthy, 1 indicates trustworthy. The larger the value is, the higher the trust degree is.

The trust degree of the services is evaluated by the users. The users give scores to the trust degree of the services after using services. The computation process can be clarified into two steps: firstly computing the score a user gives to a service, then combining the scores that all of users give and thus obtaining the whole trustworthy value of the services. The specific steps are as follows:

(1) Computation of the local trust degree

In order to compute the local trust degree of a service, we firstly let the score the user i gives to service j be $r_{i,j}$, $r_{i,j} \in [0,1]$. When the user i considers that the service j leaks much information, the score $r_{i,j}$ would be relatively low. Otherwise, if the user i considers that there is little information leaked, the score $r_{i,j}$ would be relatively high.

Then we introduce a history trust degree $R_{i,j}$, which refers to the score the users gave to the service j in the past. Based on $r_{i,j}$ and $R_{i,j}$, we use the following formula to compute the local trust degree of the user i to the service j:

$$R_{i,j} = \partial R_{i,j} + (1-\partial)r_{i,j}$$

(1)

Where, the parameter ∂ is a history factor, $\partial \in (0,1)$ shows the proportion of the history trust degree score in the computation of the local trust degree. If ∂ approaches 1, it indicates that the influence of the history trust degree score on the computation of the new trust degree is great, while when ∂ approaches 0, it indicates that the latest trust degree score play the center role.

(2) Computation of the globe trust degree

Let td be the globe trust degree of the service j. through combining the local trust degree scores other services gives to the service j, we can compute the globe trust degree of the service j. The formula is as follows:

$$td = \sum_{k=1}^{N} R_{k,j} / N$$

(2)

Through the above steps, we can obtain the trust degree of a service and the value of the trust degree is sure to be between 0 and 1.

3   Trust-Based Service Composition Privacy Authorization Model

In order to fine-grained protection the privacy of consumers, we set a trust level for every privacy privilege. Only when the trust degree of a service is higher than this trust level, can it access the privilege. Trust level actually limits the qualification of the services to access privilege.

When the services receive or send a message, they may request to access not only one privilege, but a set of privileges. Hence, we use the authorization policies to specify a set of access privileges granted to the services. Each authorization policy has a corresponding authorization policy matrix, for short, authorization matrix, where the row vectors of the matrix denotes a set of privacy privilege types, the column vectors of the matrix denotes a set of private data objects, the elements of the matrix denote the trust level required by granting a type of privilege of a data object to the services. Fig. 1 is the description about an authorization matrix.

	o_0	o_1	$\cdots$	o_n
t_0	tl_{00}	tl_{01}	$\cdots$	tl_{0n}
t_1	tl_{10}	tl_{11}	$\cdots$	tl_{1n}
$\vdots$	$\vdots$	$\vdots$	$\ddots$	$\vdots$
t_n	tl_{n0}	tl_{n1}	$\cdots$	tl_{nn}

Fig. 1. The description of authorization matrix

Definition 2: Authorization Policy. Let S be a finite set of services, M be a finite set of messages,

OP be a finite set of operations, O be a finite set of private data objects and T be a finite set of privacy privilege types, a authorization policy is defined as $plcy:=<s, op, am>$, where:

- $s \in S$ is a service;
- $op \in OP$ is an operation of s, it may be a sending operation or a receiving operation of the message msg, which are defined as type(op)=msg! or type(op)=msg? respectively, where $msg \in M$;
- am is an authorization matrix, it is formed by $|T|$ rows and $|O|$ columns. The elements of the matrix $am[i, j]$ $(0 \leq i < |T|, 0 \leq j < |O|)$ denote the trust level required by granting the privilege with the data object as j and the privilege type as i to service s, $am[i, j] \in [0,1]$, where 0 indicates to authorize this kind of privilege and 1 indicates not.

Based on the definition of authorization policy, we can present the authorization specification of a service composition as follows.

Definition 3: Authorization specification. A authorization specification is defined as $as:=<S, OP, AM, PLCY, F_{am}>$, Where:

- S is a finite set of services;
- OP is a finite set of operations;
- AM is a finite set of authorization matrices;
- $PLCY \subseteq S \times OP \times AM$ is a finite set of authorization policies. For any authorization policy $(s, op, am) \in PLCY$, it denotes that the service s has the privileges granted by authorization matrix am for operation op, where $s \in S$, $op \in OP$, $am \in AM$;
- $F_{am}: (S, OP) \rightarrow AM$ is a funcation that takes as input a $s \in S$ and a $op \in OP$ and returns the authorization matrix am, where $am \in AM$.

4   Privacy Authorization Enforcement Process

Based on the above privacy authorization model, now we can describe the architecture of the privacy authorization enforcement system. This system involves four components: authorization control manager (ACM), authorization decision maker (ADM), authorization policy repository (APR) and trust repository (TR). When a role requests for the privacy privilege, it firstly sends the request to the ACM, which includes the id of service and the name of operation. After the ACM receives the request, it asks the ADM to make the decision. The ADM firstly finds the APR according to the service id and the operation name and gets the correspondent privacy authorization matrix. Then it finds the TR and gets the correspondent trust degree of the service. Finally it makes the authorization decision according to the authorization matrix and the trust degree of service, and sends the authorization result to the ACM. The ACM sends the service about the result that whether the request is accepted or denied. The privacy authorization enforcement system is as follows:

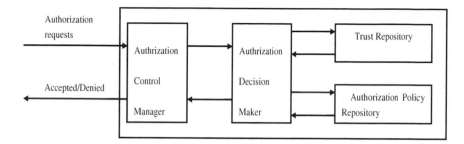

Fig. 2. The architecture of privacy authorization enforcement system

In the above authorization process, the authorization decision-maker makes the authorization decision according to the authorization matrix and the trust degree. The specific steps are as follows:

1) Let *op* is an operation of service *s*, set privacy-satisfied mark *Psatisied* as 0, where *Psatisied* is an integer variable.
2) According to the *op* and *s*, we are obtains the corresponding authorization matrix *am* and iteratively takes the trust threshold of every privacy privilege out of *am*; Then compares the trust threshold with the trust degree of *s*, if the trust threshold is lower than or equal to the trust degree, then *Psatisied* is decreased by 1.
3) Finally it checks whether the value of *Psatisied* is 0, if yes, then the authorization request is accepted, otherwise it is denied.

The following is the specific description of the privacy authorization decision algorithm.

Algorithm 1: The privacy authorization decision
Input: s; op;
Output: True; False;
    d= $f_{tl}(s)$; //get the trust degree of the service
    am:=f_{am}(s, op);   //get the authorization matrix
    For(each t in am.|T|){   //make the authorization decision
        For(each o in am.|O|){
            If(pm[t,o]:<=d){Psatisfied:= Psatisfied -1}
    }}
If(Psatisfied ==0){Return true;} Else{Return false;}

5 Related Work

In recent years, increasing attention has been paid to privacy-aware technologies and mechanisms to protect data privacy in the Web Services. The World Wide Web Consortium is advocating P3P (Platform for Privacy Preferences) [7] as the standard format for expressing data-collection and data-use practices on the web. The XACML (Extensible Access Control Markup Language) [8] is an XML-based access control language. It provides an application-independent policy language which enables the use of arbitrary attributes in different types of policies, including privacy policies.

Many other proposals can be found in current literature. For instance, Byun et al. [2] proposed a purpose- based access control framework extending RBAC along the lines given by Agrawal et al. [1] in their Hippocratic database systems. The aim of this framework is to enforce privacy promises encoded in privacy policy languages in database management systems. The framework is based on the notion of intended purpose and the notion of access purpose. The problem of those methods is that they just focus on the privacy within single organizations rather than in a distributed system. Another question of these models is that they use the "all-or-nothing" authorization decision mechanism, which may cause the unexpected privacy leakage.

Different from previous models, the novelty of our access control approach mainly includes two aspects: Firstly, our approach is constructed according to the collaborative environment of Web services. It is not limited in the inside of the organizations. Secondly, our approach has introduced the trust relationships between services and made the fine-grained authorization based on the trust relationships. In our approach, the trust level of every piece of privacy privilege has been set. Only when the trust degree of the service is higher this level, can it access the privilege.

6 Conclusions

Based on the demand for fine-grained privacy authorization, this paper proposes a trust-based privacy authorization model. First, it uses privacy authorization policies to specify the privacy privileges of service composition. Second, it proposes the method of computing the trust degree of services and utilizes the trust degree of services to make the authorization decisions. The trust-based authorization mechanism provides a feasible and effective method to protect the privacy privileges with fine granularity.

The protection of data privacy in Web services involves research in other branches. Several improvements to our current work can be foreseen. First, this paper considers the collection, usage and disclosure of private data. It has not yet considered the time property of privacy data. Therefore, more work can be done to investigate the time factor relevant to the retention time of private data. Second, in order to meet the personalization needs of service consumers for the protection of private data, the privacy policies may have to change dynamically. It requires the service composition to possess an active adapting and adjusting capability that provides suitable service composition in a timely and dynamic manner.

References

1. Agrawal, R., Kiernan, J., Srikant, R., Xu, Y.: Hippocratic databases. In: Proceeding of the 28th International Conference on Very Large Data Based, Hong Kong, China, pp. 143–154 (2002)
2. Byun, J.W., Bertino, E., Li, N.: Purpose based access control of complex data for privacy protection. In: Proceedings of 10th ACM Symposium on Access Control Models and Technologies, pp. 102–110. ACM Press, New York (2006)

3. Guarda, P., Zannone, N.: Towards the development of privacy-aware systems. Information and Software Technology 51(2), 337–350 (2009)
4. Karjoth, G., Schunter, M., Herreweghen, E.V.: Translating privacy practices into privacy promises -how to promise what you can keep. In: Proceeding of The 4th IEEE International Workshop On Policies For Distributed Systems And Networks, pp. 135–146 (2003)
5. Liu, L., Huang, Z., Zhu, H.: Role-based consistency verification for privacy-aware Web services. In: Proceeding of The 7th Int. Symposium On Collaborative Technologies And Systems, Irvine, CA, USA, pp. 399–407 (2009)
6. Rezgui, A., Bouguettaya, A., Eltoweissy, M.: Privacy on the Web: facts, challenges, and solutions. IEEE Security & Privacy 1(6), 40–49 (2003)
7. W3C. The Platform for Privacy Preferences 1.0 Specification, P3P (2002),
   `http://www.w3.org/P3P`
8. OASIS Standard. Extensible access control markup language version 2.0 (XACML), OASIS Standard (2005),
   `http://docs.oasis-open.org/xacml/2.0/`
   `access_control-xacml-2.0-core-spec-os.pdf`
9. Xu, W., Venkatakrishnan, V.N., Sekar, R., Ramakrishnan, I.V.: A Framework for building privacy-conscious composite Web services. In: Proceeding of the International Conference on Web Services, pp. 655–662 (2006)
10. Yee, G., Korba, L.: Privacy policy compliance for Web services. In: Proceedings of 2004 IEEE International Conference on Web Services, pp. 158–165 (2004)
11. Zhang, J., Chang, C.K., Zhang, L.J., Hung, P.C.K.: Toward a service-oriented development through a case study. IEEE Transaction on Systems, Man, Cybernetics, Part A 37(6), 955–969 (2007)

Research on Quality Management and Monitoring System of Post Practice Process in Higher Vocational Colleges

Wan Li[1], Yuan Ning[2], and Huiying Zhang[2]

[1] Guizhou Communication Polytechnic, Guiyang, Guizhou, China, 550001
HuaZhong University of Science & Technology,
wan20150@126.com
[2] Electrical Engineering College, Guizhou University, Guiayng, Guizhou, China

Abstract. Post practice is very important teaching mode combining learning with working through school -enterprise cooperation in training high skilled talents, which is the practice of teaching and learning activities participated by students, schools and businesses with purposes and plans. In order to enhance the effect of the post practice, it is necessary to build the quality management and monitoring system. In this paper, the connotation and construction of the quality management and monitoring system in post practice process will be introduced, the implementation result in Guizhou Communication Polytechnic shows that the students' internship , career development, base construction, curriculum teaching could be more effectively docked with the management and monitoring system, also, the school competitiveness be more strengthening.

Keywords: post practice, quality management, monitoring, higher vocational education.

1 Introduction

Vigorously developing higher vocational education is particular important for the promotion of economic growth, expanding employment size and improving the quality of employment [1]. More and more professionals with certain skill has been needed in China with the deepening economic reforms and industrial restructuring, Chinese higher vocational education has continued to grow and develop and it supplied a large number of technical personnel for the country [2]. In order to meets the needs of the citizen, the labor market and the society, The talent training goal of higher vocational college is to train application-oriented and front-line professional talents who adapt to production, construction, management and service, etc. There are many recognized vocational talent development models such as "dual-track system" of Germany, the educational and training pattern based on the ability in Australia and Canada, the Employment Education Structure advocated by the World Labor Organization. Domestically, the most commonly exist model is "2+1" model, in which three years vocational education are divided into two stages. In the first stage, students spend first two years in campus learning basic theory and accepting basic professional skill training. In the second stage, they will as a prentice spend one year in enterprises doing field trail [3] .In a sense, post

M. Zhu (Ed.): ICCIC 2011, Part V, CCIS 235, pp. 416–421, 2011.
© Springer-Verlag Berlin Heidelberg 2011

practical process is one of the main contents in higher vocational colleges practice teaching, whether quality management and monitoring system of post practice process can be established or not show whether the higher vocational colleges have significant characteristics. However, Most of the management and monitoring system of post practice process, which are random inspection and emergency handling, involve high randomness. It is lack of the systematic, institutionalized, and standardized. Therefore, to explore and exploit quality management and monitoring system is the inevitable choice of improving post practice process quality higher and strengthening school competitiveness in the circumstances of forward development of higher vocational and technical education scope, and continued improvement of social requirement level.

In section 2 of this paper, we talk about the connotation of quality management and monitoring system of post practice process in higher vocational college. The construction of quality management and monitoring system of post practice process in Guizhou Communication Polytechnic will be described in section 3. The system application results and analyzing the statistical data will be given in section 4, the conclusion can be found in the last.

2 The Connotation of Quality Management and Monitoring System of Post Practice Process in Higher Vocational College

The quality guarantee system of practical teaching in higher vocational colleges is a theory or method which, according to required quality standards and certain operation rules, utilizes specific monitoring system and management strategy or management measure to assure the quality of practical teaching in order to guarantee and improve the quality of practice teaching on the basis of quality assurance activities in higher vocational colleges. [4,5]

Post practice process is a crucial stage in the entire higher vocational education because training objectives are application-oriented talents that have related technical theoretical knowledge and practical ability in higher vocational education, which is a particular education that refers to learning scientific, technical subjects and related skills and focusing on vocational skills training and related theoretical study. It is vulnerable to be affected by many factors. Therefore, the quality management and monitoring system of post practice plays an important role in the formation of students' vocational capacity and the accumulation of working experience. The main tasks are to organize, lead, promote and coordinate the implementation of post practice teaching activities between enterprise and higher vocational colleges to ensure the coordinated development of social education mechanism, promote the combination between enterprise and higher vocational colleges, identify and guide teaching in post practice process.

3 Construction of Quality Management and Monitoring System of Post Practice Process

The construction of management and monitoring system of post practice in higher vocational college is like the figure1. This is an organization structure of three levels. The organization function details of the three levers are as following:

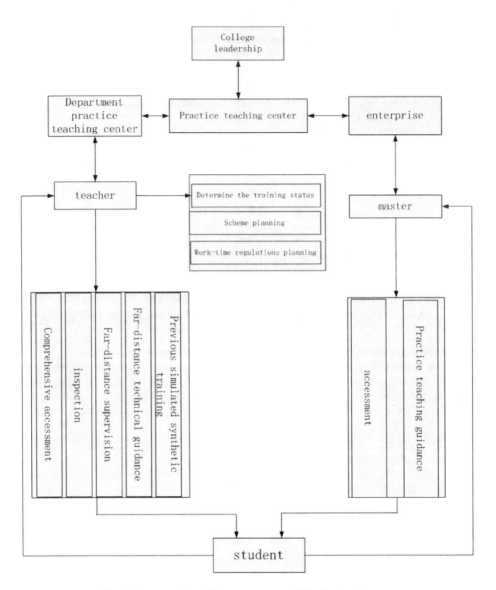

Fig. 1. Construction of Management and Monitoring System

3.1 Decision Layer of Management and Monitoring System in Post Practice Process

The top level of management and monitoring system in post practice process is decision layer, the chief chairs the executive council to realize macro-control and be in charge the whole post practice process quality. From the structure, It can be seen that the colleges should build "Practice teaching center" who is mainly in charge of post practice process quality .The leadership of college who is mainly in charge of post practice process quality is the chief of the practice teaching center, the office is set in the teaching affair office.

3.2   Coordination Layer of Management and Monitoring System in Post Practice Process

The second level of management and monitoring system in post practice process is coordination layer which lead by practice teaching center. It consists of department practice teaching center and enterprise. The specific duties of this layer are: to enact the policy measures of post practice teaching activity and coordinate activities of post practice teaching quality management as well as various conflicts in the post practice process management. Different departments set correspondent "department practice teaching center" in each department teaching affair office. The enterprises we chose to take post practice are those efficient and advanced companies which possess a large number of high skilled workers who have helped solve many high level technical problems. Its perfect mastery of technical skills and dedication will give the students a greater space for study.   Students can also get paid by the companies and sign employment contracts after they finish the post practice. The cooperative network between the school and enterprises should be built.

3.3   Implementation Layer of Management and Monitoring System in Post Practice Process

The third lever is implementation layer in which teachers in different departments whose duties are: to determine the training status, to write post practice scheme plan, to formulate work-time regulation plan, to give distance guidance and inspection.

The three levels of organization structure are interrelated, which is one of the basic conditions to guarantee post practice process teaching quality. The whole management and monitoring system construction of post practice process is the guarantee of improving post practical process teaching quality. Firstly, It have the integrity and systematic which have covered the overall situation of management system in college. Secondly, the implementation of it have clear rules to follow which have bound together into book form to guarantee the post practice teaching can be developed smoothly.

4   Application Results

As one of the National model higher vocational colleges from 2006, Guizhou communication polytechnic has a profound accumulation of experiences both in talents learning and education reform. It timely adjusted its education goal from technology-oriented to develop highly skilled frontline operators and managers. Initiated in 2006, post practice teaching model has attached great importance to developing talents by offering employees a real work environment.

Statistics shows that both the number of graduate student and employment are increased after the implementation post practice model. It can be seen from figure2 that since the implementation in 2006 the number of graduate students and employment rate was increased steadily.

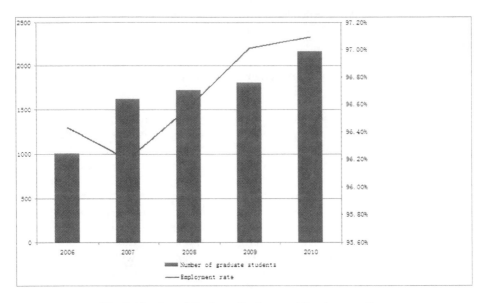

Fig. 2. Number of Graduate Students and Employment Rate

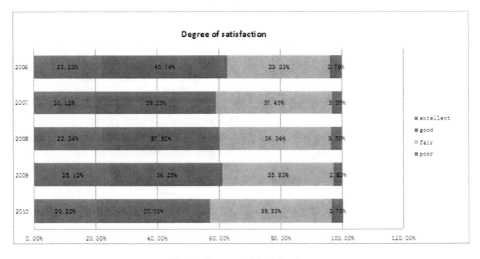

Fig. 3. Degree of Satisfaction

Since its adoption, the confusions of students at the early stage of the employment are vanished. They are more flexible and more adaptive to new environment. They usually get used to new work environment within a short time. Some of them are paid by the companies and can self-support. More than 50% of the students can sign employment contracts during post practice processing. Most of them can be an assistant to their master. Also, they can get relevant work experience. It can be seen from figure2 that employment rate is above 96% since the implementation, whereas, it is all below 90% before the implementation. It is worthy to note that the employment rate improves stable, which can be seen from figure2, in spite of the ever-increasing number of higher education graduates. Besides, many of whom have grown into the backbone of the enterprise. Enterprise comments that the post practice model is a win-win model, which beneficial to students, college and enterprise. From figure 3, it can be found that investigated enterprises are satisfied with most of students.

5 Conclusion

Schools adopting the post practice model for four or more years have seen their students' employment remains improved. With the realization of management and monitoring system of post practice process, the contradiction between the professional environment authenticity and the controllability has been eliminated, the smooth transformation from school training to work engagement also has been realized, The students will be qualified in their work after graduation. A substantial number of students have begun to close gaps from school training to work. The post practice realized the smooth transformation from school training to work engagement, laid a solid foundation for being employed.

References

1. Jiao, Y.-Y., Fei, H.-H., Li, M., Du, J., Wang, Y.: A Customized Training Model Evaluation System of Higher Vocational Education. In: Proceedings of International Conference on Management and Service Science, p. 1 (2010)
2. Li, G., Jiao, Z., Liu, S.: Tutoring Strategy Study on Game-Based Experiential Learning in Vocational School. In: Proceedings of First International Workshop on Education Technology and Computer Science (2009)
3. Zhu, Y.: Development and Continuation of Foreign Vocational Education Curriculum Models in Comparative Perspective. In: Proceedings of International Conference on Education and Network Technology (2010)
4. Xu, F.: Research on quality system of practice teaching in higher vocational colleges. Journal of Zhejiang University of Technology 11, 10 (2008)
5. Yu, X.: Three Units in A Whole:Construction of Higher Education Quality Assurance's New Mode. Journal of Heilongjiang Higher Education Research 6, 8 (2007)

Training Students' Engineering Practice Innovation Capability through Academic Competition

JiaLian Wang

School of Automation, Hangzhou Dianzi University, Hangzhou Zhejiang 310018, China
wang25263@126.com

Abstract. This paper analyzes the importance of teaching engineering practice and problems, and current automation academic competitions and engineering practice, then raised the academic competition as the carrier, is combined with technological innovation, construct the "three-level-academic-competition" engineering practice of three-dimensional system. Which explore effective competition practices, means, ways for our actual practices, and provide a good platform to train the abilities of automation students to analyze and solve practical problems, creativity and cooperative spirit. Therefore, that enriches and improves the content and form of practice teaching, practical trains students' engineering practice innovation.

Keywords: discipline competition, engineering practice, innovation ability.

1 The Importance of Engineering Practice Teaching

Engineering practice teaching is the important part of teaching, and is an important part of colleges to improve students' innovative ability, practical ability and overall quality. Only through practice, the learned knowledge changed into their knowledge structure and quality structure [1-2]. However, there is no perfect means of engineering teaching practice; the main engineering practice teaching should be student rather than teachers; practical means of teaching shouldn't be taken the way by instilling and established procedure [3].

Discipline competition of science and engineering, from a certain perspective, is actually a process, using the original foundation of knowledge, reorganizing knowledge proposing new ideas. This can effectively develop students' ability to innovate, team spirit and practical ability [4]. Some problems can be seen from analyzing academic competition in recent. Academic competition separated from the teaching system and practice teaching in some extent, the guidance of teachers in academic competition change into extra help of the participating students, which ignore the academic competition that is the guiding role of professional services, result the lack of clarity in the purpose of student participation. To solve this problem, we raised the academic competition as the carrier, which is combined with technological innovation, construct the "three-level-academic-competition" engineering practice of three-dimensional system, to enrich and improve the content and form of practice teaching, practical training students' practical and creative abilities.

M. Zhu (Ed.): ICCIC 2011, Part V, CCIS 235, pp. 422–427, 2011.
© Springer-Verlag Berlin Heidelberg 2011

2 Promotion of Academic Competition in Engineering Practice Teaching

Academic competition is series activities which closely connect with daily teaching or based on new technology, it can inspire students to integrate theory with practice and to work independently through contest way, students complete the competition task to discover and solve problems, so that it enhance students' interest in learning and research initiative, team spirit and innovative. Academic competition is a viable education, teaching behavior, with regular education hasn't special function in innovative education.

In 2005, National Undergraduate Computer Simulation Contest is launched by the Department of Higher Education, the Chinese Association of Automation, China Computer Users Association, the Beijing Aerospace Automatic Control Research Institute jointly organized in China; National Undergraduate Smart Car Contest is launched by the Ministry of Education Automation Teaching Guide Students sponsored in 2006. Academic competition as a special form of higher education has been increasingly recognized by society and the university.

In recent years, we attended or organized many academic competitions. In National Undergraduate Smart Car Contest, College won one first prize, two second prize, one first prize in an East Division; In National Undergraduate Electronic Design Contest, College won one second prize, one first prize in Zhejiang Province race; In National Undergraduate football robot Contest, College won third in three on three matches. To this end, we summarise Automation participate or self-organized in various academic competitions in recent years, proposed to strengthen academic competitions, practical training students of engineering practice innovation.

3 Academic Competition and Innovation Engineering Practice

In this paper, study object is automation academic competition of engineering teaching practice, which combined with our practical and school characteristics, and based on National Undergraduate Electronic Design Contest, National Undergraduate smart car Contest, National Undergraduate football Robotics Contest, and which explore the characteristics of automation with our professional engineering practice teaching mode such as in Figure 1.

National Undergraduate smart car Contest covers control, pattern recognition, sensor technology, electronics, electrical, computer, mechanical and other disciplines. National Undergraduate Electronic Design Contest is the application of analog circuits and digital circuit design as the main content, related to mixed analog-digital circuits, programmable logic devices, EDA software tools and application of PC. National Undergraduate football Robotics Contest involves artificial intelligence, robotics, communications, sensing, precision machinery and biomimetic materials, and many other areas of cutting-edge research and technology integration, which is a reflection of a national information and automation of basic research and high level of development.

424   J. Wang

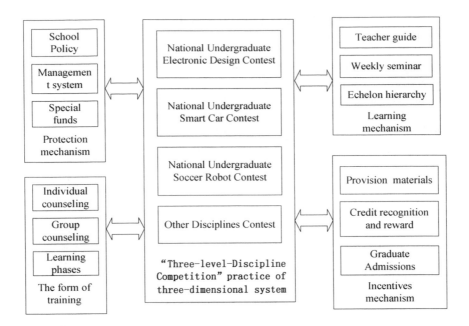

Fig. 1. "Three-level-academic-competition" engineering practice of three-dimensional system

1. "three-level-academic-competition" engineering practice of three-dimensional system is build, National Undergraduate Electronic Design Contest as a leader, National Undergraduate smart car Contest as the key, National Undergraduate football Robotics Contest as basis, these composite the   basic framework and is an integral part of engineering teaching system. Three levels complement each other, not only for students to participate in innovation activities, and exercise capacity provide a platform, but also in the campus to create a good atmosphere, to stimulate students interest in learning and teaching. finally, we achieve the purpose of promoting style in study.

2. Student academic competition based on the frontier, which covers many interdisciplinary topics courses teaching. Contest subject should comply with courses teaching the basic requirements, emphasizing the combining of system and knowledge, its content is often related to a course group, but also focus on improving the abilities of students, requiring participating teams were designed, produced a specific subject disciplines. On the other hand, the contents of contest can be transformed into teaching, but also can be transformed into a design subject.

3.There are set up appropriate management institutions in engineering   practical teaching   academic competitions, that implement individual responsibility and private venues, and be changed into accomplishing routine activities. Special funds set up to ensure adequate funding in practical teaching academic competition, all kinds of recognition and reward mechanisms are established and improved (including the organizer, teachers, students).

4.It is high require for teachers in engineering practice teaching academic competition, both a high professional level of theory, but also have strong engineering practical ability to operate. Through optimizing the structure, education and training,which can attract some outstanding young teachers participate, so that we can get a reasonable instructor echelon. According to the characteristics of different contest it is reasonable to attract teachers to participate in different disciplines, which broaden students' vision and ideas, the guiding team is determined and then can discuss specific plans and training guidance in order to ensure steady progress throughout the training.

4   Academic Competition on the Role of Practical Ability of Students

We believe that innovative talents of modern engineering should be available in six capacities as show in Figure 2. Social activities are proposed, which is an integrated of the concept comprehensive and aesthetic value in major projects, if it is no these capabilities the project back to the traditional engineering view.

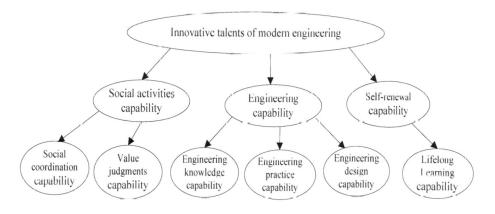

Fig. 2. Innovative talents of modern engineering

1. The students' hands-on capacity is exercised. The knowledge can help acquisition of skills and develop ability, but it is not happen automatically, and must resort to practice. Through academic competition, hands-on capacity is enhanced in engineering practice. For example, the actual problems changed into mathematical models and mathematical model results will be interpreted as the actual phenomena, using computer to solve the mathematical model, using all kinds of application software, design or debug electronic circuits and so on.

2. The students' basic research capabilities are trained. Academic competition can train students for a basic understanding of scientific research and interest, develop a rigorous scientific attitude and spirit of bold exploration in the competition process, and the competition itself follow the scientific method, helping to train students research capacity.

3. The ability of initial innovation is shaped. College students are the new force of the country's social and economic development, innovative ability is one goal of

university education. Through the contest, students generally recognize the fundamental role of innovation, students can discovery problems in the work through the analytical methods and knowledge, and propose the suggestions for improvement, train students' innovation and creative thinking.

4. the psychological quality and team spirit are improved. Academic competition improve student learning theory courses with fun, challenging and training, at the same time, improve students to pursue scientific discovery indomitable mental quality, pro-active sense of innovation and the spirit of innovation, training the students the collective spirit of unity and cooperation and coordination organizational skills, and take active part in awareness and aren't afraid of competition, difficulties and has the indomitable will in research, which is a great spiritual wealth for their future out of school and social services.

5   Conclusion

In this paper, we have discussed the importance of teaching engineering practice, and analyzed current automation academic competitions and engineering practice, then raised the academic competition as the carrier, is combined with technological innovation, construct the "three-level-academic-competition" engineering practice of three-dimensional system. Which explore effective competition practices, means, ways for our actual practices, and provide a good platform to train the abilities of automation students to analyze and solve practical problems, creativity and cooperative spirit. Therefore, that enriches and improves the content and form of practice teaching, practical trains students' engineering practice innovation.

Acknowledgements. This work was supported by the Education of Zhejiang Province under grant Y200804975, Y200907366, Higher Education of Zhejiang Province under grant Y201008. New Century Education Reform of Zhejiang Province under grant YB09025.

References

1. Zhang, R.C., Chen, Z.K., Wang, F.B.: Exploration on the conversion from disciplinary contest content to practice teaching. Experimental Technology and Management 27(7), 130–132 (2010)
2. Yi, S., Xiao, K.: Construction of multidisciplinary competition platform for cultivation of new type of top-notch talents. Experimental Technology and Management 26(5), 121–124 (2009)
3. Che, T.H., Wen, X.M., Ge, L.W., et al.: Developing students' practical and innovative ability through discipline competition–Take the university student structure competition as an example. Journal of Zhejiang University of Science and Technology 20(2), 136–138 (2008)
4. Wang, W., Zhang, Y.M., Ge, Y.: Development of Comprehensive Experiment in Automation Specialty with Engineering Awareness Enhancement. Research and Exploration Laboratory 29(8), 94–96 (2010)
5. Zhao, Y.X., Tang, Y., Huang, W.: Investigation for Integration between Automation Experiment Teaching and Engineering Application. Journal of Southwest China Normal University (Natural Science Edition) 34(1), 173–176 (2009)

6. Xu, Y.Q.: The discussion on the model between Applied Talent cultivating and subject contest. Journal of HuBei Adult Education Institute 14(2), 12–14 (2008)
7. Zhu, C.P., Huang, B., Zhu, C.S., et al.: Training Students' Practice Innovation Capability Through "Three-Level -Experiment", vol. 26(7), pp. 5–8 (2007)
8. Liang, H.K.: Subject Contest an Important Carrier of Cultivating Innovative Talents. Journal of Hubei University of Education 27(9), 106–109 (2010)
9. Li, S.B.: Driving the Curriculum Constructs and the Student Innovation Ability Raising by the Discipline Competition. College Mathematics 25(5), 8–10 (2009)

CDIO-Based Exploration and Practice of "Computer Network Design and System Integration" Course*

Wei Guo[1] and Hong Lu[2]

[1] College of Mathematics and Computer Science, Jianghan University, Wuhan, China
guo21390@126.com
[2] Network Department of Library, Jianghan University, Wuhan, China

Abstract. This paper analyzes the engineering and practice characteristics of "Computer Network Design and System Integration". After that, for training and exercise the engineering practice ability of students, this paper use CDIO education ideal as guide, present instantiation theoretical teaching and engineered experiment to reform the model of teaching to improve quality and effectiveness.

Keywords: CDIO; Computer Network Design and System Integration; Teaching Reform.

1 Introduction

With the rapid development of information technology and increasingly competitive market, computer networks present a development trend of complex and "big project" to pursuit multi-function, high efficiency, high efficiency and high quality. As one of the professional core courses for university computer network engineering major, the course of "Computer Network Design and System Integration" cover the network design, integration, and maintenance. However, too much emphasis on traditional higher education to the neglect of academic research capacity-building projects makes it difficult to meet the needs of "Computer Network Design and System Integration" course teaching, which has a strong engineering, comprehensive and practical. Therefore, for training the ability of student in professional and engineering, it has great significance directed toward to characteristics of the course and the current problems of teaching to explore using CDIO engineering education model to reform the course teaching in "Computer Network Design and System Integration".

2 Overview of CDIO Engineering Education Model

CDIO is developed by the education reform and research team of engineering education which composed of four Universities, including Massachusetts Institute of Technology

---

* Biography: Wei Guo (1966-), male, Ph.D., Senior Engineer, research direction: Networks Engineering.

M. Zhu (Ed.): ICCIC 2011, Part V, CCIS 235, pp. 428–434, 2011.
© Springer-Verlag Berlin Heidelberg 2011

of United States and Swedish Royal Institute of Technology. After four years of exploration and study, the team created the CDIO idea of the engineering education with the goal of capacity-building. CDIO is on behalf of the four stages from research and development of life cycle products, which are Conceive, Design, Implement, and Operate [1].

As an innovation models of international higher engineering education, CDIO combine the project development with course theory and practice teaching organically to change the current engineering education in the presence of heavy theory and practice of light status. Based on that, it try to training high-level professional engineers with a solid grasp of engineering the basic theory and professional knowledge, a life-long learning, large-scale system control capacity, and high moral character [2-4]. CDIO approach focuses on integrated innovation ability, and coordinated development with social environment; at the same time, more concerned with engineering practice to enhance practical ability of students. Nowadays, there are more than 50 universities have joined the CDIO co-operation program, including Denmark, Finland, France, South Africa, Singapore, China and other countries, and jointly continue to develop and improve the CDIO teaching. CDIO has an important instructive significance in Chinese university education reform, and the current reform exploration is in the initial stage [5-6].

CDIO education model is lead by industry demand, and integrate the training objectives into the course teaching. Implementing each capability points in specific teaching and experimental activities, which allow students to learn professional theory, technology and engineering experience with the initiative, practical, course between the organic contact way. The capacity training model of CDIO, which cyclic from practice to experience, experience to theory, and finally back to the practice, has an important instructive for the current reform of higher engineering education.

3 Characteristics and Problems of "Computer Network Design and System Integration" Course

3.1 Characteristics of Computer Network System Design and Integration

To share the resources plenty and achieve centralize, efficient and convenient management, Computer network systems design and integration use the structured cabling system and computer network technology to integrate the various separate devices, features and information into a interrelated, integrated and coordinated system. Computer network systems integration including equipment system integration and application integration:

1) **Equipment System Integration,** also known as hardware system integration. In order to design and build the information management and support platform within a organization, which use integrated wiring technology, communications technology, networking technology, multimedia technology, security technology, and network security technology to integrate multi-protocol related equipment of various vendors.

2) Application System Integration. It provides a system model and specific technical and operational solutions to achieve the model for the customer demands from the perspective of system architecture. Application system integration services and applications is the advanced stage of system integration, which related to specific aspects of the user to provide a comprehensive system solution.

The core of computer network systems design and integration is maximizing the organic composition, efficiency, integrity, flexibility and simplify complexity, ultimately for the system, to provide a complete set of practical Solution to the organization or enterprises.

3.2 Characteristics of Teaching Contents

As the network systems design and integration involves solving the matching among the devices interface, protocol, system platforms, application software, and subsystem integration, which need resolve various issues that related the management and integration, include built environment, construction with, organizing and staffing, and other. Thus, according to application demands, the course teaching of "Computer Network Design and System Integration" should cover the whole process of integrating hardware, networks, databases and the corresponding application software to a computer application information system with good cost-effective systems. The course has the following characteristics:

1) The Novelty of the Professional Knowledge. Computer network technology is a new subject that is closely and growing of computer technology and communication technology. The basic principle and content is the formation of new theoretical results and practical experience from the past two decades the development of computer technology and communication technology. Network systems design and integration has novel and academic characteristics, how to understand their nature and characteristics are still many issues worth exploring.

2) The Abstract of the Theoretical Teaching. As the methods and strategies to comprehensive planning and gradual implementation an information system, the teaching of computer network system design principles and integrated approach not only involves specific functional, hardware, software and various specific technology, but also the ideas and concepts that summarize from the past experience of system design and implementation. It has abstraction.

3) The Innovative of the Experimental Teaching. As an engineering innovation, on the one hand, the design of computer network systems need to consider the function of specific user requirements, quality requirements and other business factors. Thus, each computer systems integrated project has different characteristics and demands, and should tailor to the requirement. On the other hand, some conflict may exist between the function and quality, that mean there is no perfect network structure, and designer need trade-offs and compromise the various elements according to the actual situation in the specific design and implementation process to meet in general users.

3.3   Problems in Classroom Teaching

As large-scale systems, which has very complex structure, broad coverage, and widely used, the professional teaching for computer network systems design and integration should correspond to its characteristics. However, the course teaching of "Computer Network Design and System Integration" in current university is the model that combine the theoretical teaching with experiment of equipment operation. Usually, the theoretical teaching is explained by teacher, and the practice teaching is done accordance with the reservation. In this method, students act as "audience" role, follow the teacher's ideas to understanding, memory knowledge passively, and the traditional teaching methods did not change. The classroom teaching has the following characteristics:

1) The Theoretical Teaching Is too Abstract. The network systems design and integration mainly consider the design and implementation issues for the overall structure of complex information systems from the architecture level. That means the course teaching should not be the theoretical teaching for a simple seven layers protocol model. However, the faced the school students which without practical experience in projects, the abstract theory in classroom teaching not only difficult to understand, but also could not connect the elements of the layered protocol model of specific projects with the network communications system, application software and hardware systems. The result is the empty and boring theoretical teaching.

2) The Experimental Teaching Is too Shallow. On the one hand, it is less the perceptual knowledge of network systems analysis, design and implementation. The other hand, due to the time for experiment teaching is limited, the existing experiment is the teacher introduces the experiment design and implementation method, and students verify the experiment. Without necessary cognition and experiencing, any initiative exploring experience is out of the question. Because the network design could not be verified exactly and opportunely, the experiment teaching is at a low level, and the students are difficult to form the profound experience.

4   CDIO-Based Teaching Exploration of "Computer Network Design and System Integration" Course

Introduce CDIO model "Computer Network Design and System Integration" course, which simulating the network system project development process can enable students to apply the professional knowledge in practice and get experience. With comprehensive simulation exercises, students can understand the role of collaboration, comprehensive use of professional knowledge and skills, ideas to design and implement a complete network system.

4.1   Instantiate the Theoretical Teaching

The curriculum system and teaching content is the basis for theoretical teaching, which determines the structure of knowledge and ability of students. Instantiate the theoretical teaching can make classroom teaching pay more attention to the social requirement. The circumstances can be adjust depends on the specific situation of student opportunely to update teaching content, optimize the structure of professional knowledge, and strengthen the connection among the courses knowledge. The theoretical teaching is no longer a cramming education, which can help students to understand the theoretical knowledge more in-depth. Combine theory with practice in the specific theoretical knowledge explanation, it can enhance interest and initiative in learning. For the professional knowledge that is important and difficult understand, it can be addressed through interactive discussions.

In the specific teaching model, introducing CDIO that change the traditional teaching mode, which penetrates the important and difficult understand professional theoretical knowledge into the explanation of specific case. The learning purpose of student is no longer memorized the principles and methods of network design and systems integration. Teacher arranged the topic, students collect, finish and analysis data and information, in order to deepen understanding of knowledge. In this interactive teaching method, students are the subject, but no longer the teacher, and self-learning ability has been train.

In the specific teaching method, introducing CDIO that analyze the problem of specific case to lead inquiry-based learning method into classroom. The teaching methods of explain, inspire and discussion the specific case of network design and integration, which can stimulate students curiosity, arouse the enthusiasm of the students so that students learn by example and discussion of the initiative to master the network design and systems integration principles and methods.

In the specific teaching assessment method, introducing CDIO that make knowledge assessment system pay more attention to the practice of the usual time but exams, to ensure the realization of the concept CDIO engineering education. Students learn and master the professional knowledge and skills, and gradually develop independent study habits to enhance the learning ability, which can provide professional development potential for the future.

4.2 Engineered the Experimental Teaching

The introduction of CDIO teaching, not only in theoretical teaching, but also penetrate to experimental teaching of the specific professional courses. Simulating the implementation of engineering project in experimental teaching, which could makes students to understand the process and methods of the project implementation by the experimental teaching. Students should reduce its current emphasis on results, the specifications and process quality sustainable will growth, and thus enhance the ability of students to the practice of comprehensive.

For realistic simulating the implementation process of the engineering project, experimental teaching in the "Computer Network Design and System Integration" course needs to refer to the industry standards and architectures. The experimental teaching should cover the full life cycle of network project (including project start, requirement analysis, design, configuring, testing, operation, and maintenance), so that the process closer to the realistic project. As the engineering design and realization is based on the specification and network architecture, which include the project implementation process, technical specifications, engineering documents, and operational procedures, etc., all of these should be accorded to the realistic engineering standards. The experimental teaching should be operational so that the goal can be achieved really.

5 The Course Teaching Practice

Implementing the CDIO ideal in a specific course teaching, the students are the subject during the teaching, and teacher plays the role of organizer, inductor, and monitor in this process. The most important thing is to let students play to their ability in this stage, and the team cooperate implement the project by communication, wisdom share, and efforts. The process is shown as Figure 1.

1) Propose a Project. Teacher submits some simulation of network engineering projects, which is well-chosen according to the school environment that the students are familiar to arouse the interest of students. Not only the purpose and requirements of teaching has been embodied, but also the actual technology that will use in the engineering projects should be integrated. The difficulty is properly, so that students enable achieve the result of inquiry-based learning by implement the experiment with their practice.

2) Necessary Theoretical Knowledge and Practical Experience. The students have accumulated theoretical knowledge and practical experience that is necessary by classroom teaching and experimental teaching. The teacher also inspires students to gather and accumulate professional theoretical knowledge and practical experience that is necessary for the topic them choose.

3) Planning the Project. Students compose the team freely. The teacher analysis of customer requirement and guide the internal discussions in the group. The students analysis the project to development a specific design, and assign the tasks and labor to the specific team members clearly.

4) Engineered the Experimental Realization. The team members perform their duties according to their respective mandates, to complete their specific tasks. As the network engineering achieve process is not one step, that may need students adjust and improve solution constantly, and change the division of labor within the team. This is the process that student consolidate the learned knowledge by cooperation and continuous among the team members. The ability can be improved, not only the team spirit and for mutual cooperation and interpersonal communication, but also the active learn the knowledge to solve practical problems.

5) Evaluate and Improve the Result. Student explains the result of analysis and the achieve strategy their own formulation for the project. Teacher evaluates the result according to the customer requirements, industry standards and specification. This evaluation will be one of the assessment criteria.

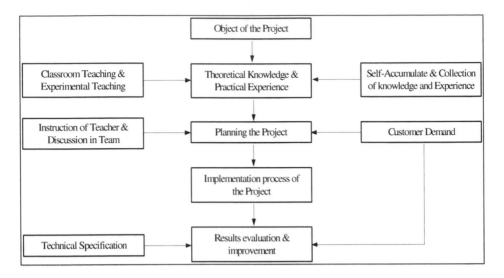

Fig. 1. Engineering project executing processes

6 Conclusions

For the characteristics of the "Computer Network Design and System Integration" course, this paper proposed to introduce the CDIO education ideal in order to achieve the reform of engineering education. Practice shows the model can better stimulate enthusiasm for learning, and improve the ability of independent learning. While training the ability to analyze and solving problems, it also can improve ability of student to actual engineering practice and the team cooperation. As the new personnel training ways of engineering innovative, CDIO could also be research and promotion in other courses teaching at the further.

References

1. Worldwide CDIO Initiative, CDIO Knowledge Library. Information on, http://www.cdio.org
2. Tao, Y., Shang, C.: Revelation on The Teaching Innovation of Higher Engineering Education Based on CDIO Outline. China Higher Education Research 11, 81 (2006)
3. Zhang, H., Dai, B., Liu, N.: The Reform and Practice of Automation Main Course Based on CDIO Model. Journal of Electrical & Electronic Education 31, 138 (2009)
4. Gu, P., Shen, M., Li, S.: From CDIO to EIP-CDIO: A Probe into the Mode of Talent Cultivation in Shantou University. Research in Higher Education of Engineering 1, 12 (2008)
5. Wang, G.: Interpretation and Thinking for CDIO Engineering Education Model. China University Education Research 5, 86 (2009)
6. Zhuang, Z., Shen, M.: Design and Practice for Project Level One Based on CDIO Idea. Research in University education of Engineering 6, 19 (2008)

Using Fishbone Diagrams in Inquiry-Based Teaching and Learning for Engineering Education

Wei Guo [1] and Hong Lu [2]

[1] College of Mathematics and Computer Science, Jianghan University, Wuhan, China
guo21390@126.com
[2] Network Department of Library, Jianghan University, Wuhan, China

Abstract. Inquiry-based teaching theory is a pedagogical approach that invites students to explore academic content by posing, investigating, and answering questions, which provide an alternative theoretical foundation for rethinking and redesigning teaching practices. This paper presents using fishbone diagrams as the method in inquiry-based teaching and learning for engineering education to develop problem-solving skills for students. An example of teaching practices which is based on the theory also has been offered for the computer network course to troubleshoot failure network link.

Keywords: Fishbone Diagrams, Inquiry-based Teaching and Learning, Engineering Education, Teaching Methodology.

1 Introduction

Engineering is a very diverse profession that requires different skills. An engineer has to perform various tasks, such as technical supervision, project development, diagnostics, and etc [1]. Therefore, engineering education is the activity of teaching knowledge and principles related to the professional practice of engineering. It is not sufficient to train a specialist who has the special skills that the profession should be obtained all by engineering education that just providing basic theoretical knowledge in the field. However, the conventional teaching strategies mainly train students to store and retrieve mastered information, that mean it could not satisfy the demand of engineering education in the information age that is based on the rapid development of technology.

Inquiry-based teaching or learning is not a simple concept, which is an approach that focuses on the process of learning, rather than outcomes. In inquiry-based teaching and learning, the traditional roles of student and teacher are changed to a collaborative relationship. However, in most classrooms, if the teacher follows the traditional teaching approach and some students were not able to understand what they will understand, they would rather just to complete the experiment, than to develop skills to solve practical problems by inquiry them. Most research on inquiry-based teaching has often focused on its application in science education.

M. Zhu (Ed.): ICCIC 2011, Part V, CCIS 235, pp. 435–442, 2011.
© Springer-Verlag Berlin Heidelberg 2011

As an intriguing and exciting method, inquiry-based teaching and learning involves students as active learners, learning real practical skills, inquiry approach is equally well-suited to the teaching of the engineering education. Therefore, how to put the wondering and the questions of students at the center, and make them naturally emerge when engaged in active learning is significance for the inquiry-based teaching in engineering education.

This paper presents using fishbone diagrams to arouse the interest, self-awareness and creative thinking in inquiry-based engineering education to develop practice experience and skills for students. In the next section, the paper first discusses the characteristics of inquiry-based teaching and learning. In section 3, the paper describes how to use fishbone diagrams to develop problem-solving skills in inquiry-based teaching to enhance the teaching and learning qualities. As examples, a teaching practice in the computer network course has been proposed, in which the fishbone diagrams approaches has used for the pre-engineering students of computer to troubleshoot failure network link.   Finally, conclusions and future work are summarized in section 4.

2   Inquiry-Based Teaching and Learning in Engineering Education

2.1   Characteristics of Inquiry-Based Teaching and Learning

In traditional teaching, the teacher is at the center of the learning process and determining what the students learn and how they learn it [2]. The primary method of traditional teaching was to have student memorize, and note taking it. The effectiveness of this way is regarded as a distribution of information from an outward source to a learner, and has frequently been criticized.

Inquiry is a process that gathers facts and observations and uses them to solve problems. Inquiry-based teaching and learning is particularly valuable for giving students practice in defining problems, gathering data to solve the problems and developing their higher-order and critical thinking abilities [3]. The teacher may pose the problem and give guidance in how to solve the problem, and the students generate the questions and determine how to research them through independent research. Therefore, inquiry-based teaching and learning has been identified as one way in which institutions can provide an explicit link between their research activity and student education[4][5].

There are numerous approaches to inquiry-based teaching and learning, and many categories of them. The typical approaches include:

The Constructivist Approach to Inquiry-Based Teaching and Learning, is problem-based teaching or learning, which often perceived as a constructivist approach where the teaching or learning is anchored around a specific problem and context, and students work from that in identifying what to learn and develop in order to solve the problem [6]; another is Project based teaching and learning built around the concept of projects, where students again work in teams, to develop on a completing project and have to solve numerous problems [7].

The Receptive Constructivist Approach to Inquiry-Based Teaching and Learning, is enquiry-based teaching and learning, where students are typically presented with a task to do and have to discover for themselves, such as what knowledge gaps and deficiencies they may have, along with skills they may need to develop.

The Discovery Approach to Inquiry-Based Teaching and Learning, the critical theory in here is that if students discover a concept for themselves, they will have better understanding of the thing being learnt rather than having a third party models foisted upon them.

Inquiry-based teaching approach advocates student learning via observation and concrete experiences instead of rote memorization, which encourages students through supports to build research skills that can be used throughout their educational experiences. The inquiry-based teaching and learning have characteristics as fellow:

1. The teaching and learning encircle an open problem to spread out – open in the sense that there are numerous methods to solution;

2. For solving the problem, the students must discover for themselves the nature of the problem, and in particular to identify what knowledge and skills they will need to investigate and develop in order to solve the problem;

3. The students are required to demonstrate self analysis and critical thinking in order to choose between a number of possible solutions and methods;

4. The teacher acts as a facilitator in the process – but avoids simply providing solutions or being prescriptive in methods.

2.2   Inquiry-Based Teaching and Learning for Engineering Education

The objectives of engineering education are providing the skill for engineering use of front line techniques. That means a student after some years undergraduate learn should have professional practical capability of engineering to develop new products, troubleshoot practical problems. He should be able to gather new knowledge from the international technical-scientific literature in the professional area and to transform such knowledge into technical applications. For this reason, students need to be taught how to develop the skills, and engineering education should provide a method that student can link the basic knowledge and skills from the teaching and experimental of classrooms to the professional practical experience. The development of engineers requires both the learning of concepts and the acquisition of inquiry skills such as scientific thinking and problem troubleshooting.

Using inquiry method in engineering education, the classrooms should are open systems where students are encouraged to search and make use of resources beyond the classroom and the school. It involves making observations, posing questions, reviewing what is already known, planning and designing experiments, collecting data, proposing answers, making predictions, and communicating the results of the work[8].

Obviously, the above characteristics make the inquiry-based teaching and learning can be applied on engineering education, and which has been confirmed through different researches. At first, the inquiry-based teaching and learning need educators not only data and information accumulation, but also the useful and applicable knowledge. Second, as there is not the best solution in many times, inquiry is not so much seeking the right answer, but rather seeking appropriate resolutions to questions and issues. This means that using inquiry-based teaching and learning in engineering education will provide more experience for students. Third, inquiry strategies in engineering education enhance learning based on increased student involvement in the process, which allows students to make some choices based on learning styles and multiple intelligences. This means students can choose learning based on a topic (usually within a set range) that is of interest to them, which will lead to active construction of meaningful knowledge rather than passive learning of facts.

Unfortunately, inquiry-based teaching and learning is not just asking questions, which is a way of converting data and information into useful knowledge. Inquiry-based teaching and learning need the teachers organize their lesson plans according to the teacher-student interaction model in class. As a purest form, if there are misgivings that traditional ways of teaching may discourage the process of inquiry. Due to the lack of understanding of inquiry based teaching and learning, which would make the student get less prone to asking questions as they move through their grade levels, they are just expected to listen and repeat the expected answers. Obviously, the approach is important for using inquiry-based teaching and learning in engineering education, which can develop independent and critical thinking skills, positive attitudes and curiosity toward science and increased achievement in engineering practice.

3   Using Fishbone Diagrams as the Inquiry Method in Engineering Education

3.1   Fishbone Diagrams Is an Effective Inquiry Tool

Fishbone diagram is invented by Kaoru Ishikawa in 1943, which is sometimes called "Cause and Effect Diagrams" and the template for constructing them is in Visio software. The design of the diagram looks much like the skeleton of a fish. Therefore, it is often referred to as the fishbone diagram. As an analysis tool, the fishbone diagram can provide a systematic way of considering a problem and the causes that create or contribute to the problem[9]. Because of the function of the fishbone diagram, it may be referred to as a cause-and-effect diagram. The value of the fishbone diagram is to assist teams in categorizing the many potential causes of problems or issues in an orderly way and in identifying root causes.

The main goal of the Fishbone diagram is to illustrate in a graphical way the relationship between a given outcome and all the factors that influence this outcome. Using a Fishbone diagram for synthesizing information, synthesis involves putting parts together to form a new whole. In a typical Fishbone diagram, the effect is usually a problem needs to be resolved, and is placed at the "fish head". The causes of the effect are then laid out along the "bones", and classified into different types along the branches, and the head or topic must be discovered. Synthesis also occurs when the related factors are combined into different categories. Bones, such as big bones, medium bones, and small bones can establish the impact of the cause. The larger bones closer to the head of the fish show a great impact, while small bones further away from the head have a lesser impact. When used as a cause-and-effect diagram, a Fishbone diagram can be used to represent the extent of influence of each cause.

Using Fishbone diagrams in inquiry-based teaching and learning, meaningless unconnected pieces of information can be make a meaningful whole when they are synthesized or combined, which is helpful in clearly identifying the relationship between a topic and all of the possible factors that relate to it. In this way, learners should present the factors or bones for a problem to combine related pieces of information, which will help them to explore the relationships that form the complete knowledge architecture.

3.2 How to Create a Fishbone Diagrams

Fishbone diagrams can be effectively combined with other analysis tools, such as Hierarchical Maps (if there is a structured relationship between the levels of information in the fishbone diagram), and Six Thinking Hats. Six Thinking Hats can be used to synthesize the information in a fishbone diagram to determine the head[10]. Following is the step to create a fishbone diagrams:

Step1: Define the problem statement in a box on the right-hand side of the diagram and create the "fish" backbone by drawing a line to the problem.

Step 2: Identify potential causes for the problem by function or by process sequence and categorize them as the "bones" of the fish. Use brainstorming to identify causes.

Step 3: Continue to brainstorm and identify sub categories for each bone with more details. Three levels of detail are usually enough.

Step 4: Analyze potential causes, and then circle the one that most likely contributing to the problem.

Step 5: Identified root cause.

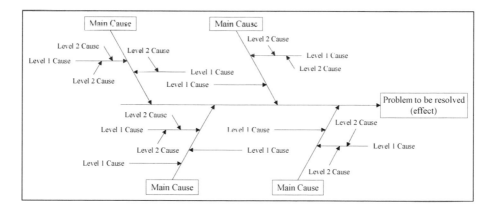

Fig. 1. Fishbone Diagram structure

3.3 Using Fishbone Diagram in Inquiry-Based Teaching and Learning to Troubleshoot Failure Network Link

Today, Computer networks and the Internet have already become the most critical infrastructure for information dissemination, business transactions, human communications, and even national security. "Computer Networks" is a strong theoretical and technical course, and have played an important role in the professional teaching of engineering. Therefore, it is important that the practitioners have a solid foundation in the field in order to further foster and flourish its development and applications. As a result, there is a pressing need to explore computer networking education in many ways, and the goal of these studies, which are still in an exploratory stage is how to training the graduates to have the ability of using multiple, complex skills to solve practical problems.

The capacity of a network is usually expressed in terms of the data transfer rate. The data transfer rate between two points on a network is simply the number of bits or bytes which can be transferred from the first point to the second in a given time interval. If a computer is unable to connect to a network or see other computers on a network, it may be necessary to troubleshoot the network link. However, to the student or even the engineer without extensive computer network operational experience, how to sort out the causes of failure network link may be difficult when there are so many possible factors, such as fellow reasons:

1. The problem of source computer (such as network card not connected properly, wrong software settings, etc.)

2. The problem of destination computer (such as server hardware fault, denial of service, etc.)

3. Firewall preventing computers from accessing each other

4. Connection related issues (such as bad network hardware, wrong routing settings, etc.)

Each of these factors contains several sub-factors, and any one of which could cause network link failure. Working through this myriad of possible causes for a failure network link can be daunting to all but the highly experienced professional.

3.4   Organize the Class Teaching to Draw a Fishbone Diagram

This section describe how to organize the inquiry-based teaching in classroom to create a fishbone diagram, which is used to identify problems with network link performance, such as connection related issues, bad network hardware, and etc. This represents the fishbone diagram is an efficacious and familiar approach that is much helpful to inquiry-based teaching and learning. The specific process of how to troubleshoot a failure network link in classroom is described step by step as follows.

Step 1: Assemble the student team members of the process outcome under study, as well as writing or drawing materials (such as flip chart, black board, markers, etc.) to get started.

Step 2: Write the problem to be solved as descriptively as possible on one side of the work space in black board, and then draw the "backbone of the fish", record the process outcome under study in a few words.

Step 3: Ask team members to identify the major causes and categories them by function, or by process sequence. Draw in the major categories of variables along diagonal lines that intersect the horizontal line to the left of the arrowhead, and label the lines.

Step 4: Taking one category of variables at a time, ask team members to brainstorm all of the variables within the category that have an effect on the outcome under study.

Record the variables as horizontal lines that intersect the diagonal "fishbone" lines and are parallel to the first horizontal line.

Step 5: Continue to add detail to the branches ("fishbones") of the diagram.   For each variable ask, "Why does that happen? ", and draw the responses as additional side branches.

Step 6: Analyze the diagram of relationships displayed.

Step 7: Choose the major categories of variables about which the group will acquire additional information and detail.

Step 8: Focus process and systems improvements in the areas identified by the team as the major "causes" of undesirable variation in the area under study.

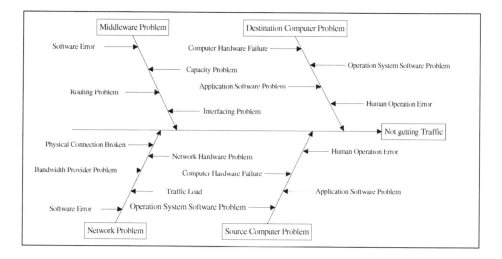

Fig. 2. Using Fishbone Diagram to troubleshoot failure network link

4   Conclusions

Inquiry is a highly effective teaching method that develops both content and process skills in students for engineering education, if it can identify, sort, display and analyze possible causes of a specific problem. Therefore, to use inquiry-based teaching and learning effectively, it requires effective approach and practice on the part of the teacher and the student. As a graphic analyze tool, the fishbone diagram permits a rigorous analysis that teacher can implement inquiry-based teaching in classroom to solve problems by conducting an analysis of a situation in a diagram. Using fishbone diagrams in inquiry-based teaching and learning for engineering education, students can actively engaged in constructing knowledge and accumulating important problems-solving skills. Even after the problem is resolved, the link design also could help student to training scientific thought way and experience for the future practice work.

References

1. Osipov, P., Ziyatdinova, J.: Humanities in Engineering Education for Character Development. In: International IGIP-SEFI Annual Conference 2010, Slovakia (2010)
2. Haggerty Dorothy, L.: Engaging Adult Learners in Self-Directed Learning and its Impact on Learning Styles. The University of New Orleans, New Orleans (2000)
3. Colburn, A.: Inquiring Scientists Want to Know. Educational Leadership 62(1), 63 (2004)
4. Tsaparlis, G., Gorezi, M.: A Modification of a Conventional Expository Physical Chemistry Laboratory to Accommodate an Inquiry/Project-Based Component: Method and Students' Evaluation. Canadian Journal of Science, Mathematics and Technology Education 5(1), 111 (2005)
5. Jenkins, A., Healey, M.: Institutional Strategies to Link Teaching and Research, Higher Education Academy. Information on,
   http://www.heacademy.ac.uk/resources.asp
6. Savery, J., Duffy, T.: Problem Based Learning: An Instructional Model and Its Constructivist Framework. Educational Technology 35(5), 31 (1995)
7. Thomas, J.: A Review Of Research On Project - Based Learning, Information on,
   http://www.bie.org/tmp/research/researchreviewPBL.pdf
8. Buch, N.J., Wolff, T.F.: Classroom Teaching Through Inquiry. Journal of Professional Issues in Engineering Education and Practice 126(3), 105 (2000)
9. Using Fishbone Diagrams as Problem Solving Tools. Information on,
   http://www.ilofip.org/GPGs/FishboneDiagrams.pdf
10. Fishbone Diagram, Information on,
   http://www.improhealth.org/fileadmin/Documents/
   Improvement_Tools/Fishbone_diagram.pdf

Professional Experiment Teaching Should Pay More Attention to the Cultivation of Students' Creative Spirit

Ying Li

Key Laboratory of Urban Stormwater System and Water Environment
(Beijing University of Civil Engineering and Architecture),
Ministry of Education, Beijing, 100044, China
liyingcase@163.com

Abstract. In view of present requests of college professional experiment teaching, this paper discusses several aspects including teaching contents, teaching methods, teaching means and the relationship between experiment teaching and scientific research. Based on the present situation and existing problems of current professional experiment teaching in college, as well as the needs of current development of social science and technology and requirements for talents of society, this paper provides a brief introduction of how to cultivate creative and explorative graduates through professional experiments, and hoped to be effective in practice.

Keywords: colleges, professional experiment teaching, creative spirit.

1 Introduction

Innovation remains as the soul of the progress of a nation. [1] The core of the quality-oriented education in the 21st century is to cultivate all kinds of creative talents, which relies exactly on the innovation of education.

2 The Importance of the Cultivation of Creative Spirit and Application Ability

Educational innovation is a means based on the purpose of cultivating students' creative spirit and practical ability. It enables students to achieve mastery of their prior knowledge through new teaching mode, and understand how the predecessors analyzed and solved specific problems, which helps to learn from their correct ways of thinking and thinking habits. Then students are supposed to gather experience in practice, broaden horizons, develop their ability of innovation, and form their own habits of thinking, thinking modes as well as innovative patterns. That is to say, the essence of educational innovation is assuring the students can truly learn the methods of analyzing and solving problems through new teaching modes, rather than knowledge itself. Therefore, educational innovation should not be a mere resounding slogan, but a concrete that set in our daily teaching works.

M. Zhu (Ed.): ICCIC 2011, Part V, CCIS 235, pp. 443–448, 2011.
© Springer-Verlag Berlin Heidelberg 2011

Currently, colleges and universities are in a key period of evolution, faced with both opportunities and challenges. Colleges in China are constantly carrying forward all sorts of reform and innovation activities in order to strengthen the cultivation of high-quality and creative talents. In order to conform to this trend, especially at this very moment when the employment tendency is changing, it is of great importance to cultivate students' creative ability and comprehensive quality.[2]

It is of vital significance to the cultivation of educational innovation and application ability. From the perspective of developing our country through science and education, such cultivation is of great necessity to improve our overall national strength, to adapt to knowledge economy era as well as international competition. The trend of international education reform shows that the recognition of innovative education and cultivation of ability is where the values of modern education lie in. Therefore, the cultivation of creative spirit and application ability in today's colleges becomes an urgent and hard task. Meanwhile, the training of creative talents with high quality is also the primary goal of higher education of the 21st century.

3   Professional Experiment Teaching and Innovation

The cultivation of creative spirit and application ability for students is a multi-channel and gradual process and it exists in every aspect of students' study and life, among which professional experiment teaching acts as a very crucial link.

Professional experiment is the soul of the development of a subject, and professional experiment teaching is a subject based on observation and experiment, focused on cultivating students' thinking ability, analytical ability and ability of scientific technology innovation. Meanwhile, the innovation of professional experiment is a crucial stage to cultivate high-quality creative talents. It is supposed to adopt open teaching methods and base mainly on students' self-study, and teachers' instructions should remain as a complementary role.[3]

In order to adapt to the needs of the development of this era, teachers are supposed to attach great importance to modernity, openness and comprehensiveness in the professional experiment teaching, and add the latest scientific achievement to the teaching timely, realizing an effective combination of basic knowledge, basic skills, basic methods and new technologies, new methods, new theory. This can effectively avoid the phenomenon of knowledge aging, method outdated and the separation between theory and practice. 85% of previous professional experiment teaching is filled with verification experiments, which means that those experiments are used to validate whether the theory is correct or not. Students in the process are in passive states, mechanically repeating procedures of the experiment, and writing down the already-learnt experimental phenomena and summary, which constitute all the tasks of the experiment. This mode of experiment teaching can no longer keep up with the needs of development of this era. Take students majoring in science and engineering for example. They will directly contact the social science and technology right after their graduation, faced with realistic and professional problems needed to be resolved and the field of the latest research. If the content of professional experiment teaching is merely confined to theoretically experiments, lacking of the cultivation of the ability of analyzing and solving for practical problems, students will be deficient in the ability of professionally practical application, which may block them in the way paved with certain requirement of current social development and wash them out.

4 Cultivate Students' Creative Spirit via the Medium of Professional Experiment Teaching

Students are the ones who receive education and act as main parts of education at the same time. All the teaching methods should fully reflect the students' subjectivity, which means students should apply independency, activity and creativity to their studies. In light of this statement, teachers are supposed to make extensively use of such teaching methods as questioning, guiding and discussing to mobilize students' learning initiative and consciousness, and to train the students to handle the ability of analyzing and solving problems. During professional practice teaching process, large-scale comprehensive experiment can be properly conducted according to certain teaching situation. Although there may be obstacles such as huge investment, plenty of teaching organizers, long lasting time, and possible risks in some of these comprehensive experiments, we cannot deny that there are essential differences between teaching mode and means of comprehensive experiments and confirmatory experiments. This kind of teaching can fully show the heuristic method of teaching and the cultivation of students' creative thinking, stimulating students' practical ability and creative ability. Teachers can also encourage students to ask questions, search relevant technical data, discuss in groups (or even argue), and bring forward unconventional ideas, stimulating students' enthusiasm, initiative and creativity in the process of comprehensive experiments. At the same time, students should also be encouraged to continuously explore the problems unsettled in the experiments, developing their scientific research spirit.

As to teaching means, teachers should actively make use of computers, multimedia, closed-circuit television systems, simulation software and other modern teaching tools. Through voice and image, as well as many other kinds of forms, teachers can make the professional experiment teaching "live", making students realized that hands-on experience teaching and theory teaching are different, enabling them to acquire the knowledge more thoroughly and vividly, and stimulating their all-round creative ability. Meanwhile, building relaxing academic atmosphere, respecting students' initiative, and encouraging students' innovation consciousness can help them learn from each other, exchange ideas freely, fully display themselves and improve together in good academic atmosphere.[4]

Modern experiment teaching and scientific research should coexist, and they should drive each other mutually, forming a benign circulation. Research is the study of the level of a certain professional technology, and its function is small in the past experiment teaching. Traditional teaching holds the concept that scientific research is just for graduate students, teachers and doctoral studies, and undergraduates are outsiders. The teaching excludes trends of scientific research, and the content of scientific research is not involved as well. When students step into society, employers will not be satisfied with their poor research ability, and the students themselves will feel self-abased. Therefore, modern experiment teaching should include the trends of scientific research, and strengthen the motivation, consciousness, involvement and creation of scientific research, and enable students to be aware of the necessity of innovation and constant development of knowledge, and make them realized the great needs for creative talents. Blending scientific research with experiment teaching can also improve teachers' ability of scientific research, stimulating and urging them to remain enthusiasm and creativity in scientific research. Thus, this kind of combination possesses great meaning of both multi-level and multi-dimension in teaching.

5   Build New Concepts between Teachers and Students in Experiment Teaching

Set up the Concept of the Importance of Experiment Teaching. The reform of experiment teaching is attached to the pattern of theory teaching, Listing experiment courses separately, and forming relatively independent experiment teaching system. The significance of experiment should be highlighted, which helps arouse students' attention to the experiment teaching, and avoid some of them considering it not indispensable. Through the experiment, students can strengthen the skill of basic operation, arouse thirst for knowledge and professional identity, and practice operating ability and strengthen innovative consciousness, forming a scientific, standardized, and rigorous work style and the ability of analyzing and solving problems.

Establish the Concept that Students are the Subject in Experiment Activities. In traditional teaching activities, teachers are the center, or the "leading role". On many occasions, the determination of teaching content, arrangements of activities, as well as design of methods are all from teachers, and students are just "costars", obeying and cooperating with the teacher passively, lacking initiative. According to the new concept of modern vocational education teaching, student-centered concept should be established in innovative experiment teaching. Teaching activity is a two-way activity including both teaching and learning. It is neither a one-way process of cognition for students nor a simple procedure of acceptance for knowledge. It is also definitely not a process conducted by teachers who set steps, modes and results in advance for students. Not only teachers, but also students should be guided to build up the concept that students are the subject in experiment activities. In teaching practice, students not only learn the basic knowledge, methods and skills of scientific experiments, but acquire strict scientific attitude and foster scientific world outlook and methodology. In this way they can form the ability of independent thinking, the comprehensive capability of analyzing and solving problems, and the innovation capacity which the innovative talents are supposed to possess.

Build the Concept that Ability Training is Crucial in Experiment Teaching. Teaching in earlier days is a kind of mode in which teachers "teach textbook". The root of this mode is the mastery of the content of teaching materials and reaching of target. And the new teaching mode, which is supposed to change, tries hard to form a mode in which teachers "teach basing textbook". Teachers should consider textbook as a tool, rather than a purpose. Through the use of such tools teachers can show students the process of forming knowledge, and reveal the internal law of learning. In such ways students can master the methods of learning, and improve the ability of knowledge application, which helps settle foundation for future study. In this manner students will be clear about the goal and requirements of the vocational education, and transfer from "learn" to "the ability to learn", thus making the teaching materials a new platform for them, based on which they can reach for higher goals, and lay a solid foundation to realize autonomous learning and lifelong learning. Therefore, under the guidance of this new concept, we are able to realize the transformation of the modes of experiment teaching.[5]

6   Give a Boost to the Innovation of Professional Experiment Teaching

Along with the development of educational reform and the booming of market economy, professional experiment teaching in colleges should connect with market and enterprise in a multi-channel and multi-dimension way, establishing fixed or random base for professional experiments or practice, in order to assure the practicality of teaching and the continuous improvement of technical application ability of both teachers and students and the utility and novelty in teaching and learning. Or colleges can provide appropriate convenience to attract enterprise or department of research and development to build their links of practice in internship, experiment and center of research and development on campuses. This can not only make full use of resources in colleges, but can provide more opportunities of experimental teaching and experimental research for teachers and students, improving their practical ability, which is beneficial in the cultivation of innovative talents.

In view of present situation, colleges should lay equal emphasis on practice teaching and theory teaching, at the same time, strengthening management, achieving the goals of strict requirement, management and quality in experiment teaching. Universities have already strengthened the management in experiment teaching by the means of greater investment in both manpower and material resources. However, standardized management is still lacking, resulting in the poor effect in experiment teaching. If a student fails to preview the experiment before class, he actually cannot know anything about the contents, procedures and conclusion of the experiment. How can there be innovation just by operating blindly and mechanically, without any thinking process? What is worse, some students just watch others operating the experiments, and they themselves don't work at all, believing that watching can be equal to doing. This kind of phenomenon widely exists. The management of experiment teaching still needs to be studied intensively.

Anyhow, the teaching and management of professional experiment in colleges should be explored and discussed continually. Based on the cultivation of students' creative spirit and the ability of analyzing and solving problems, professional experiment teaching can help students to explore knowledge initiatively. So far, the purpose of college professional experiment teaching can be achieved.

Acknowledgements. Beijing Academic Innovation Group in Urban Stormwater System and Water Environmental Eco-Technologies (PHR201106124).

References

1. Innovation is the Soul of a Nation's Progress[OL]. Information on (August 28, 2000), http://www.china.com.cn/chinese/2000/Aug/2707.Htm
2. Hao, Z., et al.: Brief Analysis on Strengthening the Cultivation of High-quality Creative Talents in Professional Experiment Teaching (October 2010)
3. Xu, H.: Constructing Experiment Teaching System of Cultivating Innovative Talents in Electrical Field (2010)
4. He, X., et al.: Research and Practice in Professional Experiment Teaching System for the Cultivation of Innovative Talents (2009)
5. Tong, S.: Research Experiment Teaching, and Realize the Innovation of Experimental Skills Teaching (2010)

The Cultivation of Research Capability for Undergraduate

Ying Li and Ting Wang

Key Laboratory of Urban Stormwater System and Water Environment
(Beijing University of Civil Engineering and Architecture),
Ministry of Education, Beijing, 100044, China
liyingcase@163.com

Abstract. Based on the advanced institutes undergraduate's scientific research ability of analyzing the status, analyzes the importance of undergraduate's research ability and guide college from the teaching content, teaching way, teaching means and other aspects of reform and innovation to improve current universities' and colleges' teaching situation, to adapt to the new requirements for education era, cultivate innovative spirit and grinds only undergraduate, make the good spirit of the students become truly useful person who have contributed to society.

Keywords: undergraduate student, scientific research ability, educational reform.

1   Status of the Undergraduate Ability in Scientific Research

Obviously, the majority of our capacity of colleges students lack of training now. The lack of activities in schools is the necessary attention and strong support, resulting in poor research capability [1]. Specific performances are: lack of research on gathering information for the initiative, and the single method of gathering information, inability to obtain the valid information; independently identify problems and problem-solving capacity is weak, poor in combining theory and practice, resulting in practical project with the completion of very poor quality; lack of scientific literature analysis, induction, generalization and summation of the capacity, resulting in a large number of practical courses like the achievement is copied. Not have their own thinking on the issues, ideas and suggestions resulting in the illusory creation of practical courses. When undergraduate students graduated, except for some graduate students have the opportunity to obtain access to the one to one specific training by advisor, the vast majority of students which obtain employment are very difficult to be under the standard scientific research training again, it not only affects the overall quality of the future improved, but also results in a predicament that employers are reluctant about engaging graduating students.

The reasons why research capability for Undergraduate is poor are: first, the traditional exam-oriented education system in China largely hindered the overall development of students. At present, education has become a machine for testing,

M. Zhu (Ed.): ICCIC 2011, Part V, CCIS 235, pp. 449–454, 2011.
© Springer-Verlag Berlin Heidelberg 2011

such as school quiz, midterm and final exams, some types of qualification certificate, work permit, grading certificates and many other social exams, students are busy for them so that rush into the slaves of that machine. Students are no longer considered how much they understand, whether to link the learning and practice, but rather managed to get a high score or a passing grade on the test as the only way of judge the comprehensive ability of students, naturally, including research capacity. Secondly, the school teaching methods and curriculum are conservative. The management of teaching should keep pace with the advancement of era, and no longer use those old teaching system. About courses, it should not set up the massive foundation teaching curriculum again primarily, should not be almost controlled all the students in the domain of campus cultural study, transform to the curriculum which unifies by the foundation and the practice primarily, and increase students outside class activities suitably, combine learning with practice, the practical ability of students strengthened, and scientific research ability enhanced naturally. Furthermore, from the social cognitive perspective, the whole society pay no attention to research capability, they tend to only care about the students education, which good universities graduation. This has created a deviation of social cognition.

2   Importance of Cultivation of Research Capability

China "Higher Education Law" second paragraph of Article XVI provides that: "Undergraduate education should enable students to systematically grasp the disciplines which are required of professional theory, and basic knowledge, to grasp the basic skills, methods and knowledge which are necessary for their expertise, to have the preliminary capability of the practical work." [2] The Law has a very specific requirements on the academic standards of undergraduate training, and it has a very clear objectives, to make which are engaged in the own major "the initial capacity of research" as one of the important goals of teaching, and with its position in the target distinct it from the requirements of the graduate students and junior college students. The emphasis is "the initial" capacity of researching on work of undergraduate. In this way, from a legal point of view the provision makes the cultivation of the students' ability as a basic assignment, and has its force. At the same time, this provision also fit for the basic rule of the development of education [3].

Of course, national legislation is essential, but it is not enough that education just depend on the national legislation, and it needs our education employees dedicated in the work, try our best to complete which of education should achieve the aims, cultivate the person who is excellent on intelligence and morality. That is a real educator.

3   Students' Self-development

There are two whereabouts for undergraduate student when they graduates. One is further study, the other is employment. No matter is the former or the latter, the formation of the preliminary research capacity is a solid foundation for its further development. From the study perspective, preliminary research capacity is benefit to adapt a new educational environment more quickly, the more achievements, the better results. From the employment point of view, the preliminary research capacity, some scientific research can increase their competitiveness. "Ministry of Education, the Ministry of Finance on the implementation of undergraduate teaching quality and teaching reform project of the opinion" pointed out that: "it is urgent to take effective measures to further deepens teaching reform and improve the capacity and level of training to satisfies the economic Social development needs of high quality innovative talents." [4]

As the undergraduate student, to participate in research projects can not only enhance the research capacity of students, but also is a rare exercise opportunity. In this process, students begin to understand the project content, data collection, literature review, analysis and understanding of current situation, identify problems, discuss issues, solve problems, make suggestions or suggestion, and so on, and end with they shared the achievement with the students. At the same time, the students experienced the confusion, puzzling, joy, realized the power of the cooperation, the own potential, and the endless power of learning felt that they grow and mature imperceptibly. Therefore, it's said that the undergraduate student involved in undergraduate research or scientific activities as soon as possible will both improve the students' comprehensive ability.

4   Social Needs

With the development of China's economic and society and the demands of the technological progress, the employment units' requirements about the talents are also transformed day by day. From focusing on education to focusing on ability, focusing on ethics and values, and having rich content of the talents, namely "professional loyalty, responsibility, and professional progress and innovation, teamwork and professional standards etc" the professional ethics, attitudes and values which regard as its core. All these have become the important criterion for the modern enterprises and the employer to choose employees. Therefore, our education can no longer blindly strive for the high score. We should strengthen the comprehensive ability of students, the solid foundation, the spirit of exploration, the moral standards, and improve their research capabilities.

5   Solution

The Aspect of Teaching. The guidance of research thought in classroom teaching: Most of the teachers are always teaching while researching, so we associate the imparting knowledge and the spirit of exploration, scientific method, philosophy and organic relationship with society, meanwhile, to excite the passion of science, to cast the spirit of science, and to point out the correct attitude of science. In addition, when teaching in the classroom, we should train student about the paper writing, and to catch the key of the knowledge, and to raise a question to make the student to be independent thinker, and also require them to write thesis. Changing the model of the homework which is" known, find, solution, and answer", regarding each work as a subject and answering it according the requirement of paper writing. All of these don't require the length, no uniform or the right answer, but beg the ways of thinking and research spirit [2]. About the teaching method, we must emphasize students' main body role, we should allow students to participate in the teaching process, encourage the curiosity of students to explore the desire to listen to teachers, in addition to their teaching, but to learn how to search tools and find the right tools they need to hunt for knowledge, and know how to sort, synthesis, extraction and processing of information, enhance the creativity of the core logic; reform the curriculum and teaching materials, the establishment of innovation to improve the quality of students curriculum and teaching materials for the target system, the quality of creative talent from the starting structure, optimize the course structure, updating teaching material, thicker wider foundation courses, students have a solid knowledge of the structure, culture and creative abilities of students capacity. In teaching management, we will put quality training into the teaching objectives, and treat it as an important indicator of teaching and assessment of an important basis for teaching quality [5].

In terms of scope from the content of thesis writing, treating teaching content as the center, and radiate the range of the students interested in. The basic knowledge of undergraduate are more fixed, their thinking may be more agile, and they have increasing passion of the connection between society and theoretical knowledge to deepen and widen the writing content without separating out of teaching content. Teachers can arrange one or two essay writing which should have the spirit of the writing process in terms of quality, scientific research's caution, integrity, innovation, practical-minded, the spirit of cooperation and many other ability should be equipped, and to develop a good style in scientific research. Teachers can arrange for students to get together to finish a paper in a conscious way and let students continue to grow in the collective cooperation [6].

Establishment of innovational funds and items for undergraduates' scientific researches: In order to educate undergraduates' ability to do scientific researches more effectively and directly, the institutions of higher learning are supposed to establish particular funds and items for undergraduates' scientific researches. Colleges' and universities' laboratories should assume the responsibility to set aside a small sum of particular funds in the field of scientific researches for undergraduates, encouraging them to join these researches.

Responsibility of Teachers. According to the new teaching plan (including the class teaching and research requirements), to improve the teachers' duty, the teaching responsibilities of teachers should to redefine and assessment into teaching with them. It should be clear that undergraduate's research is a necessary part of teaching, and guiding the undergraduate fixed, the regular instruction is the responsibility that the teacher must undertake. In practice, they can be equipped with fixed instructor for designed research topics, and pre-scheduled time, guidance, instruction methods and evaluation methods. Instructor is responsible for students' research studying guidance according the teaching plan, and grade for the effect. And related research funds may point to the form of performance of stroke related instruction teachers [7].

Secondly, the institutions of higher learning should have the strict selection of the best and recruit good teachers for teaching, assessment in-service teachers regularly in teaching method, teaching achievements, student assessment and so on, the most importance is the moral standard. Because only with morality, they are not to become a form in the whole teaching link and it can truly teach the students.

6 Activity of Student

Doing research is an innovative activity itself. It needs to arouse and mobilize students' initiative and motivation in the teaching, then students will participate in it. Schools and teachers should take measures as many as possible to stimulate students' realization in research and cultivate their spirit of it. If students are not interested in the project, it will not be easily to release their potential. Therefore, educators should try their best to create a better environment for students' spirit of exploring. Meanwhile, students need to realize the importance of experience in research and participate initiatively in it.

7 Summary and Prospect

The development of undergraduates research ability is a new teaching method that be put out to follow the needs of knowledge economy and for the drawbacks of traditional receptive learning model. From the sixties of last century, the American is the earliest and the most extensively carrying out researching activities country of the world up to now. Discussing and researching the changing, development status and the tendency have an essential inspiration and reference significance for the establishing and developing of our country's undergraduates' researching activities [8].

Tsinghua University is the earliest university of our country to carry out undergraduate researching activities. Then many key universities followed with similar undergraduate researching plan. In 2007, the ministry of education began to develop "Innovative pilot project of national university student", and now more than 120 universities have been allowed to participate in at present. Comparing with America, obviously, we are still at the primary stage, although it has developed about 10 years. We can't be relax because we have a long we to go, we must take the developed countries' education experience as reference to improve ourselves.

Acknowledgements. Beijing Academic Innovation Group in Urban rainwater System and Water Environmental Eco-Technologies (PHR201106124).

References

1. Wang, F.X., et al.: Liberal arts university undergraduate research ability condition investigation report. J. Education Inquiry (March 2008)
2. The higher education law of the People's Republic of China [EB/OL]
3. Jiang, C.B.: Undergraduate research approaches and methods of cultivating the ability of discussed technological management (August 2010)
4. The ministry of education, the ministry of finance of higher school. Concerning the implementation of undergraduate teaching quality and teaching reform project, opinion, teach high, 1 (2007)

5. Gong, W., et al.: Training institute of technology innovation ability of undergraduate research exploration of higher education (September 2009)
6. Chen, Y.D.: Training in the teaching of undergraduate research ability (2010)
7. Wu, G.Y., et al.: On undergraduate research training problems and solution. Journal of Chinese Higher Education Research (2009)
8. Lee, Z.D.: The United States and potential undergraduate research. The Enlightenment of Higher Engineering Education Research (September 2009)

Promoting the Formation of the Students' Learning Pattern Effectively

Ying Li and Ting Wang

Key Laboratory of Urban Stormwater System and Water Environment
(Beijing University of Civil Engineering and Architecture),
Ministry of Education, Beijing, 100044, China
liyingcase@163.com

Abstract. Several kinds of main learning pattern of university students were introduced, analyzed and summarized. The building of the learning pattern can improve the ability of analyzing, solving problems, forming a good study atmosphere, and helping the students finish the education. So, it's significant for the students to build the learning mode, what's more, it's also an important way to improve teaching quality.

Keywords: universities, university students, learning pattern, study.

1 Introduction

Everybody has several exclusive patterns to know the things, understand the things and process information or stimulate. Learning pattern assumes a study method that everyone can reach the top of the learning state. This theory argues that the teacher should estimate the learning pattern of their students and make sure that their teaching can be adapt to every students' learning pattern. It's important for the university students to build an effective learning pattern.

2 Models of Learning Pattern

Cooperative Learning. Cooperative learning originated in the United States in 1970s. It mainly makes individual and the mutual cooperation between individuals and promotes each other to achieve common learning goals and a teaching theory through the group's form. Students can participate in activities that have a clear collective task, such as various types of social practice, production practice, metalworking practice, and military training, and so on. This form of learning only plays a guiding role in the teacher. Activities focused on the team members of interdependence, mutual communication, mutual cooperation and shared responsibility, so as to achieve common goals. This mode of learning is widely used in teaching in many countries.

Self-study. Self-study is essentially a process of individual choice, regulation, controlling. It is a kind of learning pattern planed by the students and guiding their self-study learning. Independent learning can initially assess their learning needs with

M. Zhu (Ed.): ICCIC 2011, Part V, CCIS 235, pp. 455–460, 2011.
© Springer-Verlag Berlin Heidelberg 2011

other's help or not, identify learning objectives, look for favorable learning resources, execute their own learning plan strictly, continuously introspect study situation and analyze learning process. Self-study also emphasizes that students to creatively study, which means in the process of knowledge integration and building, students should pay great attention to the learning initiative and exploratory, aiming at forming a learning situation with students self-centered. Thus, self-learning mode is a targeted, planned way that is designed by students. Therefore, the ability of independent study is necessary for students.

Network Learning. Network Learning mode is a way based on the network. Network learning mode is a result of combination of computer assisted learning theory and computer technology, but also a new way that teaching learners learn to accomplish a specific task.

The background of Network Learning's theoretical is constantly updated with the science and technology, and the rise of the lifelong learning. The social public especially adult has come to feel the importance of lifelong learning gradually, but the traditional education's school doesn't meet the learning needs of all people. Computer, network solved the problem. With its diversity, alternation, real-time and object of universality, and many other advantages, it make everyone can accept education wishes to become a reality, and especially for many has lost the adult education opportunity, they can graduate, acquire new knowledge through the network [1].

Questions Leading Learning. Problem leading learning model is a series of learning process for the students to understand a problem or solve some doubts. Through this learning mode, it can gradually training students to think and reasoning ability, encourage students to regard the exploration of question as the core, comprehensive collection, and analysis organize related information, to promote the timely solve problems. Problem leading learning emphasizes active learning students to be able to around the problem, repeated scrutiny, collate and analyze in-depth ways to explore problems, and comprehensive utilization of the knowledge to be able to break through the boundaries of disciplines, thinking the problem with the development view, and ultimately enhance the ability of the problem leading learning and lifelong learning.

3   Importance of Learning Model

About the education of college students' learning, the learning of students regards as a key point of education and teaching, and the colleges are cultivating high-quality talents at the same time. The outline of twelve five plan puts forward that we should vigorously implement the strategy of qualified talents, insist on the guidelines of servicing development powers, talents first, treating the function as the basic, the innovation mechanism, high-end leading, overall development, strengthen modernization requires all kinds of talents team construction, to accelerate the transformation of the mode of economic development, provide personnel guarantee for scientific development. The Sixteenth Congress of Party first treats building a learning-oriented society as the comprehensive construction well-off society's important targets and tasks for education, and puts forward the basic way to insist on innovation. Insist on education innovation, necessarily involves learning innovation, and is an indispensable important aspects.

The formation of effective learning pattern can make students more independent in the study life, master knowledge learned effectively, consolidate update existing knowledge and improve their comprehensive ability to meet the new requirements of social development and contribute themselves to national development and social progress. Albert Einstein, a Famous scientist, thought that success equals hard work plus correctly method and cutting the crap. From this formula which is generally accepted, we can know that accurate method is one of the three key elements of success. Similarly, correct effective learning mode will effectively promote the students' success.

4   The Formation of an Effective Model for Learning

Improve Teaching Methods. Teacher is the main participator and administer of the teaching. They are the key part of education which always impact on the trend of a generation of students. So the whole quality' and the teaching theory' increase is very critical. Firstly, teachers are supposed to learn, suck in and explore new teaching method. Now most of college always takes old teaching method. Teacher is only talk class, not teach class, and students is only listening class, but can't take active part in it. This way of teaching must result in allowing a discount in teaching performance. So, as a excellent teacher, they must update their teaching methods and make their class active in order to get more students in, at the same time, the model of question guiding will be a very useful way of teaching. Through giving the question, students can think over themselves, and solve the problems, that students explain their own ideas and show their attitude will cultivate the ability of solving problem, and then model the concept that they are the class leader, from the concept, change the rigid teaching way inside out. Then we should enrich our instruction content, meanwhile delete some old content. Teacher should combine new environment and new educational demand to update their instruction content. And pay attention to combine the content with practice. Furthermore teacher should have the strong conscientiousness and soul into teaching so that can make innovation and breakthrough, cultivate great students. In the end, teacher should be initiative and good at communicating with students in dealing relationship management.

5   School Construction, Management

To Strengthen the Attention of College Teaching Work. Currently, many schools that are affected by the impact of teaching evaluation criteria are pursuing some rigid target like the professor, PhD., and the quantity of papers published, one-sided emphasis on research and neglect of the teaching, pay no attention to the teaching staff training and incentives to make teachers feel that teaching has become offer but have to complete the task. Teachers lost the interest of school and studying teaching force, at last it will inevitably lead to neglect the ways and means of teaching content, pay no attention to training and stimulate students' interest in learning, and thus lose the attractiveness to students. The fundamental task of the University of personnel training should educate people, student talent as the center, and personnel training must rely on teachers. Therefore, universities need to develop more willing to perform teaching duties and good talent. Government and university should take some measures like giving the outstanding teaching staff, or promotion, professional title at preferential terms to vigorously improve the front-line school teachers enthusiasm, so that they can be willing to study teaching and improve teaching of knowledge, interest, and thus stimulate students learning initiative[2]. At the same time, colleges and universities should continue to improve their teaching conditions, the trend continued enrollment, teaching colleges and universities should increase the investment timely, as more students with quality learning resources. Specific into practice is to update the books and purchase the materials, acquisition of new experimental equipment for the students to create more learning spaces, to establish a scholarship system to encourage students to innovation.

To Strengthen the Construction of Campus Culture. The atmosphere of good campus culture can not only promote the teaching proceed smoothly, and enrich the campus life so that students learn a deeper understanding of cooperation. Today, the development of colleges and universities is not only the size and the number of professors, but also the construction of the campus to the overall cultural atmosphere. Campus culture conducive to good throughout the school condensed into an organic whole, where we progress together, sharing weal and woe, exchange and mutual assistance, so that each feels is a better college life full of hope. Of course, this requires the educators, administrators and students work together to make suggestions and actively participate in the construction of campus culture, to form a good learning atmosphere.

6   Students Themselves

Paying Attention to the Cultivation of Students' Comprehensive Quality. The duty of college is to train outstanding construction talents constantly for the country, and the talents mentioned here are not only to master domain knowledge, but also good moral character, it's so called the talents have both ability and political integrity. The school should always adhere to training qualified high- quality comprehensive talents. As a student, they must shoulder the mission historical gave, during school, not only to strengthen their professional knowledge, but also improve their own moral standards, being a qualified college students and a country's excellent builder.

To Encourage Students to Record Their Learning Situation, Foster a Responsible Attitude Towards Their Own Learning. Students need to have a better understanding of their lessons, and consider how to become a more independent learner. Students write their own learning experience regularly, write their own success or failure, and analyze the reasons. After a period of time, teachers can help students to analyze the records of students of their learning and put forward reasonable suggestions. This method helps students to develop their learning strategies adopted by the achievements of study by the understanding, self-assessment and monitoring, make learners to their own learning situation responsible; understand their current level and hope to achieve the gap between the level; see the superiority and weakness so that clearly understand their comprehensive ability.

Strengthening Career Planning. Harvard University's Dr. Edwant Barfield conducted a research on the propulsion of the American social progress and found that successful people are often the one who have the concept of long-term time, and pay attention to professional planning [3]. Strengthen college students' career planning consciousness is to make every college students adequate attention to their career planning, make it throughout the whole process of college students' life and understanding, and pay close attention to this professional and relevant professional information, a large number of challenges are still be there, there's a lot of work waiting us to exploit and innovate constantly [4].

Student is the main body of the study, to make students really play their autonomous learning enthusiasm, we must respect students' individual differences, respect their personality, through cultivating students' interest, stimulate the students' initiative and creativity gradually, while encouraging students to choose their own learning methods and learning mode, only in this way can effectively promote the learning efficiency and learning effect.

7 Summary

In short, all kinds of learning mode have their own advantages and disadvantages, for different groups of students, their learning should also be variedly .Compared with domestic students, the European and American students have a stronger ability of operation, independent thinking and problem solving skills, and also have a wider range of knowledge. Because, from primary school, the class of students in Europe and America is in an open situation, students in the classroom can ask any questions that include everything, when the teacher cann't solve, the students will try to find the answer by themselves; While most of their teaching contents involves practical ability and independent ability with a wide range of courses, but not so deep. In high school, the emphasis of teaching is placed on the cultivation of the students' solidarity consciousness and the integration of theory with practice ability. In college, in addition to some professional courses, other course content are synchronized with the leading edge of knowledge Teachers will promptly absorb the newest knowledge into their daily teaching. So, their teaching is varied with your own factors, students also choose the corresponding learning mode for themselves.

Our education has fallen behind most European and American countries, it is an indisputable fact, but we cannot deny the country's education system completely. Nowadays, the Chinese education is experiencing a transformation period, therefore, our educators must grasp the opportunities and challenges to retain the essence of their education while actively learn from the experience of the European and American countries, efforts to promote the development of education in China, "all the things for the students, for everything of students" as our aim has always been, Using more effective teaching way and learning mode encourage students' study and create a good learning atmosphere for students.

Acknowledgements. Beijing Academic Innovation Group in Urban Stormwater System and Water Environmental Eco-Technologies (PHR201106124).

References

1. Gao, Y.: Adult learning model and human resource development. Adult Education (April 2010)
2. Su, Y.: The research of university students' positive status and strategy.. Hu Bei Adult Education Learning Report (March 2009)
3. Li, L.: The American college students career planning guidance in the development and innovative practice. Yue Yang Vocational and Technical College Learning Report (2009)
4. Shen, L.: The discussion of Effective promotion of environmental engineering training model of professional employment (2010)

Generalization and Application of Case Teaching in Marketing Courses

Zhang Cui-lin, Zhou Bo, and Wang Xing

Department of Economy & Management, Xi'an Aerotechnical College,
Xi'an 710077, China
zhanglin994@tom.com

Abstract. Firstly, the existing problems of traditional teaching mode in marketing courses are analyzed. Secondly, based on the features of marketing courses, the generalization mode and application method of case teaching are presented from the view of the whole teaching process including teaching materials selection, lessons preparation, class teaching, experiment and practical training and testing. Thirdly, the corresponding countermeasures of case teaching in marketing courses are advised in terms of t teaching syllabus, case library, examination library, school-based training and competition base, enterprise training base, case seminar. Finally, the practice concerns of case teaching in marketing courses are given.

Keywords: case teaching, marketing courses, teaching practice.

1 Introduction

Marketing courses, featuring in comprehensive, practical, and strong social characteristics, are the elemental courses for the marketing and management major. The teachings focus on marketing theory and method and foster the students' practice ability for the future marketing work.

Now there is too much theory and method teaching class, but there has litter practice for students in using the corresponding theory and method in real environment to gain the marketing experience. The traditional teaching mode not only cannot make students have a good understanding and absorption of various marketing theories and methods, but also lowers the teaching effects and gives rise to a lot of complaints although teacher pays more effortfulness. How to change the traditional teaching mode to improve students' ability and quality becomes an urgent requirement and hot issue for marketing teaching.

In recent years, case teaching has been widely explored and used. It has become an important means of teaching till to now because the case teaching can let the learners initiatively obtain a general knowledge, ability and attitude from some limited marketing case. Therefore case teaching can establish a bridge between theory and practice, which vividly take market behavior and activity on the front of students.

M. Zhu (Ed.): ICCIC 2011, Part V, CCIS 235, pp. 461–467, 2011.

Through directed by market case, students' enthusiasm and initiation are fully activated. It is good for students to develop their creative thinking and ability, improve their practical operational method and skill, which will lay students a solid foundation to better adapt to the requirements of future work.

On the basis of analysis of existing problems in the traditional marketing teaching mode, the generation and application method of case teaching in marketing courses are presented. Also, some measures and steps of using case teaching in marketing course are given. Finally, the corresponding practice concerns of case teaching in marketing course are highlighted.

2   Existing Problems of Traditional Teaching Mode in Marketing Courses

There exist some problems in traditional teaching mode of marketing courses.

Emphasizing Theory but Ignoring Practice. In traditional teaching mode, theory teaching is the core. Therefore more attention of teaching is paid for introducing the theory and corresponding method, while how to use it and how to resolve the real problem, especially the new emerging problem encountered in current social and economic activities, are neglected, which cause a big gap between theory and practice.

Emphasizing Content but Ignoring Form. In traditional teaching mode, the teaching materials always focus on theory and method. However the rigid form and content reduce the students' interest in marketing course and easily transfer their attention to key points in order to pass the course exam. They don't pay more attation to analyze and think during the normal teaching process.

Uneven Application Level of Case Teaching. Some marketing courses have accumulated good and plentiful cases, but others are limited, especially the new emerging marketing course, such as Network Marketing, Services Marketing, Stores Marketing, Real Estate Marketing, Tourism Marketing.

Aging Case. Some cases tell the old story long time ago. If the backgrounds are distant from the time, it will make students hard to understand these cases. Also if patial cases cannot frequently update with times, the course will gradually lose its charming attraction to absorb students' interest to participate.

Insufficient Interaction between Teachers and Students. During the traditional teaching process, the teacher's role is to convey information and knowledge of book while the student's role is to receive them in passive. Due to prolonged exposure under the education system which emphasizes cramming and unidirectional teaching, most students do not like to speak out or ask questions in class.

3   Generalization Mode and Application Method of Case Teaching in Marketing Courses

From the systematic point of view, the generalization mode and application method of case teaching are analyzed and designed. Usually the teaching process is often divided into five parts, teaching materials selection, lessons preparation, class teaching, experiment and practical training and testing. Here take the teaching process of marketing courses for example, it is illustrated that how to start and carry out the case teaching in detail.

Teaching Material Selection. Teaching materials should follow closely the teaching program, and particularly embody the principal points of knowledge, which is the fundamental basis of "teaching "and "learning". Therefore teaching material selection is the first step to be considered. For the teaching material selection, there are some points and rules that should be grasped.

Teaching Materials Should Follow Teaching Outline. Teaching materials should emphasize the basic theory and method of marketing, simultaneously equip with some proper cases to illustrate the theory and methods. Therefore the selection of materials should enable students to better understand the corresponding knowledge and accurately grasp the basic content of the courses.

Teaching Materials Should Emphasize Practice. Before selecting teaching materials of marketing courses, we should know the relationship between theory and case, which always complement each other and rely on each other. Emphasizing practical case will develop students' thinking, enhance students' learning initiative and improve students' learning effects.

Teaching Materials Should Emphasize Students' Education Objectives. There are many teaching materials in book store list. The only selection criteria is whether the materials meet the students' education objectives, while not blindly choice some so-called high-quality materials, not to mention some commercial promotion materials. Of course, some materials can be used as auxiliary resources.

Lessons Preparation. Lessons preparation is an important step and guarantee before teaching. All contents and cases must be prepared in advance, which help to form the teaching ability for completing the teaching task. Only having a good preparation can have a good lesson. Specifically, for the corresponding case selection and lessons preparation, the following rule should be obeyed.

Case Should Be accord with Theoretical Knowledge. The chosen case should be able to help students understand theory and method better, so as to enhance students' learning interest and effect.

Case Should Be Targeted Aiming at Student Feature. Considering that the education receiver is student, it is hard to understand for students if the case is departed from the students' situation and horizon. Therefore, in order to preferably attract students' interesting and thus to arise their sympathy, some cases should be prepared from students' viewpoint according to their learning, study and life.

Case Should Be Typical. General speaking, principle and concept are more abstract and hard to understand for students. It needs some help from the concrete cases to quickly analyze and understand it during the teaching process. Providing some representative case is a right path to meet the teaching goal and requirements.

Case Should Be Novel. With the quickly development of society, science and technology, the environment in which students stay, such as family, society and teaching facilities, have changed wildly. The marketing case must be constantly updated. Therefore it requires the teacher to not only learn new marketing mode, new knowledge, and new information, but also select and update the corresponding case. Closer the relationship between case and times is, more excited the students is. Thus higher enthusiasm to participate in the discussion can motivate better teaching effect.

Case Should Be as Real as Possible. Fictional case may mislead students. Only real case is the most convincing. When the reliability of case improves, the validity will naturally raise, which can improve to achieve the best results of case teaching.

Here special remind that these five rules are not isolated. When choosing the case we should put these five rules together to consider.

Class Teaching. Teaching is a process in which teacher, using right and appropriate means, teach the prepared materials to students in a certain period of time. In the class, in order to make students better understand course content and further inspire students' interest in reading textbooks, it is absolutely necessary for teaching to equip with some typical cases analysis and discussion. In order to achieve good teaching effect, two key points during class teaching should be grasped.

Combination of Theory and Case. During the teaching process of marketing courses, theory and case are complementary with each other. Therefore the teacher in the lesson teaching could not teach just theory or case but should combine both of them. Introducing theory focuses on knowledge, while case teaching illustrates principle to understand how theory is practiced in cases.

Combination of Teaching and Discussion. During case teaching, students and teachers should be more interactively communicate with each other. Teachers play an important rule, not only a good director, but also a good actor. Through the selection of cases, reasonable grouping, appropriate guide, and timely comments, combination of teaching and discussion help to improve students' enthusiasm to participate in and further study.

Experiment and Practical Training. Compared with traditional teaching method, the case teaching specially emphasizes analysis ability, information searching, report writing, group discussion and solving problem ablity. Also these activities should be done by the students themselves to get their own best solution. When students under the guidance of the teacher complete the whole process of the case teaching, they will get more harvest, such as independent thinking, information-obtained skills, language and presentation skills and collaboration with others. It is the traditional teaching methods that can not be gained.

Examination. In traditional test mode, theory examination or a closed book examination is the main way to check the teaching effect. This test mode will make the students' learning initiative establish on passing examination, not on improving the study ability. However most of marketing courses have strong practical feature, the test should be directed to improve the marketing quality and ability of students. Therefore examination form should be changed. The combination of classroom learning and case analysis, discussion, and presentation is a good test mode. In addition, some open-book and practical application test question also can be added into the traditional theory knowledge examination.

These five parts, teaching materials selection, lessons preparation, teaching, training and examination are interrelated and progressive process. The right application can improve the effect of teaching and learning.

4 Generalization and Application Countermeasures of Case Teaching in Marketing Courses

The generalization and application measure and step of case teaching in marketing courses is given as follows.

Teaching Syllabus. The syllabus is the main basis of all teaching activities. The syllabus of marketing courses should be given clear requirements in teaching guideline, teaching content and curriculum design, case study, practice activity, etc.

Case Library of Marketing Courses. Establishing case library can help provide students with application cases of marketing. Novel and appropriate case library closely related to course content can better help understand the corresponding theory and method of student learning content.

Examination Library of Marketing Courses. Examination library is composed of multi-types of test question that assess students study and learning situation. Examination library has the function of an online test, exam review, answer check and result analysis. When establishing marketing examination library, we should put the same position of practice test with the theory test. Sometimes we should give more concerns on the students' practical ability.

School-based Training and Competition Base. The training center is setting for a variety of marketing courses competition at school. On the one hand students can understand the company's business mode by case operation and competition in advance, on the other hand case competition can test students' learning effects and feedback teaching effects. Integrating theory study with practice application and multi-method combination assist make students easily master the basic theory, methods and tools of marketing courses as soon as possible.

Enterprise Training Base. Enterprise training base provides a another wide platform for students with practical training in the cooperative enterprise. For marketing courses there can never have too many enterprises training base. The enterprise may be a manufacturing enterprise, or a service enterprise, or a commercial trade. Students are allowed to visit the enterprises' real operation and take part in some activities to enrich their knowledge and experience in a regulated period of time.

Case Seminar. It is a large course system for marketing courses. Although the different marketing course has different emphases, there still exists some relevance among them. Case study and discussion are not only a process of collision of thinking, but also one of sharing experiences and case reuse between different marketing courses. Through timely and warmly seminar, the two sides, either teachers or students, can not only expand their knowledge, enlightenment their thoughts, and strengthen their skills, but also can obtain the fresher firsthand information and response from the case seminar.

Recently the training platform including the teaching syllabus, examination library and school-based training and competition base have been established and put into practice in Xi'an Aerotechnical College, China. In addition case library, enterprise-based training base, training competitions and case seminar have finished and gradually opened for students. Teachers and students give a strong enthusiastic and positive response.

5   Practice Concerns of Case Teaching in Marketing Courses

Gradually Increase Case Difficult and Depth. Case selection should be from simple to complex. If start with a complex case, the related concepts and basic principles should be pre-explained before the case teaching. The students will feel confused and cannot clearly grasp the key point, which may dilute the teaching effectiveness. Therefore case should be chosen step by step along with the teaching progress.

Appropriately Handling Relationship Between Theory and Case Teaching. Currently theory learning still is predominant in the classroom teaching of marketing courses. However the call should not be an over-reaction or even an attempt to go from one extreme to the other. If marketing courses is taught only using case teaching, it makes students lack the systemic marketing knowledge. Even if the cases are good for the students to understand the marketing content deeply, the case teaching is a part of teaching owning to each case always is limited to explain a knowledge point. Case teaching is only one mean to some extent to cultivate students' thinking way and ability to analyze problems. Therefore the role of case teaching is played only when the theoretical teaching and case teaching is correctly arranged.

Timely Case Adjustment according to Teaching Situation. Appropriate and correct case can improve students' learning effects, but different form and emphasis of case should be revised or changed according to different curriculum contents and teaching program. Therefore on one hand in teaching process, we should explore and perfect the new teaching mode in practice. On the other hand, we should adjust the length and the number of the cases according to student level and teaching level.

Tightly Link among at all Stages of Practice Training. Although many stages is composed the practice training and many measures for each stage are independent in form, they are interrelated in content. Therefore these stages should be linked together and the corresponding case library and teaching way should be adjusted and updated in a timely manner.

6   Summary

One of the most important feature in case teaching is how to select right cases and use suitable cases for the students and class teaching during the teaching process, which is different from other traditional methods. Marketing courses are the courses that are closely related to practical marketing. Therefore using appropriate cases, establishing a good case platform, updating timely case library, and formulating strict training requirements can improve teaching result and quality, raise students' interest in learning process, furthermore enhance the practice and application ability. Thus the case teaching method builds a bridge not only between teaching and learning, but also between theory and practice.

References

1. Bonoma, T.V.: Journal of Marketing Research 22(2), 199–208 (1985)
2. Perry, C.: The Marketing Review 1(3), 303–323 (2000)
3. Little, V., Brookes, R., Palmer, R.: Journal of Business & Industrial Marketing 23(2), 124–134 (2008)

ESaaS: A New Education Software Model in E-learning Systems

Md. Anwar Hossain Masud and Xiaodi Huang

School of Computing and Mathematics, Charles Sturt University,
Albury, NSW 2640, Australia
FINEREN@TOM.COM

Abstract. SaaS solutions have recently been gaining in popularity. As a software distribution model in which applications are hosted by a vendor or service provider, SaaS is available to users over the Internet in a form of the "Cloud." Introducing a new concept of ESaaS that is defined as Education Software-as-a-Service, this paper compares it with traditional education software, and discusses how such software can support the education system as a tool for enhancing information, and learning inquiry skills. The paper then focuses on the considerations that should be taken into account in deploying successful ESaaS for IT professionals, and educators of the future, if the SaaS usage becomes widespread.

Keywords: SaaS, Cloud Computing, e-learning, Learning Management System, Content Management System.

1 Introduction

There has been much interest in the notion of software as a service (SaaS) as a new model for delivering software to end users. With the advancement of tools for web application development there has been a shift in the way that software is acquired. The SaaS model, which is supported by a service oriented architecture (SOA) design, has led to a shift of ownership of software. Most of the discussion on SaaS focuses on business-to-business and business-to-consumer services. In the education sector current implementations of supporting information technology (IT) based systems face many challenges. This is equally true in many K-12 Schools in the United States that lack funding to support their IT systems and are short on IT technical staff to manage the IT infrastructure and many applications running on it [1]. In recent years there has been a large increase in Internet usage worldwide [2]. It is apparent that the Middle East and Africa are at the top of the growth trend. The Internet has become accessible to more people in the world in the past decade. This trend has led to many changes in the maturity of web application technologies. Part of this research has examined SaaS in relation to E-Learning Systems.

The task of managing an IT system in an educational institutional environment poses unique challenges. For example, one of the greatest challenges facing individual

M. Zhu (Ed.): ICCIC 2011, Part V, CCIS 235, pp. 468–475, 2011.
© Springer-Verlag Berlin Heidelberg 2011

institute is the lack of integration between various educational information systems [3]. The present situation in many educational institutes is that there are many disconnected systems managing many different tasks. Systems with differing levels of functionality run independently of one another causing multiple problems for the overall IT system [4]. In addition, the task of maintaining each individual system is time consuming. The challenges described above have prompted this research study. This study examines the system architecture of several educational systems, and a comprehensive understanding of the instructional needs of SaaS for education.

This paper considers the impact that Software as a Service (SaaS) is likely to have on the demand for IT professionals and the consequences for education providers who are preparing future IT professionals [5]. Before it does this however it explains what SaaS is, and why it is likely to become an important force in the IT industry in the future. Section 2 presents an overview of SaaS and its popularity. Section 3 also describes the relation of SaaS with E-learning. Section 4 describes the difference of traditional education software with ESaaS and Section 5 presents the conceptual system of ESaaS with integrated functionality and the connectivity scenario for a large system and section 6 offers some conclusions.

2   What Is SaaS and What Is Its Popularity?

According to Wikipedia Software as a Service (SaaS) is a software application delivery model where a software vendor develops a web-native software application and hosts and operates (either independently or through a third-party) the application for use by its customers over the Internet. Customers do not own the software but pay an ongoing fee for its use. SaaS in cloud computing is depicted in Fig. 1. There is a significant difference between the hosting of traditional applications and true SaaS applications. The hosting of traditional software applications simply changes who manages the IT behind the delivery of the application. Hosting providers typically support more hardware and software versions and are not able to quickly increase capacity as user demand grows.

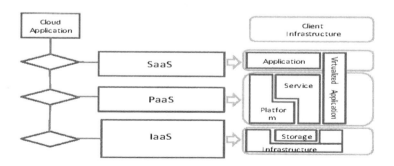

Fig. 1. SaaS in Cloud Environment

Many people who are already using service-based solutions perhaps do not realise this. For example, all hosted Email, Skype, Goto Meeting and Microsoft Live Meeting can be considered as service-based applications. By subscribing to a SaaS provider, users can still utilise software applications to run their business and consult SaaS subject experts avoiding set-upping and managing a large, complex and costly in-house IT infrastructure.

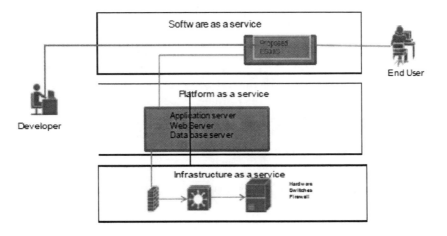

Fig. 2. ESaaS in Cloud Structure

The reason for its popularity is that SaaS provides a fundamentally different service to anything that preceded it.   The benefits of SaaS are listed:

- Even though a particular application uses the same code base (to reduce maintenance costs) it can be configured to suit the needs to each of each subscriber.
- Rather than appealing to a horizontal market, the SaaS provider can target a vertical market. This means that the application is much more likely to suit the needs of the customer and removes many of the traditional disadvantages to using packaged solutions.
- The SaaS provider takes responsibility for ensuring the application is relevant. This reduces the burden on the subscriber to maintain in-house knowledge in the specialist employment area.
- The SaaS provider can add value to their offering and case studies on employment matters.
- The SaaS subscriber can pay for the application from their operating budget without the need for a capital purchase and the budgeting problems that it entails.
- If the SaaS subscriber is no longer happy with their SaaS provider they can easily move to another.
- The SaaS provider does not need to worry about old versions of the application software running on client's sites, this simplifies maintenance and reduce their maintenance costs enabling them to pass these savings onto their subscribers.

- The support mechanism from the SaaS provider does not need to include support for configuration and installation problems or different version etc, it can concentrate on ensuring the customers gets the best out of the application.
- Some SaaS providers are offering a "try before you buy" option that is very suitable for companies who are hesitant to enter into a long term commitment.
- Flexible licensing arrangements such as weekly options can also mean that SaaS solutions can be used for short-duration or ad-hoc projects.

2.1 Why ESaaS is ideal for E-Learning?

In this day and age we want everything right now without the wait or fuss. Education Software-as-a-Service (ESaaS), is perfect for E-learning because of its fast implementation. Within hours or just a few days ESaaS is up and running alleviating the need to wait. More importantly, ESaaS lessens the burden of maintenance and support from the educational institution to the vendor, allowing them to focus on their core business. Furthermore ESaaS is perfect for E-learning since educational institutions will receive the latest updates and features without any extra financial obligation. Another advantage with ESaaS is that it helps administration and teachers to share key resources all with the simple click of a button, using Web 2.0 technology.

2.2 ESaaS vs Traditional Education Software

In this section, we compare the proposed ESaaS with tradition Education software, as shown in the following Table 1.

Table 1. Difference between Tradition software vs ESaaS

	Traditional Education Software	ESaaS
Platform	Multi version	Single Platform
Pricing	Maintenance + License	Subscription (all inclusive)
Delivery	Installed	Hosted
Development	Longer Cycle	Continuous Cycle
Allocation	Capitalised	Expensed
Additional Cost	Installation, Maintenance, Customization & Upgrades	Configuration
Profits	Initial Sale	Ongoing
Sales Focus	Close the deal	Prove Value
Feedback Cycle	Long	Short
Success	New License revenue	Lack of Churn
Updates	Longer, less frequent	Shorter, Frequent

In the following Table 2, we further list the main features of ESaaS, and its consequences and implications, particularly for education settings [6].

Table 2. ESaaS, its consequence & Implications

Feature	Consequence	Implications
Accessed via Web	Ease of access	Anywhere, any time and any one can access the application, greater demand for Web Development skills.
No client-side software needed	Reduced costs for subscriber: no installation, software maintenance, deployment and server administration costs.	Lower total cost of ownership, reduced time-to-value, fewer IT staff needed by the institution
Pay by subscription based on usage	Suitable for SME market	SMEs can gain access to more sophisticated applications.
SaaS server must support many educational institutions	Application running on a server farm	Scalability: as student usage grows, the software performance will not degrade.
All subscriber data held on SaaS server	Very high level of security needed by SaaS [7] provider in order to gain trust of subscribers and sophisticated multi-tenanted software architecture.	Subscriber data distributed between many providers and must be integrated in order to gain overview of business, higher demand for system and data integrators.

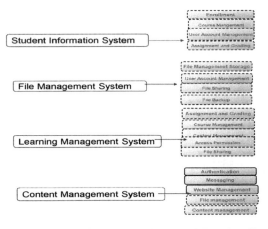

Fig. 3. Conceptual System with Integrated Functionality

3   Expected Functionality of ESaaS

Applications of ESaaS (Fig. 3) will be based on the four pillars into one integrated solution with features that eliminates overlapping functionality, enhance data consistency by having one source of data, and also provides a cost effective solution by eliminating the separate solutions from different vendors. The ability to access the system using a single-sign-on enables the end-user to access the system, and manage all functionalities according to responsibility and authority.

The expectation is that the proposed ESaaS will help education authorities in developing countries in the following ways:

• Reduce the cost of ownership of software solution by eliminating the purchase of individual system and integration cost to connect these systems i.e., technology cost savings;
• Increase the number of educational websites by providing every district, school, teacher, and course within a province region with website to enhance student learning (Fig. 4);
• Allow family and community involvement through institutional website [8] (Fig. 5);
• Improve teachers' ability in a school to communicate, and monitor student progress [9];
• Improve the school administration's ability to manage multiple systems from one integrated E-Education System; and
• Encourage and increase sharing of resources and best practices.

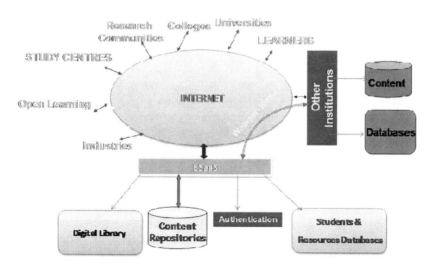

Fig. 4. Connectivity Scenario of ESaaS for a large system

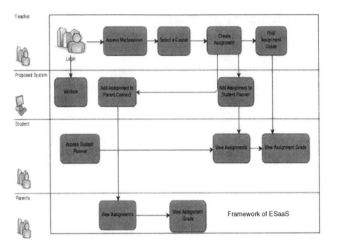

Fig. 5. ESaaS functionality as a part of Interaction

4 Summary

Educational institutions, from local schools to colleges and universities, face daunting technology challenges. Explosive growth in the number and types of devices used by students, staff and instructors, along with the difficulty of tracking and managing those devices, is just the beginning. In addition to the various software applications installed by individual departments, districts and schools within any educational institution, students, professors and teachers often bring their own software with them. On college campuses in particular, that can mean a huge influx of new software each fall. All businesses struggle with tracking assets and data, but in education, the challenge is even greater.

Fortunately, the computer industry is in the midst of a massive shift in how software is delivered. Under a new model of SaaS, vendors offer software and SaaS-enabled IT services not as a one-time purchase, but as a service delivered over the Internet [10] and supported as part of an ongoing, regularly renewed contract. The benefits of ESaaS will be immense. ESaaS is expected to be a new delivery method and choice available for Higher Education Enterprise Systems. ESaaS solution is expected to become an important alternative, not only for smaller companies with low budgets for IT, but also for larger companies as a form of outsourcing and for many services for individuals as well [11]. It is a massively scalable, offsite infrastructure accessible on demand across the internet on a pay-per-use basis eliminating upfront investment costs. In this challenging economic environment, ESaaS will enable institutions to drastically reduce their IT costs involved in automating their administrative and academic processes. [12].

In this paper, we have introduced the new concept of ESaaS based on SaaS, and compared with the traditional software, as well as described the desired functionalities of ESaaS. Our future work will try to implement it.

References

1. Steenkamp, A.L., McCord, S.A.: Teaching Research Methodology for Information Technology. Journal of Information Systems Education 18-2, 1–30 (2007)
2. Internet world status on (2009), http://www.internetworldstats.com/
3. Mckeown, N., Anderson, T., Balakrishnan, H., Parulkar, G., Peterson, I., Rexford, J., Shenker, Turner, J.: Open Flow: Enabling innovation in campus networks. ACM SIGCOMM Computer Communication Review 38-2, 69–74 (2008)
4. Aymerich, F.M., Fenu, G.: An approach to a Cloud Computing network. In: Applications of Digital Information and Web Technologies Conference, ICADIWT, pp. 113–118 (2008)
5. Bhattacharya, I., Sharma, K.: India in the knowledge economy –an electronic paradigm. International Journal of Educational Management 21-6, 543–568 (2007)
6. Manford, C.: The impact of the SaaS model of software delivery. In: 21st Annual Conference of the National Advisory Committee on Computing Qualifications, New Zealand, pp. 283–286 (2008)
7. Gerard, B., Marinos, A.: Digital Ecosystems in the Clouds: Towards Community Cloud Computing on (2009), http://msdn.microsoft.com/en-us/library/aa905332.aspx
8. Basal, A., Steenkamp, A.L.: Building an Integrated Student Information System in a K-12 School System. In: The Proceedings of ISECON 2009, Washington, DC, United States (2009) ISSN: 1542-7382
9. Basal, A., Steenkamp, A.L.: A Saas-Based Approach in an E Learning System. International Journal of Information Science and Management, Special Issue, 27–40 (January/June 2010)
10. Kwok, T., Nguyen, T., Lam, L.: A Software as a Service With Multi-tenancy Support for Electronic Contract Management Application. In: Proceedings of IEEE Conference on Services Computing, pp. 149–156 (2008)
11. Anand, S., Gupta, S., Fatnani, S., Sharma, V., Jain, D.: Semantic Cloud for Mobile Technology. International Journal of Computer Applications 8-12, 1–4 (2010)
12. Noor, S.A., Mustafa, G., Chowdhury, S.A., Hossain, M.Z., Jaigirdar, F.T.: A Proposed Architecture of Cloud Computing for Education System in Bangladesh and the Impact on Current Education System. IJCSNS International Journal of Computer Science and Network Security 10-10, 7–13 (2010)

Design and Research of SOPC Embedded Digital Frequency Meter Based on FPGA

Hu Bing and Liu Xijun

School of Electric and Information Engineering of XiHua University, ChengDu, China
hm123746@163.co

Abstract. The paper proposed a design scheme about the SOPC embedded digital frequency meter which based on the programmable chip system. The design adopts FPGA of the Cyclone series as the core and embedds the 8051 IP core as the MCU to complete the generation and detection of the system frequency. The digital frequency meter system uses Bresenham algorithm to produce appointed frequency and uses the measuring method of measuring frequency and the measuring of the week to complete the frequency measurements. The range of frequency determination is 0.1Hz-10MHz. The whole system designs miniaturization and uses single chip to complete the mainly logical functions of the system. The system runs stably and has an important role for application of the SOPC technology in the industrial design.

Keywords: SOPC, Digital frequency plans, The 8051 IP core.

1 Introduction

Frequency measurement is one of the most key technical of the electronic measurement field and digital frequency meter is the indispensable measuring tool for the measuring technology engineering personnel. There are many physical quantities of measurement can be converted to frequency measurement, such as flow, vibration, speed and so on [1,2]. High precision digital frequency meter is much more expensive and not facilitate popularization using. Putting forward a design scheme of digital frequency meter which embedds within the 8051 IP core and bases on SOPC. The system is frequency measurement range, high precision measurement, and already get practical application in a certain frequency measuring system.

2 Structure of the Digital Frequency Meter System

The structure of SOPC digital frequency meter which bases on FPGA shows as figure 1. The digital frequency meter makes up of system frequency produce and measurement two parts. The system frequency setting finishes through 4 * 4 keyboards and program scanning method. It reads keyboard status level, gets key features coding and determine the press or pop-up of button by the high or low level signals. The setting frequency completes the address decode through the I/O control module and the

M. Zhu (Ed.): ICCIC 2011, Part V, CCIS 235, pp. 476–482, 2011.

exclusive of I/O input port to make the corresponding data into 8051IP core to finish the operation. The 8051IP core uses VHDL language to write, the inside integrates timer, counter, asynchronous serial, suspend and so on to realize the most operation of the AT89C52. And displaying the setting frequency on LED. It completes the data exchange and instructions transmission by the UART module and software handshake method. Bresenham algorithm is the straight line scan conversion algorithm. The pixel is decided by error term symbols, and the system realize the decimal divider by FPGA. The system uses a 20MHz crystal oscillator as the system clock, and generates the required frequency for the reference signal. The time base-band signal and the under-test signal(analyte signal which is 1KHz-10KHz need 10 division first) complete frequency measurements by using the method of measuring frequency and measuring week into the controller by state agencies. The measurement data is treated also by the I / O control module and the 8051 IP core and displayed on LED. The generating frequency error of the SOPC digital frequency meter is less than 0.1%, and measures the high and low frequency error all less than 0.05%. The system has high measurement accuracy and runs stablly.

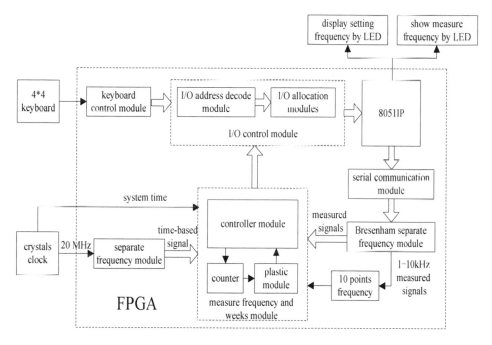

Fig. 1. Structure of SOPC digital frequency meter

3   Design of Digital Frequency Meter Core Module

3.1   Design of Frequency Integrated Survey

The frequency measurement range of system digital frequency meter is 0.1Hz-10MHz, and uses the method of measuring frequency and measuring week to measure. The

SOPC digital frequency meter is measurement range automatic conversion, uses the state machine control to realize, and uses counter to complete the counting and measurement of frequency or period[3,4].The programming flowchart of system frequency measurement shows as figure 2.

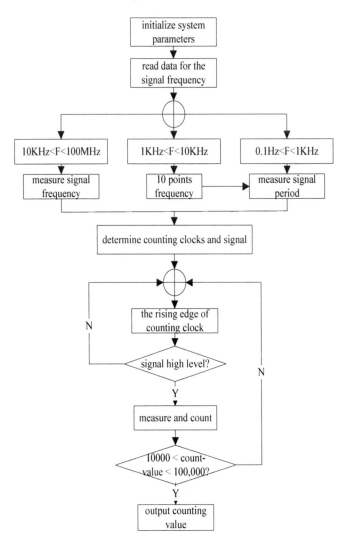

Fig. 2. System frequency measurement flowchart

Due to the measurement error of frequency counter is less than 0.05%, for the relation of analyte signal and relevant time-based signal, high-frequency signal uses frequency measurement method, lower frequency signal uses method of measuring weeks [5,6], and frequency which between 1Hz and 10KHz is not suitable of frequency measurement method or method of measuring weeks. It should be 10-points frequency before using method of measuring weeks to measure. The system state transfer is decided by 'over-range signal(Over)' and 'owe-range signal (Low)'. Using 'counting clock' to count for the signal which should be counted. The count is greater than or equal to 100,000 for the 'super-range', less than 10,000 mean 'less-span'. Settling the super-range and less-span in order to avoid a signal is read twice by state machine. Then passing it to the controller and converting range of the two signals by the controller to complet the measure of test signal.

3.2 Design of MC8051IP Core

SOPC digital frequency meter embedds 8051 IP core, and completes the assignment of frequency setting, frequency of measurement and data display. The execution time of 8051 IP core is 1-4 clock cycles, and the execution performance is 8 times better than the standard 8051 microcontroller. The design of the digital frequency meter uses LPM_RAM_DQ IP core to produce 128Bytes internal RAM and 2Kbytes extended RAM, and uses LPM_ROM IP core to produce 8Kbytes extended ROM. It can deploys the ROM, RAM and various hardware resources free. Top-level structure of 8051 IP core shows as figure 3.

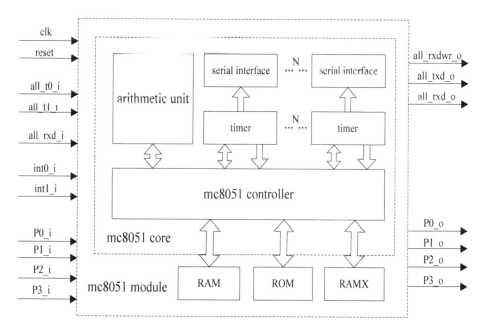

Fig. 3. Top-level structure of 8051 IP core

The workflow of 8051 IP core shows as figure 4. The setting frequency data transmittes to the 8051 IP core by the two groups of I/O ports. The 8051 IP core completes the display and serial output of the setting frequency by determining the status and coding of button. The frequency measurements are transmitted to the 8051 IP core by three groups of I/O ports. The 8051 IP core completes the showing of the measurement data and unit by judging the data of I/O ports.

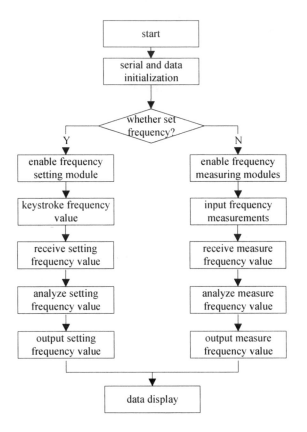

Fig. 4. Workflow of 8051 IP core

4   Simulation Results

The design of system uses Cyclone Ⅱ series EP2CT144C8 for master chip. The reaction time can reach natrium seconds level, and ensure accuracy of system measurement. The FPGA without internal clock network, therefore, the design uses a frequency of 20M, 3.3V power supply for the active crystal. FPGA constitutes the logical behavior by using look-up table structure way. It is without E2PROM or FLASH technology and the program would lost when power-down. The design uses the special configure chip EPCS4 which made by Altera to store the FPGA programming information in the external memory, and deploy the FPGA chip when power. The design makes nCONFIG, CONF_DONE, nSTATUS high to 3.3 V power supply by external pulling up 10kΩ resistor to make the system work in user mode. The system has many settings and measurements for the different frequency bands and the simulation shows as figure 5 and figure 6.

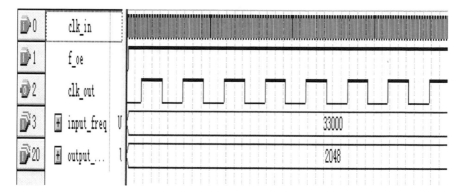

Fig. 5. Simulation of generation frequency

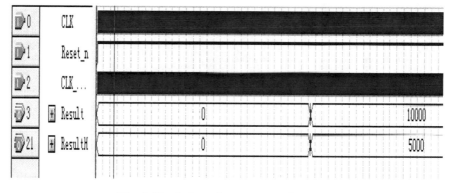

Fig. 6. Simulation of measurement frequency

5 Conclusion

The design of SOPC embedds digital frequency meter which bases on FPGA has completed the task of generation and measurement of the system frequency. It uses line scan conversion algorithm to achieve the system fractional, and displays the setting and measuring frequency by LED. The whole system uses FPGA to achieve the integrated design of the 8051 IP core and digital frequency meter. The 8051 IP core has compatible with the 8051 microcontroller, and executes instruction faster. The RAM and ROM can expand to 64KB maximum, multiply and divide instruction can be abolished, and saves 10% of the available resources. Using SOPC to complete the data processing, the system upgrades more convenient. The design achieves range converting automatically and automatic measurement, on the basis of measuring reaction time and accuracy. The design of the entire system has broad market and strong practical value on the Electronic measurement field.

6 Summary

Hu Bing: is currently working as an associate professor of School of Electrical and Information Engineering of Xihua University, china. His research interests are modern measurement and instrumentation, signal process and embedded system Etc.

Liu Xijun: is currently working toward the M.A. degree a graduate in School of Electrical and Information Engineering of Xihua University, china. His special fields of interest include modern measurement and control technology.

Acknowledgment. The work is supported by the Key Laboratory of Signal and Information Processing and the application foundation project on science and technology agency of Sichuan province (NO:05JY029-137) and the key scientific research project of Xihua university (NO:zg0720901).

References

1. Chen, S., Hu, R., Hu, H.: Auto-adjusting digital cymometer based on FPGA. Measurement and Technology of China 3, 141–144 (2007)
2. Lin, J., Song, Y.: The design and realizing of high-accuracy digital cymometer in FPGA. Electrical Measurement and Instrumentation 12, 5–7 (2001)
3. Zhang, Z., Cai, Y., Wang, Y.: Design and realization of digital frequency meter based on FPGA. Automated Instrumentation 11, 10–17 (2006)
4. Ji, B., Liu, J.: LabVIEW 7.1 programming and virtual instrument design, vol. 8, pp. 84–85. Qinghua University Press, Beijing (2006)
5. Yan, Y., Ma, Z., Yang, M.: Method of design digital on dometer on FPGA. Electronic Test Technology 21(5), 153–154 (2005)
6. Yu, S.: SCM in the frequency of high-precision measurement. Electronic Test Technology 3, 25–29 (1994)

Assessment of the Application of Wii Remote for the Design of Interactive Teaching Materials

Chien-Yu Lin[1,2], Yen-Huai Jen[2,4], Li-Chih Wang[2],
Ho-Hsiu Lin[2], and Ling-Wei Chang[2]

[1] Graduate Institute of Assistive Technology, National University of Tainan, Tainan, Taiwan
[2] Department of Special Education, National University of Tainan, Tainan, Taiwan
[3] Tainan Municipal Shengli Elementary School, Tainan, Taiwan
[4] Department of early childhood, TransWorld University, Yunlin, Taiwan
lp1232@126.com

Abstract. This research is based on the concept of operation by a child to apply interactive technology on body movements. Based on the core technology of interactive technology, the wii remote and homemade infrared emitter are used in conjunction with the teaching material; the interactive design is infused into teaching, thereby bringing the children the experience of the interactive technology application. There are two cases on this study, they are actually applied on children with developmental disabilities, and the overall equipment cost is approximately US$50.Case 1 and 2 are children took an infrared emitter to control the interactive teaching materials. The teaching materials design by customer made for the children with developmental disabilities, all the interactive teaching materials design by flash software and power point. The participants took infrared pen as a pc mouse through wii remote and laptop. In this research, the devices relied upon user-center design, reducing the learning loading from their teaching materials and enhance their learning motivation and interest. The research applies wii interactive technology into the design of teaching materials; technically, the concept is derived from the infrared receiver on the wii remote, the main purpose is to teach children in the resource classes an interactive learning method. Through the application of low cost interactive technology, the emphasis is placed on aspects such as ease of learning by resource class teachers, low equipment cost and ease of promotion etc. Based on the fundamentals of making the operating interface simpler and burden-free, the interactive technology is applied on elementary school students and kindergarten children to produce fun learning.

Keywords: human computer interaction, interface design, infrared emitter, teaching materials, children, developmental disabilities.

1 Introduction

The design of interactive information interface takes the individual differences of children into consideration, as different children have different cognitive abilities and learning methods. Conventional teaching material only presents a singular structure,

M. Zhu (Ed.): ICCIC 2011, Part V, CCIS 235, pp. 483–490, 2011.
© Springer-Verlag Berlin Heidelberg 2011

which is in turn difficult to make adjustments for individual requirements. Through well designed interactive teaching material presentations, the study intends to provide customized teaching materials for children with different handicaps and requirements, in order to make adjustments to conform to different requirements. Children with developmental disabilities which prevent them from using standard computer control devices, but custom made alternative devices could be more expensive, one kind of solution is to explore the application of devices used in contemporary gaming technology [1], such as the Nintendo Wii [2] or air mouse [3].Infrared camera is generally used in tracking systems and this leads to costs often not affordable, particular, wii remotes used as infrared cameras [4].Some research combined wii remote and infrared emitter to create low-cost interactive whiteboard [5], so that teachers enable to design teaching materials enhance learning interest for children with developmental disabilities. Through the demonstration of multimedia design, teachers have enough ability to produce the learning materials of custom made design in order to support children to absorb knowledge and teaching interaction procedure is a systematic form of teaching where teachers use to describe their behavior [6].The interactive technology consists of a wii remote, infrared emitter ,a laptop and a projector. Combined low-cost gear to create a cheaper device , the laptop could be controlled by the infrared emitter that functions much like a mouse [7]. The purpose of this research is to help children with developmental disabilities have chance to learn more interested. Assistive technology is a helpful method for learning, which has prominent influences on helping teachers explain difficult concepts, giving access to a huge range of examples and resources, and inducing pupils to engage in learning [8]. Computer-mediated communication facilitates the understanding of communication patterns, forms, functions and subtexts, which can in turn engender an understanding of how to derive meanings within such context [9]. The application of an infrared light emitter is similar as a mouse, the design of learning interfaces adopts an interactive design while the design of teaching materials adopts flash software and power point that could invent interesting display in order to raise children learning interested. In addition, children with developmental disabilities not only could taste new teaching method but also are impressed by them. Interactive interface design has an advantage in that the application software is able to make corrections to the content, while the assistive tool may also be designed according to children with different handicap categories. Taking this research as an example, the teaching course material may be presented via ppt or swf, however, through the wii remote and infrared emitter, the operating process becomes simpler; just like a magician practicing magic, the enjoyment of using the product is easily generated in others.

2   Method

This research showed appreciation with many experts who devote their technology about interactive whiteboards using the wii remote [10][11]. Wii remote, is a handheld device just like a television remote, a high-resolution high speed IR camera and wireless Bluetooth connectivity. Wii remote camera is sensitive only to bright sources of infrared light emitter, tracked objects must emit a significant amount of near infrared light to be detected [12]. With infrared emitter and wii remote could be create an effect just like pc mouse, it's a low-cost custom made device [13]. Therefore, the study is able to integrate the feedback of flash software and power point and to develop teaching materials for children with developmental disabilities.

3   Hardware Set-Up

A projector projects onto wall that children with developmental disabilities could control the display by using the relative devices. The devices include one kind of infrared emitter pen and a wii remote, the principle of infrared emitter pen built on the user press the micro switch on the pen, the pen will emit infrared light, the wii remote will receive the message. It cost so cheap and portable, so it is useful for teachers to use the devise in different places even they are Itinerant teachers.The theory that the study applies is making use of blue tooth to connect a laptop, wii remote and infrared emitter. By means of infrared light pen, wii remote can track the location of infrared emitter, the function of the infrared pen just as a pc mouse, so the children with developmental disabilities could only take a pen in his hand as a controller, the interface design could be an interactive teaching materials.

Fig. 1. The principle of this research

The display mode of this method is an intuitive learning tool. The operator not needs to use a PC mouse as a tool, children with developmental disabilities will raise their interest and motivation toward lessen their frustration during their learning processes. Since the wii remote can track sources of infrared light emitter, so the research could apply this technology to make a low-cost device. According to the requirement and preference of children, participating teachers in the study proceed to devise and adjust the design of infrared light emitter.

Interaction Design. In this research, the wii remote displays the function of infrared receiver. It is a simple tool for children to control one kind of interactive teaching materials. For instance, in the research ,the researcher use flash software and powerpoint to design interactive interface, when the research set up the device in the classroom, the children with developmental disabilities only take an infrared pen could control the interactive effect. Participants from the resource classroom could recognize how to operate this infrared pen, because it is easy to operate the micro switch than a pc mouse.

4   Case Study

The learning materials are custom made for children themselves so as to improve their learning interest and motivation. This study begins from assistive teaching, which provides lower loading. Using infrared light emitter and reflected stickers can link to corresponding information, which is able to increase the attraction and intimacy of teaching materials. Here are 2 cases and explanations of this study.

Case 1. The participant of case 1 is a girl with intellectual deficit and speech disability who is belongs to moderate multiple retarded. She is a 6th grade student at elementary school. In this case, she hold a infrared emitter pen, a wii remote is located in front of her seat, then, when the girl press the micro switch, just like she press the left button of a PC mouse. When we performed the initial probing of their interactive activity, the child was asked to hold the infrared pen in her hand, while the teachers asked him to perform continual actions of moving her hand. When she press the micro switch of the infrared pen and move it in the air, she could see the reflections on the wall.

Fig. 2. A girl participant the interactive teaching material(To protect the handicapped child, all the pictures have used masaic effect on their face)

Case 1 is one kind of teaching materials for customer made, the unit of course is an interactive teaching materials focus on understanding campus, the researcher design interactive teaching materials by the campus pictures, so, when the girl operate the pen, the projector will show the campus pictures appear gradually projected on the wall, and she know who control the situation. The case study is a real time feedback for her.

Fig. 2. show the experiment process. This case focuses on using low-cost assistive technology that included of wii remote and infrared light emitter, children are offered with digital presentation of designing and learning concepts for easier ways to operate, and it enables children to train their body active ability by interface design with interaction. The signals were emitted to the computer, and then the corresponding synchronized screen would be displayed immediately. To put it simply, we used an infrared emitter pen as a mouse, therefore we can design different teaching module courses. The main purpose is to instruct children in the application of physical activities. This case is an activity-based technological teaching material.

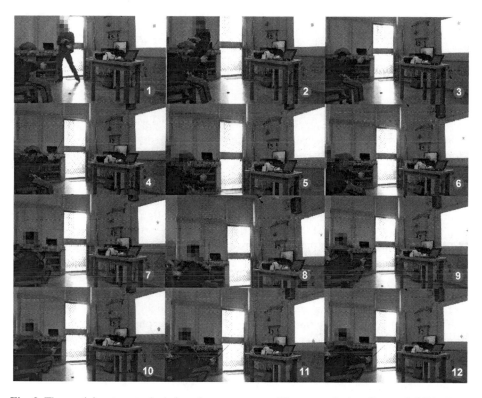

Fig. 3. The participant control a infrared pen as a mouse(To protect the handicapped child, all the pictures have used masaic effect on their face)

Case 2. The participant of case 2 is a boy with intellectual deficit who is also belongs to moderate intellectual retarded. He is a 3rd grade student at elementary school. Case 2 is one kind of teaching materials for tracking the moving objects, in case 2, the researcher work the interactive interface design by powerpoint, when the participant point the correct position of the moving object, the object will change another shape, it's one kind of real time feedback to the participant, when the participant operate the teaching materials, he will know whether the moving track of his hand follow the object. The child with developmental disabilities hold the infrared emitter pen, when he press the micro switch, the function just like we control a computer with left button of a mouse, when he moved her hands and kick the object, her images on the screen would change another shape on the projective screen.

n this interactive interface design, he must to move his position of his hand to follow the moving objects, the process could train the child's attentive ability. In case 2, the researcher design different shape in this teaching materials, the child could use a pen to control the content of an interactive interface, in the learning process, the participant didn't use pc mouse, it's means that decrease the load for the child. The case could improve the attention of children's activity; because the real-time feedback could attract children's willing to do such training of physical ability. Furthermore, because the image design used by power point, the software is very easy, teachers could change different teaching materials for different courses, Fig. 3.shows the application on shape unit, when the children with developmental disabilities, they could control the message only by an infrared pen, the wii remote will receive the message through blue tooth transfer to laptop, then control the output in the real-time on the wall.

5   Conclusion

This article has described the case study results of special education that was designed to investigate the use of low-cost interactive interface design. The research utilizes a wii remote and infrared emitter to design interactive teaching material, which is in turn is applied on the design of teaching materials for the resource class. Since the low-cost electronic white boards are widely used and cheap, it may be promoted to schools with insufficient budgets to continue the promotion information education; in terms of assistive technology application, this has demonstrated significant results.

Digital interactive teaching material would be popular in the future is a trend, because the interface focus on easy learn and easy use, moreover, the research provide real-time feedbacks and low price, it is real assistance to design interactive teaching materials for resource teacher. Children with developmental disabilities have limitations due to difficulties in the development of sufficient physical, emotional or intellectual capacities. Developmental disabilities include physical disorders such as cerebral palsy and limited vision, as well as language and speech disorders and so on. Special for children with developmental disabilities who exhibit different levels of understanding and emotional reactions, they need more feedbacks and multiple stimulus, which increases their motivation of learning.

In this research, interactive teaching materials are more attractive than regular textbook, according to the feedback and the processes, children like to participant the research's activities. The researcher also found the process could add the attention for the children. Through the low-cost device, it can truly apply on design interactive interface design more extensive, and the teaching materials will be more flexible. Teachers work for special education could design the teaching materials according to the needs of students with developmental disabilities from different courses. By the way, teachers could give efforts to design the contents of the materials because they can just apply powerpoint or flash software, it doesn't increase their loading. This research used low-cost device, this teaching material is presented through different courses, which makes the contents become more multi-development, and adds the interactive interface effect on the process of learning.

In particular, since the resource class children experience different levels of handicaps during the process of studying, ordinary teaching materials and equipment are not suitable for them; especially for the design of multimedia interactive medium, interfacing tools such as mice and keyboards become an immense burden for them. Through assistance from assistive technology, the research will provide the children with tools that are suitable for them and a learning opportunity with immediate feedback.

In the field of information interface research, the element of interactive technology has become the latest trend. In terms of the presentation of interactive design, wii remote interaction is introduced to develop easy teaching materials, so that the elementary teachers' willingness to participate in the design and development of teaching materials is increased, thereby materializing interactive teaching for the benefit of the students.

Within the research framework, the homemade interactive teaching equipment consists of a wii remote, infrared emitter and Bluetooth, the total cost is roughly NT$1,500. With this budget, it may be popularized to all classrooms; in particular, the equipment is light and compact, making it extremely portable and practical for touring teachers who travel to different classes to teach.

Acknowledgement. This work was partially supported by the National Science Council, Taiwan , under the Grant No. 98-2410-H-024-018-and 98-2515-S-024-001-.

References

1. Liu, C.Y., Lin, H.H., Jen, Y.H., Wang, L.C., Chang, L.W.: Interactive technology application program of experience learning for children with developmental disabilities. Key Engineering Materials (2011) (accepted)
2. Standen, P.J., Camm, C., Battersby, S., Brown, D.J., Harrison, M.: An evaluation of the Wii Nunchuk as an alternative assistive device for people with intellectual and physical disabilities using switch controlled software. Computers & Education 56, 2–10 (2011)
3. Shih, C.-H.: Assisting people with attention deficit hyperactivity disorder by actively reducing limb hyperactive behavior with a gyration air mouse through a controlled environmental stimulation. Research in Developmental Disabilities 32, 30–36 (2011)
4. De Amici, S., Sanna, A., Lamberti, F., Pralio, B.: A Wii remote-based infrared-optical tracking system. Entertainment Computing 1, 119–124 (2010)
5. Lee, J.C.: Hacking the Nintendo Wii Remote. Pervasive Computing, 39–45 (2008)
6. Leaf, J.B., Dotson, W.H., Oppeneheim, M.L., Sheldon, J.B., Sherman, J.A.: The effectiveness of a group teaching interaction procedure for teaching social skills to young children with a pervasive developmental disorder. Research in Autism Spectrum Disorders 4, 186–198 (2010)
7. Lin, C.Y., Lin, C.C., Chen, T.H., Hung, M.L., Liu, Y.L.: Application infrared emitter as interactive interface on teaching material design for children. Advanced Materials Research (2011) (accepted)
8. Waite, S.J., Wheeler, S., Bromfield, C.: Our flexible friend: The implications of individual differences for information technology teaching. Computers & Education 48, 80–99 (2007)

9. Bower, M., Hedberg, J.G.: A quantitative multimodal discourse analysis of teaching and learning in a web-conferencing environment–the efficacy of student-centred learning designs. Computers & Education 54, 462–478 (2010)
10. Coyle, Y., Yañez, L., Verdú, M.: The impact of the interactive whiteboard on the teacher and children's language use in an ESL immersion classroom. System 38, 614–625 (2010)
11. Slay, H., Siebörger, I., Hodgkinson-Williams, C.: Interactive whiteboards: Real beauty or just "lipstick"? Computers & Education 51, 1321–1341 (2008)
12. Standen, P.J., Camm, C., Battersby, S., Brown, D.J., Harrison, M.: An evaluation of the Wii Nunchuk as an alternative assistive device for people with intellectual and physical disabilities using switch controlled software. Computers & Education 56, 2–10 (2011)
13. Lin, C.Y., Wu, F.G., Chen, T.H., Wu, Y.J., Huang, K., Liu, C.P., Chou, S.Y.: Using interface design with low-cost interactive whiteboard technology to enhance learning for children. In: Stephanidis, C. (ed.) HCII 2011 and UAHCI 2011, Part IV. LNCS, vol. 6768, pp. 558–566. Springer, Heidelberg (2011)

The Improved Genetic Algorithm Based on Fuzzy Controller with Adaptive Parameter Adjustment*

Daohua Liu and Xin Liu

School of Computer & Information Technology,
Xinyang Normal University, Xinyang 464000, China
dlx14535@163.com

Abstract. In order to improve the performance of the genetic algorithm, the fuzzy dynamic regulator for mutation and crossover operators is constructed, the adjusting process of parameter is specified, and the implementing tactics as well as the controlling process are also provided in detail. The performances of the improved genetic algorithm and simple genetic algorithm are compared by the standard Benchmark testing function. The results indicate that the proposed method has many advantages such as higher optimization accuracy, higher optimization efficiency and less evolution steps.

Keywords: genetic algorithm, fuzzy logic controller, operator analysis, adaptive parameter adjustment.

1 Introduction

Genetic algorithm is a global random search evolutionary algorithm, its performance largely depends on the balance of the exploitation or exploration relationship (EER), namely taking advantage of the foregoing individuals with good performances and exploring some individuals which possibility evolve into more excellent ones [1]. To find out the optimal solution that may exist, "exploration" makes the search space of algorithm as large as possible. It corresponds to strategies of keeping group diversity, which belongs to a global searching process. It uses effective information in group and surroundings so that the algorithm can converge to the global optimal solutions at rapid speed. It corresponds to strategies of improving group convergence, which belongs to a partial searching process. The operator is one of the main factors that influence the balance of EER, which plays an important role in improving the performance and the efficiency of the algorithm. However, among the three operators of the genetic algorithm, especially crossover and mutation operator, which exists the inherent contradictions in exploration and utilization of optimizing process. Therefore, in order to obtain the global optimal solution, operator's probability value needs have a dynamic

---

* This work was supported by the National Science Foundation of Henan Province (112300410234), and the Fundamental Research Funds of Education Department of Henan (2010A520034), and Henan Province University Youth Prominent Teacher (2009GGJS-075).

M. Zhu (Ed.): ICCIC 2011, Part V, CCIS 235, pp. 491–497, 2011.
© Springer-Verlag Berlin Heidelberg 2011

adjustment in the evolution process. Based on this, after analyzing the influence of the three operators on group diversity as well as search ability and applicable scope, the authors construct the adaptive parameter controller of crossover operator and mutation operator, so it provides a good realizing way in achieving global optimization solutions of the complex multi-peak optimization problems by genetic algorithm.

2   The Performance Analysis of Genetic Operator

The design for the crossover and mutation operators has great influence in the standard genetic algorithm. The authors will analyze each operator's performance through the relationship between operator and group diversity as well as search ability and applicable scope of three operators.

The performance analysis of crossover operator

To explore the relationship between crossover operator and group diversity, first we present a method to calculate the group diversity.

Assuming that binary coding space of any optimization problem is $\{0,1\}^l$, population size is N, individuals collection contained in a group is $P = \{a_1, a_2, \cdots, a_N\}$, among them $a_j = (a_{j1}, a_{j2}, \cdots, a_{jl})$, $j = 1, 2, \cdots, N$, the measure of its diversity is

$$m(p) = 1 - \frac{1}{l \times N} \sum_{i=1}^{l} (\max\{\sum_{j=1}^{N} (a_{ji}), \sum_{j=1}^{N} (1 - a_{ji})\} - \min\{\sum_{j=1}^{N} (a_{ji}), \sum_{j=1}^{N} (1 - a_{ji})\}) \tag{1}$$

From the Eq.1, we can know $m(p) \in [0,1]$; when $m(p) = 0$, the diversity of group disappears completely; when $m(p) = 1$, the measure of group diversity reaches the maximum [2].

To analyze the relationship between crossover operator and group diversity, assumed two random individuals $a_1, a_2 \in P, a_1 \neq a_2, a_1 = (a_{11}, a_{12}, \cdots, a_{1l}), a_2 = (a_{21}, a_{22}, \cdots, a_{2l})$; and using single point mode of crossover, the position of crossover point is set at the first string. After been intercrossed calculation, the two new individuals are produced, which are $a_1' = (a_{11}, a_{22}, \cdots, a_{2l})$ and $a_2' = (a_{21}, a_{12}, \cdots, a_{1l})$, at the same time, progeny group is obtained, which is $P' = \{a_1', a_2', \cdots, a_N'\}$, among them when $2 < j \leq N, a_j' = a_j$. According to Eq.1, we can find out

(1) when $i = 1$, $\sum_{j=1}^{N} a_{j1}' = a_{11}' + a_{21}' + \cdots + a_{N1}' = a_{11} + a_{21} + \cdots + a_{N1} = \sum_{j=1}^{N} a_{j1}$

Similarly, $\sum_{j=1}^{N} (1 - a_{j1}') = \sum_{j=1}^{N} (1 - a_{j1})$ can be gotten.

(2) when $i = 2$, $\sum_{j=1}^{N} a_{j2}' = a_{12}' + a_{22}' + \cdots + a_{N2}' = a_{22} + a_{12} + \cdots + a_{N2} = \sum_{j=1}^{N} a_{j2}$

Similarly, $\sum_{j=1}^{N} (1 - a_{j2}') = \sum_{j=1}^{N} (1 - a_{j2})$ can be gotten.

(3) when $2 < i \leq l$, $\sum_{j=1}^{N} a_{ji}' = \sum_{j=1}^{N} a_{ji}$, $\sum_{j=1}^{N} (1 - a_{ji}') = \sum_{j=1}^{N} (1 - a_{ji})$.

From the above calculation, the measure of group diversity is $m(p) = m(p')$, that is to say, the crossover calculation of the single point mode has no effect on group diversity. So we have proved that any random multipoint crossover calculation can't change the group diversity, but crossover operator can strengthen restructuring ability of mode and improve search efficiency.

In order to explore the search ability of crossover operator, assumed the model space is $\{0,1,*\}^l$, the model whose order is R and define distance L, adopting single point mode of crossover operator, the largest probability limit, which is destroyed by single point mode of crossover operator, is $p_d(R,L) = p_c \times L/(l-1)$, and the smallest survival probability limit is $p_s(R,L) = 1 - p_c \times L/(l-1)$. Assumed r_1, r_2 for two low order patterns which are not at the intersection and distributed in different father mode. They form a new mode $r = r_1 + r_2$ order which doesn't contain father mode, whose probability is p_r, namely, $p_r = 1 - p_s(r_1, p_c) \times p_s(r_2, p_c)$. When crossover probability is bigger, the restructuring ability of the individual is strengthened, which improves the ability of opening up new searching space. If the crossover probability is low, it leads to the low individual restructuring rate, so the search of algorithm may become a dull state. Therefore, crossover probability is the key factor which affects the search ability of operator.

The performance analysis of mutation operator

As for the relationship between mutation operator and the diversity of the population, by calculating from the Eq.1, we can conclude that population diversity measure $m(p) \neq m(p')$, in other words, single point mutation arithmetic has influence on population diversity and other mutation methods can also improve population diversity.

For the search ability of mutation operator, as mutation operator is used to ensure the diversity of the population operator. Similar to crossover operator, mutation operator has the dual role of reconstruction and destruction. Under the control of the single point mutation operation, the survival probability and reconstruction probability of the mode with R order are $p_s(R, p_m) = (1 - p_m)^R$ and $p_r(R, p_m) = 1 - p_s(R, p_m) - 1 - (1 - p_m)^R$. With the addition of evolutionary time, any random mode can be searched under the effect of mutation operator; whose search ability is irrelevant with the mutation probability and the initial population.

To sum up, in the early evolution period, the reconstruction ability of the mode needs to be improved to enlarge the search space, so that we can find the subspace in which the optimal solution lies, and jump out of local extreme value point. The survivability of the mode should be improved during the late evolution period in order to realize local search in the subspace. Therefore, the self-adaptive adjustment of the crossover rate and mutation rate should be needed, in order to make full use of the search ability of crossover operator and mutation operator. In practical application, crossover calculation is the main method to generate new individual which determines the global search ability of the evolutionary. In the beginning of the evolution, crossover operator p_c should adopt large value, at the end of the evolutionary, p_c should adopt small probability. In this way, it's easy to achieve the global convergence value. When mutation probability is very small, groups have the good stability, but once getting into a local value, it is difficult to jump out, and will be easy to produce immature convergence value, while increase the value of P_m, it may destroy the assimilation of the optimal group, and make the solution space diverse, while the searching process can jump out from local extreme value point and converge to global optimal solution. In the process of working out problems, variable P_m also can use alterable value. That is to say, during the early period, P_m is larger, which extends the search space, but during the late period, P_m is smaller, which speeds up the convergence [3].

4   The Adaptive Parameter Adjusting Method for Genetic Algorithm

The parameter adjusting process for genetic algorithm

In the genetic evolution process, the system is sensitive to the parameters of evolution, and adopting a fixed parameter is not conducive to converge to the global optimal solution. In order to dynamically adjust the crossover probability P_c and mutation probability P_m, the system used two fuzzy controllers to adjust it [4]. In the evolution process, the systems continuously calculate the average fitness value of three generations. That is $k - 2\Delta \overline{eval}(V;k-2)$, $k - \Delta \overline{eval}(V;k-1)$ and $k - \Delta \overline{eval}(V;k)$.

$$\Delta^2 eval(V;k-1) = (\Delta \overline{eval}(V;k-2), _{-\Delta \overline{eval}(V;k-1))} = [\frac{\sum_{j=1}^{N} eval(v_j;k-2)}{N} - \frac{\sum_{j=1}^{N} eval(v_j;k-1)}{N}] \times \lambda$$

$$\Delta^2 eval(V;k) = (\Delta \overline{eval}(V;k-1) - \Delta \overline{eval}(V;k)) = [\frac{\sum_{j=1}^{N} eval(v_j;k-1)}{N} - \frac{\sum_{j=1}^{N} eval(v_j;k)}{N}] \times \lambda$$

Where $V = [v_1 \cdots v_2 \cdots v_j]^T$, λ is the fuzzy factor.

Thus, the dynamical adjusting process for the parameter P_c, namely, the following rules are judged in order.

if $\varepsilon \le \Delta^2 eval(V;k-1) \le \gamma_c$ and $\varepsilon \le \Delta^2 eval(V;k) \le \gamma_c$

then Increase P_c and produce the next generation;

if $-\gamma_c \le \Delta^2 eval(V;k-1) \le -\varepsilon$ and $-\gamma_c \le \Delta^2 eval(V;k) \le -\varepsilon$

then Reduce P_c and produce the next generation;

if $-\varepsilon \le \Delta^2 eval(V;k-1) \le \varepsilon$ and $-\varepsilon \le \Delta^2 eval(V;k) \le \varepsilon$

then Increase P_c rapidly and produce the next generation.

In those above-mentioned rules, ε is a pre-given nearly zero value; γ_c is a pre-set maximum value of fuzzy attribute function, $-\gamma_c$ is the minimum of fuzzy attribute function.

The dynamical adjusting process for parameters P_m and P_c is similar, except for transforming $\pm\gamma_c$ to $\pm\gamma_m$.

The implementation strategy for fuzzy logic controller

The implementation strategies of P_c are divided (P_m is similar to P_c).

① The input for fuzzy controller P_c is $\Delta^2 eval(V;k-1)$ and $\Delta^2 eval(V;k)$; its output is the changing value $\Delta P_c(k)$. ② set attribute function $\Delta^2 eval(V;k-1)$, $\Delta^2 eval(V;k)$ and $\Delta P_c(k)$, where the linguistic variables for the inputting and the outputting are shown in Fig.1 and Fig.2, at the same time, let $\Delta^2 eval(V;k-1)$ and $\Delta^2 eval(V;k)$ be standardized to the range [-1.0, 1.0] in advance, $\Delta P_c(k)$ is standardized to the range [-0.1, 0.1]. ③ The fuzzy decision table is established on the basis of experience and views of experts in the field [5], which is shown in Table 1. ④ The anti-fuzzy information table for the controller is established, the specific information is shown in Table 2. In the Fig.1 and Fig.2 , NR is negative big; NL is negative large; NM is negative middle; NS is negative small; ZE is zero; PS is positive small; PM is positive middle; PL is positive large; PR is positive big.

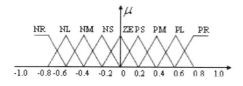

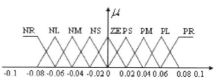

Fig. 1. Attribute function of $\Delta^2 eval(V;k-1)$ and $\Delta^2 eval(V;k)$

Fig. 2. Attribute function of $\Delta P_c(k)$ and $\Delta P_m(k)$

Table 1. The fuzzy decision table for parameter P_c and P_m

$\Delta^2 eval(V;k)$	\multicolumn{9}{c}{$\Delta^2 eval(V;k-1)$}
	NR	NL	NM	NS	ZE	PS	PM	PL	PR
NR	NR	NL	NL	NM	NM	NS	NS	ZE	NE
NL	NL	NL	NM	NM	NS	NS	ZE	ZE	PS
NM	NL	NM	NM	NS	NS	ZE	ZE	PS	PS
NS	NM	NM	NS	NS	ZS	ZE	PS	PS	PM
ZE	NM	NS	NS	ZE	PE	PS	PS	PM	PM
PS	NS	NS	ZE	ZE	PS	PS	PM	PM	PL
PM	NS	ZE	ZE	PS	PS	PM	PM	PL	PL
PL	ZE	ZE	PS	PS	PM	PM	PL	PL	PR
PR	ZE	PS	PS	PM	PM	PL	PL	PR	PR

Table 2. The anti-fuzzy table for parameter P_c and P_m

$Z(i,j)$	\multicolumn{9}{c}{i}
j	-4	-3	-2	-1	0	1	2	3	4
-4	-4	-3	-3	-2	-2	-1	-1	0	0
-3	-3	-3	-2	-2	-1	-1	0	0	1
-2	-3	-2	-2	-1	-1	0	0	1	1
-1	-2	-2	-1	-1	0	0	1	1	2
0	-2	-1	-1	0	2	1	1	2	2
1	-1	-1	0	0	1	1	2	2	3
2	-1	0	0	1	1	2	2	3	3
3	0	0	1	1	2	2	3	3	4
4	0	1	1	2	2	3	3	4	4

The controlling process for the fuzzy logic controller

The specific control process for the parameter P_c and P_m is :

(1) Input the average fitness value of continuous three generations ($k-2, k-1, k$) for $\Delta^2 eval(V;k-1)$ and $\Delta^2 eval(V;k)$.

(2) Standardize P_c and P_m, and then assign these values to the indexes i and j corresponding to the control actions in the anti-fuzzy information table, which is shown in Table 2.

(3) Calculate the variation value $\Delta P_c(k)$ and $\Delta P_m(k)$ for the control parameter P_c and P_m, where $\Delta P_c(k) = Z(i, j) \times 0.02$, $\Delta P_m(k) = Z(i, j) \times 0.002$, the contents of $Z(i, j)$ are the corresponding values of $\Delta^2 eval(V;k-1)$ and $\Delta^2 eval(V;k)$. The specific mapping is shown in Table 2. The values 0.02 and 0.002 are given to regulate the increasing and decreasing ranges of the P_c and P_m.

(4) Update the value of P_c and P_m.

$$\begin{cases} P_c(k) = P_c(k-1) + \Delta P_c(k) \\ P_m(k) = P_m(k-1) + \Delta P_m(k) \end{cases} \tag{2}$$

The Eq.2 provides that the adjusted rates should not exceed the range [0.5,1.0] for the P_c and the range [0.0,0.1] for the P_m.

5   Make Use of Benchmark Test Functions to Test the Improved Genetic Optimization Algorithm

In order to verify the solving ability of the improved optimization method, we use Benchmark test functions to test it, namely

$$^{\min} f(x, y) = 0.5 + \frac{\sin^2 \sqrt{x^2 + y^2} - 0.5}{[1.0 + 0.001(x^2 + y^2)]^2}, -100 \le x, y \le 100 \tag{3}$$

By the analysis of Benchmark function (3), the function $f(x, y)$ is an extremely difficult multimodal function, it has the minimum value in the point (0,0), whose minimum value is 0. Although the function only contains a minimum solution, there are a lot of local solutions in the vicinity of this one, so that the searching method is difficult to obtain the optimal solution[6]. The specific image of the function is shown in Fig.3. The traditional genetic algorithm and the improved genetic algorithm respectively solve the function to contrast the result. The test results are shown in Table 3. From Table 3, we can see that the maximum value is 0.03 from the 4 times optimization results, and the optimization results are within the allowed range. Its results have a higher precision compared with the result of the simple genetic algorithm. The comparison of used time shows the time of

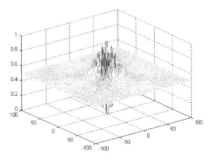

Fig. 3. The image of testing function

improved algorithm is basically in 25 seconds or less, while the simple genetic algorithm spends more than 40 seconds. Furthermore, in terms of the final convergence, the improved evolutionary algorithm used much less generations than traditional genetic algorithm.

Table 3. The comparison of test function value

Simple genetic algorithm					The improved genetic algorithm				
Evolution step	x	y	Evolution time (s)	f_{min}	Evolution step	x'	y'	Evolution time (s)	f'_{min}
1013	-0.006	0.092	41.18	0.084	297	0.002	0.029	23.07	0.028
1089	-0.016	0.000	50.57	0.062	301	-2.026	-0.017	21.64	0.030
927	0.008	-0.004	45.35	0.095	287	-0.014	0.000	23.91	0.019
1102	-0.045	0.008	47.80	0.045	276	-0.003	-0.020	20.56	0.021

6 Conclusions

When using genetic algorithm to solve optimize function problems, in order to obtain the complex function optimization results, it is better to increase the value of crossover operator P_c and mutation operator P_m in the beginning of the evolution, and reduce the value in the end of the evolution,. This paper proposes two fuzzy logic controllers to adaptively adjust them which are based on the evolutionary individual changed value. By comparing the results of optimization test functions, we can see that the improved genetic algorithm based on fuzzy controller with adaptive parameter adjustment obtains the optimal solution with higher accuracy, reduced steps and less time than simple genetic algorithm.

References

1. Lv, J., Gao, H., Yang, H.: Application in neural network design of hierarchical genetic particle swarm optimization algorithm. Computer Engineering and Applications 46(33), 227–229 (2010)
2. Yang, G., Cui, P., Li, L.: Applying and realizing of genetic algorithm in neural networks control. Journal of System Simulation 13(5), 567–570 (2001)
3. Bian, X., Mi, L.: Development on genetic algorithm theory and its applications. Application Research of Computers 7, 2425–2429 (2010)
4. Mitsuo, G., Young, S.Y.: Soft computing approach for reliability optimization: State-of-the-art survey. Reliability Engineering & System Safety 91(9), 1008–1026 (2006)
5. Guo, R., Hong, X., Su, W.: The control arithmetic for the double inverted pendulum based on the fuzzy control theory. Journal of Xidian University 33(1), 111–115 (2006)
6. Le, C., Yao, X.: Evolutionary programming using mutations based on the levy probability distribution. IEEE Transactions on Evolutionary Computation 8(1), 1–13 (2004)

Smart Home System Network Architecture and Implementation

GaoHua Liao and JieBin Zhu

Nanchang Institute of Technology, Nanchang, China
lxm1984852@163.com

Abstract. According to research and problems of the current smart home systems, the smart home of the system architecture has been research. By distributed control, all systems are architecture and designed. The whole system smart disassemble into intelligent comprehensive of every family subsystem. Individual subsystems of control actions by the nodes to implement. The method has been put forward that we can transform the smart home controller using the technology of the fuzzy neural network. It solved that the home controller how to get self-learned and self-adaptive capacity and intelligence analyze-judge capacity, satisfy domestic demands of the intelligent control and have better economy and practicality.

Keywords: Smart home, Intelligent controller, Intelligent Building, Control-bus.

1 Introduction

With green ecological and environmental health and sustainable development, energy conservation and intellectualized are housing development trend and theme [1].Along with the society and economic level's continualenhancement, various appliances enter the ordinary family, which is constituted of all forms of modernized rooms with appliances as the basic hardware. However, in some kind of degree, the popularization of appliances has acontradiction with the strengthening safety consciousness and reliability request of the residents. Under this social background, how to guarantee an effective control to the appliances and ensure the safety of the living environment has become the society matter of concern [2]. In this paper, the intelligent systems of domestic research use distributed control. The whole system intelligence break into a comprehensive intelligent for the families of the subsystem. Individual subsystems of control actions implement by the nodes and study communication means and wisdom node control of the principles, structures, implementation and the control rules of the system. Whole system of the architecture and design.

2 The Home Systems Structure

The overall structure parts are compose of hardware platforms, network system structure and the gateway,As shown in Fig.1. The home system achieve the following functions [3]:

M. Zhu (Ed.): ICCIC 2011, Part V, CCIS 235, pp. 498–503, 2011.

• Smart burglar—auto setting(There was nobody at home or to lock the door, or press the button when the night) ; Wireless and cable the emergency button.

• Smart environment climate—the room temperature, humidity and air quality monitoring and control, auto open in the room and shut automatically when you out.

•   Smart sound—turn on in the room, turn left when you out.

• smart phones—if don't have call, all the telephone shrilled, only asks a bell rang for the short distance of people.

• Lighting system—according to the brightness and close automatically, automatic and get up at night. When you leave, shut automatically and manual controls with priority.

• Carrying electrical curtain.

• Automatically control function—according to the master will combine the control scheme, if somebody, turn the water, sound the gently music in the living room. When the television on, automatically turn off the sound. when call on, the volume automatically to the smaller. Summer after midnight, the temperature outside is below the room temperature auto open the window air flow.

• Remote function—use the internet and mobile phone remote.

• Open of system—convenient connected with the housing estate or a lan.

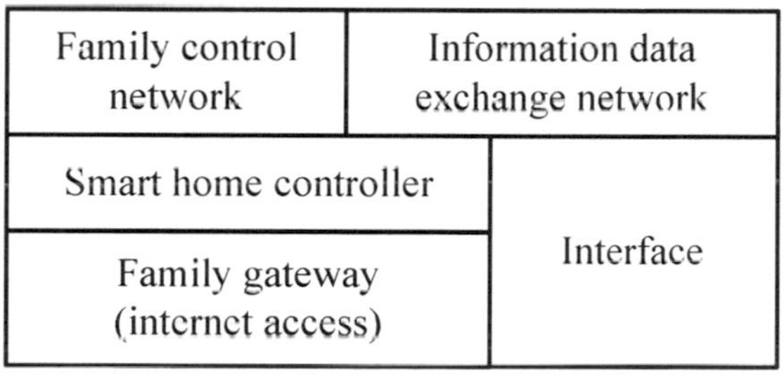

Family control network	Information data exchange network
Smart home controller	Interface
Family gateway (internet access)	

Fig. 1. Overall chart of the smart home system

3   Smart Home Communications Media

In family network, the media of transmission is important because it is crucial to the system availability, scalability and practicality after product.

• RS-485 is the most commonly interface standard, used for communication data among the computers and between computer with peripheral devices. Design of the data communication is for intelligent the smart home controller and among gateway. According to realities select the drive, through investigation has chosen the price relatively low SN75176A/D [4].

• RF wireless adopt relatively cheap nFR401 modules, combined with the peripheral devices, realize the wireless data communication for family control network.

• Infrared transport now is a kind of transmission technology and almost used in every remote controller. In the design,infrared remote controller adopt a variety of infrared remote control realize the signal identification, storage and reproduce, thus realize multiple electric remote control. As the public network, the design the controller based on dtmf (the two-tone more frequent) signals, then easy to implement the home networking remote monitor [5]. The controller of the system in Fig.2. Using 89c51 as Main Control Unit, including the rings detest and simulated picks circuit, the two-tone more frequent, the receiving and sending circuit, voice control circuit, 24C02 serial storage. Also use the wireless interface with the upper realize information exchange. The circuit can control the receiving and sending circuit automatically make the preset phone call.

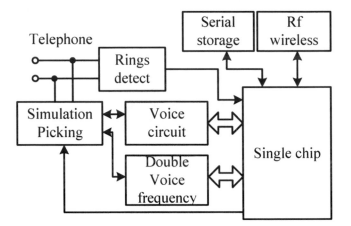

Fig. 2. The network interface circuit

4   Construction Home Monitoring System

Family Automation Subsystem

Family Lighting Subsystem. The system to function including:According to the brightness automatically regulate the light of the brightness or turn off; Get up automatically open and brightness at night; Automatically turn off the lights if leaving the room and turn on lights if entering the room; Manual or the home system unified action has the priority; Fault alarm. the circuit shown in Fig.3.

Curtains Control. Its function including: Achieve any man when he left home, automatically closethe curtain; people at home,automatically open the curtains; People during the break ,automatically open the curtain; people get up, automatically open the curtains; Manual or the unified action has the priority; Fault alarm.

Smart Environment of the Climate System. According to indoor environment of temperature, humidity, the inhalation of dust content and CO_2 gas saturation indoor. Equipment of the air conditioner, the air domestic purify union regulate air indicators to achieve a desirable in existence. That can create a moderate family, fresh and healthy living environment; Automatically closes when people leave the room and open into the room; Manual or the unified action has the priority. ④ Fault alarm.

Smart Sound and Smartphone. The function including: People in the sound on, after leave sound off; If don't call, all the telephone shrilled, only asks a bell rang for the short distance of people; Manual or the unified action has the priority;Fault alarm.

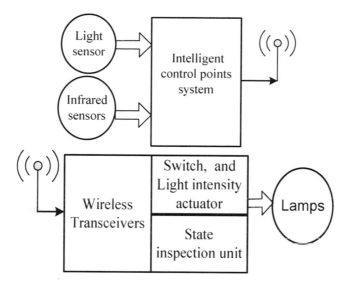

Fig. 3. The lighting systems of control structure

Safety Precautions against Module. Modules to be achieved including: If detect the gas, smoke, the temperature changes over, automatically safety guidelines to the area security and the alarm,open the window, start a fire control facilities and audible visual type; When detect the damage to window, glass, the door, send audible and visible warning to the area security and the remote alarm, and start the video surveillance system; Home owners have an emergency, press the cable and wireless and the community centre to help; There was nobody at home and lock the door, or press the night button, automatically an exemplary; Anyone coming, start the visual and interphone function. By the logical control, the node in the system of fuzzy logic rules library to store a series of control regulations. If the status detected by the sensor system or device satisfy the rules control, the node implement conclusion of the control rules. The executive orders issued by radio to the actuator,subsystem or the other. Actuator operations or other manner unified action system for the operation,thus the implementation of security, preventing fire alarm functions and winding.

Home Electronic Information System. In addition to a control signal, transportation between information appliances or with the internet are primarily a lot of audio, video signal. The information appliances system including computers, televisions sets, the sound, the telephone, cameras, water, the vcd [6]. The manner unified action system to control, control mainly have: Cameras opening and closing; The TV channel switch, and the regulation, the recording; Sound of the switch and the volume adjustment; Switch of the water heater; Records-sent and the long transmission for three meters; The remote control and monitoring network video; Detection the work state of equipment for all the information systems and;

Manual Operation Platform. Through radio and infrared remote the RF wireless remote controller   control equipment, as shown in Fig4. Manual operation: Variety of devices opening, closing and sizes adjustment can carry out by equipment its operating platform or the controller and other intelligent control the operation platform; To the rules of the manual amend, you can access the smart home operating system by   computer.

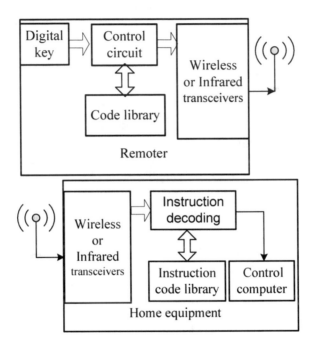

Fig. 4. RF wireless, infrared remote control block

5   System Intelligently Implemented and Gateway

Intelligent home system has the function for analysis, study, adaptive accept and training the expert knowledge, also with   copy of the people, human, study, adaptive master family life and run regular of various family equipment. Try to monitor equipment in the home. "Understanding" home owners provid multiple services, find the exceptional condition and appropriately handling or alarm. The the core of functions is the home controller. Smart home control additional in the family automation network, the implementation these functions is using the fuzzy nerve network control technology to monitoring and regulation the of family intelligence network node.

The needs of agreement for the home networking communication is simple, and embedded systems have a small volume, technical, configuration low, simple and timely strong and low cost etc, there offer an the scheme that interconnect the family network with internet by embedded gateway. Use 89C51 monolithic integrated circuits and network card TE-2008 lord chip RTL8019AS to research singlechip application in the ethernet card data communications. Embedded gateway is the TCP/IP protocol stack in singlechip, and singlechip have access to ethernet of a cheap network meet to the device. As long as a controller of the network interface chips to control and communication, and by independent developing TCP/IP protocol stack. The standard network technology (TCP/IP) applied to embedded devices, and then can monitor at any time from any place in the internet environment. Using of traditional web and the internet for monitoring mechanism realize the data control and the operation.

6 Summary

The smart home control network has established in this paper. The overall smart home studied from the overall and distributed. Design the overall aspect of the network system and communications media, and the gateway , give the the principles and methods of soft-hardware. Adopt a decentralized system in line with the feature and application smart home, has good stability and flexibility, the home systems consistent reached home life of health and safety purposes. For some special features, can greatly increase the energy efficient, effective and better than the system of performance. Special feature set, the implementation of the building of real changes, the house of the ecological environment of coordination, automatically identify of the burglar alarm system set up.

Acknowledgement. It is a project supported by Jiangxi education department of science and technology.

References

1. Peng, X.o., Li, R.: Research on Embedded Smart Home Control System Based on ARM. Low Voltage Apparatus (18), 42–45 (2009)
2. Xu, Y.: The Control System for Smart Home Based on GSM and the Radio. In: 2010 International Conference on Computer, Mechatronics, Control and Electronic Engineering, pp. 134–137 (2010)
3. Wang, K.: The Study of Smart Home System. Xi'an University of Science and Technology, XI'an (2005)
4. Zhang, Z.-q.: Research and Realization of Smart Home System in double-deck House. Xi'an University of Science and Technology, XI'an (2006)
5. Gao, Q., Qin, W., Ni, Z.F., Huang, W.X., Chen, S.M., Yao, Q.: Design and Realization of Electrical Appliances and Home Monitor System Base on GSM. Journal of Zhejiang Sci.-tech. University 26, 391–394 (2009)
6. Cao, W.: Design and Implementation of a Street Lamp Monitoringand Management System with SMS/GPRS/USSD and GIS. Acta Scientiarum Naturalium Universitatis Neimongol. 40, 722–727 (2009)

Study of Numerical Control Machining Parameter Optimization

GaoHua Liao and Jia Liu

Nanchang Institute of Technology, Nanchang, China
xli84@yahoo.cn

Abstract. Choosing the numerical control processing cutting parameters is an important problem to solve in modern technuque of manufacture, for it relates to the system productivity, the cost of production as well as the product quality in processing. A new optimizations of cutting parameters method was put forward. Using three targets control parameters, machining time, machining accuracy and machining cost, multiple targets nonlinear programming model was established. The multiple targets nonlinear constraint program problem was transformed to single target nonlinear no constraint program problem. Based on the model, the optimal cutting parameters are generated with improved particle swarm optimization (PSO). An example shows that the optimal cutting parameters are easier to satisfy the optimizing object than the empirical ones, and PSO is applicable for solving complicated nonlinear problem. It provided a scientific method for the reasonable choice of cutting quantity.

Keywords: Numerical control machining, Particle swarm optimizer, Cutting parameter, Optimization.

1   Introduction

In numerical control(NC) processing, right to choose a reasonable cutting parameters is play very important role to ensure the quality of products, improve productivity and reduce production cost. In recent years, the NC of general application and all sorts of advanced manufacturing technology has developed rapidly. By greatly reducing the production time and correspondingly the amount of time, the proportion of greatly improved. Shorten processing time for cutting to increase productivity plays an important role [1]. Traditional selection cutting parameters are with reference to the production of some of the empirical data, supplemented by the necessary calculation. By the people of the objective condition restrict, the design cycle is long. In order to avoid and minimize abnormal generally select the more conservative values, utilizing the data are generally not optimal result, but also difficult to ensure quality of design. It is no longer suited to the new product research and development necessary. Cutting parameter selection is an important issue for processing. The use of metal cutting theory, mathematical modeling and model optimization algorithm to find optimal values of cutting parameters, is one of the major directions in current cutting parameters selection [2]. In this paper, turning roughing optimization of cutting parameters was studied. Taking into account the actual machine tool and tool constraints, and set up a mathematical model of cutting parameters.

M. Zhu (Ed.): ICCIC 2011, Part V, CCIS 235, pp. 504–510, 2011.

It has the greatest productivity and the lowest production costs for the optimization goal. Application of particle swarm optimization, optimization of cutting parameters based on the set up mathematical model, and verified by example.

2   Parameter Optimization Model

Reasonable cutting parameters selection to ensure quality, improve productivity, reduce costs play an important role. The use of optimization theory to shorten machining time can effectively improve productivity, avoid use their experience to select cutting parameters and cutting parameters to achieve the best optimization. For turning, two important parameters are the processing time T and cost C [3]. When the workpiece, cutting tool, machine tool parameters are determined, the impact on production efficiency are the main factor cutting speed v, tool feed rate f. In general, cutting depth and cutting width of the workpiece identified by the process according to the processing headroom and specific requirements, generally considered of a known quantity in the calculation. Therefore, the main consideration is cutting speed v and tool feed rate f as a model of decision-making variables, set x1 and x2.

Set up the Objective Function. Refers to processing a part at least the time spent to set up the goal to optimize the function relationship.

$$Tw = \frac{\pi DL}{1000vf} + t_{ct}\frac{\pi DL}{1000T(X)} + t_{ot} \quad ,\, C = C_0\frac{\pi DL}{1000vf} + (C_0 t_{ct} + C_t)\frac{\pi DL}{1000T(X)} + C_0 t_{ot} \quad (1)$$

Where, t_{ct} is the tool change time (min). t_{ot} is the tool change time in addition to other than the auxiliary time. T (X) is the tool life function. C_0 is the share of the whole plant expenditure (yuan/min) of processes per unit time. C_t is modao cost, D is the tool diameter. L is cutting length.

Constraint Conditions. By restrictions such as the machine tool spindle speed, feed rate, feed force, cutting torque, machine power, workpiece quality, decision-making variables bound by the following conditions in working hours [4][5].

- Cutting speed to meet the constraints of machine tool spindle speed, that is

$$g_1(X) = \frac{\pi Dn_{min}}{1000} - x_1 \le 0 \quad ,\, g_2(X) = x_1 - \frac{\pi Dn_{max}}{1000} \le 0 \quad (2)$$

Where n_{min}, n_{max} are separately for minimum and maximum machine tool spindle speed.

- Feed rate to meet the feed rate per tooth constraint, that is

$$g_3(X) = \frac{\pi Dv_{f\,min}}{1000Zx1} - x_2 \le 0 \quad ,\, g_3(X) = x_2 - \frac{\pi Dv_{f\,max}}{1000Zx1} \le 0 \quad (3)$$

Where v_{fmin}, v_{fmax} are respectively for the smallest and the largest machine tool cutting feed speed.

• Parts processing to meet the requirement of its surface roughness, that is

$$g_4(X) = x_2 - \sqrt{R_{max}/(8r_\varepsilon)}$$ (4)

Where R_{max} is the largest surface roughness, r_ε is   tool tip radius.
• Cutting machine tool power is less than effective power, that is

$$g_5(X) = \frac{F_c x_1}{1000} - \eta P_{max} \leq 0$$ (5)

Where P_{max} is maximum power of the machine tool, F_c is the cutting force and η is effective coefficient of the machine tool.

3   Problem Solution

Determination of R (f),T (X). T(X) and R(f) of the empirical formula is difficult to meet specific site of the actual situation, in this method fitting a similar function to replace so that can make working conditions in line with the requirements. As BP neural network is essentially a set of sample input and output of the nonlinear mapping problem, it can be applied to neural network training of test data derived T(X) and R (f).

Using neural network fitting R(f) and T (X), the number of nodes depends on the data source dimension, that the input feature vector dimension, the network input nodes, respectively, for two and one, sometimes used for function fitting the output node for one. Neural network base on BP algorithm, select the number of nodes on each floor has a great influence on network performance. Therefore, the layer number of nodes required to carry out appropriate choice. If too few hidden layer units, the network may not be trained, this is because the use of hidden units is low, on many local minima. However, a few too many hidden units makes studying for too long, the error is not necessarily the best. Therefore there are an optimum number of hidden units. Literature[6] give the hidden layer units is calculated as follows: $nl = \sqrt{m+n} + a$. Where m is the number of output neurons, n is the number of input neurons and the selection of a between 1~10. So fitting for the R (f) and Tw (X) check hidden layer nodes are 9 and 11.

Multiobjective Programming Problem to Solve. This paper addresses a multi-objective optimization problem. At present, this type of problem there is the solution: linear weighting method, constraint target method, fuzzy programming method and so on. According to the characteristics of optimization of cutting parameters, we have adopted the first method, the multi-objective into a single objective to solve the problem. Question therefore becomes the minimum value for the next type.

$$\min f(X) = w_1 T + w_2 C$$ (6)
$$s.t. R(f) - Ra_{max} < 0, v - v_{max} \leq 0$$
$$v_{min} - v \leq 0, f_{min} - f \leq 0$$

Because by the neural network give a function of more complicated and difficult to use analytic expressions for their express, so we use artificial intelligence algorithms PSO (Particle Swarm Optimizer). Nonlinear function is a great value as an example to introduce the basic PSO algorithm. Set f (x) as defined the D element function in the D-Dimensional Euclidean Spaces E^D on a region S. where $x = (x_1, x_2,...,x_D)^T$. Set N express the particle number, $xi = (x_{i1}, x_{i2},..., x_{iD})^T \in S$, $v_i = (v_{i1}, v_{i2},..., v_{iD})^T$ and fitness = f (x_i) are express separately the ith particles position, speed, and fitness value at that time in the S. where i = 1, 2,...,N, while pbest$_i$ and $X_i^{best} = (X_{i1}^{best}, X_{i2}^{best},..., X_{iD}^{best})^T$ are express separately once the maximum fitness value and its corresponding location for the ith particle neighboring particles.

In spite of the particles are good, but in an experiment was found in the process, Sometimes in the local, are not made optimal solution to the direction of development, thus the whole system is present premature phenomenon.

Improved Particles of Algorithms. The particles of algorithms are carried out improvement. Main idea is that carry genetic algorithms and particles of algorithms that two types of optimization are derived from biotechnology bionics to combine. Local solutions by using of the particles are genetic disorders and make it out of local area [7].

For optimization problem:

$$\text{Min } Z = f(x) \qquad x \in [a, b] \tag{7}$$

Get a group of local minimum x_k by using the particles of algorithms and the value to a binary value, then the value to mutate into x_p by using genetic algorithm. The process of variations in is as follows.

$$X_k = [X_{k1}, \cdots X_{ki-1}, X_{ki}, X_{ki+1}, \cdots, X_{kj}, \cdots]$$

$$X_p = [X_{k1}, \cdots X_{ki-1}, X_{ki}, X_{ki+1}, \cdots, X_{kj}, \cdots]$$

Through this variation, you can jump very small part, makes the solution of the quality improved. Fig.1 shows this variation in the process, a local minimum x_k translate into x_p through variation, and out of the local areayou can continue to the best solution, thus enhancing the quality.

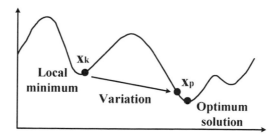

Fig. 1. The value variation of local minimum

Examples of Optimization

Design of System Structure. Base on actual testing of the data collation, and the formation of BP neural network training samples, and the network will be trained to survive, transferred PSO algorithm, enter the appropriate parameters (requirements of the processing time, processing costs) to derive the optimal cutting parameters selection program. Optimal cutting parameters of the system as shown in Fig.2. System consists of four components including: training data, BP neural network, PSO optimization module, the output display module.

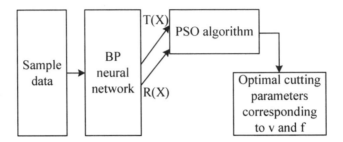

Fig. 2. The optimal cutting parameters of the system

NC Rough Milling Processing Parameter Optimizition. Machine tools is five coordinates the horizontal processing center. Tools rating power 35kw, a spindle speeds n= 20~3000r min; To give a speed vf_{max}=15200mm /min; the materials chosen 7045- T7451 (aluminium); Tool is JH420, D= 20mm, r_ε = 3mm; Processing requirements: a rough surface of the ra milling shape Ra= 6.3μm, L = 1000mm. The results shown in table1.

Table 1. The form milling optimizition

Parameter	Spindle speeds (r/min)	Feedrate (mm/min)	Cutting width (mm)
Field production	2500	1000	20
PSO optimal	3268. 291	1173. 926	19. 231
Improved PSO optimal	3488. 342	1201. 018	19. 935
Ra(μm)	Cutting depth(mm)	Cutting power(kW)	Time(s)
6	6. 2	14. 1	6
6. 013	5. 814	19. 284	5. 298
6. 002	5. 587	22. 385	5. 073

BP Neural Network Training. Using Matlab programming respectively roughness, tool life neural network training. Neural network hidden layer node is 9, and after 255 training error is 0.01. Tool life of neural network hidden layer nodes is selected as 12. After training 9652, the error is 0.01. The result shows that the training is satisfactory. Training error of neural network and Particle Swarm computing process shown in Fig.3.

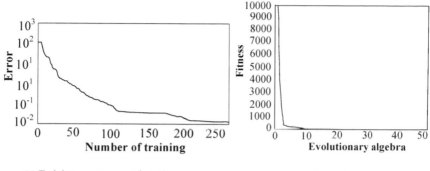

(a) Training error curves of roughness   b) PSO convergence curve

Fig. 3. Optimization of the process of curve

In the matlab environment to prepare the optimal cutting parameters systems, the known parameters substituted into obtain the best fitness value when f=0.2mm/r, v= 164.78m/min. Other conditions the same with the front experimental conditions, the surface roughness of the workpiece obtained by the conversion of a Ra214μm.It can be seen using this cutting can be an ideal surface roughness. Particle Swarm computing through 25 on behalf of the operator to find the best fitness value. We can see the convergence rate of algorithm is relatively fast.

4   Summary

Study cutting parameters optimization and set up optimization model that the optimization objective with the greatest productivity and the lowest production costs. The model convert into single-objective optimization model, model join a variety of restrictive conditions of the machine and add the actual processing. Particle swarm algorithm applied to the complex under the conditions of multi-constrained multi-parameter, multi-objective optimization problem solving. Model using Improved PSO algorithm to optimize calculation, the objective function value optimized v, f is much smaller than the value calculated by the experience of the objective function value. The results of optimization of cutting parameters transition from the general theory of optimal values to production under the conditions of a specific optimal value. This shows that the optimized cutting parameters values are better meet the user's optimization goals than obtained from the experience or manuals on the recommended values and more reference value.

Acknowledgement. Jiangxi Province scientific and technological support projects, item number is 2009BGB02600.

References

1. Hu, D.: Establishment of numerical control processing cutting parameter model and optimization algorithm. Journal of Inner Mongolia University of Science and Technology 26(3), 431–434 (2007)
2. Liu, H., Huang, W.: Computer Numerical Control Machining Parameter Optimization Based on Particle Swarm Optimization. Journal of Tongji University (Natural Science) 36(6), 803–806 (2008)
3. Guo, W., Zhao, S.f.: Using Network and Particle Swarm Optimizer to Realize Optimization of cutting Parameter Real Time in Workplace. Machine Tool & Hydraulics (5), 54–56 (2005)
4. Qin, J.h., Li, Z.: Application of Improved Particle Swarm Algorithm in NC Machining Parameter Optimization. Modular Machine Tool & Automatic Manufacturing Technique (5), 9–11 (2005)
5. Wu, M., Zhai, J., Liao, W.: Research on NC Machining Parameter Optimization. China Mechanical Engineering 15(3), 235–237 (2004)
6. Yuan, Z.: Artificial neural network and its application. Tsinghua University Press, Beijing (1999)
7. Qin, J., Li, Z.: Application of Improved Particle Swarm Algorithmin NC Machining Parameter Optimization. Modular Machine Tool & Automatic Manufacturing Technique 5 (2005)

Cooperative Learning Using Social Network Analysis

Wei Hantian[1] and Wang Furong[2]

[1] School of Software, NanChang University, China
[2] School of Foreign Language, JiangXi University of Finance and Economics, China
wht2879@126.com

Abstract. Cooperative learning is an effective education method. Social network is used to analyze the knowledge sharing, interaction in cooperative learning group. Explain Structural factors of study group knowledge sharing through viscosity and strength, structure hole, the concentration of network, and groupuscule. And a case study is examined to explain the influence of knowledge sharing in interaction of members. Quantitative evaluation by Social network will evaluate and improve organizational knowledge management structure and improve the efficiency of team learning.

Keywords: Cooperative learning, social network analysis, tacit knowledge, knowledge sharing.

1 Introduction

Cooperative learning is origin from United States in the early 70s of 20th century, it is important to improve the psychological atmosphere and student academic achievement, promote non-intellectual aspects of students significantly. So it becomes a mainstream teaching theories and strategies in many counties of the world. Cooperative learning is not a simple absorption of information, but in a specific environment and exchange of knowledge, collaborative process. Learning process includes the explicit knowledge, and also including tacit knowledge acquisition, so the cooperation between team members can not avoid the interaction. It should consider the socialization process of knowledge through personal communication to the organization, and the individual absorb knowledge through interaction with others. The interaction between the members of the group is a collaboration of social behavior. The effects of cooperative learning can be evaluated by building networks, analyze the relationship between individuals in the network. Social network analysis is developed among anthropology, psychology, sociology, mathematics and statistics. It is in line with the study. The research of cooperative learning from the perspective of building relationships in the team for issues related to tacit knowledge through a case study.

2 Related Works

Cooperative Learning. There are many different theoretical supports for Cooperative learning.

M. Zhu (Ed.): ICCIC 2011, Part V, CCIS 235, pp. 511–517, 2011.
© Springer-Verlag Berlin Heidelberg 2011

Social Interdependence Theory. The core of cooperative learning theory can be used to express the very simple words. When all the people have a common goal or work, it relies on the power of solidarity. Rely on each other can provide the impetus for individuals, and enable them mutual encourage, mutual help, mutual love.

Choice Theory. According to this theory, students who do not love learning, the vast majority are not "stupid head", but he was "unwilling to learn." Only by creating conditions for students to meet the needs of belonging and self-esteem, they will be fell the learning is meaningful, be willing to learn, be possible to achieve academic success.

Development Theory. Children complete appropriate tasks for the interaction can promote their mastery of important concepts.

Elaboration Theory. It is believed that if you want to keep the information in memory, and linked with the information in memory, learner must do some form of reorganization or the knowledge elaboration.

Contact Theory. It focuses on social interaction research, to promote different racial, ethnic, gender, students in interactive learning and exchange, which reached harmonious group relations.

Social Network. Social network refers to social actors (ACTOR) and the relationship between the collections. It can also say that a social network is composed of multiple points (social actors) and the connection between points (the relationship between actors). The "point" in Social network is the various social actors; "edge" refers to a variety of actors in social relations. Relationship can be directed, or undirected. At the same time, social relations can be expressed in multiple forms. For example, it stands undirected s for communication and relationships between members, or trade relations between countries. Social network analysis (SNA) is the quantitative research to the relationship between of actors in the social network. Graph theory is the basis of social network analysis of mathematical theory, the formal description of social networks can be divided into social network maps and social matrix. In graph theory, social network can also be divided into digraph and undirected graph. Social network graph is composed by a set of nodes $N = \{n_1, n_2, ..., n_k\}$, and the connection between nodes $L = \{l_1, l_2, ... l_m\}$. In undirected graph, the connection between nodes uses line, and in digraph (fig.1) connections between nodes are directional, with arrows. Matrix of social relations (fig. 2) is converted from the network of social relations. The matrix element represents the relationship between actors. Matrix of social relations is more standardized, which will help computer for processing, is the basis for quantitative analysis for computer.

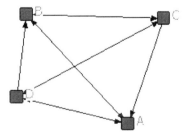

	A	B	C	D
A	0	1	0	1
B	1	0	1	0
C	1	1	0	1
D	1	1	1	0

Fig. 1. Digraph of social network   **Fig. 2.** Matrix of social relations

Learning group is an organization with a common scientific goals and commitments related to the task. the inherent complexity of knowledge of Learners in most cases can not be clear in the document, describe and record, this tacit knowledge combined with "Acquired knowledge" is impossible and the separation of individual actions. Tacit knowledge is personal protection for the whole team, shows the close interaction between members of knowledge sharing. Granovetter (1985) believed that put the intellectual activity embedded in social relations system is important to observe the behavior of economic agents based on a specific real-time by social networks. Social network will affect the organization of knowledge generation and sharing, social networking is the main access to information, resources, social support to identify and exploit opportunities opportunity structure. The social structure is constituted by nodes, a series of social relations, a relatively stable pattern of relationships.

2.1 Case Analysis

Case Introduction. A software development training group with 16 students is selected, they are co-design an information systems development.

Data Collecting. To survey knowledge sharing by questionnaire as table 1, and daily activities of team communication.

Table 1. Questionnaire of survey knowledge sharing

Network type	question
Evaluate Network	Understanding Knowledge and skills of others?
Communicate Network	Get in touch with others?
Interact Network	Who give substantial help to you?

Draw Network diagram. Arrange the data as fig 3, and input data to organize a network by SNA tool UCINET, as fig. 4.

```
    A B C D E F G H I J K L M N O P
    - - - - - - - - - - - - - - - -
A   1 0 1 1 0 0 0 1 0 1 0 0 0 0 0 0
B   1 1 1 0 0 0 0 0 0 0 0 0 0 0 0 0
C   1 1 1 1 0 0 0 1 0 0 0 0 0 1 0 0
D   1 1 1 1 0 0 0 1 0 0 1 0 0 0 1 0
E   0 0 0 1 1 1 1 0 0 0 1 1 0 0 1 0
F   0 1 0 1 1 1 1 1 0 1 0 1 0 1 0 0
G   0 0 0 0 0 1 1 1 1 0 0 0 0 0 0 1
H   0 0 0 0 1 0 1 1 1 0 0 0 0 0 0 0
I   0 0 1 0 0 0 0 1 1 1 0 1 0 0 0 0
J   0 1 0 0 1 0 0 0 1 1 1 1 1 0 1 0
K   0 0 0 0 0 0 0 1 1 1 1 0 1 0 0 0
L   0 1 0 0 0 0 0 1 1 0 1 1 0 0 0 0
M   0 1 0 0 0 0 0 1 0 0 0 0 1 1 1 1
N   0 0 0 1 0 0 0 0 0 1 0 0 0 1 1 1
O   0 1 0 1 0 0 0 0 1 0 1 0 1 1 1 1
P   0 1 0 0 0 0 0 0 1 0 0 0 1 1 0 1
```

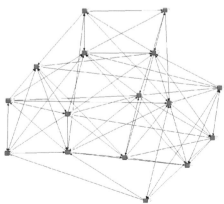

Fig. 3. Data collecting   **Fig. 4.** Social Network of the Interaction

Analysis of Network Density and Distance. Density and distance indicate the interactive relationship, the dissemination of knowledge need to have sticky network. Use the interactive network as example, after calculation, the network density is 0.3250. Geodesic Distance between the points is as fig. 5, the average length is 1.867 and it means an average of nearly 2 people to find other members. For example, N needs 4 people to interact with F. The lower density declares a negative interactive network, but the distance value stands for short length in mutual effect. Network viscosity is lower, but the average distance between nodes is shorter, it is because the distribution of the relationship. The group is divided into 4 team work, due to the different division of labor, the result confirmed this point that members of different sub-topics has a weak link. This shows that the team as a whole is not quite sufficient in terms of internal communication, lack of motivation to share tacit knowledge of the interaction measures.

```
   A B C D E F G H I J K L M N O P
A  0 2 1 1 2 3 2 1 2 1 2 2 2 2 2 3
B  1 0 1 2 3 4 3 2 3 2 3 3 3 2 3 3
C  1 1 0 1 2 3 2 1 2 2 2 3 3 1 2 2
D  1 1 1 0 2 3 2 1 2 2 1 2 2 1 2 2
E  2 2 2 1 0 1 1 2 2 2 1 1 2 2 1 2
F  2 1 2 1 1 0 1 1 2 1 2 1 2 1 2 2
G  3 2 2 2 2 1 0 1 1 2 2 2 2 2 3 1
H  3 3 2 2 1 2 1 0 1 2 2 2 2 3 2 2
I  2 2 1 2 2 3 3 2 0 1 1 2 1 2 2 2
J  2 1 2 2 1 2 2 2 1 0 1 1 1 2 1 2
K  3 2 2 2 2 3 2 1 1 1 0 1 2 1 2 2
L  2 1 2 3 2 3 2 1 1 2 1 0 2 3 3 1
M  2 1 2 2 3 2 1 2 3 2 3 2 0 1 1 1
N  2 2 2 1 3 4 3 2 1 2 2 3 2 0 1 1
O  2 1 2 1 3 4 3 2 1 2 1 2 1 1 0 1
P  2 1 2 2 3 4 3 2 1 2 2 3 1 1 2 0
```

	Degree	EffSize	Efficie	Constra	Hierarc
A	6.000	2.722	0.454	0.579	0.111
B	10.000	6.167	0.617	0.362	0.079
C	7.000	3.455	0.494	0.497	0.113
D	10.000	5.821	0.582	0.361	0.076
E	9.000	5.500	0.611	0.402	0.063
F	9.000	4.917	0.546	0.401	0.111
G	6.000	3.167	0.528	0.558	0.108
H	11.000	7.462	0.678	0.333	0.078
I	11.000	7.071	0.643	0.340	0.087
J	10.000	6.154	0.615	0.369	0.094
K	9.000	4.731	0.526	0.400	0.077
L	8.000	4.150	0.519	0.448	0.071
M	7.000	4.389	0.627	0.474	0.084
N	9.000	5.500	0.611	0.407	0.097
O	10.000	5.643	0.564	0.361	0.068
P	7.000	3.250	0.464	0.502	0.098

Fig. 5. Geodesic Distance between the points   **Fig. 6.** Structural hole index

Structural Hole Measures. Sharing of tacit knowledge is related to the strength of mutual relations between members, but also related to the position of network. Burt proposed the concept of structural holes in 1992, if an actor in the network by linking the other two who have no direct connection between them, the location of the actors is a structural hole. Structural holes mark the interests of a network. When a member of the team to establish relationships with its partners are in a structural hole position, it means that the member had access to two types of heterogeneous information flow, which will bring information richness through across structural holes. Structural holes have different effects on sharing of tacit knowledge. If the structural holes embedded in a general advisory network, it is not enough to offset the structural holes to the members with information superiority due to lack of trust and mutually beneficial relationship network. And the members are apt to do opportunistic behavior - the tacit knowledge of individual monopoly. If the member is a reciprocal relationship between the embedded network, the relationship will be stronger in the absence of other transfer information between two parties, the member's role to change as a "bridge". It can stimulate the circulation of knowledge and shared location. Bridge is an important channel to acquire new knowledge and it can expand weak. In fig 6. "EffSize" is

Effective Size; the actor has greater value means more freedom in the network. "Efficie" is efficiency; greater value means higher operational efficiency. "Constr" is constraint, greater value means actor is more constrained, "Hierarc" is hierarchical, higher value means centre of network. So the actor H is freedom point, and has a high efficiency in the network, G is the most constrained actor, and C is the centre of network, so it must pay more attention to these actors, they play a more important role in the group.

Concentricity of Network. Network index system is concentricity which can be divided into node concentration (Centrality) and whole network concentration (Network Centralization). Concentration indicates the individual nodes in the network occupied a strategic position; the whole network is a measure of central tendency of the concentration of the overall network. When a member has high concentration, it marks it has core resources in whole team, such as the important view, resources, and core technology. So that other members within the team will have a dependent on the member, and it has the right to resource allocation in the network. Similarly, high whole network concentricity indicated that a few has the right to call the information resources. Knowledge sharing occurs mainly in a small number of persons, will inevitably lead to atrophy and lower the efficiency of knowledge sharing. But the low concentration can't guarantee the smooth progress of the tacit knowledge sharing for distributed knowledge. In fig.7, Degree Centrality is the node centrality, Betweenness Centrality is the whole network centrality, measuring influence and control of an actor plays between the actors attached to it, Closeness Centrality is most important centrality. From the result, node H is the centre of the network, it play most important role.

	Degree	Closeness	Betweenness	Eigenvector
A	33.333	60.000	0.771	23.233
B	60.000	71.429	6.603	37.530
C	40.000	62.500	1.619	27.420
D	60.000	71.429	4.540	39.612
E	53.333	68.182	2.723	36.669
F	53.333	68.182	3.565	35.900
G	33.333	60.000	1.460	22.831
H	66.667	75.000	8.063	41.632
I	66.667	75.000	6.930	42.519
J	60.000	71.429	4.603	40.242
K	53.333	68.182	2.120	38.807
L	46.667	65.217	1.390	34.057
M	46.667	65.217	1.707	33.036
N	53.333	68.182	3.619	35.511
O	60.000	71.429	3.778	41.175
P	40.000	62.500	1.746	26.494

Fig. 7. Normalized Centrality Measures

Groupuscule Analysis. The groupuscule appear is due to too closed strong ties and the existence of structural holes. The cluster result is as fig 2. So they are 4 cluster formed in the group, as table 2.

Table 2. Cluster of actors

1	A,B,C,D
2	F , E, H, J , L
3	N, M, I , K , O, P
4	G

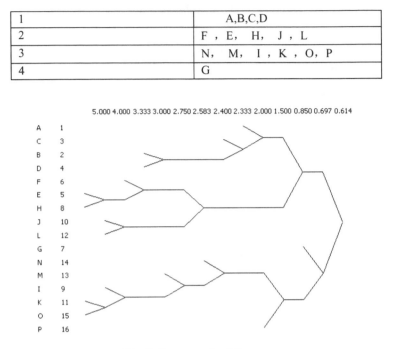

Fig. 7. Groupuscule of the group

3   Strategy

It is need to develop mechanisms to ensure their smooth communication when there are no management of direct absorption of knowledge sharing. In this paper, cooperative learning management team members as the object of knowledge sharing, some strategies are proposed to mitigate some of the structural barriers, and promote teamwork, knowledge sharing.

Improve the knowledge transfer mechanisms, and improve member interaction frequency. There is a need for the creation of a research team that can be connected to each member. Such as network platform for discussion, meetings, create a forum for related issues, encouraging team members publish their own in practice the problems encountered and problem-solving method of empirical knowledge, and encourage members to exchange between different groups.

Identify the central figure in the team, weakening the advantage of small groups. Use social network analysis to identify key figures in the network, identifying their skills, knowledge and situation interact with other network members. As much as possible to explicit knowledge of core members, avoid damage and the interruption of tacit knowledge exchange when they leave the group.

Concern about the bridge of team. If the groupuscule appears in team, it must pay attention to the location of the member. Adopt certain incentive measures to promote the knowledge sharing of the members, and improve the efficiency of other members.

4   Conclusion

The research use social network analysis that focus on the impact of structural factors of study group knowledge sharing. It includes relationships between the viscosity and strength, structure hole, the concentration of network, and groupuscule. And use a case study to explain the influence of knowledge sharing in interaction of members. To strengthen interpersonal relationships, and implement stimulation measures related to personnel adjustments are proposed to the possible obstacles. Application of SNA and appropriate software tools in knowledge-based interactive network analysis and visualization for quantitative evaluation of this work to evaluate and improve organizational knowledge management structure will certainly improve the efficiency of team learning.

References

1. KMR. Knowledge management review survey reveals the challenges faced by practitioners. Knowledge Management Review 4, 8–9 (2001)
2. Kochikar, V.P., Suresh, J.K.: Towards a knowledge-sharing organization: Some challenges faced on the infosys journey. Infosys Technologies Limited, India (2004)
3. Perry-Smith, J.E., Shalley, C.E.: The social side of creativity: A static and dynamic social network persperctive. Academy of Management Review 28, 89–106 (2003)
4. Liu, L., Antonopoulos, N., Mackin, S.: Managing peer-to-peer networks with human tactics in social interactions. Journal of Supercomputing 44, 217–236 (2008)
5. Bowles, S., Gintis, H.: The Evolution of Strong Reciprocity: Cooperation in Heterogeneous Populations. Theoretical Population Biology 65, 17–28 (2004)
6. Roy, L.: Tacit knowledge and knowledge management: The keys to sustainable competitive advantage. Organizational Dynamics 29, 164–178 (2001)
7. Cross, R., Borgatti, S.P., Parker, A.: Beyond answers: Dimensions of the advice network. Social Networks 23, 215–235 (2001)
8. Cross, R., Prusak, L.: The people who make organizations go or stop. Harvard Business Review 6, 5–12 (2002)
9. Ailing, W.: Ethic Pursuit in Cooperative Learning. Education Science 24, 41–45 (2008)
10. Tan, W.: Cooperative learning introduction. Journal of the Chinese Society of Education 2, 32–35 (2002)

An Enhanced Recommendation Algorithm Based on the Count of Common Rated Items

Gao Jianxin, Huang Yongsheng, and Wang Huan

Hebei United University, Tangshan, 063009, China
gjx128976@yahoo.cn

Abstract. Collaborative filtering is a widely-used recommendation algorithm. Neighbor selection is an important step in collaborative filtering recommendation. Selected neighbors will have direct influence to the recommendation. In traditional collaborative filtering algorithm, similarity is the only factor to determine which users should be selected as neighbors. However, the count of common rated items can indicate the effect of the similarity of both users. In this paper, an improved approach to collaborative filtering algorithm is proposed in which the count of common rated items is taken as an important factor in neighbor selection. Experimental results demonstrate the approach can achieve better recommendation quality.

Keywords: collaborative filtering, common rated item, similarity calculation.

1 Introduction

With the development of information technology, especially the development of internet, the information-overload problem becomes a challenge confronted by researchers. Personalized recommendation is one of the methods to ravel out the problem. In the field of recommendation research, collaborative filtering is the most popular approach, at the same time, content-based filtering and hybrid filtering are also two key approaches, and more and more researchers start to pay their attention to them. Content-based filtering compares profile of users with that of items using designated model, and offer similar products to users or provide a user with products that similar users have purchased [1-3]. Hybrid filtering is approaches which can enhance performances of recommendation quality by combining more than two recommendation techniques [4, 5].

In recommendation field, collaborative filtering is hot spot research. Due to the importance of neighbor selection to the recommendation quality, it attracts researchers more attention from the forepart of the research of collaborative filtering. The technique of k-nearest neighbors of collaborative filtering algorithm is a frequently-adopted method [6, 7]. The word, "nearest", means that these neighbors have the largest similarity value with the designated user. K nearest neighbors are selected to predict unrated items in this technique if there are enough users who have common rated items. If the count of the users who have common rated items is less than the number k, these users are all selected as nearest neighbors. Although this technique is simple, it can also alleviate the effect of data sparsity.

M. Zhu (Ed.): ICCIC 2011, Part V, CCIS 235, pp. 518–522, 2011.
© Springer-Verlag Berlin Heidelberg 2011

The cluster-based technique is another neighbor selection approach and has attracted more attention from the researchers in recent years. Commonly, cluster-based technique selects neighbors according to some specific rules. These rules can alleviate the problem of data sparsity, or can improve the quality of recommendation, or else can affect both of them. In order to improve predict precision when data is sparse, R. Wang proposed a novel algorithm and resolve the data sparsity problem via the novel clustering approach-modified Bisecting K-means [8]. Quan et al proposed an approach based on stability of user similarity. As the diversity of items, users can have different preferences to them. In the approach these factors are all taken into account when clustering neighbors are selected [9]. S. Gong provides an method that utilizes the fuzzy similar-priority comparison to calculate the similarity of users and uses the fuzzy clustering technology to select neighbors, and the experimental results demonstrate that this algorithm can improve the quality of recommendation [10]. Incorporating content-based rules into cluster-based technique is another hot spot of research [11-13]. In these methods, content-based predictor is used to enhance existing user and item data and help to improve the quality of neighbor selection.

This paper will analyze the similarity calculation and neighbor selection. As item-based technique is similar to user-based technique, this research will focus on one technique, user-based collaborative filtering. Utilizing experiments demonstrate the effects which the count of common rated items imposes to the quality of recommendation. By the analysis of experimental results, an improved method to collaborative filtering is proposed and experiments indicate it can enhance the recommendation quality of collaborative filtering.

The Effect of the Count of Common Rated Items to Collaborative Filtering. Undeniably, similarity can reflect the relationship of two users and is an important factor in neighbor selection. However, similarity computed on small count of common rated items can not well indicate the relationship of two users. Accompanying with the count of common rated items which similarity computation is based on increasing larger, the similarity can reflect the relationship of two users better. To analyze the effect of the count of common rated items to collaborative filtering, the process of recommendation should be researched firstly.

Collaborative Filtering Algorithm. In order to describe data of collaborative filtering, two kinds of sets are defined, $U = \{u_1, u_2, ... u_m\}$ which represents users, and $I = \{i_1, i_2, ... i_n\}$ which denotes items. If a user u_x rates a item i_y with a score, the value of the score can be recorded r_{xy} which represents that the user u_x has rated item i_y and the rating score is r_{xy}. The rating scores of all items rated or unrated by all users can be denoted as a matrix $R = \{r_{xy}\}$. One common method to compute the similarity between two users is called correlation similarity and can denotes as [14]:

$$sim(u_a, u_b) = \frac{\sum_{c \in I_{ab}} (r_{a,c} - \overline{r_a})(r_{b,c} - \overline{r_b})}{\sqrt{\sum_{c \in I_{ab}} (r_{a,c} - \overline{r_a})^2} \sqrt{\sum_{c \in I_{ab}} (r_{b,c} - \overline{r_b})^2}} \qquad (1)$$

I_{ab} is a set which includes all items which is the common rated items of u_a and u_b. c is a item in the set I_{ab}. The notations $\bar{r_a}$ and $\bar{r_b}$ denote the average rating of the items rated by the users u_a and u_b, respectively. After similarities between users computed, the predicting score of $r_{a,y}$, if the item i_y has not rated by the user u_a, can be calculated by the following equation:

$$p(r_{a,y}) = \bar{r_a} + \frac{\sum_{b \in U_N}(r_{b,y} - \bar{r_b}) \times sim(u_a, u_b)}{\sum_{b \in U_N} sim(u_a, u_b)} \tag{2}$$

$p(r_{a,y})$ denotes the predicting score of $r_{a,y}$, and U_N is a set of the u_a's neighborhood users whose preferences are similar to u_a.

Probability of CCRI in Stochastic Conditions. From view of probability, to any of two users, the count of common rated item(CCRI) of them can be simulated as poison distribution. The Poisson distribution is a discrete probability distribution that expresses the probability of a number of events occurring in a fixed period of time if these events occur with a known average rate and independently of the time since the last event. Typical poison distribution depicts the following event: the number of customs who enter a bank in a fixed period of time. Disregarding of the preference of users, any of two users can be considered as a bank, and films (objects users rate) as customs. The count of films which "enter" the two users in a fixed period of time conforms to poison distribution.

In collaborative filtering, the probability of CCRI of two users can be expressed as follows disregarding of the preference:

$$p(CCRI) = \frac{\cdot e^{\lambda} \lambda^{CCRI}}{(CCRI)!} \tag{3}$$

To a given period of time, rating scores from users are stored in collaborative filtering system. The mean number of CCRI between two users can be achieved, and then the $p(CCRI)$ can also be achieved. The $p(CCRI)$ is the probability of CCRI disregarding of preference of users, and the CCRI of given two users indicates the CCRI does occur and it has preference information of users. If the CCRI of two users is k, and $p(k) = p$. If p is small and the CCRI of the two users k do occur, this means small probability event has occurred. On the contrary, if p is large, it means large probability event has occurred. In collaborative filtering, these two events represent important information. If a user a has two neighbor users, b and c, who have same similarity with a, the probability of CCRI of a and b is much smaller than that of a and c indicates a is more similar than a and b. The following two reasons can explain it. Firstly, the smaller probability of CCRI at stochastic condition has occurred infers special relationship between a and c. The more similar preference of a and c results in the occurrence of the events of smaller probability. Secondly, the same similarity is different in deed. The similarity between a and c is difficult to occur in stochastic condition, and it is more similar preferences that result in that.

Neighbors Selection. As two factors, similarity and CCRI, are taken into consideration in neighbor selection. How to determine the weight of them in neighbor selection is an important problem to solve. A neighbor selection index $I_{i,j}$ is chosen which combines the influence of similarity and CCRI and denotes the degree of preference similar of two user, i and j. $I_{i,j}$ is a comparative value, in other words, if the preferences of the users i and j is more similar than that of the users i and k, then $I_{i,j} > I_{i,k}$, the index is appropriate. $I_{i,j}$ is expressed as follows:

$$I_{i,j} = sim(u_i, u_j) f(p(CCRI_{i,j})) \qquad (4)$$

Accordingly, a new prediction approach of unrated items by equation (2) can be modified as follows:

$$p(r_{a,y}) = \overline{r_a} + \frac{\sum_{u_b \in N_a} (r_{b,y} - \overline{r_b}) \times I_{a,b}}{\sum_{u_b \in N_a} I_{a,b}} \qquad (5)$$

2   Experimental Results

Recommender systems provide recommendation by prediction of unrated items. If the prediction to unrated items is more accurate, the recommendation quality will be better. The commonly employed method to measure the quality of prediction in collaborative filtering is calculating the value of MAE (Mean Absolute error). MAE can be computed by the following equation:

$$MAE = \frac{1}{t} \Sigma_{y \in T} \left| r_{a,y} - p(r_{a,y}) \right| \qquad (6)$$

T is a set of unrated items, t is the total number of unrated items in the set T. $r_{a,y}$ and $p(r_{a,y})$ are the actual and the predicted ratings, respectively.

Data sets used in these experiments are provided by MovieLens. In the experiments, The designated number of rating scores of the designated users to a certain items are abstracted as Table 1 and 80% of the rating scores are taken as training set which is used to predict the other 20% rating score. The experimental results are listed as Table 1 and indicate the proposed algorithm can always enhance the recommendation quality.

Table 1. Experimental Data and Experimental Results

Count of Users	Count of movies	MAE of the Traditional Algorithm	MAE of the Proposed Algorithm
235	420	0.76382	0.75663
310	580	0.76138	0.75224
470	820	0.75867	0.75109
785	1266	0.75239	0.74827

3 Conclusion

The count of common rated items is an important fact which has great influence to the recommendation quality in collaborative filtering. It means the similarity computed by it is more effective with its value larger. In the paper, an improved approach has been proposed which takes count of common rated items into account in neighbors selection and experimental results demonstrate it has better recommendation quality.

References

1. Phuong, N.D., Thang, L.Q., Phuong, T.M.: A graph-based method for combining collaborative and content-based filtering, Heidelberg, D-69121, Germany, pp. 859–869 (2008)
2. Pasi, G., Bordogna, G., Villa, R.: A multi-criteria content-based filtering system, New York, NY 10036-5701, United States, pp. 775–776 (2007)
3. Wen, Z.-F., Yuan, H.: Novel algorithm for content-based image filtering. Tongxin Xuebao/Journal on Communication 27, 280–284 (2006)
4. Bezerra, B., De Carvalho, F.D.A.T.: A Symbolic hybrid approach to face the new user problem in recommender systems, Heidelberg, D-69121, Germany, pp. 1011–1016 (2004)
5. Li, C., Liang, C., Ma, L.: Collaborative filtering recommendation algorithm based on domain nearest neighbor. Jisuanji Yanjiu yu Fazhan/Computer Research and Development 45, 1532–1538 (2008)
6. Chen, B., Zhou, M.: Rater maturity oriented k-nearest neighbor collaborative filtering algorithms. Chinese Journal of Electronics 16, 584–590 (2007)
7. Rashid, A.M., Lam, S.K., LaPitz, A., Karypis, G., Riedl, J.: Towards a scalable kNN CF algorithm: Exploring effective applications of clustering, Heidelberg, D-69121, Germany, pp. 147–166 (2007)
8. Wang, R.: Improve recommendation quality via a novel clustering algorithm. Journal of Computational Information Systems 3, 1963–1970 (2007)
9. Quan, T.K., Fuyuki, I., Shinichi, H.: Improving accuracy of recommender system by clustering items based on stability of user similarity, Piscataway, NJ 08855-1331, United States, p. 4052704 (2007)
10. Gong, S.: The collaborative filtering recommendation based on similar-priority and fuzzy clustering, Piscataway, NJ 08855-1331, United States, pp. 248–251 (2008)
11. Puntheeranurak, S., Tsuji, H.: A multi-clustering hybrid recommender system, Piscataway, NJ 08855-1331, United States, pp. 223–228 (2007)
12. (k)Bezerra, B., Carvalho, F., Alves, G.: Collaborative Filtering based on Modal Symbolic user profiles: Knowing you in the first meeting, Heidelberg, D-69121, Germany, pp. 235–245 (2004)
13. Tiraweerakhajohn, C., Pinngern, O.: Finding item neighbors in item-based collaborative filtering by adding item content, New York, NY 10016-5997, United States, pp. 1674–1678 (2004)
14. Karypis, G.: Evaluation of item-based top-N recommendation algorithms, Atlanta, GA, United states, pp. 247–254 (2001)

Design and Implementation of Security Reverse Data Proxy Server Based on SSL

Jiang Du and GuoXin Nie

Department of Computer Science and Technology, Chongqing University of Posts and
Telecommunications, Chongqing 40065, China
gxn327867@126.com

Abstract. In order to solve the database security access through the network,
according to analysis of the characteristics of the security applications of
SSL/TLS(Secure Sockets Layer/Transport Layer Security) protocol and reverse
proxy server, the paper presents a prototype system of security reverse data proxy
server based on SSL is designed and implemented. Through testing, the
prototype scheme is feasible and has some reference value to improve the
security of database application.

Keyword: security, SSL, reverse proxy server, database, JDBC.

1 Introduction

With the rapid development of the technology of the computer network and database,
more and more information is stored in the database, and much of information is
conveyed through the network. The security transmission of some key information is a
vital problem. Once the key information was leaked, it could have serious consequence.
Therefore, to guarantee the important data in the database safely transmitted through
the network is one of the most important security problems which enterprises and
government institutions faces. As a kind of network security transfer protocol, SSL
protocol can better be applied to protecting the data transmission through the network,
the technology of reverse proxy server is a important means of protecting the server of
the application system, the paper is to discuss how to combine these two security
technologies to protect database applications.

2 Introduction of SSL

SSL is a network security transfer protocol developed by the Netscape Company, and
mainly uses public key encryption and X.509 digital certificate technology to protect
the transmission of information. Now SSL protocol is widely used in HTTP, FTP,
TELNET and SMTP, and currently one of the most important security protocols in
point-to-point data communications on Internet. Due to a wide range of application, the
implementation of low cost, security, efficiency, and simple operation etc., SSL has
become most widely used protocol in the application of e-commerce systems. The
current version of SSL is version 3.1, also known as TLS (Transport Layer Security).

M. Zhu (Ed.): ICCIC 2011, Part V, CCIS 235, pp. 523–528, 2011.
© Springer-Verlag Berlin Heidelberg 2011

SSL protocol above the TCP/IP protocol, is completely transparent to the application service based on TCP/IP, in order to achieve secure transmission of the network data provides the following security services:

1) Confidentiality: The client and server of SSL negotiate through the handshake, and determine the cryptographic algorithm and session key during the communication process, and then establish a secure connection, later the transmission data of the transceiver is transmitted over the network after using the session key to encrypt. In addition, The SSL handshake negotiation process is also processed with encryption and digital signature, to prevent illegal eavesdropping and decoding.

2) Authentication of the Endpoint: SSL using X.509 (current version is 3) certificate technology, supports the two-way authentication mechanism of the client and server to ensure the legitimacy of the communicating parties' identities.

3) Reliability: SSL protocol uses the technology of a very strong message authentication code called MAC (message authentication code), for example: SHA-1.And the authentication code is placed in the tail of the data packet, encrypted and transmitted with data. Thus, if the data is modified, the hash value can not match the original authentication code, which can detect whether data has been modified. MAC can also be used to protect SSL connection from interference.

4) Protection of data against replay-attack: SSL uses serial numbers to protect communication sides from the message replay attack. The serial number is encrypted as the data packet payload. During the whole SSL handshake, there is a unique random number to mark the SSL handshake, so replay-attack will be no exploits.

5) Protection of data against the recorder attack: the serial number mentioned above can also prevent from recording packets and sending them in a different order.

3   Data Security Transmission and Reverse Proxy Server Technology

Reverse Proxy mode refers to that the proxy server accepts the request of connection from the Internet, and then forwards the request to a special server on the internal network, and the results obtained from the server back to the client which requests the connection from the Internet. At this point, the proxy server is representing as a external server.

A reverse proxy server can act as an application layer firewall of an application server on the Internet. In fact, it contains two aspects: the access request is constrained by the rules and policies configured in the proxy server, while the application server is closed, isolated from the outside network, thus effectively enhances the difficulty of external attacks.

A reverse proxy server, also often takes responsibility for content filters, although content filters and firewall are more closely related, but the reverse proxy has better performance. Most of vendors of the proxy server implement a mechanism to block certain keywords or content types. This is to prevent malicious code against the real server to another level.

Among the proxy server and other machines there are one or more connections using SSL protocol to encrypt, then the reverse proxy server will become a security reverse proxy server.

The main uses of a security reverse proxy server are as follows:

1) A security reverse proxy server can provide a encrypted connection from the external network to a internal content server through a firewall.

2) A security reverse proxy can allow the client to safely connect to the proxy servers, thus it is helpful to safely transmit data and important information (such as credit card numbers).

3) In addition to SSL-encrypted data transmission, the proxy server can also use the mechanism of client verification, which requires the computer requesting a connection to the proxy server to provide a certificate to verify its own identity.

A security reverse proxy could cause slower secure connection because of the system overhead to encrypt the data. However, because SSL provides a caching mechanism, both sides of the connections can reuse security parameters negotiated previously, thus greatly reduce the overhead of the subsequent connections.

Design and Implementation of Security Reverse Data Proxy Server. With the development of the network and database technology, many databases provide the remote connectivity, some of which taken some protective measures to the connection of the application system and database server, such as encryption and authentication, while some of another can not guarantee the security of data communications for various reasons. In general, if the data transmission is not encrypted between the application system and the database server, it is very easy to sniff the important and sensitive information, such as the username and password, which brings great security risks to the application. SSL protocol can be combined with reverse proxy server technology to establish a SSL reverse proxy server between the application system and database server, through SSL encryption tunnels combination with identity authentication to protect the data communication between the systems, but also which can has least negative effect to other applications on the original system.

Overall Design of the Security Reverse Data Proxy Server. The SSL reverse data proxy server is deployed behind the firewall in the enterprise, as shown in Fig. 1. One remote client and the SSL reverse data proxy server locate in different networks, to form a secure channel between both sides, it is necessary to use SSL to encrypt data communications, resulting in the formation of a encrypted tunnel between the remote Internet client and the SSL reverse data proxy server. The SSL reverse data proxy server and database servers are in the different hosts within the same security domain in the internal network, and the data among them can be transmitted with plaintext. The remote client can only directly communicate with the SSL reverse data proxy server. When the remote client communicates with the database server in the internal network, the SSL reverse data proxy server handles the request of the client and forwards the request to the database server. In order to avoid the internal server being attacked, the SSL reverse data proxy server need to taken some security measures, such as strict identity authentication, access control, information hiding and so on, to protect the security of the internal network resources.

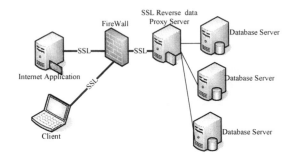

Fig. 1. Security reverse data proxy server topology

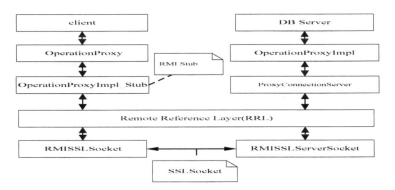

Fig. 2. Security reverse data proxy server Framework

Partial Important Codes of the Security Reverse Data Proxy Server. Based on RMI、SSL technology and proxy design pattern, the prototype system is written in Java to implement a JDBC security proxy driver server to agent a client to the data access request of the target database server [1,2,3,4,5], to realize the proxy server forwarding requests to the database and the two-way authentication between the client and the reverse proxy server. The overall framework of the SSL reverse data proxy server is shown in Fig.2. Some important code as follows (refer with: Fig.3, Fig.4):

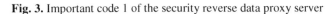

```
/*ProxyConnectionServer*/
public class ProxyConnectionServerImpl extends UnicastRemoteObject
    implements ProxyConnectionServer{
private DatasourceManager mDatasourceManager;/* manager datasource */
    public ProxyConnectionServerImpl( DatasourceManager datasourceManager,
    int port,RMISSLClientSocketFactory clientFactory,RMISSLServerSocketFactory serverFactory )throws RemoteException{
    ....
super( port, clientFactory, serverFactory );
    mDatasourceManager = datasourceManager;
    }
    public Connection getConnection(Properties props)
        throws RemoteException, SQLException{    ///get connection
    ....
    Connection conn = mDatasourceManager.getConnection(dataSource, props.getProperty("user"), props.getProperty("password"));

    OperationProxy impl = new OperationProxyImpl(conn);
    ConnectionProxy proxy = new ConnectionProxy();
    ....
    proxy.setOperationProxy( impl );
    return proxy;
    }
}
```

Fig. 3. Important code 1 of the security reverse data proxy server

```
/*implementation of the DatasourceManager*/
public class SimpleDatasourceManager implements DatasourceManager(
  public SimpleDatasourceManager (XMLProperties props)
  throws ConfigurationException(
  ......
    XMLProperties dsProps = props.getProperty("dataSource").iterator();;
  }
  public Connection getConnection ()
  throws SQLException(
  ......
    Class.forName(props.getProperty("driver"));
    return DriverManager.getConnection(props.getProperty("url"));
  }
}
```

Fig. 4. Important code 2 of the security reverse data proxy server

Running Interface of the Security Reverse Data Proxy. The running interface of the security reverse data proxy as below (refer with: Fig.5):

Fig. 5. Running Interface of the security reverse data proxy

4 Conclusion

To some extent, SSL protocol and reverse proxy server technology can strengthen communication security between two nodes on the network. This paper combines the two technologies using in protecting the database applications. Through testing, the system can provide a good forwarding service for the data request for the database, and because of the communication based on SSL, the data transmission is encrypted. Even though eavesdropped, sensitive information will not be exposed, to a certain extent, which improved the security of database applications, to achieve the desired purpose. However, because the database applications needs to access through the SSL proxy server, the efficiency that the remote client accesses the database server is decreased inevitably. To improve the hardware of the SSL proxy server, to use cache, and to apply load balancing and other means can improve the system performance; The SSL reverse proxy server as the endpoint of the application system and the database server can also be added more rich access control strategy and information filtering and other security features to, to enhance their own performance against a variety of complex attacks, and to further enhance application security and reliability.

Acknowledgement. Thanks for the partial support of the network security key laboratory project of the Ministry of Public Security of China (C09608) for this work.

References

1. Konstantinou, A.V.: Java Security, on (2002),
   http://www1.cs.columbia.edu/dcc/nestor/presentations/
   java-security/java-security-slides.pdf
2. Pistoia, M., et al.: Java 2 Network Securit, on (1999),
   http://domino.research.ibm.com/comm/research_projects.nsf/
   pages/javasec.resources.html/$FILE/java2network_security.pdf
3. Zhang, X., Jaeger, J., Koved, L.: Applying static analysis to verifying security properties. In: Proceedings of the 2004 Grace Hopper Conference (October 2004)
4. Porat, S., Biberstein, S., Koved, L., Mendelson, B.: Automatic Detection of Mutable Fields in Java. In: Proceedings of CASCON 2000 (2000),
   http://www.research.ibm.com/people/k/koved/papers/
   MutabilityCASCON2000.pdf
5. EUROSEC: Secure Programming in Java, on (2005),
   http://www.secologic.org/downloads/java/
   051207_Draft_EUROSEC_Whitepaper_Secure_Java_Programming.doc

A New Workforce Cross-Training Policy for a U-shaped Assembly Line

Jun Gong[1], Lijie Wang[1], and Sen Zhang[2]

[1] School of Information Science and Engineering, Key Lab of Integrated Automation of Process Industry of MOE, Northeastern University, Shenyang, 110004
[2] School of Mechanical and Aeronautical Engineering, Singapore Polytechnic, Singapore, 139651
GONG08089@163.com

Abstract. This study addresses a U-shaped assembly line staffed by partially cross-trained workers with skill chaining. When a worker is absent, the performance of the production system must become worse. Cross-trained workers can improve the performance by replacement. The present paper proposes a new training policy called workload-balanced chaining policy for the workers in a U-shaped assembly line. A mixed integer quadratic programming (MIQP) model is used to realize this policy by assigning workers to be cross-trained for particular stations. The numerical examples are developed to compare the new chaining policy with the traditional chaining policy. Some managerial insights are derived from the analysis of the experiments.

Keywords: a U-shaped assembly line, cross-training, mean flow time, MIQP.

1 Introduction

In recent competitive global environment increasingly sophisticated customers demand customized products of high quality with fast response and reasonable cost. Variability in the demand for operations and the availability of trained workers make staffing decisions a challenge. Powerful approaches to creating flexibility via multi-functional sources of production have been proposed [1]. One way to facilitate this is by cross-training workers, thereby enabling each worker to act as a source of flexible capacity to yield high throughput (TH), low Work-In-Process (WIP), and short cycle time.

A training strategy called chaining in which workers are trained to perform a second task, and the assignments of task types to workers are linked in a chain. It is shown that chaining is a practical and effective strategy for prioritizing cross-training to compensate for absenteeism in the lines. A variety of skill chaining strategies have been proposed to be robust and efficient methods for implementing workforce agility in serial production lines except the U-shaped production line [1, 2, 3, 4].

A U-shaped production line can be described as a special type of cellular manufacturing used in just-in-time (JIT) production systems and Lean Manufacturing. The U-shaped line arranges machines around a U-shaped line in the order in which

M. Zhu (Ed.): ICCIC 2011, Part V, CCIS 235, pp. 529–536, 2011.

production operations are performed (see in Fig1). In the present paper, a new training policy called workload-balanced chaining among the workers for a U-shaped line is proposed to compensate the loss of the performance by the negative effects of absenteeism. A MIQP model is developed to implement this policy by selecting workers to be cross-trained for particular stations.

The rest of the paper is organized as follows. In Section 2, we describe the problem, the new cross-training policy, and the mathematic model. In Section 3, the experiments are designed to compare the new policy with traditional chaining policy and analyzed to illustrate this new training policy more practical and effective to compensate for absenteeism on a U-shaped line. In Section 4, discusses the applicability of the approach and makes suggestions for further research.

2   A Workload-Balanced Chaining Policy for U-shaped Lines

The U-shaped production line can be described as a special type of cellular manufacturing used in just-in-time (JIT) production systems and Lean Manufacturing (see Fig. 1) [5]. The U-shaped line arranges machines around a U-shaped line in the order in which production operations are performed. Operators work inside the U-line. One operator supervises both the entrance and the exit of the line. Machine-work is separated from operator-work so that machines work independently as much as possible. Standard operation charts specify exactly how all work is done. U-lines may be simple or complex, depending on the number of tasks to be performed, the production volume and setup times. U-lines are rebalanced periodically when production requirements change. The U-line satisfies the flow manufacturing principle. This requires operators to be multi-skilled to operate several different machines or processes. It also requires operators to work standing up and walking because they need to operate different machines.

Line balancing is the process of assigning sets of tasks to stations to accomplish a worker. The duration to perform a task is called the task time. The sum of the times of tasks assigned to a station is called the station time. Precedence constraints specify the permissible sequences of the tasks. This sequence can be influenced by several technological and managerial considerations. Fig. 1 illustrates how the tasks assigned to a station to balance the workload of each station. Actually, workers' absenteeism is a negative effect on the balanced U-line. According to [5], multifunctional workers can reinforce overloaded workers whereas specialized workers often cannot. A particular benefit of cross-training in lines is reducing the negative impact of absenteeism. Cross-training can help to ensure that all operations on a line are fully staffed.

A variety of cross-training policies based on skill structures have been proposed in the different environment to improve the production system performance, e.g. "cherry picking", "chaining", "hierarchy" [6, 7, 8, 9, 10]. To this day, chaining is a popular cross-training approach. Based on previous research on chaining, a new chaining policy called workload-balanced chaining is proposed in this paper to improve the production performance further.

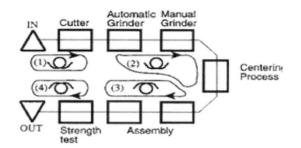

Fig. 1. Fishing rod production line in Japan

When the U-shaped line is balanced based on the workload of each station, the total workload of each station including several takes is almost the same. The station with the maximum workload will decide the throughput of this line. In the U-shaped line, a worker is responsible for a station. Fig. 2 illustrates the balanced U-shaped line with 5 stations, 5 workers and 9 tasks. The cycle time is decided by station 3 (worker 3). In other words, the throughput of a U-shaped line is related to the slowest worker's performance.

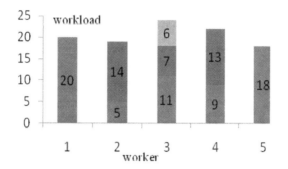

Fig. 2. The workload of each worker in the balanced U-shaped line

In practice, the workers are often absent by different reasons. When a worker is absent, management must scramble quickly to find a replacement to compensate the loss of the throughput. The concept of chaining in the context of a set of plants producing a set of products is introduced by [1]. The concept of chaining is applied by [2] to cross-training on a line to mitigate the negative effects of absenteeism (see Fig 3). In this paper this kind of chaining is called traditional chaining. For a U-shaped line, every worker will be cross-trained for stations in the next station by the traditional chain. To some degree, this policy of the cross-training improves the throughput of the line with absenteeism. However, this cross-training policy also destroys the balance of each station by increasing the workload to each worker. In this way, the throughput of the line is going to bad. For improving the performance of the production system, a new policy called workload-balanced policy is proposed to not only maintain the balance of each station as possible as we can, but also mitigate the negative effects of absenteeism.

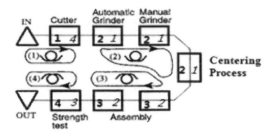

Fig. 3. The distribution of cross-trained workers based on the traditional chaining policy

In a U-shaped line, a worker can process products in the previous station or the next station without affecting the throughput of the line. In other words, a task in one station can be assigned to a worker in the previous or next station, but a worker in the previous by the traditional chaining policy. A MIQP model is developed for the workload-balanced cross-training policy for maintaining the balance of the whole line. This policy improves the balance level of the production system based on the characteristics of the U-shaped line by increasing the flexibility of the chaining. Fig. 4 illustrates a feasible solution based on the new cross-training policy. For example, worker 2 can process task 2, 3 and 4 before cross-training. Worker 2 will be able to process task 2, 3, 4, 5 and 6 according to the tradition policy. Worker 2 will be able to process task 2, 3, 5, and 1.

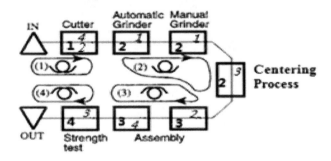

Fig. 4. The distribution of cross-trained workers based on the workload-balanced chaining policy

Notation

i Index set of workers.(station) $(i = 1,2,.....,I)$

j Index set of tasks $j = (1,2,....J)$.

● Parameters :

T_j Process time of task j.

C_{ij} A 0-1 binary variable where $C_{ij} = 1$, if task j is the primary station to worker i ; otherwise0.

E_{ij} A 0-1 binary variable where $E_{ij} = 1$, if task j is not the task in the previous

station or not the

task in the next station to worker i ; otherwise0.

- Decision variable

X_{ij} If worker i is decided to be trained for task j , otherwise 0.

- Model

$$\min \sum_{i=1}^{I} \left(\sum_{j=1}^{J} X_{ij} T_j - \sum_{i=1}^{I} \sum_{j=1}^{J} X_{ij} T_j / I \right)^2 / I \tag{1}$$

Subjection to:

$$\sum_{i=1}^{I} X_{ij} (1 - C_{ij}) = 1 \qquad \forall j \tag{2}$$

$$\sum_{j=1}^{J} X_{ij} E_{ij} = 0 \qquad \forall i \tag{3}$$

$$X_{ij} = 1 \qquad \{(i, j) | C_{ij} = 1\} \tag{4}$$

The objection function (1) represents minimizing the square error of the workload of the whole U-shaped line. Constraint (2) concerns every task is only assigned to a worker for cross-training. Constraint (3) forces the tasks which aren't in the previous or next station can't be assigned to the worker in this station. Constraint (4) concerns workers to be trained for the tasks which are in the primary station.

3   Analysis and Discussion of the Experiments

The example concerns a small U-shaped line consisting of five stations (workers) and nine tasks. Table 1 shows process time of each task in the U-shaped line. Table 2 shows the workers' distribution in the balanced U-shaped line. Table 3 shows the tasks that some workers can't be trained according to the new chaining policy.

Table 1. Process time of each task in the U-shaped line

	Task1	Task2	Task3	Task4	Task5	Task6	Task7	Task8	Task9
Process	2	5	1	1	7	6	9	1	1
time(min.)	0		4	1				3	8

Task means station.

Table 2. The workers' distribution in the balanced U-shaped line

	Task1	Task2	Task3	Task4	Task5	Task6	Task7	Task8	Task9
Worker1	1	0	0	0	0	0	0	0	0
Worker2	0	1	1	0	0	0	0	0	0
Worker3	0	0	0	1	1	1	0	0	0
Worker4	0	0	0	0	0	0	1	1	0
Worker5	0	0	0	0	0	0	0	0	1

Table 3. The tasks that the workers can't be cross-trained

	Task1	Task2	Task3	Task4	Task5	Task6	Task7	Task8	Task9
Worker1	0	1	1	0	0	0	0	0	1
Worker2	1	0	0	1	1	1	0	0	0
Worker3	0	1	1	0	0	0	1	1	0
Worker4	0	0	0	1	1	1	0	0	1
Worker5	1	0	0	0	0	0	1	1	0

Table 4. The workers' workload according to the different cross-training policies

Cross-training policy	Worker1	Worker2	Worker3	Worker4	Worker5	Average workload	Square error workl oad
*balanced line	20	19	24	22	18	20.6	4.64
Traditional chaining	38	45	43	40	40	41.2	8.56
Workload-balanced chaining	39	43	46	40	38	41.2	6.16

*balanced line means the U-shaped line is only balanced but chained.

The model of the workload-balanced chaining policy is mixed integer quadratic programming and solved optimally by means of the ILOG CPLEX 10.0 optimizer. Table 4 shows the results of each worker's workload in the different situations consisting of no chaining policy, the traditional chaining policy and the workload-balanced chaining policy. Fig.4 shows the workers' workload distribution after they are cross-trained based on two chaining policies.

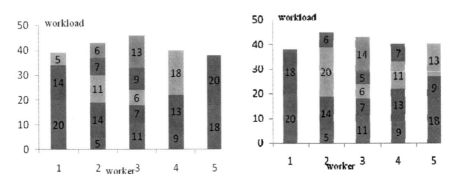

A. The traditional chaining policy   B. The workload-balanced chaining policy

Fig. 4. The workers' workload distribution based on two chaining policies

We investigate the impact of the unbalancing level of the U-shaped line on the distribution of workers' workload based on two cross-training chaining polices. Six experiments are developed for comparisons of two chaining polices. Each experiment consists of five workers and nine tasks. The number of the tasks in each station in each experiment is the same, but the workload of each station in each experiment is different. Square error of the workload of the whole line is chosen to present the unbalancing level of the line. Fig. 5 shows that the unbalancing level of the line based on traditional chaining is worse than that of the workload-balanced chaining policy with the increasing unbalancing level of the balanced U-shaped line. In other words, the workload-balanced chaining policy is a more robust method for implementing workforce agility.

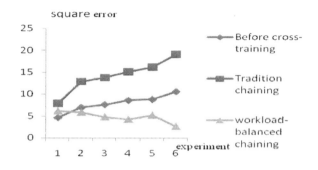

Fig. 5. The results of square error of six U-shaped lines after two chaining cross-training

The impact of the length of the U-shaped line on the distribution of workers' workload based on two cross-training chaining polices is also investigated. Five different length lines are analyzed for two chaining polices. The length of line consists of four, six, eight, ten and twelve workers (stations) and each station consists of two tasks. Fig. 6 shows that the unbalancing level of the line based on traditional chaining is worse than that of the workload-balanced chaining policy in five different size lines, but the bad degree becomes smaller with the increasing size of the length of the balanced U-shaped line. In other words, the workload-balanced chaining policy is better than the traditional chaining policy, especially to the shorter U-shaped line.

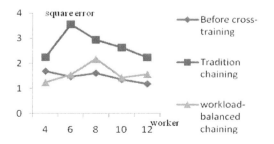

Fig. 6. The results of square error of five different size U-shaped lines after two chaining cross-training

4 Conclusions

This study addresses a U-shaped line staffed by partially cross-trained workers with skill chaining. When a worker is absent, the performance of the production system must become worse. Cross-trained workers can improve the performance by replacement. This study proposes a new training policy called workload-balanced chaining for the workers in a U-shaped line. A mixed integer quadratic programming (MIQP) model is used to for this policy. The numerical examples are developed to compare this new policy with the traditional policy. The results show that the new training policy can robustly support more balanced line than the traditional chaining after considering the effects of absenteeism. Another major issue that requires further investigation is how to affect the operational performance of a U-shaped line with the new chaining policy considering the absenteeism rate.

Acknowledgements. This paper is financially supported by the Natural Science Foundation of China (NSFC) funded projects (70971019, 71021061) and the Fundamental Research Funds for the Central Universities (N100404026).

References

1. Jordan, W.C., Graves, S.C.: Principles on the benefits of manufacturing process flexibility. Management Science 41, 577–594 (1995)
2. Jordan, W.C., Inman, R.R., Blumenfeld, D.E.: Chained cross-training of workers for robust performance. IIE Transactions, 953–967 (2004)
3. Brusco, M.J., John, T.R.: Staffing a multiskilled workforce with varying levels of productivity: an analysis of cross-training policies. Decision Sciences 29, 499–515 (1998)
4. Hopp, W.J., Tekin, E., Van Oyen, M.P.: Benefits of skill chaining in serial production lines with cross-trained workers. Management Science 50, 83–98 (2004)
5. Miltenburg, J.: Balancing and scheduling mixed-model U-Shaped production lines. The International Journal of Flexible Manufacturing Systems 14, 119–151 (2002)
6. Billionnet, A.: Integer programming to schedule a hierarchical workforce with variable demands. European Journal of Operational Research 114, 105–114 (1999)
7. Emmons, H., Burns, R.N.M.: Off-day scheduling with hierarchical worker categories. Operations Research 39, 484–495 (1991)
8. Zavadlav, E., McClain, J.O., Thomas, L.J.: Self-buffering, self-balancing, self-flushing production lines. Management Science 42(8), 1151–1164 (1996)
9. Narasimhan, R.: An algorithm for multiple shifts scheduling of hierarchical workforce on four-day, and three-day workweeks. INFOR 38(1), 14–32 (2000)
10. Anuar, R., Bukchin, Y.: Design and operation of dynamic assembly lines using work-sharing. International Journal of Production Research 44, 4043–4065 (2006)

Author Index

Ai, Shengli   VI-480
Aithal, Himajit   IV-351
AliHosseinalipour   V-36
Anil kumar, A.   IV-351
Aslam, Mohammed Zahid   IV-260

Babaei, Shahram   V-36
Bailong, Liu   III-39, III-47
Bangjun, Lu   VI-124
Bangyong, Hu   II-60
Bao, Liwei   IV-93
Bi, Guoan   IV-224
Bin, Dai   II-436, II-443
Bin, Li   III-151
Bing, Hu   V-476
Bingxue, Han   IV-265
Bo, Qi   VI-282
Bo, Sun   I-526, II-475
Bo, Wu   V-74
Bo, Yang   IV-1
Bo, Zhou   V-461
Bu, Yingyong   I-335

Cai, Nengbin   IV-402
Cai, Ning   II-87
Cai, Xiaonan   I-519
Cai, Xiaoqing   VI-166
Cao, An-Jie   IV-376
Cao, Fengwen   IV-189
Cao, Jianbo   VI-398
Cao, Jianshu   VI-536
Cao, Qiang   VI-417
Cao, Yukun   III-232
Chang, Henry Ker-Chang   VI-500
Chang, Ling-Wei   V-483
Chang, Yinxia   IV-427
Chang, Zhengwei   IV-167
ChangJie, Hu   VI-461
Chang-ping, Zhao   VI-290
Changxi, Ma   VI-282
Changyuan, He   V-211
Chao, Hu   IV-42
Chao, Yan   II-530
Chaoshi, Cai   I-395, III-321

Chen, Bin   V-170, V-175
Chen, Cheng   II-157
Chen, Chuan   IV-369
Chen, Chun   IV-376
Chen, Haijian   III-508
Chen, Haiyuan   III-9
Chen, Hong-Ren   III-407
Chen, Huiying   V-201
Chen, Lingling   V-125
Chen, Weiping   III-508
Chen, Xiaodong   V-175
Chen, Xinglin   VI-110
Chen, Yan   VI-152
Chen, Yanhui   VI-84, VI-89
Chen, Yu-Jui   V-10
Cheng, Jiaji   IV-280
Cheng, Li   V-321
Cheng, Shih-Chuan   VI-436
Cheng, Yingjie   III-74
Chengcheng, Jiang   I-288
Chenguang, Zhao   IV-136, IV-144,
    IV-151
Chi, Xiaoni   I-143
Chiang, Yea-Lih   III-407
Chong, Guo   VI-50
Chuan, Tang   I-29
Chuang, Li   VI-404
Chujian, Wang   I-191, I-366
Chun, Huang   I-36
Chun, Yang Chang   VI-511
Chunhong, Zhang   II-326
ChunJin, Tian   III-207
Chunling, Zhang   V-381
Chunqin, Zhang   III-369
Congdong, Li   I-288
Congmei, Wan   V-321
Cui, Kang   IV-59
Cui, Yanqiu   I-550
Cui-lin, Zhang   V-461

Da, Zheng   V-94
Dai, Minli   VI-424, VI-430
Dai, Wei-min   V-100
Danxia, Bi   V-105

Dasen, Li   II-405
Deng, Fang   II-294
Deng, Hui   V-201
Deng, Jianping   IV-189
Deng, Nan   IV-402
Deng, Xianhe   II-396
Deng, Xiaoyun   VI-343
Deng, Xubin   VI-26
Deng, Yibing   V-316
Deqian, Xue   VI-383
Ding, Feng   II-350
Dong, Hao   VI-1
Dong, Liu   III-292
Dong, Xu   III-39, III-47
Dong, Yu   VI-50
Dong-Ping, Liu   II-303
Du, Jiang   V-523
Du, Maobao   V-365
Du, Wencai   III-1

E., Shiju   VI-398

Fan, Hongda   VI-1
Fan, Jihua   III-515
Fan, Tongliang   IV-433
Fan, Zhao   IV-441
Fang, He   II-172
Fang, Ligang   VI-430
Fang, Qiang   VI-166
Fang, Sun   IV-242
Fang, Yuan   II-274
Fanjie, Bu   II-382
Fei, Zhou   II-281
Feng, Lei   V-304
Feng, Lou   III-312
Feng, Lv   II-101
Feng, Pengxiao   IV-172
Feng, Wenlong   III-1
Feng, Yuan   II-194
Fengling, Wang   I-262
Fengxiang, Chen   V-234
Fu, Wenzhi   IV-172
Fu, Xixu   V-43
Fu, Yizhe   VI-179
Fuhua, Xuan   I-275
Furong, Wang   VI-445, V-511

Gaijuan, Tan   V-234
Gai-ning, Han   VI-39
Gan, Jing   III-427

Gang, Chen   I-492
Gao, Cheng   I-359
Gao, Fei   III-427
Gao, Haiyan   III-433
Gao, Jin   IV-306
Gao, Junli   VI-166
Gao, Li   VI-357
Gao, Shuli   V-226
Gao, Wei   VI-188, VI-197
Gao, Xin   II-391
Gao, Xiuju   V-365
Gao, Zhijie   III-17
Gong, Jun   V-529
Gong, Xiaoyan   II-194
Gong, Xizhang   V-43
Gu, Caidong   VI-424, VI-430
Guan, Xianjun   I-21
Guangyu, Zhai   IV-503
Guilin, Lu   VI-232
Guo, Changgeng   III-442
Guo, Fachang   IV-382
Guo, Lejiang   II-194
Guo, Lina   III-494
Guo, Lu   VI-452
Guo, Shuting   V-288
Guo, Wei   V-428, V-435
Guo, Wenping   III-488
Guo, Xinbao   I-403, I-409
Guo, Yanli   V-226
Guo, Zhiyun   III-284
Guo, Zirui   I-359
Guohong   V-64
Guohong, Li   I-248
Guojin, Chen   III-299, III-305
Guojing, Xiong   II-267
Guo-song, Jiang   I-320, I-328

Haicheng, Xu   IV-10
Hailong, Sun   I-161
Hai-qi, Feng   V-374
Haitao, Hong   VI-50
Haiwen, Li   IV-335
Haixia, Wan   I-484
Haixia, Yu   VI-522
HamidehJafarian   V-36
Han, Baoyuan   IV-450
Han, Dong   IV-464
Han, Hua   I-478
Han, Xinchao   III-401
Han, Xu   V-100

Hang, Ling-li   V-268
Hantian, Wei   VI-445, V-511
Hao, Fei Lin   V-304
Hao, Hong   VI-551
Hao, Yitong   II-143
Hau, Chuan-Shou   V-239
He, Jilin   V-137
He, Juan   III-103
He, Li   III-174
He, Lijuan   III-337
He, Siqi   II-420
He, Weisong   VI-94, VI-100
He, Xiangguang   VI-188, VI-197
He, Yang   II-312
He, Yinghao   IV-32
He, Yong   V-304
He, Zhuzhu   II-458
Heng, Chen   III-89
Hengkai, Li   I-213
Hong, Liang   IV-181
Hong, Lu   I-465
Hongbing, Zhang   VI-551
Hongjun, Liu   I-533
Hong-li, Zhang   I-302
Hongmei, Jiang   IV-159
Hongmei, Tang   III-345, III-355, III-363
Hongwei, Luo   III-183
Hou, Shouming   III-337
Hou, Xuefeng   IV-369
Hu, Caimei   IV-81
Hu, Jianfeng   IV-456
Hu, Jun   V-409
Hu, Wenfa   V-281, V-288
Hu, YongHong   VI-452
Hu, Zhigang   V-246
Hu, Zhiwei   IV-392
Hu, Zong   IV-54
Hua, Wang Guo   VI-157
Huan, Wang   V-518
Huang, Changqin   V-258
Huang, De-Fa   V-239
Huang, Haifeng   I-428
Huang, Hanmin   I-94
Huang, Hexiao   III-508
Huang, Jun   V-268
Huang, Qiong   II-287
Huang, Tao   III-174
Huang, Weitong   V-117
Huang, Xiaodi   V-468
Huang, Yu-Chun   V-239

Huang, Zhiqiu   V-409
Huanhuai, Zhou   V-334
Huijuan, Ying   V-334
Hui-li, Wang   VI-370
Huili, Zhang   I-161
Huixia, Wang   II-150, II-172
Huixin, Jin   I-248

Jangamshetti, D.S.   IV-351
Jen, Yen-Huai   V-483
Ji, Jia   VI-398
Jia, Guangshe   V-125
Jia, Zhiyang   VI-188, VI-197
Jian, Wang   V-374
Jian, Zhou   III-143
Jiang, Fuhua   II-396
Jiang, Jia   VI-398
Jiang, Xuping   III-482
Jiang, Yuantao   II-17, II-95
Jian-Hao, Xu   VI-34
Jianhong, Sun   IV-1, IV-10
Jian-Min, Yao   III-151
Jianping, Li   I-395, III-321
Jianping, Tao   III-143
Jianqi, Han   VI-50
Jian-tong, He   VI-290
Jianwen, Cao   IV-503
Jianxin, Gao   V-518
Jianzheng, Yi   IV-342
Jiao, Linan   V-189
Jia-xin, Lin   VI-224
Jie, Jin   II-303
Jie, Quan   I-413
Jie, Xu   V-82
Jie, Yu   VI-467
Jieping, Han   I-132
Jin, Haiyi   V-328
Jin, Min   II-73
Jin, Wang   V-82
Jinfa, Shi   III-453, III-465
Jinfang, Zhang   VI-467
Jing, Liang   V-207
Jing, Tu   I-184
Jing, Zhao   III-292
Jing, Zhou   I-66, I-71
Jing-xin, Chen   I-343, I-351
Jingzhong, Liu   II-318
Jin-hai, Wang   VI-319
Jinhui, Lei   III-207
Jinwei, Fu   IV-10

Jinwu, Yuan   III-420
Jiuzhi, Mao   I-313
Jou, Shyh-Jye   V-10
Jun, Li   VI-148
Jun, Song   V-137
Jun, Wang   V-82
Jun, Zhang   VI-45
Jun-qi, Yang   VI-297
Junsheng, Li   IV-1
Jyothi, N.M.   III-328

Kai, Zhang   V-133
Ke, Xiaoyu   II-73
Kebin, Huang   II-150
Kewen, Geng   VI-124
Kun, Shi   VI-66

Lai, Herbert Hsuan Heng   VI-500
Lan, Jingli   II-518
Lee, Xuetao   II-226
Lei, Xu   VI-232
Lei, Yang   II-109
Lei, Yu   V-193
Li, Chen   II-303
Li, Cungui   II-499
Li, Deyang   III-263
Li, Dou Hui   VI-157
Li, Fengri   VI-20
Li, Fengying   IV-101, IV-110
Li, Guanglei   III-433
Li, Guangzheng   III-81
Li, Haibin   I-115
Li, Haiyan   IV-233
Li, Hongli   VI-424
Li, Houjie   I-550
Li, Hua   I-380
Li, Hui   III-174
Li, Jia-Hui   IV-316
Li, Jianfeng   IV-297
Li, Jianling   IV-233
Li, Jinglin   III-502
Li, Jinxiang   VI-430
Li, Kuang-Yao   V-239
Li, Li   VI-458
Li, Liwei   III-241
Li, Luyi   III-192, III-394
Li, Mingzhe   IV-172
Li, Na   II-202
Li, Peng   V-56
Li, Qi   I-359

Li, RuZhang   V-18
Li, Shaokun   VI-335
Li, Shenghong   IV-441
Li, Shijun   IV-233
Li, Wan   V-416
Li, Wang   V-346
Li, Wenbin   IV-392
Li, WenSheng   I-101
Li, Xiangdong   III-401
Li, Xiumei   IV-224
Li, Yang   IV-42
Li, Yanlai   IV-297
Li, Ying   V-443, V-449, V-455
Li, Yu   II-128
Li, YuJing   V-18
Li, Zhenlong   III-488
Lian, Jianbo   I-451
Lianbo, Jiang   VI-551
Liang, Wen-Qian   II-450
Liang, Yuechen   III-232
Liang-feng, Shen   I-255
Liangtao, Sun   I-492
Liao, GaoHua   VI-7, V-498, V-504
Liao, Jiaping   III-174
Lieya, Gu   I-8
Lifen, Xie   II-34
Li-jia, Chen   VI-297
Lijun, Shao   V-105
Li Jun, Sun   II-428, II-436, II-443
Liminzhi   I-513
Lin, Chien-Yu   V-483
Lin, Haibo   II-414
Lin, Ho-Hsiu   V-483
Lin, Jing   VI-179
Lina, Wang   IV-59
Ling, Chen   I-29, IV-59
Ling, Shen Xiao   VI-511
Lingrong, Da   II-373
Li-ping, Li   V-221
Liping, Pang   V-82
Lisheng, Wang   V-234
Liu, An-Ta   VI-500
Liu, Bao   IV-427
Liu, Bingwu   I-437
Liu, Bojia   V-111
Liu, Bosong   IV-32
Liu, Chunli   III-255
Liu, Daohua   V-491
Liu, Deli   II-181
Liu, Gui-Ying   II-342

Liu, Hong   VI-74
Liu, Hongming   III-116
Liu, Hongzhi   VI-335, VI-343, VI-357
Liu, Jia   V-504
Liu, Jiayi   II-1
Liu, Jingwei   IV-491
Liu, Jixin   IV-360
Liu, June   I-143
Liu, Jun-Min   II-493
Liu, Li   V-258
Liu, Lianchen   III-158
Liu, Lianzhong   II-164
Liu, LinTao   V-18
Liu, Linyuan   V-409
Liu, Shiwang   II-181
Liu, Tao   III-442
Liu, Wenbai   V-316
Liu, Xiaojing   V-117
Liu, Xiaojun   I-59, II-164
Liu, Xin   V-491
Liu, XingLi   IV-181
Liu, Yang   VI-110
Liu, Yanzhong   II-235
Liu, Yongsheng   I-471
Liu, Yongxian   III-337
Liu, Yuewen   II-458
Liu, Zhaotian   IV-233
Liu, Zhi-qiang   III-112
Liu, Zhixin   I-177
Liurong, Hong   V-389
Liuxiaoning   V-64
Lixia, Wang   VI-267
Lixing, Ding   V-50
Li'yan   II-22
Li-yan, Chen   I-76, I-83
Liyu, Chen   I-166, I-172
Liyulong   I-513
Long, Chen   VI-50
Long, Hai   IV-25
Long, Lifang   II-181
Long, Shun   II-450
Long, Xingwu   IV-252
Lu, Hong   V-428, V-435
Lu, Hongtao   IV-392, IV-402
Lu, Jing   I-519
Lu, Ling   V-258
Lu, Xiaocheng   II-294
Lu, Y.M.   V-353, V-359
Lu, Zhijian   II-47
Luo, Rong   I-222

Luo, Yumei   II-414
Lv, Qingchu   IV-93
Lv, Rongsheng   II-211
Lv, Xiafu   IV-280

Ma, Chunlei   I-471
Ma, Jian   V-164
Ma, Lixin   V-328
Ma, Qing-Xun   II-116, II-122
Ma, Sen   IV-369
Ma, Yuan   V-189
Ma, Zengjun   IV-93
Ma, Zhonghua   III-103
Mai, Yonghao   VI-417
Mamaghani, Nasrin Dastranj   III-22
Maotao, Zhu   VI-210, V-211
Maoxing, Shen   VI-148
Masud, Md. Anwar Hossain   V-468
Meilin, Wang   V-181
Meng, Hua   V-69
Meng, Yi-Le   V-10
Mengmeng, Gong   V-82
Mi, Chao   VI-492
Miao, J.   V-353
Milong, Li   I-457
Min, Ye Zhi   VI-511
Ming qiang, Zhu   I-150, I-206
Mingqiang, Zhu   II-81
Mingquan, Zhou   VI-528

Na, Wang   I-233
Naifei, Ren   V-133
Nan, Li   I-533
Nan, Shizong   IV-476
Nie, GuoXin   V-523
Nie, Zhanglong   VI-138
Ning, Ai   V-334
Ning, Cai   I-36
Ning, Yuan   V-416
Nirmala, C.R.   III-328
Niu, Huizhuo   IV-369
Niu, Xiaoke   IV-289

Pan, Dongming   V-43
Pan, Min   I-446
Pan, Rong   II-1
Pan, Yingchun   V-170
Pan, Zhifang   IV-392
Pei, Xudong   VI-105

Peng, Fenglin   III-482
Peng, Hao   IV-335
Peng, Jianhan   III-508
Peng, Jian-Liang   II-136
Peng, Yan   V-309
Pengcheng, Fan   VI-528
Pengcheng, Zhao   II-405
Piao, Linhua   VI-239, VI-246, VI-253, VI-261
Ping, Li   VI-273
Pinxin, Fu   V-181

Qi, Lixia   I-124
Qi, Zhang   IV-219
Qian, Minping   IV-491
Qiaolian, Cheng   V-370
Qin, G.H.   V-89
Qin, Zhou   I-302
Qingguo, Liu   III-130
Qinghai, Chen   IV-335
Qingjia, Geng   V-105
Qingling, Liu   IV-273, V-24
Qingyun, Dai   V-181
Qinhai, Ma   I-238
Qiong, Long   VI-467
Qiu, Biao   VI-179
Qiu, YunJie   IV-402
Qiuhe, Yang   VI-267
Qiyi, Zhang   VI-124
Qu, Baozhong   III-255
Qun, Zhai   III-143
Qun, Zhang   III-377, III-386

Ramaswamy, V.   III-328
Rao, Shuibing   V-137
Ren, Chunyu   VI-218
Ren, Hai Jun   V-56
Ren, Honge   VI-131
Ren, Jianfeng   III-494
Ren, Mingming   I-115
Ren, Qiang   III-276
Ren, Shengbing   V-246
Ren, Wei   III-81
RenJie   VI-376
Rijie, Cong   I-132
Rubo, Zhang   III-39, III-47
Rui, Chen   II-303
Rui, Zhao   I-248, I-313
Ruihong, Zhang   II-253
Ruirui, Zhang   IV-204, IV-212

Runyang, Zhong   V-181
Ru'yuan, Li   II-22

Saghafi, Fatemeh   III-22
Samizadeh, Reza   III-22
San-ping, Zhao   VI-13, VI-410
Sha, Hu   IV-470
Shan, Shimin   IV-32
Shang, Jiaxing   III-158
Shang, Yuanyuan   IV-369, IV-450
Shangchun, Fan   V-321
Shao, Qiang   I-109
Shaojun, Qin   VI-210
Shen, Ming Wei   V-304
Shen, Qiqiang   III-95
Shen, Yiwen   II-47
Shen, Zhang   VI-370
Sheng, Ye   VI-232
Shi, Danda   V-316
Shi, Guoliang   IV-48
Shi, Li   IV-289
Shi, Ming-wang   V-143
Shi, Wang   V-105
Shi, Yan   II-414
Shi, Yi   VI-131
Shidong, Li   V-296
Shou-Yong, Zhang   II-428, II-436, II-443
Shu, Xiaohao   III-95
Shu, Xin   V-164
Shuai, Wang   V-221
Shuang, Pan   III-30
Song, Haitao   VI-166
Song, Meina   III-284
Song, Yichen   IV-73
Song, Yu   IV-73
Sreedevi, A   IV-351
Su, Donghai   V-404
Sun, Qibo   III-502
Sun, Zhaoyun   V-189
Sun, Zhong-qiang   V-100
Sunqi   I-513
Sunxu   I-484
Suozhu, Wang   I-14

Tan, Liguo   VI-110
Tang, Dejun   V-328
Tang, Fang Fang   V-56
Tang, Fei   I-478
Tang, Hengyao   II-274
Tang, Peng   II-1

Tang, Xin   II-17
Tang, Xinhuai   V-1
Tang, Yong   V-258
Tanming, Liu   II-331
Tao, Li   IV-204, IV-212
Tao, Zedan   II-357
Tian, Fengbo   IV-280
Tian, Fengqiu   VI-430
Tian, Ling   III-241
Tianqing, Xiao   IV-10
Ting, Chen   I-387
Tong, Guangji   II-499, II-510, II-518
Tong, Ruo-feng   IV-198
Tu, Chunxia   I-46, I-59

Wan, Hong   IV-289
Wan, Wei   VI-452
Wan, Zhenkai   III-9, IV-484
Wang, Bing   II-484
Wang, Chen   V-328
Wang, Chengxi   I-451
Wang, Chonglu   I-222
Wang, Chunhui   I-500
Wang, Dan   IV-433
Wang, Dongxue   IV-297
Wang, Fei   I-88
Wang, Feng   V-201
Wang, Fengling   II-128
Wang, Fumin   I-198
Wang, Haiping   III-224
Wang, Hongli   VI-315
Wang, Huasheng   II-350
Wang, Hui-Jin   II-450
Wang, JiaLian   V-252, V-422
Wang, Jian   II-211
Wang, Jianhua   IV-48
Wang, Jianqing   V-111
Wang, Jie   V-404
Wang, Jing   V-100
Wang, Jinyu   I-335
Wang, Li-Chih   V-483
Wang, Lijie   V-529
Wang, Linlin   V-275
Wang, Luzhuang   IV-93
Wang, Min   VI-424
Wang, Qian   III-166, III-284
Wang, Ruoyang   VI-398
Wang, Ruo-Yun   IV-376
Wang, Shangguang   III-502

Wang, Shanshan   II-458
Wang, Shijun   IV-464
Wang, Shi-Lin   IV-376, IV-441
Wang, Shimei   I-428
Wang, Shuyan   II-10
Wang, Tiankuo   II-510
Wang, Ting   V-449, V-455
Wang, Weiliang   VI-544
Wang, Xia   I-21
Wang, Xiaohong   III-241
Wang, Xiaohui   I-269
Wang, Xiaoya   II-420
Wang, Xiaoying   V-117
Wang, Xing   VI-239, VI-246, VI-253,
        VI-261
Wang, Yan   IV-508
Wang, Y.C.   V-359
Wang, Yiran   III-247
Wang, Yongping   III-276
Wang, YouHua   V-18
Wang, Yu   IV-252
Wang, Yude   VI-480
Wang, Yuqiang   V-170
Wang, Zhenxing   III-166
Wang, Zhizhong   IV-289
Wei, Cai   II-150, II-172
Wei, Cheng-Wen   V-10
Wei, Fengjuan   II-235
Wei, Guo   IV-252
Wei, Li   III-30
Wei, Lin   VI-79
Wei, Ling-ling   III-212, III-218
Wei, Liu   I-351
Wei, Ou   V-409
Wei, Xianmin   IV-418, IV-422
Wei, Yang   II-253
Wei, Yu-Ting   III-407
Wei, Zhou   VI-305
Weihong, Chen   III-89
Weihua, Liu   III-183, III-369
Weihua, Xie   V-30
Weimin, Wu   IV-242
Weiqiong, He   IV-219
Weiwei, Fang   III-321
Weixi, Han   I-465
Wen, Chengyu   I-177
Wen, Jun Hao   V-56
Wendi, Ma   II-364
Wenping, Zhang   I-184
Wu, Bin   V-246

Wu, Caiyan   VI-424
Wu, Di   II-143
WU, Guoshi   III-247
Wu, Hao   I-380
Wu, Kaijun   V-43
Wu, Peng   VI-452
Wu, Xiaofang   IV-32
Wu, Xiwei   II-357
Wu, Xue-li   V-69
Wu, Yanqiang   IV-470
Wu, Yong   II-493
Wu, Zhongbing   I-109

Xi, Ba   IV-325
Xi, JunMei   VI-7
-xia, Gao   VI-297
Xia, Li   IV-273, V-24
Xiang, Hongmei   VI-94, VI-100
Xiang, Jun   II-181
Xiang, Qian   V-215
Xiang, Song   VI-305
Xiang_Li, Wang   II-428
Xianzhang, Feng   III-453, III-465
Xiao, Weng   III-130
Xiao-hong, Zhang   IV-411
Xiaolin, Chen   II-281
Xiao-ling, He   I-320, I-328
Xiaona, Zhou   I-313
XiaoPing, Hu   VI-350
Xiaosai, Li   V-340
Xiaosheng, Liu   I-213
Xiaowei, Wei   VI-391
Xiaoxia, Zhao   III-207
Xiaoya, He   II-259
Xiaoyan, Xu   VI-528
Xiao-ying, Wang   I-343
Xiaoyong, Li   II-364, II-382
Xie, Dong   IV-25
Xie, Hualong   III-337
Xie, Li   V-1
Xie, Lihui   II-218
Xie, Luning   III-122
Xie, Qiang-lai   III-212, III-218
Xie, Xiaona   IV-167
Xie, Xing-Zhe   IV-316
Xie, Zhengxiang   IV-280
Xie, Zhimin   I-21
Xifeng, Xue   VI-148
Xijun, Liu   V-476

Xilan, Feng   III-453, III-465
Xiliang, Dai   VI-124
Xilong, Jiang   IV-219
Xin, Xiao   IV-204, IV-212
Xin, Zhanhong   I-222
Xing, GuiLin   VI-357
Xing, Wang   V-461
Xing, Xu   VI-210
Xinhua, An   II-40
Xinling, Wen   VI-66, VI-474
Xinzhong, Xiong   II-52
Xinzhong, Zhang   I-373
Xi ping, Zhang   I-150, I-206
Xiucheng, Dong   V-340
Xu, Dawei   IV-450
Xu, Jing   III-166
Xu, Kaiquan   II-458
Xu, Li   VI-305
Xu, Ming   III-95
Xu, Shuang   I-550
Xu, Wanlu   VI-398
xu, Wenke   VI-20
Xu, Zhifeng   II-17
Xu, Zhou   III-64
Xuan, Dong   VI-305
Xue, Qingshui   IV-101, IV-110
Xuemei, Hou   V-193
Xuemei, Li   V-50
Xuemei, Tang   V-158
Xuhua, Chen   IV-342
Xuhua, Shi   V-148, V-153
Xuhui, Wang   II-22
Xun, Jin   IV-252
Xuxiu   IV-521
Xu-yang, Liu   V-207

YaChao, Huang   V-30
Yachun, Dai   V-133
Yamin, Qin   I-373
Yan, Fu   I-14
Yan, Jun   I-115
Yan, Peng   V-74
Yan, Qingyou   II-420
Yan, Shou   III-158
Yan, Yunyang   IV-120
Yan, Zhang   IV-325
Yanbin, Shi   VI-517, VI-522
Yang, Chen   VI-210
Yang, Fangchun   III-502

Yang, Fei   IV-88
Yang, Hao   III-122
Yang, Lianhe   IV-476
Yang, Li Chen   III-292
Yang, Liming   V-365
Yang, Qian   II-164
Yang, Qin   VI-458
Yang, Renfa   II-287
Yang, Song   I-238, I-395
Yang, Wei   III-112
Yang, Xinhua   IV-450
Yang, Xue   I-101, I-124
Yang, You-dong   V-164
Yang, Yue   II-87
Yanli, Shi   VI-517, VI-522
Yanli, Xu   IV-136, IV-144, IV-151, IV-159
Yanping, Liu   III-369
Yan-yuan, Zhang   VI-79
Yanzhen, Guo   I-248
Yao, Lei-Yue   III-218
Yaqiong, Wei   I-132
Yazhou, Chen   V-211
Ye, H.C.   V-89
Yi, Cui   V-82
Yi, Jing-bing   III-54
Yi, Ru   VI-474
Yifan, Shen   III-312
Yihui, Wu   IV-335
Yin, Jinghai   IV-456
Yin, Qiuju   IV-66
Yin, Zhang   I-313
Yinfang, Jiang   V-133
Ying, Mai   I-280
Yingfang, Li   IV-1
Yingjun, Feng   IV-144, IV-151
Yingying, Ding   III-89
Ying-ying, Zhang   IV-42
Yixin, Guo   VI-282
Yong, Wu   I-156
Yong-feng, Li   VI-39
Yongqiang, He   III-413, III-420
Yongsheng, Huang   V-518
Yong-tao, Zhao   VI-224
Yongzheng, Kang   I-161
You, Mingqing   III-200
Youmei, Wang   IV-18
Youqu, Lin   II-326
Yu, Chen   VI-66, VI-474
Yu, Cheng   III-377, III-386

Yu, Chuanchun   IV-120
Yu, Deng   I-8
Yu, Jie   VI-398
Yu, Liangguo   VI-488
Yu, Quangang   VI-239, VI-246, VI-253, VI-261
Yu, Shuxiu   II-226
Yu, Siqin   II-95
Yu, Tao   I-244
Yu, Tingting   V-281
Yu, Yan   IV-48
Yu, Yao   II-143
Yu, Zhichao   I-52
Yuan, Fang   I-76, I-83
Yuan, Feng   III-473
Yuan, Qi   III-312
Yuan, Xin-wei   III-54
Yuanqing, Wang   II-530
Yuanquan, Shi   IV-204, IV-212
Yuanyuan, Zhang   V-374
Yue, Wang   VI-328
Yue, Xi   VI-204
Yu-han, Zhang   VI-319
Yuhong, Li   I-465
Yuhua, He   I-1
Yujuan, Liang   VI-173
Yun, Wang   V-133
Yun-an, Hu   VI-224
Yunfang, Chen   IV-242
YunFeng, Lin   VI-350
Yunna, Wu   IV-325
Yuxia, Hu   VI-364
Yuxiang, Li   V-105
Yuxiang, Yang   VI-267

zelong, Xu   VI-551
Zeng, Jie   III-433
Zeng, Zhiyuan   VI-152
Zhai, Ju-huai   V-143
Zhan, Yulong   II-143
Zhan, Yunjun   I-421
Zhang, Bo   I-437
Zhang, David   IV-297
Zhang, Fan   IV-32
Zhang, Fulin   III-200
Zhang, Haijun   I-437
Zhang, Haohan   IV-172
Zhang, Hongjing   II-10
Zhang, Hongzhi   IV-297

Zhang, Huaping   VI-1
Zhang, Huiying   V-416
Zhang, Jian   VI-131
Zhang, Jianhua   V-69
Zhang, Jie   IV-93
Zhang, Kai   V-404
Zhang, Kuai-Juan   II-136
Zhang, Laishun   IV-464
Zhang, Liancheng   III-166
Zhang, Liang   IV-484
Zhang, Liguo   IV-508
Zhang, Ling   II-466
Zhang, Minghong   III-135
Zhang, Minghua   I-451
Zhang, Qimin   VI-376
Zhang, RuiTao   V-18
Zhang, Sen   V-529
Zhang, Shu   V-43
Zhang, Shuang-Cai   II-342
Zhang, Sixiang   IV-427
Zhang, Tao   VI-179
Zhang, Tingxian   IV-360
Zhang, Wei   II-350
Zhang, Wuyi   III-64, III-74
Zhang, Xianzhi   II-194
Zhang, Xiaolin   I-500
Zhang, Xiuhong   V-404
Zhang, Yi   III-268
Zhang, Yingqian   II-414
Zhang, Yong   I-269
Zhang, Yu   IV-189
Zhang, Yuanliang   VI-117
Zhang, Yujin   IV-441
Zhang, Yun   II-66
Zhang, Zaichen   IV-382
Zhang, Zhiyuan   III-135
Zhangyanpeng   I-513
Zhanqing, Ma   V-399
Zhao, Hong   V-275
Zhao, Huifeng   II-244
Zhao, Jiyin   I-550
Zhao, Liu   V-321
Zhao, Min   IV-306
Zhao, Xiaoming   III-488
Zhao, Xiuhong   III-433
Zhao, Ying   III-276
Zhaochun, Wu   II-26
Zhaoyang, Zhang   II-530
Zhe, Yan   VI-273
Zhen, Lu   II-187

Zhen, Ran   V-69
Zhen, Zhang   VI-232
Zhen-fu, Li   VI-290
Zheng, Chuiyong   II-202
Zheng, Fanglin   III-394
Zheng, Jun   V-409
Zheng, Lin-tao   IV-198
Zheng, Qian   V-321
Zheng, Qiusheng   III-401
Zheng, Xianyong   I-94
Zheng, Yanlin   III-192, III-394
Zheng, Yongliang   II-181
Zhenying, Xu   V-133
Zhi, Kun   IV-66
Zhi'an, Wang   II-22
Zhiben, Jie   II-259
Zhibing, Liu   II-172
Zhibo, Li   V-193
Zhi-gang, Gan   I-295
Zhi-guang, Zhang   IV-411
Zhijun, Zhang   II-109
Zhiqiang, Duan   IV-342
Zhiqiang, Jiang   III-453, III-465
Zhiqiang, Wang   I-262
Zhisuo, Xu   V-346
Zhiwen, Zhang   II-101
Zhixiang, Tian   II-373
Zhiyuan, Kang   I-543
Zhong, Luo   III-442
Zhong, Shaochun   III-192
Zhong, Yuling   II-181
Zhongji, Tan   VI-517
Zhongjing, Liu   VI-370
Zhonglin, He   I-1, I-166
Zhongyan, Wang   III-130
Zhou, Defu   VI-430
Zhou, De-Qun   II-466
Zhou, Fang   II-493
Zhou, Fanzhao   I-507
Zhou, Feng   I-109
Zhou, Gang   VI-417
Zhou, Hong   IV-120
Zhou, Jing-Jing   VI-58
Zhou, Lijuan   V-309
Zhou, Wei   IV-427
Zhou, Yonghua   VI-492
Zhou, Zheng   I-507
Zhu, JieBin   V-498
Zhu, Jingwei   III-508
Zhu, Libin   I-335

Zhu, Lili   II-420
Zhu, Linlin   III-135
Zhu, Quanyin   IV-120, IV-189
Zhu, Xi   VI-152
Zhuanghua, Lu   V-389

Zhuping, Du   V-193
Zou, Qiong   IV-129
Zunfeng, Liu   V-381
ZuoMing   IV-514
Zuxu, Zou   II-81